An Annotated Glossary of Arabic Musical Terms

An Annotated Glossary of Arabic Musical Terms

COMPILED BY
Lois Ibsen al Faruqi

Forewords by Ali Jihad Racy and Don Michael Randel

Greenwood Press
Westport, Connecticut • London, England

Library of Congress Cataloging in Publication Data

Faruqi, Lois Ibsen.
An annotated glossary of Arabic musical terms.

Bibliography: p.
1. Music—Terminology. I. Title.
ML108.F27 781.7'2927'014 81-4129
ISBN 0-313-20554-X (lib. bdg.) AACR2

Library of Congress Catalog Card Number: 81-4129
ISBN: 0-313-20554-X

First published in 1981

Greenwood Press
A division of Congressional Information Service, Inc.
88 Post Road West, Westport, Connecticut 06881

Printed in the United States of America

10 9 8 7 6 5 4 3 2 1

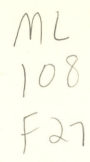

Contents

Foreword

by Ali Jihad Racy
University of California at Los Angeles

Musical scholarship is a cumulative and perpetual process. In each historical era we find works which function as scholarly "rechargers." The writings of Ptolemy, Ikhwan al-Safa', al-Farabi, Hawkins, and Fetis all capture the past, record the present, and project into the future. In his Kitab al-Musiqa al-Kabir (The Great Book on Music), the tenth-century philosopher al-Farabi analyzed ancient Greek musical doctrines and presented a broad range of musical concepts current at his time. Eventually, his compendium became a vital source of information for other theorists and an exemplar for succeeding writers on music. Nearly a millennium later, a comparable contribution was undertaken by a visionary composer and theorist from Egypt, Kamil al-Khula'i. In his Kitab al-Musiqa al-Sharqi (The Book of Eastern Music, ca. 1904), al-Khula'i expressed his desire to follow the path of al-Farabi and al-Isfahani and to produce a practical anthology for the modern Egyptian musician. His book discussed established Arab and Turkish musical principles and explained European music theory. It also advocated open-mindedness towards music of the West. In more recent decades, comparable contributions appeared in Arabic and in other languages.

Professor Lois I. al-Faruqi's An Annotated Glossary of Arabic Musical Terms is both a continuation of this scholarly tradition and a breakthrough in the field of Near Eastern musical research. Her work introduces musical traditions from a long historical period extending from the seventh century A.D. to the present. It informs the reader about a relatively unexplored, but fundamental, body of knowledge: medieval treatises, melodic modes, systems of tuning, doctrines of aesthetics, instruments, and performance techniques. Rooted in antiquity, this body of knowledge constitutes the main musical background of Arab and other west Asian countries. Throughout history, its impact has proliferated farther into parts of Africa, Europe, and Central and South Asia.

Al-Faruqi's glossary bridges the gap which has existed between Arab music and musical scholarship in the West. The two have been separated by musical, cultural, and language barriers, a fact which gives further tribute to pioneering works by Villoteau, Farmer, d'Erlanger, and others. Written in English, the present glossary serves a large number of Western and Third World readers. It provides a thorough musical orientation for the less specialized investigator. It also renders unique assistance to scholars and students pursuing the study of Arab or Near Eastern music in general. The topics discussed range from medieval finger modes to contemporary musical instruments in Upper Egypt. The material is properly researched and documented, and the presentation is both systematic and stimulating.

The reader soon realizes the enormous task undertaken by the author in preparing this work. It is apparent that she does more than define specific musical concepts. She investigates central musical phenomena such as the relationship between theory and practice, the link between music and other disciplines, the intermixing of various ethnic groups and musical systems in medieval Islam, and the influx of Greek, Persian, Turkish, and later, French and Italian musical nomenclature into the Arabic language. Al-Faruqi deals with these and other questions with due perceptiveness and caution. Whenever necessary, the entries provide alternative definitions which consider factors of time and place. The entries also allude to the written works in which the terms have been discussed. This provides the reader with a clear contextual perspective and possibilities for pursuing further research. The number of works consulted is impressive. Also to be mentioned is the glossary's use of the standard form of transliteration. Such standardization will undoubtedly facilitate communication among writers.

Professor al-Faruqi is one of the few scholars today whose knowledge encompasses both past and present Arab musical traditions. As her many publications demonstrate, she has unique expertise in the area of Islamic decorative arts and in the aesthetic relationship between these arts and the music. This background is complemented by her impressive command of the Arabic language and her personal affinity for the cultural heritage which this work represents. Comprehensive and well researched, this work deserves to be studied in its entirety by anyone who is seriously interested in music of the Arab and Islamic Near East. Al-Faruqi's An Annotated Glossary of Arabic Musical Terms marks the beginning of a new phase in the study of an old legacy.

Foreword

by Don Michael Randel
Cornell University

Dictionaries are usually made from other dictionaries. Each new one, if it justifies its existence at all, adds new material, new emphases, new perspectives. However objective or scientific, it reveals a new set of prejudices about its field. Nevertheless, it is almost certain to have identifiable ancestors, even if it is a particularly rebellious offspring. But what must it be like to write the first one--to have no ancestors either to venerate or to rebel against? Most of us can only be grateful that someone else has spared us the experience. The present glossary calls for just such gratitude.

It is the first. And it is the first in a particularly difficult field. Not the least of the difficulties is the field's vast extent, both chronological and geographical. In consequence, even the most mechanical aspect of such a work--spelling the words and presenting them in an alphabetical list--is unusually difficult. Given the variety of schemes of transliteration and the variety of mistranslations or partial translations to which the field has given rise, it is frequently quite hard to determine whether two words in different sources are intended to be the same or different. And then there is the problem of understanding the nature of the intersections (and discontinuities) between an early, large, highly developed theoretical literature and a living musical tradition whose modes of transmission are largely oral. The labor of making the first charts for such a vastness requires courage and patience in considerable measure along with all of the relevant scholarly equipment.

There can be no doubt about the importance of this labor, however. Its value for the study of the living musical traditions of Arabic-speaking peoples is self-evident, as is its value for the study of the early treatises. In short, the specialist in Arabian music and music theory of any period will find this glossary an essential aid to navigation. But just as important is its value for the study of neighboring fields. Alas, not all of these fields have taken full account of the extent to which they are neighbors--in some cases because the frontiers have seemed impenetrable, in some cases for reasons less easily forgiven. But there are at least two groups of scholars who must take hold of this glossary with both hands and begin to mine the treasures to which it can lead them: students of the music of Classical Antiquity and students of the music of the European Middle Ages. No complete account of either of these fields will be possible without a thorough exploration of Arabic materials.

The crowning virtue of this glossary is precisely the way in which it can lead scholars in all fields to the materials on which it draws, for it is an index to these materials as much as it is a glossary with which to read them. Thus, it serves not only the reader interested in finding a definition of a particular Arabic word. It serves the reader who wishes to know where that word occurs in the literature. And, with its index of English musical terms, it serves the reader who wishes to know the Arabic equivalents of English terms and where in the literature these Arabic terms have been used or discussed. Thus, for example, the student of scales or tetrachords of whatever period or culture can quickly gain entry to relevant Arabic materials.

In this respect the glossary encourages readers to question it and go beyond it. In so doing, it not only provides the first necessary step toward a better and more general understanding of Arabian musical culture, it provides a means and a stimulus toward further steps as well. Our considerable debt to Lois Ibsen al Faruqi will best be repaid as we attempt those further steps.

Introduction

This is the first Arabic-English glossary of musical terms to be published for the Western student or investigator of Arabian music. Such a tool is a necessity for acceptable advance in the field. No foreign area study can be efficient if every person pursuing it must go through the time-consuming task of deciphering on his own the subject's foreign language terminology, a knowledge of which is a prerequisite for any contribution to the study.

To add to this general need for lexicographical assistance in a foreign area discipline, it is well known to anyone who has stepped even superficially into the field of Arabian music study, that there are substantial problems of terminology to be encountered there. First, many musical terms in the Arabic language have had differing musical meanings over the centuries. Secondly, various terms have often been used for a single musical phenomenon. At times, different meanings for a particular term or different terms for one specific meaning have been used during the same period, by different authors or even by the same author. Thirdly, whenever Western scholars have written about Arabian music, they have been forced to transliterate the musical terminology into one of the Western languages. No consistent transliteration rules were used by these writers, even in the works written in any single non-Arabic language. When the Arabic terms are compared in their transliterated forms in different European languages as used by different authors, they are often not only confusing, but even unrecognizable (e.g., roudjouʿou = rujūʿ = رجوع, chtîḥ' = shaṭḥ = شطح, ḫafī = khafī = خفي, r'eçen = rhoçn = ghuṣn = غصن, etc.). Fourthly, among the Arabs themselves, a great deal of variety in pronunciation of musical terms has developed because of the colloquialization of these terms. In turn, these pronunciations have found their way into the transliterated forms (e.g., aba for qabā or قبا ; 'emrabbaʿ for murabbaʿ or مربع ; tnia for thāniyah or ثانية ; etc.). In addition dialectical variations in different regions of the Arab World change the spoken sound of a word or words and thus often make it difficult to know their correct literary form. When that pronunciation is rendered in transliteration to a European language, the difficulty is complicated further (e.g., bu-rhanim for abū ghanam or أبو غنم; neqlabāt for inqilābāt or إنقلابات; etc.).

Despite these difficulties and the general need for assistance, only a limited number of musical terms are defined in the standard Arabic or Arabic-English dictionaries available to Western students and researchers. If we look to the English language dictionaries of music, we find the available materials even less helpful. Some of these include only the most superficial treatment of the terminology needed for a study of Arabian music. Others, limited by size considerations, intentionally include no items from the Arabic musical vocabulary.

Eric Werner and Isaiah Sonne evidently sensed the great need of any researcher for assistance in this problem of Arabic musical terminology, for they included a glossary of musical terms in their article on the writings of Judaeo-Arabic musical theorists of the Middle Ages (Werner and Sonne 1941:305-311). That work, however, contains only thirty-some transliterated entries, and confines itself to terms used during the Middle Ages.

Another attempt to provide lexicographical assistance for the student of music was made by Magdi Wahba in his An English-Arabic Vocabulary of Scientific, Technical and Cultural Terms (Wahba 1968:68-70). Definitions in Arabic of one hundred and thirty-seven verbs, nouns, adjectives and phrases of the contemporary English musical vocabulary are included. The entries reveal a strong Western music orientation of the work. Such words as fugue, leitmotiv, libretto, magnificat, march, oratorio, sonata, symphony, and brass band form a large portion of that glossary. The compiler has given Arabic equivalents for some terms, defined others briefly (e.g., "magnificat" becomes in Arabic "panegyrics to the Virgin Mary for the sake of God"), and simply transliterated other English terms into Arabic characters (e.g., "sonata" becomes ṣūnātah; "symphony," sīmfūniyyah). The three-page section on "Music" includes no coverage of terms used in the theoretical works of earlier centuries. The glossary is obviously one which may assist the Arab who has some interest in the music of the Western World; it offers little help to the person (Arab or non-Arab) who wishes to do research in the native music and chant of the Arab peoples.

It is possible to find definitions of over two hundred Arabic musical terms by consulting the "Subject and Geographical Index" in H. G. Farmer's A History of Arabian Music to the XIIIth Century (Farmer 1967) and then looking up individual references. That method, unfortunately, involves many difficulties: 1) Many important Arabic musical terms are omitted. 2) The terms found there and mentioned in the text are only those used in the historical period covered by the book. There is no treatment of musical vocabulary used since 1300. 3) It is difficult for all but the experienced researcher to distinguish musical from other Arabic terms, for all are presented in the Index in italics. 4) To find a definition of an Arabic term sometimes necessitates looking up several references and reading many pages of material, a laborious and time consuming task.

Two unpublished dissertations should also be mentioned: the doctoral dissertation of JaFran Jones (1977) includes a glossary with 137 Arabic entries and their English definitions, drawn from the author's work among the ʿĪsāwiyyah musicians of Tunisia. These terms are important for the region, but they make no attempt, and could not be expected, to go beyond that very limited regional coverage of Arabic musical terminology. The doctoral dissertation of the present author (al Faruqi 1974) contains a 47-page glossary of Arabic musical terms in Appendix II. That student work proved to be a useful but very preliminary exercise for preparation of the present glossary.

We understand that an English-Arabic dictionary of musical terms is being produced by the Ministry of Education of the Government of Lebanon, but that work is meant for the Arab student or teacher who is involved in the study of the music of Western culture. It therefore has a much different body of materials to cover from that included in the present work, though a few terms would be applicable in both areas of study.

As far as publications in Arabic are concerned, five works available in some of the more specialized libraries of North America should be mentioned. The first of these is the Arabic dictionary of musical terms which was prepared by Ḥusayn ʿAlī Maḥfūẓ and published by the Ministry of Culture, Government of ʿIrāq, in connection with the Conference on Arabian Music held in 1964 in Baghdād. A similar dictionary was published by the same author in Baghdād in 1977. Efforts to acquire a copy of the more recent work have been unsuccessful, but a review in an Arabic language journal (Al-Qītharah, Vol. V, No. 54, May, 1978) carries a description which suggests that the 1977 publication is an updating or enlargement of the earlier work. Ibrahīm al Dāqūqī translated to Arabic the Turkish musical dictionary of A. Kāẓim (Kāẓim 1964). This book was also published by the Ministry of Culture in connection with the Baghdād conference of 1964. A supplement to the Kāẓim dictionary was translated by al Dāqūqī and published the following year (al Dāqūqī 1965). Surprisingly, these translations of a foreign musical dictionary and its supplement are indeed relevant to a study of Arabic musical terms, for there is much overlap in terminology and practice between the Turkish and Arabic music traditions. For the purposes of this glossary, only the terms in the Kāẓim-al Dāqūqī works which seemed unequivocably relevant for Arabic musical practice were included. Finally, lists of musical terms used in Tunisia are included in the specialized indices of al Rizqī's Al Aghānī al Tūnisiyyah (1967). The relevant lists for our study are those on "Instruments and Provisions" (pp. 360-366), "Sounds and Tones" (pp. 367-371), and "Singing and Music" (p. 399).

None of the works published in the Arab World is readily accessible to the American ethnomusicologist, nor are their Arabic materials penetrable except by the experienced Arabist. There is therefore genuine need for a lexicographical work dealing with Arabic musical terminology which could be used by a wider segment of the Western readership. It is hoped that the present volume will assist in filling that gap.

The purpose of this glossary is to provide ready access to definitions of musical terms necessary for an understanding of Arabian music as discussed and practiced in both the historical and contemporary Arab World. It seeks to fulfill as many as possible of the requirements of the specialist, without the inclusion of materials, methods or techniques which would make it unusable by the non-specialist. In the attempt to satisfy both types of reader, each decision regarding the inclusion of materials and the form of their presentation was made with much hesitation and, in some cases, inevitable misgivings. For example, use of the Arabic script rather than transliterations for entries would have been a desirable addition for the Arabist, but would have precluded the glossary's use by the non-Arabist. Alphabetization of terms according to the Arabic alphabet would have been more consistent with the language itself than an English alphabetization. The latter requires not only a reordering of the Arabic alphabet but the inclusion under some English letters of the transliterated forms of two and even three Arabic letters (e.g., d for د , ḍ for ض , and dh for ذ , all under the letter "D"; s for س , ṣ for ص , and sh for ش , all under "S", etc.). Yet, given the varying transliteration systems used in Western languages and a lack of acquaintance with the Arabic alphabetic order of roots, an Arabic alphabetization would have made location of terms exceedingly difficult--and perhaps even impossible--for the non-Arabist. The Arabist will be able to find both dāl (د) and ḍāḍ (ض) under letter "D", but the non-Arabist would never locate the definition of sawt (a much used, though careless, transliteration of ṣawt) if confronted with a glossary arranged according to Arabic alphabetization. And how would the latter ever know that mutaṣawwat was to be found under "S" since its root is (ṣ-w-ṭ)? The inclusion of chrestomathic passages drawn from the sources as illustration for each entry, however desirable for precise clarification of usages, would have increased the size and scope of the glossary inordinately, making its publication costs unacceptable, not only to the publisher, but also, in turn, to users.

These are just a few of the difficult choices that had to be made. In all such decisions, I have chosen to "tilt" in favor of the wider readership and to include the non-experts who I felt were more in need of the assistance that such a work provides. The present glossary therefore lays no claim to precluding the necessity for other kinds of works dealing with Arabic musical terminology. Instead, it hopes merely to provide an initial lexicographical tool which could assist and further a much delayed but newly evolving field of ethnomusicological study.

Scope and Coverage:

"Arab" and "Arabian" have sometimes been narrowly defined as pertaining to the Semitic peoples of the Arabian Peninsula. This is not the definition of these terms which applies to this work. Instead, "Arab" and "Arabian" are used here for the musical phenomena of all the Arabic-speaking peoples, regardless of the racial background of the practitioners or theorists, or the location of their homelands.

Prior to the seventh century of the Christian era, these terms referred to the people of the Arabian Peninsula. In later times they were applied to all the people of the Fertile Crescent region. Still later, these terms were considered applicable to the peoples in a wide region stretching from as far as the Iberian Peninsula and the Atlantic coast of Africa in the West, across North Africa and the Near East to Central Asia in the East. Today the relevance for these two terms has shrunk to an area bordered by Morocco in the West and ʿIrāq in the East. This does not preclude the fact that there are many musical terms from that region that have a much wider relevance beyond the contemporary boundaries of "Arabia"--in Iran, Turkey, Central Asia,

Africa, and even farther afield; and that terminology and practices common to the surrounding regions are often used within the Arab World as here delineated. Perhaps the difference between this Arab World and its neighbors is not intrisically different from that which differentiates one region within the Arab World from another. It is only greater in degree.

In attempting to make a systematic presentation of such a vast and comprehensive subject as Arabic musical terminology, it was necessary to divide the fourteen or more centuries covered by the terms of this glossary into three subdivisions. These not only reveal the above-mentioned differences in geographic coverage, but also acknowledge some fundamental differences in musical materials and terminology despite the threads of correspondence and commonality in this long tradition. Providing names for each of these periods made reference to them in the definitions a quick indicator of an entry's relevance.

The "Early Period" represents Arab history from approximately the seventh to the tenth centuries. It is roughly equivalent to the prominence of the "Old Arabian School," as the theorists of that period have been designated by Henry George Farmer (1965b:x-xi). Following and interpenetrating with this Early Period is a second, extending from the ninth to the late seventeenth century. It will be called the "Classical Period." "Classical" here applies to that segment of Arab-Islamic history which has been regarded as having provided the major flowering and standard of civilizational excellence. Although signs of deterioration became evident in the latter part of that period, the eight centuries it covered have generally been regarded as a golden age for the culture. It was a period which saw great creativity in every aspect of civilization as well as political and economic strength for the Arabic-speaking peoples, regardless of their racial background. It is certainly misleading to designate it as "medieval," as is often done. The qualifying "baggage" which inescapably accompanies that term borrowed from Western European history is quite inapplicable for the parallel Arab-Islamic period.

Farmer and others have preferred to divide this long span, the Classical Period, into two subdivisions: one (from the ninth to the thirteenth century) which they called the period of the Greek Scholiasts (Ibid.:xi-xiii), because of the important influence they felt that philosophical body of ideas played on the Arab music theorists of the time; the other subdivision of the Classical Period (i.e., from the thirteenth to the seventeenth century) taking its name, the "Systematist School," from another group of Greek philosophers who were seen as influential on later Arab theorists (Ibid.:xxiii-xxv). I have some difficulty with the postulation of separate "schools" to the writers of this span of time. In fact, there seems little reason to differentiate between such writers as al Fārābī and Ibn Sīnā on the one hand, and Ṣafī al Dīn and his followers on the other. For example, Ṣafī al Dīn and other so-called "Systematists" were as much prone to use the knowledge and terminology that had been acquired by the Arabs from the ancient Greeks as al Fārābī and the other so-called "Scholiasts." The theoretical works of the later writers were actually closely influenced, were even based on those of their predecessors. The Systematists, on the other hand, were no more "systematic" than the writers of the earlier centuries, as even the most superficial perusal of the works of al Fārābī and Ibn Sīnā would reveal. A third distinction between them maintained by many writers is that the theoretical scale of the Arabs and Muslims changed significantly at the time of Ṣafī al Dīn. This argument is also open to question. Instead of a drastic change in the tonal materials of the music of that time, the works of Ṣafī al Dīn and other writers who followed him present a more specific, a more practice-descriptive, or even a regionally-determined statement of the musical theory of their times. Works of the earlier Classical Period theorists had treated their subject matter in a more general and inclusive way which would be relevant over the wider geographic territory to which those writers spoke. For example, there is no melodic mode described by Ṣafī al Dīn which would be excluded from the modal system as described by al Fārābī. There is no name for any of the "famous rhythmic modes of the Arabs" (<u>al Īqā'āt al ʿArabiyyah al mashhūrah</u>) described by al Fārābī which is not included in the list given by Ṣafī al Dīn. It is true that the descriptions of the rhythmic modes by the later theorist differ from those of al Fārābī. But this is perfectly understandable, given the centuries and territorial expanse which separated the two writers, without positing a distinct change in the theory of music or its practice. Al Fārābī was a ninth-tenth century resident of regions west of the capital of Baghdād (primarily Syria); Ṣafī al Dīn lived in thirteenth century Baghdād and other centers to the east. The differences between al Fārābī and Ṣafī al Dīn, between Ibn Sīnā (d. 1037) and al Lādhiqī (15th C.) seem not to warrant our crediting the later theorists with the presentation of drastically new theoretical statements, divorced from those which preceded them. Rather, their statements vary from the earlier ones because of the particular regional and time-dictated differences between the situations known to their authors. Similar differences can be documented between al Fārābī and Ibn Sīnā.

The third time division which has significance for this glossary is called the "Modern Period." This period covers musical practice from the late seventeenth to the twentieth century. We are close enough to this Modern Period to have access to more of the details of musical terminology in various parts of the Arab World. For this reason, it was also necessary to divide the Modern Period geographically, distinguishing and naming two contemporary musical traditions which evidence a good deal of terminology variance. These will be called the "Maghribī" and the "Mashriqī" traditions. The former term, Maghribī (literally "pertaining to the West"), applies to the musical traditions of North Africa as far eastward as to include Lībyā. Mashriqī (literally "pertaining to the East") refers to the musical traditions known in Egypt and eastward to ʿIrāq. Of course even within each of these two subdivisions, further differences in musical terminology are discoverable. Wherever these differences seemed to provide useful information for the readership, they were indicated by citing the country or the sub-region where the term and/or a particular tradition have been relevant. In addition, the bibliographical reference dates the use of the term or the particular definition in question by providing the name of the author who used it.

<u>Works Consulted:</u>

The entries for this glossary are gleaned from over one hundred and fifty works on Arabian music in Arabic, English, French and German.

Of course, the Arabic works have been given priority for determining transliterations and meanings, but it was also considered advisable to include non-Arabic works in the field in order to relate the terms used in works written in Western languages to their Arabic equivalents. Thereby, this work attempts to bridge the gaps between the classical Arabic and the colloquial and dialect terminology, as well as between the classical Arabic and the varying systems of transliteration in three different Western languages. It is hoped that this glossary will be able to alleviate, if not eradicate, many problems 1) by including the correct, written form wherever possible of every Arabic term rather than only its colloquialized version; 2) by relating variant transliterations and pronunciations to these literary terms; and 3) by including cross references to many of the variant spellings which are found in the translated or original works using Western languages. All variant spellings could not be included in this work. This would have constituted an enlargement of the work not comparable with the derived benefit. A sufficient number of items, however, are included and cross referenced with their more correctly transliterated forms to give the observant user a key for deciphering the identity of other spellings when he comes in contact with them in the future.

A list, alphabetized by authors, of the works from which the entries in the glossary are derived can be found under Authors and References Cited (pp. 498-511). Readers will notice that this title (instead of the usual References Cited) presents a departure from standard practice. This departure was dictated by the need to distinguish the terminology and definitions of original authors of past centuries, first, from those of editors and translators in recent times, and second, from the transliterations of later writers. In some cases the recent editions contain works of several earlier theorists, either in Arabic or in translation, or in both forms. To identify them with the name of the contemporary translator/editor would have been to hide the identity of the user of any term and/or definition. It became evident that a twentieth century translation or edition of an al Kindī work, for example, must be included both under that theorist's name and under the name of the man who has translated and/or edited that work, if the bibliographical references were to convey accurate information concerning the provenance of a term or its meaning. Therefore, the list of sources is more a list of authors and their works than it is simply a list of books or references. The obvious benefits for quick identification of the period of relevance for the entry and its definition seemed to outweigh the complication of double listing of those works for which it was necessary. A translated work will generally reveal the Arabic term in transliteration used either in the text as a loan word or inserted as parenthetical material immediately following its translation. Rarely, reference has been made to materials where the term used is translated rather than transliterated. This occurs only where the compiler is assured that the terminology used by the translator is indeed referent to that of the entry in question, and where the translated materials are deemed especially important for the reader's understanding.

Except for authors of the Modern Period, dates of publication are utterly unreliable for determining the period in which terms or definitions were used. To counteract this difficulty, a date or dates after the name of the author will assist the reader in identifying the period of relevance for the terms and meanings in question. If no date is included, the publication year of the work will indicate the approximate production period of the author.

The sources consulted for entries includes a selection of the writings of Arab music theorists and Modern Period Western writers on Arabian music rather than an exhaustive covering of the field. In making this selection, there was a consistent attempt to include those works which are accessible to the Western student of Arabian music in the university libraries of this country and Canada, or accessible through the standard practices and technical facilities provided by such institutions (e.g., inter-library loan, microfilm). It only includes works difficult to acquire when they were considered to provide terminology or definition additions which were not available in the more readily accessible materials. It is always possible to argue that some additional work should have been included or that some work included was not necessary for achieving a truly comprehensive study. Such criticisms are difficult to counter, since it is almost impossible to document the benefit achieved from reading this or another article, from investigating this or another book. But since such criticisms are equally difficult to prove, we present the work thus far completed, with confidence that the inclusion or exclusion of single works does not drastically affect the success or failure of the project.

Because of the extensive additions that would have been necessitated, it was decided not to cover the names and specifications of melodic and rhythmic modes in this glossary. A few modal names have crept into the work because they are also used in other senses. But no systematic inclusion was intended. It is important that future research be devoted to such materials, in order to make the resultant data accessible.

Presentation of the Materials:

Each entry will begin with the Arabic word or expression carefully and consistently transliterated according to a system described in Appendix III (pp. 493-496). All entries are given in capital letters, as are all other transliterated Arabic words and phrases, as well as their variant spellings. Adjectival entries are generally given in their masculine form, with the alternative -AH feminine ending understood rather than cited. Irregular feminine forms for musical terms are, however, often included, especially when they differ markedly in spelling from the masculine form. Users should be advised that all Arabic plural nouns, except those designating human beings, take feminine singular modifiers. This accounts for the variant adjectival forms in multi-word entries. Plural forms will be given separate entries only if they diverge significantly from the singular spellings. The definite article has been omitted at the opening of entries to clarify alphabetization, except in such cases where its omission would have drastically altered the meaning of the Arabic expression. In all cases, the definite article is rendered "AL," regardless of its case-governed pronunciation in the Arabic language. The multiple spelling entry, i.e., one in which two Arabic spellings of the term are considered correct, is alphabetized according to the first of the two forms, the second spelling appearing again in its properly alphabetized position, with cross referencing (equiv. of _______) to the compound entry.

As mentioned earlier, entries are arranged according to English alphabetization. The ordering of entries is governed word by word, thus, ABŪ GHANAM and ABŪ AL ZULUF precede ABŪDHIYYAH. Hyphenated words are treated as single words, thus ABŪ-D-Duluf precedes ABŪDHIYYAH but follows ABŪ AL ZULUF. The hamzah (') and ʿayn (ʿ), letters of the Arabic alphabet which have no equivalent letter symbol in English, will be disregarded for the purposes of alphabetization (thus, TA'ALLUF will appear before TAAR) except when the entries are otherwise identical. In such cases, the entry with hamzah or ʿayn will follow the one without these letters. Some Arabic musical terms borrowed from other languages are adaptations of words including letters whose sounds have no equivalent in the Arabic alphabet (e.g., the "p", the "v" and the hard "g" sounds). Such letters occur most frequently in borrowings from the Persian and Turkish languages. In every case, these words have been transliterated to conform as closely as possible with the written Arabic form, with other spellings using the non-Arabic letters given as variants when they occur in the references consulted. Therefore, the reader will find BISTAH rather than PISTAH, BASHRAF rather than PEŚREV, BUZURK rather than BUZURG, DŪKĀH rather than DŪGĀH given in the main entry. It has not been feasible to include original forms or literal meanings for all of these loan words.

In no case should the definite article be regarded as affecting alphabetization. Particles (i.e., prepositions, conjunctions, pronouns) are considered for alphabetization only where their exclusion would erase the distinction between two entries (e.g., BUʿD ALLADHĪ BIL ARBAʿ precedes BUʿD BIL ARBAʿ) or where the particle is the initial word in the entry (e.g., ʿALĀ ITTIṢĀL and ʿALĀ INʿIṬĀF). Short voweled letters will be entered prior to long voweled ones, all other things being equal (e.g., ZIR precedes ZĪR, NIM precedes NĪM). Letters without pointing are alphabetized before those with pointing when the entries are otherwise identical (e.g., TĀR precedes ṬĀR). Otherwise, pointing is not taken into consideration in alphabetization.

Following the entry title, the plural form, wherever applicable and available, has been enclosed in parentheses. Where variant spellings of the entry are available and their inclusion is considered instructive, these are placed in the next position on the opening line and preceded by an equivalency sign (=). This is followed by the root letters of any noun, verb, adjective or adverb contained in the entry title. These are enclosed in parentheses in the following manner: (ḍ-r-b) or (k-t-b). If the entry or part of it is a foreign (i.e., non-Arabic) word which does not proceed from an Arabic root, the position of root letters is taken by an abbreviation of the language from which the word comes, for example, (Pers.), (Turk.), or (Eng.). Sometimes words were borrowed at such an early date and so thoroughly Arabicized that it is difficult to distinguish them from those derived from Arabic roots. Such words have been treated as Arabic words. When the word is not governed by a known Arabic root, derivation information is included in the place of the root letters, e.g., (geog.) for a geographic term, (onom.) for a word onomatopoetically derived, (ethn.) for the name of an ethnic group, etc. All such abbreviations, as well as others used in this glossary, are included in the list of

Abbreviations included as Appendix IV (p. 497). The last item of the opening line materials is the literal meaning of the entry title. It is enclosed by quotation marks.

The definition itself begins on a new line, with consecutive numbering for multiple definitions. In cases where no inconsistency of meaning is known to have existed over the centuries, and the entry has been very widely used, no bibliographic reference was deemed necessary. Otherwise, location of the source from which the term, spelling or information was drawn appear enclosed by parentheses following the relevant data. These references determine for the reader the source of the term as regards writer, period, and approximate geographic area. Where multiple references to a particular term were available, these are given only if such information was deemed important to the reader in establishing relevancy of the entry or its definition, or in providing a key to important materials on the use of that musical expression. Bibliographic references are therefore meant to be informative of the period in which this word and/or the given meaning was used and not to be exhaustive of the term's inclusion in the more than 150 works consulted. In the case of multiple occurrences of a particular term or expression in a single work, all instances will not be documented in the bibliographical references. Instead, the reference will, wherever possible, direct the reader to a significant and definitive use of the term in that work. Ibid. will refer to a previous bibliographical reference only within the same entry or, in the case of multiple definitions, only within the same numbered definition. Cross listing will direct the reader to related materials. When the only meaning to be conveyed is that the entry is the plural of a term with a very different spelling (a common phenomenon in Arabic and one which causes no small amount of confusion to beginning students), that information will be presented as the definition of the term. When the musical meaning to be presented is more detailed or even quite different from a purely etymological connection with the singular form of the word, the designation of the term's plural relation to another term will be given in the opening line of the entry, in the place where the plural of a singular entry is normally found; and the more significant meaning will appear as body of the definition. When words are repeated in successive compound entries, repetition of plurals are not deemed necessary.

All references to lexicographical works which alphabetize their materials from beginning to end, rather than according to topically arranged sections (e.g., Marcuse, Maʿlūf, Wehr, Madina, Elias and Elias), will provide only the compiler's name, pagination in such cases being superfluous. References to Arabic lexicographical works which utilize systems of organization which make location of terms difficult (e.g., Maḥfūẓ, al Zabīdī) will be provided with volume number and pagination.

Punctuation:

The asterisk (*) immediately following an Arabic word or expression will direct the reader to another entry, under that title, which furnishes materials that are deemed pertinent to an understanding of the term defined. Only the first such entry title used within a numbered definition will be thus marked. A diagonal (/) and a number following an Arabic word or expression will indicate the specific definition under that entry which is relevant. If no diagonal and number appears, the cross reference applies to the definition generally, rather than to one particular part of it.

Musical Notation:

Pitch Notation: The usual conventions will be followed with the addition of 𝄳 indicating a half flat or a lowering of approximately ¼ tone, and the 𝄲 for a half # or a raising of approximately ¼ tone. The Arabian scale (JADWAL) is essentially a three octave combination of tones beginning on the G below Middle C, and extending upward. The tones of the various octaves will be identified by the addition of subscript numbers in the following way:

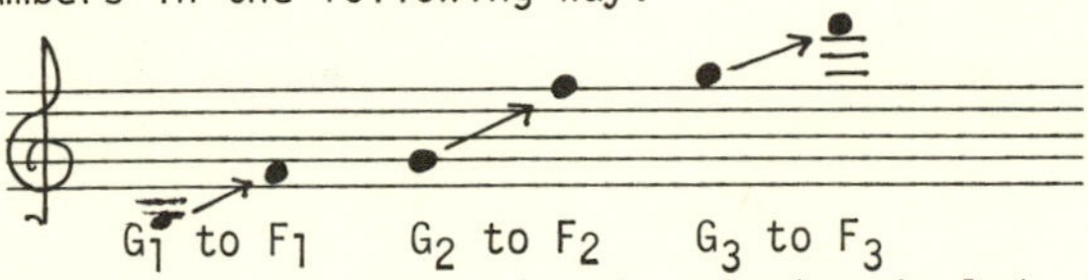

Rhythmic Notation: Notation for rhythms includes a note with descending stem (𝅘𝅥) to represent the DUM, a deep, "wet" stroke, and a note with ascending stem (♩) to represent the TAK, a light, "dry" stroke.

Supplementary Materials:

To prepare the photo-ready typescript for such an extensive work without missing any items or materials proved to be a difficult undertaking. Every effort has been made to achieve as accurate and comprehensive a product as was possible, without necessitating too many retypings to maintain space limitations and proper alphabetization. Given these demands, it was found necessary to include a Supplement immediately following the body of the glossary, which includes those items inadvertently omitted from the main body of the work. This Supplement follows the same system for presentation of materials. Reference to its entries, whether in the main body of the glossary or in the indices, is always followed by the abbreviation (supp.).

Five appendices complete the work. Appendix I comprises an Index of English Musical Terms which will facilitate location of Arabic equivalents in the glossary.

An Index of Arabic Roots is found in Appendix II. Since Arabic words are generally created by adding different prefixes, suffixes or internal consonants and/or vowels to a basic trilateral root, it is helpful to be aware of the basic letter combination from which a musical term is derived and the cognates of that term. For the advanced Arabist, these connections may sometimes be self-evident, but for the student or non-specialist, the index provides an important tool for deeper understanding and investigation. The need for distinguishing between the letters necessitated an arrangement by Arabic alphabetical order for this index. Both the letter subdivisions (e.g., alif, bā', tā', thā', etc.) and the letters within the roots themselves are arranged according to an Arabic alphabetization. Entry titles included under those roots, however, appear in the order in which they occur in the glossary text.

Appendix III provides a Guide to Pronunciation and Transliteration used for the preparation of this glossary. Generally, transliteration rules follow those of the Library of Congress (Bulletin 118/ Summer, 1976). Any alterations are specified in the Appendix, with cross referencing to the relevant portion of the Library of Congress Bulletin.

Appendix IV comprises a List of Abbreviations used in the glossary.

An alphabetical list of Authors and References Cited in this work is contained in Appendix V. Multiple listings for any one author are included in chronological order of publication dates. Items on this list will generally be identified in bibliographical references by the author's last name, the date of publication, the volume number (where applicable), and the page(s), as in (Ibn Zaylah 1964:42) or (Shiloah 1965:I, 69). Two groups of references within this list are identified in a slightly different manner in order to avoid the confusion of listing each a large number of articles using a single publication date. One group includes the numerous articles written by Hency George Farmer for The Encyclopaedia of Islam. The main volumes of this encyclopedia were published between 1913 and 1934, and a supplement followed in 1938. See the entry under Farmer 1913-1938 in Appendix V for a list of all the articles in this category which have been consulted. Reference to the Farmer articles in that encyclopedia will contain the author's last name, EI(Eng) or EI(Fr) to indicate whether the English or French edition was consulted in the case of any particular article, the title of the article (e.g., "Rabāb" or "Ṭabl") and the page number(s) which are appropriate. This information appears in the following manner: (Farmer EI(Eng), "Ghinā'":1074). The second group of articles referred to collectively in the Authors and References list includes all those written by Farmer for the 1954 edition of Grove's Dictionary of Music and Musicians. These articles are enumerated in Appendix V under Farmer 1954. Reference to them in the definitions contains the following information: author's last name, publication date, title of article, vol. no. and page(s), e.g., (Farmer 1954, "Nawba":V, 386).

Anmār Faruqi is gratefully credited for initial preparation of the Index of Arabic Roots, Taymā' and Līnā Faruqi for their updating of that index and alphabetization of its entries. My husband, Isma‘īl, helped immeasurably with proof reading of the manuscript. He was both patient and generous in furnishing much needed advice, encouragement and linguistic assistance throughout the preparation of the glossary. Without that help, the work could never have been completed. To all of these people, therefore, I offer my sincere thanks and appreciation. I share with them credit for whatever success the glossary may achieve, while absolving them of responsibility for any inaccuracies or inadequacies of the project. For those shortcomings, I alone am responsible.

Glossary

A

"A" (abbrev. for "aleph," the first letter of the Ar. alphabet)

1. This letter was used by theorists of the Classical Period to designate the shortest duration used as one percussion or unit of a rhythmic mode. It was also known as ZAMĀN AL AWWAL*, and was described as having a duration so short that no additional percussion in that space was possible (Ṣafī al Dīn 1938b:161; al Jurjānī 1938: 477; Anonymous Treatise 1939:159; al Lādhiqī 1939:459). A conjunct rhythm utilizing this length of percussion was designated as HAZAJ KHAFĪF* (Ṣafī al Dīn 1938b:160).
2. Al Kindī's designation for the lowest tone of the theoretical scale and the lowest tone on the lute (ʿŪD*) was abbreviated thus (al Kindī 1966:144; Ḥāfiẓ 1971:93). The unabbreviated term was MAFRŪDAH/1*.

ABA

A double-reed aerophone used in contemporary Egypt. It is a larger instrument than the SIBS* (Sachs 1940:248). Colloq. var. of QABĀ*.

ABʿĀD LAḤNIYYAH (pl. of BUʿD LAḤNĪ*) (b-ʿ-d) (l-ḥ-n) "melodic intervals"

As reported by al Fārābī (1930:101; 1967:270), a name given by "the ancient scholars" to all those intervals smaller than a perfect fourth. Syn. of NAGHAM ṢUGHRĀ* or MUTTAFIQĀT ṢUGHRĀ*. In the d'Erlanger translation, the equivalent is "intervalle de modulation (emmèles)" (d'Erlanger 1930:101). Al Fārābī designated them as the intervals used for creating melodies (1967:273), thus showing the importance of the stepwise melodic progression in the Arabic music of a period whose musical examples are lost to us. According to Ṣafī al Dīn and al Jurjānī, these intervals were divided further into three sub-categories: large, including intervals with ratios 5/4, 6/5 and 7/6; medium, with ratios of 8/7, 9/8 and 10/9; and small, with ratios from 11/10 to 16/15 (Ṣafī al Dīn 1938b:26-27; al Jurjānī 1939:244).

ABʿĀD MUTASHĀBIHAH AL NAGHM (pl. of BUʿD MUTASHĀBIH AL NAGHM) (b-ʿ-d) (sh-b-h) (n-gh-m) "intervals that resemble each other in tone"

Intervals having the same ratio (NISBAH*) but varying from each other in pitch by a perfect octave, a perfect fifth, or a perfect fourth (al Fārābī 1967:356).

ABʻĀD MUTASHĀKILAH AL NAGHM (pl. of BUʻD MUTASHĀKIL AL NAGHM*) (b-ʻ-d) (sh-k-l) (n-gh-m) "intervals resembling each other in tone"

As reported by al Fārābī, a name given by "the ancient scholars" to the intervals of a perfect fourth and a perfect fifth, as well as to the octave plus fourth or fifth. In the 10th C. these intervals were called MUTTAFIQĀT WUSṬĀ* or NAGHAM WUSṬĀ* (al Fārābī 1967: 270; 1930:101; Ibn Sīnā 1935:124).

ABʻĀD MUTTAFIQAH AL NAGHM (pl. of BUʻD MUTTAFIQ AL NAGHM*) (b-ʻ-d) (w-f-q) (n-gh-m) "intervals harmonious in tone"

The intervals of an octave and double octave, a name given to them by "the ancient scholars," according to al Fārābī (1967:270; 1930: 101). They were also called MUTTAFIQĀT ʻUẒMĀ* or NAGHAM ʻUẒMĀ*.

ABAḤḤ (b-ḥ-ḥ) "more hoarse or husky (of voice)"

Descriptive term for the lowest pitched string of the lute, a low-pitched lute or a low-pitched singing voice.

ABBŪBAH (thought to be a derivative of the ancient Babylonian term, IMBŪBŪ)

Syrian name for a variety of end-blown flute (Farmer 1954, "Syrian Music":251; 1931:49; ʻArnīṭah 1968:60).

ABJADĪ (derived from the first four letters of the Ar. alphabet)

Alphabetic pitch notation (Farmer 1957:454). See ʻADADĪ*.

ABRÛÂL

Single-headed cylindrical drum made of pottery, of the same type but larger than the TAʻRĪJAH/1* (Mor.) (Chottin 1939:165).

ABṬA' (b-ṭ-') "slower"

1. Slower in tempo.
2. Descriptive term for any disjunct (MUNFAṢIL/3*) rhythmic mode in which the shorter percussion(s) come after the longer in the cycle (Ibn Sīnā 1930:93; al Ḥafnī 1930:38). See ASRAʻ/2*.

ABŪ GHANAM = BU-RHANIM, BURHANIM ('-b-w) (gh-n-m) "father of the reed, or shepherd's flute"

An entertainer and player of the double clarinet folk instrument known as the ZAMR/2* among the Zemmour tribesmen, or GHANAM* (ARHANIM*) by mountain Berbers (Mor.). Among the Zemmour tribesmen, the player of the ZAMR is also known as MAWLĀ AL ZAMR* (Chottin 1939:33).

ABŪ ḲURŪN

Var. of ABŪ QURŪN* (Farmer EI(Fr), "Būḳ":45).

ABŪ QURŪN = ABŪ ḲURŪN ('-b-w) (q-r-n) "father of horns"

A very large horn thought to have been of conical bore which is mentioned in a 13th C. ms. from Moorish Spain.

ABŪ AL ZULUF ='ABŪ-Z-ZELŪF, ABU-D̲-D̲ULUF ('-b-w) (z-l-f) "father of ZULUF"

A melismatic, recitative-like folksong of Lebanon which is similar to the MAWWĀL/1*. It is a musical setting of dialect poetry with strophes of four lines and a characteristic monorhyme "-AYYAH" or "-IYYAH" (Jargy 1978:86-87). There are numerous repetitions of the latter part of the musical lines as well, thus giving the impression of an alternation between free and regular rhythm as has been described by Reichow (1971:141). Also UMM AL ZULUF* ("mother of ZULUF") (Jargy 1970:40).

ABU-D̲-D̲ULUF

Var. of ABŪ AL ZULUF* (Reichow 1971:19-20).

ABŪDHIY̲YAH = ABŪDĪYA, ABŪZIYYAH, ABŪD̲IYYA, BŪḌIYA ('-b-w) ('-dh-y), from ABŪ ADHIYYAH (?), "father of trouble, grievance"

A variety of folksong enjoying great popularity in ʿIrāq. It is similar to the ʿATĀBĀ* in being a musical setting of strophes containing four poetic lines, the final line always ending with the characteristic assonance--in this case "-IYYAH" or "-IYYĀ." It also resembles the ʿATĀBĀ in the recitative-like character of its melodic line. Nostalgia and sadness are usual topics, but other themes such as love, courage, praise, etc., are also found (al Ikhtiyār n.d.:111-112). The generally sad character of the themes may account for its name, if our hypothesis of derivation is correct (see above). It has been defined as a piece having no end (Jargy 1970:43).

ABŪDĪYA

Var. of ABŪDHIYYAH* (Farmer 1954, "Iraqian and Mesopotamian Music": IV, 532).

ABŪD̲IYYA

Var. of ABŪDHIYYAH* (Jargy 1970:222).

'ABU-Z-ZELUF

Var. of ABŪ AL ZULUF* (Jargy 1970:73).

ABŪZIYYAH

Var. of ABŪDHIYYAH* (Bashīr 1978:76).

ABWĀQ (b-w-q)

Pl. of BŪQ*.

ABYĀT (b-y-t) "verses of poetry"

1. Pl. of BAYT/1*.

2. A vocal number of the NAWBAH/1* suite (Tun.), which is a musical setting of classical poetry. The ABYĀT is comparable to the QAṢĪDAH/1* of the Mashriq and is sometimes replaced by it. This movement, considered to be the most noble segment of the NAWBAH, begins with a short instrumental prelude (DUKHŪL*) in rapid 2/4 rhythm followed by the solemn ABYĀT in slow 4/4 with a minimum of embellishment (d'Erlanger 1959:147).

ACHTÂR EL-ÛWLIN

Var. of ASHṬĀR AL ŪLĀ* (Chottin 1939:160).

AÇL

Var. of AṢL/6* (Chottin 1939:140).

ADĀ' AL ALḤĀN (pl. ADĀ'ĀT) ('-d-y) (l-ḥ-n) "rendering, performance"

Musical performance (al Fārābī 1967:51ff).

A'DĀD (pl. of 'ADAD) ('-d-d) "numbers"

A category of TAḤSĪN AL LAḤN* (Ibn Sīnā 1930:99; Ibn Zaylah 1964:18).

'ADADĪ ('-d-d) "numerical"

A durational notation utilizing numbers (Farmer 1957:454). See ABJADĪ*.

AḌ'AFA (ḍ-'-f) "to make (something) double"

To "double" a tone by playing its octave equivalent (Ibn al Munajjim 1976:219).

(al) ADAQQ (d-q-q) "most tight"

Said of strings of a musical instrument which are tightened to produce the high pitches (al Khwārizmī 1968:238).

ADHĀN = ADZÂNE ('-dh-n) "hearing; proclamation"

The call to prayer which is cantillated five times a day from the minaret of the mosque. There are two ways of doing the ADHĀN, according to el Helou (1961:201): 1) LAYTHĪ*, the older form which is close to recitative and is popular in the villages; and 2) SULṬĀNĪ*, a less recitative-like rendering which is popular in Egypt. In Indonesia the sound of a drum is sometimes added to the human voice in order for the signal for prayer time to be heard through the forest. Trumpets and drums have been used during the annual pilgrimage to Makkah in order to assure the announcement's being heard by the great crowds of people (El-Kholy 1954:59). Today, of course, loudspeakers preclude the need for other means to insure that the call is audible to all concerned.

ĀDHĀN AL 'ŪD ('-dh-n) ('-w-d) "ears of the 'ŪD"

Pl. of UDHN AL 'ŪD*. Tuning pegs of the lute.

ADID ('-d-d?) "number, quantity"?

General name for music of the Arabian/Persian Gulf region performed at weddings and healing ceremonies (Touma 1977a:122).

ADJAM

Var. of ʿAJAM* (Touma 1977b:37).

ADOR

Var. of DAWR/7* (Ribera 1970:87-88).

AḌRAB AL NĀS BIL WATAR (ḍ-r-b) (n-w-s) (w-t-r) "the most capable of the people who strike the string"

The best of performers on stringed instruments (Ibn ʿAbd Rabbihi 1887:III, 190; 1943/44:58).

ADUFE

Var. of (al) DAFF or DUFF* (Ribera 1970:92; Perkuhn 1976:179).

ADZÂNE

Var. of ADHĀN* (Rouanet 1922:2940).

AFERDI (f-r-d?)

A Berber song used in the music-poetry-dance performance of the Middle Atlas mountain areas (Mor.). Its rhythm is somewhat different in emphasis from that of the IZLI*, but it retains the 5-beat measure (Chottin 1939:22).

AGHĀNĪ (gh-n-y)

Pl. of UGHNIYAH*. See also GHINĀ'*.

AGHANIM

Var. of (al) GHANAM* (Marcuse).

AGHÂNÎM

Var. of (al) GHANAM*, a woodwind instrument of Morocco (Chottin 1961: Band IX, col. 1565).

AGHANN, f. GHANNĀ' (gh-n-n) "nasal"

Melodious (said of a voice).

AGRĪ

A type of harp with pronounced "hump back," described by ʿAbd al Qādir ibn Ghaybī in the 15th C. It was strung similarly to the Persian harp but had a wooden instead of a skin face (Farmer EI(Eng), "Miʿzaf":529).

AGWĀL

Var. of AQWĀL/1* (Chottin 1961:Band IX, col. 1567) and AQWĀL/2* (Grame 1970:86).

AḤADD (ḥ-d-d) "more sharp"

Higher in pitch. See also QAWĪ DHŪ AL TAḌʿĪF*.

ĀHANG or ĀHANK (Pers.) "song, tune, gamut"

1. Range or compass (e.g., of a melodic mode) (Anonymous Treatise 1939:237).
2. Vocal range (Anonymous Treatise 1939:251-252).
3. A coda-like section near the end of the DAWR/5*, a vocal genre of modern Egypt. In this section of repetitions and improvisation within the contrast segment (GHUṢN/1*) of the DAWR, the vocal soloist performs elaborate vocalise-like passages on the syllable "ĀH" or on certain phrases of the poem. After each solo improvisation, the chorus (MADHHAB/3*) responds with repetitions and complementary phrases at a lower register (d'Erlanger 1959:179). Also called ĀHĀT* (al Helou 1961:191), HANK/1* (Maḥfūẓ 1964:107; Ḥāfiẓ 1971:206; Touma 1977b:84).
4. The good effect brought about in the listener from metered musical sounds (Kāẓim 1964:23).
5. The sound or pitch used as a tuning standard for musical instruments (Kāẓim 1964:23).

ĀHĀT (pl. of the exclamation "ĀH")

1. Repetitions of the syllable "āh" as verbal content of an improvised or composed melodic passage (Ḥāfiẓ 1971:198).
2. Syn. of ĀHANG or ĀHANK/3*.

AḤAṬṬ (ḥ-ṭ-ṭ) "lower"

Lower in pitch (al Fārābī 1967:794).

AHĀZĪJ (h-z-j)

Pl. of UHZŪJAH*.

AHELLEL (h-l-l?)

A kind of popular Berber song which resembles TAHLĪL* or religious chant (Chottin 1939:22).

AHIDOUS = 'AHIDUS, AH'IDOUS (h-d-w) or (h-d-y)

The music-poetry-dance performance of the Berber peoples of the Middle Atlas Mountains (Mor.). If accompanied by beatings of the feet and/or hands, it is called TAMHAWST*. If accompanied with percussion instruments, it is called TAMSERALIT* (Chottin 1939: 15-22).

AH'IDOUS

Var. of AHIDOUS* (Chottin 1939:16).

'AHÎDÛS

Var. of AHIDOUS* (Chottin 1961:Band IX, col. 1564).

AḤJĀL (ḥ-j-l)

Pl. of ḤIJL* (Farmer 1945:37).

AHOUACH or AH'OUACH

Vars. of AḤWĀSH* (Chottin 1939:13).

AHOUZI

Var. of (al) ḤAWZĪ* (Delphin and Guin 1886:30), both spellings given (one in Ar. script, the other in transliteration).

AḤWĀSH (ḥ-w-sh)

A music-poetry-dance performance of the Berbers of the southern regions of the Atlas Mountains (Mor.). It is similar to AHIDOUS* in its combination of an undulating choral chain dance of men or women, its improvised vocal numbers and poetry, and its sharply defined rhythms (Chottin 1939:23-31).

ʿAIR

Drum mentioned by a 14th C. writer. Farmer suggests that the text may have been misread and that the instrument is actually the KABAR* (Farmer 1978:II, 31).

'AÏTA

Var. of ʿAYṬAH* (Chottin 1939:163).

AʿJAL (ʿ-j-l) "more hurried"

A tempo faster than ʿĀJIL*, and comparable to Allegro (al Ḥafnī 1946:287; Maḥfūẓ 1964:177).

ʿAJAM = ADJAM, 'AJEM (ʿ-j-m) "foreigner; Persian"

1. Contemporary tetrachord (JINS/1*) of 1-1-½ division.
2. Contemporary melodic mode (MAQĀM/1*) utilizing the tetrachord of the same name as fundamental or lower member of the octave scale.
3. Name for a note of the contemporary Arab scale, Bb_2 or $A\#_2$

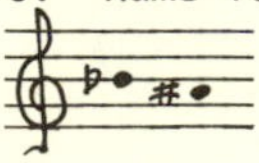 .

'AJEM

Var. of ʿAJAM* (Smith 1847:182).

AJHAR (j-h-r) comp. of "loud"

Louder in instrumental or vocal sound.

ʿĀJIL (ʿ-j-l) "immediate"

A lively tempo comparable to Allegretto (al Ḥafnī 1946:287; Maḥfūẓ 1964:177).

ʿAJJALA (ʿ-j-l) "to hurry"

To accelerate; to play or sing rapidly.

AJNĀS MUFRADAH (j-n-s) (f-r-d)

Pl. of JINS MUFRAD*. Also see JINS/1*.

AJRĀS (j-r-s)

Pl. of JARAS*.

ʿAJZ (ʿ-j-z) "backside, rear; last part"

Second hemistich of a line of poetry, also called MIṢRĀʿ* (el Helou 1961:196).

AKHLĀQ (pl. of KHULQ or KHULUQ*) (kh-l-q) "tempers, natures"

Term used by al Kindī, al Masʿūdī, Ikhwān al Ṣafā' and others to apply to the natures (black bile, blood, phlegm, yellow bile), each of which the theorists of the early centuries of the Classical Period associated with one or more of the melodic modes. In the Maghrib, the term ṬABĀ'Iʿ (s. ṬABĪʿAH*) was used to convey the same meaning (Farmer 1933b:11; see also p. 39).

AḲWĀL

Var. of AQWĀL/1* (Farmer EI(Fr), "Ṭabl":231).

'ÂLA

Var. of ʿĀLAH* or syn. of ʿĀLAH ANDALUSIYYAH* (Chottin 1939:107-108).

ʿALĀ INʿIṬĀF (ʿ-ṭ-f) "indirect; inclined, bent"

Transverse, e.g., said of the flute. See also INTIQĀL ʿALĀ INʿIṬĀF*.

ʿALĀ ITTIṢĀL (w-ṣ-l) "with connection"

Syn. of MUTTAṢIL/1*, a category of melodic movement (INTIQĀL/1*) described by al Fārābī as comprising steady movement in one direction without leaps (al Fārābī 1967:967).

ĀLAH, (pl. ĀLĀT) ('-w-l) "tool, instrument; apparatus"

1. Musical instrument.

2. Syn. of ĀLAH ANDALUSIYYAH*.

ĀLAH ANDALUSIYYAH (ʿ-w-l) (geog.) "Andalusian shelter or umbrella"

The classical vocal and instrumental music of Morocco which is said to be derived from the Andalusian tradition. In its widest sense, the term represents all classical music of the area, but above all the secular rather than religious vocal music (Chottin 1939:107-108). Syn. of ṢANʿAH* (Mor.) and MA'LŪF* (used in other parts of the Maghrib).

ĀLAH DHĀT AL AWTĀR ('-w-l) (w-t-r) "instrument possessing strings"

Stringed musical instrument, i.e., a chordophone.

ĀLAH DHĀT AL NAFKH ('-w-l) (n-f-kh) "instrument possessing breath"

Wind instrument, i.e., an aerophone.

ĀLAH DHĀT AL RIQQ ('-w-l) (r-q-q) "instrument possessing a membrane"

Any membranophone (al Ḥafnī 1971:27).

ĀLAH ĪQĀʿ ('-w-l) (w-q-ʿ) "instrument of rhythm"

Any percussion instrument.

ĀLAH ĪQĀʿIYYAH ('-w-l) (w-q-ʿ) "rhythmic instrument"

Any percussion instrument.

ĀLAH LAHW ('-w-l) (l-h-w) "instrument of amusement or diversion"

Any musical instrument.

ĀLAH MALĀHĪ ('-w-l) (l-h-w) "instrument of places of diversion"

This term was used for musical instrument in the 1001 Nights (Farmer 1945:25).

ĀLAH MUṢAWWITAH BI DHĀTIHĀ ('-w-l) (ṣ-w-t) "instrument sounded with itself"

Any idiophone (al Ḥafnī 1971:27).

ĀLAH MŪSĪQĀ ('-w-l) (Gr.) "instrument of music"

Any musical instrument.

ĀLAH MŪSĪQIYYAH ('-w-l) (Gr.) "musical instrument"

Any musical instrument.

ĀLAH MŪSĪQĀRIYYAH ('-w-l) (Gr.) "a musician's instrument"

Any musical instrument (Shiloah 1968a:237, 245).

ĀLAH NAFKH ('-w-l) (n-f-kh) "instrument of breath"

Any wind instrument, i.e., an aerophone.

ĀLAH NAQR ('-w-l) (n-q-r) "instrument of percussion"

Any percussion instrument.

ĀLAH ṢINĀʿIYYAH ('-w-l) (ṣ-n-ʿ) "constructed instrument"

Any musical instrument (al Fārābī 1960:11, 14). Opp. of ĀLAH ṬABĪʿIYYAH*.

ĀLAH ṬABĪʿIYYAH ('-w-l) (ṭ-b-ʿ) "natural instrument"

Any of the vocal "instruments" of the human body, e.g., vocal chords, larynx (al Fārābī 1960:11, 14). Opp. of ĀLAH ṢINĀʿIYYAH*.

ĀLAH ṬARAB ('-w-l) (ṭ-r-b) "instrument of musical delight"

Any musical instrument (Ibn Abī al Dunyā 1938:19, 41; al Khulaʿī 1904: 47).

ĀLAH WATARIYYAH ('-w-l) (w-t-r) "stringed instrument"

Any musical instrument with strings, i.e., a chordophone.

ĀLAH ZAMR ('-w-l) (z-m-r) "wind instrument"

A mechanical device similar to the organ (Farmer 1945:33).

ʿALĀMAH ʿĀRIḌAH (ʿ-l-m) (ʿ-r-ḍ) "sign of something non-essential, accidental"

Grace note (el Helou 1961:55).

ʿALĀMAH ILGHĀ' (ʿ-l-m) (l-gh-w) "sign of cancellation"

Natural sign in musical notation (al Ḥafnī 1946:286; Maḥfūẓ 1964: 187).

ʿALĀMAH AL KHAFḌ (ʿ-l-m) (kh-f-ḍ) "sign of lowering"

Flat sign (al Ḥafnī 1946:286; Maḥfūẓ 1964:192).

ʿALĀMAH MANQŪṬAH (ʿ-l-m) (n-q-ṭ) "dotted sign"

Dotted note (Maḥfūẓ 1964:187).

ʿALĀMAH MŪSĪQIYYAH (ʿ-l-m) (Gr.) "music sign"

Sign for a note in musical notation (Maḥfūẓ 1964:187).

ʿALĀMAH RAFʿAH (ʿ-l-m) (r-f-ʿ) "sign of raising"

Sharp sign(al Ḥafnī 1946:286; Maḥfūẓ 1964:195).

ʿALĀMAH AL TAḤWĪL (ʿ-l-m) (ḥ-w-l) "sign of transformation"

Any accidental in musical notation (el Helou 1961:36; Maḥfūẓ 1964:187).

ʿALĀMAH AL TAḤWĪL AL MUḌĀʿAF (ʿ-l-m) (ḥ-w-l) (ḍ-ʿ-f) "sign of double transformation"

Double sharp or double flat (Maḥfūẓ 1964:187).

ʿALĀMAH AL TANAZZUL (ʿ-l-m) (n-z-l) "sign of lowering"

Decrescendo sign (Maḥfūẓ 1964:187).

ʿALĀMAH AL TAṢAʿʿUD (ʿ-l-m) (ṣ-ʿ-d) "sign of going up"

Crescendo sign (Maḥfūẓ 1964:187).

ĀLĀT AL ḤARAKĀT ('-w-l) (ḥ-r-k) "instruments of motion"

Category of unidentified musical instruments which make a plaintive sound, according to al Khwārizmī. Farmer speculates that they may have been automatic hydraulic instruments (Farmer 1931:117). See ḤANNĀNAH*.

ĀLĀTĪ (pl. ĀLĀTIYAH) ('-w-l) "belonging to instruments"

1. Instrumentalist.
2. A male professional musician, either vocalist or instrumentalist (Lane 1973:354).

ALATYE

Var. of ĀLĀTĪ* (Kieswetter 1968:94).

ALḤĀN (l-ḥ-n)

Pl. of LAḤN*.

ALḤĀN BIL IṬLĀQ (l-ḥ-n) (ṭ-l-q) "tunes with the release or setting free"

A melody without sections (al Ḥafnī, introduction to al Fārābī 1967:13).

ALḤĀN JUZ'IYYAH (l-ḥ-n) (j-z-') "partitioned melodies"

A melody or song with sections or divisions (al Fārābī 1967:880). See ṬARĪQAH/3*.

ALḤĀN KĀMILAH (l-ḥ-n) (k-m-l) "perfect melodies"

Vocal music (al Fārābī 1967:68; 1960:13, 16).

ĀLĪ (pl. ĀLIYYUN) = 'ÂLÎ, 'ĀLI 'ALÎ

Professional musician (Mor.), both vocalist and instrumentalist (Chottin 1939:108).

ʿĀLIM (pl. ʿULAMĀ') (ʿ-l-m) "learned man"

1. Religious learned man and teacher who instructs students in Qur'ānic cantillation.
2. Professional male dancer or musician.

ʿĀLIMAH (pl. ʿAWĀLIM) (ʿ-l-m) "learned woman"

Professional female musician or singer (Farmer 1945:20; Lane 1973: 355; Ḥāfiẓ 1971:192; Racy 1978a:51). The name is indicative of the many accomplishments of these singing girls.

ALLUN

Berber name for the BANDĪR*, a large frame drum of the Maghrib (Chottin 1939:33).

ʿAMAD and ʿAMĀD

Var. of ʿIMĀD/1* (Rouanet 1922:2701). As ʿAMĀD, var. of ʿIMĀD/2*.

ʿAMAL (ʿ-m-l) "work; performance, execution"

1. A genre of song setting Persian poetry to music which had a short rhythmic cycle and a lively tempo. Each composition of this genre opened with an introduction (MAṬLAʿ/1* or ṬARĪQAH/3*), then a second prelude (JADWAL/2*), followed by a melismatic section called ṢAWT AL WASAṬ* or MIYAT KHĀNAH*, and one or two refrain sections (TASHYĪʿAH* or BAZKISHT*) (ʿAbd al Qādir ibn Ghaybī, quoted in Anonymous Treatise 1939:244).
2. The performance of vocal or instrumental music.

ʿAMALĪ (ʿ-m-l) "pertaining to work"

Practical as opposed to theoretical (NAẒARĪ*), in regard to the art of music (Farmer 1943:15).

AMESSAD

The poet-singer of the Berber music-poetry-dance performance known as AHIDOUS* (Chottin 1939:21).

AMEZ'AD or AMEZʿAD

South Algerian bowed chordophone. The illustration in Chottin and Hickmann 1949-1951:Band I, col. 584) shows a short necked, single stringed bowed instrument with a round face. The bow is hemispheric in shape. See AMZ'AD*.

AMGHAR = AMRHAR

Leader of a group of Berber musicians (Mor.) (Chottin 1939:33). Also MAWLĀ AL ZAMR*, SHAYKH/5*.

AMHAL (m-h-l) "more leisurely"

A more leisurely tempo than MĀHIL*, and comparable to Adagio (al Ḥafnī 1946:287; Maḥfūẓ 1964:177).

Aʿ MIDAH (ʿ-m-d)

Pl. of ʿAMŪD/3* (Farmer 1926a:244, taking information from Ibn Zaylah).

ʿAMILA (ʿ-m-l) "to do ; to execute"

To perform musically (Farmer 1945:43).

AMRHAR

Var. of AMGHAR* (Chottin 1939:33).

ʿAMŪD (pl. AʿMIDAH) = ʿUMŪD (ʿ-m-d) "support, prop; centerpole"

1. The fundamental time unit (basic beat) (Ikhwān al Ṣafā' 1957: I, 198). The Ikhwān mention four basic time units: 1) ʿAMŪD AL AWWAL*; 2) ʿAMŪD AL THĀNĪ*; 3) ʿAMŪD AL THĀLITH*; and 4) ʿAMŪD AL RĀBIʿ*, proceeding from shortest to longest.
2. Neck of a lute or viol (Egypt) (Farmer 1978:II, 63).
3. Support for the strings of a psaltery or dulcimer (Ibn Zaylah in Farmer 1926a:244).

ʿAMŪD AL AWWAL (ʿ-m-d) ('-w-l) "first ʿAMŪD"

The shortest of possible fundamental time units. Also called KHAFĪF* (Ikhwān al Ṣafā' 1957:I, 200), it is notated by Shiloah (1964-1965: 146) as "O". See ʿAMŪD/1*.

ʿAMŪD AL RĀBIʿ (ʿ-m-d) (r-b-ʿ) "fourth ʿAMŪD"

The longest of the four possible fundamental time units described by the Ikhwān al Ṣafā'(1957:I, 200). Also called THAQĪL AL THĀNĪ*, it is notated by Shiloah as "O..." (1964-1965:146). See ʿAMŪD/1*.

ʿAMŪD ṬARĪQAH (ʿ-m-d) (ṭ-r-q) "fundamental ṬARĪQAH"

A kind of instrumental prelude mentioned in Kitāb al Aghānī. See ṬARĪQAH/3*.

ʿAMŪD AL THĀLITH (ʿ-m-d) (th-l-th) "third ʿAMŪD"

The third unit of the four possible fundamental time units described by the Ikhwān al Ṣafā' (1957:I, 200). Also called THAQĪL AL AWWAL*, it is notated by Shiloah as "O.." (1964-1965:146). See ʿAMŪD/1*.

ʿAMŪD AL THĀNĪ (ʿ-m-d) (th-n-y) "second ʿAMŪD"

The second unit of the four possible fundamental time units described by the Ikhwān al Ṣafā' (1957:I, 200). Also called KHAFĪF AL THĀNĪ*, it is notated by Shiloah as "O." (1964-1965:146). See ʿAMŪD/1*.

AMZ'AD

A single-stringed spike fiddle of the North African Tuareg, with a body made from a gourd and covered with goatskin. It is either plucked or bowed (Marcuse). According to Shiloah (1965:I, 30), it is only played by women. See AMEZ'AD*.

ĀNĀ MAQĀM (?) (q-w-m)

The melodic mode considered to be the basic one from which all other modes are derived. In recent centuries, this has usually been RĀST/2* (al Dāqūqī 1965:14). Also MAQĀM AL UMM*.

ANĀBĪB (n-b-b)

Pl. of UNBŪB*.

ʿANĀṢIR AL ARBAʿ (s. ʿUNṢUR) (ʿ-n-ṣ-r) (r-b-ʿ) "four elements"

The four elements or temperaments which were related to the four strings of the lute by the theorists of the Classical Period (d'Erlanger 1939:519-520).

ANF (pl. UNŪF) ('-n-f) "nose; pride"

1. The nut of a stringed instrument, such as the long or short necked lute, which marks the upper end of the vibrating portion of the string or strings. It is a thin piece of ivory, wood or plastic fastened to the upper end of the neck of the instrument over which the strings pass in order to avoid touching the fingerboard.
2. A piece of wood fixed firmly to the sound box of the QĀNŪN* at the inside of the mount for the tuning pegs. The strings pass through thin grooves in this ANF before being fastened to the tuning pegs (Lane 1973:358-359).

ANFĀR (n-f-r)

Pl. of NAFĪR* (Farmer 1954, "Egyptian Music":893).

ANFUR (n-f-r)

Pl. of NAFĪR* (Marcuse).

ANGALYŪN

A musical instrument which al Hujwīrī (d. ca. 1072) says was used by Gr. doctors for its therapeutic effect (Robson 1938c:4).

ANGHĀM (n-gh-m)

Pl. of NAGHAM*, NAGHM*.

ʿANQĀ' (ʿ-n-q) "a legendary bird, griffon or phoenix; something or some-one long-necked"

Ancient instrument mentioned by Ibn Sīnā (1935:233, where the final

HAMZAH is unfortunately missing) and Ibn Zaylah (Farmer 1926a:244). It is thought that this instrument was a trapezoidal psaltery with strings of different lengths. It was not mentioned after the 11th C. (Farmer EI(Eng), "Miʿzaf":529-530).

ANSHADA (n-sh-d) "to recite, chant"

1. To sing.
2. To recite poetry or chant it.

ANSHŪDAH (n-sh-d)

Regularly rhythmed song according to Farmer (1945:43). Probably a var. of UNSHŪDAH*.

ANWĀʿ (n-w-ʿ)

Pl. of NAWʿ*.

AOUADAH

Var. of ʿAWWĀDAH/2*, the musical ensemble (Tun.) (Touma 1977b:111).

AOUDJ

Var. of AWJ* (Touma 1977b:37).

AQĀWĪL (pl. of QAWL*) (q-w-l) "sayings, utterances"

Lyrics (al Fārābī 1967:1093; Ikhwān al Ṣafā' 1957:I, 218).

ʿAQD (pl. ʿUQŪD) (ʿ-q-d) "tie; knotting; circle"

1. Any tetrachordal or pentachordal segment with its internal intervallic division from which modal scales are composed. The term was first used in this sense by Iskandar Shalfūn, an early 20th C. Egyptian musician. See ʿIQD*, a word with identical Ar. spelling.
2. A contemporary term for a JINS/1* that has five tones rather than the usual four, i.e., a pentachord (Ṣalāḥ al Dīn 1950:100).

ʿAQĪRAH (pl. ʿAQĪRĀT) (ʿ-q-r) "core, center"

1. The sound of a vocalist, wailer or QĀRI'/1*.
2. The end of a musical sound (Maḥfūẓ 1964:118).

AQLIGH

Castanets used by the dancers of Egypt, according to Villoteau (Farmer EI(FR), "Ṣandj":210).

AQRAʿ (q-r-ʿ) "bald"

Said of a MUWASHSHAḤ/1* which lacks an opening presentation of the refrain (al Ṣafadī 1966:21).

AQSĀM BUʿD DHĪ AL ARBAʿ or AQSĀM BUʿD DHĪ AL KHAMS (s. QISM BUʿD . . .) (q-s-m) (b-ʿ-d) (r-b-ʿ) or (kh-m-s) "partitions of the tetrachord" or "partitions of the pentachord"

The seven tetrachordal or twelve pentachordal species from which the 84 octave scales or ADWĀR (s. DAWR/4*) of Ṣafī al Dīn were derived by changes in position or order (Ṣafī al Dīn 1938b:Chaps. 5, 6).

AQṢĀQ (Turk.) "lame"

Said of a rhythmic mode (ĪQĀʿ/1*) which includes both binary and ternary subdivisions of the repeated cycle (d'Erlanger 1959:33). Also known as AʿRAJ*.

AQWĀL = AGWĀL, AḲWĀL, ABRÛÂL (q-w-l) "words, utterances"

1. A goblet drum, with clay body and single head, of the Maghrib. Similar to the DARABUKKAH*, this drum has been known since medieval times. Today it is double the size of the TAʿRĪJAH* (Marcuse).
2. According to Grame (1970:8), this name is given to the BANDĪR* by the Berbers of Morocco.

ʿARABAH (pl. ʿARABĀT) (ʿ-r-b) "a river which runs swiftly; a vehicle"

1. Any of the intermediary notes between the tones of the scale of mode RĀST*, the fundamental scale of the contemporary Arabs of the Mashriq. These are the quarter tone intervals into which the scale had already been theoretically divided by the time of Villoteau (d. 1839) (Maḥfūẓ 1964:89). A more precise definition is found in el Helou (1961:68) and Ṣalāḥ al Dīn(1950:90), where the ʿARABAH applies only to the notes halfway between the extremities of the whole tone interval of the contemporary fundamental scale of the Arabs (RĀST). Since three quarters occur between some tones of that scale, and four quarters between others, the ʿARABĀT do not always fall precisely at the midpoint between scale tones. Farmer has equated the ʿARABAH with "quarter-tone" (1954, "Iraqian and Mesopotamian Music":IV, 531), while Spector (1970:244) uses it as an equivalent of "semitone." See also NĪM ʿARABAH* and TĪK ʿARABAH*.
2. Any of the small metal pieces (pl. ʿURAB*) fastened near the strings at the left side of the QĀNŪN* which permit pitch adjustments.

ʿARABĪ DŪDUK (ʿ-r-b) (Turk.) "Arabian DUDUK"

A woodwind instrument, probably of the recorder type, invented at Nablus and played by the monks of the Holy Sepulchre at Jerusalem (Farmer 1976b:20). Farmer suggests that it may have been identical to the ṢAFFĀRAH* or ṢUFFĀRAH* of Egypt which was mentioned by Villoteau (d. 1839).

ʿARABĪ ZŪRNĀ ('-r-b) (Turk.) "Arabian oboe"

This woodwind instrument with double reed is said to have been invented in Syria, but was used in various regions of the Mashriq (Farmer 1976b:26).

ʿARĀḌĀ

Var. of ʿARḌAH* (Jargy 1970:145).

ʿARĀḌAH (ʿ-r-ḍ) "act of widening; displaying"

Syn. of ʿARḌAH* (Jargy 1970:112-113).

ARĀḌĪ ('-r-ḍ) "basic things; lands"

Tonic of a melodic mode (Maḥfūẓ 1964:185); al Ḥafnī 1947:290).

ARĀGHĪL (r-gh-l)

Pl. of ARGHŪL*.

ARĀGHIN (r-gh-n)

Pl. of URGHAN or URGHANŪM* (Ikhwān al Ṣafā' 1957:I, 202).

AʿRAJ (ʿ-r-j) "lame"

Said of a rhythmic mode (ĪQĀʿ/1*) which includes both binary and ternary subdivisions within the repeated cycle (d'Erlanger 1959:33). Also known as AQṢĀQ*.

ARBAʿAH MUTATĀLIYAH (r-b-ʿ) (t-l-w) "a succession of four"

A scalar segment of four successive tones (al Kindī 1966:143, 161). Cowl's definition, "chain of fourths" (1966:143, 150), is not tenable. In this reference, it is not the fourths that al Kindī is considering as consecutive; rather, he speaks of a unit in which there are four consecutive tones.

ARBĀB (r-b-b) "masters"

A folk instrument of the double clarinet type (Mor.) (Chottin 1939: 37).

ʿARḌAH = ʿARĀḌAH, ARDHA, ʿARĀḌĀ (ʿ-r-ḍ) "a demonstration or presentation"

A folk dance with war theme performed by the Bedouins of the Arabian Peninsula or the Gulf area (Touma 1977a:122). Some versions of this dance are also found among sedentary Arab peoples, e.g., the ʿARĀḌAH* of Syria (Jargy 1970:112-113).

ʿARḌĀWĪ (ʿ-r-ḍ)

1. A NAWBAH/1* or suite in the musical tradition of the ʿĪsāwiyyah brotherhood of Tunisia (Jones 1977:290).
2. A folkish melodic mode (Tun.) (Jones 1977:290).
3. A folkish rhythmic mode (Tun.) (Jones 1977:290).

ARDHA

Probably a var. of ʿARḌAH* (Olsen 1967:28).

ARDIN or ARDINE

A 10-12 stringed angular harp of the Moors of Mauretania. It has a calabash resonator covered with skin which is drummed upon as accompaniment to the plucking of the strings. This instrument is played exclusively by women (Marcuse).

AREDDAD (r-d-d) perhaps a var. of (al) RADDĀD, "the one who returns or repeats"

Accompanists in the ensemble of professional, itinerant musicians of Morocco. There are generally three of them. One plays the large circular frame drum (BANDĪR*), while the others play the popular single headed drum known as TAʿRĪJAH* (Chottin 1939:33).

ARGHAN or ARGHANŪM

Vars. of URGHAN or URGHANŪM/1* (Farmer 1978:I, 56; al Lādhiqī 1939: 269; Marcuse).

ARGHOÛL

Var. of ARGHŪL or URGHŪL* (Hickmann 1958:17).

ARGHŪL or URGHŪL = ARGHŪN, ARGŪL, ʿARQŪN, ARGHOÛL, ARGOUL, ʿARḲŪN, YARGHOUL, YARGHŪL, ARǦUL

A single reed aerophone (clarinet type) with two pipes of different lengths. The longer pipe has no fingerholes and is used as a drone. It is made of several detachable extensions so that its pitch can be adjusted according to need. It can reach a length of over 2 m The shorter pipe is called RA'ĪS/4* because it is the "leader" or melody producer. This folk instrument is used today in the Mashriq (al Ḥafnī 1971:178) and the Maghrib (el Mahdi 1972:52) and is known in earlier centuries as well (Farmer EI(Eng), "Mizmār":541). It produces a very harsh sound (Lane 1973:367-368).

ARGHŪN

Var. of ARGHŪL or URGHŪL* (Farmer EI(Eng), "Mizmār":541).

ARGOUL

Var. of ARGHUL OR URGHUL* (Touma 1977b:105).

ARGŪL or ARǦUL

Vars. of ARGHŪL or URGHŪL* (Marcuse).

ARHANIM

Var. of GHANAM* (Chottin 1939:33, 37-38).

ʿARḲUN

Var. of ARGHŪL or URGHŪL* (Farmer EI(Eng), "Mizmār":541).

ARMŪNĪQĪ (Gr.)

Panpipes in ʿAbbāsī Period and subsequent centuries (Farmer 1967:210; Ikhwān al Ṣafā' 1957:I, 202).

ARNABAH "female hare"

Egyptian spike fiddle (El-Kholy 1978:13). According to ʿArnīṭah (1968:54), it has fallen into disuse.

A'ROUBIA

Var. of ʿARŪBIYYAH* (Delphin and Guin 1886:35-36).

ARRABIL

An instrument similar to the RABĀB or RABĀBAH/1*, according to Farmer (1976a:231).

ʿARṬABAH

A synonym for the short-necked lute (ʿŪD/2*), according to Ibn Salamah and a 14th C. treatise (Ibn Salamah 1951:82; Farmer 1978: II, 31). In Farmer 1967:209, the word is spelled AWṬABAH. Some Arab lexicographers maintained that it was used for a drum as well (Farmer 1978:II, 31). See Ibn Salamah 1938a:11, n. 2.

ʿARŪBĪ (ʿ-r-b) "eloquent; Arabizing"

1. A quatrain in which the even numbered hemistiches end with a particular rhyme, and the odd numbered ones have a contrasting rhyme.
2. A musical setting of such a poem (ʿARŪBĪ/1*) (d'Erlanger 1959: 167-168).
3. One of the genres of Moroccan folk music (GHRĪḤAH*) and consisting of a musical setting of a short poem containing an enigma or allegory (Chottin 1939:163).

ʿARŪBIYYAH = A'ROUBIA (ʿ-r-b) f. of "eloquent; Arabizing"

The opening couplet of a QAṢĪDAH/2* (Alg.). Also called HADDAH* or MAṬLAʿ/2*.

ʿARŪḌ (ʿ-r-ḍ) "prosody"

1. Prosody.
2. First hemistich of a poetic line or BAYT/1* (Farmer 1933b:6).

ʿARŪḌĪ (ʿ-r-ḍ) "pertaining to prosody"

Metrical (Cowl 1966:154).

ARYATH (r-y-th) comp. of RĀ'ITH

Slower than RĀ'ITH, comparable to Largo (al Ḥafnī 1946:287).

ʿAṢĀ (pl. ʿUṢĪ) (ʿ-ṣ-y) "stick"

The wooden part of the bow of the KAMĀN or KAMĀNJAH* (Maḥfūẓ 1964: 159; al Ḥafnī 1971:68).

AṢĀBIʿ (pl. of IṢBAʿ) (ṣ-b-ʿ) "fingers"

1. The melodic modes said to have been organized into a system by IBN MISJAḤ*. They were described by Ibn al Munajjim in Risālah fī al Mūsīqī (Shawqī 1976:853, 868ff). See also Farmer 1957:448; Wright 1978:41). These modes were named for the finger or fret positions used for producing their starting tones--MUṬLAQ* (open string), SABBĀBAH* (first finger), WUSṬĀ* (second finger) or BINṢIR* (third finger)--and the MAJRĀ* which determined their use of a major third (MAJRĀ AL BINṢIR*) or a minor third (MAJRĀ AL WUSṬĀ*). By the 13th C., this use of the term was already considered QADĪM ("ancient"), and the term AṢĀBIʿ then designated the six octave modes/scales mentioned as a group by Ṣafī al Dīn (1938b:179-180) and ʿAbd al Qādir ibn Ghaybī (Wright 1978:249-250). These six scales (MUṬLAQ/2*, MAZMŪM*, MUSARRAJ*, MUʿALLAQ/2*, MAḤMŪL* and MUJANNAB/3*) included both diatonic and non-diatonic (with the 3/4 tone interval) combinations. They were also called the "six laws" (Ṣafī al Dīn 1938b:179). Also known as MAWĀJIB*, these six modes were at one stage related to six of the rhythmic modes to produce a corpus of 36 ṬURUQ (s. ṬARĪQAH/5*) (Wright 1978:250-251).
2. Finger positions on the fingerboard of a chordophone (al Kindī 1966:150).

AṢAF

A single headed drum mentioned in a 14th C. treatise on music and equated with the KABAR* (Farmer 1978:II, 29).

AṢAFĪ ZŪRNĀ

A double-reed aerophone (oboe type) described in a 17th C. Turkish ms. as having been invented by a governor of Baṣrah (ʿIrāq) (Farmer 1954, "Iraqian and Mesopotamian Music":530).

ASĀMAR (s-m-r)

Syn. of MUSĀMARAH*. We are told that the word was used by Burckhardt, the 19th C. traveler (Farmer 1954, "Iraqian and Mesopotamian Music":532). The latter actually has ASAMER, which is probably a var. of (al) SAMAR, meaning "the joyful evening entertainment." See Burckhardt 1967:82-83, 253.

ASĀS (pl. USUS) ('-s-s) "foundation"

Contemporary term for the tonic (Jones 1977:66, 290).

AṢBAʿ

Var. of IṢBAʿ* (Farmer 1965b:1).

ASHGHĀL (pl. of SHUGHL*) (sh-gh-l) "works"

1. A kind of TAWSHĪḤ/1* with many embellishments (Tun.).
2. A grouping of MUWASHSHAḤĀT (s. MUWASHSHAḤ/1*) in the Maghribī suite (NAWBAH/1*) using different melodic and rhythmic modes. It is preceded by a classical QAṢĪDAH/1* and ends with a folkish one

(d'Erlanger 1959:200-201). This group within the NAWBAH is considered to be lighter than the other portions and shows influence from the Mashriq.

ASHṬUR AL ŪLĀ (pl. of SHAṬR AL AWWAL) = EL-ACHTÂR EL-ÛWLÎN (sh-ṭ-r) ('-w-l) "first lines"

The introductory part of the SARRĀBAH*, a genre of popular music (Mor.) (Chottin 1939:160). This is the first of the three segments which make up the piece, each comprising setting for three poetic lines, each of which has three sub-sections.

AṢL (pl. UṢŪL) =AÇL ('-ṣ-l) "principle"

1. A root or primary melodic mode (Farmer 1925:15), i.e., any of the four (Farmer 1967:204) or five (Farmer 1933b:8) principal melodic modes of Andalusian and Maghribī practice and theory. In a 16th C. ms. however, it seems to have applied to any melodic mode (Farmer 1965b:64).
2. The main tetrachord (JINS/1*) of a melodic mode (Collangettes 1904:169-170) or the lowest JINS in its scale (de Vaux 1891:329).
3. The intervals into which the tetrachords or pentachords making up a melodic modal scale are divided (al Jurjānī 1938:376).
4. The fundamental melody of a song denuded of its ornamentation (Chottin 1939:140).
5. A rhythmic mode according to al Kindī (Farmer 1967:151), al Jurjānī (1938:472), and contemporary Maghribī (Farmer 1954, "Moorish Music":871) and Mashriqī (al Ḥafnī 1946:220) theorists.

ASRAʿ (s-r-ʿ) "faster"

1. A tempo faster than SARĪʿ*, and comparable to Vivace (al Ḥafnī 1946:287; Maḥfūẓ 1964:177).
2. Descriptive term for a disjunct (MUNFAṢIL/3*) rhythmic mode in which the shorter percussion(s) come before the longer in the cycle (Ibn Sīnā 1930:94). See ABṬA'*.

ASṬŪKHŪSIYAH (Gr.)

Syrian theorists of the 8th C. (Farmer 1954, "Syrian Music":255; 1929a:57).

AṢWĀT (ṣ-w-t)

Pl. of ṢAWT*.

AṢWĀT MUḤZINAH (ṣ-w-t) (ḥ-z-n) "saddening sounds"

Tragic music (al Kindī 1966:156).

ʿATAB or ʿATABAH (pl. ʿATAB, ʿUTAB, ʿATABĀT) (ʿ-t-b) "step; stair; doorstep"

1. Ar. equiv. of the Pers. DASTĀN/1* or fret (Ibn Salamah 1951:83; 1938a:31; al Ḥafnī 1946:289).
2. From at least the 9th C. to the 15th, this term was used as the

name for the nut of a stringed instrument, the small piece of wood between the end of the neck and the pegbox, which marks the end of the vibrating string(s) (Farmer 1978:II, 64).

ʻATĀBĀ or ʻATĀBAH (ʻ-t-b) "mild scolding of a friend"

One of the most popular genres of folk song in Lebanon, Palestine, Syria and ʻIrāq. Said to have originated long ago in the desert (Weil EI(Fr), "ʻArūḍ":475), it is considered a folkish version of the MAWWĀL/1*. It comprises a vocal setting of quatrains in which the first three short lines rhyme and the fourth line always ends with the syllable(s) "āb," "ābā," or "ābah." Even when that ending has no actual meaning in the poem, the convention is maintained, its function being to emphasize the end of the quatrain. In Lebanon a variant "nā" ending is sometimes used (Jargy 1978:84). The musical setting has a recitative-like character with free rhythm and many descending phrases to tones of modal stability. Sometimes it is combined with a MAYJANĀ*, a vocal genre with regular rhythm, to become ʻATĀBĀ WA MAYJANĀ. Originally the ʻATĀBĀ was a song of friendship. Later it made use of a great variety of other themes, especially love and melancholy (Jargy 1970:35).

AṬABAL (colloq. of AṬBĀL, "drums")

Kettledrums of the Maghrib, which are played with a pair of drumsticks (Salvador-Daniel 1976:118, see also Farmer 1976a:224). This term is undoubtedly a var. of (al) ṬABL

AṬAMBOR

A large double-headed drum used for the military and religious processions in the Maghrib. It is played with an animal's bone (Salvador-Daniel 1976:118). This term is undoubtedly a var. of (al) ṬAMBŪR*.

ATEMCHI

Syn. of IZLI* (Chottin 1939:21).

ATHQAL ṬABAQATAN (th-q-l) (ṭ-b-q) "on a lower level"

With lower pitch level. See also QAWĪ DHŪ AL TAḌʻĪF* and ATHQAL*.

ʻATĪDAH (pl. ʻATĪDĀT) (ʻ-t-d) f. of "venerable; prepared"

A large drum known in the Sudan.

AṬLAQA (ṭ-l-q) "to free; to set free"

To perform vocal or instrumental music (Kāẓim 1964:21).

AṬRAB (ṭ-r-b) "more delightful"

1. More melodious.
2. More delightful (of music).

AṬRABA (ṭ-r-b) "to delight someone through music"

To sing or play for someone.

AṬSARA (s-ṭ-r?)

Syn. of SAṬṬARAH*, according to Chottin (1939:46).

AUJ

Var. of AWJ* (Smith 1949:181).

AʿWĀD (ʿ-w-d) "sticks, twigs; reeds, canes"

1. Sticks or reeds for beating a rhythm.
2. Pl. of ʿŪD*.

AWADAH

Var. of ʿAWWĀDAH/2* (Touma 1977b:111).

ʿAWĀLIM (ʿ-l-m)

Pl. of ʿĀLIMAH* (Jargy 1971:84).

AWĀNĪ (pl. of ĀNIYAH) ('-w-n) "vases"

Vase-like idiophones mentioned by the Ikhwān al Ṣafā' (late 10th C.) (Farmer EI(Fr), "Ṣandj":211).

ĀWĀZ (pl. ĀWĀZĀT) (Pers.) "voice, sound"

1. Generic for melodic mode.
2. Any of the six secondary melodic modes derived from the twelve primary or SHADD* modes (Ṣafī al Dīn 1938a and al Jurjānī 1938:387-388; Anonymous Treatise 1939:123-131). According to al Lādhiqī, six melodic modes were known to his predecessors, the "anciens," as ĀWĀZ modes, while seven were included in this category by his contemporaries, the "modernes" (al Lādhiqī 1939:437-440). Most of these modes were notated in descending order and had a compass of less than an octave (al Lādhiqī 1939:395-399; see also d'Erlanger 1939:pt. 2, p. 394, n. 36). While all those modes which had a scale divisible into conjunct tetrachords or tetrachord-pentachord combination were classified as SHADD/2* modes, the others were considered to be of either ĀWĀZ or MURAKKAB/1* varriety. The categorization seems to have been based primarily upon the type of species (i.e., diatonic, non-diatonic, or JINS MUFRAD*) and the arrangement of the species within the octave, but some inconsistencies suggest that extra musical factors also played a role in assignment of modes to particular classes (Wright 1978:Chap. III). In the 15th C. Anonymous Treatise (d'Erlanger 1939:101), ĀWĀZ is equivalent to the derivative modal type, SHUʿBAH*.
3. A tune.
4. A sound that has an effect on the feelings of the listener (Kāẓim 1964:67).

ʿAWD or ʿAWDAH (pl. ʿAWDĀT) (ʿ-w-d) "return"

1. The whole tone interval (9/8) (al Jurjānī 1938:237). Al Fārābī described this interval as the difference between the perfect fourth and the perfect fifth intervals. He informs us that it was called MADDAH/1* or BUʿD ṬANĪNĪ* by his predecessors (al Fārābī 1930:54; 1967:144).
2. A return to a note previously sounded in a melodic progression (INTIQĀL/1*) (Ibn Sīnā 1930:96).
3. A poetic or musical repetition (al Fārābī 1935:64; 1967:1090-1091), and by extension, a refrain.

AWḤĀ (w-ḥ-y) comp. of WAḤĪ* "rapid"

A tempo faster than WAḤĪ* and comparable to Prestissimo (Maḥfūẓ 1964:177; al Ḥafnī 1946:287).

AWJ = AOUDJ, AUJ ('-w-j) "high"

1. A melodic mode mentioned from the 15th C. until the present day (Anonymous Treatise 1939:140).
2. A tone of the contemporary scale equivalent to B♭$_2$ 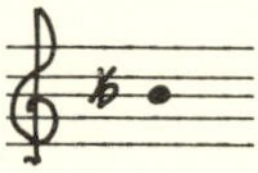 .

AWNĀ (w-n-y) comp. of WĀNIN* "weaker, more tired"

A tempo designation used by contemporary musicians, meaning a little slower than Andante or its equivalent WĀNIN (al Ḥafnī 1946:287; Maḥfūẓ 1964:177). This term retains the literal meaning of Andantino (i.e., a little slower than Andante), though generally Andantino designates a tempo quicker than Andante.

AWQAʿA (w-q-ʿ) "to make fall in proper place"

1. To tune an instrument.
2. To sing music governed by a rhythmic mode.

ʿAWṬABA

See ʿARṬABAH*.

AWTĀR (pl. of WATAR*) (w-t-r) "strings"

1. Any stringed instrument or chordophone (Ibn Taymiyyah 1966:II, 319).
2. The wire strings used as snares on a drum or tambourine.

AWTĀR MUṬLAQAH (w-t-r) (ṭ-l-q) "freed strings"

The "open strings" found on such instruments as the lyre, harp, psaltery and dulcimer (Farmer EI(Eng), "Miʿzaf":528).

ʿAWWĀD = AWAD (ʿ-w-d) "one who performs on the ʿŪD*"

1. Lutenist, performer on the ʿŪD*.
2. A long flute with low droning sound which is used by the camel drivers of North Africa. See ʿAWWĀDAH/3*.

ʿAWWĀDAH (ʿ-w-d) "f. of ʿAWWĀD*"

1. Female performer on the ʿŪD*.
2. A musical ensemble (Tun.) (Rizqī 1967:63), which generally comprises an ʿŪD, a QĀNŪN*, a DARABUKKAH*, and a ṬĀR/2* or RIQQ*.
3. A vertical reed flute used by the North African Berbers, and having six equidistant fingerholes and a rear thumbhole (Marcuse). Chottin localizes the use of this term in the south of Morocco (Chottin 1939:34). In the north, the instrument is called LĪRAH* or NĪRAH*.

AWZĀN (pl. of WAZN) (w-z-n) "weights"

1. A long-necked lute, probably of Turkish origin, which was introduced into Egypt during the Ayyūbī dynasty (12th-13th C.) and remained popular in the Mamlūk period. It had three strings and was played with a wooden plectrum (Farmer 1967:209). It has also been designated as a drum, but this is probably a mistake (Farmer EI(Eng), "ʿŪD":987).
2. Pl. of WAZN/1*.

ĀYAH (pl. ĀYĀT) ('-w-y) "sign"

A verse of the Qur'ān.

AYALA

War dances of "la côte des Pirates" (Olsen 1967:28).

ʿAYṬAH (pl. ʿIYĀṬ) = 'AÏTA (ʿ-y-ṭ) "a cry, scream, shout"

A genre of Moroccan folk music (GHRĪḤAH*) (Chottin 1939:163). This vocal genre is similar to a QAṢĪDAH/1*, a strophic song of the Moroccan folk tradition, but uses the vocabulary, musical setting and course sounds of the Bedouins. It is usually sung by women, and is associated with their dances.

ʿAYN (pl. ʿUYŪN) (ʿ-y-n) "eye"

Any of the sound holes on the face of the long- or short-necked lutes (Farmer 1945:13; al Khwārizmī 1968:239).

ʿAZAFA (ʿ-z-f) "to play"

1. To play a musical instrument.
2. To play a tune.

ʿAZFĪ (ʿ-z-f) "pertaining to musical performance"

Instrumental (Ḥāfiẓ 1971:120).

ʿAZF (ʿ-z-f) "playing; performance"

1. Playing or performing on a musical instrument. While ʿAZF is a general term for such performance, specific terms can vary according to the instrument: e.g., ḌARB* for the ʿŪD*; ZAMR* for the aero-

phones; NAQR* for the tambourine or drum; or WAQʿ* for the rhythm stick (QADĪB*) (Kitāb al Aghānī in Shawqī 1976:279).
2. An unidentified open-stringed instrument of the period from the 9th to the 14th C. (Farmer 1978:II, 31).
3. Generic term for any member of the lute family (Farmer 1978:II, 31). Also MIʿZAF*.
4. Voice or sound of the JINN (Chottin 1939:85).
5. A kind of primitive harp (Chottin 1939:85).

ʿĀZIF (pl. ʿĀZIFŪN) (ʿ-z-f) "the one who plays or performs"

1. Instrumentalist.
2. The voice or sound of the JINN (Ibn ʿAbd Rabbihi 1941:136, n. 4).

ʿĀZIF MUNFARID (ʿ-z-f) (f-r-d) "single person who plays or performs"

Instrumental soloist (Wahba 1968:69).

B

"B" (abbrev. for "bā'" the second letter of the Ar. alphabet)

1. This letter designated a duration or percussion which was twice as long as "A"* time or ZAMĀN AL AWWAL* for theorists of the Classical Period (Ṣafī al Dīn 1938b:161; 1938a:478; al Jurjānī 1938: 478; Anonymous Treatise 1939:159; al Lādhiqī 1939:459). A conjunct rhythm utilizing this length of percussion was designated as HAZAJ KHAFĪF* (Ṣafī al Dīn 1938b:161).
2. An abbreviation for the interval BAQIYYAH* (Ṣafī al Dīn 1938a: 238). By the 14th C., al Jurjānī writes that this letter served as symbol among the musical experts for both the limma, for which he retained the name BAQIYYAH, as well as the comma or FAḌLAH* (al Jurjānī 1938:238). See also Anonymous Treatise 1939:37-38; al Lādhiqī 1939:302; de Vaux 1891:336).

BACHRAF

Var. of BASHRAF/1* (Touma 1977b:87).

BADANIYYAH (pl. BADANIYYĀT) (b-d-n) "body"

Name for the main section of the MUWASHSHAḤ/1* or other similar compositions, which is sung by the chorus in main melodic mode (MAQĀM/1*) and rhythmic mode (ĪQĀ'/1*). Sometimes two of these sections are used, one called B. AL ŪLĀ*, and the other called B. AL THĀNIYAH*.

BADANIYYAH AL ŪLĀ (b-d-n) ('-w-l) "first body"

The opening vocal segment or phrase of the MUWASHSHAḤ/1* or similar composition, which is sung by the chorus (Ḥāfiẓ 1971:110). See B. AL THĀNIYAH*.

BADANIYYAH AL THĀNIYAH (b-d-n) (th-w-n) "second body"

The second vocal segment or phrase of a MUWASHSHAḤ/1* or similar composition. It utilizes the opening musical material of the BADANIYYAH AL ŪLĀ*, with a change in poetic content. It is followed by the KHĀNAH* (Ḥāfiẓ 1971:110).

BAḌḌA (b-ḍ-ḍ) "to tune"

To tune a musical instrument (Maḥfūẓ 1964:185).

BADOUAH

Var. of BADWAH* (Touma 1977b:72).

BADWAH (b-d-'?)

A vocal portion sometimes used to introduce a performance of MAQĀM AL ʿIRĀQĪ* instead of the TAḤRĪR*. It is characterized by very long and very short vocal sounds in alternating high and low vocal registers.

BAGHLAMAH = BAGLAMA (Turk.) "tied, bound"

A very small long-necked lute (ṬUNBŪR/1*) with three strings and pear shaped body, described by an 18th C. traveler in the Mashriq. According to Villoteau (d. 1839), it was the smallest of five types of ṬUNBŪR known in Egypt at his time (Farmer EI(Fr), "Ṭunbūr":270). Also called ṬUNBŪR BAGHLAMAH*.

BAGLAMA

Var. of BAGHLAMAH* (Marcuse).

BAḤR (pl. BUḤŪR or ABḤĀR) "sea; zone; period"

1. Any tetrachordal or pentachordal segment with its four or five tones which is used in combination with other like or different segments to create a melodic mode (Ṣafī al Dīn 1938a and al Jurjānī 1938:351ff).
2. Any four consecutive tones which can be found in the scale of a melodic mode, e.g., CDEF, DEFG, EFGA, etc. (Ṣafī al Dīn 1938a and al Jurjānī 1938:351ff; Anonymous Treatise 1939:91).
3. Melodic mode (al Irbalī 1951:107).
4. Rhythmic mode (Kāẓim 1964:25; Farmer 1933b:5).
5. Poetic meter.
6. Tetrachordal or pentachordal species. See NAWʿ/1*.

BAIAT

Var. of BAYĀTĪ* (Gerson-Kiwi 1970:70).

BAIT

Var. of BAYT*.

BĀJ

Another name for the BAMM* or lowest string of the ʿŪD* (al Atharī 1950:4, n. 4; Maḥfūẓ 1964:28).

BAḲĪYA

Var. of BAQIYYAH* (Farmer EI(Fr), "Mūsīḳī":751).

BALABĀN

A popular aerophone of the Tīmūrī period (Farmer 1954, "Zamr":396). This oboe-type instrument (i.e., with double reed) was mentioned by ʿAbd al Qādir ibn Ghaybī (15th C.), as well as by the 17th C. writer Chelebi (Farmer 1976b:26).

BALŪṢĀ (b-l-ṣ)

The reed of an aerophone (Maḥfūẓ 1964:163).

BAMM (pl. BUMŪM) (Pers.) "thick, low sound"

The lowest pitched string of the ʿŪD* or other lute.

BANĀDRĪ (pl. BANĀDRIYYAH)

BANDĪR* performer (Jones 1977:44).

BANDAIR or BANDAÏR

Vars. of BANDĪR* (Marcuse; Sachs 1940:247, resp.)

BANDĪR (pl. BANĀDĪR) = BANDAIR, BANDAIR, BENDAÏR, BENDIR, ABENDAIR

A large, circular frame drum which has been used over a widespread area and for a long period of time. It was known to the Moors of Spain and is still played in the Maghrib and Egypt (Touma 1977b:108; al Rizqī 1967:360; al Ḥafnī 1971:176). This frame drum with its single membrane has a diameter of approximately 40 cm. and a depth of about 10 cm. The frame has an opening into which the player's thumb fits in order to aid in holding the instrument upright. Two chords or snares are mounted across the inner surface of the membrane. Like the MIZHAR or MAZHAR/1*, this instrument is often used by religious brotherhoods for their DHIKR* and processional music. It is also known as AQWĀL/2* (AGWĀL*) among the Berbers of Morocco (Grame 1970:85).

BANJAQ

The "head" of the ʿŪD/2*, that ending piece of the neck which is bent back and holds the tuning pegs (al Ḥafnī 1971:75). Also RA'S/1*.

BĀQ

Var. of BŪQ* (ʿAbd al Qādir ibn Ghaybī, according to Farmer EI(Eng), "Mizmār":540-541).

BAQIYYAH (pl. BAQĀYĀ) = BAḲĪYA (b-q-y) "remainder, remnant"

An interval equivalent to the Pythagorean limma (256/243 or 90 c.) or the approximation of that interval used by Arab theorists (20/19) (al Fārābī 1930:109; 1967:145; Ibn Sīnā in Farmer 1926a:252, 254). This minor semitone was also known as FAḌLAH* and was abbreviated as "B"/2*. Others assigned this term as well as FAḌLAH to another interval which was comparable to the Pythagorean comma (approximate ratio 81/80) (d'Erlanger 1939:502-503, n. 12). Recognizing the confusion that was caused by this varying terminology, Arab theorists of the school of Ṣafī al Dīn al Urmawī chose to use the term BAQIYYAH for limma only, and FAḌLAH exclusively for the comma (al Jurjānī 1938:238).

BARADAH

Var. of BARDAH* (Spector 1970:244).

BĀRBAD or BĀRBUD

1. A famous performer on the lute (BARBAṬ*) in the days of Khusrau Parwiz (d. 628 A.C.), the Sasanid king of Persia (al Khwarizmi 1968).
2. Vars. of BARBAṬ* (al ʿAzzāwī 1951:10; Marcuse, resp.).

BARBAKH

A peasant version of the popular single-headed goblet drum of the Arabs. It is made of pottery and is used in ʿIrāq (al Dāqūqī 1965:39). See DUMBALAK*.

BARBAṬ (pl. BARĀBĪT) = BARBAT, BĀRBAD, BARBIT, BARBET, BĀRBUD (Pers.) "chest (BAR) of the duck (BAṬṬ)"

1. A Persian short-necked lute famous at least as early as the 3rd C. of The Christian era. Its neck and sound box were made of a single piece of wood, unlike the Arabian lute (ʿŪD/2*). In that early period, it had two strings, a pear-shaped body and a hollow neck (Ḥāfiẓ 1971:18; Robson 1938a:6, n. 5). Later it developed characteristics similar to those of the ʿŪD of the Classical Period, of which it is thought to be a forerunner.
2. Generic term for lutes used in early centuries of Islamic period. For that period, it designated a short-necked lute with four strings and a wooden face. It often seems to have been used synonymously with ʿŪD*, its name in Arabic (al Khwārizmī 1968:238). Sachs claims that Ibn Sīnā was the only writer to use this term for the short-necked lute (1940:253), but references to it can be found in many Arabic sources from the 7th C. and later (e.g., al Khwārizmī 1968:238; Ibn Salamah 1938a:11; Ibn ʿAbd Rabbihi 1887: III, 105), It is often difficult to know whether an author of those centuries used it as synonym of the earlier skin-faced lutes (also known as KIRĀN*, MIZHAR*, and MUWATTAR*), of the Persian instrument (BARBAṬ/1*), or of the wooden-faced ʿŪD/2*.
3. A tambourine with cymbals in its frame (Hickmann 1947:21).
4. Playing on the lute, according to Ibn Abī al Dunyā (Robson 1938c:49). See also Ibid.:27, n. 5, where Robson comments on the strange textual definition of this word.

BARBAṬĪ (Pers.)

BARBAṬ* player (Farmer 1929a:57).

BARBET or BARBIT

Vars. of BARBAṬ* (Rouanet 1922:2745).

BARDAH (pl. BARADĀT) = BARADAH, BARDĀH, BORDA, PARDAH (Pers.) "curtain"

1. The interval between two consecutive degrees of the fundamental scale (RĀST/2*) of the contemporary Arabs. Sometimes this interval will be a major whole tone, sometimes approximately a 3/4 tone. Between the extremities of the BARDAH interval, therefore, will be either two or three intermediary notes known as ʿARABĀT, s. ʿARABAH/1*. According to Aḥmad al Dīk, a 20th C. Egyptian theorist, there are two kinds of BARADĀT: BARDAH KABĪRAH*, equivalent to a whole tone; and BARDAH ṢAGHĪRAH*, equivalent to a semitone (Shawqī 1969a:37). This accords with Villoteau's description of the BARADĀT as the seven diatonic intervals of the octave scale (Farmer 1954, "Egyptian Music":895). For el Helou (1961:68), BARDAH applies only to the whole tone interval, while ʿARABAH/1* designates the semitone. See also TĪK ʿARABAH*, NĪM ʿARABAH*.
2. Some contemporary theorists use this term to designate all the possible scale steps (al Dāqūqī 1965:85).
3. Any of the twelve principal melodic modes, according to a 14th C. theorist (Shiloah 1968a:237, 244). The ms. (Ibid.:237) uses BARDĀH, and the translator uses BARDAWĀT*. I have considered both to be variant spellings rather than new terms.

BARDĀH (pl. BARDAWĀT)

Var. of BARDAH/3*(Shiloah 1968a:237).

BARDAH KABĪRAH (Pers.) (k-b-r) "large BARDAH"

The whole tone interval (Shawqī 1969a:37). See BARDAH/1*.

BARDAH ṢAGHĪRAH (Pers.) (ṣ-gh-r) "small BARDAH"

The half tone interval (Shawqī 1969a:37). See BARDAH/1*.

BARDAWĀT

Pl. of BARDĀH*(Shiloah 1968a:244). See BARDAH/3*.

BARHIA

Var. of BUGHYAH* (Chottin 1939:126).

BAROUEL

Var. of BARWĀL* (Jargy 1971:94; el Mahdi 1972:14).

BARWĀL (pl. BARĀWĪL) = BAROUEL, BEROUAL

1. A vocal number in the Maghribī suite (NAWBAH/1*). It has a joyous mood and utilizes the rapid 2/4 rhythmic mode of the same name. Two or more of these vocal numbers, which resemble the MUWASHSHAḤ/1*, are often performed in a NAWBAH. See also NŪBAH/1*.
2. A rapid 2/4 rhythmic mode of Maghribī NAWBAH/1* performance. In d'Erlanger (1959:149), it is described as a Tunisian rhythm with an Andante(*sic*) 2/4 measure.

BARWĀLAH (pl. BARĀWĪL) = BERWÂLA

A genre of Moroccan folk music or GHRĪḤAH*, which is a musical setting for a kind of popular poetry composed of strophes of unequal length (e.g., a quatrain alternating with a six-line strophe). Because the melodies are so similar to those of the classical music, the BARWĀLAH is sometimes included in the last sections of the NAWBAH/1* (Chottin 1939:154-155).

BASHRAF (pl. BASHĀRĪF) = BACHRAF, BASHRŪ, BĒCHERAF, BASHRAU, BĪSHRŪ, BĪSHRAW (Pers.) "prelude; to go before"

1. A contemporary instrumental prelude with regular rhythm, usually based on a relatively long rhythmic cycle. Some theorists say that it should have sixteen or more basic beats per cycle (el Mahdi 1972:20). It is one of the numbers of the suite in most regions of the Arab World. In its early stages of development, the BASHRAF conformed to few rules regarding rhythm or form and was bound only by the limitations of the chosen melodic mode. Later it developed the following characteristics: a) It should be composed of four KHĀNAH/2* segments, each of which is followed by a refrain section of the same number of measures as the KHĀNAH. This refrain is called TASLĪM/1*. Sometimes five KHĀNĀT are used, and rarely one hears a BASHRAF with only three of these parts. b) In the first KHĀNAH, the character of the chosen melodic and rhythmic modes is established. c) In the second KHĀNAH, modulations and variations of the first KHĀNAH's melodic and rhythmic material are exposed. d) The music of the third KHĀNAH moves to the higher reaches of the modal scale. e) In the fourth KHĀNAH the principle theme reappears. f) If five KHĀNĀT are used, both the second and third involve variations and modulations. g) The TASLĪM should repeat the core of the main theme of the first KHĀNAH. h) The principal rhythmic mode of the refrain section should be different from the rhythms of the contrasting KHĀNAH sections (el Mahdi 1972:20; d'Erlanger 1959:181).

2. In Tunisia, a measured instrumental overture comprising two parts. The first is of moderate tempo, and the second, called ḤARBĪ/1*, is of very rapid tempo. An instrumental solo may be interjected between the two parts. These orchestral overtures are often replaced today by the more recent version of BASHRAF described above (d'Erlanger 1959:199-200).

BASHRAF SAMĀʿĪ (Pers.) (s-m-ʿ) "heard prelude"

A precomposed, regularly rhythmed orchestral number of the contemporary Mashriq and Maghrib. It has been used as part of the suites of both regions, as an introduction to vocal or instrumental solos, or as a separate composition. Like the BASHRAF* and the SAMĀʿĪ/1*, it is made up of sections. It uses the SAMĀʿĪ/2* rhythmic modes. Often TAQĀSĪM (s. TAQSĪM*) are used between the major sections of this composition (Farmer 1954, "Nauba":34; EI(Fr), "Nawba":947; Racy 1979:19).

BASHRAU

Var. of BASHRAF* (Farmer 1954, "Nauba":32-34).

BASHRŪ

Var. of BASHRAF* (al Ḥafnī 1946:254).

BASĪṬ or BASĪṬAH (pl. BASĀYIṬ, BUSŪṬ) (b-s-ṭ) "simple"

1. Describes a melodic mode (MAQĀM/1*) in which only one variety of tetrachordal/pentachordal segment (JINS/1*) is found (d'Erlanger 1949:101). Opp. of MURAKKAB or MURAKKABAH/1*.
2. Describes a contemporary rhythmic mode (ĪQĀʿ/1*) in which the beats are organized in duple combinations (al Ḥafnī 1946:222).
3. Used by theorists of the Classical Period to describe a rhythmic mode when its basic percussions were of the same length. Such a mode could include a longer or shorter duration between the last percussion of one cycle and the beginning of the next. This duration separating cycles is known as a FĀṢILAH/4* (al Fārābī 1930:31ff; 1967:999ff). See also MUFAṢṢAL AL BASĪṬ*.
4. A genre of vocal music described in a 15th C. treatise and involving one of the following rhythms in its setting of the poetry: THAQĪL AL AWWAL*, THAQĪL AL THĀNĪ* or THAQĪL AL RAMAL*. It comprised an instrumental prelude (called ṬARĪQAH/3* or PISHRŪ/1*) and a refrain section (called TASHYĪʿAH* or BĀZKISHT*) with or without poetic content. Sometimes a modulatory passage (ṢAWT/2*, ṢAWT AL WASAṬ*, MIYAT KHĀNAH*)was added (Anonymous Treatise 1939:235-236; Farmer 1957:452). According to the 14th C. commentary of al Jurjānī, this vocal number consisted of an alternation between vocal and instrumental segments. All poetic syllables were to occur on a new tone of the melody (al Jurjānī 1938:552-553). Se also TARĀNAH*.
5. The first of the five movements of the NAWBAH/1* or suite, as performed in Morocco (Ḥāfiẓ 1971:128). It comprises a series of vocal MUWASHSHAḤ/1*-like numbers constructed on a slow ternary rhythmic mode. This group of songs follows the two instrumental overtures of the Moroccan NAWBAH (d'Erlanger 1959:189).
6. A rhythmic mode of the contemporary Maghrib used in the NAWBAH/1* movement of the same name. See definition 5 above.
7. A variety, one of three, of the folkish genre of vocal music of Egypt known as INSHĀD/2* (Ḥāfiẓ 1971:199).
8. Descriptive term for those graces that comprise a single tone rather than multiple tones (MURAKKAB or MURAKKABAH/3*) preceding a longer main tone (al Faruqi 1978:24).
9. A category of melodic movement (INTIQĀL/1*) as described by Ibn Sīnā. It involved steady movement in a single direction, i.e., either ascending or descending (Ibn Sīnā 1930:95).

BASĪṬ AL AWWAL (b-s-ṭ) ('-w-l) "first simple"

A disjunct (MUNFAṢIL/3*) rhythmic mode (ĪQĀʿ/1*) which contains only one percussion followed by a time unit known as a FĀṢILAH/4* which separates it from the next cycle (al Fārābī 1935:32; 1967:1002).

BASĪṬ AL THĀNĪ (b-s-ṭ) (th-w-n) "second simple"

A disjunct (MUNFAṢIL/3*) rhythmic mode (ĪQĀʿ/1*) which contains two percussions plus a disjunctive time unit known as a FĀṢILAH/4* which separates them from the next cycle (al Fārābī 1935:32; 1967:1003).

BASĪṬ AL MURAKKAB (b-s-ṭ) (r-k-b) "simple composed"

A variety, one of three, of the folkish genre of vocal music of Egypt known as INSHĀD/2* (Ḥāfiẓ 1971:199).

BASM (b-s-m) "smiling"

A technique for achieving a loud sound on the lute (ʿŪD/2*). It involves striking the string with two fingers of the right hand rather than with the plectrum. This technique is used by musicians of many regions but is especially popular in Egypt (Touma 1977b:95).

BASSEH

One of the work songs (AHĀZĪJ, s. HAZAJ/7*) of the Arab/Persian Gulf region used to accompany the raising of the small sails on the boats (Touma 1977a:122).

BASṬĀ (b-s-t)

Var. of BASṬĪ* (Cowl 1966:137).

BASTAH

Equiv. of BISTAH*.

BASṬĪ = BASṬĀ (b-s-ṭ) "cheerful"

One of the three moods of a musical composition, as mentioned by al Kindī (Farmer 1926b:16). See also QABḌĪ*, MUʿTADIL*, KARAM*.

BAṬAIḤ

Var. of BAṬĀYḤĪ* (Farmer 1967:200).

BAṬĀYḤĪ = BAṬĪḤ, BAṬAIḤ, BTAYḤYAH, BTAYḤĪ, BTÂIH'Î, BETAÏHH, BIṬAYḤĪ, MAṬĀYḤĪ (b-ṭ-ḥ) "of the desert" (colloq.)

1. A vocal number similar to the MUWASHSHAḤ/1* used in the Maghribī suite (NAWBAH/1*). It is based on a rhythmic cycle of the same name (def. 2). The number of these in a NAWBAH varies.
2. A four-beat rhythmic cycle of moderate tempo, utilized in the BAṬĀYḤĪ movement of the suite (NAWBAH/1*) (Tun., Alg.). It has also been described as very slow (Alg.) (Rouanet 1922:2855). In Morocco it designates a rhythm with eight beats to the cycle (Ḥāfiẓ 1971:132).

BAṬĪʾ (b-ṭ-ʾ) "slow"

Very slow in tempo, comparable to <u>Grave</u> (Maḥfūẓ 1964:177).

BAṬĪḤ (b-ṭ-ḥ) "of the desert" (colloq.)

Equiv. of BAṬĀYḤĪ* (al Rizqī 1967:367).

BAṬN (pl. BUṬŪN) (b-ṭ-n) "stomach, belly"

The face of the lute (ʿŪD*) (Bulos 1971:19).

BAWWAQA (b-w-q) "to blow the trumpet"

To play the BŪQ*.

BAYĀḌ (b-y-ḍ) "white; whiteness"

The skin covering of the spike fiddle of Egypt. This skin is made from the skin of a special fish (Lane 1973:356).

BAYĀTĪ = BEYÂTY, BAIAT, BAYYĀTĪ (b-y-t) "pertaining to student boarder"

1. A contemporary tetrachordal scalar segment (JINS/1*) of 3/4-3/4-1 intervalic division.
2. An important melodic mode (MAQĀM/1*) utilizing the BAYĀTĪ tetrachord. This name has been used for a MAQĀM as early as the 15th C. (Anonymous Treatise 1939:137).

BAYḌĀ' (b-y-ḍ) f. of ABYAḌ, "white; clean"

A half note used in contemporary notation (el Helou 1961:20).

BAYT (pl. ABYĀT) = BAIT, BEIT, BIT (b-y-t) "house; tent"

1. One line of poetry. The BAYT generally comprises two hemistiches, the first known as SHAṬR/1* or ṢADR/2*; the second, as MIṢRĀʿ* or ʿAJZ* (al Faruqi 1975:14).
2. Musical setting of any line of poetry. Therefore, it names the vocal phrase sung in unison by the choir and then repeated by the orchestra in its answer or JAWĀB/2* in the Moroccan suite (NAWBAH/1*) (Chottin 1939:132). In Algeria, this term is used to designate the second couplet of the QAṢĪDAH/1* (Delphin and Guin 1886:36). Also FIRĀSH/2*, GHUṢN/2*.
3. Any one of the five openings in the rim of the tambourine which hold the pairs of metal cymbals (Mor.) (Chottin 1939:117).

BAYT AL MALĀWĪ (b-y-t) (m-l-w) "house of the instruments of turning"

The wooden receptacle for the tuning pegs of a chordophone. See MILWĀ or MILWĪ*.

BAYTĀN (dual of BAYT) = BITAÏN, BAYTAYN (b-y-t) "two houses"

1. A musical setting of a couplet of poetry. In the Maghrib, it is an unmetered introductory song (Chottin 1939:126, 128).
2. A couplet of poetry. In the 14th C. it was a syn. of MAWĀLIYĀ/2*, a popular poetry of Baghdād and Egypt (Ibn Khaldūn 1967: III, 475-476).

BAYTAYN (dual of BAYT in the dative case) (b-y-t)

Var. of BAYTĀN* (Chottin 1939:126, 128).

BĀZ or BĀZAH (pl. BĀZĀT) (b-w-z) "falcon"

A small kettledrum (6-7 inches in diameter) used in recent centuries for religious processions, begging, hawking and to awaken the people for the dawn meal during the month of fasting (Lane 1973:365; ʿArnīṭah 1968:51). Earlier known as ṬABL AL BĀZ*, this instrument hangs from or is held by a small projection or handle on its back. It is played with a leather or fabric strap.

BĀZKISHT

Syn. of TAṢHYĪʿAH*, the refrain section of certain genres of vocal music (BASĪṬ/4* and ʿAMAL*) described in a 15th C. treatise, or of any movement of the NAWBAH/1* suites of that time (Anonymous Treatise 1939:235-236, 244).

BĒCHERAF

Var. of BASHRAF* (Farmer 1976a:201).

BEIT

Var. of BAYT* (Chottin 1939:117; Jargy 1970:29).

BENDAÏR

Var. of BANDĪR* (Delphin and Guin 1886:37; Rouanet 1922:2931).

BENDIR

Var. of BANDĪR* (Touma 1977b: Rouanet 1922:2931).

BEROUAL

Var. of BARWĀL* (Rouanet 1922:2880).

BERWÂLA

Var. of BARWĀLAH* (Chottin 1939:154-155).

BESTE

Var. of BISTAH or BASTAH* (Touma 1977b:73).

BETAÏHH

Var. of BAṬĀYḤĪ* (Farmer 1976a:195).

BEYÂTY

Var. of BAYĀTĪ* (Smith 1847:182).

BI TAKHAṬṬĪ

See (BI) TAKHAṬṬĪ under "T".

BI IZLĀQ

See (BI) IZLĀQ under "I".

BIDĀYAH (pl. BIDĀYĀT) (b-d-') "beginning"

Starting tone of a melodic mode (MAQĀM/1*) (el Helou 1961:79).

BIKĀ'

Var. of BUKĀ'* (Farmer EI(Eng), "Ghinā'":1073).

BILLĪQ (b-l-q) "always spotted"

Genre of popular song known during the Classical Period (Farmer EI(Eng), "Ghinā'":1074).

BINṢIR (pl. BANĀṢĪR) (b-n-ṣ-r) "ring finger"

The fret position corresponding to the tone made by the ring finger on the lute (ʿŪD*) string and producing the major third above the open string. This term was used from the early centuries of the Islamic period until the 19th C.

BINṢIR AL MASHHŪRAH (b-n-ṣ-r) (sh-h-r) "famous ring finger"

The fret position (see BINṢIR*) which produces the major third (81/64) interval above the open string of the lute (al Fārābī 1967:813).

BIQA'

Var. of BUKĀ' (Farmer 1957:424).

BĪSHAH (Pers.) "grove, thicket"

Panpipes, Pers. equiv. for the Chinese MUSTAQ* or MUSTAQ ṢĪNĪ* (al Khwārizmī 1968:237; Ibn Salamah 1951:86; see Robson 1938a:15, n. 4).

BĪSHRAW

Var. of BASHRAF* (Farmer EI(Fr), "Nawba":947).

BĪSHRŪ (Pers.) "going forward"

Var. of BASHRAF* (al ʿAzzāwī 1951:40; al Khulaʿī 1904:46).

BĪSHRŪN

Var. of BASHRAF* (al ʿAzzāwī 1951:40).

BISTAH or BASTAH = BESTE, PASTA, PASTĀ, PESTE (Pers.) "tie; tied"

A genre of regularly rhythmed vocal music of strophic variety sung in contemporary ʿIrāq. It is generally heard following segments of the MAQĀM AL ʿIRĀQĪ* performance (Kāẓim 1964:26). It serves as a kind of rest period for the soloist (Ḥāfiẓ 1971:168). Jargy describes the BISTAH as a setting for strophic poetry with a refrain which is repeated regularly by a chorus (Jargy 1971:92). This name is also sometimes given to the MUWASHSHAḤ/1* in the Mashriq (al Khulaʿī 1904:46).

BIT

Var. of BAYT/1* (Rouanet 1922:2862).

BITAÏN

Var. of BAYTAYN* (Chottin 1939:126, 128).

BIṬAYḤĪ

Var. of BAṬĀYḤĪ* (Rouanet 1922:2855).

BÔQ

Var. of BŪQ* (Chottin 1939:71).

BOQUE

Var. of BŪQ* (Rouanet 1922:2745).

BORDA

Var. of BARDAH* (Rouanet 1922:2715).

BORHIA

Var. of BUGHYAH* (Chottin 1939:126).

BOUSALIK

Var. of BŪSALĪK* (Rouanet 1922:2725).

BOUZOQ

Var. of BUZUQ*(Touma 1977b:103).

BOUZOURK

Var. of BUZURK*(Touma 1977b:37).

BOUZROUK

Var. of BUZURK* (Rouanet 1922:2720).

BSÎT

Var. of BASĪṬ/5*, the first of the five movements of the NAWBAH/1* suite (Mor.) (Chottin 1939:118).

BTÂÎH'Î

Var. of BAṬĀYḤĪ* (Chottin 1939:118).

BṬAYḤĪ

Var. of BAṬĀYḤĪ* (d'Erlanger 1959:189, 194; el Mahdi 1972:11, 14, 30; Jargy 1971:94).

BUʿD (pl. ABʿĀD) (b-ʿ-d) "distance; interval"

Musical interval, i.e., the distance between any two tones of different pitch. See chart below on "Principal ABʿĀD of Classical and Contemporary Terminology."

PRINCIPAL ABʿĀD (s. BUʿD) OF CLASSICAL AND CONTERMPORARY TERMINOLOGY
(in order of increasing size)

Intervals	Arabic Terms		Ratios (approx.)	Cents (approx.)
1/8 tone (Pythagorean comma)	FAḌLAH BAQIYYAH		81/80	22-23
1/4 tone (enharmonic diesis)	IRKHĀ' RUBʿ RUBʿ ṬANĪNĪ RUBʿ MASĀFAH	NĪM NĪM ʿARABAH	36/35	45-50

Intervals	Arabic Terms	Ratios (approx.)	Cents (approx.)
Semitone (limma)	BAQIYYAH		
	FAḌLAH	256/243 or 20/19	90
Semitone (of tempered scale)	NIṢF BARDAH		100
	NIṢF BUʿD, NIṢF ṬABʿ		
	MUJANNABĀT (s. MUJANNAB)		
Semitone (limma plus comma)	BUʿD ṢAGHĪR	16/15	112
	MUTAMMAM		
	MUJANNAB AL ṢAGHĪR		
Major semitone (apotome)	INFIṢĀL	2187/2049	114
	FAḌLAH AL ṬANĪNĪ		
3/4 tone	BUʿD AL ʿARABĪ	12/11	146
	TĪK ʿARABAH/2, BUʿD MUTAWASSIṬ		
Tone (minor)	TATIMMAH, BUʿD KĀMIL AL AQALL, MUJANNAB AL KABĪR	10/9	182
Whole tone (major)	ṬANĪNĪ, ʿAWDAH, MADDAH, BUʿD ṬANĪNĪ, BUʿD KĀMIL, BUʿD KABĪR, ṬABʿ, TĀMM BARDAH	9/8	204
Thirds	DHŪ AL THALĀTHAH		
	BUʿD AL THULĀTHĪ		
Minor:	WUSṬĀ AL QADĪM MUJANNAB AL WUSṬĀ	32/27	294
	WUSṬĀ AL FURS	81/68	318
Neutral:	WUSṬĀ AL ZALZAL	27/22	355
Major:	BUʿD KULL WA RUBʿ	81/64	408
Perfect fourth	DHŪ AL ARBAʿ	4/3	498
	DHŪ QUWĀ AL ARBAʿ		
	BUʿD BIL ARBAʿ		
	BUʿD ALLADHĪ BIL ARBAʿ		
	BUʿD DHŪ ITTIFĀQ AL THĀLITH		
	BUʿD MUTTAFIQ AL THĀLITH		
Perfect fifth	DHŪ AL KHAMS	3/2	702
	DHŪ QUWĀ AL KHAMS		
	BUʿD BIL KHAMS		
	BUʿD ALLADHĪ BIL KHAMS		
	BUʿD DHŪ ITTIFĀQ AL THĀNĪ		
	BUʿD MUTTAFIQ AL THĀNĪ		
Octave	DHŪ AL KULL	2/1	1200
	BUʿD MUTTAFIQ AL AWWAL		
	BUʿD ALLADHĪ BIL KULL		
	BUʿD BIL THAMĀN, BUʿD BIL THAMĀN		
	BUʿD AL AʿZAM		
	BUʿD BIL KULL		

BUʿD ALLADHĪ BIL ARBAʿ (b-ʿ-d) (r-b-ʿ) "interval which is with four"

Perfect fourth interval.

BUʿD ALLADHĪ BIL KHAMS (b-ʿ-d) (kh-m-s) "interval which is with five"

Perfect fifth interval.

BUʿD ALLADHĪ BIL KULL (b-ʿ-d) (k-l-l) "interval which is with the whole"

Octave interval. According to al Fārābī (1967:14), this expression was used by his predecessors while in his time the expression DHŪ AL KULL* was more common.

BUʿD ALLADHĪ BIL KULL MARRATAYN (b-ʿ-d) (k-l-l) (m-r-r) "interval which is with the whole twice"

Double octave interval.

BUʿD AL ʿARABĪ (b-ʿ-d) (ʿ-r-b) "Arab interval"

Three-quarter tone interval (Shawqī 1969a:14).

BUʿD AL AʿẒAM (b-ʿ-d) (ʿ-z-m) "greater interval"

Any interval smaller than a minor third (el Helou 1961:201).

BUʿD AL BASĪṬ (b-ʿ-d) (b-s-ṭ) "simple interval"

Any interval smaller than a minor third (el Helou 1961:201).

BUʿD BIL ARBAʿ (b-ʿ-d) (r-b-ʿ) "interval with four"

Interval of a perfect fourth (Maḥfūẓ 1964:186).

BUʿD BIL KHAMS (b-ʿ-d) (kh-m-s) "interval with five"

Interval of a perfect fifth (Maḥfūẓ 1964:186).

BUʿD BIL KULL (b-ʿ-d) (k-l-l) "interval with all"

Interval of a perfect octave (Maḥfūẓ 1964:186).

BUʿD BIL KULL MARRATAYN (b-ʿ-d) (k-l-l) (m-r-r) "interval with all twice"

Interval of a double octave (Maḥfūẓ 1964:186).

BUʿD BIL THAMĀN (b-ʿ-d) (th-m-n) "interval with the eight"

Interval of an octave (al Dāqūqī 1965:21).

BUʿD DHŪ ITTIFĀQ AL THĀLITH (b-ʿ-d) (w-f-q) (th-l-th) "the interval possessing the third consonance"

Interval of a perfect fourth (al Fārābī 1967:141).

BUʿD DHŪ ITTIFĀQ AL THĀNĪ (b-ʿ-d) (w-f-q) (th-n-y) "the interval possessing the second consonance"

Interval of a perfect fifth (al Fārābī 1967:141).

BUʿD AL IRKHĀ' (b-ʿ-d) (r-kh-w) "relaxation interval"

Interval of a quarter tone (36/35) (d'Erlanger 1939:616-617, n. 27).

BUʿD KABĪR (b-ʿ-d) (k-b-r) "large interval"

Interval of a whole tone (Al Ḥalqah 1964:11).

BUʿD KĀMIL (b-ʿ-d) (k-m-l) "complete interval"

The interval of a whole tone (contemporary theorists). This interval is distinguished from BUʿD KĀMIL AL AQALL*, the minor whole tone (Ḥāfiẓ 1971:95).

BUʿD KĀMIL AL AQALL (b-ʿ-d) (k-m-l) (q-l-l) "lesser complete interval"

Minor whole tone interval (Ḥāfiẓ 1971:95).

BUʿD KULL WA RUBʿ (b-ʿ-d) (k-l-l) (r-b-ʿ) "interval of all plus a fourth"

The major third interval (d'Erlanger 1935:297).

BUʿD LAḤNĪ (b-ʿ-d) (l-ḥ-n) "melodic interval"

See definition under pl. form, ABʿĀD LAḤNIYYAH*.

BUʿD MUTANĀFIR (b-ʿ-d) (n-f-r) "dissonant interval"

Dissonant interval.

BUʿD MUTASHĀBIH AL NAGHM (b-ʿ-d) (sh-b-h) (n-gh-m) "interval similar in tone"

See definition under pl. form, ABʿĀD MUTASHĀBIHAH AL NAGHM*.

BUʿD MUTASHĀKIL AL NAGHM (b-ʿ-d) (sh-k-l) (n-gh-m) "interval which is similar (regarding shape or form) in tone"

See definition under pl. form, ABʿĀD MUTASHĀKILAH AL NAGHM*.

BUʿD MUTAWASSIṬ (b-ʿ-d) (w-s-ṭ) "median interval"

Three-quarter tone interval (Al Ḥalqah 1964:11).

BUʿD MUTTAFIQ AL AWWAL (b-ʿ-d) (w-f-q) ('-w-l) "first consonant interval"

Interval of the perfect octave.

BUʿD MUTTAFIQ AL NAGHM (b-ʿ-d) (w-f-q) (n-gh-m) "interval which is harmonious in tone"

See definition under pl. form, ABʿĀD MUTTAFIQAH AL NAGHM*.

BUʻD MUTTAFIQ AL THĀLITH (b-ʻ-d) (w-f-q) (th-l-th) "third consonant interval"

Interval of the perfect fourth (al Fārābī 1967:141).

BUʻD MUTTAFIQ AL THĀNĪ (b-ʻ-d) (w-f-q) (th-n-y) "second consonant interval"

Interval of the perfect fifth (al Fārābī 1967:140).

BUʻD ṢAGHĪR (b-ʻ-d) (ṣ-gh-r) "small interval"

Semitone interval (Al Ḥalqah 1964:11).

BUʻD ṬANĪNĪ (b-ʻ-d) (ṭ-n-n) "resounding interval"

Whole tone interval (al Khwārizmī 1968:242).

BUʻD AL THULĀTHĪ (b-ʻ-d) (th-l-th) "third interval"

Interval of a third (Shawqī 1969a:115).

BUʻD AL THAMĀN (b-ʻ-d) (th-m-n) "eighth interval"

Octave interval (al Dāqūqī 1965:25).

BUʻD AL ZĀ'ID (b-ʻ-d) (z-y-d) "interval of increase"

Interval of one and a half tones (6 quarter tones) (Al Ḥalqah 1964: 11; Ḥāfiẓ 1971:185; Shawqī 1969a:162).

BUGHIA

Var. of BUGHYAH* (Schuyler 1978:38).

BUGHIYAH

Var. of BUGHYAH*.

BUGHYAH (pl. BUGHYĀT) = BUGHIA, BUGHIYAH, BUĠYAH, BORHIA, BURHIA (b-gh-y) "object of desire"

A short, non-metered instrumental prelude for the suite (NAWBAH/1*) which reveals the tones of the melodic mode chosen for performance (Mor.) (d'Erlanger 1959:189; Ḥāfiẓ 1971:130). A long version is known as MASHĀLIYAH*.

BUĠYAH

Var. of BUGHYAH* (d'Erlanger 1959:189).

BUKĀ' = BIḲĀ', BIQĀ' (b-k-y) "crying, weeping"

Funeral lamentation of women, which has been known since pre-Islamic times.

BŪMA

The lowest pitched of the five strings of the SIMSIMIYYAH*, a contemporary harp-like folk instrument of the regions near the Red Sea and the Arab/Persian Gulf (Shiloah 1972:19).

BŪQ (pl. BŪQĀT or ABWĀQ) = BĀQ, BÔQ, BOQUE (b-w-q)

1. Generic for any instrument of the horn or trumpet family.
2. More specifically, any horn with conical bore (Farmer 1945:33). Originally it was a natural horn without keys or valves. Later the BŪQ was made of metal and included many improvements. As a metal instrument, it became an important military instrument, sometimes reaching tremendous lengths. By the 10th C. one BŪQ was described as being 1.80 meters long.
3. Since the term BŪQ was used for any wind instrument with a conical bore, it has also been applied to certain single and double reed aerophones with a bell. A woodwind instrument with a double reed and fingerholes and carrying this name was known in 10th C. Spain. It was also called BŪQ ZAMRĪ* (Ibn Khaldūn 1967:II, 396). See also BŪQ BIL QAṢABAH*.

BŪQ AL NAFĪR (b-w-q) (n-f-r) "swelling trumpet"

Large metal trumpet, i.e., with cylindrical bore, used in the military bands of ʿAbbāsī period (Farmer 1967:154; EI(Fr), "Ṭabl Khāna":233).

BŪQ BIL QAṢABAH (b-w-q) (q-ṣ-b) "trumpet with reed"

Woodwind instrument used in late ʿAbbāsī times (Farmer 1967:210).

BŪQ ZAMRĪ (b-w-q) (z-m-r) "blowing trumpet"

A woodwind instrument with double reed, known in 10th C. Spain (Ibn Khaldūn 1967:II, 396). See also BŪQ/3*.

BURĜEL (ABŪ RIJL?)

A form of QAṢĪDAH/1* in the Maghrib (Chottin 1961:Band IX, col. 1564).

BURGHŪ or BŪRGHŪ

A large horn with conical bore used under the Mughal and Tatar rulers, according to ʿAbd al Qādir ibn Ghaybī (d. 1435). It is said to have been longer than the usual NAFĪR* (Farmer EI(Fr), "Būḳ":46).

BURHIA

Var. of BUGHYAH* (Chottin 1939:126).

BU-RHANIM or BURHANIM

Vars. of ABŪ GHANAM* (Chottin 1939:33).

BŪRĪ or BŪRŪ (Pers.) "marsh-reed"

A horn with conical bore used in modern Egypt and Syria (Farmer EI(Fr), "Būḳ":46).

BURJ (pl. BURŪJ or ABRĀJ) (b-r-j) "castle; constellation"

Any of the seven steps of the fundamental scale of the Arabs (Mashaqah 1847:175). The ABRĀJ are of two sizes: with four or with three quarters of a tone (Mashāqah n.d.:fol. 4).

BŪSALĪK = BOUSALIK, BÛSELIK, BŪSALIK (Turk.) "light kiss"

1. Name of a melodic mode (Ṣafī al Dīn 1938b:135; el Helou 1961: 128).
2. A tone of the contemporary scale of the Arabs, D#˥ or Eb˥

.

BÛSELIK or BŪSALIK

Vars. of BŪSALĪK* (Smith 1847:182; Ṣafī al Dīn in de Vaux 1891: 340-341).

BUSṬĀ

Var. of BASṬĪ* (Cowl 1966:137).

BUZRAK or BUZRUK

Vars. of BUZURK* (Mashāqah n.d.:fol. 3; de Vaux 1891:319, resp.).

BUZUQ = BOUZOQ (pers.) from BUZURK*? "large"

A long necked lute with small piriform body, fretted fingerboard and two or three pairs of metal strings. This instrument is especially popular in Syria and Lebanon. It is related to what treatises of earlier centuries have referred to as ṬUNBŪR AL BAGHDĀDĪ*. Its thin neck is about two feet long and has some 27 nylon string frets tightly wrapped around it. Its steel strings are arranged in two or three courses, with each course having two or three strings tuned in unison or at the octave. One course may serve as a drone, the other course(s) for performing melodies. A plectrum made from a soft piece of animal horn is used to strike the strings (Nettl and Riddle 1973; al Ḥafnī 1971:85). The instrument's name ("large" ?) is thought to have arisen because of the great length of the neck in relation to the saml1 soundbox or to the neck of the ʿŪD/2* (al Ḥafnī, loc. cit.). See BUZURK/3*.

BUZURG

Var. of BUZURK* (d'Erlanger 1938:136).

BUZURK = BUZURG, BOUZROUK, BOUZOURK, BUZRAK, BUZRUK, BUZUQ (Pers.)
"large"

1. Name of a melodic mode mentioned from at least the 13th C. (Ṣafī al Dīn 1938b:136).
2. Name of a tone of the contemporary Arab scale, E$\not\flat_2$  . (al Khulaʿī 1904:35).

3. A stringed instrument of Turkish origin (al Rizqī 1967:360). See BUZUQ*.

C

CADHIBA

Var. of QAṢABAH/1* (Rouanet 1922:2745).

CANK

Var. of JANK* (Sachs 1940:259).

ÇAN'A

Var. of ṢANʿAH* (Chottin 1939:127).

ÇDA

Plectrum of the lute (Mor.) (Chottin 1939:138).

CEDEF

Var. of ṢADAF* (Delphin and Guin 1886:48).

CENA'A and ÇENA'A

Vars. of ṢANʿAH* (Delphin and Guin 1886:61-62; Rouanet 1922:2941 resp.).

ČENK

Var. of JANK* (Sachs 1967:244).

CHABBABAH

Var. of SHABBĀBAH/1* (Touma 1977b:105).

CHAÏKH

Var. of SHAYKH/1* (Chottin 1939:218).

CHĀLGHĪ (Turk.) "musical instrument"

1. A suite of music (Maḥfūẓ 1964:17).
2. A vocalist (Maḥfūẓ 1964:17).
3. An instrumentalist (Maḥfūẓ 1964:17).

CHĀLGHĪ BAGHDĀDĪ (Turk.) (geog.)

Var. of JALGHĪ BAGHDĀDĪ* (Maḥfūẓ 1964:17).

CHANC and CHANG

Vars. of JANK* (Ribera 1970:93; Farmer 1976b:32-33, resp.).

CHANGAL

Var. of SHANGHAL* a drumstick with curved head (Rouanet 1922:2933).

CHATH'

Var. of SHATḤ* (Chottin 1939:50).

CHATR

Var. of SHAṬR/2* (Chottin 1939:155).

CHEBIL

Var. of SHABĪL*, a straight drumstick for the left hand (Delphin and Guin 1886:44; Rouanet 1922:2933). See SHANGHAL*.

CHEDDÂD

Var. of SHADDĀD* (Chottin 1939:160).

CHEDDÂDA

Var. of SHADDĀDAH* (Chottin 1939:160).

CHEKCHEK

Var. of SHAQSHĀQ*, a small tambourine having five sets of jingles (Rouanet 1922:2932).

CHÉKH

Var. of SHAYKH* (Chottin 1939:33, 218).

CHEMSA

Var. of SHAMSAH* (Chottin 1939:138).

CHENGAL

Var. of SHANGHAL* (Delphin and Guin 1886:44).

CHÎKH

Var. of SHAYKH* (Chottin 1939:159-160).

CHITHARA

Var. of QITHĀRAH* (Farmer 1931:4).

CHOʿBA

Var. of SHUʿBAH* (Rouanet 1922:2715).

CHOUQRA

Var. of SHUQRAH* (Chottin 1939:89).

CHTÎH'

Berber var. of SHATḤ* (Chottin 1939:50).

CHUBCHIQ

Described by ʿAbd al Qādir ibn Ghaybī (d. 1435) as the MŪSĪQĀR/4* (panpipes) of Khaṭā. Made of a number of reed pipes bound together, the instrument was blown through a tube and the wind stored in a wind-chest (JAWF*). It had finger holes to change the pitch (Farmer 1978:II, 16-17).

CHŪMLAK DUNBALAGĪ

An earthenware kettledrum said to have been invented in Egypt and played in the procession which takes the elaborately decorated covering for the Kaʿbah to Makkah for the pilgrimage (Farmer 1976b: 16).

CHURHL

Var. of SHUGHL/1* (Chottin 1939:128-129).

ÇÎKA

Var. of SĪKĀH* (Chottin 1939:61).

CITARA

Var. of QĪṬĀRAH* (Ribera 1970:109, 111).

CITHARA

Var. of QĪTHĀRAH* (Farmer 1931:48).

ÇÛTU DÎL

Var. of ṢAWT DHAYL* (Chottin 1939:132).

ÇÛTU H'SIN

Var. of ṢAWT ḤUSAYN* (Chottin 1939:132).

ÇÛTU JHIR

Var. of ṢAWT JAHĪR* (Chottin 1939:133).

ÇÛTU MÂÏA

Var. of ṢAWT MĀ'IYAH* (Chottin 1939:132).

ÇÛTU RAMAL

Var. of ṢAWT RAMAL* (Chottin 1939:132).

D

"D" (abbrev. for "dāl," one of the letters of the Ar. alphabet)

This letter designated a percussion or beat which was four times as long as ZAMĀN AL AWWAL* or "A"* time (Ṣafī al Dīn 1938b:161; 1938a: 478; al Jurjānī 1938:478; Anonymous Treatise 1939:59; al Lādhiqī 1939: 459; see also d'Erlanger 1938:608, n. 46). A conjunct rhythm utilizing this length of percussion was designated as HAZAJ THAQĪL* (Ṣafī al Dīn 1938b:161).

ḌABAṬA (ḍ-b-ṭ) "to regulate, adjust, correct"

To tune a musical instrument (Maḥfūẓ 1964:151; Wahba 1968:68).

DABBŪS (pl. DABĀBĪS) = DEBBŪS, DUBBŪS (d-b-s) "pin"

Idiophone used by the Ṣūfī dervishes which consists of a stick or lash to which chains and pellet bells are attached (Farmer EI(Fr), "Sandj":211).

DABDĀB (pl. DABĀDĪB) (onom.)

Syn. of DABDABAH/1* (Farmer 1978:I, 87).

DABDABAH = DEBDEBE, DERDEBA, DABDAB, TABDABA, TAPDEBA (onom.) "sound of footsteps"

1. A kettledrum which was used in military parades in the ʿAbbasī period (Ikhwān al Ṣafā' 1957:I, 192; 1964/65:137; Farmer 1967:154, 207).
2. A small drum used by the Berbers of North Africa and also known as DARDABAH*(Marcuse). Rouanet describes a drum with similar name (TAPDEBA*) as a member of the DARABUKKAH family (1922:2794).

ḌĀBIṬ AL ĪQĀʿ (pl. ḌUBBĀṬ AL ĪQĀʿ) (ḍ-b-ṭ) (w-q-ʿ) "officer or controller of the dropping or falling"

Another name for the RIQQ*, a small frame drum with jingles (ʿIrāq) (Touma 1977b:106).

DABKAH = DABKE (d-b-k) "stamping the feet"

The most popular form of folk dance in Palestine, Lebanon, Jordan and Syria. This open circle or line dance is performed by men or women who link themselves together by their arms and hands and strike the floor with their feet in regular sound patterns (Jargy 1970:31). In Palestine the MIJWIZ/1*, the SHABBĀBAH/1* and a singer known as QAWWĪL* often accompany this dance (ʿArnīṭah 1968:65).

DABKE

Var. of DABKAH* (Jargy 1970:31).

ḌABṬ (ḍ-b-ṭ) "adjustment; correction"

Tuning (of a musical instrument) (Shawqī 1976:350).

DAF

Var. of DAFF or DUFF/1* (Perkuhn 1976:175).

DAFF or DUFF (pl. DUFŪF, DAFĀF, DAFFAFAH) = DOF, DEFF, ADUFE, DOUFF, DOUF, DOUFE, DIF, DOF (d-f-f) "flapping the wings, fluttering"

1. Generic for frame drum or tambourine. There are many kinds varying in size, shape, and use or not of cymbals and/or snares.
2. A single-headed round frame drum with metal cymbals (ṢUNŪJ/1*) attached to its frame. This instrument is used widely for art and folk music. It differs from the RIQQ* by having a larger diameter (ca. 30 cm.) and shallower frame. It is mounted with five pairs of cymbals instead of the ten pairs of the RIQQ (Touma 1977b:107).
3. A square frame drum of the Mashriq (Delphin and Guin 1886:41).
4. A square or octagonal tambourine with two membranes instead of one. We have evidence of such an instrument from pre-Islamic times, during the ʿAbbāsī period, as well as in the contemporary Maghrib where it is mounted with snares or jingles (Kitāb al Aghānī, cited in Farmer 1967:47; Ibn Salamah 1938a:7, n. 3; Sachs 1940:246; Farmer 1945:34). Also DAFF MURABBAʿ*.

DAFF MUDAWWAR (d-f-f) (d-w-r) "round tambourine"

Syn. of DAFF or DUFF/2*.

DAFF MURABBAʿ (d-f-f) (r-b-ʿ) "square tambourine"

Syn. of DAFF or DUFF/4*.

DAFF SINDJARI

Var. of DAFF SINJĀRĪ* (Touma 1977b:106).

DAFF SINJĀRĪ = DAFF SINDJARI, DAFF ZINJĀRĪ (d-f-f) (geog.) "DAFF of Sinjār"

Syn. of DAFF or DUFF/2*.

DAFF ZINJĀRĪ

Var. of DAFF SINJĀRĪ*. Tsuge describes it as syn. of RIQQ*(1972:63).

DAFFĀF (d-f-f) "master of the DAFF"

Tambourine (DAFF or DUFF*) performer.

ḌAFĪR (ḍ-f-r) "plait, braid"

One of the sub-categories of melodic movement (INTIQĀL/1*) as described by al Kindī (1966:135-136; 146-148). It comprises both ascending and descending movements of alternating small and large intervals. There are two further sub-categories of the ḌAFĪR melodic patterning: 1) the "bound braided" (ḌAFĪR AL MUSHTABIK or ḌAFĪR AL MUTTAṢIL), and 2) the "unbound braided" (ḌAFĪR AL MUNFAṢIL). These seem to be differentiated by the restriction to use of tones not exceeding an octave by the ḌAFĪR AL MUNFAṢIL (1969:107-108).

DAFQAH (pl. DAFQĀT) (d-f-q) "outpouring, effusion"

The aesthetic release at the end of a literary segment (e.g., line, strophe, etc.). It has also been used to designate analogous points of aesthetic resolution of tension in the musical and visual arts (al Faruqi 1974:36, 184, 234ff, 305ff).

ḌĀGHIṬAH (pl. ḌĀGHIṬĀT) (ḍ-gh-ṭ) "that which exerts pressure"

A plectrum worn on the finger, e.g., that of the QĀNŪN* performer (Maḥfūẓ 1964:186).

DAḤḤIYYAH (d-ḥ-w) "that which is spread out, unrolled"

A popular song-dance of the Bedouins of the Sinai Peninsula (Shiloah 1972:17).

ḌAHR (colloq. of ẒAHR*)

The back side of the soundbox of the QĀNŪN* (Lane 1973:358).

DAINAK

A drumstick (Farmer EI(Fr), "Ṭabl":231).

DĀ'IR (d-w-r) "circulating, turning"

Designation for a type of melodic patterning (INTIQĀL/1*) which evidenced a coincidence of kinds of movement, number of notes and ratio of the intervals (Ibn Sīnā 1930:95-96; 1935:162ff).

DĀ'IRAH (pl. DAWĀ'IR) = DA'IRE, DAÏRAT (d-w-r) "circle; cycle"

1. Generic for all round frame drums (Sachs 1940:246), and even for all frame drums, according to Farmer (EI(Fr), "Duff":80).
2. Small round tambourine with pairs of cymbals inserted at intervals in its wooden frame. This tambourine had both cymbals and pellet bells attached to its frame in the early centuries of the Islamic period and in Moorish Spain. According to some authorities, it is still found in modern times with pellet bells (Farmer 1954, "Iraqian and Mesopotamian Music":531; Marcuse).
3. Tetrachordal species according to Ṣafī al Dīn (de Vaux 1891:330).

4. One of the numbers included in the North African suite (NAWBAH/1*) (Alg.). It comprises a short prelude of free rhythmed style which can be vocal, solo instrumental or orchestral. It is described as musical segments separated by silences. If sung, it utilizes stock phrases or nonsense syllables (d'Erlanger 1959:190; Touma 1977b:77; Rouanet 1922:2846).
5. A modal scale. With this meaning, the term was used over a wide historical period. It designated any of the seven-note scalar successions in the theory of Isḥaq al Mawṣilī (767-850) (Shawqī 1976:469) and the 16th C. theorist al Lādhiqī (1939:259). See also d'Erlanger 1939:509.
6. Cycle of a rhythmic mode according to Ṣafī al Dīn (1938b:164ff). See also Ṣafī al Dīn 1938a:489ff; al Jurjānī 1938:489ff; Anonymous Treatise 1939:183ff; al Lādhiqī 1939:468ff; d'Erlanger 1959:2). These, like the melodic modes, were often presented in a circular representation which accorded with their name.
7. The face of the lute (ʻŪD/2*) (Maḥfūẓ 1964:151).

DAÏRAT

Var. of DĀ'IRAH* (Rouanet 1922:2736).

DA'IRE

Var. of DĀ'IRAH/3* (Touma 1977b:77).

DĀJINAH (pl. DĀJINĀT) (d-j-n) "one who is dusky, dark; one who stays"

A professional singing girl of pre-Islamic and early Islamic times (Farmer 1967:11-12; 1957:424; EI(Eng), "Ghinā'":1073). Farmer argues that this name was given to these girls because they used to sing and play when the sky was overcast, in order to conjure rain (Farmer 1967:11, n. 4). A more likely reason for the designation may have been the color of the girls' skin.

ḌALĀL = ḌILĀL

The daughter of LAMAK*. She was traditionally held to be the inventor of the MIʻZAF* or harp (Ibn Khurdādhbih 1969:16, n. 3; al Masʻūdī 1874:VIII, 89).

DALĪL (pl. DALĀ'IL) (d-l-l) "path; guide; method"

Key signature (el Helou 1961:92).

DALĪL AL KABĪR AL ʻARABĪ (d-l-l) (k-b-r) (ʻ-r-b) "big, i.e., major, Arab method"

A category for all those melodic modes utilizing the key signatures and notes of the fundamental, contemporary Arabian scale (RĀST/2*), i.e., including intervals of 3/4 tone size (Al Ḥalqah 1964:15).

DALĪL AL KABĪR AL ʻAMM (d-l-l) (k-b-r) (ʻ-m-m) "big, i.e., major, general method"

A contemporary category for all those melodic modes utilizing the key signatures and notes of the major and minor scales of Western music, i.e., with half, whole, and one and half steps (Al Ḥalqah 1964:15).

DALĪL AL MAQĀM (d-l-l) "method of the MAQĀM"

Key signature.

DĀMĀ "checkers"

Bridge for the QĀNŪN*, called so because of its resemblance to the pieces of the checkers game (Touma 1977b:102).

DAMMAMĀT (perhaps from DAMMĀM, a seaport on the Arabian/Persian Gulf)

A women's ensemble (ʿIrāq) made of drummers and singer which performs in urban areas. Their music is "halfway between folk and art music" (Shiloah, presentation at Princeton University seminar, 1979:5). If the spelling is with Ḍ, the root may be (ḍ-m-m)"to join".

DANBAK

A single-headed, goblet-shaped drum used in Tunis and ʿIrāq (Maḥfūẓ 1964:33). Syn. of DUMBALAK*.

DANDAFAH

A stringed instrument with a metal neck used by the people of the African Sūdān (al Rizqī 1967:361).

DAOUR

Var. of DAWR/5* (Touma 1977b:82-84).

ḌĀQA (ḍ-w-q) "to become narrow"

To raise in pitch (al Khwārizmī 1968:237). Opp. of WASSAʿ*.

DAQĪQAH (pl. DAQĀ'IQ) (d-q-q) "degree;

Any one of the 70 degrees into which the scalar octave was divided in the system of Tawfīq al Sabbāgh, the 20th C. Syrian theorist. This theoretical division of the octave produced a major tone of 12 DAQĀ'IQ, and two minor tones of 9 and 8 DAQĀ'IQ (Farmer 1954, "Syrian Music":257). Even earlier (mid-19th C.) Mashāqah (n.d.:fol. 4-5) speaks of an octave divided into 68 DAQĀ'IQ.

DAQQA (d-q-q) "to pound, knock; to be thin, subtle and intricate"

1. To play a musical instrument.
2. To ring, sound (a bell).
3. To beat a percussion instrument.

DAQQĀQ (d-q-q) "the one who beats or strikes"

The instrumentalist, esp. the percussionist.

DAQQ-IL-ḤABB (d-q-q) (ḥ-b-b) "pounding the kernel of grain"

Singing and dancing performed during the harvest (Touma 1977a:122).

DARĀ (Pers.)

Clapper bell hung on the necks of elephants and camels (Marcuse).

ḌARABA (ḍ-r-b) "to strike"

To play percussion or plucked musical instrument (Farmer 1945:44).

ḌARABJĪ (ḍ-r-b)

Colloq. of ḌĀRIB*.

DARĀBKĪ (d-r-b-k)

DARABUKKAH* performer (Tun.) (Jones 1977:44; al Rizqī 1967:399).

DARABOUKKA

Var. of DARABUKKAH* (Touma 1977b:109).

DARABUKA

Var. of DARABUKKAH* (Marcuse).

DARĀBBUKKAH or DARĀBUKKEH

Vars. of DARABUKKAH* (Lane 1973:366-367).

DARABUKKAH (pl. DARABUKKĀT) = DARBŌKA, DARĀBUKKAH, DIRBAKKA, DARBŪKA, DARABUKA, DERBUGA, DERBOUKA, DARBOUKA, DARABOUKKA, DARBUKKA, DOURBAKKÉ, DURBAKKEH (d-r-b-k) der. from DARBAKAH, "drum beating; noise; din or uproar"

Goblet-shaped, single-headed drum used in the performance of art and folk music. Made of terracotta, glass, wood or metal, it is held by the performer under his left arm or on his left thigh and is played with both hands. The DUM* strokes are performed at the center of its head by the right hand, the TAK* strokes by the fingers near the edge of the drumhead. In the Maghrib, this drum is used primarily in the folk tradition, larger models being familiar in the desert regions, smaller ones among the people near the coast. In Egypt and some other parts of the Mashriq, this drum is also known as ṬABLAH/2* (el Mahdi 1972:52). The instrument varies in size over the wide geographic area and historic period of its use.

DARAJ (pl. ADRĀJ) = DARJ, DRAJ, DĀRIJ, DERDJ, DERJ (d-r-j) "course, way; staircase, stairs"

1. One of the movements of the suite (NAWBAH/1*) of the Maghrib. It varies slightly from country to country but is usually a lively vocal number similar to the MUWASHSHAḤ/1* with an introductory instrumental prelude known as KURSĪ/1* (Alg.) or DUKHŪL* (Tun.) (d'Erlanger 1959:189-196). It makes use of the rhythmic mode of

the same name, generally a ternary rhythm but of varying tempi.
2. Gradation of time values within a rhythmic mode (Farmer 1943:81).
3. A rhythmic mode of contemporary Maghribī and Mashriqī practice which varies from country to country: e.g., see el Mahdi 1972:30; Touma 1977b:65; d'Erlanger 1959:31, 151; el Helou 1961:158-160.

DARAJAH (pl. DARAJĀT) (d-r-j) "step, course"

1. Scale step.
2. Note or pitch.
3. Sound (musical).

DARAJAH AL BIDĀYAH (d-r-j) (b-d-') "starting step"

Starting tone of a scale (often syn. of tonic) (Shawqi 1976:470).

DARAJAH AL IBTIDĀ' (d-r-j) (b-d-') "starting step"

Starting tone of a scale (often syn. of tonic) (Shawqi 1976:550).

DARAJAH AL ILTIQĀ' (d-r-j) (l-q-y) "step of meeting"

The common tone between two conjunct tetrachordal scalar segments (s. JINS/1*) in the scale of a melodic mode (MAQĀM/1*), that is, the tone highest in the lower JINS and lowest in the upper JINS (al Dāqūqī 1965:78).

For example:

DARAJAH AL ISTIQRĀR (d-r-j) (q-r-r) "step of rest, stability"

Tonic note (al Rajab 1967:13).

DARAJAH AL RUKŪZ (d-r-j) (r-k-z) "step of resting"

Tonic note (Al Ḥalqah 1964:12; Shawqī 1976:550).

ḌARB (pl. ḌURŪB, ḌARABĀT) (ḍ-r-b) "percussion, strike, beat"

1. A percussion or beat on a percussion or stringed instrument.
2. A rhythmic mode (Farmer 1945:45; al Ḥafnī 1946:220).
3. A period or cycle of a rhythmic mode (Bulos 1971:15).
4. Playing a musical instrument, especially a percussion instrument (Majd al Dīn al Ghazālī 1938:127; Robson 1938c:75; Shawqī 1976:346).
5. Beating time for the music with handclapping or the hand striking the thigh (Kāẓim 1964:69).
6. A genre of music utilizing two different rhythmic modes simultaneously (Anonymous Treatise, drawing from ʿAbd al Qādir ibn Ghaybī, 1939:243).

ḌARB AṢLĪ (ḍ-r-b) ('-ṣ-l) "principal or fundamental beat"

1. A pattern of fundamental rhythmic accentuation within the cycle of a rhythmic mode by which its percussions or time units are divided

into two groups, each beginning with an accent. This term is cited by Ṣafī al Dīn in Kitāb al Adwār (1938a:488), but is virtually ignored in Risālah al Sharafiyyah (1938b). In the 15th C. Anonymous Treatise (1939:184ff) and the work of al Lādhiqī (1939:469ff), it gets much fuller treatment. Today this accentuation pattern is known as NAQARĀT AṢLIYYAH*.
2. Name given to the rhythmic mode THAQĪL AL RAMAL* by the Persians in the 13th-16th C. because of its importance in theory and practice (Ṣafī al Dīn 1938a:501; Anonymous Treatise 1939:196). This mode was designated as a 24-beat rhythm with fundamental beats on 1 and 19 (4 4 2 2 2 2 2 2 4) (Anonymous Treatise 1939:196ff).
+ +

DARBĀKA

Var. of DARABUKKAH* (d'Erlanger 1959:12).

DARBŌKA

Var. of DARABUKKAH* (Lackmann 1929:79).

DARBOUKA

Var. of DARABUKKAH* (Touma 1977b:108; Shiloah 1965:30; el Mahdi 1972:52).

DARBŪKAH (pl. DARBŪKĀT) (d-r-b-k)

1. A frame drum of North Africa (Marcuse; Lachmann and Fox-Strangways 1938:578).
2. Var. of DARABUKKAH* (d'Erlanger 1959:12; Touma 1977b:108; al Rizqī 1967:361).

DARBUKKA

Var. of DARABUKKAH (Farmer EI(Fr), "Ṭabl":231).

ḌĀRIB (pl. ḌIRĀB) (ḍ-r-b) "one who strikes"

Instrumentalist, e.g., ḌĀRIB AL ṬABL would be a synonym for "drummer."

DĀRIJ (d-r-j) "growing, spreading; current, popular"

1. Descriptive term used in the titles of contemporary rhythmic modes of rapid tempo.
2. Rapid vocal number of the Mashriqī suite (WAṢLAH/1*), with short rhythmic cycle and a rapid tempo which is gradually accelerated (d'Erlanger 1959:187-188).
3. Musical practice connected with the MAWLID/3* (i.e., the birthday celebrations of the Prophet Muḥammad) in Egypt. A vocal group sings a QAṢĪDAH/1*, followed by the leader (RA'ĪS/1*) singing a portion of the same poetic QAṢĪDAH/2* to a different tune. The chorus utilizes the leader's tune for the rest of the piece (Maḥfūẓ 1964:76).
4. One of the numbers of the suite (NAWBAH/1*) mentioned in 1001 Nights (Farmer 1967:199). See def. 5.

5. A rhythmic mode similar to the contemporary DARAJ/3*, which was used in earlier times, probably not before the 15th C. (Farmer 1945:47). It was utilized for and gave its name to the movement of the NAWBAH/1* of the same name (def. 4).

DARJ

Var. of DARAJ* (Farmer 1933b:24; Touma 1977b:77).

DARRĀZĪ

One of the optional ending movements of the NAWBAH/1* as performed in Tunisia. It is characterized by a particular folk rhythm (Jones 1977:76). According to el Mahdi, the term means a type of folk rhythm or form.

DASĀTĪN AL JĀHILIYYAH (pl. of DASTĀN AL JĀHILĪ) (Pers.) (j-h-l) "frets of the Jāhiliyyah (pre-Islamic) period"

Fretting of the ṬUNBŪR AL BAGHDĀDĪ* which was reported by al Fārābī to have been used in pre-Islamic times. It had become obsolete by the 9th C. (al Fārābī 1967:662; Collangettes 1904:401).

DASS (d-s-s) "putting, insertion"

Stopped-string execution of tones on the lute (ʿŪD*) (Farmer 1933b: 3). This was contrasted with the ḌARB*, or open string execution.

DASSAH = DESSA (d-s-s) "insertion"

An embellishing musical passage played on the KAMĀNJAH* at a high pitch level (Mor.). It is also known as THANIYYAH* or JUMLAH/1* (Chottin 1939:147).

DASTABĀN = DESTEBAN (Pers.)

Fret or fret position (al Masʿūdī 1874:VIII, 99).

DASTAH (d-s-t) "a place or seat of honor"

The wide, flat neck of the MUGHNĪ*, an ancient stringed instrument (Farmer 1926a:251).

DASTĀN (pl. DASĀTĪN, DASTĀNĀT) (Pers.) "fret"

1. Any of the modes or, more likely, tunes (ALḤĀN, s. LAḤN*) ascribed to BĀRBAD*, a famous musician of the 7th C. This group of regularly rhythmed melodies was known at the time of ʿAbd al Qādir ibn Ghaybī (d. 1435) (Farmer 1967:198-199).
2. Fret or fret position on the neck of a stringed instrument where the finger is placed in order to achieve a desired tone. Such frets are either lines marked on the fingerboard or strings tied around the neck at precise locations. The main frets on the ʿŪD*, according to al Fārābī, are given in the diagram on the next page. Al Khwārizmī (1968:238) uses the DASĀTĪN plural form; Farmer uses DASTĀNĀT in commenting on the passage from al Khwārizmī's Mafātīḥ al ʿUlūm. DASTĀNĀT is also found in Tāj al ʿArūs (al Zabīdī 1965) and in a work of Ibn Zaylah (d. 1143), according to Farmer (1926c:95), though an edition of Ibn Zaylah's Al Kāfī fī al Mūsīqā (1964:73) shows DASĀTĪN.

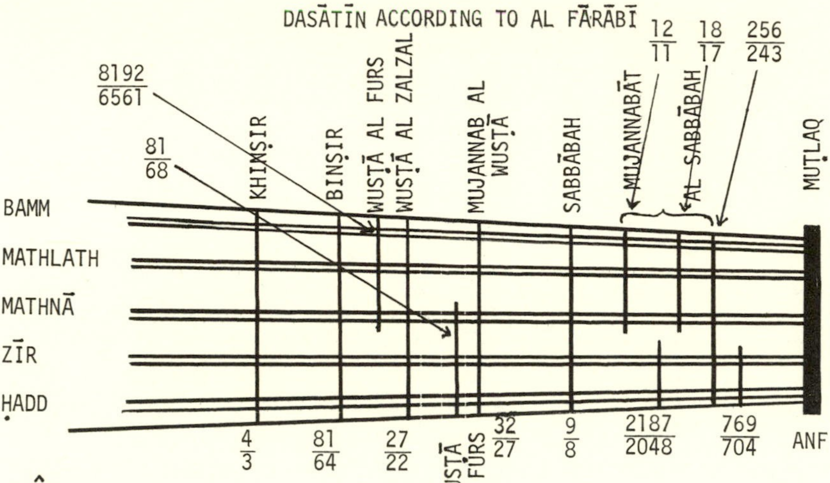

DAÛR

Var. of DAWR/1* (Chottin 1939:80, 101).

DAWR (pl. ADWĀR) = DOR, DŌR, ADOR, DAÛR (d-w-r) "turn, cycle"

1. Cycle of a rhythmic mode (ĪQĀʿ/1*) (Ṣafī al Dīn 1938b:164ff; 1938a:490ff; al Rajab 1967:23).
2. Melodic mode. The term was used in this sense at least as early as the 12th C. (Farmer 1965b:43). In the 13th-14th C., it was synonymous with SHADD/2*, i.e., a primary melodic mode.
3. A compound melodic mode, i.e., one drawing one of its tetrachords from one mode, and another from a different mode (according to al Iṣfahānī in Kitāb al Aghānī (Farmer 1967:106).
4. Any of the 84 octave species of the melodic modes, as described by Ṣafī al Dīn(1938a:312ff).
5. A vocal form especially popular in Egypt. It is similar to the MUWASHSHAḤ/1*, but utilizes much more colloquial Arabic in the poetic content. The term has been used in this sense at least since the 15th C. (Farmer 1965b:62). The contemporary DAWR has three distinct parts: 1) The MADHHAB/1* in which the theme is exposed by a soloist and then repeated by two or more choristers in unison. This is followed by an instrumental repetition of the same tune. 2) The DAWR/6*, which includes solo improvisations based on the original theme and ending with virtuoso passages on the upper registers of the mode. The chorus echos the soloist on a lower register or by singing complementary phrases. This richly ornamented construction is sung to the syllable "AH" and is known as ĀHANG or ĀHANK/3*. Sometimes it is called simply HANK* (Ḥāfiẓ 1971:205). Each section of variation or modulation by the soloist is followed by an orchestral repetition of the MADHHAB, each phrase by a short instrumental motif known as a LĀZIMAH*. 3) The QAFLAH/1* in which the instrumentalists and singers join to perform in unison a number of phrases recapitulating the MADHHAB and gradually descending to the tonic (Bulos 1971:30-31; d'Erlanger 1959:178-179). This is the longest genre of the Mashriqī suite or WAṢLAH/1* (Racy 1978b:2-3). According to Ḥāfiẓ, the first segment of the DAWR

(the MADHHAB) was formerly a choral refrain which alternated with contrasting segments (AGHṢĀN, s. GHUṢN*) sung by the soloist. According to him the melodic content of the MADHHAB and GHUṢN were identical. More recently, he continues, the soloist repeats the words of the first GHUṢN or poetic segment many times with different tunes. The chorus may repeat any of these new tunes in response to a solo segment. Hickmann describes another type of DAWR done by a vocal soloist and instrumentalists only. He compares it to a suite of several songs separated by instrumental interludes. The melody is accompanied in unison or at the octave by the SIBS* or one or two other aerophones. When one instrument plays a melody, the other provides drone-like support (Hickmann 1958:42).
6. One of the three major sections of the DAWR/5*, MUWASHSHAḤ/1* or similar genre.
7. The "turn" of a musician for performing (Ribera 1970:87-88).

DAWR AL QUWĀ (d-w-r) (q-w-y) "cycle of strength"

Each octave span in the range of an instrument or voice (al Fārābī 1967:124).

DAWZANA (d-w-z-n) "to tune"

To tune a musical instrument.

DAWZANAH (d-w-z-n) "tuning"

Tuning of a musical instrument.

DAYĀLŪJ (Eng.) "dialogue"

A contemporary term for musical "discussion" or interplay between two vocalists.

ḌAYYAQA (ḍ-y-q) "to narrow; to tighten, pull tight"

To be or become high in pitch (al Khwārizmī 1968:237).

DEBBŪS

Var. of DABBŪS* (Marcuse).

DEBDEBE

Var. of DABDABAH* (Kieswetter 1968:93).

DEBLAK

Syn. of NUQAYRAH* kettledrums (Shiloah 1965:30).

DEFF

Var. of DAFF or DUFF* and described as a frame drum of very ancient times (Chottin 1939:116, 164). Rouanet describes it as a tambourine having two membranes. In some parts of the Maghrib, it is square in shape; in others places, it is round (Rouanet 1922:2935).

DEHOL

Var. of DUHUL* (Marcuse).

DERBOUKA or DERBOÛKA

Vars. of DARABUKKAH* (Salvador-Daniel 1976:118; Chottin 1939:116).

DERBUGA

Var. of DARABUKKAH* (Schuyler 1978:40).

DERDEBA (d-r-d-b)

A drum used by by the negroes of Algeria (Delphin and Guin 1886: 61). Syn. of DABDABAH/2* and var. of DARDABAH* (supp.) (Marcuse).

DERDJ

Var. of DARAJ/1* (Delphin and Guin 1886:64-65).

DERJ

Var. of DARAJ/3* (Chottin 1939:11, 118); DARAJ/1* (Rouanet 1922:2855).

DESSA

Var. of DASSAH* (Chottin 1939:147).

DESTEBĀN

Var. of DASTABĀN* (de Meynard 1874:VIII, 99).

DHABDHABAH (pl. DHABDHABĀT) (onom.) "vibration"

The beats of a musical vibration; musical vibration (Shawqī 1976: 277).

DHĀHIR

Var. of ẒĀHIR* (d'Erlanger 1938:366; 1939:375).

DHAHĪR

Var. of ẒAHĪR* (d'Erlanger 1949:106-108).

DHAIL

Var. of DHAYL* (Farmer 1933b:35).

DHĀQINAH (pl. DHĀQINĀT) (dh-q-n) der. from DHIQN, "chin"

A piece of wood fastened to the top end of the sound box on which rests the player's chin at the time of playing a violin or viola type instrument (Maḥfūẓ 1964:159).

DHARRAH ṢAWTIYYAH (pl. DHARRĀT ṢAWTIYYAH) (dh-r-r) (ṣ-w-t) "tiny sound particle"

Syn. of "cent," the unit of measurement for musical intervals which is equal to 1/100 of the semitone of the equal tempered or well-tempered scale. Thus each octave equals 1200 cents (or DHARRĀT) and each semitone of the tempered scale equals 100 cents (or DHARRĀT). Also SANT* (Allawerdi 1949:142-146).

DHĀT ʿAWDĀT (ʿ-w-d) "possessor of returns"

A poetic or musical passage with repetitions of segments.

DHĀT al AWTĀR (w-t-r) "possessor of strings"

Any chordophone.

DHĀT QAWĀFĪ (q-w-f) "possessor of rhymes"

Measured rhymed verse.

DHĀT AL SINN (s-n-n) "possessor of teeth"

1. Eighth note in contemporary notation (el Helou 1961:20; Maḥfūẓ 1964:186).
2. Said of any woodwind instrument that is blown with a reed (al Fārābī 1967:787, n. 3).

DHĀT SINNAYN (s-n-n) "possessor of two teeth"

Sixteenth note in contemporary notation (el Helou 1961:20).

DHAYL = DHAIL, DHĪL, DĪL (dh-y-l) "tail"

1. The lowest or BAMM* string of the lute (Farmer 1933b:35) or of the Maghribī rabāb (Chottin 1939:145-146).
2. One of the principal melodic modes of the contemporary Maghrib.

DHEKR

Var. of DHIKR* (Touma 1977b:134ff).

DHIKR = DHEKR, DÎKR, ZIKR (dh-k-r) "remembrance"

Religious ritual performed by mystics of the Muslim World which involves recitation of the Qur'ān, the chanting of religious prayers, formulas and poetry, in an effort to reach a religious ecstasy or trance. Other practices which are often involved are meditation, group singing and body movements, use of incense and instrumental music, and less often dance and self-torture. The prime goal is to "remember" God. DHIKR takes place usually at a public or private gathering place other than the mosque. The event is known as a ḤAḌRAH*. See Gardet 1965:II, 223-227.

DHĪL

Var. of DHAYL*, mentioned in a copy of an anonymous treatise from the Maghrib, whose original source probably dates from before 1504 (Farmer 1933b:3).

DHŪ AL ʻANQĀ' (ʻ-n-q) "having a long neck"

Syn. of ʻANQĀ'*. This ancient instrument was mentioned by Ibn Sīnā (1935:233) and is described as having its open strings stretched across the surface of the resonance box.

DHŪ AL ARBAʻ = DOUL ʻARABAʻ (r-b-ʻ) "possessor of four"

Perfect fourth interval.

DHŪ AL KHAMS (kh-m-s) "possessor of five"

Perfect fifth interval.

DHŪ AL KULL (k-l-l) "possessor of all"

Octave interval. Also DHŪ BIL KULL.

DHU AL MADDATAYN (m-d-d) "having two whole tones"

Said of a tetrachordal scalar segment (JINS/1*) having two whole tones, i.e., the diatonic JINS of two whole tones and a semitone (al Fārābī 1967:824, n. 2; 892).

DHŪ QUWĀ AL ARBAʻ (q-w-y) (r-b-ʻ) "possessor of the strengths of four"

Perfect fourth interval (al Fārābī 1967:141-142).

DHŪ QUWĀ AL KHAMS (q-w-y) (kh-m-s) "possessor of the strengths of five"

Perfect fifth interval (al Fārābī 1967:141-142).

DHŪ AL TAḌʻĪF (ḍ-ʻ-f) "possessor of doubling"

One of the three types of strong (QAWĪ*) tetrachordal scalar segment (JINS/1*), and described as that in which two intervals are equal in size (al Fārābī 1967:293-298; 892). Also QAWĪ DHŪ AL TAḌʻĪF*.

DHŪ AL THALĀTHAH (th-l-th) "possessor of three"

Any interval of a third, including two kinds of minor third, a neutral third and a major third, which have been used in Arabian music.

DIANEI

Var. of DIYĀNĀY* (de Meynard 1874:VIII, 90).

DIF

Var. of DAFF or DUFF/1* (el Helou 1961:135; Perkuhn 1976:115).

ḌIʿF (pl. AḌʿĀF) = DUʿF (ḍ-ʿ-f) "double, a multiple"

Octave equivalent (Ibn al Munajjim 1976:218; al Kindī 1966:153).

ḌIʿF ALLADHĪ BIL KULL (ḍ-ʿ-f) (k-l-l) "the double of that which has all"

The double octave (al Fārābī 1967:964).

ḌIʿF DHŪ AL KULL (d-ʿ-f) (k-l-l) "the double of the possessor of all"

The double octave (al Khwārizmī 1968:244).

DĪH (pl. DĪHĀT)

Syn. of DUM* or TUM* (Massignon EI(Fr), "Tik":765).

DĪK

Syn. of TĪZ* (Kāẓim 1964:34).

DÎKR

Var. of DHIKR* (Chottin 1939:169).

DĪL

Var. of DHAYL* (Farmer 1933b:3; Chottin 1939:145-146).

ḌILʿ (pl. ḌULUʿ, AḌLĀʿ, AḌLUʿ) (ḍ-l-ʿ) "rib, side"

Rib of the ʿŪD*. See Rouanet 1922:2926, 2944 (pl. DALʿAĀT).

DILAL

Var. of ḌALĀL* (de Meynard 1874:VIII, 89).

DIQQAH (d-q-q) "thinness; subtlety"

1. Fineness or smallness of tone (Ibn al Munajjim 1950:6).
2. Highness of pitch (Shawqī 1976:347).

DIRBAKKAH

Var. of DARABUKKAH* (Syr.) (Madina).

DIRRĪJ (d-r-j) "one who is always advancing"

Drum with a single face, similar to the DARABUKKAH*, which was known at the time of Ibn Salamah (1938a:14). It was similar to the contemporary Maghribī drum known as DURRAIJ or DURRAYJ*. Except for diacritical marks, these terms are spelled identically. Another use of the same Ar. spelling, given without diacritical marks which could determine its proper transliteration, is found in Maḥfūẓ (1964:32). There, it is defined as a ṬUNBŪR*, i.e., a long-necked lute. Robson denies this extension of the meaning of the term to be legitimate (1938a:14, n. 3, 15; 1938b:244).

DĪWĀN (pl. DAWĀWĪN) (d-w-n) "council"

The eight consecutive steps (notes) comprising one octave of a modal scale. It is also used for the eight notes comprising one octave of the two-octave gamut of contemporary Arabian music theory (Mushāqah 1849:175; Shihāb al Dīn in Collangettes 1904:414).

DĪWĀN ASĀSĪ (d-w-n) ('-s-s) "fundamental register, collection"

Contemporary designation for the fundamental octave of a melodic mode (MAQĀM/1*), constituting two tetrachordal segments (s. JINS/1*) --the JIDHʿ* and the FARʿ/1* (d'Erlanger 1949:100).

DĪWĀN AWWAL (d-w-n) ('-w-l) "first collection"

1. G_1-G_2, the lower octave in the two-octave gamut of tones used by the Arabs (el Helou 1961:69; al Khulaʿī 1904:34).
2. The lower octave of a modal scale (el Helou 1961:94).

DĪWĀN FARʿĪ (d-w-n) (f-r-ʿ) "branch collection"

Contemporary designation for the second or higher octave of a modal scale.

DĪWĀN JAWĀBĪ (d-w-n) (j-w-b) "answering collection"

The notes of the upper octave of the two-octave scale of contemporary Arabian music theory (Allawerdi 1949:589).

DĪWĀN KĀMIL (d-w-n) (k-m-l) "complete collection"

Octave scale (al Rajab 1967:16).

DĪWĀN QARĀRĪ (d-w-n) (q-r-r) "bottom, or most stable collection"

The notes of the lower octave of the two-octave gamut of contemporary Arabian music theory (Allawerdi 1949:589).

DĪWĀN THĀNĪ (d-w-n) (th-n-y) "second collection"

1. G_2-G_3, the higher octave in the two octave gamut used by the contemporarh Arabs (el Helou 1961:69; al Khulaʿī 1904:35).
2. The second or higher octave of a modal scale (el Helou 1961:94).

DĪWĀNĪ (d-w-n) "recorded"

Notated (music) (al Dāqūqī 1965:40).

DIYĀNAI or DIYĀNĀY

Vars. of DŪNĀY* (Farmer EI(Eng), "Mizmār":541; 1978:I, 57-58). Farmer claims these are more authentic forms than DŪNĀY, and that they are the ones used by al Fārābī and al Masʿūdī. The 1874 Ar. edition of al Masʿūdī (VIII:90) uses DIYĀNĀY, but the 1967 edition of al Fārābī's Kitāb al Mūsīqī al Kabīr has DŪNĀY (p. 795). The editor, Khashabah (1967:795, n.2) gives other forms found in various manuscripts.

DIYAYZ (pl. DIYAYZĀT) (Fr.) "sharp sign"

The sharp sign (#) for raising the pitch of a tone by one semitone. For the contemporary Arab musician or theorist, there are three kinds of DIYAYZ: DIYAYZ AL KŪMĀ*, DIYAYZ AL BAQIYYAH*, DIYAYZ AL MUJANNAB AL ṢAGHĪR* (al Dāqūqī 1965:40).

DIYAYZ AL KŪMĀ (Fr.) (Eng.) "sharp sign of the comma"

Sharp sign raising the pitch of a note by 22 c. (ǂ or ⸸ or ∓) (al Dāqūqī 1965:40).

DIYAYZ AL BAQIYYAH (Fr.) (b-q-y) "sharp sign of the remainder"

Sharp sign raising the pitch of a note by 92 c. (#) (al Dāqūqī 1965:40).

DIYAYZ AL MUJANNAB AL ṢAGHĪR (Fr.) (j-n-b) (ṣ-gh-r) "sharp sign of the small neighbor"

Sharp sign raising the pitch of a note by 114c. (丰丰 or ⁘) (al Dāqūqī 1965:40).

DJAHLAH (j-h-l?)

A water jar of 60 cm. height which is used as a percussion instrument in the Arabian/Persian Gulf region to accompany the vocalists of a type of folk music called FIDJRI*. This instrument is played by the open hand beating on the jar's mouth and by scraping the jar with finger rings (Touma 1977a:124-127).

DJALADJIL

Var. of JALĀJIL* (Touma 1977b:15).

DJALGHI BAGHDADI

Var. of JALGHĪ BAGHDĀDĪ* (Touma 1977b:71).

DJAOUAB

Var. of JAWĀB/1* (Touma 1977b:38).

DJAOUAK

Var. of JUWĀQ/1* (Salvador-Daniel 1976:16, 116, 220-221).

DJENK

Var. of JANK* (de Meynard 1974:VIII, 90).

DJILDAH

Var. of JILDAH* (Farmer EI(Fr), "Rabāb":1160).

DJIRBEH

Var. of JIRBAH* (Touma 1977a:122).

DJNBRI

Var. of JUMBRĪ* (Touma 1977b:96).

DJNOUDJ

Var. of ṢUNŪJ* or ZUNŪJ*, the finger cymbals (Salvador-Daniel 1976: 189, 243).

DJORKA

Var. of JIHĀRKĀH*.

DJOUAK

Var. of JUWĀQ/1* (Delphin and Guin 1886:45; Shiloah 1965:30).

DJOUMBRI

Var. of JUMBRĪ* (Touma 1977b:96).

DJOZE

Var. of JAWZ or JAWZAH* (Touma 1977b:71).

DJULDJUL

Var. of JULJUL* (Farmer EI(Fr), "Ṣandj":210).

DKHEL

Var. of DUKHŪL* (Chottin 1939:128).

DKHOUL

Var. of DUKHŪL* (el Mahdi 1972:14).

DOF

Var. of DAFF or DUFF* (Salvador-Daniel 1976:109).

DOHOL

Var. of DUHUL* (Marcuse).

DOM

Var. of DUM* (Chottin 1957:41).

DOR or DŌR

Vars. of DAWR/5* (Jargy 1970:34; Touma 1977b:82-84, resp.).

DOUF

Var. of DAFF or DUFF* (Chottin 1957:41; Rouanet 1922:2744-2745).

DOUFE

Var. of DAFF or DUFF* (Rouanet 1922:2744-2745).

DOUFF

Var. of DAFF or DUFF* (Chottin 1939:60; Touma 1977b:107).

DOUKAH

Var. of DŪKĀH* (Touma 1977b:37).

DOUL ʿARABAʿ

Var. of DHŪ AL ARBAʿ* (Rouanet 1922:2706).

DOULAB

Var. of DŪLĀB* (el Mahdi 1972:19; Touma 1977b:90).

DOUM

Var. of DUM* (Touma 1977b:64).

DOUNBAK

Var. of DUMBALAK*, the goblet-shaped drum (Touma 1977b:71).

DOU-NEÏ

Var. of DIYĀNĀY* or DŪNĀY* (de Meynard 1874:VIII, 90).

DOURBAKKE

Var. of DARABUKKAH* (Touma 1977b:108).

DRABGĪ

Var. and colloq. of ḌĀRIB* (ḌARABJĪ*) (Chottin 1939:143).

DRABGUÎ

Var. and colloq. of ḌĀRIB* (ḌARABJĪ*) (Chottin 1939:142).

DRAJ

Var. of DARAJ/1* (Tun.) (el Mahdi 1972:12, 14; Jones 1977:291) and DARAJ/3* (d'Erlanger 1959:151; Jones 1977:291).

DRŪB

Var. of ḌURŪB* (d'Erlanger 1959:151).

DŪBAYT (Pers.) (b-y-t) "two-line"

1. Genre of poetry with paired lines.
2. Genre of ʿATĀBĀ* found in the Sūdān.

DUBBŪS

Var. of DABBŪS* (Marcuse).

DUF

Var. of DAFF or DUFF* (Lachmann and Fox-Strangways 1938:578).

DUʿF

Var. of ḌIʿF* (Collangettes 1904:405).

DUFE

Var. of DAFF or DUFF* (Rouanet 1922:2744-2745).

DŪFĀY

Var. of DŪNĀY* (Farmer 1978:57).

DUFF

Equiv. of DAFF* (al Rizqī 1967:361).

DŪGĀH

Var. of DŪKĀH/1* (Smith 1847:181).

DUGHAH

Var. of DŪKĀH/3* (Shiloah 1972:19).

DUHUL = DEHOL, DOHOL (Pers.)

Drum used in a military band of Fāṭimī and Mamluk periods (Farmer 1967:208; 1954, "Egyptian Music":893). A barrel-shaped drum with two laced heads was known by this name in Persia (Farmer 1978: II, 13).

DUḪŪL

Var. of DUKHŪL* (Perkuhn 1976:107).

DŪKĀH = DŪGĀH, DOUKAH, DUGHAH (Pers.) "position two"

1. Name for D_1 , a note of the contemporary Arabian scale.
2. A melodic mode mentioned in the 15th C. (Anonymous Treatise 1939: 399).
3. The second (moving from lowest to highest in pitch) of the five strings of the SIMSIMIYYAH*, a contemporary harp-like folk instrument (Shiloah 1972:19).

DUKHŪL = DKHEL, DKHOUL, DUḪŪL (d-kh-l) "entrance"

A short optional instrumental prelude which precedes some of the songs of the NAWBAH/1* or suite (Tun.) (el Mahdi 1972:14; d'Erlanger 1959: 193-196).

DULAAB

Var. of DŪLĀB* (Bulos 1971:36).

DŪLĀB (pl. DAWĀLĪB) = DULAAB, DOULAB "wheel"

A short instrumental introduction, a sort of refrain which separates the vocal sections of the suite (WAṢLAH/1* or NAWBAH/1*). It is played by the orchestra in unison in a rapid tempo which utilizes a rhythmic mode (ĪQĀʿ/1*) of short binary cycle, usually WAḤDAH ṢAGHĪRAH*. It is generally composed of a short melodic phrase which is repeated once or twice, after which contrasting phrases are added before one or two repetitions of the whole piece. The final cadence retards the movement as this introductory piece ends on the tonic of the melodic mode (MAQĀM/1*). This number is comparable to the KURSĪ* of Algeria and the FĀRIGHAH* of Tunisia (d'Erlanger 1959:180-181; el Mahdi 1972:19).

DUM = DOUM, DOM, TUM, DUMM (onom.)

A heavy, dense percussion stroke (d'Erlanger 1959:10). See DUMM*, TAK*.

DUMBALAK = DANBAK, DUNBAK, DUMBAK, DŪMBŪK, DUMBŪK, DOUMBAK, DONBAG

Contemporary drum of goblet shape, usually made of metal and covered by a single membrane. In some regions it is played with a metal pipe or wooden drumstick for accompanying dancers. Otherwise it is played with the fingers (Ḥāfiẓ 1971:162, 164). In ʿIrāq, it is generally used in connection with the NĀY/1*, as part of an instrumental ensemble to accompany the vocalist in MAQĀM AL ʿIRĀQĪ* (Touma 1977b:71). The peasant version of this instrument used in ʿIrāq can be made of pottery and called BARBAKH*; made of wood, it is called KHASHABAH* (al Dāqūqī 1965:39). According to Ḥāfiẓ, it is known as DŪMBŪK* in Eygpt. The name goes back to pre-Islāmic times.

DŪMBŪK, DUMBŪK or DUMBUK

A small goblet-shaped, single-headed drum played with the fingers (Mashriq) (Ḥāfiẓ 1971:162, 164, 169). Vars.of DUMBALAK*.

DUMM (pl. DUMUM) (onom.)

Equiv. of DUM* (el Helou 1961:134). One of the two qualitatively variant percussion strokes, the other being TAK*. The DUMM stroke is heavy, dense and sonorous. It is produced a) at the center of the drum or tambourine membrane, b) by the open and slightly hollows palms if clapping, or c) by the right foot stamping if dancing (Massignon 1913-1934:765-766).

DŪNĀY = DIANEÏ, DOU-NEÏ, DIYĀNAI, DIYĀNĀY (Pers.) "two nays"

Double reed pipe described by al Fārābī, al Masʿūdī and other theorists of the Classical Period. Both pipes were furnished with fingerholes (Farmer EI(Eng), "Mizmār":541; al Fārābī 1967:795, also see n.2; al Mas'ūdī 1874:VIII, 90). The instrument is said to have been invented by the Persians to accompany the ṬUNBŪR/1*. See Farmer (1928a:513-514; 1978:I, 57-58) for a discussion of the various spellings or terms for this instrument. See DIYĀNAI or DIYĀNĀY*.

DUNBAK

Var. of DUMBALAK* in 'Irāq (Touma 1977b:71, 109). This name goes back to ancient Persia, when it designated a goblet-shaped drum similar to that which carries the name today (Farmer EI(Fr), "Ṭabl": 231).

DŪRĀY

Var. of DŪNĀY* (Farmer 1978:I, 57).

DURBAKKEH

Var. of DARABUKKAH* (Jargy 1978:81).

ḌURRĀB (ḍ-r-b) "those who always strike"

Syn. (pl. form) of ḌĀRIB* (al Kindī 1965:9).

DURRAIJ or DURRAYJ (d-r-j) "dim. of DIRRĪJ"

A contemporary single-faced goblet drum of the Maghrib (Marcuse). See DIRRĪJ*.

ḌURŪB (ḍ-r-b) "strikings"

1. Method of gradual acceleration near the end of a tune. It is followed, after a moment of silence, by a return to the original tempo and/or rhythm (Tun.) (Ḥāfiẓ 1971:120).
2. The first of two codas for the MUṢADDAR/1*, an instrumental movement of the Tunisian suite (NAWBAH/1*) (d'Erlanger 1959:192). Also ṬAWQ/1* or ḤURŪB*.
3. Pl. of ḌARB*.

DŪSĀY

Var. of DŪNĀY (Farmer 1978:I, 57).

DŪZĀN (d-w-z-n)

Syn. of DAWZANAH* (Wehr).

DŪZĀY

Var. of DŪNĀY* (Farmer 1978:I, 57).

E

ECH-CHREUL

Var. of SHUGHL/2* (Rouanet 1922:2942).

ECHREUL

Var. of SHUGHL/2* (Rouanet 1922:2877, 2881).

'EMʿANNĀ

Var. of MUʿANNĀ* (Jargy 1970:40).

EMM-Z-ZULUF

Var. of UMM AL ZULUF* (Jargy 1970:40).

'EMRABBAʿ

Var. of MURABBAʿ/4* (Jargy 1970:45).

F

FACELA

Var. of FĀṢILAH/5* (Delphin and Guin 1886:49).

FAḌLAH (pl. FAḌLĀT) (f-ḍ-l) "surplus, remainder"

An interval equivalent to the Pythagorean limma (256/243 or 90 c.) or the approximation of that interval used by Arab theorists (20/19) (al Fārābī 1930:109; 1967:145; Ṣafī al Dīn 1938b:26). This minor semitone was also known as BAQIYYAH* and was abbreviated as "B"/2*. Other theorists assigned the name FAḌLAH, as well as BAQIYYAH, to an interval comparable to the Pythagorean comma with approximate ratio of 81/80 (d'Erlanger 1939:502-503, n. 12). Later writers alleviated the confusion by using the term BAQIYYAH for the limma, and FAḌLAH for the comma (al Jurjānī 1938:238; al Lādhiqī 1939:301).

FAḌLAH AL ṬANĪNĪ (f-ḍ-l) (ṭ-n-n) "surplus of the resonant"

Major semitone interval (2187/2049, or 114 c.) according to Ibn Sīnā (Farmer 1937a:252, 255; 1978b:52).

FAḤL (pl. FUḤŪL) = F'HAL (f-ḥ-l) "male animal; stallion; master"

A single pipe, end-blown flute mentioned by a 13th-14th C. writer (Shawqī 1976:281). Also ZĪR/2*. A contemporary version of this instrument improvised from a metal tube is described as a folk instrument of the Maghrib (el Mahdi 1972:49).

FANN AL NAGHAM (f-n-n) (n-gh-m) "art of tones"

Art of music (Shiloah 1968a:239, 246).

FAQQĀSHĀT (f-q-sh) "broken pieces"

An unidentified percussion instrument of Moorish Spain (el Helou 1965:39). Today the term is applied to a percussion instrument of the folk tradition (Palestine and Egypt) which comprises two pieces of wood or dried bone fastened to the fingers. It is generally played only by women to accompany the dance and is used as a double pair, one in each hand. This contemporary version is often made of metal as well as of wood or bone (ʿArnīṭah 1968:45-46).

FARʿ (pl. FURŪʿ) (f-r-ʿ) "branch"

1. Second or upper of two main tetrachordal segments (JINS/1*) making up the scale of a melodic mode (MAQĀM/1*) (Al Ḥalqah 1964: 17; Ṣalāḥ al Dīn 1950:103).
2. Derivative melodic mode (Anonymous Treatise 1939:131; see also Touma 1976:17). In the Maghrib, it has meant any of the 19 secondary modes derived from the 5 principal modes or UṢŪL of North African-Andalusian practice and theory (Farmer 1933b:8).

FARAS (pl. AFRĀS) (f-r-s) "horse, mare; knight (of the chess game)"

The bridge to support strings of a chordophone. For the QĀNŪN* it is a wooden stick of triangular shape affixed to the face of the sound box near its perpendicular end, at right angles with the two parallel sides (al Ḥafnī 1971:49). For the lute (ʿŪD/2*) the name is given to a piece of wood attached to the lower end of its face. The instrument's strings are fastened in the holes bored in this FARAS (al Ḥafnī 1971:74).

FARDIYYAH (pl. FARDIYYĀT) (f-r-d) "singular"

Designation for the time units of an AʿRAJ* rhythmic mode, denoting their non-paired organization (el Helou 1961:135).

FĀRIGHAH AL NAGHAM (f-r-gh) (n-gh-m) "empty notes"

Vocal performance in which one syllable of the text is sung to each pitch or tone of the melody or to more than one tone (al Fārabi 1967: 1133; d'Erlanger 1935:250, n. 2). Opp. of MAMLUWWAH AL NAGHAM*.

FĀRIGHAH = FARIGA (f-r-gh) "empty (of lyrics); wide"

A short instrumental interlude played between vocal numbers or verses of sung poetry in the NAWBAH/1* suite (Tun.) (el Mahdi 1972: 14; Jones 1977:197). Also used as an instrumental overture.

FĀṢIL (pl. FAWĀṢIL) (f-ṣ-l) "division"

1. Any of the 53 units of measurement into which some of the Syrian theorists of this century have divided the octave. Each FĀṢIL is equal to 1/9 of a whole tone, or a comma (KŪMA or KŪMĀ*) (d'Erlanger 1949:28-30).
2. Syrian form of the instrumental and vocal suite known in other parts of the Arab World as WAṢLAH/1* or NAWBAH/1*, FAṢL/1*.

FĀṢILAH (pl. FAWĀṢIL) = FACELA, FÂÇIL (f-ṣ-l) "that which separates"

1. The silence separating two musical phrases or sections (al Fārābī 1935:63; 1967:1090).
2. The distance separating two tones, i.e., an interval.
3. The silence between phrases of Qur'ānic psalmody (Boubakeur 1968:

394).
4. The time between the last percussion of a disjunct rhythmic cycle and the beginning of the first percussion in the following cycle (al Fārābī 1967:455-456, 478). The same source describes it as the longest separating duration between percussions of a rhythmic mode.
5. The wooden ring (see FAṢL/4*) mounted at the top of the GHAYṬAH/1* into which the ḍouble reed is placed (Alg.) (Delphin and Ġuin 1886:49).
6. A prosodic term borrowed by the Arab music theorists to indicate the duration of a member (RIJL/1*) within the rhythmic cycle (DAWR/1*). This term stands for a member with four beats (comparable to a poetic member with four consonants, three moving and the other quiescent--TANANAN). It has been notated in various ways (e.g., ♫♪𝄾; ♪♩♩𝄽; etc.) with varying tempi (Farmer 1943: 72; al Fārābī 1967:1076ff). See also SABAB*, WATAD*.

FĀṢILAH ṢUGHRĀ (f-ṣ-l) (ṣ-gh-r) "small separator"

A linguistic term used by the Arab music theorists to designate a member (RIJL/1*) of the rhythmic cycle having four basic time units (s. ZAMĀN AL AWWAL*) (d'Erlanger 1959:4-5).

FĀṢILAH KUBRĀ (f-ṣ-l) (k-b-r) "large separator"

A linguistic term used by the Arab theorists to designate a member (RIJL/1*) of the rhythmic cycle having five basic time units (s. ZAMĀN AL AWWAL*) (d'Erlanger 1959:4-5).

FĀṢILAH ʿUẒMĀ (f-ṣ-l) (ʿ-ẓ-m) "largest separator"

The longest percussion in the cycle of a rhythmic mode (al Fārābī 1967:999, also n. 4).

FĀṢILAH WUSṬĀ (f-ṣ-l) (w-s-ṭ) "medium or middle separator"

A species of scalar combination (JAMʿ/1*) in which the separating whole tone is at the middle of each octave of the two-octave scale (Ṣafī al Dīn in de Vaux 1891:323).

FAṢL (pl. FUṢŪL) (f-ṣ-l) "section"

1. Suite of instrumental and/or vocal movements based primarily on a single melodic mode (MAQĀM/1*). It contains improvised as well as composed numbers (d'Erlanger 1959:185). Each FAṢL takes its name from the MAQĀM on which it is based. In ʿIrāq, the FAṢL is generally three to four hours in duration. In the course of an evening's musical entertainment, several FUṢŪL may be performed (Touma 1977b:73-74). See also FĀṢIL/2*.
2. Syn. of MURAṢṢAʿ/1*, a musical section or movement described by theorists of the Classical Period (al Kindī 1966:154; ʿAbd al Qādir ibn Ghaybī in <u>Anonymous Treatise</u> 1939:246-247).
3. Any of the many musically accelerating sections of the DHIKR* ceremony which involve repetitive chanting of formulae by the general participants and solos (s. MADĪḤ*) by a male vocalist (MUNSHID*). A four-beat rhythm known as WAḤDAH/2* underlays the

melodic creation. The chosen melodic mode (MAQĀM/1*) is maintained until near the end of the segment, where a modulation and quickening change of tempo foretell the abrupt conclusion of the FAṢL (Poche 1978:68).
4. The head of the GHAYṬAH/1*. This wooden cylinder is approx. 9 cm. long; 7.5 cm. of it are fitted into the upper end of the tube of the instrument (Farmer 1978:I, 81). See FĀṢILAH/5*.

FAṢL MŪSĪQĪ (pl. FUṢŪL MŪSĪQIYYAH) (f-ṣ-l) (Gr.) "musical section, partition"

Musical selection, piece (al Ḥafnī 1946:290).

FERACHE

Var. of FIRĀSH/2* (Delphin and Guin 1886:34).

F'HAL

Var. of FAḤL*, a folk instrument of the Maghrib. It is made today from a metal tube (el Mahdi 1972:49).

FIDJRI

Var. of FIJRĪ* (Touma 1977a).

FIJRĪ = FIDJRI (f-j-r) "breaking through, as a sunrise"

A musical term designating all "sea musics," but specifically a genre of Baḥrayn folk music performed by the men who are involved with pearl diving. It is mainly a vocal music accompanied by clapping, percussion, and dance movements. The people of Baḥrayn distinguish many types of FIJRĪ, e.g., MEYDAF*, BASSEH*, QAYLEMI*, and KHRAB*, which are sung at sea as well as for evening entertainment on shore. Instruments include double-headed drums (ṬABL/2* and MIRWĀS*), single-headed frame drums (s. ṬĀR/1*), small cymbals (ṬŪS*) and water jars (DJAHLAH*). The performance consists of a series of sections by a male soloist (NAHHĀM*) or soloists and a male chorus. Each section is characterized by and named after a particular rhythmic structure (Touma 1977a).

FIKRAH MŪSĪQIYYAH (pl. FIKRĀT MŪSĪQIYYAH) (f-k-r) (Gr.) "musical idea"

Musical theme.

FIQRAH (pl. FIQRĀT, FIQAR) (f-q-r) "section, paragraph"

A women's NAWBAH/1* or suite (Tun.) (Maḥfūẓ 1964:93).

FIRĀSH (pl. FURUSH, AFRISHAH) = FERACHE, FRÂCH (f-r-sh) "pillow; blanket; bed; mattress"

1. First two segments of the poetic line (SHAṬR/2*) of the QAṢĪDAH/2* set to music of the same name in Morocco. Each line is actually a "triplet," with the first two parts constituting the FIRĀSH, the third and last being known as the GHIṬĀ'/2* (Chottin 1939:155).

2. The second couplet (also called BAYT/2* or GHUṢN/2*) of the QAṢĪDAH/2* (Alg.). It usually presents a commentary on the first couplet or HADDAH* (HEUDDA*) (Delphin and Guin 1886:34).
3. The opening tune in the performance of each movement of the NAWBAH/1* (Mor.) (Ḥāfiẓ 1971:130). Also called DUKHŪL*.

FIRQAH (pl. FIRAQ) (f-r-q) "division, section; party, group"

1. An instrumental ensemble. Today it usually includes four or more violins, two celli, one bass, two QĀNŪN*s, two ʿŪD/2*s, two NĀY/1*s, one RIQQ* and one ṬABLAH/3* (Egypt) (el-Shawan 1978).
2. Any musical performing group (instrumental and/or vocal).

FRÂCH

Var. of FIRĀSH/1* (Chottin 1939:155).

FRUDĀSHT

Var. of FURŪDĀSHT* (Anonymous Treatise 1939:236).

FUḲAISHĀT

Var. of FUQAYSHĀT* (Farmer EI(Fr), "Ṣandj":209).

FUNDU

A genre of popular song using colloquial language, though the musical setting is in classical style (Tun.). This music is described as QADĪM ("ancient") by al Rizqī (1967:370).

FUQAYSHĀT (pl. of FUQAYSHAH) = FUḲAISHĀT (f-q-sh) dim. of "broken pieces"?

Metal cymbals (Hickmann 1947:21). See also FAQĀSHĀT*.

FURŪDĀSHT = FRUDĀSHT (Pers.)

A free rhythmed vocal number characterised as the fourth movement of the NAWBAH/1* suite in a 15th C. ms. (Anonymous Treatise 1939: 236).

FUSḤAH (f-s-ḥ) "open plain"

1. Face or flat area of a musical instrument.
2. The length of the string of a chordophone (from Mashāqah in Collangettes 1904:417; Mashāqah n.d.:fol. 40).

G

GADWAL

Var. of JADWAL* (Egypt) (Spector 1970:246).

GAITA

Var. of GHAYṬAH* (Marcuse).

ǴAMRAH

See GHAMZAH* (d'Erlanger 1935:27).

GANK

Var. of JANK* (Sachs 1940:259).

GAOUACHT

Var. of KAWASHT or KUWASHT* (Touma 1977b:36).

ǴARRADA

Var. of GHARRADA* (d'Erlanger 1939:190).

GASĀA

Var. of QAṢʿAH* (el Mahdi 1972:52-53).

GASPAH

Var. of QAṢABAH* (Jargy 1971:120; Farmer 1976a:220; el Mahdi 1972: 49).

ǴAWĀQ

Var. of JUWĀQ* (Sachs 1940:248; Chottin 1961:Band IX, col. 1565).

GAWASHT

Var. of KAWASHT or KUWASHT*, using the hard "g" which has no equivalent in Arabic.

GEMBRI

Var. of GUNBRĪ*(Chottin and Hickmann 1949-1951:Band I, col. 583).

GENBRÎ

Var. of GUNBRĪ* (Chottin 1961:Band IX, col. 1566).

GEṢʿAH and GESʿÂAH

Var. of QAṢʿAH* (Chottin 1961:Band IX, col. 1567-1568).

GESBA

Var. of QAṢABAH* (Marcuse).

GHĀB or GHĀBAH (pl. GHĀBĀT) (gh-y-b) "forest, reed stick"

1. Ancient name for the vertical flute (Marcuse).
2. Generic term for instruments made from reed cane (al Ḥafnī 1971:25).

GHĀDĪ BIL ʿAKS = RHĀDĪ BEL-'ĀKS (gh-d-w) (ʿ-k-s) "going in the opposite direction"

The syncopations and counter rhythms executed by the RABĀB* performer of a Maghribī (Mor.) ensemble during the response or refrain (JAWĀB/2*) to vocal segments (Chottin 1939:147).

GHAIDA

Var. of GHAYṬAH* (Marcuse).

GHAIṬA

Var. of GHAYṬAH* (Farmer 1929a:142).

GHALĪẒAH (gh-l-ẓ) "burly, thick"

Bass or low pitched (Isḥaq al Mawṣilī in Shawqī 1976:346).

GHAMMĀZ (pl. GHAMMĀZĀT) (gh-m-z) "that which makes the eye blink, i.e., that which pleases"

Note of importance in a MAQĀM/1* or melodic mode. It is located a fifth, a fourth or a third above the tonic, and is comparable to a "dominant" in Gregorian chant (el Helou 1961:79).

GHAMZAH (pl. GHAMZĀT) (gh-m-z) "a wink, sign, hint"

A weak beat or percussion (al Fārābī 1967:987). See also NAQRAH/5* and MASḤAH*. D'Erlanger's translation (1935:27) has ʿAMRAH*.

GHANAM = ARHANIM, AGHANIM, AGHĀNĪM (gh-n-m) "sheep"

A folk instrument of double clarinet type (Mor.). See ABŪ GHANAM*

GHANNĀ (gh-n-y) "to sing; to nasalize"

1. To sing.
2. To chant.
3. To sing the praises of, to eulogize.

GHANNĀ bi ________ (name of an instrument or genre of song) (gh-n-y) "sang with ________ "

To play an instrument or sing a particular kind of song.

GHANNĀ' (gh-n-n) f. of "nasal"

Melodious (of a voice).

GHANNĀ'Ī = R'ENNAI (gh-n-y) "one who nasalizes or sings"

Professional vocalist who sings non-religious songs of love and pleasure accompanied by various instrumentalists (usually woodwinds and tambourines) (Delphin and Guin 1886:31-32). According to Farmer (1954, "Maghribi Music":506), this singer performs the light, popular music known as KALĀM AL HAZL* (Alg.).

GHANNĀYAH (gh-n-y) "those who nasalize or sing" (masc.)

Pl. of GHANNĀ'Ī* (al Rizqī 1967:399).

GHANNĀYĀT (gh-n-y) "those who nasalize or sing" (f.)

Professional women singers (al Rizqī 1967:399).

GHARAD (gh-r-d) "singing, twittering like a bird"

Singing; song.

(AL) GHARĪD (d. ca. 716-717)

Nickname for Abū Yazīd (or Abū Marwān) ʿAbd al Malik. Born a slave of Berber origin, he became a freedman in Makkah where he was trained as a NĀ'IH* by IBN SURAYJ*. Later he sang at the court of Damascus. He is listed as one of the "four great singers" of his time. He was also a lutenist, a tambourinist and player of the QADĪB* (Farmer 1967:80-81; EI(Fr), "Al Gharīd":86).

GHARNĀṬĪ

Var. of GHURNĀṬĪ or GHURNĀṬIYYAH* (al Rizqī 1967:194, 370).

GHARRADA = ǴARRADA (gh-r-d) "to sing or twitter"

To sing (Ṣafī al Dīn 1938a:190).

GHĀYAH AL SURʿAH (gh-y-y) (s-r-ʿ) "goal of a fast tempo"

Accelerando (el Helou 1961:59). This expression is usually preceded by the particle "bi" ("with").

GHAYAṬAH or GHĀYAṬAH (colloq.)

Vars. of GHAYṬAH* (Delphin and Guin 1886:47, 49; Rouanet 1922:2943).

GHAYDĀ

Var. of GHAYṬAH* (Hickmann 1947:8).

GHAYR MUNTAẒIM (gh-y-r) (n-ẓ-m) "not ordered"

One of two types of "soft" (LAYYIN/1*) tetrachordal scalar segments (s. JINS/1*). It has its large interval positioned between the two smaller ones rather than having the three intervals arranged in accordance with progressively increasing or decreasing size (al Fārābī 1967:280ff). See also de Vaux 1891:309.

GHAYR MUTALĀ'IM (gh-y-r) (l-'-m) "not suitable; not mended or corrected"

Dissonant.

GHAYR MUTASHĀBIHAH (gh-y-r) (sh-b-h) "other than resembling"

A category of melodic movement (INTIQĀL/1*) described by al Kindī as that in which the size and pitch level of intervals in not similar from motif to motif (Ibn Sīnā 1930:96). Opp. of MUTASHĀBIHAH/3*.

GHAYR ZIYĀDAH NAQRĀT (gh-y-r) (z-y-d) (n-q-r) "other than an addition of percussions"

One of the two basic types of alteration (TAGHYĪR/2*) of a rhythmic cycle in order to form new modes (ĪQĀʿĀT). As the expression indicates, it involves no addition of new percussions. Four kinds of such TAGHYĪR are mentioned by al Fārābī:

a) TAWṢĪL AL MUFAṢṢAL*, the combination of two or more cycles into one;
b) TAFṢĪL AL MUWAṢṢAL*, adding extra space between percussions of a cycle;
c) TAKRĪR/2*, multiple successive repetitions of one percussion of the cycle;
d) TARKĪB/2*, repetition of one percussion from the cycle at another place within that cycle (al Fārābī 1967:1012-1016).

This expression is usually preceded by the particle "bi" ("with"). See also ZIYĀDAH NAQRĀT MIN KHĀRIJ*.

GHAYRWĀRAH (pl. GHAYRWĀRĀT) = GUIRWARAT

Ancient instrument similar to the ṬUNBŪR/1*, or long-necked lute (Ibn Khurdādhbih 1969:17, n.4; al Masʿūdī 1874:VIII, 91). Also given as GHUNDŪRĀT*(Ibn Khurdādhbih 1969:17) and QUNDHŪRĀT* (Farmer 1928:512, 515).

GHAYṬAH (pl. GHAYĀṬ) = GHAYDĀ, GHAITA, GHĀYATAH, GHETA, GHAIDA, GAIDA, GHĪTA, RAICA, RAITA, RHAITA, RHEITA, R'AITA (gh-y-ṭ), said to be a Spanish term meaning "that which disturbs" (Poche 1978:69)

1. Double-reed, conical aerophone about 36 cm. in length, normally having 7 fingerholes, one thumb hole, and a conical bell about 10 cm. in diameter (Maghrib). It is used in connection with pilgrimage or other religious and folk occasions. It was known at least as early as Ibn Baṭṭūṭah (d. 1377), who identified it with the SURNĀY* of the Mughals (Farmer 1978a:81; Delphin and Guin 1886:47, 49; Sachs 1940:248).
2. Reedpipe with cylindrical bore and single reed (Egypt), rendered by Farmer as GHĪTAH*, a term with identical spelling in Ar. (Farmer EI(Eng), "Mizmār":540).
3. A bagpipe in 13th C. Spain (Marcuse).

GHAZAL (gh-z-l) "flirt; flirtation; love"

A genre of free rhythmed vocal music described as early as the writings of ʿAbd al Qādir ibn Ghaybī (d. 1435). At that time, it was a setting of Persian verses on the subject of love, and was designated as the second movement of the NAWBAH/1* or suite. A prelude (ṬARĪQAH/3*) and a refrain (TASHYĪʿAH*) were considered obligatory for this movement (Anonymous Treatise 1939:236).

GHAZĀL or GHAZĀLAH (Pl. GHAZĀLĀT) (gh-z-l) "gazelle"

Bridge of the KAMĀNJAH* (Lane 1973:356).

GHETA

Cylindrical clarinet of Egypt with metal bell and six or seven fingerholes (Marcuse). Var. of GHAYṬAH/2*.

GHICHAK

Var. of GHISHAK (Farmer 1954, "Iraqian and Mesopotamian Music": 530). See SHĪSHAK or SHĪSHAL*.

GHILẒ (gh-l-ẓ) "thickness"

1. The thickness (of the vibrating string of a chordophone) (al Kindī 1965:17; Ikhwān al Ṣafā' 1957:I, 194).
2. Thickness or roughness in musical performance, the opp. of gentleness (Ibn al Munajjim 1976:208).

GHINĀ' (gh-n-y) "song, singing"

1. Music in a generic sense, including both vocal and instrumental music. This meaning is said to be a very old one which was widespread before the translation of Greek theoretical works on music and the subsequent borrowing of the term MŪSĪQĀ or MŪSĪQĪ*. It was still used in this way by the Ikhwān al Ṣafā' (1957:I, 192; 1964/65:135, 138).
2. The practical art of music in opposition to the theoretical art (MŪSĪQĀ or MŪSĪQĪ*).

3. Singing or vocal music as opposed to instrumental music. Used from the early centuries of the Islamic period, this meaning is still the most generally accepted one today (Ibn ʿAbd Rabbihi 1887: III, 187; Ibn Abī al Dunyā 1938:46).
4. That vocal music which is based on a rhythmic mode, said to have originated in the Arab states of al Ḥīrah (ʿIrāq) and Ghassān (Syria) in the first century of the Islamic period (d'Erlanger 1959:158-159). This new form of song (also GHINĀ' AL MUTQAN*) was originated, we are told, by ṬUWAYS* (d. 710), a famous singer of Madīnah.
5. The music of the Arabs as contrasted to that of the ancient Greeks (Ibn al Munajjim in Br. M. ms. Or. 2361).
6. The vocal music for enjoyment, as opposed to that for mourning or religious purposes (e.g., NIYĀḤAH*, QIRĀ'AH*, the ADHĀN* (al Fārābī 1967:68).

GHINĀ' AL ʿARAB (gh-n-y) (ʿ-r-b) "Arab singing"

The early cameleer's songs of the Arabs, e.g., the ḤIDĀ'/1*, NAṢB*.

GHINĀ' AL AWWAL AL THAQĪL (gh-n-y) ('-w-l) (th-q-l) "first heavy singing"

Slow songs or singing, i.e., utilizing the slow rhythmic mode known as THAQĪL AL AWWAL* (Ibn ʿAbd Rabbihi 1887:190; Farmer 1943/44:58).

GHINĀ' AL MAWQIʿ (gh-n-y) (w-q-ʿ) "song that has been made to fall in the proper place"

Song or singing with regular rhythm (al Iṣfahānī as reported in Farmer 1967:51). Syn. of GHINĀ' AL MUTQAN*. Although Farmer transliterated the term as MAWQIʿ, it is more likely that the Ar. spelling should instead be rendered MUWAQQAʿ ("rhythmed").

GHINĀ' AL MURTAJAL (gh-n-y) (r-j-l) "improvised song"

Improvised song (Farmer 1957:436).

GHINĀ' AL MUTQAN = RHINĀ EL MOUTQĀN (gh-n-y) (t-q-n) "perfect singing or song"

A genre of vocal music introduced in the first century of the Islamic period which involved a musical rhythm (ĪQĀʿ/1*) which was different from the meter (ʿARŪḌ*) of the poem of which it was a setting but was nevertheless an offshoot from metrical principles. This genre was in contrast to the older NAṢB*. The first ĪQĀʿ introduced in this music was the HAZAJ/2*. Others claim it was the THAQĪL AL AWWAL*. ṬUWAYS* was the first to sing in this genre, we are told (Ibn ʿAbd Rabbihi 1887:III, 187; Farmer 1967:49-51). Also called GHINĀ' AL RAQĪQ*. See GHINĀ' AL MAWQIʿ*.

GHINĀ' AL RAQĪQ (gh-n-y) (r-q-q) "refined song or singing"

Syn. of GHINĀ' AL MUTQAN* (al Iṣfahānī in Farmer 1967:51; Farmer 1954, "Syrian Music":VIII, 254).

GHINĀ' AL RUKBĀN (gh-n-y) (r-k-b) "song of travellers or cameleers"
Vocal music of the cameleers (Ibn ʿAbd Rabbihi 1887:III, 130).

GHINĀ'Ī (gh-n-y) "pertaining to song or singing"

Pertaining to song or singing.

GHINĀR

An unidentified musical instrument mentioned in a 13th C. treatise of Moorish Spain (Farmer 1926a:247).

GHĪRBĀL (pl. GHIRĀBĪL) = GIRBĀL (gh-r-b-l) "sieve"

Frame drum known from the first century of the Islamic period (Sachs 1940:246) as well as later in the ʿAbbāsī period (Farmer 1967:211). It is also mentioned by al Ghazālī (1902:743) and an anonymous 15th C. treatise (see Farmer 1965b:62). It is believed to have been a round instrument with snares similar to the contemporary Maghribī BANDĪR*. The term is still used for a tambourine of Egypt (Marcuse; Shiloah 1965:30) and the Maghrib (al Rizqī 1967: 363).

GHIRRĪD (gh-r-d) "singing; twittering"

Singing.

GHIROUARAT

Var. of GHAYRWĀRAH* (Rouanet 1922:2683).

GHISHAK = GHICHAK, GHIZHAK

A chordophone, probably a bowed instrument, known at the time of ʿAbd al Qādir ibn Ghaybī (d. 1435) (Farmer 1954, "Iraqian and Mesopotamian Music":530). At that time it was a large instrument with two main strings and eight sympathetic strings (Farmer 1954, "Kamancha":695-696). Farmer writes that it was probably equivalent to the SHAUSHAK* (Farmer 1967:210). See also SHĪSHĀK or SHĪSHĀL* and Farmer 1978:II, 32.

GHĪṬAH

Single-reed aerophone with cylindrical bore, used in Egypt (Farmer EI(Eng), "Mizmār":540; Marcuse). Var. of GHAYṬAH/2*.

GHIṬĀ' (pl. AGHṬIYAH) (gh-ṭ-w) "cover"

1. The third of three main sections of the MUWASHSHAḤ/1*, also known as QAFLAH/1* or RUJŪʿ/3* or TAQFIYYAH/2* (al Faruqi 1975; see also Ḥāfiẓ 1971:130). This term is used for any final segment.
2. The third and concluding line of the poetic strophe in a popular vocal form of QAṢĪDAH/1* (Mor.). The first two lines are known as FIRĀSH/1* (Chottin 1939:155).

GHIZHAK or GHIŽAK

Vars. of GHISHAK* (Farmer 1978:II, 32). See also SHISHAK or SHISHAL*.

GHŪGHĀ

Bowed chordophone of Algeria and Morocco with bowl-shaped body and skin face. It has a single string secured with a tuning ring (Marcuse; Wright 1979:501). See GUGHE*.

GHUNDŪRAH

Syn. of GHAYRWĀRAH* (Ibn Khurdādhbih 1969:17).

GHUNNAH (gh-n-n) "nasal sound"

A nasal vocal sound, described by al Fārābī (1967:1070, esp. n. 2) as a less nasal sound than the ZAMM*.

GHURNĀṬĪ or GHURNĀṬIYYAH ± GHARNĀṬĪ, GIRNATI (geog.) "Granadan"

Classical music of Alg. and Mor., syn. of MA'LŪF*, ṢANʿAH* (Touma 1977b:77; Rizqī 1967:194).

GHUṢN (pl. AGHṢĀN) = GOUSN, R'EÇEN, RHOÇN (gh-ṣ-n) "bough"

1. One of the parts of the DAWR/5*, SĀMIR* and similar compositions (Egypt) (Ḥāfiẓ 1971:196-198). The AGHṢĀN are segments of new and/or contrasting musical materials which are separated by repetitions of a refrain-like segment usually called the MADHHAB/1*.
2. A couplet or segment of the poetic QAṢĪDAH*. In Morocco it comprises a strophe of a certain number of lines which alternates with a short refrain known as ḤARBAH* (Chottin 1939:104). In Algeria, it is the second couplet of the QAṢĪDAH, also called BAYT/2* or FIRĀSH/2*, which usually presents a commentary on the first couplet or HADDAH* (Delphin and Guin 1886:34). In the MUWASHSHAḤ/2*, it is the name often given to the opening and recurring segment of poetry, also called MAṬLAʿ/3* or MADHHAB/4* (d'Erlanger 1959:165).

GINBRĪ

Var. of GUNBRĪ* (Shiloah 1965:I, 30).

GIRNATI

Var. of GHURNĀṬĪ or GHURNĀṬIYYAH* (Touma 1977b:77).

GNBRI

Var. of GUNBRĪ*. In Morocco this plucked lute has two or three strings with a soundbox made from wood or tortoise shell and covered with skin (Touma 1977b:96).

GNÎBRÎ

Var. of GUNĪBRĪ* (Chottin 1961:Band IX, col. 1566).

GONGOLAH

Var. of KINKULAH* (de Meynard 1874:VIII, 92). The Ar. text in that work of al Masʿūdī has KINKULAH.

GOSBA

Var. of QAṢABAH* (Farmer 1976a:220; Delphin and Guin 1886:37; el Mahdi 1972:49). It has been described as having three finger holes, at other times as possessing five or six (Salvador-Daniel 1976:109, 116).

GOUAL

Var. of QAWWĀL*, the itinerant musician or singer of Algeria (Delphin and Guin 1886:2).

GOUSN

Var. of GHUṢN* (Touma 1977b:82).

GRĪḤAH = GRÎH'A, probably a colloq. of QARĪḤAH* (q-r-ḥ) "natural talent; intuition"

General term for folk music in Morocco (Chottin 1939:14, 153; 1961: Band IX, col. 1559, 1563). Chottin describes it as a simplified and popular form of music which has many of the characteristics of the classical art ("une sorte d'adaptation ou de vulgarisation de la musique andalouse à des besoins nouveaux" (Chottin 1939:153). It was born in the 17th C. as a national reaction to the artistic influence of the immigrating Andalusians. In its sense of "artistic inspiration," the word fits well this type of music which, in contrast to the classical music of the region, is free to deviate from the rules of the ancient tradition. This local Maghribī music is susceptible to continuous inspired innovation. The classical music uses the classical Arabic and the meters of classical poetry which are based on the combination of long and short syllables, whereas GRIḤAH or QARĪḤAH employs the popular language (LUGHAH ZINQAWIYYAH*) and ignores the quantity based ancient meters in favor of an accentual system. There are many kinds of GRĪḤAH, all being songs with regular rhythm and percussion accompaniment. These include the BARWALAH*, QAṢĪDAH/1*, SARRĀBAH*, ʿAYṬAH*, ʿARŪBĪ/3*, as well as other light songs and processional music. The following percussion instruments are used to accompany these songs: 1) ṬĀR/1*, 2) TAʿRĪJAH/1*, 3) BANDĪR*, 4) AQWĀL* (ABRÛÂL*), and 5) ṬABLÂH/4* (Chottin 1939:154-168).

GUANGUA or GUENGOU

A large double headed drum used by the negroes (Alg.) (Delphin and Guin 1886:44). Despite its two heads, only one is used for playing. A hooked drumstick is used by the right hand, a straight stick or the fingers provide the sound made by the left (Rouanet 1922:2934). The Arabic of this instrument is given as DANDŪN* (supp.) (*Ibid.*).

GUD

Unidentified musical instrument mentioned in the translation of Ibn Abī al Ṣalt (Avenary 1952:52).

GUEBLI or GUEBLIA

An end-blown flute played in the mountain regions of southern Algeria. It is generally 49-50 cm. in length, with six fingerholes (Delphin and Guin 1886:45; Rouanet 1922:2922).

GUEÇAʿA

Var. of QAṢʿAH* (Rouanet 1922:2944).

GUEDIHA

Var. of QADĪḤAH* (Delphin and Guin 1886:36).

GUELLAL (probably var. of QULLĀL*)

A single headed terracota drum of the Maghrib having an embroidered covering (ZAWWĀDAH* or ZUWWĀDAH*). This long drum (ca. 60 cm.) with one end larger than the other (diameters 25 cm. and 15 cm.) is placed horizontally on the knee of a seated performer or carried under the arm of the standing drummer (Delphin and Guin 1886:39-40; Rouanet 1922:2944). See GULLĀL*.

GUEMBRI

Var. of GUNBRĪ* (Chottin 1939:17).

GUENBRI

Var. of GUNBRĪ* (Chottin 1939:138; Marcuse).

GUENEBRI

Var. of GUNIBRI* (Rouanet 1922:2944).

GUENIBRI

Var. of GUNĪBRĪ*, a small long necked lute of the Maghrib with two strings, soundbox made from a tortoise shell or a coconut, and a skin face (Delphin and Guin 1886:60-61; Rouanet 1922:2929).

GUESBA

Var. of QAṢABAH* (Chottin 1939:34; 1957:I, 41; Delphin and Guin 1886:37).

GUGHE

Algerian spike fiddle with membrane face and single horsehair string attached to a tuning ring (Marcuse), probably var. of GHŪGHĀ*.

GUIRWARAH

Var. of GHAYRWĀRAH* (de Meynard 1874:VIII, 91).

GULLĀL

A cylindrical single headed drum of the Maghrib (Alg.) (Farmer EI(Fr), "Ṭabl":230), var. of QULLĀL*. Also QUWWĀL* in other parts of the Maghrib. Marcuse defines it as a frame drum, repeating the error in Farmer 1978:I, 45.

GUNBRĪ (pl. GANĀBIR) = QUNBRĪ, QANBRĪ, GUEMBRĪ, GUENBRI, GEMBRI, GINBRI, GENBRĪ, GNBRI, GUNBURI (q-n-b-r)

A large version of a folk instrument of long necked lute type used in the Maghrib and the Sudan. GUNĪBRĪ* is the name often used for a smaller instrument of this type. The GUNBRĪ has a skin face and a cylindrical, fretless neck which penetrates the body. Most instruments bearing this name have three strings, but sometimes they are found with two or four. The strings are tuned in fifths. The sound box is constructed of a great variety of materials. Since there is no Ar. letter for "G," this word is spelled with a "QĀF" in many works--QUNBRĪ*. Much has been written about the various names for this instrument (see Farmer 1978:I, 39-49).

GUNĪBRĪ (pl. GANĀBIR) = GUENEBRĪ, GUENIBRI, QANĪBIRĪ, GNÎBRÎ, QUNĪBRĪ (q-n-b-r) "dim. of GUNBRĪ"

A small long necked lute, similar to the GUNBRĪ* (Grame 1970:81, 84; see Farmer 1978:I, 39). In addition to being a smaller instrument, the GUNIBRĪ differs from the GUNBRĪ in having cone-shaped, cylindrical or flat tuning pegs. Its sound box is made of various materials (e.g., wood, tortoise shell, coconut, gourd, even metal), and is covered with a skin face. The instrument rarely has a nut. Instead, a piece of gut or leather is tied round the neck and strings to mark the end of the vibrating string. Sometimes a bamboo plectrum is used on this fretless instrument. The strings (generally two or three) are tuned in fifths (Farmer 1978:I, 44). Since there is no Ar. letter for "G," this word is spelled with a "QĀF" in the Ar. script, QUNIBRĪ*. Some authors make a regional distinction between GUNĪBRĪ AND GUNBRĪ, the former said to apply to the lute of the north, the latter to the south (Delphin and Guin 1886:60-61).

GUNBURĪ

Var. of GUNBRĪ* (ʿArnīṭah 1968:54). The Ar. text has QUNBURĪ* followed by this transliteration in parentheses.

ǦUWĀK

Var. of JUWĀQ/2* (Marcuse).

GUWASHT

Var. of KAWASHT or KUWASHT*, using the hard "g" which has no equivalent in the Ar. script.

GWAB

Var. of JAWĀB/1*, evidencing the Egyptian colloquialization of this term (Spector 1970:247).

H

"H" (abbrev. for "HĀ'," one of the letters of the Ar. alphabet)

1. This letter designated one of the frets or finger positions on the neck of the lute (ʿŪD/2*) used by the early theorists, as well as the tone governed by it.
2. A percussion of duration 5 times as long as the basic time value ("A"* time or ZAMĀN AL AWWAL*) (Anonymous Treatise 1939:159; al Lādhiqī 1939:459).

"Ḥ" (abbrev. for "ḤĀ'," one of the letters of the Ar. alphabet)

One of the frets or finger positions on the neck of the lute (ʿŪD/2*) which was used by theorists of the Classical Period, as well as the tone governed by it.

ḤABBAH (ḥ-b-b) "seed; grain"

Sound box of the hydraulic organ described by 9th C. writers (Farmer 1931:85, 105). Equiv. of ḤABBAH AL MUṢAWWITAH*.

ḤABBAH AL MUṢAWWITAH (ḥ-b-b) (ṣ-w-t) "seed that makes sound"

The sounding device of a musical instrument, whether the mouthpiece of a wind instrument or the sound box of an organ (Farmer 1931:92).

ḤĀDĀT AL ḤĀDĀT

Cowl (1966:152) gives its meaning as "highest (register)," but this seems to be a mistranslation of the text of al Kindi (1966: 161) as well as a mistransliteration. See ḤĀDDAH AL ḤĀDDĀT*.

HADAYĀ or HADĀYE (h-d-y), perhaps vars. of HIDĀYAH "guidance"

A lullaby (Jargy 1970:37). Also given as HADĪ*.

ḤĀDD (pl. ḤUDŪD) (ḥ-d-d) "sharp; at the edge"

1. Name given in Classical Period to fifth and highest pitched string of the lute (ʿŪD*) (al Fārābī 1967:126). Al Fārābī presented most of his theoretical discussion of pitches and accordature with use of a four-stringed ʿŪD, but he admitted the advantage of having a fifth string in order to complete the double octave range without changing hand positions (al Fārābī 1967:588-591; 1930:204-207; see Ibn Sīnā 1935:236). This was the ḤĀDD (or ZĪR AL THĀNĪ* string, which is thought to have been first adopted in Moorish Spain by ZIRYĀB* and in the Mashriq by al Kindī (Farmer 1937a:247; 1978:II, 47).
2. High in pitch (Isḥaq al Mawṣilī in Shawqī 1976:346).

HADDAH = HEUDDA (h-d-d) "heavy fall"

The first couplet of a QAṢĪDAH*, which is followed by the FIRĀSH/2* (Alg.) (Delphin and Guin 1886:34). Also ʿARŪBIYYAH* or MAṬLAʿ/2*.

ḤĀDDAH AL ḤĀDDĀT = ḤĀDĀT AL ḤĀDĀT (ḥ-d-d) (ḥ-d-d) "highest of the high"

The uppermost tone of the scalar collection (JAMʿ/1*) of tones. It is two octaves above the lowest tone and is one of the unalterable tones (NAGHAM AL RATĪBAH*) within the collection (al Fārābī 1967:372; al Kindī 1966:151; see Ḥāfiẓ 1971:94).

H'ADDARAH (ḥ-ḍ-r?) ḤAḌḌĀRAH (?) "assistant"

Older professional female singer (Mor.) who performs for family gatherings (Chottin 1939:40, 165).

ḤADHF (ḥ-dh-f) "cancellation; omission"

Elimination of percussions of a rhythmic cycle (Ibn Sīnā 1935:181; Anonymous Treatise 1939:165).

HADĪ (h-d-y)

Lullaby of Jerusalem (Jargy 1970:10). See HADAYĀ or HADĀYE*.

ḤĀDĪ (pl. ḤUDAH) (ḥ-d-w) or (ḥ-d-y) "caravan leader; cameleer; singer"

The person who urges camels forward by singing; the singer of a ḤIDĀ' or ḤUDĀ'*, a caravan song.

ḤADOU

Var. of ḤADW* (Burckhardt 1967:86).

ḤADR (ḥ-d-r) "lowering"

1. Slight acceleration of the tempo in measured musical performance (al Fārābī 1967:1177).
2. One of the three ways of reciting the Qur'ān, according to Jalāl al Dīn al Suyūṭī (15th C.) and other writers on TAJWĪD* (al Suyūṭī 1941:I, 172; Shaqriyyah n.d.:6). It designated a

rapid reading but was never incorrect despite the tempo. See also TAḤQĪQ*, TADWĪR*.

ḤAḌRAH (ḥ-ḍ-r) "presence"

The gathering of Ṣūfīs for performing their religiously oriented, poetic-musical-movement rituals (DHIKR*) which have as goal and culmination the ecstatic mystical experience of intuiting the "presence" of the Divinity.

ḤADW = ḤADOU (ḥ-d-w) or (ḥ-d-y) "urging forward by singing"

1. A war song (Burckhardt 1967:86).
2. A camel driver's song (Burckhardt 1967:86).

H̬AFĪ

Var. of KHAFĪ* (d'Erlanger 1938:336; 1939:375).

H̬AFĪF

Var. of KHAFĪF* (Perkuhn 1976:107).

H̬AFIYYUN

Var. of KHAFĪ* with full nominative ending (KHAFIYYUN) (d'Erlanger 1939:375).

ḤĀFIẒ (pl. ḤUFFĀẒ, ḤAFAẒAH) (ḥ-f-ẓ) "guardian; memorizer"

An older musician who has learned the music directly from its composer, through a recording, or from an earlier generation of performers (Egypt), according to el-Shawan 1978. Through the centuries, ḤĀFIẒ (HAFIZ, HAFFIZ and ḤĀFIZ in El-Shawan's handout) has meant any "memorizer." It has been used for the person who committed to memory literary, musical, scientific--in fact, any type of knowledge. In a more specific sense, it has also meant the person who has committed the Qur'ān to memory. As a technical musical term, it is first used, according to our knowledge, in the El-Shawan reference, where the author maintains that the term now designates a specific role and personage in the transmission of the music of contemporary Egypt.

ḤAFLAH (pl. ḤAFLĀT) (ḥ-f-l) "party"

Syn. of ḤAFLAH MŪSĪQIYYAH*.

ḤAFLAH MŪSĪQIYYAH (ḥ-f-l) (Gr.) "music party"

Musical performance, concert. Also ḤAFLAH*.

HAK

A percussion stroke considered to be a double TAK*, i.e., two TAK strokes executed simultaneously or nearly so (d'Erlanger 1959:11). It is used only when preceded by the weak and dry TĀ* stroke, and is found only near the end of a long rhythmic cycle in order to announce its completion (d'Erlanger 1959:10-11).

HALĀHIL (h-l-l) colloq.

Syn. of ZAGHĀRĪD*.

ḤALLAH or ḤILLAH = HELLA (ḥ-l-l) "large cooking pot"

Percussion instrument of the Mashriqī folk tradition. It is made of a large pottery water jar covered with a skin (Jargy 1971:125).

HALLĀL = HELLÂL (h-l-l) "chanter"

A chanter of religious poetry and scripture (Mor.) (Chottin 1939:169).

ḤALQ (pl. ḤULŪQ, AḤLĀQ) (ḥ-l-q) "throat"

1. Neck of a stringed instrument (al Kindī 1965:22ff).
2. Unidentified musical instrument mentioned by Ibn al Munajjim (1950:3; 1976:191). Al Atharī mentions another instrument (ʿUNQ/2*) which was known in the early centuries of the Islamic period and went under a name with similar literal meaning (al Atharī 1950:3, n. 5; also see Shawqī 1976:191).

ḤAMĀS (ḥ-m-s) "enthusiasm, zeal; courage"

War poem, chant or song (Jargy 1970:30).

ḤAMD (ḥ-m-d) "thanks"

A genre of Islamic religious music giving thanks to God.

ḤĀMIL or ḤĀMILAH (pl. HAWĀMIL) (ḥ-m-l) "carrier"

Bridge for a chordophone, comprising a piece of thin wood which is placed standing on the face of the instrument and on which the strings rest. This notched piece of wood also holds the strings separate from each other. This term used in the 20th C. has also been used at least as early as al Fārābī (1967:485, 499, 631, 800). See ZĀMILAH*, probably a misreading or misprint of this term.

HAMZAH (pl. HAMAZĀT) (h-m-z), the letter of the Ar. alphabet corresponding to the glottal stop

1. Abrupt glottal stop of the consonant sound at the end of a word, phrase or section or vocal music.
2. Sharp attack, accent in vocal music. Also called NABRAH*.

HANA

Var. of KHĀNAH/2* (Touma 1977b:87-88).

ḤANAFĪ (ḥ-n-f) "pertaining to Banū Ḥanīfah (the tribe)"

One of the two kinds of song sung in the Yaman (a region of S.W. Arabian Peninsula) in pre-Islamic times (Farmer 1967:15). See ḤIMYARĪ*.

ḤĀNAH

A large frame drum with bells (Egypt) (Hickmann 1958:44).

HANBAQAH

Unidentified aerophone mentioned by Ibn Salamah (1951:86, n. 3; 1938a:16, n. 6). Another spelling of this term is HUNBŪQAH*.

HANK

1. Equiv. of ĀHANG or ĀHANK/3* (Maḥfūẓ 1964:107; Ḥāfiẓ 1971:206; Touma 1977b:84).
2. Repetition (Maḥfūẓ 1964:107).

ḤANNĀNAH (ḥ-n-n) "always twanging"

A musical instrument of a class described as "instruments of motion" (ĀLĀT AL ḤARAKĀT*), which were said to make a plaintive sound (al Khwārizmī 1968:254).

ḤARAKAH (pl. ḤARAKĀT) (ḥ-r-k) "movement"

1. Melodic or rhythmic movement.
2. Tempo (Ḥāfiẓ 1971:120).

ḤARAKĀT (pl. of ḤARAKAH) (ḥ-r-k) "movements"

The second part of the musical segment of contrast (GHUṢN/1*) of the SĀMIR*, a vocal genre of modern Egypt. This part is devoted to repetitions and variations of the opening tune of the MADHHAB/1* or opening refrain (Ḥāfiẓ 1971:198). See HANK/1*, AHANG or AHANK/3* for a similar feature in the DAWR/5* and other compositions.

H'ARBA

Var. of ḤARBAH* (Chottin 1939:155).

ḤARBAH (pl. ḤIRĀB) = H'ARBA (ḥ-r-b) "the head of the arrow"

The short refrain section of one or two lines which alternates with strophes (AGHṢĀN, s. GHUṢN/2*) of the popular form of vocal QAṢĪDAH/1* (Mor.) (Chottin 1939:104). It usually contains the name or some other indication of the identity of the poet, and a resume of the subject of the poem being sung (Chottin 1939:155).

ḤARBĪ (ḥ-r-b) "warlike"

The concluding part of the Tunisian BASHRAF/2* or the SAMĀʿĪ/1*, orchestral genres much used as overtures. It is characterized by a very rapid tempo (d'Erlanger 1959:200; el Mahdi 1972:21).

ḤASABA (ḥ-s-b) "to calculate, reckon"

To play (an instrument), according to a 9th-10th C. ms. (Farmer 1931:59).

ḤASHW (ḥ-sh-w) "filling, stuffing"

Extra percussions of extemporaneous variety that "fill in" the basic cycle of a rhythmic mode (ĪQĀʿ/1*), therefore, the percussions of secondary importance as contrasted to the NAQARĀT AṢLIYYAH* (d'Erlanger 1959:3).

ḤASS (ḥ-s-s) "sensation, feeling"

Equiv. of ḤISS*.

ḤASSĀS (ḥ-s-s) "sensitive; readily affected"

The leading tone or seventh of the scale (al Ḥafnī 1946:290).

ḤATHĪTH = ḤAṮIṮ (ḥ-th-th) "incitement"

1. Shortening the shortest percussion of a rhythmic cycle (al Fārābī 1967:1019).
2. Embellishment or improvement of the melody by speeding up the tempo (Ibn Sīnā 1930:99). See TAḤĀSĪN*.

ḤATHTH (ḥ-th-th) "acceleration"

Acceleration of the tempo of a rhythmic mode without the addition of supplementary percussions (al Fārābī 1967:1019, 1177; al Kindī 1965:10).

HAṮIṮ

Var. of ḤATHĪTH* (al Ḥafnī 1930:52).

ḪATM

Var. of KHATM* (Perkuhn 1976:107).

ḤAṬṬ (ḥ-ṭ-ṭ) "lowering, diminishing; descending"

Lowering (in pitch) (al Khwārizmī 1968:240).

ḤAṬṬAṬA (ḥ-ṭ-ṭ) "to put down, to lower"

To lower in pitch (al Fārābī 1967:619).

HAWĀ' (pl. AHWIYAH) (h-w-y) "air, atmosphere"

A short song, melody or tune, with or without words (al Khulaʿī 1904:46). This term is used for a melodic theme in both Maghrib and Mashriq (d'Erlanger 1959:169). See Maḥfūẓ 1964:107.

HAWĀ'Ī (h-w-y) "pertaining to a tune or air"

A musical fantasy improvised on a melodic motif. This genre of indefinite length was the fastest of genres mentioned by ʿAbd al Qādir ibn Ghaybī (d. 1435) (Anonymous Treatise 1939:245).

ḤAWJ (ḥ-w-j) "need, want"

The chanted magical sayings of the soothsayer (Chottin 1939:85).

ḤAWZĪ = AHOUZI, HAOUZI (ḥ-w-z) "pertaining to surroundings, city limits"

A category of simple music heard in family festivals and cafes of the Maghrib. The songs comprising this category are primarily songs of love, the poetry of which is often more important than its musical setting (Rouanet 1922:2866, 2942).

HAYKAL ṢAWTĪ (h-y-k-l) (ṣ-w-t) "framework for sound"

Sounding board of a musical instrument (Ḥāfiẓ 1971:20, 22).

HAZADJ

Var. of HAZAJ* (Touma 1977b:15).

HAZAJ (pl. AHZĀJ, AHĀZĪJ) = HAZADJ, HEZEJ, HEZEDJ (h-z-j) "the disturbance caused by thunder; a very ancient Arabic prosodic meter"

1. One of the three kinds of singing in ancient Arabia. It was characterized by a quick, dance-like rhythm and a light-hearted feeling (Ibn ʿAbd Rabbihi 1887:III, 186; Farmer 1941:25; Ibn Salamah 1938a:19; 1938b:249). See also SINĀD*, NAṢB/3*.
2. Name for one of the "famous Arab rhythmic modes" (ĪQĀʿĀT AL ʿARABIYYAH AL MASHHŪRAH*) described by the Classical Period theorists. For some, the term designated any conjunct (MUTTAṢIL/4*) rhythmic mode (Ibn Sīnā 1930:92). According to al Fārābī, this was an outmoded usage, and that the term was more correctly applied only to those conjunct (MUWAṢṢAL*) modes of moderate tempo (al Fārābī 1967:453, 1022; see also Ṣafī al Dīn 1939a:510; Anonymous Treatise 1939:163). It was thought to have been the first rhythmic mode (ĪQĀʿ/1*) introduced in the new genre of song of the 7th C. known as GHINĀ' AL MUTQAN*.
3. In contemporary theory, any lively rhythmic mode.
4. A song with HAZAJ/2* rhythm (Ibn Khurdādhbih 1969:26).
5. The sound of the singer (Maʿlūf).
6. Vocal sound in which there is a desired huskiness (Maḥfūẓ 1964:119), or one in which there is a highness in pitch (Ibid.)
7. General term for any of the work songs (AHĀZĪJ) included in the FIJRĪ* folk music of the Baḥrayn pearl divers (Touma 1977a:122).

HAZAJ KHAFĪF (h-z-j) (kh-f-f) "lively HAZAJ"

Name given by the theorists of the Classical Period to the conjunct (MUTTAṢIL/4*) rhythmic mode using only "B"* time units or percussions.

HAZAJ KHAFĪF AL THAQĪL (h-z-j) (kh-f-f) (th-q-l) "fairly slow HAZAJ"

Name given by the theorists of the Classical Period to the conjunct (MUTTAṢIL/4*) rhythmic mode using only "J"* time units or percussions.

HAZAJ SARĪʿ (h-z-j) (s-r-ʿ) "rapid HAZAJ"

Name given by the theorists of the Classical Period to the conjunct (MUTTAṢIL/4*) rhythmic mode using only "A"* time units or percussions.

HAZAJ THAQĪL (h-z-j) (th-q-l) "slow HAZAJ"

Name given by the theorists of the Classical Period to the conjunct (MUTTAṢIL/4*) rhythmic mode using only "D"* time percussions.

ḤAZQ (ḥ-z-q) "straining, tightening"

1. Tightening of a string to raise the pitch (Ikhwān al Ṣafā' 1957: I, 204; al Khwārizmī 1968:240).
2. Stringing a musical instrument.

ḤAZZĀB (ḥ-z-b) "one who continually forms a party or group"

A professional cantillator of the Qur'ān who chanted with others in chorus (Maghrib) (El-Kholy 1954:50). This unusual practice astonished Ibn Jubayr, the famous traveler of the 12th C. The derivation of this usage may relate to the 60 AḤZĀB ("parts") into which the Qur'ān is divided.

ḤEJĀZ

Var. of ḤIJĀZ* (Smith 1849:181).

ḤELLA

Var. of ḤALLAH or ḤILLAH* (Jargy 1971:125).

HELLĀL

Var. of HALLĀL* (Chottin 1939:169).

HESS

Var. of ḤISS or ḤASS* (Poche 1978:66).

HEUDDA

Var. of HADDAH* (Delphin and Guin 1886:34).

HEZEDJ

Var. of HAZAJ (de Meynard 1874:VIII, 93).

HEZEJ

Var. of HAZAJ* (Ribera 1970:31, n. 2).

ḤIDĀ' or ḤUDĀ' = HIDÉ, HOUDA' (ḥ-d-w or ḥ-d-y) "urging forward"

1. Camel driver's song of pre-Islamic and early Islamic periods. According to al Masʿūdī, this genre was the earliest of songs among the Arabs (1874:VIII, 92).
2. Chanting of poetry.
3. Singing of poetry with regular rhythms and agreeable sounds (al Ghazālī 1901-1902:217). See HIJJANIYE*.

ḤIDDAH (ḥ-d-d) "sharpness; highness"

Highness of pitch.

ḤIDDAH AL ṢAWT (ḥ-d-d) (ṣ-w-t) "highness of sound"

Highness of pitch (Ibn al Munajjim 1976:343).

HIDÉ

Var. of ḤIDĀ' or ḤUDĀ'* (Ribera 1970:31).

HIǦǦON (h-j-j?)

Syn. of HIJJANIYYE* (Jargy 1970:36). This popular Lebanese version of the ancient ḤIDĀ' or ḤUDĀ'* is found chiefly in the Zaḥlah region. It comprises a long, free-rhythmed melody setting one verse of poetry which is repeated over and over. The melody, not the words, are the important element.

HIJĀ' (h-j-w) "satire"

Satirical poem or song.

ḤIJĀB (pl. ḤUJUB, AḤJIBAH) (ḥ-j-b) "veil; veiling"

Small ornament, usually of ivory, with which the joining of the instruments neck covering and the body of the lute (ʻŪD/2*) are covered (Maḥfūẓ 1964:151; al Ḥafnī 1971:75).

ḤIJĀZ (ḥ-j-z) "varrier; a geographic region in the Western part of the Arabian Peninsula; the chain of mountains separating the desert from the Red Sea"

1. Contemporary tetrachordal scalar segment (JINS/1*) of ½-1½-½ division.
2. An important melodic mode (MAQĀM/1*) utilizing the ḤIJĀZ JINS. This MAQĀM has been mentioned from at least the 13th C. (Ṣafī al Dīn 1938b:135-136).
3. Name of a note of the contemporary Arab scale, $F\#_1$, Gb_2, which is also known as ṢABĀ*  .

HIJJANIYYE (h-j-j?)

Syn. of HIǦǦON*, a popular Lebanese version of the ancient ḤIDĀ' or ḤUDĀ'* (Jargy 1970:36).

ḤIJL (pl. AḤJĀL, ḤUJŪL) (ḥ-j-l) "anklet"

A metal ring or anklet worn by women, according to the 1001 Nights stories (Farmer 1945:37). The term is usually found in the plural, as part of a dancer's accoutrement. Syn. of KHALKHAL or KHALKHĀL*.

ḤILLAH (ḥ-l-l) "large cooking pot"

Equiv. of ḤALLAH*.

ḤIMĀR (ḥ-m-r) "donkey"

Bridge for a musical instrument in the Maghrib (Farmer 1978a:42, n.2).

ḤIMYARĪ (geog.), adj. from ḤIMYAR, an ancient people and culture of south Arabia

One of two kinds of song sung in the Yaman (southwest region of the Arabian Peninsula) in pre-Islamic times. See ḤANAFĪ* (Farmer 1967:15).

HINDĪ DARĀY

Unidentified percussion instrument of pre-Islamic times (Farmer 1957:425).

ḤIṢĀR (ḥ-ṣ-r) "siege, blockade"

1. Melodic mode of eight tones mentioned from the 15th C. to today (Anonymous Treatise 1939:139; el Helou 1961:130).
2. Name of a note of the contemporary Arab scale, $G\#_2$ or Ab_2,  .

ḤISS or ḤASS = HESS (ḥ-s-s) "sensory perception, sound"

1. Musical sound, tone (al Fārābī 1967:822).
2. A voice endowed with subtlety and capable of transmitting religious feeling (Poche 1978:66).

ḤIWĀR (ḥ-w-r) "debate"

A genre of folk song characterized by an acceleration of movement and emphasis on the basic structure of the melodic line. It has four, or sometimes eight, lines per strophe (Shiloah 1974:55).

ḤIZB (pl. AḤZĀB) (ḥ-z-b) "party, group"

1. A series of invocational texts upon the names and attributes of God (Tun.), sung by members of the ʿĪsāwiyyah brotherhood without instrumental or hand clapping accompaniment. This set of devotional texts is designed for repetition in order to fix the concentration of the participants on God. Their recitation has melodic and rhythmic properties, but is not considered musical. It is performed before or after a musical program as an optional addition. Sometimes it is recited with Qur'ānic cantillation (Jones 1977:24, 31-32, n.9).
2. The small local group or "cell" of ʿĪsāwiyyah brothers (Tun.) (Jones 1977:24).

Ḫ̮LAS

Var. of KHALĀṢ* (Perkuhn 1976:106).

ḤŌRĀB (ḥ-r-b)

Songs of war in the Mashriq (Jargy 1970:30).

HŌSĀ (ḥ-w-s?)

A folk song of ʿIrāq which sets four-line or seven-line verses of poetry. It is partly sung and partly recited. Originally it named a dance rhythm of an essentially religious character. Later it gained political themes and was used to incite courage and patriotism. Among some Shīʿī groups, it continued to involve only religious themes (Jargy 1970:45-46).

HOSAÏNI

Var. of ḤUSAYNĪ* (Rouanet 1922:2735).

HOUDA'

Var. of ḤIDĀ' or ḤUDĀ'* (Touma 1977b:14; Rouanet 1922:2714).

HOUSSAÏNI

Var. of ḤUSAYNĪ/2* (Touma 1977b:37).

HOUZAM

Var. of HUZĀM* (Touma 1977b:37).

ḪRŪB

Var. of ḤURŪB* (Perkuhn 1976:107).

ḤSĪN

Var. of ḤUSAYN* (Chottin 1939:145-146).

ḤUDĀ' (ḥ-d-w or ḥ-d-y)

Equiv. of ḤIDĀ'*.

HUǦAYNĪ

Var. of HUJAYNĪ*(Shiloah 1972:17).

HUJAINI

Var. of HUJAYNĪ* (Farmer 1954, "Iraqian and Mesopotamian Music":532).

HUJAYNĪ = HUǦAYNĪ, HUJAINI (h-j-n) dim. of "racing camel"?

A solo song of narrative and nostalgic character sung by the Bedouin inhabitants of the Sinai Peninsula. It is believed to be a cameleer's or caravan song. This very ancient genre is now performed in social gatherings as well as while traveling in the desert. It is performed by a soloist who sometimes accompanies himself on the one-stringed stick fiddle (RABĀBAH*) (Shiloah 1972:17).

HUNBŪQAH (pl. HANĀBIQ) = HANBAQAH

An unidentified aerophone (MIZMĀR*). This is one spelling of the name of an instrument mentioned but not described by Ibn Salamah (1951:86, n. 3; 1938a:16, n. 6).

ḤUQQAH (pl. ḤUQAQ, ḤIQĀQ, AḤQĀQ) (ḥ-q-q) "small box"

The coconut soundbox of the KAMANJAH* of Egypt as described in the 19th C. (Lane 1973:356).

ḤURŪB (pl. of ḤARB*) = ḪRŪB (ḥ-r-b) "wars"

This plural form of ḤARB* is used for the first of two codas for the MUSADDAR/1*, an instrumental movement of the NAWBAH/1* suite (Tun.) (d'Erlanger 1959:192). Also TAWQ/1*, ḌURŪB/2*.

ḤURŪF AL HIJĀ' (ḥ-r-f) (h-j-w) "letters of spelling"

The letter names for the musical tones as determined by the fret positions or finger positions on the ʿŪD/2* according to Isḥaq al Mawṣilī (Shawqī 1976:330). See also pp. 336-337 of the same work, for comparison between the ḤURŪF of al Kindī and al Mawṣilī, and of Ibn al Munajjim in 1950:5-6. Later theorists continued to use letter names for notes until the Modern Period, when a system of descriptive names became widely accepted. Syn. of ḤURŪF AL JUMAL*.

ḤURŪF AL JUMAL (pl. of ḤARF AL JUMLAH) (ḥ-r-f) (j-m-l) "letters of the group"

The letters used to name the tones of the musical gamut (Ibn al Munajjim 1950:5). Syn. of ḤURŪF AL HIJĀ'*.

ḤUSAIN

Var. of ḤUSAYN* (Farmer 1933b:3).

ḤUSAYN = ḤUSAIN, ḤSĪN (ḥ-s-n) "dim. of handsome; excellent"

1. Syn. for ZĪR/1*, one of the lute strings (Farmer 1933b:3).
2. The higher of the two strings of the Maghribi RABĀB* (Chottin 1939:145-146).

ḤUSAYNĪ = HUSAINI, HOSAÏNI, HUSEINY, HUSEINI (ḥ-s-n) "pertaining to dim. of handsome; excellent"

1. A melodic mode mentioned from the 13th C. (Ṣafī al Dīn 1938b: 126) until today (el Helou 1961:91).
2. Name for a note of the contemporary Arab scale, A_2, 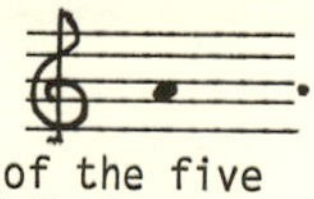.

3. Moving from lowest to highest in pitch, the fourth of the five strings of the SIMSIMIYYAH*, a contemporary harp-like folk instrument (Shiloah 1972:19).

ḤUSAYNĪ SHADD (ḥ-s-n) (sh-d-d) "pulled or stretched ḤUSAYNĪ"

Name for a note of the contemporary Arab scale, E_2, Fb_2, 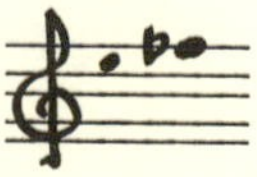.

ḤUSEINI or ḤUSEINY

Vars. of ḤUSAYNĪ* (Shiloah 1972:19; Smith 1847:181, resp.).

HUZĀM = HOUZAM (h-z-m)

1. A tetrachordal scalar segment (JINS/1*) of 3/4-1-½ division.
2. An important melodic mode (MAQĀM/1*) of contemporary practice utilizing the HUZĀM/1 tetrachord. Also known as SĪKĀH MUTAWASSIṬ*.

I

ʿIBĀRAH (ʿ-b-r) "explanation"

Musical phrase or theme (Ḥāfiẓ 1971:126). See ʿIBĀRAH MŪSĪQIYYAH*.

ʿIBĀRAH MŪSĪQIYYAH (pl. ʿIBĀRĀT MŪSĪQIYYAH) (ʿ-b-r) (Gr.) "musical phrase"

Musical phrase or theme (al Ḥafnī 1946:292).

IBDĀL (b-d-l) "substitution"

A tonal embellishing technique involving the substitution of one tone for its octave equivalent. When the octave equivalent is used in combination with the main note, instead of as substitution for it, the embellishment is called TAḌʿĪF /1*; but it remains a variety of IBDĀL, according to Ibn Sīnā (1930:98-99).

IBDĀL AL SHUḤĀJĀT (b-d-l) (sh-ḥ-j) "substitution of low notes"

An embellishing technique in which melody notes are replaced by their upper octave equivalents (al Fārābī 1967:1174). According to the translation in d'Erlanger (1935:91), the IBDĀL AL SHUḤĀJĀT could also involve the use of notes a perfect fourth or fifth higher than the melody tone.

IBN MISJAḤ, ABŪ ʿUTHMĀN SAʿĪD (d. ca. 715)

One of the first famous musicians of the Islamic period. Born at Makkah as a slave, he won his freedom as a result of his beautiful singing of poetry. He lived later in Syria and Persia before returning to the Peninsula. He is included among the "Four Great Singers" of his time and is believed to have formulated the eight melodic modes called AṢĀBIʿ/1* as well as six rhythmic modes. His pupils included IBN MUḤRIZ* and IBN SURAYJ*.

IBN MUḤRIZ, ABŪ AL KHAṬṬĀB MUSLIM (or SALM) (d. ca. 715)

One of the "Four Great Singers" of the early Islamic period. He is supposed to have taken features of Persian and Byzantine music and combined them with Arab elements. He is credited with two musical innovations: the rhythmic mode RAMAL/1* and the singing of couplets (ZAWJ/2*). He was born in Makkah where his father, a Persian freedman, was one of the guardians of the Kaʿbah. One of his teachers was IBN MISJAḤ*. He had leprosy so made no formal musical appearances. Despite a life of wandering due to his illness, he had a wide reputation as a performer and composer.

IBN SHUKLAH

Another name for IBRAHĪM IBN AL MAHDĪ*.

IBN SURAYJ, ABŪ YAḤYĀ ʿUBAYDULLAH (ca. 634-726)

One of the "Four Great Singers" of the early Islamic period. He was the son of a Turkish slave born at Makkah. As a freedman, he studied music with IBN MISJAḤ* and ṬUWAYS*. His fame derived from his beautiful singing of elegies and improvisations (GHINĀ' MURTAJAL*) accompanied by the rhythm stick (QADĪB*). About 684 he began playing the ʿŪD AL FĀRISĪ* and is said to have been the first to sing Arabic poetry while accompanying himself on the ʿŪD*.

IBRAHĪM IBN AL MAHDĪ (770-839)

Musician (vocalist and instrumentalist) and member of the caliphal family. He was son of the ʿAbbāsī caliph, al Mahdī, and half-brother of Hārūn al Rashīd. He had a voice of tremendous power and wide range which was supposed to have been so beautiful that it tamed wild beasts (Maḥfūẓ 1964:138). He became the leader of the opposition to ISḤAQ AL MAWṢILĪ* in the latter's endeavor to preserve the traditional Arabian music. He was also known as IBN SHUKLAH*.

IBRAHĪM AL MAWṢILĪ (742-804)

Famous musician (singer, instrumentalist and composer) of the ʿAbbāsī court, founder of a music school which advocated preservation and renewal of the traditional Arabian music, as opposed to the innovatory musical movement led by IBRAHĪM IBN AL MAHDĪ*. He trained many eminent pupils: e.g., ZALZAL* and his son, ISḤAQ IBN IBRAHĪM AL MAWṢILĪ*.

IBRĪQ (b-r-q) "pitcher, jug"

Syn. of ʿUNQ*, the neck of the lute (ʿŪD*) (al Khwārizmī 1968:239).

IBTIDĀ' (b-d-') "starting"

Starting or opening tone of a melodic mode or a performance of music (Ibn Sīnā 1930:96; Shawqī 1976:968).

IBTIDĀ' BI TAMAHHUL TADRĪJĪ (b-d-') (m-h-l) (d-r-j) "beginning to proceed slowly step by step"

Ritardando (el Helou 1961:59).

IBTIHĀL (b-h-l) "supplication"

Prayer to God as performed with the aid of chant or song in the Ṣūfī DHIKR* ceremony (Poche 1978:67).

IBZĪM (pl. ABĀZĪM) (b-z-m) "buckle, clasp"

Peg box which holds the tuning pegs of a chordophone (Ibn Salamah 1938a:9; 1938b:239).

IÇBA or IÇBA'OU

Vars. of IṢBA'* (Rouanet 1922:2725, 2808, resp.).

ICITALI (Turk.) "two metal strings"

An 18th C. long-necked lute with two metal strings (Farmer EI(Fr), "ṬUNBŪR":270).

IḌ'ĀF (ḍ-'-f) "doubling"

1. Doubling of a tone with its octave equivalent (Ibn al Munajjim 1976:218; Maḥfūẓ 1964:111).
2. A process which creates disjunct (MUNFAṢIL/3*) rhythmic modes out of conjunct (MUTTAṢIL/4*) ones (al Fārābī 1967:1008).

'IDĀN ('-w-d)

Pl. of 'ŪD*.

IDRĀJ (d-r-j) "inclusion; gradation"

The introduction of supplementary percussions between the fundamental percussions of a rhythmic mode (ĪQĀ'/1*) to increase the feeling of movement without actually accelerating the tempo (al Fārābī 1967: 1019). Ibn Sīnā designated this practice as TAḌ'ĪF/2* (1930:99; see also 1935:176).

ÎFERRED (f-r-d?), perhaps a colloq. form of FARD (pl. AFRĀD) "one of a pair" or of FARRADA "to single out, isolate"

The basic beats of the Moroccan percussion style known as UMM WA HASHIYAH* ("mother and stuffing"). These basic beats are the UMM or "mother" of the rhythmic cycle, while the counter beats are the "stuffing (Chottin 1939:165). See ITHELLETH*.

IFTITĀḤ (pl. IFTITĀḤĀT)(f-t-ḥ) "opener"

Instrumental introductory piece, an overture or musical introduction.

IFTITĀḤIYYAH (f-t-ḥ) "that which opens"

Syn. of IFTITĀḤ*.

IHTIZĀZ (pl. IHTIZĀZĀT) (h-z-z) "shaking, vibration"

Sound vibration; vibration of the string or air column of a musical instrument (Ibn Sīnā 1930:98; Allawerdi 1949:140-141).

IJRĀ' AL ʿAMAL (j-r-y) (ʿ-m-l) "performance of the work"

The characteristic melodic treatment of the scale of a melodic mode (MAQĀM/1*). It includes the order of exposition for constituent tetrachordal segments (s. JINS/1*), possible modulations, starting and ending tones, etc. (el Helou 1961:94). Syn. of UṢLŪB AL ʿAMAL* or SAYR AL ʿAMAL*.

IKHTILĀF (kh-l-f) "difference, disagreement"

Dissonance (Shiloah 1968a:236, 240).

IKHTIRĀʿ (kh-r-ʿ) "invention"

1. Composition of a melody (Kāẓim 1964:15).
2. Creation of a new melodic mode (MAQĀM/1*) (Kāẓim 1964:16).

IKHTIṢĀR (kh-ṣ-r) "abbreviation; tapering to the waist"

1. Rallentando or ritardando, i.e., a gradual slowing of the tempo (el Helou 1961:58).
2. Diminuendo, i.e., a gradual softening of the volume (el Helou 1961:58).

IKHTIYĀRĪ (kh-y-r) "pertaining to choice, preference"

Descriptive term for the unmeasured music of the ancient Arabs (Farmer 1929a:254). Opp. of MAWZŪN*.

ʿILM AL MŪSĪQĀ (ʿ-l-m) (Gr.) "knowledge of music"

The theory or science of music, as differentiated from its practice (Farmer 1965b:22, from a 9th C. ms.).

ʿIMĀD (pl. ʿAMAD) = ʿAMĀD (ʿ-m-d) "pole, support"

1. Lowest tone of the Arab musical scale as described by IṢHAQ AL MAWṢILĪ* and Ibn al Munajjim. It was equivalent to the open string tone produced on the MATHNĀ* string of the lute. Its name ("pole, support") was fitting since the other tones and tuning of instruments depended upon it (Ibn al Munajjim 1950:3; 1976:192; Shawqī 1976:273).
2. Syn. of TAṢDĪR*. See TAḤSĪN AL LAḤN* and Ibn Sīnā 1930:99.

IMBŪBŪ

An ancient pre-Islamic woodwind instrument similar to the MANJĪRAH* (ʿArnīṭah 1968:60). Also JANJARAH*, JANJIRĀS*, JANJĪRAH*.

IMDYAZEN

The troups of ambulant professional musicians of the Zemmour tribe (Berbers of the plains of Morocco) (Chottin 1939:32).

IMTIZĀJ (m-z-j) "combination"

1. The combination of tones (Farmer 1925:5).
2. Musical concordance or harmony (Ikhwān al Ṣafā' 1957:I, 194ff). Opp. of TANĀFUR* or discord.

INCHĀD

Var. of INSHĀD/1*, a genre of chanted vocal music (Chottin 1939: 132, 133, 136).

INCIRAF or INÇIRĀF

Vars. of INṢIRĀF (Chottin 1939:113, 126).

INFIRĀD (pl. INFIRĀDĀT) (f-r-d) "solitude, isolation"

A vocal or instrumental solo; solo performance (Ḥāfiẓ 1971:130).

INFIṢĀL (f-ṣ-l) "separation"

1. The interval which, when added to the two tetrachords of a scale, completes the octave (al Fārābī 1967:330). It may be placed below the two tetrachords (AJNĀS), above them or between them.
2. The interval produced by a fret added by al Kindī anterior to the SABBĀBAH* fret (Farmer 1937a:248). The tone produced by this fret was 114 c. above the open string tone. See MUJANNAB/2* (Ibid.)

INḤIRĀF (ḥ-r-f) "slant, inclination"

Oblique, rather than parallel, melodic movement (Maḥfūẓ 1964:194).

INQILĀB (pl. INQILĀBĀT) = NEKLAB, NEKLĀB (q-l-b) "transformation"

1. Generic for song (Maghrib) (Farmer 1976a:194).
2. A genre of semi-classical songs, usually on a love theme (Alg.) with rapid 2/4 rhythm, modulations and numerous returns to a refrain segment (Chottin 1961: Band IX, col. 1561). See NAWBAH INQILĀBĀT*.

INSHĀD (pl. ANĀSHĪD, INSHĀDĀT) = INCHĀD (n-sh-d) "recitation"

1. A genre of vocal solo (Mor.). It is a vocal declamation or floriated, non-measured recitative setting of a couplet of classical Arabic poetry. This genre is also called BAYTAYN*, which means "two lines" or "couplet." Theorists speak of twenty INSHĀDĀT or BAYTAYNAT, five of which are no longer used. Each one belongs to a suite (NAWBAH/1*) closely corresponding to it in mood and mode. This musically rendered poetry is devoted to the expression of noble moral or religious themes which are sung with gravity and majesty by the soloist or MUNSHID* (Chottin 1939:133). It has been called a vocal equivalent of the TAQSĪM* (Chottin 1939:66).

2. A folkish genre of vocal music (Egypt), which is composed of two parts: a MADHHAB/1* and a GHUṢN/1*. It used to be opened by the soloist singing the initial poetic segment, followed by an immediate choral repetition. Now, however, it conforms to one of the following three varieties:

a. BASĪṬ/7* in which the soloist sings the opening segment (MADHHAB/1) which is repeated by the chorus. The soloist then sings a second segment (GHUṢN/1) utilizing the melodic material of the MADHHAB/1 to accompany a new poetic line. This is followed by a choral repetition of the musical/poetic MADHHAB. Additional poetic contrasting segments may be added, each followed by the MADHHAB repetition, but the same melody is utilized for all.

b. BASĪṬ AL MURAKKAB* in which each GHUṢN segment introduced by the soloist is sung to new melodic materials and followed by a choral repetition of the musical/poetic MADHHAB.

c. MURAKKAB/5* in which the soloist presents the MADHHAB followed by a choral repetition, as usual. Each GHUṢN is then introduced with a new tune sung by the soloist, but this variety differs from the BASĪṬ AL MURAKKAB form by ending the GHUṢN with a TASLĪM/2* or repeated phrase which acts as a coda (Ḥāfiẓ 1971:199).

3. Chanting or chanted poetry (Jargy 1971:13).

INSIJĀM (s-j-m) "fluency, order"

Harmony or concordance (al Ḥafnī 1946:286).

INṢIRĀF (pl. INṢIRĀFĀT) = INÇIRĀF, INCIRAF, NEÇERAF (ṣ-r-f) "departure"

1. One of the vocal movements of the Maghribī suite (NAWBAH/1*). It is described as fourth of the five main movements, and it comprises a series of MUWASHSHAḤĀT (s. MUWASHSHAḤAH*) (Maḥfūẓ 1964: 106). In Algeria, this series of songs has a ternary rhythm and rapid tempo (d'Erlanger 1959:191; Ḥāfiẓ 1971:126). Strangely enough, other sources writing about the Algerian NAWBAH describe the INṢIRĀF as a movement which is characterized by a slow tempo and the quality of a triumphal march (Delphin and Guin 1886:64). According to el Mahdi, it has a 5/8 or 10/8 rhythmic cycle (1972: 12, 29).

2. The second of two parts into which each of the five major segments (MAWĀZĪN, s. MĪZĀN/3*) of the Moroccan NAWBAH/1* is divided--the first slower, the second more rapid (Schuyler 1978: 37). Chottin writes that this part is also known as MĪZĀN MUṢARRAF* (1939:112). Also MUṢARRAF*.

3. A Maghribī rhythmic mode with 5/8 or 10/8 cycle (Alg.) (el Mahdi 1972:29), 5/8 in Tunisia (Chottin 1939:119; Ḥāfiẓ 1971:132), 3/8 in Morocco (Ḥāfiẓ 1971:132).

INTIQĀL (n-q-l) "transporting"

1. Melodic movement or patterning as described by the theorists of the Classical Period.

According to al Kindī (1966:135-136, 146-148; 1969:107-108), it included the following divisions:

I. MUTATĀLĪ* ("successive"): ascending or descending stepwise movement

II. LA MUTATĀLĪ* ("not successive"): alternating ascending and descending movement with leaps

A. LAWLABĪ* ("spiral")

1. LAWLABĪ DĀKHILĪ ("inner spiral"): in which the movement proceeds from an initially large interval and becomes gradually smaller in its ascending and descending leaps, e.g.,

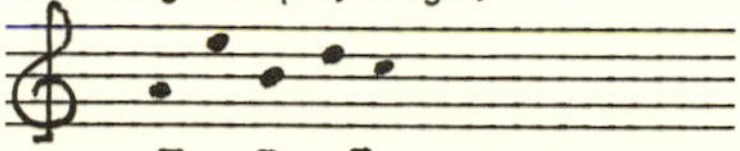

2. LAWLABĪ KHĀRIJĪ ("outer spiral"): in which the movement proceeds from a smaller interval to progressively larger ascending and descending leaps, e.g.,

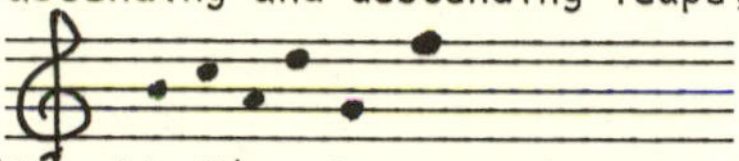

B. ḌAFĪR* ("braided"): interweaving of alternating large-small, ascending-descending intervals

1. ḌAFĪR AL MUSHTABIK or AL MUTTAṢIL ("bound or connected braided"): in which the notes of more than one octave are "connected" or involved, e.g.,

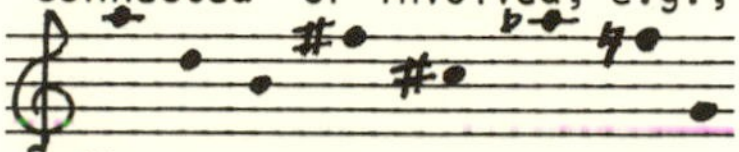

2. ḌAFĪR AL MUNFAṢIL ("unbound braided"): in which the notes of only one octave are involved, e.g.,

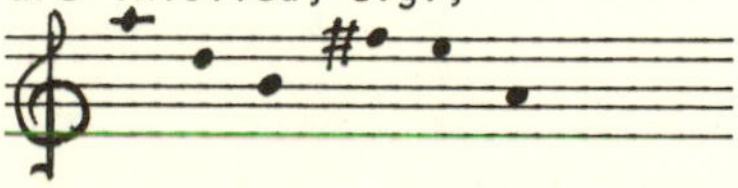

According to al Fārābī, there were four basic varieties of INTIQĀL (1967:418ff; 967-983; 1930:145-149; 1935:24-25). A translation of the passage in 1967:967-983 can be found in al Faruqi 1974:428-433.

I. INTIQĀL ʿALĀ ISTIQĀMAH* ("direct INTIQĀL"): steady movement in one direction--either ascending or descending

A. MUTTAṢIL* or ʿALĀ ITTIṢĀL* ("conjunct"): progressing without leaps, e.g.,

B. ṬĀFIR* or BI TAKHAṬṬĪ* ("disjunct"): progressing with leaps of various sizes, e.g.,

II. INTIQĀL ʿALĀ INʿIṬĀF* ("INTIQĀL with deviation"): with returns to the starting tone after one or more tones and utilizing tones sounded previously or not

A. Leaping back to the starting tone after one or more tones progressing in the opposite direction, e.g.,

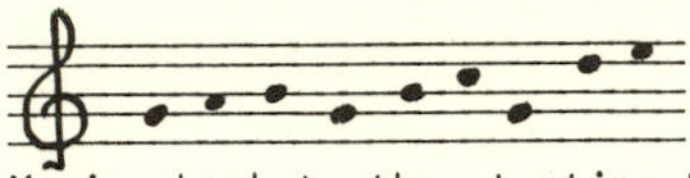

B. Moving back to the starting tone in a stepwise progression after moving in the opposite direction for varying numbers of tones, e.g.,

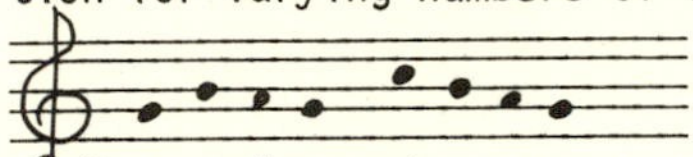

III. INTIQĀL ʻALĀ ISTIDĀRAH* ("cyclical INTIQĀL"): symmetrical patterns executed in both directions from the starting tone. Returns to that starting tone may occur after every tone, after 2 tones, after 3 tones, etc., e.g.,

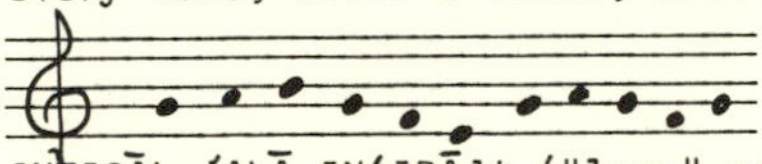

IV. INTIQĀL ʻALĀ INʻIRĀJ* ("lame" or "crooked INTIQĀL"): ascending-descending patterns which alternate direction freely and make returns to other than starting tone, e.g.,

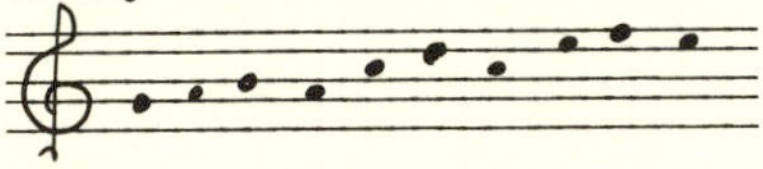

According to Ibn Sīnā, there were two basic varieties of INTIQĀL, each with two subdivisions (1930:95-96; 1935:162ff).

I. BASĪṬ/9* ("simple"): without returns to notes sounded previously, therefore, steady movement in one direction
    A. MUTTAṢIL/1* ("conjunct"): progressing diatonically instead of with leaps
    B. ṬĀFIR* ("disjunct"): with leaps

II. MURAKKAB/4* ("compound, complex"): involving alternating ascending and descending movement
    A. MUTTAṢIL/1* or ʻALĀ ITTIṢAL* ("conjunct"): without leaps
    B. ṬĀFIR* or ʻALĀ ṬĀFIR* ("disjunct"): with leaps

MURAKKAB INTIQĀL, according to Ibn Sīnā, could include patterns which were identical (MUTASHĀBIHAH*) or not identical (GHAYR MUTASHĀBIHAH*) in their kind of movement (i.e., in KAYF*), in the number of notes (KAMM*) and/or in ratio of its intervals (NISBAH*). If the patterns created were similar in all these three ways, the progression was designated by Ibn Sīnā as DĀ'IR*.

Other descriptions and classifications of INTIQĀL as melodic patterning can be found in Ṣafī al Dīn 1938b:152-158; *Anonymous Treatise* 1939:152-153; al Lādhiqī 1939:426-427; Ibn Abī al Ṣalt 1952:64-67, 73; de Vaux 1891; Rouanet 1922:2726; de Vaux 1891:342-343, Ibn Zaylah 1964:41-44.

2. The art of passing from one mode, whether that be melodic or rhythmic, to another (Farmer 1943:88; Ikhwān al Safā' 1957:I, 233). It is used to designate melodic modulation most often, however.

3. Moving the tonic of a mode to form a new tetrachordal or octave species (al Fārābī 1967:959-966).

4. Moving from one tune to another, with modulations or without.

INTIQĀL ʻALĀ INʻIRĀJ (n-q-l) (ʻ-r-j) "movement with lameness or crookedness"

Ascending-descending melodic patterning which alternates direction freely but does not return to the starting tone (al Fārābī 1967: 416-434, 967-982; 1930:145-149; 1935:24-25). See al Faruqi (1974: 428-433) for a translation into English of the al Fārābī passage.

INTIQĀL ʻALĀ INʻIṬĀF (n-q-l) (ʻ-ṭ-f) "movement with deviation"

Melodic patterning which moves back to the starting tone after moving away from it. The return can be done with stepwise movement or with a leap (al Fārābī 1967:416-434, 967-982; 1930:145-149; 1935:24-25). See al Faruqi 1974:428-433.

INTIQĀL ʻALĀ ISTIDĀRAH (n-q-l) (d-w-r) "cyclical movement"

Symmetrical melodic patterning executed in both directions from the starting tone. Returns may occur after every tone, after two tones, three tones, etc. (al Fārābī 1967:416-434, 967-982). See al Faruqi 1974:428-433.

INTIQĀL ʻALĀ ISTIQĀMAH (n-q-l) (q-w-m) "direct movement"

Melodic patterning which moves steadily in one direction, either ascending or descending. It can be done without leaps (MUTTAṢIL/1*) or with leaps of various sizes (ṬAFIR*) (al Fārābī 1967:416-434, 967-982). See al Faruqi 1974:428-433.

INTIQĀL MIN LAḤN ILĀ LAḤN (n-q-l) (l-ḥ-n) (l-ḥ-n) "transporting from tune to tune"

Modulation (al Kindī 1976:104).

ĪQĀʻ (pl. ĪQĀʻĀT) = YIQĀʻ (w-q-ʻ) "falling, causing to fall"

1. Rhythmic mode, i.e., a succession of percussions of like or varying lengths arranged to constitute a cycle which is repeated for the length of a vocal or instrumental segment or number. The type and arrangement of its accents help give the rhythmic mode its special character. The ĪQĀʻĀT varied from period to period as to composition, names and number of modes in use. For al Kindī and al Fārābī, for example, there were eight rhythmic modes in common usage (Farmer 1943:19-22; al Fārābī 1967:1022-1055, tr. in al Faruqi 1974:443-455). Ṣafī al Dīn and al Jurjānī listed six rhythms which were frequently performed (d'Erlanger 1938:485), while al Khwārizmī described seven ĪQĀʻĀT (al Khwārizmī 1968:245-246). See ĪQĀʻĀT AL MASHHŪRAH*. Today over 100 are known (d'Erlanger 1959:138-140), though a much smaller number is common in the repertoire of any performer. The term ĪQĀʻ today often applies to the rhythm as performed, while another term (MĪZĀN/2*) is used more often in contemporary Moroccan parlance for the theoretical rhythmic mode (Chottin 1939:115).
2. A beat produced on a percussion instrument, as opposed to the NAQRAH* produced on a chordophone (Ikhwān al Ṣafā' 1957:I, 200).
3. Playing (on a musical instrument) (Ibn Khurdādhbih 1969:17; al Masʻūdī 1874:VIII, 91).

ĪQĀʿĀT AL ʿARABIYYAH AL MASHHŪRAH (w-q-ʿ) (ʿ-r-b) (sh-h-r) "famous Arab fallings"

The famous rhythmic modes described by the Classical Period theorists. According to al Fārābī, there were eight of these modes: HAZAJ/2* (1967:1022ff); 2) KHAFĪF AL HAZAJ* (1022ff); 3) KHAFĪF AL RAMAL* (1029ff); 4) RAMAL* (1033ff); 5) THAQĪL AL THĀNĪ* (1038ff); 6) MĀKHŪRĪ* or KHAFĪF AL THAQĪL AL THĀNĪ* (1042ff); 7) THAQĪL AL AWWAL* (1045ff); and 8) KHAFĪF AL THAQĪL AL AWWAL* (1048ff).

ĪQĀʿĀT MUFAṢṢALAH (w-q-ʿ) (f-ṣ-l) "disconnected fallings"

A disjunct rhythmic mode, i.e., one in which the percussions are of different lengths (al Fārābī 1967:999).

ĪQĀʿĀT MUWAṢṢALAH (w-q-ʿ) (w-ṣ-l) "connected fallings"

A conjunct rhythmic mode, i.e., one in which the percussions are of equal length (al Fārābī 1967:997-998; 1935:30-31). Al Fārābī writes that there are nine of these, seven in which each percussion is followed by a period of rest (WAQFAH/1*) and two which move at such rapid tempo that no pause is evident between beats.

ʿIQD (pl. ʿUQŪD) (ʿ-q-d) "collar, necklace"

A melodic genre or scalar segment which is tetrachordal or pentachordal in extent (d'Erlanger 1949:71). See ʿAQD/1*, which has an identical spelling in Arabic, and an identical plural form.

IQLIQ

An obsolete spike fiddle with two, three or four strings known in Turkestan, Arabia and Turkey at least as early as the 15th C. (Marcuse). It was a small instrument, with hemispherical sound chest. It was thought in the 17th C. to have been invented in Egypt. Farmer thinks it may have corresponded to the KAMĀNJAH FARKH* described by Villoteau (Farmer 1976b:44-45).

IQTIRĀḤ (q-r-ḥ) "improvisation"

Musical improvisation (early ʿAbbāsī period) (Farmer 1967:122).

IQTIRĀN (q-r-n) "combining"

Combining of two or more tones simultaneously (al Fārābī 1967:111).

ʿIRĀN (geog.)

Unidentified woodwind instrument mentioned by Ibn Salamah (1951:86). Maḥfūẓ defines it as the MIZMĀR* (Maḥfūẓ 1964:42). This would also fail to clarify whether it was a single reed, double reed, whistle or end-blown instrument, since that term has had many definitions.

ʿIRĀQ (geog.)

1. A tetrachordal scale segment (JINS/1*) of 3/4-1-3/4 division

which is known in contemporary practice and theory.
2. A melodic mode (MAQĀM/1*) utilizing the JINS/1* of the same name. A MAQĀM with this name has been mentioned in theoretical works as early as the 13th C. (Ṣafī al Dīn 1938b:136). Today it is also called SĪKĀH TĀMM*.
3. Name for one of the tones of the contemporary Arabian scale, Bb_1, 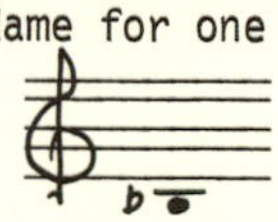 .

ʿIRĀQIYYAH (pl. ʿIRAQIYYĀT) = ʿIRĀQYA, ʿIRĀQĪYA, ʿIRAQIYA (geog.) "pertaining to ʿIRĀQ"

A foreshortened oboe-like instrument with cylindrical tube and bore and a domelike head. This instrument was played with a very wide reed. It had seven front fingerholes and two rear thumbholes and was 18-23 cm. in length (Marcuse). Farmer thinks it was a descendant of the NĀY AL ʿIRĀQĪ* mentioned by al Ghazālī (d. 1111) (Farmer EI(Eng), "Mizmār":541). It was still found in 18th C. Egypt by Villoteau (Farmer 1954, "Egyptian Music":895).

ʿIRĀQYA

Var. of ʿIRĀQIYYAH* (Farmer 1929a:142).

IRKHĀ' (r-kh-w) "relaxation"

1. The quarter tone interval (al Fārābī 1967:260; 1930:97; al Kindī 1966:145). In al Khwārizmī, it is described as approximately half the FAḌLAH* (limma), thus the Arab approximation of the Pythagorean comma (al Khwārizmī 1968:243). See also Ibn Abī al Ṣalt 1952:34, and BUʿD*.
2. Loosening of a string to lower the pitch on a chordophone (Ikhwān al Ṣafā' 1957:I, 233).

ʿIRQ (pl. ʿURŪQ) (ʿ-r-q) "vein"

Formerly used to designate a string of a chordophone. Syn. of the contemporary term, WATAR* (Bulos 1971:19).

IRTAJALA (r-j-l) "to extemporize"

To improvise vocally or instrumentally.

IRTIJĀL (pl. IRTIJĀLĀT) (r-j-l) "extemporizing"

Improvising.

IṢBAʿ (pl. AṢĀBIʿ) (ṣ-b-ʿ) "finger"

See AṢĀBIʿ*.

ISḤAQ IBN IBRAHĪM AL MAWṢILĪ (767-850)

A famous musician of ʿAbbāsī times. He was trained by his father, IBRAHĪM AL MAWṢILĪ* and his uncle, ZALZAL*, as well as other famous musicians of his time. He succeeded his father as court musician in Baghdād. Systematizer of the old Arabian music style and theory, he was leader of the classicists of his time. Isḥaq al Mawṣilī is thought to have been the first to establish an organization of the various melodic and rhythmic modes. He was reknowned as a performer, a theorist, a talented literary figure, and was even knowledgeable in philology and law. He is credited with writing forty works in various fields.

ISHĀRAH ḤULYAH (pl. ISHĀRĀT ḤULYAH) (sh-w-r) (ḥ-l-w) "sign of ornament"

Grace note (al Ḥafnī 1946:287).

ISHĀRAH AL ISTIMRĀR (pl. ISHĀRĀT AL ISTIMRĀR) (sh-w-r) (m-r-r) "sign of continuity"

Pedal point (Maḥfūẓ 1964:185).

ISHĀRAH AL RUJŪʿ (pl. ISHĀRĀT AL RUJŪʿ) (sh-w-r) (r-j-ʿ) "sign of return"

Repetition sign (Maḥfūẓ 1964:185).

ISHĀRAH AL TAKRĀR (pl. ISHĀRĀT AL TAKRĀR) (sh-w-r) (k-r-r) "sign of repetition"

Repetition sign, a notation borrowing from Western music (Maḥfūẓ 1964:185).

ISHMĀM (pl. ISHMĀMĀT) (sh-m-m) "the pronunciation of 'u' with a trace of 'i'"

Percussion of medium force (al Fārābī 1967:987).

ISJĀḤ (pl. ISJĀḤĀT) (s-j-ḥ)

Lower tone of an octave interval (Shawqī 1976:282; Farmer 1937a:253, 255). Al Khwārizmī mentions this term as well as SAJĀḤ*, but labels ISJĀḤ as an incorrect usage (1968:240).

IṢLĀḤ (ṣ-l-ḥ) "reform; restoration"

Tuning (of a musical instrument).

IṢLĀḤ AL NAGHAM (ṣ-l-ḥ) (n-gh-m) "reform of the tune"

Tuning of a musical instrument.

ISTAHALLA (h-l-l) "to begin, introduce"

1. To raise one's voice (Madina).
2. To intone (a tune) (Madina).

ISTAKHBAR

Var. of ISTIKHBĀR* (Lachmann).

ISTIʿĀDAH (pl. ISTIʿĀDĀT) (ʿ-w-d) "substitution"

Playing a note on another string when the string on which it is usually played is broken in performance (Ibn al Munajjim in Shawqī 1976:352ff).

ISTIDHKĀR (pl. ISTIDHKĀRĀT) (dh-k-r) "self-reminding"

One type of LĀZIMAH* or instrumental punctuation phrase at the end of a section. This type repeats the final phrase of the preceding vocal section. It is also called ṢADĀ* (el Helou 1961:180).

ISTIFTĀḤ (pl. ISTIFTĀḤĀT) (f-t-ḥ) "opening"

1. An improvisatory, free rhythmed overture for the NAWBAH/1* suite (Tun.) (el Mahdi 1972:13). It is played by the orchestra in unison (d'Erlanger 1959:191-192). Counterparts in other regions of the Maghrib are DĀ'IRAH/3* (Alg.) and MASHĀLIYAH* (Mor.).
2. A religious song or instrumental overture with many variant parts (TABDĪLĀT, s. TABDĪLAH*), which is performed by religious brotherhoods of the Maghrib (d'Erlanger 1937:11).

IṢṬIḤĀB (pl. IṢṬIḤĀBĀT) (ṣ-ḥ-b) "company, accompanying"

1. Accordatura (according to a 13th C. ms., Farmer 1965b:49).
2. Instrumental accompaniment of vocal numbers, including introductions, repetitions, additions, as well as standard underlay of the vocal line (Khashabah in Preface to al Fārābī 1967:24).

ISTIḤĀLAH (pl. ISTIḤĀLĀT) (ḥ-w-l) "change, transformation"

Pitch alteration (al Kindī 1966:150).

ISTIḤĀLAH ṢAWTIYYAH (ḥ-w-l) (ṣ-w-t) "self-transformation of sound"

Pitch alteration (al Kindī in Cowl 1966:150), or more precisely, the musical "transitions" of which al Kindī speaks can be from one note (NAGHMAH*) to another, one interval (BUʿD*) to another, one tetrachordal scalar segment (JINS*) to another, one scalar collection (JAMʿ*) to another, etc. (al Kindī 1969:67, 100ff).

ISTIHLĀL (pl. ISTIHLĀLĀT) (h-l-l) "to raise one's voice"

An overture or prelude. More specifically, al Fārābī describes it as a short vocal prelude using only a portion from the opening line of poetry (al Fārābī 1967:1162; 1935:85). Khashabah (in al Fārābī 1967:1162, n. 2) writes that it is usually MAMLŪ' AL NAGHAM* ("full noted"), i.e., having one tone per syllable in order that the listener would be able to understand the words perfectly. The definition of al Jurjānī (1938:540) is similar. He adds, however, that it can be done either with free rhythm or a rhythmic mode, and instead of the opening words of the poem of the song, it may utilize stock words or phrases. If it sets one or two full poetic lines, he writes, it is known as NASHĪD/3*.

ISTIKBAR

Var. of ISTIKHBĀR* (el Mahdi 1972:14).

ISTIKHBĀR (pl. ISTIKHBĀRĀT) = ISTAKHBAR, ISTIKBAR (kh-b-r) "inquiry"

Solo instrumental prelude of the Maghrib. It is improvisatory and free rhythmed, thus can be considered a Maghribī equivalent of the TAQSĪM* (d'Erlanger 1959:180). Syn. of MUSTAKHBIR/1*.

ISTIQRĀR (q-r-r) "permanent settlement"

One of the types of LĀZIMAH* or instrumental punctuation phrase, this type occurring between a vocal section and a refrain (el Helou 1961:180).

ISTIRĀḤAH (pl. ISTIRĀḤĀT) (r-w-ḥ) "rest, relaxation"

The final long, steady tone of a song which terminates on a quiescent "H" (al Fārābī 1967:1166; 1935:86; al Jurjānī 1938:541). See also SHARQAH* and IʿTIMĀD/1*.

ITÂMAH

Var. of YATĀYIM* (Chottin 1939:124).

ITHELLETH (th-l-th) (colloq.)

Those beats of the Moroccan percussion style known as UMM WA HASHIYAH* which provide the filler rather than its basic beats (IFERRED*) (Chottin 1939:165).

IʿTIMĀD (pl. IʿTIMĀDĀT) (ʿ-m-d) "support, prop"

1. A steady vocal tone terminating a song which does not terminate on a quiescent "H" (al Fārābī 1967:1166; 1935:86; al Jurjānī 1938:541). See also ISTIRĀḤAH*.
2. Supplementary percussion(s) added prior to the beginning of a rhythmic cycle (Ibn Sīnā 1935:181; Anonymous Treatise 1939:165; al Rajab 1967:23). Also called TAṢDĪR* (al Rajab, loc. cit.). See MAJĀZ*, ʿIMĀD*.

IṬLĀQ (pl. IṬLĀQĀT) (ṭ-l-q) "freeing; dispatching"

Vocal or instrumental musical performance.

IṬRĀB (ṭ-r-b) "delight, pleasure"

1. Singing.
2. Performing music.

ITTIFĀQ (w-f-q) "agreement"

1. Consonance (al Fārābī 1967:112; Shiloah 1968a:236, 240).
2. Coordination of the vocal and instrumental parts (Maḥfūẓ 1964:57).

ITTIFĀQ AL AʿẒ̣AM (pl. ITTIFĀQĀT AL ʿUẒMĀ) (w-f-q) (ʿ-ẓ-m) "agreement of the largest; largest agreement"

Consonance of the perfect octave (al Fārābī 1967:824).

ITTIṢĀL (pl. ITTIṢĀLĀT) (w-ṣ-l) "connection"

Stepwise melodic progression (Ibn Sīnā 1930:96; al Kindī 1966:156).

(BI) IZLĀQ (z-l-q) "with sliding"

A slide or glissando-like ornament (al Ḥafnī 1946:297).

IZLI (pl. IZLAN)

A short song used in the Berber AHIDOUS*. It comprises a musical setting for a poetic phrase divided into two unrhymed hemistiches and expressing a simple idea. It is repeated by a chorus. This song is always performed to a 5-beat rhythm. It is also called ATEMCHI* or TARHIULT*. A variety of the IZLI with four hemistiches, but without refrain, is known as AFERDI* (Chottin 1939:21-22).

J

"J" (abbrev. for "jīm," one of the letters of the Ar. alphabet)

1. A duration or percussion three times as long as "A"* time or ZAMĀN AL AWWAL* (Ṣafī al Dīn 1938b:161; 1938a:478; al Jurjānī 1939: 478; Anonymous Treatise 1939:159; al Lādhiqī 1939:459). A conjunct rhythm utilizing only this length of percussion was designated as HAZAJ AL KHAFĪF AL THAQĪL* (Ṣafī al Dīn 1938b:161).
2. An abbreviation for the MUJANNAB/1* interval (Ṣafī al Dīn 1938a: 238; al Jurjānī 1938:238; Anonymous Treatise 1939:37; al Lādhiqī 1939:302). This interval was of two sizes: 1) MUJANNAB AL KABĪR* (10/9); and 2) MUJANNAB AL ṢAGHĪR* (16/15). See also TATIMMAH*, an equivalent for the larger "J" interval; MUTAMMAN*, equivalent for the smaller.

JABHAH (j-b-h) "forehead, brow"

The curled end piece of the contemporary bowed instrument (KAMĀN*) which is beyond the tuning pegs (Maḥfūẓ 1964:159).

JADHB (j-dh-b) "pulling, tugging"

PLucking to achieve sound from the string of a musical instrument (Ḥāfiẓ 1971:87).

JĀDHBIYYAH LAḤNIYYAH (j-dh-b) (l-ḥ-n) "melodic attraction, gravitation"

Melodic direction or contour (ʿArnīṭah 1968:42).

JADWAL (pl. JADĀWIL) (j-d-w-l) "list, schedule"

1. The gamut or scale of musical tones used by the contemporary Arabs. In the writings of the Classical Period theorists, the term JAMʿ/1* was used. See p. 117.

THE TONES OF THE CONTEMPORARY ARABIAN JADWAL

DĪWĀN AWWAL ("First DĪWĀN")

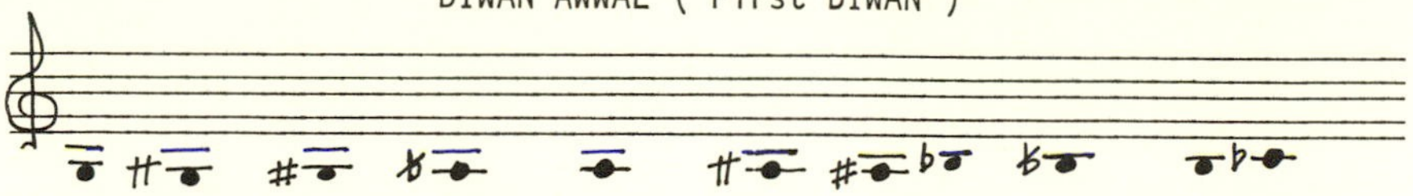

YAKĀH | QARĀR NĪM ḤIṢĀR | QARĀR ḤIṢĀR | QARĀR TĪK ḤIṢĀR | ʿUSHAY-RĀN | QARĀR NĪM ʿAJAM | QARĀR ʿAJAM, or ʿAJAM ʿUSHAYRĀN | ʿIRĀQ | KAWASHT, or SUZDĀK

TĪK KAWASHT | RĀST | NĪM ZIRKŪLĀH | ZIR-KŪLĀH | TĪK ZIRKŪLĀH | DŪKĀH | NĪM KURD | KURD | SĪKĀH

BŪSALĪK | TĪK BŪSALĪK | JIHĀRKĀH | NĪM ḤIJĀZ | ḤIJĀZ, or ṢABĀ | TĪK ḤIJĀZ | NAWĀ, or JAWĀB YAKĀH

DĪWĀN THĀNĪ ("Second DĪWĀN")

NAWĀ | NĪM ḤIṢĀR | ḤIṢĀR | TĪK ḤIṢĀR | ḤUSAYNĪ | NĪM ʿAJAM | ʿAJAM | AWJ | NIHUFT | TĪK NIHUFT

KIRDĀN, or MAHŪR | NĪM SHĀHNĀZ | SHĀHNĀZ | TĪK SHĀHNĀZ | MUḤAYYIR | NĪM ZIWĀL | ZIWĀL, or SUNBULAH | BUZURK

ḤUSAYNĪ SHADD | TĪK ḤUSAYNĪ SHADD | MĀHŪRĀN | JAWĀB NĪM ḤIJĀZ | JAWĀB ḤIJĀZ | JAWĀB TĪK ḤIJĀZ | JAWĀB NAWĀ, or RAMAL TŪTĪ

2. A second introductory segment of the ʿAMAL/1*, a vocal composition described by a 15th C. theorist (Anonymous Treatise, drawing from ʿAbd al Qādir ibn Ghaybī 1939:244).

JAGHĀNAH (j-gh-n?) or ṢAGHĀNAH (ṣ-gh-n)

An instrument comprising small cymbals or bells attached to the body of various forms, e.g., a stick or a pavilion-like construction. A version of this used by the Christians was known as MIRWAḤAH* (Farmer EI(Fr), "Ṣandj":210).

JAHARA (j-h-r) "to raise the voice"

To sing.

JAHĪR (j-h-r) "loud of voice"

1. Intense in sound, i.e., opp. of KHAFĪF/5*.
2. Low in pitch.

JAHURA (j-h-r) "to be loud and clear of voice"

To sing loudly and clearly.

JAHWARĪ (j-h-r) "loud of voice"

Intense in musical sound (Wehr).

JALĀJIL (pl. of JULJUL*) (j-l-j-l) "bells"

1. Bells used as a musical instrument.
2. Cymbals of the tambourine.

JĀLGHĪ BAGHDĀDĪ = DJALGHI BAGDADI, CHĀLGHĪ BAGHDĀDĪ(Turk.) (geog.) "Baghdad ensemble"

The small instrumental ensemble used to accompany a vocalist (QĀRI'/2*) or instrumental soloist (ʿIrāq). The ensemble is usually composed of three musicians who play the SANṬŪR*, the JAWZ* and the ṬABLAH/2* or DUNBAK*. Sometimes a RIQQ* is added to the ensemble (Touma 1977b:71; Maḥfūẓ 1964:17).

JAMʿ (pl. JUMŪʿ) (j-m-ʿ) "collection, group, set"

1. Any scalar combination of three or more notes from which melodies are composed or improvised (Ṣafī al Dīn 1938b:17; Quṭb al Dīn al Shirāzī in Wright 1978:169). Other theorists define it as a combination of five or more tones to form a scale (al Fārābī 1967:121; 1930:117; al Khwārizmī 1968:241; el Helou 1961:84). Also see d'Erlanger 1930:312, n.7). Today the term is generally used for the seven-tone octave scale (Ṣalāḥ al Dīn 1950:99). See JAMAʿAH*.
2. A composed or performed arrangement of tones, i.e., a motif or musical phrase (Maḥfūẓ 1964:112).

JAMʿ AL AKMAL (j-m-ʿ) (k-m-l) "most perfect collection"

The scalar combination of tones with extent of a double octave (al Fārābī 1967:327).

JAMʿ AL AʿẒAM (j-m-ʿ) (ʿ-ẓ-m) "largest collection"

A scalar combination of tones with extent greater than double the perfect fourth and less than the double octave (al Fārābī 1967:325).

JAMʿ IFTIRĀQ (j-m-ʿ) (f-r-q) "combination of separation"

Disjunct, two-octave scalar combination of tones (al Kindī 1969:64). For example:

Syn. of JAMʿ AL MUNFAṢIL/2*, JAMʿ INFIṢĀL*.

JAMʿ AL IJTIMĀʿ (j-m-ʿ) (j-m-ʿ) "collection of the gathering"

A double octave scalar collection in which the whole tone interval of disjunction is found between the two tetrachords (AJNĀS, s. JINS/1*) of each octave (al Fārābī 1967:332). See JAMʿ AL MUTTAṢIL.

JAMʿ AL INFIṢĀL (j-m-ʿ) (f-ṣ-l) "disjunct collection"

Disjunct, two-octave scalar combination (al Kindī 1969:64). Syn. of JAMʿ AL MUNFAṢIL/2*, JAMʿ IFTIRĀQ*.

JAMʿ AL JAMʿ (j-m-ʿ) (j-m-ʿ) "combination of the collection"

1. Name given to the 91 melodic modes used in the 15th C. (Anonymous Treatise 1939:240).
2. Syn. of KULL AL NIGHAM/1* (Anonymous Treatise 1939:240).

JAMʿ AL KĀMIL (j-m-ʿ) (k-m-l) "the perfect collection"

1. A scalar combination of tones with extent of a double octave (al Fārābī 1967:327; 882; Ibn Zaylah 1964:36).
2. According to al Fārābī, his predecessors had considered the octave plus a perfect fourth as the extent of the JAMʿ AL KĀMIL (1967:327).

JAMʿ AL KĀMIL ʿALĀ IṬLĀQ (j-m-ʿ) (k-m-l) (ṭ-l-q) "the most perfect collection"

A double octave scalar collection of tones, syn. of JAMʿ AL KĀMIL/1* and JAMʿ AL TĀMM* (al Fārābī 1967:1056; Collangettes 1906:160).

JAMʿ AL KĀMIL BIL QUWWAH (j-m-ʿ) (k-m-l) (q-w-y) "the perfect collection which has strength"

A scalar combination of tones of one octave range (al Fārābī 1967: 1056; Ibn Zaylah 1964:38).

JAMʿ AL MUNFAṢIL (j-m-ʿ) (f-ṣ-l) "disjunct collection"

1. A scalar combination of two AJNĀS (s. JINS/1*) without a common tone (Ṣalāḥ al Dīn 1950:103; el Helou 1961:92). Also known as JAMʿ AL MUNFAṢIL AL AWSAṬ* (Khashabah in al Fārābī 1967:329-330, n. 4). For example:

RĀST MAQĀM

2. A scalar combination of the AJNĀS (JINS/1*) of a double octave in such a way that a whole tone separates the two inner AJNĀS (Ibn Sīnā 1930:91). Syn. of JAMʿ INFIṢĀL*, JAMʿ IFTIRĀQ*. Al Fārābī defines it as a scalar combination of the AJNĀS of a double octave in such a way that a whole tone interval of disjunction is at the lowest possible position in both octaves (al Fārābī 1967:331).
For example:
See also Ibn Zaylah 1964:40.

JAMʿ MUTADĀKHIL (j-m-ʿ) (d-kh-l) "mutually penetrating collection"

A scalar combination of AJNĀS (s. JINS/1*) in which the two tetrachords share more than one common tone (Al Ḥalqah 1964:17; Ṣalāḥ al Dīn 1950:103).
For example:

ṢABĀ MAQĀM

JAMʿ AL MUTAGHAYYIR (j-m-ʿ) (gh-y-r) "changed collection"

A scalar combination of two octaves' extent in which the succession of intervals is not the same in both octaves (Collangettes 1906:169; al Fārābī 1967:332-335).

JAMʿ AL MUTTAṢIL (j-m-ʿ) (w-ṣ-l) "conjunct collection"

1. A scalar combination of two AJNĀS (s. JINS/1*) with one common tone (Ṣalāḥ al Dīn:103: el Helou 1961:92).
For example:

NAHĀWAND MAQĀM

2. A scalar combination of the AJNĀS (JINS/1*) of a double octave in which the whole tone interval of disjunction does not separate the two octaves (al Kindī 1969:63; Ibn Sīnā 1930:91). Syn. of MUTTAṢIL/3*, JAMʿ AL IJTIMĀʿ*, according to Ṣafī al Dīn (de Vaux 1891:323). Ṣafī al Dīn describes JAMʿ AL IJTIMĀʿ as an already outmoded designation for the JAMʿ AL MUTTAṢIL. See Ibn Zaylah 1964:40 for another definition of JAMʿ AL MUTTAṢIL.
The definition of al Fārābī is: A scalar combination of the AJNĀS of a double octave in such a way that a whole tone interval of disjunction is at the highest possible position in both octaves (al Fārābī 1967:331).
For example:

JAM' AL MUTTAṢIL AL NĀQIṢ (j-m-') (w-ṣ-l) (n-q-ṣ) "the deficient conjunct collection"

A scalar combination of an octave plus a perfect fourth in extent. In the early centuries of the Islamic period, it was called JAM' AL TĀMM* because the lutes of the time had only four strings and thus could not produce the full two octave range without change of position (al Fārābī 1967:838).

JAM' AL NĀQIṢ (j-m-') (n-q-ṣ) "the deficient collection"

A scalar combination of tones with an extent greater than a perfect fourth and less than an octave (al Fārābī 1967:325; Ibn Zaylah 1964: 39).

JAM' AL TĀMM (j-m-') (t-m-m) "the complete collection"

A scalar combination of tones with the extent of a double octave (al Fārābī 1967:331; Maḥfūẓ 1964:186). According to al Fārābī, this name was given, in the early centuries of the Islamic period, to a scalar combination of an octave plus a fourth, which, for that time, was "complete" since the lutes of time had only four strings and could not produce the full two octaves without change of hand position (al Fārābī 1967:838). Syn. of JAM' AL MUTTAṢIL AL NĀQIṢ*.

JAMĀ'AH (pl. JAMĀ'ĀT) (j-m-') "grouping"

Syn. of JAM'*, which can be substituted in any of the above compounds by adding the feminine ending "-ah" to the descriptive terms.

JAMĀ'ĀT AL MASHHŪRAH (j-m-') (sh-h-r) "the famous collections"

The famous melodic modes of the Classical Period (Ibn Sīnā in Farmer 1967:203, n. 5).

JANĀḤ (pl. AJNIḤAH) = JENĀH, JINĀ (j-n-ḥ) "wing"

1. A tetrachord (Allawerdi 1949:136).
2. A woodwind instrument mentioned by Mushāqah 1849:211. It consisted of seven or more tubes of different lengths set in a collar, i.e., like panpipes. Each tube produces a different pitch.
3. Lyre with four strings or sometimes five (Pal.)(Rouanet 1922:2788).

JĀNIB (pl. JAWĀNIB) (j-n-b) "direction, side"

A direction (either ascending or descending) for melodic progression or movement (al Kindī 1966:144, 162); or either of the two pitch extremities (high or low) of the modal scale (al Kindī 1969:95ff).

JANJARAH

Syn. of JANJĪRAH* ('Arnīṭah 1968:60).

JANJIRĀS

Syn. of JANJĪRAH* ('Arnīṭah 1968:60).

JANJĪRAH

An ancient pre-Islamic woodwind instrument, similar to the MANJĪRAH* (ʿArnīṭah 1968:60). See also JANJARAH*, JANJIRĀS*.

JANK (pl. JUNUK) = DJENK, JENK, ČENK, CHANG (j-n-k), from name for earlier Pers. harp known as "chang"

A harp with upper sound chest and varying number of strings (as few as 13 and as many as 40 mentioned), which was said to have been invented by Pythagoras. According to some, the instrument was made so that every note had a solitary string (Farmer EI(Eng), "Miʿzaf": 529); however, the strings could also be arranged in pairs or even in triplets according to other sources (Sachs 1940:259), depending on the region and century. The strings were plucked with the fingers of both hands, to which plectra (s. ZAKHMAH*) were sometimes affixed. Some examples of this instrument had a humped, some a straight back. The face of the sound box was of skin (Farmer EI(Eng), "Miʿzaf":529). It was used as late as the 15th C. in Egypt; and in 17th C. Turkey, it was described as a large instrument in the form of an elephant's trunk with forty strings and an astonishing sound (Farmer 1976b:32-33). Syn. of ṢANJ or ṢINJ*. Also called JUNK*.

JANK ʿAJAMĪ (j-n-k) (ʿ-j-m) "Persian harp"

Name given to a variety of harp mentioned in the <u>1001 Nights</u> and distinguished from the JANK MIṢRĪ*. It had a resonator of wood at the side of the strings. This term was used as late as the 15th C. (Farmer 1945:29-30; 1965b:62).

JANK MIṢRĪ (j-n-k) (geog.) "Egyptian harp"

Name given to a variety of harp having two sets of strings, with a wooden sounding board between them (Farmer 1954, "Egyptian Music": 894). This instrument was known at least as early as the 15th C., when it was mentioned in an anonymous manuscript (Farmer 1965b:62). Other references maintain that it was distinguished from the JANK ʿAJAMĪ at a much earlier date (Farmer 1945:29-30).

JAOUADA

Var. of JAWWADA* (Touma 1977b:126).

JARĀD (pl. JARĀDĀT) (j-r-d) colloq. "locust"

Male singer (Maḥfūẓ 1964:17).

JARĀDATĀN (dual of JARĀDAH) (j-r-d) f. of "locust" (colloq.)

Two famous singing girls of the Arabian tribe of ʿĀd in the 7th C. (Ibn ʿAbd Rabbihi 1887:III, 26).

JARĀNAH (j-r-n)

Syn. of KAMĀNJAH* (Tun.) (al Rizqī 1967:360).

JARAS (pl. AJRĀS) (j-r-s) "bell"

A bell, usually a large cone-shaped or square one with an interior oscillating striker (Farmer 1945:36).

JĀRIYAH (pl. JĀRIYĀT, JAWĀRĪ) (j-r-y) "slave girl; maid"

Syn. of QAYNAH*, a singing girl or female musician.

JARKAH

Var. of JIHĀRKĀH/2* (al Rizqī 1967:367).

JARRA (j-r-r) "to draw forward, to pull"

To draw the bow across the strings of a musical instrument.

JARRĀYNĪ (j-r-n)

Player of the KAMĀNJAH* (JARĀNAH*) in Tunisia (al Rizqī 1967:399).

JASS (j-s-s) "fingering, thrumming"

Plucking of the strings of a chordophone such as the lute (ʿŪD*) with the first finger and the thumb, instead of striking them with a plectrum (al Khwārizmī 1968:239-240). According to al Kindī, one century earlier, there were two distinct types of JASS: 1) that which consisted of three distinct tones produced, for example, by the thumb, then first finger and thumb successively  ;

2) that consisting of simultaneous striking of two strings with the thumb and first finger as in  (Farmer 1929a:104).

JASSA (j-s-s) "to finger, thrum"

To pluck the strings of a chordophone (al Kindī 1965:27).

JAWĀB (pl. AJWIBAH) = DJAOUAB, JUÂB, GWAB (j-w-b) "answer"

1. Upper octave equivalent of a tone. The contemporary musician or theorist uses this term in combination with names of tones of the fundamental or lower octave (DĪWĀN*), in order to name notes of the upper octave. For example, JAWĀB ḤIJĀZ*  is one octave higher then ḤIJĀZ*  (ʿArnīṭah 1968:24, el Helou 1961:69-70). See QARĀR/2*.
2. A musical answer or consequent phrase. It could be a choral or instrumental response. In contemporary music it is often an orchestral segment which repeats the vocal phrase of a soloist or chorus (Chottin 1939:32; Ḥāfiẓ 1971:126). See SU'ĀL*.
3. Lowest pitched string of the four of the Maghribī lute known as QUWAYTARAH* (KOUITRA*) (Rouanet 1922:2927).

JAWĀB ḤIJĀZ (j-w-b) (ḥ-j-z) "answer of ḤIJĀZ"

A note of the contemporary Arabian scale, $F\#_2$ or Gb_3,  .

JAWĀB NAWĀ (j-w-b) (n-w-w) "answer of NAWĀ"

A note of the contemporary Arabian scale, G_3,  , also called RAMAL TŪTĪ*.

JAWĀB NĪM ḤIJĀZ (j-w-b) (Pers.) (ḥ-j-z) "answer of lowered ḤIJĀZ"

A note of the contemporary Arabian scale, F𝄲_2,  .

JAWĀB TĪK ḤIJĀZ (j-w-b) (Pers.) (ḥ-j-z) "answer of raised ḤIJĀZ"

A note of the contemporary Arabian scale, G𝄳_3, 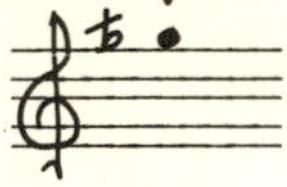 .

JAWĀB YAKĀH (j-w-b) (Pers.) "answer of YAKĀH"

A note of the contemporary Arabian scale, G_2 ,  ; also called NAWĀ*.

JAWF (pl. AJWĀF) = JAUF (j-w-f) "hollow cavity; center"

The wind chest of the CHUBCHIQ*, a variety of panpipes (Farmer 1978: II, 17).

JAWQ (pl. AJWĀQ) or JAWQAH (pl. JAWQĀT) (j-w-q) "troupe, group"

A musical group or troupe. Sometimes it is a vocal group, i.e., a choir. At other times it means an instrumental ensemble, as in contemporary ʿIrāq where it usually comprises the following instruments: the SANṬŪR*, JAWZAH*, DUMBUK* and ṬUNBŪR/1* (Ḥāfiẓ 1971:114, 162). In ̇the Maghrib, it is a combination instrumeṅtal and vocal ensemble for performing the suite (NAWBAH/1*) (Ḥāfiẓ 1971: 118).

JAWQ GHINĀ'IYYAH (j-w-q) (gh-n-y) "singing troupe"

A chorus (Wahba 1968:68).

JAWRĀ

A double-reed, woodwind instrument of the MIZMĀR/2* type. It is the larger of a pair of these oboe-type instruments, the other being the SIBS*. The JAWRĀ in this combination plays the role of shadowing the SIBS* in its role as melody instrument (al Ḥafnī 1971:179).

JAWWADA = JAOUADA (j-w-d) "to improve"

To chant the Qur'ān.

JAWZ (pl. AJWĀZ) or JAWZAH (pl. JAWZĀT) = JOZ, JOZE, DJOZE (j-w-z) "walnut; coconut"

A bowed chordophone made from a coconut shell with skin face. In contemporary ʿIrāq, this spike fiddle is similar to the KAMĀNJAH/1*. Its four strings are tuned a fourth apart (Ḥāfiẓ 1971:164). In some regions, it is a very primitive type of folk instrument. A Nubian version has only two strings (Olsen 1977:8). See Touma 1977b:98 for another tuning of the JAWZAH (DJOZE*) used in ʿIrāq.

JAZM (j-z-m) "cutting off"

Elimination of an opening percussion of a rhythmic cycle (al Rajab 1967:23). See ṬAYY*.

JIDHʿ (pl. JUDHŪʿ, AJDHĀʿ) (j-dh-ʿ) "stem, trunk (of a tree)"

The fundamental, lowest tetrachord (JINS/1*) of a mode (Al Ḥalqah 1964:19).

JIHĀRAH (j-h-r) "loudness"

With great volume (Shawqī 1976:348).

JIHĀRKĀH = DJORKA, JARKAH (Pers.) "station or place four"

1. A note of the contemporary Arabian scale, F_1, $E\#_1$,  .

2. A melodic mode of the 15th C. (al Lādhiqī 1939:400) and contemporary practice.

JILDAH (j-l-d) "a skin"

The face of a lute made from the skin of an animal or of a fish (Farmer 1978:I, 42). This term is also used for the head of a drum or frame drum.

JINĀ

Var. of JANĀḤ/2* (Marcuse).

JINS (pl. AJNĀS) (j-n-s, Arabicized from the Gr.) "genus, kind"

1. Any tetrachordal or pentachordal scalar segment from which modal scales are composed. More rarely, other segments, larger or smaller, have been included among the AJNĀS. Theorists of different periods have categorized the AJNĀS in various ways.

According to al Kindī (1969:103ff; see also Shawqī 1969:64-66) there were:
I. JINS AL ṬANĪNĪ*, i.e., including every diatonic JINS
II. JINS AL LAWNĪ*, i.e., every chromatic JINS
III. JINS AL TA'LĪFĪ*, i.e., every enharmonic JINS.

For al Fārābī (1967:280-309), there were two principal categories with further subdivisions:

I. QAWĪ*("Strong"): in which the sum of any two intervals is greater than the size of the third
   - A. JINS AL QAWĪ DHŪ TAḌ'ĪF*: a QAWĪ tetrachordal segment in which there are two equal intervals
   - B. JINS AL QAWĪ AL MUNFAṢIL*: a QAWĪ tetrachordal segment in which the two large intervals do not have ratios which are consecutive
   - C. JINS AL QAWĪ AL MUTTAṢIL*: a QAWĪ tetrachordal segment in which the two large intervals have ratios which are consecutive

II. LAYYIN* ("Weak"): in which the sum of two intervals is less than the size of the third
   - A. JINS AL NĀẒIM*: the enharmonic JINS, also called JINS AL RĀSIM*, containing the major third
   - B. JINS AL MULAWWAN*: with the minor third, therefore the chromatic tetrachord

See also al Fārābī 1967:157-163.

Al Khwārizmī (1968:243) gives the following names to the categories of AJNĀS:

I. QAWĪ*: diatonic, also JINS AL MUQAWWĪ*
II. MULAWWAN*: chromatic
III. NĀẒIM* or RĀSIM* or TA'LĪFĪ*: enharmonic.

According to Ibn Sīnā (1930:90-91; 1935:273-274):

I. QAWĪ*: diatonic
II. LAYYIN*:
   - A. JINS AL NĀẒIM*, JINS AL TA'LĪFĪ* or JINS AL RAKHWĪ*: chromatic (sic)
   - B. JINS al MULAWWAN*: enharmonic.

The AJNĀS categories of Ṣafī al Dīn (1938b:63-64) include the following:

I. QAWĪ*: diatonic, with subdivisions as under al Fārābī
II. LAYYIN*:
   - A. JINS AL RĀSIM*: enharmonic (5/4 interval)
   - B. JINS AL MULAWWAN* or LĀWINĪ*: chromatic (6/5)
   - C. JINS AL NĀẒIM*: chromatic (7/6).

In the 15th C., al Lādhiqī (1939:345-360) utilized the same categories as Ṣafī al Dīn. See also de Vaux 1891:311.

In the modern period, a committee of Egyptian theorists (Al Ḥalqah 1964) divided the AJNĀS into two categories:

I. Those utilizing the ½ tone, whole tone and 1½ tone intervals
II. Those utilizing also the 3/4 tone interval.

Baron d'Erlanger, compiling materials presented at the international conference on music held in Cairo in 1932, lists the following categories of AJNĀS (1949:76-98):

I. The Pythagorean diatonic AJNĀS
II. The Arab diatonic, i.e., those based on the fundamental scale of the Arabs which includes the 3/4 tone in addi-

tion to the ½ tone, and whole tone intervals

III. The chromatic AJNĀS containing an augmented second interval

IV. "Special" AJNĀS (AJNĀS MUFRADAH, s. JINS MUFRAD*) which do not fit precisely into any of the above categories.

2. The basic or fundamental rhythmic modes, according to al Kindī, from which various other modes are derived (Farmer 1943:19, 78). This usage is also to be found in the writings of Ibn Zaylah (Ibid.) and Ibn Khurdādhbih (1969:54). The derivative modes were called ANWĀʿ (s. NAWʿ/2*).

JINS AL ADNĀ (j-n-s) (d-n-w) "nearer genus"

The fundamental and lowest JINS/1* of a melodic mode (MAQĀM/1*) (el Helou 1961:80; Ṣalāḥ al Dīn 1950:103).

JINS AL AʿLĀ (j-n-s) (ʿ-l-w) "higher genus"

Second or upper of two main AJNĀS of a melodic mode (MAQĀM/1*) (el Helou 1961:80).

JINS AL ASFAL (j-n-s) (s-f-l) "lower genus"

The fundamental and lowest JINS/1* of a melodic mode (MAQĀM/1*) (Ṣalāḥ al Dīn 1950:103).

JINS AL AWWAL (j-n-s) ('-w-l) "first genus"

A category of AJNĀS with interval division of 1-1-½ (al Fārābī 1967:150-152). See TAJNĪS*, TAJNĪS AL AWWAL*.

JINS KHĀLIYAH MIN ARBĀʿ AL ṢAWT (j-n-s) (kh-l-w) (r-b-ʿ) (ṣ-w-t) "genus which is empty of quarter tones"

A JINS/1* in which there are no 3/4 tones (Ḥāfiẓ 1971:182).

JINS AL LĀWINĪ (j-n-s) (l-w-n) "coloring genus"

The chromatic tetrachord, i.e., with one interval equaling an augmented second. This expression is found in translations of various works by Classical Period theorists (Ṣafī al Dīn 1938b:55; 1938a: 266; Anonymous Treatise 1939:52; al Lādhiqī 1939:347). This is strange usage in Arabic and should be checked in the various manuscripts fron which these translations are made. The more likely form is JINS AL LAWNĪ*.

JINS AL LAWNĪ (j-n-s) (l-w-n) "colored genus"

A sub-category of JINS AL LAYYIN* in which the largest interval is equal to an interval of 1½ tones, therefore, equivalent to the chromatic tetrachord. This was one of the three categories of JINS/1* defined by al Kindī (1969:103; see also 64-65). See JINS AL LĀWINĪ*.

JINS AL LAYYIN (j-n-s) (l-y-n) "weak genus"

One of the categories of JINS/1* described by the theorists of the

Classical Period. This so-called "weak" JINS contained two intervals, the sum of which was less than the size of the third (al Fārābī 1967: 160-163).

JINS AL LAYYIN GHAYR AL MUNTAẒIM (j-n-s) (l-y-n) (gh-y-r) (n-ẓ-m) "unordered weak genus"

A "weak" JINS/1* (JINS AL LAYYIN*) which has the large interval placed between the two smaller ones (al Fārābī 1967:279).

JINS AL LAYYIN AL MUNTAẒIM GHAYR MUTATĀLĪ (j-n-s) (l-y-n) (n-ẓ-m) (gh-y-r) (t-l-w) "weak, ordered, non-successive genus"

A "weak" JINS/1* (JINS AL LAYYIN*) in which the larger of the two small intervals is positioned at the opposite side of the scalar tetrachord from the largest interval (al Fārābī 1967:279).

JINS AL LAYYIN AL MUNTAẒIM AL MUTATĀLĪ (j-n-s) (l-y-n) (n-ẓ-m) (t-l-w) "weak, ordered, successive genus"

A "weak" JINS/1* (JINS AL LAYYIN*) in which the larger of the two small intervals is positioned between the largest and smallest intervals (al Fārābī 1967:279).

JINS AL MUʿALLAQ (j-n-s) (ʿ-l-q) "hanging genus"

A JINS/1* in which the melodic resting tone is on the dominant of the JINS (i.e., at its upper extremity) rather than on its lowest tone (d'Erlanger 1949:108).

JINS AL MUFRAD (pl. AJNĀS AL MUFRADAH) (j-n-s) (f-r-d) "solitary genus"

Any JINS/1* which did not fit into the standard tetrachordal pattern, either because 1) it was smaller in extent than a perfect fourth; 2) it had four rather than three internal intervals; or 3) it was a pentachord which was not divisible into a tetrachord plus a whole tone (e.g., G-Ab-Bb-C-C#-D) (d'Erlanger 1949:91-96; see also Ṣafī al Dīn 1938b:54ff).

JINS AL MULAWWAN (j-n-s) (l-w-n) "colored genus"

1. The chromatic tetrachord, i.e., one having an augmented second interval (al Fārābī 1967:161; al Khwārizmī 1968:243).
2. The enharmonic tetrachord, i.e., one having one interval equal to a major third (Ibn Sīnā 1930:90-91; 1935:143-146).

JINS AL MUNTAẒIM (j-n-s) (n-ẓ-m) "ordered genus"

Syn. of JINS AL NĀẒIM*.

JINS AL MUQAWWĪ (j-n-s) (q-w-y) "strong genus"

A "strong" JINS/1*, one of the three categories of AJNĀS mentioned by al Fārābī and other theorists of the Classical Period (al Fārābī 1967:163; al Khwārizmī 1968:243). Syn. of JINS AL QAWĪ*.

JINS AL MUTAWASSIṬ (j-n-s) (w-s-ṭ) "middle genus"

According to contemporary musicians, any JINS/1* which has nine quarter tones between its two extremities, e.g., HUZĀM* (3/4-1-½), instead of the usual ten (Ḥāfiẓ 1971:182). See JINS AL NĀQIṢ*, JINS AL SHARQĪ*, JINS AL TĀMM*, JINS AL ZĀ'ID*.

JINS AL NĀQIṢ (j-n-s) (n-q-ṣ) "decreased genus"

According to contemporary musicians, any JINS/1* which has eight quarter tones between its two extremities, instead of the usual ten, e.g., SABA (3/4-3/4-½) (Ḥāfiẓ 1971:182). See JINS AL MUTAWASSIṬ*, JINS AL SHARQĪ*, JINS AL TĀMM*, JINS AL ZĀ'ID*.

JINS AL NĀẒIM (j-n-s) (n-ẓ-m) "organizing genus"

1. The enharmonic JINS/1*, which has the major third as one of its intervals. It is contrasted with the diatonic (QAWĪ* or MUQAWWI*) and the chromatic (MULAWWAN*) tetrachords (al Fārābī 1967:163; see also 280-309; al Khwārizmī 1968:243); Ṣafī al Dīn 1938b:63; 1938a:268; Anonymous Treatise 1939:52-53; al Lādhiqī 1939:346). 2. For Ibn Sīnā, this was the chromatic JINS/1* (1930:90-91; 1935:143-146).

JINS AL QAWĪ (j-n-s) (q-w-y) "strong genus"

Any tetrachord in which the sum of two intervals was greater than the third (al Fārābī 1967:160). These were the diatonic tetrachordal segments from which the Arabs of the Classical Period composed many of their scales and melodies (Ibn Sīnā 1930:90; Ṣafī al Dīn 1938b:64; 1938a:262-263; Anonymous Treatise 1939:60-76; al Lādhiqī 1939:355-359). They were of four kinds: JINS AL QAWĪ DHŪ AL TAḌ'ĪF*, JINS AL QAWĪ GHAYR AL MUTTAṢIL*, JINS AL QAWĪ AL MUNFAṢIL*, JINS AL QAWĪ AL MUTTAṢIL*.

JINS AL QAWĪ DHŪ AL TAḌ'ĪF (j-n-s) (q-w-y) (ḍ-'-f) "strong genus with doubling"

A "strong" tetrachordal segment (JINS AL QAWĪ*) in which there were two equal intervals with ratios of 8/7, 9/8 or 10/9. Using the 8/7 interval, it was given the additional description, AL RKHĀ or TAḌ'ĪF AL AWWAL. Using the 9/8 interval, it was also called AL AWSAṬ, DHŪ AL MADDATAYN or TAḌ'ĪF AL THĀNĪ. Using the 10/9 interval, it was described as AL ASHADD or TAḌ'ĪF AL THĀLITH (al Fārābī 1967:293-298). Al Fārābī describes this JINS as the most consonant after the JINS AL QAWĪ AL MUTTAṢIL* (al Fārābī 1967:310).

JINS AL QAWĪ AL MUNFAṢIL (j-n-s) (q-w-y) (f-ṣ-l) "strong disjunct genus"

A "strong" tetrachordal segment (JINS AL QAWĪ*) in which the two large intervals do not have ratios which are consecutive (al Fārābī 1967:304-308). See JINS AL QAWĪ AL MUTTAṢIL*.

JINS AL QAWĪ AL MUTTAṢIL (j-n-s) (q-w-y) (w-ṣ-l) "strong conjunct genus"

A "strong" tetrachordal segment (JINS AL QAWĪ*) in which the two large intervals have ratios which are consecutive, e.g., 8/7 - 9/8 or 9/8-10/9. This JINS, in all its varieties, was considered by al Fārābī to be the most consonant of all the AJNĀS (al Fārābī 1967: 310). See JINS AL QAWĪ AL MUNFAṢIL*.

JINS AL RĀBIʿ (j-n-s) (r-b-ʿ) "fourth genus"

A JINS/1* category with interval division of 1½-½-½, i.e., the chromatic tetrachord. Syn. of TAJNĪS AL RĀBIʿ* (al Fārābī 1967: 150-152).

JINS AL RAKHWĪ (j-n-s) (r-kh-w) "relaxed genus"

According to Ibn Sīnā, the chromatic tetrachordal scalar segment (Ibn Sīnā 1930:90-91). See also Ibn Zaylah 1964:27.

JINS AL RĀSIM (j-n-s) (r-s-m) "ordering genus"

1. The enharmonic tetrachord, a sub-category of "weak" tetrachordal segment in which the largest interval has a ratio of 5/4 (al Fārābī 1967:161, n. 2; Ṣafī al Dīn 1938b:63; 1938a:264; Anonymous Treatise 1939:52-53; al Lāḍhiqī 1939:346; Ibn Zaylah 1964:27).
2. For Ibn Sīnā, this was the chromatic tetrachord, i.e., with one interval equaling 1½ tones in size (Ibn Sīnā 1935:144).

JINS AL SHARQĪ (j-n-s) (sh-r-q) "eastern genus"

According to contemporary musicians, any JINS/1* which contains 3/4 tones (Ḥāfiẓ 1971:182). See JINS AL MUTAWASSIṬ*, JINS AL NĀQIṢ*, JINS AL TĀMM*, JINS AL ZĀ'ID*.

JINS AL SUFLĀ (j-n-s) (s-f-l) "lower or lowest jins"

Fundamental or lowest JINS/1* of a melodic mode (MAQĀM/1*) (el Helou 1961:83). Also called JIDHʿ* or JINS AL ADNĀ*.

JINS AL TA'LĪFĪ (j-n-s) ('-l-f) "composed genus"

1. The enharmonic JINS/1*, i.e., a tetrachord whose division includes one interval of two whole tones in size (al Kindī 1969:103; and as reported by Shawqī 1969:64).
2. Ibn Sīnā used this term to designate the chromatic JINS/1*, i.e., a tetrachord whose division includes one interval of 1½ tones in size (Ibn Sīnā 1930:90; 1935:154).

JINS AL TĀMM (j-n-s) (t-m-m) "complete genus"

According to contemporary musicians, any JINS/1* which has ten quarter tones (perfect fourth) between its two extremities (Ḥāfiẓ 1971:182). See JINS AL MUTAWASSIṬ*, JINS AL NĀQIṢ*, JINS AL SHARQĪ*, JINS AL ZĀ'ID*.

JINS AL ṬANĪNĪ (j-n-s) (ṭ-n-n) "ringing genus"

The diatonic JINS/1*, i.e., any tetrachord containing whole steps and half steps (al Kindī 1969:109; see also Shawqī 1969:64-66).

JINS AL THĀLITH (j-n-s) (th-l-th) "third genus"

A JINS/1* category with intervallic division of 1¼-3/4-½. Syn. of TAJNĪS AL THĀLITH* (al Fārābī 1967:150-152).

JINS AL THĀNĪ (j-n-s) (th-n-y) "second genus"

A JINS/1* category with intervallic division of 1-3/4-3/4 (as in contemporary RĀST/1*. Syn. of TAJNĪS AL THĀNĪ* (al Fārābi 1967: 150-152).

JINS AL ZĀ'ID (j-n-s) (z-y-d) "increasing genus"

According to contemporary musicians, any JINS/1* which is larger than a perfect fourth in extent (Ḥāfiẓ 1971:182). See JINS AL MUTAWASSIṬ*, JINS AL NĀQIṢ*, JINS AL TĀMM*, JINS AL SHARQĪ*.

JINS AL ZĀ'ID NAWʿAN (j-n-s) (z-y-d) (n-w-ʿ) "increasing type of genus"

Syn. of JINS AL ZĀ'ID* (Ḥāfiẓ 1971:182).

JIRBAH = DJIRBEH, JIRBEH (j-r-b), probably colloq. of JIRĀB "bag"

A bagpipe of the Arabian/Persian Gulf region.

JISM (j-s-m) "body

The sound chest of a lute (Farmer 1978:II, 91).

JOMLA

The high-pitched, melodic ornaments of the KAMĀNJAH* player of a Moroccan orchestra (Chottin 1939:147). Var. of JUMLAH/1*.

JOUAQ

Var. of JUWĀQ* (Chottin 1939:34, n. 1).

JOZE

Var. of JAWZ or JAWZAH* (Olsen 1977:8).

JUÂB

Var. of JAWĀB/2* (Mor.) (Chottin 1939:132, 147).

JUÂK

Var. of JUWĀQ* (Chottin 1939:168).

JULJUL (pl. JALĀJIL) = DJULDJUL (j-l-j-l) "bell"

1. Musical bell, usually a spherical pellet bell, used throughout Arab history. Small JALĀJIL were sometimes attached to the tambourine instead of cymbals (Farmer EI(Fr), "Ṣandj":210).
2. Chime, in a 9th C. manuscript (Farmer 1965b:19-20).

JULJUL AL ṢAIYĀḤ

Var. of JULJUL AL ṢAYYĀḤ* (Farmer EI(Fr), "Ṣandj":210).

JULJUL AL ṢAYYĀḤ = JULJUL AL ṢAIYĀḤ (j-l-j-l) (ṣ-y-ḥ) "roaring bell"

Chimes, an instrument known at least from the 10th C.. Syn. of JULJUL AL ṢIYĀḤ* (Farmer EI(Fr), "Ṣandj":210).

JULJUL AL ṢIYĀḤ (j-l-j-l) (ṣ-y-ḥ) "crying bell"

Syn. of the chimes known as JULJUL AL ṢAYYĀḤ* (Farmer EI(Fr), "Ṣandj":210).

JUMBRI = DJUNBRI, probably a var. of GUNBRI*

A plucked lute with two or three strings, a skin face and a sound box of wood or tortoise shell (Mor.) (Touma 1977b:96).

JUMLAH = JOMLA (j-m-l) "group; sentence"

1. An ornamental musical segment played by the KAMĀNJAH* at high pitch. Also known as THĀNIYAH* (TNIA*) or DASSAH* (DESSA*) (Ḥāfiẓ 1971:198; Chottin 1939:147).
2. Syn. of JUMLAH MŪSĪQIYYAH*.

JUMLAH MŪSĪQIYYAH (j-m-l) (Gr.) "musical sentence"

A musical theme (Al Ḥalqah 1964:59). Also JUMLAH/2*.

JUMLAH RA'ĪSIYYAH (j-m-l) (r-'-s) "main sentence"

Main musical theme or idea (Ḥāfiẓ 1971:198).

JUMŪʿ ṢIGHĀR (j-m-ʿ) (ṣ-gh-r) "small species"

The modal scales that do not reach the octave in extent (al Shīrāzī 1978:188, 291).

JUNK

Equiv. of JANK* (Ikhwān al Ṣafā' 1957:I, 202).

JÛQ

Var. of JAWQ or JAWQAH* (Chottin 1939:141).

JŪRĀ ZŪRNĀ

A small Egyptian oboe described by Villoteau (d. 1839) as 31.2 cm. in length (Farmer 1976b:24-25). Also known as ZAMR AL ṢUGHAYYIR*. See JŪRAH*.

JŪRAH (pl. JUWĀR) (j-w-r) "pit"

Another name for the double reed wind instrument (Hickmann 1947:8). See JŪRĀ ZŪRNĀ*.

JUWĀQ = JUÂK, DJOUAK, DJAOUAK, ǴAWĀQ (j-w-q)

1. A small end-blown flute of the Maghrib with range greater than an octave (Farmer 1976a:116). It has been known from Crusader times and probably even earlier (Farmer 1929a:143). In Algeria it has six fingerholes and one thumb hole known as a RAJĀʿ* (REDDJAA'*) (Delphin and Guin 1886:45; Rouanet 1922:2922). It is generally made of a reed, sometimes of metal or rarely of bone. Rouanet writes that it is made in various sizes, the most usual being 30-35 cm. in length.
2. A whistle flute of the Maghrib (Tlemcen area) (Chottin 1939:34, n. 1).

JUWAYRIYYAH (pl. JUWAYRIYYAT) (j-w-r) "small singing girl or maid"

Dim. of JĀRIYAH* (Majd al Dīn al Ghazālī 1938:129).

JUZ' (pl. AJZĀ') (j-z-') "part, division"

1. One of the subdivisions of a rhythmic cycle (ĪQĀʿ/1*) which are marked and determined by its fundamental percussions (NAQARĀT AṢLIYYAH*). Each JUZ' is composed of 1, 2, 3, 4 or 5 units of the basic beat (ZAMĀN AL AWWAL*). When the member has 1, 2 or 4 of these basic beats, it is known as a JUZ' AL BASĪṬ* (d'Erlanger 1959: 3). See also JUZ' AL AʿRAJ*, JUZ' AL MURAKKAB*. Al Fārābī has a similar phenomenon in mind, but he equates it with a single percussion and its timespan within the ĪQĀʿ cycle (1967:1013ff).
2. A musical phrase or period (al Fārābī 1967:1090ff; 1935:63ff).
3. One hemistich of poetry.

JUZ' AL AʿRAJ (j-z-') (ʿ-r-j) "limping or lame division"

Any member (JUZ'/1*) within a rhythmic cycle which is composed of three basic beats (s. ZAMĀN AL AWWAL*) (d'Erlanger 1959:4).

JUZ' AL BASĪṬ (j-z-') (b-s-ṭ) "simple division"

Any member (JUZ'/1*) within a rhythmic cycle which contains one, two or four of the basic beats (s. ZAMĀN AL AWWAL*). The member is called AṢGHAR if it contains only one basic beat; ṢAGHĪR if it contains two; and KABĪR if it contains four (d'Erlanger 1959:3).

JUZ' AL MURAKKAB (j-z-') (r-k-b) "complex division"

Any member (JUZ'/1*) within a rhythmic cycle which is composed of five basic beats (s. ZAMĀN AL AWWAL*) (d'Erlanger 1959:4).

JUZULE (j-z-l?), perhaps from JAZALA, "to be or become eloquent"

Double clarinet of the Kurds of ʿIrāq (Marcuse).

K

KĀ

One of the percussion strokes used by contemporary Arabs which is between the DUMM* and TAK* in tone and intensity (d'Erlanger 1959: 10).

KAʿB (pl. KUʿŪB) (k-ʿ-b) "joint; ankle; heel"

1. The standing rib of the soundbox of the QĀNŪN* (al Ḥafnī 1971: 48; Ḥāfiẓ 1971:84).
2. A piece of wood fastened to the bottom of the ʿŪD/2* to cover the lower ends of the ribs (Maḥfūẓ 1964:151).

KABAR (pl. KIBĀR) = KEBAR, KEMER (k-b-r?)

1. Drum of DARABUKKAH* type with a single face, but with a cylindrical or semi-conical body (Ibn Salamah 1938a:14; Robson 1938b: 247). First mentioned in the 9th C., by the 14th C. it was identified with the ASAF* (Farmer 1978:I, 59; II, 29). A similar drum is known today as AQWĀL* in the Maghrib (Robson 1938b:247). Kieswetter (1968) mistakenly spells it KEMER*.
2. In an 11th C. Latin-Arabic glossary, chorus (Farmer 1978:I, 59; II, 29).

ḲABBŪṢ

Var. of QABŪS* (Farmer EI(Eng), "ʿŪd":986). See also QUBŪZ*.

KABŪS

Var. of QABŪS* (Farmer EI(Eng), "ʿŪd":986). See also QUBŪZ*.

K'ACIDA

Var. of QAṢĪDAH* (Delphin and Guin 1886:2).

ḲAḌĪB

Var. of QAḌĪB* (Farmer EI(Fr), "al Gharīd":86).

KADRIAT SENÁA

Var. of QADARIYYAH AL ṢINĀʿAH* (Farmer 1976a:195). See Rouanet 1922: 2845.

KAH

One of the percussion strokes of the Modern Period. It is less strong than the TAK* stroke which it follows. It is similar to the KĀ* stroke, but occurs when the time is shorter than to allow that stroke's use (d'Erlanger 1959:10).

-KĀH (Pers.) "position"

Termination used in combination with various Persian numbers to name tones of the contemporary Arab scale, e.g., YAKĀH* ("one or first position"), DŪKĀH* ("two or second position"), SĪKĀH* (three or third position"), JIHĀRKĀH* ("four or fourth position"), etc. Since there is no consonant equivalent to hard "G" in Arabic, the "KAF" ("K") is usually substituted.

KAITĀRA

Var. of QĪTHĀRAH* (Farmer 1978:II, 30).

KAITHĀR or KAITHĀRAH

Vars. and dim. of QĪTHĀRAH* (Farmer 1978:II, 30). Farmer has maintained that variants of this chordophone which begin with "K" were more commonly used in reference to the Arabian chordophone, whereas QITĀRAH, QIṬĀRAH, QĪTHĀRAH, etc. were used generally for the Greek or Byzantine instrument. I have found many instances of both groups of terms being used for lutes of both peoples, in earlier times as well as today.

KALĀM AL HAZL (k-l-m) (h-z-l) "jesting or profane speech"

Light or popular music (Alg.) (Farmer EI(Eng), "Ghinā'":1073). See KALĀM AL JADD*.

KALĀM AL JADD = KALĀM AL DJEDD (k-l-m) (j-d-d) "serious speech"

Serious or classical music (Alg.) (Farmer EI(Eng), "Ghinā'":1073; Delphin and Guin 1886:29-30). This expression includes two kinds of music: 1) MAWZŪNĪ* (MAZOUNI*), and 2) MAKHĀZINĪ* (MEKRAZENI*).

KALĀM MALḤŪN = KLÂM MELH'OÛN (k-l-m) (l-ḥ-n) "tuned words"

A musical setting for poetry in dialect language.

ḲALĀḲIL

Var. of QALĀQIL* (Farmer EI(Fr), "Ṣandj":210).

KAMĀLĀT AL ʿASHR (k-m-l) (ʿ-sh-r) "the ten perfections"

The ten basic principles of the science of music according to al Fārābī (1967:175-178; 1930:67, 317, n. 17). Also MULĀ'AMĀT AL ʿASHR*.

KAMALDJA

Var. of KAMĀNJAH* (Rouanet 1922:2925). This term is thought by some writers to have been derived from the combination, KAMĀL JĀ'A, signifying "the perfect has come" (Delphin and Guin 1886:56; Rouanet 1922:2925). Such a theory ignores the more plausible connection with KAMĀN*, Pers. for "bow."

KAMĀN or KAMĀNJAH (Pers.) "bow" or "small bow"

1. An unfretted spike fiddle known in Persia from ca. 900 and even earlier in Egypt and Sind. Later it spread widely among the Arab and Muslim peoples. There are two kinds of this bowed chordophone: 1) that in which the sound chest is made from a coconut shell or other round object with lamb or fish skin covering and strings of horsehair; and 2) that in which the sound chest is made from strips of wood covered both back and front with membrane and has gut strings mounted across its face (Maḥfūẓ 1964:47). The instrument's one to four strings have generally been tuned a fourth or a fifth apart and secured by lateral pegs on the long neck. In the past, as well as with many contemporary performers, the instrument was held upright on the knee with the bow grasped from the underside rather than from the top as in Western bowing technique (Chottin 1939:140-141).
2. Both terms, KAMĀN and KAMĀNJAH, have been used in the Modern Period for the Western violin and viola which, because of similar tuning and range, are often substituted for the older bowed instrument. In the Maghrib, the name KAMĀN is more frequently used for the viola in the NAWBAH/1* orchestra (Mor.), while KAMĀNJAH is used for the violin (Schuyler 1978:39; Chottin 1939:140). These instruments are played both upright on the knee or placed under the chin.
3. Formerly a generic term for all bowed instruments (Marcuse).

KAMĀN AL AWSAṬ (Pers.) (w-s-ṭ) "middle KAMĀN"

Name given to the viola by Mashriqī performers who often substitute the Western instrument for the older spike fiddle which was known by the name KAMĀN*.

KAMĀN AL JAHĪR (Pers.) (j-h-r) "persistently loud KAMĀN"

Name given to the lowest pitched KAMĀN*, or the cello which is sometimes added to the instrumental ensemble by Mashriqī performers (el Helou 1961:168).

KAMANCHA

Var. of KAMĀNJAH* (Farmer 1954, "Kamancha":694-696).

KAMANDJA

Var. of KAMĀNJAH* (Touma 1977b:86).

KAMĀNǴA

Var. of KAMĀNJAH* (Sachs 1940:255).

KAMANJĀ

Var. of KAMĀNJAH* (Wehr).

KAMĀNJAH = KAMANDJA, KAMĀNCHA, KAMĀNǴA, KEMENDJAH, KAMANJĀ, KEMENJEH, KAMALDJA (Pers.) "little bow"

Equiv. of KAMĀN*.

KAMĀNJAH AL ʿAJŪZ (Pers.) (ʿ-j-z) "old KAMĀNJAH"

A folk version of the spike fiddle (Egypt). See KAMĀN/1*. With handle projecting through the body and protruding at the lower end, this instrument has lateral tuning pegs and a skin covering the sound box. The two horsehair strings stretched on its small coconut body are tuned a fifth apart. In some parts of southwest Asia, this instrument has three or even four strings. If there are three strings, they are usually tuned to a ground tone, its fourth and its octave or ninth (Sachs 1940:255).

KAMĀNJAH AL ʿARABĪ (Pers.) (ʿ-r-b) "Arab KAMĀNJAH"

Syn. of KAMĀN or KAMĀNJAH/1* (Mushāqah 1849:210), in contrast to KAMĀNJAH AL FRĀNJĪ*.

KAMĀNJAH AL FARKH (Pers.) (f-r-kh) "KAMĀNJAH which is like a young bird or a young sprout"

Syn. of KAMĀNJAH ṢAGHĪRAH/1*.

KAMĀNJAH AL FRĀNJĪ = KAMĀNJAH AFRĀNJĪ (Pers.) (nat.) "French (i.e., Western) KAMĀNJAH"

Syn. of European type violin, a four-stringed bowed instrument (Mashāqah 1847:210). See KAMĀNJAH AL ʿARABĪ*.

KAMĀNJAH KABĪRAH (Pers.) (k-b-r) "large KAMĀNJAH"

Name given to the Western viola used in the classical orchestra of Morocco. Various tunings used can be found in Chottin 1939:143. See KAMĀNJAH ṢAGHĪRAH/2*.

KAMĀNJAH RŪMĪ (Pers.) (nat.) "Byzantine KAMĀNJAH"

Arab name for the Byzantine LĪRAH*, which was introduced into the Arabic-speaking world in the Middle Ages, we are told by Sachs (1940:275). The body was pear-shaped, tapering to a peg disc with three rear pegs. Its three gut strings are tuned to the fourth, the tonic and the fifth of the scale in use, the central string being a drone, the outer ones played in harmonics (Sachs, loc. cit.).

KAMĀNJAH ṢAGHĪRAH (Pers.) (ṣ-gh-r) "little KAMĀNJAH"

1. A variation of the spike fiddle used in Egypt. With its handle projecting through the body and protruding at the lower end, this chordophone has lateral tuning pegs and a skin covering the sound box. It has a small coconut body and two hair strings tuned a fourth

apart (Sachs 1940:255). Also known as KAMĀNJAH AL FARKH*.
2. Name in the Maghrib for the European violin often used in the NAWBAH/1* orchestra (Chottin 1939:141). Various tunings for this instrument as used in Morocco can be found in Chottin (1939:144).

KAMĀNJAH TAQṬĪʿ (Pers.) (q-ṭ-ʿ) "KAMĀNJAH of partitioning"

A variety of KAMĀN or KAMĀNJAH/1* with three strings and a trapezoidal body frame covered on top and bottom with membrane (Marcuse).

KAMĀNJĪ = KÂMENJÎ (Pers.) "player of the KAMĀN"

The KAMĀN or KAMĀNJAH* performer; a violinist.

KAMENGAH

Var. of KAMĀNJAH* (Chottin 1957:41).

KAMENJA

Var. of KAMĀNJAH* (Chottin 1939:144; 1957:41), used in various compounds, e.g., KAMENJA ÇRHÎRA, KAMENJA KBÎRA, etc.

KÂMENJÎ

Var. of KAMĀNJĪ* (Chottin 1939:142).

KĀMIL FĪ AL TALĀ'UM (k-m-l) (l-'-m) "complete in harmonization"

A category of scales used by the theorists of the 13th C. and later. It included all scales made up only of intervals which were considered to be "consonant" (Wright 1978:98-99).

KAMM (k-m-m) "quantity"

Number of tones. This term was used by Ibn Sīnā in combination with the particles BI and AL (BIL KAMM) for comparison of two melodic patterns (INTIQĀL/1*) which were said to be equal or unequal "in the number of tones" (Ibn Sīnā 1930:96). See also KAYF*, MUTASHĀBIHAH*.

KAMMIYYAH (pl. KAMMIYYĀT) (k-m-m) "a quantity"

Pitch, a term used in a 17th C. Maghribī ms. (Farmer 1933b:14; 1965b:67). See KAMMIYYAH AL NAGHAM*.

KAMMIYYĀT AL NAGHAM (k-m-m) (n-gh-m) "the quantity of notes"

The highness or lowness (pitch) of notes (al Fārābī 1967:1065).

ḲANBŪṢ

Var. of QANBŪṢ* (Farmer EI(Eng), "ʿŪd":986).

KĀNKĀN

A genre of popular song said to have been sung "later" than the 11th C. (Farmer EI(Eng), "Ghinā'":1074).

KANKARAH

A one-stringed instrument used by the East Indians and mentioned by al Jurjānī (1938:221). This seems to be a var. of KINKULAH*.

ḲÂNÔN

Var. of QĀNŪN* (Smith 1847:210).

KÂNOÛN

Var. of QĀNŪN* (Chottin 1939:89).

K'ANOUN

Var. of QĀNŪN* (Delphin and Guin 1886:56).

KĀRA

A Sudanese chordophone similar to the GUNĪBRĪ*, with pear-shaped body, leather face, cylindrical neck and two gut strings (Marcuse).

KARAM (k-r-m) "noble nature; generosity"

One of the three types of ethos attributed to al Kindī by Cowl (1966:137). See also BUSṬĪ* and QABḌĪ*. Farmer, drawing likewise from al Kindī, has instead MUʿTADIL* (1926b:16). It is this latter term that occurs in the Ar. from which Cowl is supposedly translating (al Kindī in Cowl 1966:166).

KARĀQĪB

Var. of QARĀQĪB* (Marcuse).

KARDĀN = KOURDAN (Turk.)

A note of the contemporary Arabian scale, C_2 or $B\#_2$,  . This pitch also called MĀHŪR* or MĀHŪRĪ*.

KARĪNAH (pl. KARĪNĀT) (k-r-n) "female partner"

Ancient name for singing girl, mentioned by various writers (Ibn Salamah 1938a:11, 1951:82; 1938b:241; Ibn Khurdādhbih 1969:20; al Masʿūdī 1874:VIII, 93; Ibn ʿAbd Rabbihi 1887:III, 186). See KIRĀN*.

KARJAH

A folkish instrument of the woodwind family, simlar to the SURNĀY* or ṢURNĀY*. It differed from that instrument in having a piece of bent brass near the lower end of the pipe (a conical metal bell?). It was mentioned in a 14th C. ms. (Khashabah in al Fārābī 1967:787, n. 3).

KARNA or ḲARNĀ (q-r-n) "horn"

A bent trumpet of the 14th C. (Farmer 1954, "Nafīr":3). According to ʿAbd al Qādir ibn Ghaybī, it was often of an "S" shape (Farmer EI(Fr), "Ṭabl Khāna":236). See QARNA*.

KARRANĀY or KARRANĀ (q-r-n) (Pers.) "horn NĀY"

A variety of bent trumpet in pre-Islamic times, mentioned in the Shāh-Nāmah of Firdawsī (Farmer 1957:425) and by ʿAbd al Qādir ibn Ghaybī. In the 17th C. it was a long bent trumpet (Farmer 1976b: 32).

KARSH AL ṢANʿAH = KERCH-EC-ÇAN'Ā (k-r-sh) (ṣ-n-ʿ) "belly of the art"

The development section of a ṢANʿAH/2* (Chottin 1939:128). It is also called WASAṬ AL ṢANʿAH* (Ḥāfiẓ 1971:130).

KARSĪ

Var. of KURSĪ* (Farmer 1967:200).

KĀS or KA'S (pl. AKWĀS, KU'ŪS, KA'SĀT) (k-w-s) "cup, drinking glass"

Finger cymbal, the larger bowl-shaped type as well as the flat plate-like variety (Farmer 1945:36; EI(Fr), "Ṣandj":209).

KĀSAH (pl. KĀSĀT) (k-w-s) "a cup"

1. The sound box of the MUGHNĪ*, an obsolete chordophone mentioned in the 14th C. treatise on music, Kanz al Tuḥaf (Farmer 1926a:251). Also used as sound box of other instruments (Farmer 1978:II, 16; EI(Eng), "ʿŪd":986).
2. Syn. of KĀS or KA'S* (al Lādhiqī 1939:414-415).

ḲAṢEEDAH

Var. of QAṢĪDAH* (Lane 1973:171, 217, 446).

KATHĪR AL TARANNUM (k-th-r) (r-n-m) "with much chanting or cantillation"

With much ornamentation and movement in the melody (Ḥāfiẓ 1971:122).

KAWACHT

Var. of KAWASHT/1* (Rouanet 1922:2750); of KAWASHT/2* (Collangettes 1906:186).

KAWASHT = KAWACHT, GAVAST, QAOUACHT (Pers.) "meat"

1. A note of the contemporary Arabian scale, B_1 or Cb_1,  .

2. Name of a melodic mode (MAQĀM/1*) described by the 13th-15th C. theorists.

KAYF (k-y-f) "how"

The kind of intervals, as opposed to the number (KAMM*) of intervals used in comparing two melodic patterns or motifs. This term was used by Ibn Sīnā in combination with the particles BI and AL (BIL KAYF) to describe the relationship between patterns of INTIQĀL/1* (Ibn Sīnā 1930:96). Also see MUTASHĀBIHAH*.

KAYFIYYĀT AL NAGHAM (pl. of KAYFIYYAH AL NAGHAM) (k-y-f) (n-gh-m) "the qualities of tones"

All the characteristics of tones other than pitch (al Fārābī 1967: 1065). See KAMMIYYĀT AL NAGHAM*.

KEBAR

Var. of KABAR* (Marcuse).

K'ECBA

Var. of QAṢABAH* (Delphin and Guin 1886:45).

KEMENDJAH

Var. of KAMĀNJAH* (Salvador-Daniel 1976:119).

KEMER

Var. of KABAR* (Kieswetter in Farmer 1978:II, 27).

KENNARA

An unidentified instrument mentioned in a pre-Islamic inscription from Palmyra (Farmer 1957:425). See KINNĀR or KINNĀRAH* (Farmer 1926a:246).

KERCH-EÇ-ÇAN'Â

Var. of KARSH AL ṢANʿAH* (Chottin 1939:128).

KERIFT

A wind instrument mentioned by Mushāqah (Smith 1849:211).

K'ERK'ABOU

S. of K'RAK'EB, a var. of QARĀQĪB* (Delphin and Guin 1886:61).

KERSI

Var. of KURSĪ/1* (Salvador-Daniel 1976:202; Touma 1977b:77) and KURSĪ/3* (Rouanet 1922:2924).

KESAN

Var. of KIRĀN (Kieswetter in Farmer 1978:II, 27).

KESARAT

Var. of KINNĀRAH (Kieswetter in Farmer 1978:II, 27).

KHABAB (kh-b-b) "an amble or trot"

1. The song of the caravan driver (Chottin 1939:59), or the knight (Chottin 1957:41).
2. A fast tempo for measured musical performance (al Fārābī 1967: 1172, 1177).

KHĀBĀRIYYAH (pl. KHĀBĀRIYYĀT)(kh-b-r)

A species of MAWWĀL/1* of ʿIrāq which is sung to a rhythmic mode (Maḥfūẓ 1964:75).

KHAFḌ AL ṢAWT (kh-f-ḍ) (ṣ-w-t) "lowering, softening the sound"

Decreasing the sound, especially of one's voice.

KHAFĪ = ḪAFĪ, ḪAFIYYUN (kh-f-y) "hidden, secret"

Equiv. of KHAFĪ AL TANĀFUR*, and thus a designation for a melodic mode (DAWR/2*) used by the theorists of the 13th-16th C. It was applied to those modes in which the dissonance was only slightly evident, as opposed to those labeled ẒĀHIR* (not DHĀHIR as in the d'Erlanger translation), i.e., very dissonant (al Jurjānī 1938:336; al Lādhiqī 1939:375). It was abbreviated "KH".

KHAFĪ AL TANĀFUR (kh-f-y) (n-f-r) "hidden dissonance or conflict"

A descriptive category for scales used by the theorists of the 13th-16th C. It included those scales with slightly fewer consonant intervals than it had notes. The other categories are KĀMIL FĪ AL TALĀ'UM* or MULĀ'IM*, and MUTANĀFIR/1* (Wright 1978:97-99).

KHAFĪF (pl. KHAFĀF) (kh-f-f) "light"

1. Rapid in tempo, a term often used to characterize and name rhythmic modes. The fastest of the MUWAṢṢAL* or conjunct rhythmic modes were given this name by al Fārābī (1967:449ff).
2. A species of MUWASHSHAḤ/1* sung in the Tunisian NAWBAH/1*. It is based on a slow ternary rhythmic mode of the same name, and is preceded by an instrumental prelude on the same rhythm (d'Erlanger 1959:196).
3. Name of a contemporary rhythmic mode (ĪQĀʿ*) with "very slow" tempo and ternary division: $\frac{3}{4}$  ♩ = 66 (d'Erlanger 1959:196). This is a strange usage of the term, given the widespread meaning of the term. See KHAFĪF/1*.
4. The shortest basic time unit (See Shiloah 1964:146, n. 89; Ikhwān al Ṣafā' 1957:I, 200). Also called ʿAMŪD AL AWWAL/1*.
5. Weak in intensity of sound (Ikhwān al Ṣafā' 1957:I, 194; 1964:140).

KHAFĪF AL AWWAL (kh-f-f) ('-w-l) "first rapid"

One of the three categories of rhythmic modes. This one contains the fastest rhythms. The other two are KHAFĪF AL THĀNĪ/2* and THAQĪL/3* (Kāẓim 1964:45).

KHAFĪF AL HAZAJ (kh-f-f) (h-z-j) "rapid HAZAJ"

A conjunct rhythmic mode comprising a sequence of equal percussions performed at a tempo which allows only one percussion to be fitted between any two percussions (al Fārābī 1967:451).

KHAFĪF AL RAMAL (kh-f-f) (r-m-l) "rapid RAMAL"

One of the "Famous Rhythmic Modes" (ĪQĀʿĀT AL ʿARABIYYAH AL MASHHŪRAH*) described by the theorists of the Classical Period. For al Fārābī, the term was used for a rhythmic mode with two percussions, the first short, the second long (notated 0.0.......:2-8) (al Fārābī 1967:1029, 1033). For al Kindī, KHAFĪF AL RAMAL designated a rhythmic mode of either two or three percussions (000 : 1-1-1 or 00. : 1-2) (Farmer 1943:85). For Ibn Sīnā it was made of three percussions of two different lengths (0.00. : 2-1-2) (Ibn Sina 1935:209). See Farmer (1943:84-85) and al Faruqi (1974:134-135) for descriptions of this mode by other theorists.

KHAFĪF AL THĀNĪ (kh-f-f) (th-w-n) "second rapid"

1. One of the four basic time units mentioned by the Ikhwān al Ṣafā' (1957:I, 200). See ʿAMŪD AL THĀNĪ*, also Shiloah 1964:146, n. 89).
2. One of three categories of rhythmic modes. This one contains all the medium speed rhythms (Kāẓim 1964:45). See also KHAFĪF AL AWWAL*, THAQĪL/3*.

KHAFĪF AL THAQĪL (kh-f-f) (th-q-l) "light heavy"

A rhythmic mode (ĪQĀʿ/1*) described by various theorists of the Classical Period. Also known as MUKHAMMAS/1* (Ṣafī al Dīn 1938a: 498; al Jurjānī 1938:498; Anonymous Treatise 1939:192-195). See also Farmer 1943:83). By the 16th C. (al Lādhiqī 1939:474-475), the mode was described as obsolete (Ibid.:470).

KHAFĪF AL THAQĪL AL AWWAL (kh-f-f) (th-q-l) ('-w-l) "first light heavy"

One of the "Famous Rhythmic Modes (ĪQĀʿĀT AL ʿARABIYYAH AL MASHHŪRAH*) of the Classical Period, described by al Fārābī as a three percussion cycle, two short followed by one longer (0.0.0... : 2-2-4) (al Fārābī 1967:1048). It was used by other theorists to designate different cycles. See al Faruqi (1974:134-135) for transcription of this rhythmic cycle as described by some of the important theorists from the 9th to the 16th C.

KHAFĪF AL THAQĪL AL HAZAJ (kh-f-f) (th-q-l) (h-z-j) "light neavy HAZAJ"

A sequence of equal percussions forming a rhythmic mode and performed at a tempo which allows two percussions between any two of the basic percussions (al Fārābī 1967:452).

KHAFĪF AL THAQĪL AL THĀNĪ (kh-f-f) (th-q-l) (th-w-n) "second light heavy"

One of the "Famous Rhythmic Modes (the ĪQĀʿĀT AL ʿARABIYYAH AL MASHHŪRAH*) of the Classical Period, described by al Fārābī as a fast version of THAQĪL AL THĀNĪ (00.0.. : 1-2-3) (al Fārābī 1967:1042ff). The name is used by other theorists to designate different cycles. See al Faruqi (1974:134-135) and Farmer(1943:82) for transcriptions of the rhythmic cycles of this name as described by other important theorists from the 9th to the 16th C. This ĪQĀʿ is also known as MĀKHŪRĪ*.

KHĀFITAH (kh-f-t) "low in volume"

Soft in volume (Shawqī 1976:346).

KHALĀKHIL or KHALĀKHĪL (kh-l-kh-l) "anklets"

Pls. of KHALKHAL and KHALKHĀL*, resp., and generally used in these forms to designate the metal rings or anklets worn by dancers to produce rhythmic sounds (Farmer 1945:37). Syns. of AḤJĀL* (s. ḤIJL*).

KHALĀṢ = KHLASS, KHÊLASS, KHLĀS, H̆LAS (kh-l-s) "ending" (colloq.)

The last of the five vocal movements of the Maghribī NAWBAH/1* (Farmer 1967:200; el Mahdi 1972:12-14). The variant spellings resembling KHALĀṢ are probably colloquial versions of the literary term KHULĀṢAH, "ending." It is based on a ternary rhythm.

KHALĪL IBN AḤMAD (718-791)

A famous scholar of philology and music theory of the ʿAbbāsī period. He produced two works on music: Kitāb al Nagham (Book of Tones) and Kitāb al Īqāʿ (Book of Rhythm).

KHALKHAL (pl. KHALĀKHIL) and KHALKHĀL (pl. KHALĀKHĪL) (kh-l-kh-l)

See KHALĀKHIL and KHALĀKHĪL*.

KHĀMIS AL TĀMMAH (kh-m-s) (t-m-m) "complete fifth"

The perfect fifth interval (3/2) (al Khulaʿī 1904).

KHAMSAH WA KHAMSĪN (kh-m-s) (kh-m-s) "fifty-five"

Music of the Andalusian repertory (Mor.) when played by other types of ensemble than the traditional orchestra of RABĀB/2*, KAMĀNJAH* (violin), KAMĀN* (viola), QĀNŪN*, ʿŪD/2*, ṬĀR/1* and DARABUKKAH*. The names derives from the product of the eleven melodic modes and the five rhythmic cycles used in the Maghrib (Schuyler 1978:39, n. 4).

KHĀNAH (pl. KHĀNĀT) = XANA (kh-w-n) "square of chessboard; inn, house"

Any of the sections of contrast which alternate with a refrain section in the MUWASHSHAḤ/1*, BASHRAF/1*, SAMĀʿĪ/1*, or other vocal and instrumental genres of similar form. It customarily presents a departure in register (to the higher regions), in mode, in performers, and/or in melodic theme.

KHĀQĀNĪ KŪS

Syn. of KŪS/1*, said to have gotten this name because the patron of the kettledrum players was the Chinese KHĀQĀN (Farmer 1976b:13).

KHARAK

Var. of KHARAQ* (Farmer 1978:II, 15).

KHARAQ = KHARAK (kh-r-q) "tearing, piercing"

The movable bridges of the stringed instrument YĀTŪGHĀN which was described by ʿAbd al Qādir ibn Ghaybī (d. 1435).

KHARAS (kh-r-s) "silence"

Inaudibility (of musical sound) (al Kindī 1965:21).

KHĀRIJ AL DASĀTĪN (kh-r-j) (Pers.) "outside the frets"

A fret position for the ZĪR/1* string as described by ISḤAQ AL MAWṢILĪ* and Ibn al Munajjim which was an augmented fourth above the open ZĪR string (Shawqī 1976:314).

KHARJAH (pl. KHARJĀT) (kh-r-j) "exit"

1. The last line or segment of the poetic MUWASHSHAḤ/2*, which was originally in the colloquial or non-Arabic language.
2. A street procession of the musical group of a Ṣūfī brotherhood on the occasion of an Islamic or national festival. Such a musical procession is also found in connection with private family festivals (Tun.) (Jones 1977:32-33).

KHASHABAH (kh-sh-b) "a piece of wood"

A peasant version of the DUMBALAK/2* or DARABUKKAH*, a single-headed goblet drum made of wood (ʿIrāq) (al Dāqūqī 1965:39).

KHAṢR (pl. KHUṢŪR) (kh-s-r) "waist"

The inward bend which is between the top and bottom sides of the soundbox of the KAMĀN* (Maḥfūẓ 1964:159).

KHATM (pl. KHUTŪM, AKHTĀM) = ḪATM (kh-t-m) "conclusion; seal"

1. The finale of the Maghribī NAWBAH/1* (Tun.) (Ḥāfiẓ 1971:122). It is a type of MUWASHSHAḤ/1* with fast tempo based on a very rapid ternary rhythm of the same name. See KHATM/2*. It gradually accelerates toward the end and includes much vocal embellishment (d'Erlanger 1959:196-197). It corresponds to the KHALĀṢ* or MAKHLAṢ* of the Algerian or Tunisian suite and the QUDDĀM/1* of the Moroccan suite. Its words generally treat of TAWḤĪD, the Islamic idea of the unity of God (el Mahdi 1972:14).
2. A rapid ternary rhythmic mode used in Maghribī art music: 3/8 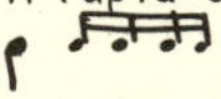 or 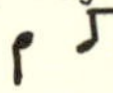, ♩ = 208. Another source designates it as a 6-beat rhythmic cycle (Tun.) (Racy 1979:20).

KHAWĀ (kh-w-y) "to be empty"

To tune a musical instrument (Delphin and Guin 1886:61). That source has KHĀWĀ, probably a spelling mistake.

KHĀWĪ (kh-w-y) "empty"

Syn. of TABRĪD* (Chottin 1939:113).

KHAZNAH (pl. KHAZNĀT) (kh-z-n) "cupboard, locker"

The head of the neck of the KAMĀNJAH* of Egypt, into which the tuning pegs are inserted (Lane 1973:356).

KHÊLASS

Var. of KHALĀṢ* (Farmer 1976a:195).

KHINÇIR

Var. of KHINṢIR* (Rouanet 1922:2701).

KHINṢIR (pl. KHANĀṢIR) = KHINÇIR (kh-n-ṣ-r) "little finger"

Fret or fret position of the Classical Period corresponding to the tone produced by the little finger on the lute (ʿŪD/2*), that is, the perfect fourth above the open string.

KHIYĀL (kh-y-l)

An unidentified musical instrument mentioned in a 13th C. treatise from Moorish Spain (Farmer 1926a:247).

KHLĀS or KHLASS

Vars. of KHALĀṢ* (Jargy 1971:94; el Mahdi 1972:11, resp.).

KHRAB (kh-r-b) colloq.?

One of the work songs (AHĀZIJ, s. HAZAJ*) of the sailors of the Arabian/Persian Gulf region. It is used to accompany the weighing of the anchor (Touma 1977a:122).

KHRŪJ

Var. of KHURŪJ/1* (Chottin 1939:131).

KHUJISTAH (pl. KHUJISTĀT)

An open-stringed instrument without frets reported to have been described by Ibn Sīnā (Farmer 1926a:244;.1978:I, 8).

KHULQ or KHULŪQ (pl. AKHLĀQ) (kh-l-q) "character, nature"

Syn. of ṬABĪʿAH*.

KHUNTHĀ or KHUNTHAWĪ (kh-n-th) "effeminate"

Terms meaning "feminine" which were used in the 10th C. for describing some forms of JINS/1* or tetrachordal scalar segment (al Khwārizmī 1968:244).

KHURŪJ = KHRŪJ (kh-r-j) "exits, excursions"

1. Final closing part of the ṢANʿAH/2*, a movement of the suite (NAWBAH/1*) (Mor.) (Chottin 1939:128). Ḥāfiẓ describes it as involving a return to the opening theme (Ḥāfiẓ 1971:130). A coda.
2. Short improvised "breaks" by the woodwind player (ZAKKĀR*) who leads the ensemble of ʿĪsawiyyah musicians (Tun.) (Jones 1977:21, 71-72). These represent "excursions" or "exits" from a dominant style.

KHWANDAGUI or KHWANANDAGUI (Pers.)

Name given to all forms of regularly rhythmed vocal music by the Persians, according to a 15th C. anonymous treatise. It was known as "simple" when the melody was based on a single melodic mode, "compound" when it contained modulations to other melodic modes (Anonymous Treatise 1939:249-250).

KIAMI-NATIK (probably QIYĀM NĀṬIQ* "standing speaker")

Unidentified vocal number with much ornamentation (Chottin and Hickmann 1949-1951:Band I, col. 594).

KINKULAH = GONGOLAH, KIRKALAH, KANKARAH

A one-stringed instrument with a gourd soundbox, reported to have been used by the East Indians (Ibn Khurdādhbih 1968:18; al Masʿūdī 1874:VIII, 92). Al Jurjānī was also familiar with the instrument, but gave it the name KANKARAH (al Jurjānī 1938:221). It is impossible to be absolutely certain about the voweling of this term.

KINNĀR or KINNĀRAH = KENNARA, KINNĪRAH

An ancient musical instrument. The name has been used for a lute (Ibn Salamah 1951:88), a pandore or long-necked lute (Farmer 1926a: 246), a tambourine, a drum (Ibn Salamah 1938a:18; 1938b:248, n.1) or a lyre (Marcuse; Wahba 1968:69). The most probable of these definitions is that it was, like the ancient Hebrew KINNŌR, an instrument similar to the SIMSIMAH* or SIMSIMIYYAH* still used in Egypt and the Red Sea area, or the ṬAMBŪRAH* of Upper Egypt and the Sūdān (al Ḥafnī 1971:46).

KINNĪRAH

An unidentified musical instrument mentioned in a 13th C. ms. from Moorish Spain (Farmer 1978:I, 11). A var. of KINNĀR or KINNĀRAH* (?).

KIRĀN (pl. AKRINAH) = KESAN (k-r-n)

A short-necked lute of the pre-Islamic period (Ibn Salamah 1938a:17; 1938b:241; 1951:82). It was used by the Jāhiliyyah poets to accompany their poetry (Ḥāfiẓ 1971:20). This leather-faced forerunner of the ʿŪD/2* was superceded by the wooden faced instrument borrowed from the ʿIrāqī or Persian lute at the close of the 6th C. (Farmer 1929a:240; al Zabīdī 1965:IX, 32Q). It is from this name that the term for a female musician (KARĪNAH*) is derived. According to al Zabīdī, KARĪNAH is the one who strikes the KIRĀN (Ibid.).

KIRĀṬ

Var. of QIRĀṬ* (Smith 1849:214).

KIRKALAH

Var. of KINKULAH (Ibn Khurdādhbih 1969:19).

KIRRĪJ

Unidentified musical instrument mentioned in a 13th C. ms. from Moorish Spain (Farmer 1926a:247).

KISTIWĀN

Var. of KUSTUBĀN* (Lane 1973:360).

KĪTĀRAH

Var. of QĪTHĀRAH* (Farmer 1978:II, 30).

KĪTHĀRAH

Var. of QĪTHĀRAH* (Farmer 1926a:246).

KLAM EL DJED

Var. of KALĀM AL JADD* (Delphin and Guin 1886:27-28; Rouanet 1922: 2686).

KLAM EL HAZL

Var. of KALĀM AL HAZL* (Rouanet 1922:2686; Delphin and Guin 1886: 27-28).

KLÂM MELH'OÛN

Var. of KALĀM MALḤŪN* (Chottin 1939:103).

KOETRRA

Var. of QUWAYṬARAH* (Touma 1977b:95).

KOUEÏTRA or KOUÎTRA

Vars. of QUWAYṬARAH* (el Mahdi 1972:56; Rouanet 1922:2927, resp.).

KOURDAN

Var. of KARDĀN* (Touma 1977b:37).

KOURKETOU

Var. of KURKATŪ* (Delphin and Guin 1886:44; Rouanet 1922:2933).

KOURSI

Var. of KURSĪ/2* (el Mahdi 1972:19).

K'RAK'EB

Var. of QARĀQĪB* (Delphin and Guin 1886:61).

KRAOUA

Var. of KHAWA* (Delphin and Guin 1886:61).

KŪBAH (k-w-b) "drinking glass"

An hourglass-shaped, single-headed drum dating from the 9th C. or earlier. Today it is known as ṬABL MUKHANNATH* or ṬABL AL SŪDĀN* (Maḥfūẓ 1964:37-38). The playing of this drum was forbidden by the Shāfiʿī jurist al Nawawī in the 13th C. because of its use by homosexuals (Robson 1938c:3). See also al Ghazālī 1901:213, 237, and illustration from a 13th C. ms. in Farmer 1965b:ix.

KUBRĀ (f. of KABĪR) (k-b-r) f. of "larger"

A category of intervals used by Ṣafī al Dīn (Kitāb al Adwār) which included the large intervals: the double octave, the octave plus perfect fifth, the octave plus perfect fourth, the octave, the perfect fifth, and the perfect fourth (Wright 1978:133). In the Risālah al Sharafiyyah, Ṣafī al Dīn subdivided the intervals in such a way that puṭ the perfect fourth and perfect fifth in an intermediate (WUSṬĀ/2*) category, between the KUBRĀ ("large") and ṢUGHRĀ* ("small") intervals (Wright loc. cit.). See (AL) KIBAR* (supp.).

KŪBRĪ (colloq.) "bridge"

A variety of instrumental passage (LĀZIMAH*) which joins two vocal segments (el Helou 1961:180). It may vary considerably in length.

KULL AL ḌURŪB (k-l-l) (ḍ-r-b) "all the rhythms"

A lengthy musical genre in which several rhythmic modes were used. There were two types of KULL AL ḌURŪB: 1) in which the different rhythms were introduced consecutively, before returning at the end to that rhythmic mode which opened the piece; and 2) in which there were simultaneous combinations of two or more rhythms. This genre of musical performance was always introduced by an instrumental overture known as ṬARĪQAH/3* and a refrain section known as TASHYĪʿAH*. A vocalise-like section known as ṢAWT AL WASAṬ* was optional (Anonymous Treatise 1939:239, quoting from ʿAbd al Qādir ibn Ghaybī).

KULL AL ḌURŪB WAL NIGHAM (k-l-l) (ḍ-r-b) (n-gh-m) "all the rhythms and tones (or tunes)"

A musical genre in which the characteristics of both KULL AL ḌURŪB* and KULL AL NAGHAM* were combined in a single performance (Anonymous Treatise 1939:243).

KULL AL NIGHAM (k-l-l) (n-gh-m) "all the notes"

The musical genre in which, in a single composition, all the melodic modes are successively used. This was also known as JAMʿ AL JAMʿ* (Anonymous Treatise 1939:240-241, quoting from ʿAbd al Qādir ibn Ghaybī).

KŪMA or KŪMĀ (Eng.) "comma"

A contemporary term for the comma, the micro-interval of 23.5 c. (Pythagorean comma) or 21/5 c. (the Didymic comma). It was known as FAḌLAH* or BAQIYYAH* by theorists of the Classical Period. Shawqī (1969a:147) describes it as 1/53 of the octave; Ḥāfiẓ (1971: 98) writes that it is achieved at 1/81 of the string length.

ḲUPŪZ or ḲŪPŪZ

Vars. of QABŪS* or QUBŪZ* (Farmer EI(Eng), "ʿŪd":986).

KURD or KŪRD (ethn.) "a person of Kurdistan"

1. A tetrachordal scalar segment (JINS/1*) of contemporary practice which has the following intervallic division: ½-1-1.
2. A contemporary melodic mode (MAQĀM/1*) utilizing the JINS/1* of the same name.
3. A tone of the contemporary Arabian scale, Eb_1 or $D\#_1$  .

KŪRDĪ (ethn.) "pertaining to KURD"

Syn. of KURD and KŪRD* (Rouanet 1922:2750).

KURGA or KŪRGĀ

Vars. of KURJAH* (Marcuse; Farmer 1954, "Iraqian and Mesopotamian Music":529, resp.). See also Farmer EI(Fr), "Ṭabl Khāna":236).

KURJAH = KURGA, KŪRGĀ, KUWARGĀ, KŪRKAH, QŪRQAH

A very large kettledrum introduced by the Mughals (15th-18th C.) which reached almost the height of a man. It was played by two persons, and was usually carried on a chariot because of its size (Maḥfūẓ 1964:46).

KŪRKA or QŪRQAH

Syn. of KURJAH*, said to have been used "later" than the 10th C. (Farmer 1978:I, 87). It is described as a "monster" kettledrum (Farmer 1978:II, 12, n. 4).

KURKATŪ = KOURKETOU

A percussion instrument of Alg., comprising an earthen plate covered with a membrane and played with drumsticks (Delphin and Guin 1886: 44; Rouanet 1922:2944).

KURSĪ (pl. KARĀSĪ) = KARSĪ, KERSI (k-r-s) "chair"

1. A short and rapid instrumental introduction for any of the vocal movements of the NAWBAH/1* (Alg.) (Maḥfūẓ 1964:98). It is comparable to the DŪLĀB* of the Mashriq and has a 2/4 rhythmic cycle known as WAḤDAH ṢAGHĪRAH* (el Mahdi 1972:19).
2. An instrumental interlude between the sections of vocal or instrumental performances, which serves to articulate and emphasize the separation of parts. It varies from only a few tones to as much as a short period of music (Maḥfūẓ 1964:98). Syn. of LĀZIMAH*.
3. The bridge for a Maghribī stringed instrument of the lute type (Farmer 1978:I, 42; Rouanet 1922:2924).
4. The tail piece of the ṬUNBŪR/1* (Egypt) (Farmer 1978:I, 42, n.2).

KURŪF

This term is used instead of ṬURUQ AL MULŪKIYYAH* in one of the editions of Ibn Khurdādhbih's Kitāb al Lahw wa al Malāhī (Ibn Khurdādhbih 1969:15). No other musical use of this term is known.

KŪRUS (Eng.)

Chorus (Ḥāfiẓ 1971:111, 197).

KURUSH (Fr.)

Croche, eighth note (Ḥāfiẓ 1971:187).

KŪS (pl. KŪSĀT) (k-w-s)

1. A large kettledrum of the villages of Khurāsān during the ʿAbbāsī period. It was used in conjunction with trumpets to call to battle or to signal the attack (Ikhwān al Ṣafā' 1957:I, 193; Shiloah 1964:139). First mentioned in mss. of the 10th C. (al ʿAzzāwī 1951: 18), it is thought to have originated in South Arabia (Farmer 1967: 3). It was the largest kettledrum used by the Muslims until the Mughals introduced the KURJAH* (Farmer 1945:35). Sachs has disputed the argument of Farmer that this drum was known at the time of the Prophet Muḥammad (Sachs 1940:250).
2. In its pl. form, small brass cymbals.

KŪSHAH

Syn. of melodic mode (Anonymous Treatise 1939:102).

KUSHTUBĀN (pl. KASHĀTIBĪN) = KISTIWĀN (Pers.) "thimble"

A metal (usually brass or silver) ring worn on the index fingers of both hands, with which the plectra for playing the QĀNŪN* are affixed (Maḥfūẓ 1964:155).

KŪSSĪ (k-w-s)

One who plays the KŪS/1* drum.

KU'ŪS (pl. of KĀS or KA'S*) (k-w-s)

Bowl-shaped cymbals of early Islamic period (Marcuse).

KUWAITARA

Var. of QUWAYṬARAH* (Marcuse).

KUWARGĀ

Var. of KURJAH* (Marcuse; Farmer EI(Fr),"Ṭabl Khāna":236).

KUWAYTARAH, KŪWAYṬARAH and KUWAITARAH

Vars. of QUWAYṬARAH* (Delphin and Guin 1886:56; Rouanet 1922:2944; Chottin 1961:Bánd IX, col. 1566). This instrument has supplanted the ʿŪD/2* in the Maghrib. A small variety used in the towns is called QARĪNADAH* or QARĪʿAH* (Rouanet 1922:2944).

KUWĪTHRA

Var. of QUWAYṬARAH* (Farmer EI(Eng), "ʿŪd":987).

KWĪTRA

Var. of QUWAYṬARAH* (Farmer EI(Eng), "ʿŪd":987; 1933b:25).

L

LĀ MUTATĀLĪ (t-l-w) "not successive"

A sub-category of melodic movement (INTIQĀL/1*) described by al Kindī (1966:135-136). It included all patterning with leaps, whether ascending or descending. See MUTATĀLĪ* and INTIQĀL/1*.

LAḤḤĀN (l-ḥ-n) "one who chants or sets to music"

1. Composer of music.
2. Musician; musical performer.

LAḤḤANA (l-ḥ-n) "to chant; to set to music"

1. To set to music, to compose.
2. To chant or sing.

LĀḤIQ = L'ÂḤ'IQ (l-ḥ-q) "reaching; connected"

According to Ṣafī al Dīn, a type of INTIQĀL/1* or melodic patterning which includes returns to the point of departure (de Vaux 1891:342; Rouanet 1922:2726, 2808).

LAḤĪẒAH (pl. LAḤĪẒĀT) (l-ḥ-ẓ) "a fleeting moment"

A term used by contemporary musicians and theorists for the eighth rest (Maḥfūẓ 1964:195).

LAḤN (pl. ALḤĀN, LUḤŪN) "song, tune"

1. Song, tune, melody, either instrumental or vocal.
2. Musical theme.
3. Melodic mode (al Kindī 1965:26; 1969:66; al Lādhiqī 1939:394).
4. Rhythmic mode (Farmer 1943:28-37). The Ikhwān al Ṣafā' (1957: I, 233) use the term in this way in a discussion of rhythmic modulation (INTIQĀL/4*). This term, however, is not used in

consistently by those writers with that meaning. In the main part on rhythm in the Rasā'il the one use of the term LAḤN may not refer to rhythmic mode. On the other hand, there are many uses of the usual term (ĪQĀʿ "rhythmic mode") in that section of the Beirut edition (Ikhwān al Ṣafā' 1957:196-202).

LAḤN AL ḤURR (l-ḥ-n) (ḥ-r-r) "free tune"

Syn. for the MŪNŪLŪJ* in its more recent forms. The orientalization of this genre originally influenced heavily by Western culture has resulted in this new name. Aspects of this orientalization include the combination of the MŪNŪLŪJ with other contemporary oriental genres, the addition of choral refrains, and the complication of rhythmic and melodic features. It has become a tune in which any combination of elements is acceptable--hence, its new name.

LAḤN MAWZŪN (l-ḥ-n) (w-z-n) "measured melody"

1. A regularly rhythmed tune.
2. A tune measured according to the prosody of its verse rather than having an independent musical rhythm. The ḤIDĀ' or ḤUDĀ'* and the NAṢB* were of this type. It was not until the late 7th C. that musical rhythm appears to have been practiced by the Arabs in such genres as the SINĀD* and HAZAJ/1* (Farmer 1967:15).

LAHW = LAHŪ (l-h-w) "entertainment"

Musical entertainment.

LAḤẒAH (pl. LAḤẒĀT) (l-ḥ-ẓ) "moment; glimpse"

A term used by contemporary musicians and theorists for the quarter rest (Maḥfūz 1964:187).

LAʿIBA (l-ʿ-b) "to play"

To play on a musical instrument.

LAÏÏN

Var. of LAYYIN/1* (Rouanet 1922:2724).

LAIWAH (l-w-y?) perhaps a colloq. of LAWYAH, "a turn, twist"

A genre of vocal-instrumental music of the Arabian/Persian Gulf region performed by vocalists, two oboe-like instruments (s. SURNĀY*) and a group of drums of various types (Touma 1977a:122). See LEIWAH*.

LAMAK or LAMK IBN MUTAWSHĪL

Said to have been the first man to play the lute (ʿŪD*), as well as the inventor and first maker of that instrument (Ibn Salamah 1938a:9; Robson 1938b:239; Ibn Khurdādhbih 1969:15). His son ṬŪBAL* was considered the inventor of the drum and tambourine; his daughter, ḌALĀL* invented the harp.

LAMḤAH (pl. LAMAḤĀT) (l-m-ḥ) "a quick look or glance"

A term used by contemporary musicians and theorists for the sixteenth rest (Maḥfūẓ 1964:187).

LAMĪḤAH (pl. LAMĪḤĀT) (l-m-ḥ)

A term used by contemporary musicians and theorists for the thirty-second rest (Maḥfūẓ 1964:187).

LAṬEM

Var. of LAṬM* (Jargy 1970:38).

LAṬM (pl. LAṬMIYYĀT) = LAṬEM (l-ṭ-m) "striking with hand on cheeks as a sign of lamentation"

A song of lament performed by women in ʿIrāq.

LAULĀ

Var. of LAWLĀ* (Farmer 1978:I, 82).

LAULYA

Var. of LAWLĀ* (Farmer 1978:I, 82).

LAUNĪ

Var. of LAWNĪ*, meaning chromatic (Cowl 1966:155).

LĀWINĪ (l-w-n) "that which colors"

A tetrachordal division (JINS/1*) in which the largest interval has a ratio of 6/5, i.e., the chromatic JINS (Ṣafī al Dīn 1938b:39; al Lādhiqī 1939:346). This is a questionable transliteration. See JINS AL LĀWINĪ*.

LAWLĀ = LAULĀ, LAULYA, LOULA, LŪLĀ

The brass staple to which the double reed (QASHSHAH*) of an oboe-like instrument is fastened. Other materials are also used for this mounting.

LAWLAB (pl. LAWĀLIB) (l-w-l-b) "screw, spiral; spring"

The screw and its place in the heel of the bow of the KAMĀN/1* or other bowed instrument (Maḥfūẓ 1964:160).

LAWLABĪ (l-w-l-b) "spiraling"

One variety of melodic patterning (INTIQĀL/1*) according to al Kindī (1966:135-136, 146-148). There are two varieties of LAWLABĪ INTIQĀL: 1) LAWLABĪ DĀKHILĪ ("Inner Spiral"), in which the movement proceeds from an initially large interval to gradually smaller ascending and descending leaps; and 2) LAWLABĪ KHĀRIJĪ ("Outer Spiral"), in which the movement proceeds from a smaller interval to progressively larger ascending and descending leaps. See summary of al Kindi's categories of melodic patterning under INTIQĀL/1*.

LAWNĪ (l-w-n) "colorful"

Chromatic, a subcategory of "weak tetrachord" (JINS AL LAYYIN*) as described by the theorists of the Classical Period. See summary of the categorizations of these theorists descriptions under JINS/1*.

LAWṬĀ (from lute?)

A comparatively modern chordophone similar to the QUWAYṬARAH*. This short-necked lute has four double strings (Farmer EI(Eng), "ʿŪd":987).

LAYĀLĪ (pl. of LAYL) (l-y-l) "nights"

A solo vocal improvisation of non-rhythmed variety using the words YĀ LAYL ("Oh night!") and/or YĀ ʿAYNĪ ("Oh my eye!"), repeated with varying melodic passages (d'Erlanger 1959:172). It is a vocal equivalent of the TAQĀSĪM* (s. TAQSĪM*) (Ḥāfiẓ 1971:206-207).

LAYLAH = LEILA (l-y-l) "night"

The night festival of music and dance of the Moors of Spain. Syn. of ZAMBRAH/1*.

LAYTHĪ (l-y-th) "lion-like"

The older way of doing the ADHĀN* or call to prayer, which is close to a recitative and is popular in the villages according to el Helou (1961:201). See also SULṬĀNĪ*.

LAYYIN (l-y-n) "weak, soft, gentle"

1. Name given to any tetrachordal division (JINS/1*) in which one interval was larger than the sum of the other two (al Fārābī 1967:280-292). This category of JINS was used by the theorists of the Classical Period. See the summary of AJNĀS categorizations under JINS/1*.
These "weak" (LAYYIN) tetrachordal segments were divided into the following sub-categories by Ibn Abī al Ṣalt:

- I. "Regular": the large interval being located at the upper or lower end of the tetrachord
    - A. "Continuous": in which the medium-sized interval was positioned between the largest and smallest
    - B. "Discontinuous": in which the smallest interval was in the central position

II. "Irregular": the large interval being located between the other two intervals. This type was not used in practice, according to Ibn Abī al Ṣalt.
(Ibn Abī al Ṣalt in Avenary 1952:40; 72).

2. Soft in volume (Maḥfūẓ 1964:181; Shawqī 1976:346). Opp. of SHADDAH/3*.

LĀZIM AL TARJĪʿAH (l-z-m) (r-j-ʿ) "that which must be repeated"

The drone string used in performing a TARJĪʿ/3* (ʿAbd al Qādir ibn Ghaybī in the Anonymous Treatise 1939:246). Also RĀJIʿ/1*.

LĀZIMAH (pl. LĀZIMĀT) (l-z-m) "necessity"

An instrumental interlude or interjection between sections of a vocal or instrumental performance used to articulate and emphasize their separation. It varies from a little as a single note (d'Erlanger 1959:178) to as much as a period of music (el Helou 1961:180). In addition to emphasizing the end of musical sections, it provides a rest period for the soloist at the end of a hemistich, line or section. There are seven kinds of LĀZIMĀT, according to el Helou (Ibid.): 1) TARJAMAH/2*, a repetition of that music which has just been sung; 2) RASM*, an orchestral performance of the vocal phrase or period which is to follow; 3) KUBRĪ*, a connecting segment between the former and next vocal parts; 4) ISTIQRĀR*, a connector passage between the end of the solo segment and the beginning of the refrain; 5) ISTIDHKĀR* or ṢADĀ/1*, an instrumental repetition of the preceding vocal music which acts as an echoing; 6) TAWḌĪḤ AL ḌARB*, an instrumental repetition of the rhythmic cycle; and 7) ṢIYĀḤAH*, a filler for the remaining beats of the rhythmic cycle.

LEILA

Var. of LAYLAH* (Ribera 1970:145).

LEIWAH

African dance of the Arabian/Persian Gulf area (Dubay and Baḥrayn) (Olsen 1967:30). See LAIWAH*.

LĪR

Syn. of LŪR or LŪRĀ* (al ʿAzzāwī 1951:101).

LIRA or LÎRA

1. An ancient Byzantine bowed chordophone, probably similar to that which is known today as KAMĀNJAH RŪMĪ* (Marcuse, Sachs 1940:275). According to Ibn Khurdādhbih, it was called LŪRĀ* (1969:19).
2. A stopped reedpipe of Morocco with a retreating reed (Marcuse).
3. A recorder type woodwind instrument of the Maghrib (Chottin 1939:planche XVI; Marcuse).
4. In Northern Morocco, a vertical reed flute (Chottin 1939:34). Also NĪRA*. In the south it is called ʿAWWĀDAH*.

LISĀN (pl. ALSĪNAH or ALSUN) "tongue"

The mouthpiece or reed of a woodwind instrument (al Fārābī 1967: 787, n. 3; ʿArnīṭah 1968:58).

LMAÏT (m-ʿ-ṭ), probably AL MAʿĪṬ "the loud-crying"

Vocalise of the Berber mountain people (Mor.) (Chottin 1939:22).

LONGA

Var. of LŪNJAH* (el Mahdi 1972:21).

LORHA ZENQÂWÎYA

Var. of LUGHAH ZINQĀWIYYAH* (Chottin 1939:154).

LOULA

Var. of LŪLĀ*(Rouanet 1922:2920).

LUGHAH ZINQĀWIYYAH = LORHA ZENQÂWÎYA (l-gh-w) (ethn.) "ZINQĀWĪ language"

A type of colloquial Arabic used in the popular music (GRĪḤAH*) of Morocco.

LŪLĀ = LOULA, LAWLĀ, LAULYA

A small cylindrical piece of leather with a very short tube, to which is attached the double reed of the GHAYṬAH/1* (Delphin and Guin 1886:48). See LAWLĀ*, a similar device made of steel.

LŪNGĀ

A kind of folk dance influenced by gypsy music and involving a 3/4 rhythmic cycle (al Dāqūqī 1965:81).

LŪNGHAH

Var. of LŪNJAH*(el Helou 1961:183).

LŪNJĀ

Var. of LŪNJAH* (<u>Al Ḥalqah</u> 1964:64).

LŪNJAH = LŪNGHAH, LŪNJĀ, LONGA (Turk.) "club; club house"

1. A rapid orchestral piece used often at the end of a FAṢL/1* or suite in the Mashriq. It is based on a simple rhythmic cycle (el Mahdi 1972:21).
2. An introductory instrumental number similar to the BASHRAF/1* (el Helou 1961:183; Ḥāfiẓ 1971:207).

LŪR or LŪRĀ = LIRA, LÎRA, LĪR

1. An ancient stringed instrument of the Byzantines which Ibn Khurdādhbih and al Masʿūdī equated with the RABĀB* of the Arabs. It was described as a bowed instrument with five strings and made

from wood (Ibn Khurdādhbih 1969:19; al Mas'ūdī 1874:VIII, 91). See LIRA or LÎRA/1*, LIR*.
2. An ancient Byzantine chordophone similar to the ṢANJ/1* or harp (al Khwārizmī 1968:236).

LUTAR

A three-stringed lute of the Maghribī Berbers (Marcuse).

M

MAÂLEM

Var. of MUʿALLIM*/1* (Rouanet 1922:2865, 2910).

MAʿANNĀ

Var. of MUʿANNĀ* (Jargy 1970:40).

MAʿĀZIF (ʿ-z-f)

Pl. of MIʿZAF or MIʿZAFAH*, and used with a variety of definitions.

MAʿBAD, i.e., ABŪ ʿABBĀD MAʿBAD IBN WAHB (d. 743)

A freedman who began his life as an accountant and later made use of his amateur musical training. He made a sort of musical pilgrimage to win first prize in a song contest organized in his native city of Madīnah. He sang later at the Umawī court in Damascus and, upon the death of IBN SURAYJ*, became famous in the court and among the people as both a composer and singer (Farmer 1967: 81-82; EI(Fr), "Maʿbad").

MABĀDI' AL ALḤAN (b-d-') (l-ḥ-n) "starting places of tunes"

The tone from which the melodic progression or patterning (INTIQĀL/1*) begins. According to al Fārābī it is either the highest tone or the lowest tone of the octave species from which the melody is to be composed, whereas the tones between the opposite extremity and this tone are designated as MABĀNĪ AL ALḤAN* (al Fārābī 1967:966).

MABĀDI' AL INTIQĀLĀT (b-d-') (n-q-l) "starting places of movements"

Syn. of MABĀDI' AL ALḤĀN* (al Fārābī 1967:959).

MABĀNĪ AL ALḤAN (pl. of MABNĀ AL ALḤĀN) (b-n-y) (l-ḥ-n) "principles of building melodies"

All the tones of the scalar row of an octave species except the highest or lowest one designated as starting tone or MABDA'* (al Fārābī 1967:966). Also see MABĀDI' AL ALḤĀN*.

MABDA' (pl. MABĀDI') (b-d-') "place of starting"

1. Starting tone of a melodic mode. Sometimes this starting tone corresponds with the tonic of the mode, but other degrees are possible as MABĀDI' in certain modes (d'Erlanger 1949:105).
2. Tonic or lowest tone of a modal scale (al Fārābī 1967:371).
3. Starting tone of a melodic pattern (INTIQĀL/1*)(de Vaux 1891:341).

MABTŪRAH (b-t-r) "fragmentary"

Descriptive term for a stop (MAQṬA'/1*) between partitions of song which is not long enough to completely satisfy the listeners (al Fārābī 1967:1166; 1935:86).

MAÇDER

Var. of MAṢDAR* (Delphin and Guin 1886:64).

MADD (pl. MADDĀT) (m-d-d) "extension"

Syn. of MADD AL WATAR* (al Kindī 1966:156).

MADD AL WATAR (m-d-d) (w-t-r) "extension of the string"

Tension of a string of a musical instrument (Shawqī 1969:52). Also MADD*.

MADDĀBAH (pl. MADDĀBĀT)

Professional wailing women to mourn the dead (Farmer 1957:434).

MADDAH (pl. MADDĀT) (m-d-d) "extension"

1. The whole tone interval. According to al Fārābī, it was a name used by the "ancients" for that interval. Syn. of BU'D AL ṬANĪNĪ* (al Fārābī 1967:144; 1930:54; al Jurjānī 1938:237).
2. Musical tie (el Helou 1965:134).

MADDĀḤ = MEDDAH (m-d-ḥ) "panegyrist"

1. A minstrel who chants praise of the Prophet Muḥammad.
2. A professional singer in Algeria, one who performs either religious or classical (KALĀM AL JADD*) music (Farmer 1954, "Maghribi Music":506). He is often accompanied by a double flute, tambourine and drum (Delphin and Guin 1886:2).

MADḤ = MEDḤ (m-d-ḥ) "praise"

Panegyric poem or song.

MADHAB

Var. of MADHHAB/1* (Touma 1977b:82; Tsuge 1972:65).

MADHHAB (pl. MADHĀHIB) = MADHAB (dh-h-b) "starting place"

1. Opening section of the DAWR/5*, SĀMIR*, MUWASHSHAḤ/1*, or other similarly constructed genres. It contains the principal melodic material which is repeated many times in the course of the piece as a refrain segment.
2. A "school" of musical performance (al Kindī 1965:26).
3. Chorus or group of vocalists.
4. Opening segment of poetry.

MADHHABJĪ (pl. MADHHABJIYYAH) (dh-h-b) "one who follows or does the MADHHAB*" (colloq. with Turk. ending)

Chorister (d'Erlanger 1959:178).

MADHHABJIYYAH (pl. of MADHHABJĪ) (dh-h-b)

1. The musical ensemble which accompanies the vocal soloist in a performance of the DAWR/5* or similar vocal compositions (Touma 1977b:144). Both vocal and instrumental performers accompany here.
2. Female chorister.

MADĪḤ (pl. MADĀ'IḤ) (m-d-ḥ) "praise, panegyric"

Poem, song or chant eulogizing Allah or the Prophet Muḥammad and used in the DHIKR* ceremony of the Ṣūfī brotherhoods as well as on other religious occasions.

MADĪḤ NABAWĪ (m-d-ḥ) (n-b-w) "praise of prophet"

Chanted rendition of rhymed prose (SAJʿ*) or poetry (SHIʿR*) in honor of the Prophet Muḥammad. It is primarily connected with the birthday of the Prophet, though it may be performed on other religious and non-religious occasions. See MAWLID*. Its performance is executed by a soloist accompanied often by a small instrumental ensemble and/or a chorus. The group, performing in unison, usually repeats a refrain section between segments of improvisation by the soloist.

MADJINA (d-j-n) (MAJINAH)

Syn. of DĀJINAH* (Roy Choudhury n.d.:55).

MADKHAL (pl. MADĀKHIL) (d-kh-l) "entrance"

Syn. of MABDA'/1* or starting tone of a melodic mode (d'Erlanger 1949:105).

MAḌRIB AL AWTĀR (ḍ-r-b) (w-t-r) "beating place of the strings"

The position on the face of the lute which is directly beneath the point where the strings are struck. It usually is covered by a piece of tortoise shell or wood affixed to the face of the instrument to protect it from the plectrum (Farmer 1978:II, 90). See RAQMAH/2*.

MAFRŪḌAH (pl. MAFRŪḌĀT) (f-r-ḍ) "the imposed"

1. The lowest tone on the lute (ʿŪD*) according to al Kindī (Ḥāfiẓ 1971:93). Al Kindī's term for the <u>proslambanomenos</u> of the ancient

Greeks, this word was given the symbol "A" in Arabic and is often equated with a theoretical A_1 of Western notation (Cowl 1966:140). See Table II in Cowl (loc. cit.), Rouanet (1922:2724), al Fārābī (1967:334ff; 1930:119ff), and others, for the Greek and corresponding Arabic names for the other tones of the double octave scale.
2. Tonic note (al Shīrāzī 1978:172).

MAǦĀZ

Var. of MAJĀZ* (Ibn Abī al Ṣalt 1952:70-71).

MAGHNĀ (pl. MAGHĀNĪ) (gh-n-y) "a place for singing"

Melody (Farmer 1945:43), but probably only applied to vocal melody.

MAGHRIBĪ (gh-r-b) "western"

Pertaining to the western part of the Arab World, i.e., to western North Africa, including Morocco, Algeria, Tunisia and Libya. In older contexts, it also included Moorish Spain.

MAĠNĪ

A kind of psaltery mentioned by al Jurjānī (d'Erlanger 1938:412). Var. of MUGHNĪ*.

MAGREFAH (gh-r-f?), perhaps var. of MIGHRAFAH, "utensil for ladeling"

An 11th-12th C. instrument which is believed to have been some kind of organ (Ibn Abī al Ṣalt 1952:52, 53, n. 11).

MAH

One of the intermediary percussion strokes which can be used in conjunction with DUMM* and TAK*. It is less strong than DUMM and is used to subdivide the time which separates a DUMM from the following stroke (d'Erlanger 1959:10).

MAH'ÂSIN AL LAH'N (var. pl. of ḤUSN AL LAḤN) (ḥ-s-n) (l-ḥ-n) "improvements of the melody"

Melodic ornaments (Chottin 1939:66). Var. of MAḤĀSIN AL LAḤN. See TAḤSĪN AL LAḤN*.

MAḤAṬṬ (ḥ-ṭ-ṭ) "stopping place"

1. A cadence (al Ḥafnī 1946:289).
2. An abbreviated suite as used by contemporary Egyptian musicians to cater to less classical tastes. In addition to being shorter in overall length than the traditional WAṢLAH/1*, it is composed generally of only two or three songs preceded by their instrumental preludes. The shortened suite uses a variety of melodic modes within a single performance. The first pieces are generally slow with long rhythmic cycles, the later ones faster and with shorter cycles. The songs of a single suite conform to either binary or ternary rhythms (d'Erlanger 1959:197-198).

MAḤBAḌ (pl. MAḤĀBIḌ) (ḥ-b-ḍ) "medium of pulsation"

Any string of the short- or long-necked lute (Farmer 1945:13). See MIḤBAḌ*.

MAḤBAR (ḥ-b-r) "embellishment"

A note of the contemporary Arabian scale, D_2,  . Also called MUḤAYYIR*.

MAHIL (m-h-l) "leisurely"

A leisurely tempo. comparable to Larghetto (al Ḥafnī 1946:287; Maḥfūẓ 1964:177). Usually with ʿALĀ (ʿALĀ MAHIL)

MAẖLAṢ

Var. of MAKHLAṢ* (d'Erlanger 1959:191).

MAḤMŪL (ḥ-m-l) "carried"

One of the six octave scales mentioned by ʿAbd al Qādir ibn Ghaybī (d. 1435), which were known collectively as the AṢĀBIʿ/1* or MAWĀJIB*. By the time of Ṣafī al Dīn, this categorization was already considered ancient (QADĪM) (Wright 1978:249-240). The other octave scales were known as MUṬLAQ/2*, MUʿALLAQ/2*, MUSARRAJ*, MAZMŪM, MUJANNAB/3*.

MAHOURAN

Var. of MĀHŪRĀN* (Touma 1977b:38).

MAḤṢŪRAH (ḥ-ṣ-r) "restricted"

A fret higher than the normal KHINṢIR* fret which produced the perfect fourth above the open string. The MAḤṢŪRAH was played by the fifth finger in an extended position (al Kindī 1965:19). It is not clear whether this fret position produced an augmented fifth or a major sixth above the open string tone.

MAḤTHŪTH (ḥ-th-th) "that which is urged or prodded"

A rhythmic mode which is performed at a fast tempo (al Fārābī 1967: 998; d'Erlanger 1935:31).

MĀHŪR or MĀHŪRĪ (Pers.) "lunar"

1. A note of the contemporary Arabian scale, C_2 or $B\#_2$,  . Also called KARDĀN* (el Helou 1961:69).

2. A note of the contemporary Arabian scale, B_2,  , (Ṣalāḥ al Dīn 1950:91).

3. Melodic mode mentioned from the 15th C. (<u>Anonymous Treatise</u> 1939: 138).

MĀHŪRĀN = MAHOURAN (Pers.), dual form of MĀHŪR*

A note of the contemporary Arabian scale, F_2 or $E\#_2$,  .

MĀHŪRĪ

Equiv. of MĀHŪR*.

MAHZŪZAH MUKASSARAH (h-z-z) (k-s-r) "shattered trembling"

An ornamentation in which a long note is broken up into a series of repeated tones of the same pitch (al Fārābī 1967:1172; 1935:90).

MÂÎA

Var. of MĀ'IYYAH* (Chottin 1939:123).

MÂÏAH

Var. of MĀ'IYYAH/2* (Rouanet 1922:2761, 2918).

MĀ'IYYAH = MÂÎA, MÂÏAH, MEÏA, MĀYA, MĀYAH (m-w-h) "sap, juice of a plant"

1. The note equivalent to "la" or "A" (Mor.), as well as the string of an instrument tuned to that pitch.
2. One of the melodic modes of earlier times (al Jurjānī 1938:391; Anonymous Treatise 1939:129; al Lādhiqī 1939:440) and the contemporary Maghrib (Rouanet 1922:2918).
3. An ancient instrument mentioned by al Fārābī, we are told (Salvador-Daniel 1976:224). No reference to this use of the term has been found in al Fārābī (1967). See MEÏA*.

MAJĀZ (pl. MAJĀZĀT) = MAǦĀZ (j-w-z) "passageway"

Supplementary percussion(s) added in the FĀṢILAH/4* rest period at the end of a rhythmic cycle (al Fārābī 1967:1018; 1935:38). Al Fārābī describes it as a process for easing the passage from one cycle to another. According to Ibn Sīnā (1930:99), such additions are a method of embellishing a melody. The author of the 15th C. Anonymous Treatise (1939:165) takes his definition of the term from Ibn Sīnā.

MAJRĀ (pl. MAJĀRĪ) = MEDJRA (j-r-y) "course; current; drain"

One of the two "courses" or "sets" by which the eight finger modes (AṢĀBIʿ*) were classified by IBN MISJAH* (d. ca. 715) and his followers during the 8th-10th C. One course, MAJRĀ AL WUSṬĀ*, made use of the middle finger (WUSṬĀ*) fret on the lute, which produced a tetrachord with minor third; the other course, MAJRĀ AL BINṢIR*, made use of a third finger (BINṢIR*) fret, thereby producing a tetrachord with major third (Ibn al Munajjim 1950:3, 7; Shawqī 1976:222; al Kindī 1966:156).

MAJRĀ AL BINṢIR (j-r-y) (b-n-ṣ-r) "course of the ring finger"

One of the two "courses" for tetrachordal division, as described by theorists of the 8th-10th C. It included the open string tone, the SABBĀBAH*, the BINṢIR* and the KHINṢIR*, i.e., a diatonic scalar segment with 1-1-½ division (Shawqī 1976:375-389). See MAJRĀ*, MAJRĀ AL WUSṬĀ*.

MAJRĀ AL WUSṬĀ (j-r-y) (w-s-ṭ) "course of the middle finger"

One of the two "courses" for tetrachordal division, as described by theorists of the 8th-10th C. It included the open string tone, the SABBĀBAH*, the WUSṬĀ* and the KHINṢIR*, i.e., a diatonic scalar segment with 1-½-1 division (Shawqī 1976:375-389). See MAJRĀ*, MAJRĀ AL BINṢIR*.

MAJRŪR (j-r-r) "pulled, drawn"

Bow for playing a musical instrument (Maḥfūẓ 1964:48).

MAJRŪRAH (pl. MAJRŪRĀT) (j-r-r) f. of "pulled, drawn"

Bowed musical instrument (Maḥfūẓ 1964:48).

MAKHĀZINĪ = MEKRAZENI (kh-z-n) "pertaining to storehouses"

A genre of popular song, one of the two kinds of KALĀM AL JADD* known in Algeria. This type of song, which is more recent than the MAZOUNI* (MAWZŪNĪ?) type, is characterized by a marked pause between verses, less tremolo, and a prolonged final assonance. It is accompanied by a drum and a woodwind instrument of flute type, and is described as an urban music (Delphin and Guin 1886:29, 37). In the text, both this form (in Ar.) and a strange transliteration (MEKRAZENI*) are given. The authors comment that this genre was also called HAWZĪ* (AHOUZĪ*) (Ibid.:30).

MAKHLAṢ = MEKLASS, MEKHLAÇ, MAHLAS, MOUKRELES (kh-l-ṣ) "place of purification, escape"

Last section of the Maghribī suite (NAWBAH/1*) (Alg), being a vocal movement characterized by a rapid triple rhythm, many vocal embellishments and use of stock phrases (d'Erlanger 1959:191). The vocalists are answered after each poetic segment by an instrumental JAWĀB/2*. The number ends with a slow, non-rhythmed musical segment (Ḥāfiẓ 1971:127). There is only one MAKHLAṢ for each NAWBAH.

MĀKHŪRĪ (pl. MAWĀKHĪR) (m-kh-r) "pertaining to a brothel"

1. Syn. of that rhythmic mode of the Classical Period known as KHAFĪF AL THAQĪL AL THĀNĪ*, one of the "Famous Rhythmic Modes" (ĪQĀ'ĀT MASHHŪRAH*) (al Fārābī 1967:1042-1044).
2. A genre of song attributed to Satan and called by this name because it was sung by IBRAHĪM IBN MAYMŪN AL MAWṢILĪ* in the brothels.

MAKHZINAH (MAKHZANAH?) (kh-z-n) "a storehouse"

Sound chest of Maghribī lutes (Farmer 1978:I, 41; Rouanet 1922: 2926).

MAKSŪR AL ǦANÂH

Var. of MAQṢŪR AL JANĀḤ* (Chottin 1961:Band IX, col. 1564).

MALĀHĪ (pl. of MILHĀ) (l-h-w) "playthings and instruments of diversion, toys or games"

1. Musical instruments (Ibn Abī al Dunyā 1938:41).
2. Forbidden pleasures, such as gambling, drunkenness and fornication, with which music and singing were linked by some Muslim writers (Ikhwān al Ṣafā' 1964/65:127, n. 4).

MALĀWĪ (l-w-w) or (l-w-y)

Pl. of MALWĀ or MILWĀ* (Ibn Salamah 1938a:9; 1938b:239; Ḥāfiẓ 1971: 86; al Khwārizmī 1968:238).

MALḤŪN = MALH'ÛN, MELH'OUN (l-ḥ-n) "tuned; ungrammatical"

1. A genre of vocal folk music in the Maghrib (esp. Mor.) setting a QAṢĪDAH/1*-like poem of the same name to music. The genre fits both its literal meanings, since it is a song which employs the colloquial rather than classical Arabic and includes some influences from the Berber language (Chottin 1939:103-104, 154).
2. A variety of QAṢĪDAH/2* poetry based on dialect Arabic (Mor.) (Chottin 1939:103-104).

MALMAS (pl. MALĀMIS) (l-m-s) "point of contact; touch"

The piece of ebony which covers the flat face of the neck of some versions of the KAMĀN or KAMĀNJAH*. It lies beneath the strings.

MALOUF or MA'LOUF

Vars. of MA'LŪF* (Jones 1977:187-188; Touma 1977b:77, resp.).

MĀLSH

A technique, described by the author of "Objéts des Melodies" and quoted in a 15th C. treatise, which involved touching the finger to the point on a vibrating string which would determine a new tone without replucking or rebowing. According to the author, such a technique could also be produced by a movement of the throat to reproduce the two extremities of the IRKHĀ'* or quarter tone interval (Anonymous Treatise 1939:146). Perhaps either a trill or a tremolo.

MA'LŪF = MALOUF, MA'LOUF ('-l-f) "familiar, usual"

1. Art music of the Maghrib. It consists of a suite or series of vocal and instrumental movements based on a single melodic mode. The term MA'LŪF is used esp. in Tunisia and Lībyā. Other terms used are GHURNĀṬĪ*, MŪSĪQĀ ANDALUSIYYAH*, ʿĀLAH*, or ʿĀLAH ANDALUSIYYAH*.
2. A popular form of musical MUWASHSHAḤ/1*, involving colloquial poetry and sung in Lebanon (Jargy 1970:95). D'Erlanger writes that this name designates the most regular and simple form of MUWASHSHAḤ, one which entails only one or two simple modulations (d'Erlanger 1959:173-174).

MALWĀ or MILWĀ (pl. MALĀWĪ) (l-w-w) or (l-w-y) "instrument of tuning"

Tuning peg of a chordophone. In al Fārābī, we find MALWĀ (1967:483), in most other sources MILWĀ (Lane 1973:356; Wehr).

MAMLUWWAH AL NAGHAM (m-l-w) (n-gh-m) "full notes"

A vocal performance in which two or more syllables are sung to each new pitch of the melody (al Fārābī 1967:1133ff; 1935:66ff; see also d'Erlanger 1935:250, n. 2). Opp. of FĀRIGHAH AL NAGHAM*.

MAMZŪJAH (m-z-j) "mixed"

Description of a rhythmic mode (ĪQĀʿ/1*) when it is made up of a combination of different cycles, i.e., affected by TAMZĪJ/4* (al Fārābī 1967:477; 1930:156).

MANFAKH (n-f-kh) "place of blowing"

Syn. of MINFĀKH* (Farmer 1978:I, 84), the mouthpiece of an instrument.

MANGHŪM (n-gh-m) "set to melody or tune"

Melodious (al Kindī, according to Cowl 1966:157).

MANJĀRAH (n-j-r)

Syn. of MANJĪRAH*.

MANJĪRAH (n-j-r) "a wood-worked piece"

A small NĀY* (end blown flute) with five fingerholes, which is used in Syria and Lebanon. It is similar to other instruments named JANJĪRAH*, JANJARAH* or JANJARĀS, and IMBŪBŪ* in ancient times (ʿArnīṭah 1968:60).

M'ANNA

Var. of MUʿANNĀ* (Shiloah 1974:58).

MANQŪṬAH (n-q-ṭ) "dotted; provided with diacritical marks"

Dotted, a term used by contemporary musicians and theorists to describe the dotted note of the Western notation system which has been adopted by Arab theorists (Allawerdi 1949:599).

MANṢŪR (n-ṣ-r) "supported; victorious"

A woodwind instrument similar to the NĀY/1* (Maḥfūẓ 1964:51).

MANṢŪRĪ (n-ṣ-r) "supported; victorious"

1. One of the sections of the MAQĀM AL ʿIRĀQĪ* performance. It involves modulation to another melodic mode (MAQĀM/1*) than that on which the performance begins and ends. It is a setting to two or more lines (ABYĀT, s. BAYT/1*) of ʿATĀBĀ* poetry. This segment goes to higher pitch regions than found in the TAHRĪR* but ends with a return to the tonic of the principal MAQĀM in the descending refrain phrase or segment known as TASLĪM* or TASLŪM* (Ḥāfiẓ 1971: 166).
2. An unidentified reed flute (Maḥfuẓ 1964:51). See MANṢŪR*.

MANTHŪR (n-th-r) "scattered; prose"

1. One of the two kinds of music. It is described as similar to TAQĀSIM* (s. TAQSĪM*) (Allawerdi 1949:548). Opp. of MANẒŪM/1*. See NATHR AL NAGHAMĀT*, a syn. of this term.
2. Prose (NATHR).

MANẒŪM (n-ẓ-m) "ordered"

1. One of the two kinds of music. It is described as including all regularly rhythymed music (Allawerdi 1949:548). Opp. of MANTHŪR/1*. Syn. of NAẒM AL NAGHAMĀT*.
2. Poetry (NAẒM).

MAOUAL

Var. of MAWWĀL* (Touma 1977b:85).

MAOUAJEB

Var. of MAWĀJIB*(Rouanet 1922:2725).

MAOULID

Var. of MAWLID* (Touma 1977b:130).

MAQĀM (pl. MAQĀMĀT) (q-w-m) "place where one stays or rises"

1. Melodic mode. Melodic modes were in use in Arabian musical theory and practice long before their connection with this term. In al Kindī's time, for example, MAQĀM was still used as "place," "position" or "station" in a non-technical way (al Kindī 1965:21). See MAQĀM/2. The term was used in the sense of melodic mode at least as early as the Durrah al Tāj of Quṭb al Dīn al Shīrāzī (1236-1310) (Wright 1978:290, tr. on p. 180). According to Farmer, the term appeared earlier with this meaning when it was used by Ṣafī al Dīn to designate the twelve principal modes of his time (Kitāb al Adwār, Br. Mus. ms. Or. 136). No evidence for this is available

in the al Jurjānī commentary on this work translated in d'Erlanger (1938), nor in the other work of Ṣafī al Dīn (Al Sharafiyyah) in the same volume. Shiloah writes that the term was used for mode from the 12th C., but he provides no bibliographical reference (Shiloah 1965:I, 27). A 12th C. usage would have even antedated the writings of Ṣafī al Dīn (d. 1294). Wright confirms that the work of al Shīrāzī is probably the earliest instance of this usage, and that there it has none of the particularized connotations that it later acquired.

According to a treatise of the 15th C., the term stood only for the fundamental or principal (as opposed to derivative) melodic modes (Anonymous Treatise 1939:102; 131). In a 16th C. treatise, Al Fatḥiyyah, it was reported to have been known in earlier times to apply to any of the twelve "consonant" melodic cycles (ADWĀR, s. DAWR/2*) which had a full octave scale. The author of that work writes that among his contemporaries the term was used only for "consonant" (MUTALĀ'IM*) modes (or, more properly, scales) of less than one octave's extent (al Lādhiqī 1939:374-375; 429-437). See also d'Erlanger 1939:519, n. 36).

Today MAQĀM applies to all melodic modes rather than to any particular subcategory. Its distinguishing elements are defined by contemporary performers and theorists as follows:

a. Constituent AJNĀS (s. JINS/1*), ascending and descending
b. Type of JAMʿ/1* or scalar combination of AJNĀS: conjunct (MUTTAṢIL/3*), disjunct (MUNFAṢIL/4*, or overlapping (MUTADĀKHIL *). This includes the proper pitch level or ambitus as well.
c. QARĀR/1* or tonic
d. GHAMMĀZ* or dominant
e. MABDA'/1* or starting tone
f. ẒAHĪR* or leading tone(s)
g. MARKAZ* (pl. MARĀKIZ) or secondary tones of stability
h. USLŪB AL MAQĀM* or rules governing succession of AJNĀS, modulations, important tones and AJNĀS, etc. (al Faruqi 1974:90-110).

2. The place where the singer stands in front of the audience or the caliph. This definition has been questioned by Touma (1976:15) because of the knowledge that the singers of the ʿAbbāsī period performed behind a curtain for the caliphal court audiences. Despite the presence of a curtain, the position of the performers may have been precisely determined, thus giving rise to this use of the term.
3. Touma uses the word as a type or technique of performance involving solo, free rhythmed, modal improvisation--that phenomenon commonly known as TAQSĪM* (instrumental) or LAYĀLĪ* (vocal) (Touma 1971).
4. Equivalent of NAWBAH/1* or suite among the Muslims of Central Asia (see Farmer EI(Fr), "Nawba":947).

MAQĀM AL ʿIRĀQĪ (q-w-m) (geog.) "ʿIrāqī MAQĀM"

A genre of musical performance with a tradition of nearly 400 years, which is executed by a vocal soloist (QĀRI'/2* or MUGHANNĪ*) and a small instrumental ensemble (JALGHĪ BAGHDĀDĪ*). It is considered to be one of the most perfect and noble of Arabic musical genres (Touma 1977b:71). A complete performance of a MAQĀM AL ʿIRĀQĪ is called a FAṢL/1* and comprises a number of units. It opens generally with a vocal TAḤRĪR* or BAḎWAḤ*, though in some cases an instrumental prelude (MUQADDIMAH AL DŪLĀBĪ*) of well defined rhythm may precede the entrance of the vocal soloist (Tsuge 1972:63). The TAḤRĪR comprises a series of free rhythmed vocal passages establishing the characteristics of the chosen MAQĀM/1* and sung to vocables peculiar to that melodic mode. The instruments respond to the vocal line at points of musical and/or poetic pause. Such an instrumental "answer" is called a MUḤĀSIBAH*. It may be only a brief phrase, or may consist of elaborate solo passages performed on one of the instruments. A BADWAH is characterized by the juxtaposition of very long and very short notes executed by the soloist in a loud voice in alternatingly low and high registers (Touma 1977b:72). The TAḤRĪR or BADWAH ends with a TASLĪM/2* or refrain phrase which descends to and ends on the tonic of the main MAQĀM. Various other segments follow, each being one in the series of musical passages of different lengths in which pitch regions of the fundamental MAQĀM are explored, or prescribed and strictly ordered modulations are developed in connection with one or more lines of poetry in classical Arabic or the ʿIrāqī dialect. A BISTAH*, an instrumental, metered composition in the fundamental MAQĀM, ends the performance and serves as a period of rest for the soloist before he begins another FAṢL/1 (Touma 1977b:71-75; Tsuge 1972; Ḥāfiẓ 1971: 162-169). The order of the most basic segments are as follows:

MUQADDAMAH AL DŪLĀBĪ* (optional instrumental overture)
TAḤRĪR (vocal unmetered improvisation establishing the characteristics of the fundamental MAQAM/1)
MANṢŪRĪ/1* (vocal segments performed at a higher pitch level than the TAḤRĪR)
MIYĀNAH (one or more vocal segments at still higher pitch)
Other optional segments
BISTAH (a metered composition performed by the instrumental ensemble)

MAQĀM AL MUTASHĀBIH (q-w-m) (sh-b-h) "similar MAQĀM"

Any of the melodic modes that have identical tetrachordal divisions (AJNĀS, s. JINS/1*) and identical combinations (s. JAMʿ/1*) of these AJNĀS, but begin from a different tone and therefore have different key signatures (Ṣalāḥ al Dīn 1950:104; Al Ḥalqah 1964:18).

MAQĀM AL UMM (q-w-m) ('-m-m) "the mother MAQĀM"

The melodic mode considered to be the basic one from which all other modes are derived. In recent centuries, this has been considered to be the RĀST/2* mode (al Dāqūqī 1965:14, 42). Also ĀNĀ MAQĀM*.

MAQBIḌ or MIQBAḌ (pl. MAQĀBIḌ) (q-b-ḍ) "handle, knob"

The end of the bow by which it is grasped for playing a chordophone.

MAQRŪN or MAQRŪNAH (q-r-n) "two things joined together, a pair, or paired"

1. A double clarinet of the contemporary Maghrib consisting of two tubes with five identically placed holes on each tube so that each of the fingers can cover two holes simultaneously. Each of the tubes is fitted with a detachable single reed at one end and a small horn as bell at the other end (al Ḥafnī 1971:178; Racy 1979:24; Farmer EI(Eng), "Mizmār":541).
2. Accompanied (said of a vocal or instrumental solo) (Ibn Taymiyyah 1966:II, 319).

MAQRŪNAH BIL KALĀM (q-r-n) (k-l-m) "paired with words"

Said of music that is set to words (Ḥāfiẓ 1971:126).

MAQṬAʿ (pl. MAQĀṬIʿ) (q-ṭ-ʿ) "division, section; crossing, passage"

1. A rest between notes, phrases or sections (al Fārābī 1967:1166; 1935:86).
2. A musical phrase or section (Wehr, Madina).

MAQṬAʿ AL ṢAWT (q-ṭ-ʿ) (ṣ-w-t) "the place of cutting the sound"

The ending tone, whether of a piece of music or of a musical phrase or section (Shawqī 1976:968-969).

MAQṬŪʿAH (q-ṭ-ʿ) "something cut"

Syn. of QIṬʿ or QIṬʿAH* (Ḥāfiẓ 1971:126).

MARABBA

Var. of MURABBAʿ/2* (Farmer 1978:II, 33, n. 4).

MARĀTHĪ (r-th-w)

Pl. of MARTHĀH or MARTHIYAH*.

MARBOUʿAH

Var. of MARBŪʿAH/2* (Hickmann 1958:8).

MARBŪʿAH (r-b-ʿ) "four-sided; quartered"

1. A variant of the DAḤḤIYYAH*, a song-dance genre of the Bedouins of the Sinai Peninsula (Shiloah 1972:17).
2. A square tambourine, syn. of MURABBAʿ/1* (Hickmann 1958:8).

MARDAMZĀD (Pers.)

Syn. of HAWĀ'Ī*, a fantasy-like musical genre (<u>Anonymous Treatise</u> quoting from ʿAbd al Qādir ibn Ghaybī:245).

MARGHŪL or MARGHŪLAH (Pers.) "curl, ringlet"

1. Melodic ornamentation involving repetitions of a note to keep the sound and movement continuous (Ibn Sīnā 1935:168; <u>Anonymous</u>

Treatise 1939:159). Also TAKARRUR/3*, TAḌʿĪF/3*, TAKRĪR/1*.
2. Immeasurably short durations (al Lādhiqī 1939:459). Among the musicians of his time, al Lādhiqī noted that the Persian-speaking ones used the term MARGHŪLAH for this musical characteristic, the Arabic-speaking ones calling it TARʿĪD/2*. To both al Lādhiqī and the author of the Anonymous Treatise (1939:159), it involved percussions which were too rapid to be perceptible by the human ear.

MARKAZ (pl. MARĀKIZ) (r-k-z) "center, pivot"

1. Contemporary term of the Mashriq for tones of melodic resolution in a melodic mode (MAQĀM/1*) which are of secondary importance to the tonic (QARĀR/1*).
2. An introductory refrain segment of the musical rendition of ZAJAL* poetry which is sung by vocalists in unison. This segment has two lines which repeat at the end of each stanza. Both lines end with a rhyme which also closes the fourth and final line of each stanza (d'Erlanger 1949:100, 636).
3. The refrain or KHARJAH/1* of a MUWASHSHAḤ* poem (el Helou 1965:91).

MARTABAH (pl. MARĀTIB) (r-t-b) "step or platform"

1. Initial and final tone of the melodic mode, i.e., the tonic (al Kindī 1976:105; Shawqī 1976:70).

MARTHĀH or MARTHIYAH (pl. MARĀTHĪ) (r-th-w) or (r-th-y) "funeral oration"

Musical lament of pre-Islamic times and later. It has usually been sung by women (Rouanet 1922:2686; Farmer 1967:10, 19).

MASĀFAH SHARQIYYAH AL AKBAR (s-w-f) (sh-r-q) (k-b-r) "largest oriental distance"

Syn. of MASĀFAH SHARQIYYAH AL KUBRĀ* (Ḥāfiẓ 1971:181).

MASĀFAH SHARQIYYAH AL KUBRĀ (s-w-f) (sh-r-q) (k-b-r) "large oriental distance"

An interval ¼ tone larger than a whole tone (Ḥāfiẓ 1971:181).

MASĀFAH SHARQIYYAH MUTAWASSIṬAH (s-w-f) (sh-r-q) (w-s-ṭ) "median oriental distance"

An interval ¼ tone smaller than a whole tone (Ḥāfiẓ 1971:181).

MASĀFAH SHARQIYYAH AL AṢGHAR (s-w-f) (sh-r-q) (ṣ-gh-r) "smallest oriental distance"

Syn. of MASĀFAH SHARQIYYAH AL ṢUGHRĀ* (Ḥāfiẓ 1971:181).

MASĀFAH SHARQIYYAH AL ṢUGHRĀ (s-w-f) (sh-r-q) (ṣ-gh-r) "small oriental distance"

An interval 3/4 tone smaller than a whole tone (Ḥāfiẓ 1971:181), i.e., the quarter tone interval.

MAṢDAR = MEÇDER, MAÇDER (ṣ-d-r) "source, origin; beginning"

One of the five movements of the Maghribī suite or NAWBAH/1* (Farmer 1967:200). See also Delphin and Guin 1886:63ff. See MUṢADDAR/1*.

MASHĀ (m-sh-w) or (m-sh-y)

Probably a var. of MĀSHĀ* (al Kindī in Cowl 1966:156).

MĀSHĀ (m-sh-w) or (m-sh-y) "to walk with"

To harmonize. See MASHĀ*.

MASHADD = MŠAD, MSHADD (sh-d-d) "action or place where reinforcement takes place"

1. One of the movements of the Tunisian NAWBAH/1* which is executed, TAQĀSĪM*-like, by the solo lute (ʿŪD*) or RABĀB*, with accompaniment only of percussion instruments. The RABĀB improvisations are unmetered, but those by the ʿŪD are based on a duple rhythmic mode of the same name. See MASHADD/2*. The MASHADD is preceded by a brief prelude executed by the full orchestra (d'Erlanger 1959:195). The improvisation moves at a fairly slow tempo to embroider and vary the motifs based on the MAQĀM/1* of the suite. MASHADD has been defined not as a separate number, but as the opening and closing solo segments of the TAWSHIYAH or TŪSHIYAH/3* instrumental number (Tun.) (Ḥāfiẓ 1971:120). In either case, it retains its essential character of an unmetered, instrumental improvisation. 2. One of the rhythmic modes of the contemporary Maghrib (Tun.), having a 2/4 or 4/4 cycle. D'Erlanger gives the following notation of this rhythmic cycle (1959:150):

Adagio

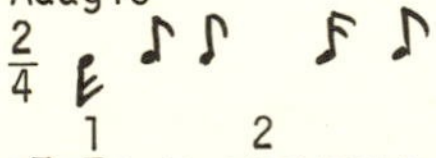

1 2

Also MĪZĀN AL MASHADD* (Ḥāfiẓ 1971:120).

MASḤAH (pl. MASḤĀT) (m-s-ḥ) "a wipe; a cleaning"

Percussion of medium force or volume struck with a flexible mallet (al Fārābī 1967:987). In the translation of this work (d'Erlanger 1935:27), we find MATH̲AH, with "T" and the symbol employed in that work for the letter "KH", undoubtedly a printer's error.

MASHĀLIYAH = MCHÂLIA, MICHALIA, MICHALYAH, MECHALAYAH, MSHELIA (sh-y-l) f. of "pertaining to carrying or transportation of loads"

An opening movement of the NAWBAH/1* (Mor. and Alg.). This unmeasured prelude to the suite is executed in unison by the orchestra or as an instrumental solo. Some short examples of this genre are known under the name BUGHYAH* (el Mahdi 1972:11). Also called DĀ'IRAH/ * (Alg.), TAQYĪD AL ṢANʿAH* (Alg.) or ISTIFTĀḤ/1* (Tun.).

MASḤÔURAH

Var. of MASḤŪRAH* (Hickmann 1958:29).

MASHRIQĪ (sh-r-q) "eastern"

Pertaining to the eastern part of the Arab World, i.e., from Egypt and eastward. Opp. of MAGHRIBĪ*.

MASḤŪRAH = MASḤOÛRAH (s-ḥ-r) "bewitched, fascinated"

A kind of double clarinet in the Mashriq having two to four fingerholes. It was used in ancient Syria (Farmer EI(Eng), "Mizmār":541) as well as in contemporary Egypt (Hickmann 1958:29). In its contemporary version, it is smaller than the ZUMMĀRAH* and has four fingerholes on each pipe and down cut reeds (Marcuse).

MASJŪʿ (s-j-ʿ) "spoken or written in rhymed prose"

Rhymed prose (al Fārābī 1967:1090; 1935:64). Syn. of SAJʿ*.

MASLŪQ (s-l-q) "boiled; lacerated"

Satirical folk song of the Maghrib (Chottin 1961:Band IX, col. 1564). See MAZLŪQ (supp.).

MASMOUDI

Var. of MAṢMŪDĪ* (Touma 1977b:66).

MAṢMŪDĪ = MASMOUDI (ethn.) "name of a Berber tribe"

Designation for two contemporary rhythmic modes (MAṢMŪDĪ KABĪR, MAṢMŪDĪ ṢAGHĪR). The term is thought to be derived from the name of an important Berber tribe of North Africa (MAṢMŪDAH). See d'Erlanger 1959:60.

MASRŪDAH (s-r-d) "that which is continuous"

1. Any song which is continuous, i.e., not marked by partitioning or separating silences (FAWĀṢIL, s. FĀṢILAH/1*) (al Fārābī 1967: 1140; 1935:77).
2. Simple prose, since it is without the partitions of poetry.
3. Lyrics of a song.

MASṬARAH (s-ṭ-r) "a place to draw lines"

The piece affixed on the face of the ʿŪD to which the lower end of the strings are fastened (al Khwārizmī 1968:239; Farmer 1978: I, 42). It would seem that the voweling of this term should be MISṬARAH* ("ruler") rather than this form given in the 1968 edition of al Khwārizmī's work.

MĀSŪL or MĀSŪLAH

A folk instrument of woodwind family, which is used in the Arabian/Persian Gulf regions and ʿUmān (Jargy 1970:124). This name is probably a var. of MAWṢŪL*.

MAṬĀRIQ (ṭ-r-q)

Pl. of MIṬRAQ or MIṬRAQAH*, the mallets for playing any dulcimer-like instrument (Ibn Zaylah, according to Farmer 1926a:245; al Dāqūqī 1965:56; Ḥāfiẓ 1971:162; Ibn Zaylah 1964:73).

MAṬĀYḤĪ = METÂÏHI

The fourth piece of an Algerian NAWBAH/1*, which has a higher pitch elevation than those movements that precede it (Delphin and Guin 1886:64). This seems to be a mistaken spelling and pronunciation of BAṬĀYḤĪ*. It is found in conjunction with BAṬĀYḤĪ in Rouanet (1922:2846).

MATḪAH

Var. of MASḤAH* (d'Erlanger 1935:27), probably a printer's error.

MATHĀLITH (th-l-th) "tripled"

Another name for the QĀNŪN* (because of its triple stringing) (Maḥfūẓ 1964:48).

MATHĀNĪ (th-n-y) "doubled"

Another name for the ʿŪD/2* (because of its double stringing) (Maḥfūẓ 1964:48).

MATHLATH or MITHLATH (th-l-th) "third place"

Name for one of the strings of the ʿŪD* in the Classical Period. It was the second string, reading from lowest pitched upwards. The apparent reversal of the names for the MATHLATH AND MATHNĀ* ("second place") strings results from the fact that the classical ʿŪD originally had four rather than five strings that were named from highest to lowest pitched (al Kindī in Farmer 1943:20).

MATHNĀ (th-n-y) "second place"

One of the strings of the ʿŪD/2* of the Classical Period. It was the third string, reading from lowest pitched upwards. See MATHLATH*.

MATHQŪB (th-q-b) "bored"

The hole in which to blow to produce musical sound on any aerophone.

MAʿṬIF (pl. MAʿĀṬIF) (ʿ-ṭ-f) "place of bending (the air)"

Any of the finger holes or the end opening of a woodwind instrument (al Fārābī 1967:777ff).

MAṬLAʿ (pl. MAṬĀLIʿ) = MET'LA' (ṭ-l-ʿ) "place of rising"

1. The instrumental introduction of 15th C. performance practice. Syn. of ṬARĪQAH/3* (ʿAbd al Qādir ibn Ghaybī quoted in Anonymous Treatise 1939:244). The word is still used for an introductory orchestral number and as syn. of BASHRAF/1* (al Ḥafnī 1946:253). 2. The opening section of music in a QAṢĪDAH/1* or MUWASHSHAḤ/1*,

which returns like a kind of refrain throughout the movement (al Rizqī 1967:371). Also MADHHAB/1*, ṬĀLIʿ/2*.
3. The opening and recurring segment of poetry in the MUWASHSHAḤ/2* (d'Erlanger 1959:165). Also MADHHAB/4*, ṬĀLIʿ/2*. In Algeria, the same term is used for the first couplet of a QAṢĪDAH* (Delphin and Guin 1886:36). HADDAH* and ʿARŪBIYYAH* are synonyms of its similar use in that country.

MAṬLŪQ (ṭ-l-q) "freed"

One of the tunings of the Moroccan KAMĀNJAH*, syn. of MUSĀWIYAH ʿALĀ AL MĀ'IYYAH (Chottin 1939:144).

MĀʿŪN (pl. MAWĀʿĪN) (m-ʿ-n) "instrument"

Any musical instrument (al Rizqī 1967:365).

MAUSSIL

Var. of MAWṢŪL* (Marcuse).

MAUSUL

Var. of MAWṢŪL* (Marcuse).

MAWĀJIB (pl. of MAWJIB, MŪJIB) (w-j-b) "consequences; necessary things"

A set of six scales known collectively by this name in the 13th C. (Ṣafī al Dīn 1938b:179-180). See Wright 1978:249, n. 2. AṢĀBIʿ/1* was an earlier synonym. Although we have little more than the scalar information about the MAWĀJIB, it is quite possible that they possessed other modal characteristics which are now lost to us.

MAWĀL

Var. of MAWWĀL* (Farmer 1954, "Iraqian and Mesopotamian Music":IV, 532; "Egyptian Music":II, 896; Weil 1913-1934:I, 475).

MAWĀLIYĀ = MAWÂLÎYÂ (m-w-l)

1. Syn. of MAWWĀL/1* (Wehr; Madina; el Helou 1961:196).
2. A kind of popular poetry of the people of Baghdād and Egypt in the time of Ibn Khaldūn (d. 1406). It had many subdivisions, each with its special name. It was also called ṢAWT/2* (Ibn Khaldūn 1967:III, 475-476).

MAWĀT (m-w-t) "a lifeless thing"?

An unidentified song form of the Maghrib (Mor.) (Chottin 1961: Band IX, col. 1562).

MAWḌIʿ AL NAGHAM (pl. MAWĀḌIʿ AL NAGHAM) (w-ḍ-ʿ) (n-gh-m) "rank or location of notes"

Construction of melodic modes (Farmer 1945:22).

MAWḌŪʿAH (pl. MAWḌŪʿĀT, MAWĀḌĪʿ) (w-ḍ-ʿ) "subject matter; question; topic

Melodic patterns or themes, according to a 13th C. treatise (Farmer 1965b:xxiii).

MAWJIB (pl. MAWĀJIB*) (w-j-b) "effect, consequence"

See MAWĀJIB*. Also possibly MŪJIB* (see de Vaux 1891:352).

MAWLĀ AL ZAMR = MOUL-EZ-ZAMR (w-l-y) (z-m-r) "master of the ZAMR"

Master performer of the double clarinet (ZAMR/2*) of tribal music (Mor.). He is usually regarded as leader or SHAYKH/1* of the ensemble (Chottin 1939:33). See also ABŪ GHANAM*.

MAWLID (pl. MAWĀLID) (w-l-d) "birthday; the Prophet Muḥammad's birthday"

1. Poems in honor of the birth of the Prophet Muḥammad (El-Kholy 1954:55).
2. Later the word was applied generally to all chanting of religious poetry in the vocal unaccompanied and free rhythmed style of cantillation. This music was performed by male voices antiphonally and in unison (El-Kholy 1954:55).
3. The celebrations and entertainments on the occasion of the Prophet's birthday.

MAWLŪʿ = MÛLÛ' (w-l-ʿ) "person strongly attached to something"

Amateur musician (Mor.).

MAWQIʿAH (pl. MAWĀQIʿ) (w-q-ʿ) "place of falling"

Rhythm (Farmer 1945:22).

AL MAWṢILĪ (geog.) "the one from MAWṢIL, the town in ʿIRĀQ"

This refers to Ibrahīm ibn Māhān al Arjānī, also called "al Nadīm," or IBRAHĪM AL MAWṢILĪ*. He was the famous musician, and the father of ISḤAQ AL MAWṢILĪ*.

MAWṢŪL = MAUSSIL, MAUSUL, MĀSŪL, MĀSŪLAH (w-ṣ-l) "joined"

A single reed, double-pipe wind instrument (i.e., double clarinet) of contemporary Egypt. It is also called ARGHŪL* or ZUMMĀRAH* (al Ḥafnī 1971:178). This term was used for a double-pipe instrument as early as the 13th C. (Egypt) (Farmer EI(Eng), "Mizmār":541) and as far away from the Arab center as Moorish Spain (el Helou 1965:39). Its use today is limited to the performance of folk music.

MAWTIR (w-t-r)

An ancient one-stringed instrument. One wonders if this is just a different voweling of MUWATTAR*, another ancient predecessor of the ʿŪD/2*. The author of the treatise in which it is found (al Rizqī 1967:366) gives no assistance in settling this question.

MAWWĀL (pl. MAWĀWĪL) = MAWĀL, MUWÂL, MUWWĀL, MAWĀLIYĀ, MAWÂLÎYÂ (m-w-l) "causing to bend, or repeatedly bending"

1. A genre of vocal, free rhythmed, improvised music which is a richly ornamented setting of a kind of popular strophic poetry of the same name. See MAWWĀL/2. This genre was formerly considered to be folk music, but in more recent years it is used in programs of art music where it can replace the classical QAṢĪDAH/1* (d'Erlanger 1959:172-173).

This form is supposed to have originated in Baghdād early in the 9th C. (el Helou 1961:196). Egypt, ʿIrāq, Palestine, Lebanon and Syria all have their versions of this popular form of poetic and musical expression. One variety is called MUSABBAʿ* ("sevened") because of its seven poetic lines. In Palestine, Lebanon, and Syria, a folkish version called ʿATĀBĀ* is very popular. The village people of ʿIrāq also sing a variety of MAWWĀL called ʿATĀBĀ*; another, NĀYALĪ*, is popular with both urban and village populations in that country (Ibid.:197). TARNĪMAH* is the name used in Egypt for still another MAWWĀL-like genre (Al Ḥalqah 1964:52). The MAWWĀL of the Mashriq usually includes only a few lines of poetry. The singer "plays" with the words of each hemistich in succession, subjecting them to a variety of complete and partial repetitions as he/she improvises on the tones of the chosen melodic mode. The MAWWĀL is usually preceded by an improvisation on the words YĀ LAYL, YĀ ʿAYN.

In Morocco the MAWWĀL is also an improvisation, but it is based on melodic motifs from the folk song materials of the area more than on original material. It has a long, almost imperceptible rhythmic mode, and it conforms to one of the melodic modes from which any specific performance of this genre takes its name, e.g., MAWWĀL SĪKĀH, MAWWĀL DHAYL, etc. It follows a clear plan: 1) The instruments give the fundamental tone of the chosen mode, which they continue to repeat slowly. 2) A vocal prelude on the stock formula, YĀ LAYL, serves as preparation for the voice and for establishing the mode. This vocalise is accompanied by one of the stringed instruments of either plucked or bowed type. The instrument shadows the vocal line and returns often to the fundamental pedal tone held by the other instruments. 3) The first line of the chosen quatrain is sung. At the end of each line, the accompanying stringed instrument repeats one by one the improvised motifs done by the singer as a kind of contest of virtuosity between vocalist and instrumentalist. 4) A rapid measured movement called GHIṬĀ'/1*, which is played by the ensemble, ends the Maghribī MAWWĀL. It is usually based on elements heard earlier in the movement. Sometimes the singer accompanies himself in the MAWWĀL performance, using one of the common stringed instruments of the area (Chottin 1939:133-136).

2. A strophic poem using colloquial rather than classical Arabic. Some authorities maintain that its strophes have 7, 14 or even more lines. These groups of 7 or multiples of 7 are subdivided into two segments of 3 lines, each with its own rhyme. The seventh line completes the idea of the first line and rhymes with it (Jargy 1970: 37, 44). Others claim that it may have as few as 4 or 5 lines per strophe. When it has 4 lines and is known as MURABBAʿ/4*, there

is a single rhyme ending lines 1, 3 and 4. When it has 5 lines and is known as MUKHAMMAS/2*, the fourth line does not follow the basic rhyme pattern (d'Erlanger 1959:167-168). Each line or BAYT/1* of the poem evidences a symmetrical division into two hemistiches.

MAWZŪN or MAWZŪNAH (w-z-n) "measured"

1. Descriptive of any music that has an underlying rhythmic mode.
2. Measured, i.e., metered (said of verse).

MĀYA (m-w-h) "juice, sap"

Syn. of the MATHLATH* string of the lute in the Maghrib (Farmer 1933b:3). Perhaps a var. of MĀ'IYYAH/1*.

MĀYAH

Var. of MĀ'IYYAH* (al Rizqī 1967:370; al Jurjānī 1938:391).

MAYANAH

Highest pitched phase of the MAQĀM AL ʿIRĀQĪ* performance (Touma 1977b:72). Var. of MIYĀNAH*.

MAYJANĀ = MĪJĀNĀ, MIJANA, MIǦANA

A genre of vocal folk music which serves as a regularly rhythmed refrain for the ʿATĀBĀ* (Reichow 1971: 6, n. 4, 20). It is especially popular in Syria and Lebanon (Ibn Dhurayl 1969:149). Al Ikhtiyār (n.d.:94) describes it as an "introduction" to the ʿATĀBĀ. This should not be counted as a new meaning for the term; it merely indicates the possibility of this genre preceding the initial rendering of the ʿATĀBĀ. The two genres alternate with each other repeatedly in such a performance.

MAZĀMĪR (z-m-r)

Pl. of MIZMĀR*. MAZĀMMĪR in Avenary (1952:80) seems to be a misspelling.

MAZHAR (z-h-r) (MAẒHAR is believed to be an incorrect var.) "blossoming"

Equiv. of MIZHAR*. MIZHAR is considered the ancient term, while the pronunciation MAZHAR is more common today (Wehr).

MAZMŪM or MAZMŪMAH (z-m-m) "tightened"

1. Tightened or tuned (said of a string on a musical instrument) (Ikhwān al Ṣafā' 1957:I, 204).
2. One of the six octave scales (or modes) mentioned by ʿAbd al Qādir ibn Ghaybī (d. 1435), which were known collectively as the AṢĀBIʿ/1* or MAWĀJIB*. By the time of Ṣafī al Dīn, this categorization was already consider ancient (Wright 1978:249-250). The other scales were MUṬLAQ/2*, MUSARRAJ*, MUʿALLAQ/2*, MAḤMŪL* and MUJANNAB/3*.

MAZOUNI (MAWZŪNĪ?)

A genre of popular song of ancient origin and marked by trembling and guttural quality in the voice, slow tempo without stops, and a final held assonance (Alg.). It is one of the two kinds of KALĀM AL JADD*, a musical category of contemporary Algeria (Delphin and Guin 1886:29-30). See also MAKHĀZINĪ* (MEKRAZENI*), MAWZŪN or MAWZŪNAH/1*.

MAʿZŪFAH (pl. MAʿZŪFĀT) (ʿ-z-f) "played"

A piece of music (performed).

MĀZŪR (Eng.) "measure"

A foot or measure of a rhythmic cycle (Al Ḥalqah 1964:43-44).

MCHÂLIA

Var. of MASHĀLIYAH* (Chottin 1939:126).

MCHERGUÎ (MUSHARQĪ?) "oriental"?

A QAṢĪDAH* of religious theme with a musical setting in the folkish GRĪḤAH* or colloq. style (Mor.) (Chottin 1939:155).

MECHALAYAH

Var. of MASHĀLIYAH* (el Mahdi 1972:13).

MEDAWAR

Var. of MUDAWWAR* (Rouanet 1922:2781).

MEDDĀH

Var. of MADDĀḤ* (Delphin and Guin 1886:31-32).

MEDH

Var. of MADḤ* (Chottin 1939:48, n. 1).

MEDJOUES

Var. of MIJWIZ*, the double-piped wind instrument (Touma 1977b:105).

MEDJRA

Var. of MAJRĀ* (Rouanet 1922:2694).

MEÏA

Var. of MĀ'IYYAH*, and equated with an ancient instrument mentioned by al Fārābī, according to Salvador-Daniel (1976:224). See MĀ'IYYAH/3*.

MEKHEZNA

Var. of MAKHZINAH* (Rouanet 1922:2926).

MEKHLAÇ and MEKLAÇ

Vars. of MAKHLAṢ* (Rouanet 1922:2846; 2858-2859).

MEKLASS

Var. of MAKHLAṢ* (Salvador-Daniel 1976:195).

MEKRAOUÏA

Var. of MUKHĀWAYAH* (Delphin and Guin 1886:61).

MEKRAZENI

Var. of MAKHĀZINĪ* (Delphin and Guin 1886:29, 37).

MELH'OUN

Var. of MALḤŪN* (Chottin 1939:104).

MERABA'

Var. of MURABBAʿ* (Delphin and Guin 1886:36).

MESAMER

Var. of MUSĀMARAH* (Burckhardt 1967:82-83, 253).

MESSRAF

Var. of MUṢARRAF* (Farmer 1976a:195).

MESTEKBER

Var. of MUSTAKHBIR* (Rouanet 1922:2914; Farmer 1976a:194).

MESTRA

Var. of MISṬARAH* (Rouanet 1922:2926).

MET'AÏAHI

Var. of MAṬĀYḤĪ* (Delphin and Guin 1886:64).

METÂÏHI or METÂÏHÎ

Vars. of MAṬĀYḤĪ* (Rouanet 1922:2846).

MET'LA'

Var. of MAṬLAʿ* (Delphin and Guin 1886:36).

MEYDAF (q-dh-f?) perhaps var. or colloq. of MIQDHĀF "oar"

One of the work songs (AHĀZĪJ, s. HAZAJ*) of the Arabian/Persian Gulf region sung to accompany the rowing of the sailors (Touma 1977a:122). See also BASSEH*, QAYLAMĪ*, KHRAB*.

MEZOUED

Var. of MIZWID* (el Mahdi 1972:49).

MEZWEG

Var. of MIZWIJ* (Jargy 1978:89).

MÂÂZENÎ (w-z-n?) perhaps a colloq. form of MAWĀZĪNĪ "the person involved with meters"

The musician who has a talent for remaining true to the rhythmic mode in his performance. This is one of the most admired of the musical talents (Mor.) (Chottin 1939:116, n. 1).

MICHALIA

Var. of MASHĀLIYAH* (Touma 1977b:77).

MICHALYAH

Var. of MASHĀLIYAH* (el Mahdi 1972:11-12).

MIDHRAB

Var. of MIḌRAB or MIḌRĀB* (Kieswetter 1968:95).

MIḌMĀR (ḍ-m-r) "field of activity"

Musical aptitude (Ibn Khaldūn 1967:II, 399).

MIḌRAB or MIḌRĀB (pl. MAḌĀRIB) = MIDHRAB (ḍ-r-b) "instrument of striking"

Plectrum.

MIḌRĀB ZIRYĀB (ḍ-r-b) (n. of pers.) "plectrum of ZIRYĀB*"

Plectrum invented by the famous musician of Moorish Spain. It was made from one of the primary quills of an eagle, rather than from wood as the earlier ones had been made.

MIFTĀḤ (pl. MAFĀTĪḤ) (f-t-ḥ) "key"

1. The small pieces of wood used as tuning pegs in chordophones of all varieties (Maḥfūẓ 1964:155).
2. The hollow metal key used to turn the tuning pegs on a QĀNŪN* or similar open-stringed chordophone (Maḥfūẓ 1964:155).
3. Very early name for the SABBĀBAH* fret or fret position, according to al Kindī (Shawqī 1976:289). However, al Kindī describes the placement for this fret at 1/10 of the string length instead of the

1/9 position used to achieve the usual whole tone SABBĀBAH (al Kindī 1965:12).
4. Clef, as borrowed in contemporary musical theory and practice from Western notation. See MIFTĀḤ JAHĪR*, MIFTĀḤ AL KAMĀN*, MIFTĀḤ FA*, MIFTĀḤ SOL*.

MIFTĀḤ FĀ (f-t-ḥ) "Fa clef"

F clef  used by contemporary theorists for musical notation (al Ḥafnī 1946:23). Syn. of MIFTĀḤ JAHĪR*.

MIFTĀḤ JAHĪR (f-t-ḥ) (j-h-r) "clef of loudness"

Syn. of MIFTĀḤ FĀ* (al Ḥafnī 1946:23).

MIFTĀḤ AL KAMĀN (f-t-ḥ) (Pers.) "clef of the KAMĀN"

Syn. of MIFTĀḤ SŪL* (al Ḥafnī 1946:22).

MIFTĀḤ SŪL (f-t-ḥ) "Sol clef"

G clef  used by contemporary theorists for musical notation (al Ḥafnī 1946:22). Syn. of MIFTĀḤ AL KAMĀN*.

MIǦANA

Var. of MAYJANĀ (Reichow 1971:20).

MIḤBAḌ (pl. MAḤĀBIḌ) (ḥ-b-ḍ)

String of the lute (ʿŪD*) (Ibn Salamah 1938a:12; 1938b:242). See MAḤBAḌ*.

MĪJĀNĀ

Var. of MAYJANĀ* (Jargy 1970:30).

MIJHAR or MIJHĀR (j-h-r) "loud voiced"

Having a loud sound, vocal or instrumental.

MIJWEZ

Var. of MIJWIZ*(Bulos 1971:23).

MIJWIZ = MEDJOUES, MEZWEG, MIJWEZ, MEZOUEJ (j-w-z) "instrument of traveling"

This term seems to be a well established colloq. of MIZWIJ*. See (j-w-z) in Wehr. It is used as syn. of both MIZWIJ/1*, the double piped folk instrument (ʿArnīṭah 1968:61; Touma 1977b:105); and MIZWIJ/2*, the contemporary small bagpipe of the folk tradition (Bulos 1971:23).

MILHĀ (pl. MALĀHĪ) (l-h-w) "instrument of diversion"

Musical instrument (Roy Choudhury n.d.:54, n. 2). See MALĀHĪ*.

MILWĀ (l-w-w)or (l-w-y)

Equiv. of MALWĀ* (Lane 1973:356).

MINFAKH (pl. MANĀFIKH) or MINFĀKH (pl. MANĀFĪKH) (n-f-kh) "instrument of blowing"

The mouthpiece of an aerophone, or the hole into which the wind player blows.

MIQBAḌ (q-b-ḍ)

Equiv. of MAQBIḌ* (Wehr).

MIQDĀR (pl. MAQĀDĪR) (q-d-r) "measure; extent; quantity"

1. Proportion or measurement between finger holes of a flute, pitches of tones, lengths of strings, or lengths of pipes (al Fārābī 1967:775).
2. Size of intervals (Ibn Sīnā 1930:98-99).
3. Length of a percussion (Ibn Sīnā 1930:98-99; Ikhwān al Ṣafā' 1957:I, 200).
4. Cycle of a rhythmic mode (Farmer 1943:24, 46), i.e., the precise pattern of mensural and dynamic succession of beats in a rhythmic mode (Ibid.:44).

MIQṬAʿ (pl. MAQĀṬIʿ) (q-ṭ-ʿ) "cutting instrument"

A stop or rest period between phrases, according to theorists of the ʿAbbāsī period (al Masʿūdī 1874:VIII, 90; Farmer 1929a:55; 1967:106). See MAQṬAʿ/1*.

MIR'ĀH (m-r-') "mirror"

The ornamental facing of the flat side of the neck (RAQABAH*) the ʿŪD* (Maḥfūẓ 1964:151; al Ḥafnī 1971:75).

MIRIÂS

Probably a var. of MIRWĀS* (Hickmann 1958:59).

MIRWAḤAH (r-w-ḥ) "a fan"

A percussion instrument comprising a stick or a construction to which bells were attached. This name was used by the Christian Arabs. Other names were JAGHĀNAH , SAGHĀNAH*, ZILLĪ MĀSHA* (Farmer EI(Fr), "Ṣandj":210).

MIRWĀS (pl. MARĀWĪS) = MIRIÂS (r-w-s) "racetrack"

A small double-headed drum similar to the ṬABL/2* and used by the folk musicians of the Sūdān and the Mashriq. The Sūdānī version is approximately 31.5 cm. in diameter and 32.5 cm. in height (Hickmann 1958:59). In the Arabian/Persian Gulf region it is described as 18 cm. in diameter, 20 cm. in height (Touma 1977a:124).

MISHQAR (sh-q-r)

Syn. of SHAQIRAH*, an unidentified musical instrument mentioned in a 12th C. ms. (Farmer 1926a:252ff).

MISHṬ

Var. of MUSHṬ* (Ikhwān al Ṣafā' 1957:I, 203; de Vaux 1891:331).

MIṢRĀʿ (pl. MAṢĀRĪʿ) (ṣ-r-ʿ) "leaf of a door"

A hemistich of poetry.

MISṬARAH (pl. MASĀṬIR) = MAṢṬARAH, MISTRA (s-ṭ-r) "ruler"

1. The piece of wood (usually beech) along the oblique end of the soundbox into which the tuning pegs (MALĀWĪ*) of the QĀNŪN* are inserted (Lane 1973:358; Ḥāfiẓ 1971:84; Maḥfūẓ 1964:155). The piece resembles a ruler, hence, its name.
2. The end piece of wood to which the lower ends of the strings of the QUWAYṬARAH* lute are attached (MESTRA*).
3. Any one of the keys of a keyboard instrument such as the URGHANŪM* of the Classical Period (Farmer 1926a:256).

MITHLATH (th-l-th)

Equiv. of MATHLATH* (al Fārābī 1967:503).

MITHQĀL (th-q-l) "a weight"

Syn. of MŪSĪQĀL* (Farmer 1976b:22).

MIṬRAQ (pl. MAṬĀRIQ) (ṭ-r-q) "hammer, mallet"

One of the pair of hammers used to strike the strings of a dulcimer-like instrument (Ibn Zaylah, fol. 235v. of Br. Mus. Or. 2361, mentioned by Farmer 1926a:245; al Dāqūqī 1965:56; Ḥāfiẓ 1971:162).

MIṬRAQAH (pl. MAṬĀRIQ) (ṭ-r-q) "a hammer or mallet"

A stick with which sound is produced on an idiophone or membranophone (Farmer 1943:77). MTAREG is a var. pl. in Rouanet 1922:2933.

MIYĀNAH = MAYANAH (Pers.) "middle"

The middle, highest-pitched portion or portions of the MAQĀM AL ʿIRĀQĪ* performance (Touma 1977b:72; Ḥāfiẓ 1971:166-168). When a series of these is included, they are called AL MIYĀNAH AL ŪLĀ, AL MIYĀNAH AL THĀNIYAH, AL MIYĀNAH AL THĀLITHAH, etc.

MIYAT KHĀNAH (colloq. of MI'AH) (kh-w-n) "100 squares"

A melismatic passage sometimes contained in the BASĪṬ/4* or AMAL* genres. It was often used as well in the four movements of the Classical Period suite (NAWBAH/1*). Syn. of ṢAWṬ/2* or ṢAWṬ AL WASAṬ* (Anonymous Treatise 1939:236, 244).

MIʿZAF or MIʿZAFAH (pl. MAʿĀZIF) (ʿ-z-f) "musical instrument"

1. Generic term for any stringed instrument (Ibn Abī al Dunyā 1938:20, 41).
2. Any one of the many instruments that use only open strings, e.g., the QĀNŪN*, the SANṬŪR*, ṢANJ or ṢINJ/1*, JANK* (al Fārābī 1967: 497, 822-877). According to Ḥāfiẓ (1971:20), the term was used in this sense in the pre-Islamic and early Classical Periods. A harp-like instrument of this name is traditionally held to have been invented by DALĀL*, the daughter of LĀMAK*. That instrument was described as having from 15-25 strings which were fastened to tuning pegs (Ḥāfiẓ 1971:20-21). See also al Khwārizmī 1968:237; Ikhwān al Ṣafā' 1957:I, 202; Ibn Taymiyyah in Haq 1944:123; Maḥfūẓ 1964:50).
3. Any stringed or wind instrument (Farmer EI(Eng), "Miʿzaf":528).
4. Any stringed instrument played with a plectrum (Farmer 1926a: 243-244; 1978:I, 7-8).
5. According to al Zabīdī 1965, the tambourine is also included among the MAʿĀZIF. This is a mistake according to Farmer (EI(Eng), "Miʿzāf":528).
6. A contemporary kettledrum (Marcuse) (doubtful).
7. An instrument for producing the sound of the JINN (Farmer 1941: 137, n. 4).

MĪZĀN (pl. MAWĀZĪN) (w-z-n) "scale"

1. Rhythm.
2. Rhythmic mode (Allawerdi 1949:479ff).
3. Any of the five large "movements" of the suite (NAWBAH/1*) of the Maghrib, each of which is based on a different rhythmic mode. These movements are subdivided into two sections in Morocco, one slow section known as MUWASSAʿ*, and the other fast section known as INṢIRĀF/2*. Each MĪZĀN is marked by a new rhythmic accentuation and a faster tempo than that preceding it. It is made up of a series of songs (ṢANʿAH/2*) which follow each other without pause (Schuyler 1978:37). Each phase thus reveals a progressive internal acceleration as well as an external acceleration from the phase or MĪZĀN before it (Chottin 1939:112).
4. A kind of musical prelude (Alg.) (Chottin 1939:125, n. 1).
5. A large frame drum, larger than the BANDĪR*. Its loud sound precludes its being used as an accompanying instrument for singers (Alg.) (Delphin and Guin 1886:42).

MĪZĀN ʿĀYIB (w-z-n) (ʿ-y-b) "faulty scale"

Name given by Tunisian musicians to any rhythmic mode corresponding to measures of 10/8, 5/4, 7/4 or 14/8. These rhythms seem foreign to the Andalusian tradition of the Maghrib and have probably been imported from the Mashriq (d'Erlanger 1959:201).

MĪZĀN AL KHAFĪF (w-z-n) (kh-f-f) "light scale"

A rhythmic mode of slow 3-beat cycle used in the KHAFĪF/2* portion of the NAWBAH/1* (Tun.) (Ḥāfiẓ 1971:122).

MĪZĀN AL MASHADD (w-z-n) (sh-d-d) "scale of the place of reinforcement"

Duple rhythm of medium speed used to accompany the improvisatory solo by RABĀB* or ʿŪD/2* which is joined to the TAWSHIYAH/3*, one of the movements of the NAWBAH/1* or suite (Tun.) (Ḥāfiẓ 1971:120). Syn. of MASHADD/2*.

MĪZĀN M'CERREF

Var. of MIZAN MUṢARRAF* (Chottin 1939:113).

MĪZĀN MUṢARRAF = MĪZĀN M'CERREF (w-z-n) (ṣ-r-f) "running scale"

The final segment of a ṢANʿAH/2* or song within the suite (NAWBAH/1*) of the Maghrib. It reveals the highest point of acceleration within the song. This coda is a preparation for the piece or ṢANʿAH to follow, in which the acceleration process continues (Chottin 1939: 113). Syn. of INṢIRĀF/2*, MUṢARRAF*.

MĪZĀN MUṬLAQ (w-z-n) (ṭ-l-q) "freed scale"

The bare percussion and silence pattern of the rhythmic cycle, as opposed to its artistic rendering (Maghrib) (Chottin 1939:116). Syn. of TAKTĪF*.

MIZAWD (misspelling of MIZWAD*?)

Identified as a bagpipe of Tunisia (Farmer EI(Eng), "Mizmār":541).

MIZHAR or MAZHAR (pl. MAZĀHIR) = MAẒHAR (z-h-r) "that which brightens"

1. A frame drum of pre-Islamic and early Islamic times (Robson 1938a:8, n. 2). As such, it was usually known as MIZHAR. Today either MIZHAR or MAZHAR is used in the Mashriq for a large circular frame drum of ca. 45-60 cm. in diameter and furnished with five pairs of jingles in the frame (Sachs 1940:246-247; ʿArnīṭah 1968: 48-49; Hickmann 1947:21). It is also described as a large frame drum without cymbals, instead equipped with a small chain fastened across the inner face of the membrane (Touma 1977b:107-108; al Ḥafnī 1971:176; Robson 1938a:8, n. 2). This instrument is used for accompanying religious music of the DHIKR* ceremony or other religious occasions. Al Dāqūqī (1965:87) has MAẒHAR (?).
2. A leather-faced, short-necked lute of pre-Islamic and early Islamic times. It was used before the wooden-faced ʿŪD* was adopted (Ibn Salamah 1951:82; Ibn ʿAbd Rabbihi 1887:26). Also KIRĀN*, MUWATTAR*. Sachs (1940:246) disputes this definition, maintaining that the word was used only for a frame drum (see def. 1); but we have the authority of Ibn ʿAbd Rabbihi and Ibn Salamah for use of the term with this meaning. Many other writers confirm this usage (Farmer 1967:4, 9, 10; Chottin 1939:60; Ḥāfiẓ 1971:20). Ḥāfiẓ even claims that the term MIZHAR was used for either the

leather- or wooden-faced lute and that the instrument had two strings (Ḥāfiẓ 1971:20). AS far as is known, the term is not used for any contemporary chordophone.

MIZMĀR (pl. MAZĀMĪR) (z-m-r) "instrument for piping a tune"

1. Generic term for woodwind instrument, from pre-Islamic times till today (Robson 1938b:240; Farmer 1967:16). Many authors use the term in this general way as well as in one or more of the following specific senses. See Farmer 1978:I, 65-67.
2. Generic term for any of the woodwind instruments played with reeds rather than those which are pipe-blown (Farmer EI(Eng), "Mizmār":539).
3. Generic term for any woodwind instrument employing a double reed like the oboe, as distinguished from the clarinet and recorder types (Robson 1938b:240; al Ḥafnī 1971:178-179). Such instruments have been used since pre-Islamic times by the Arabs. The MIZMĀR is often used today in pairs--a smaller one called SIBS* which performs the melody and a larger instrument of similar construction known as JAWRĀ* which shadows the melody (al Ḥafnī 1971:179).
4. Syn. of the NĀY/1*, or an end-blown flute, in a 13th C. ms. (Farmer 1978:I, 21).
5. The term may have also been applied by the Arabs to stringed instruments at an early period. It is so indicated in a 13th C. ms. (see Farmer 1978:I, 21, n. 2).
6. The pipe of an organ, according to a 12th C. copy of an 8th or 9th C. work (Farmer 1931:94).

MIZMĀR AL BALADĪ (z-m-r) (b-l-d) "MIZMĀR of the village"

Double-reed wind instrument used in the Mashriq (ʿArnīṭah 1968:60). It is similar to the SURNĀY/1* described by al Fārābī (1967:787-794, also see 787, n. 3).

MIZMĀR AL ʿIRĀQĪ (z-m-r) (geog.) "ʿIrāqī MIZMĀR"

An unidentified ʿIrāqī reedpipe of the 14th C. (al Ghazālī n.d.: II, 272; Farmer 1954, "Iraqian and Mesopotamian Music":580).

MIZMĀR AL JIRĀB (z-m-r) (j-r-b) "MIZMĀR of the bag"

Bagpipe, according to Ibn Sīnā and Ibn Zaylah(Farmer EI(Eng), "Mizmār":541).

MIZMĀR AL MUTHANNĀ (z-m-r) (th-w-n) "double MIZMĀR"

A woodwind instrument having two reed pipes fastened together (al Ḥafnī 1971:179).

MIZMĀR MUZĀWAJ or MIZMĀR AL MUZAWWAJ (z-m-r) (z-w-j) "paired MIZMĀR"

Any double pipe woodwind instrument known at the time of al Fārābī (1967:795-800). It was also known at that time as MUTHANNĀ*, MUZĀWAJ* or DŪNĀY* (Ibid.:795, see also n. 2). These instruments are described as having two pipes of the same length, fastened close together near the mouthpiece and spreading toward the lower extremities. Generally there were five finger holes in the right tube and four in the left (Ibid.).

MIZWAD (pl. MAZĀWID) = MIZWID, MEZOUED, MIZAWD (?) (z-w-d) "provision bag"

A bagpipe-like folk instrument with two reed pipes tuned identically (Tun.) (al Rizqī 1967:366). Unlike Scottish bagpipes, it has no drones and does not always play in an uninterrupted fashion (Racy 1979:24). Also called MIZWIJ/2* (el Mahdi 1972:49).

MIZWID

Var. of MIZWAD* (Jones 1977:6).

MIZWIJ = MEZWEG, MEZOUEJ (z-w-j) "paired instrument"

1. A double reed, oboe-like instrument with double pipes used by peasants and shepherds in the Mashriq. It can produce simultaneously a drone base and a highly ornamented melody of fairly limited range (Kāẓim 1964:91).
2. A small bagpipe of the Maghrib with two pipes of equal pitch (el Mahdi 1972:49). Syn. of MIZWAD*.

MLÂWI

Colloq. var. of the pl. of MILWĀ or MILWĪ*(Chottin 1939:138).

MOCHT

Var. of MUSHṬ* (Chottin 1939:138; Rouanet 1922:2702).

MOGHANNI

Var. of MUGHANNĪ* (Kieswetter 1968:94).

MOHAYAR

Var. of MUḤAYYIR* (Rouanet 1922:2750).

MOHASSABA

Var. of MUḤASSABAH* (el Mahdi 1972:14).

MOQADDEM

Var. of MUQADDIM* (Chottin 1939:33).

MOSADDER

Var. of MUṢADDAR/1* (Farmer 1976a:195).

MOSTAK

Var. of MUSTAQ* (Ribera 1970:93).

MOTHRIB

Var. of MUṬRIB* (Kieswetter:94).

MOUACHCHAH

Var. of MUWASHSHAḤ* (Touma 1977b:78ff).

MOUATTAR

Var. of MUWATTAR* (Touma 1977b:15).

MOUCHAMMAS

Var. of MUKHAMMAS/1* (Touma 1977b:66).

MOUDAOUAR

Var. of MUDAWWAR* (Touma 1977b:67).

MOUFRAD

Var. of MUFRAD* (Rouanet 1922:2719).

MOUHASSABAH

Var. of MUḤASSABAH* (el Mahdi 1972:14).

MOUJANNAB

Var. of MUJANNAB* (Rouanet 1922:2714).

MOUKRELES

Var. of MAKHLAṢ* (Delphin and Guin 1886:65).

MOUL-EZ-ZAMR

Var. of MAWLĀ AL ZAMR* (Chottin 1939:33).

MOUNFAÇIL

Var. of MUNFAṢIL* (Rouanet 1922:2719).

MOUNTAD'IM

Var. of MUNTAẒIM*(Rouanet 1922:2719).

MOURABBA'

Var. of MURABBAʿ* (Touma 1977b:69).

MOUSSEMI

Var. of MUSAMMIʿ (Chottin 1939:147).

MOUSTADIR

Var. of MUSTADĪR* (Rouanet 1922:2726).

MOUTALÂÏM

Var. of MUTALĀ'IM* (Rouanet 1922:2705).

MOUTRIB

Var. of MUṬRIB* (Touma 1977b:82).

MOUTTAÇIL

Var. of MUTTAṢIL/1* (Rouanet 1922:2719).

MRÂRIA

Lullaby (Mor.) (Chottin 1939:170).

MŠAD

Var. of MASHADD* (d'Erlanger 1959:150, 195).

M'SADAR

Var. of MUṢADDAR* (el Mahdi 1972:20).

MṢADDAR

Var. of MUṢADDAR/3* (d'Erlanger 1959:146).

MSHELIA

Var. of MASHĀLIYAH* (Schuyler 1978:38).

MTHELLITH

Var. of MUTHALLATH or MUTHALLITH* (Chottin 1939:144-145).

MUACHCHAH'

Var. of MUWASHSHAḤ* (Chottin 1939:14, 90, 110).

MU'ADHDHIN ('-dh-n) "caller of the ADHĀN"

Caller to prayer, who chants the ADHĀN* from the minaret of the mosque before each of the five daily prayers of the Muslims.

MU'ALLAF (pl. MU'ALLAFĀT) ('-l-f) "composition"

A musical composition.

MUʿALLAQ (ʿ-l-q) "suspended"

1. Said of a tetrachordal scalar segment (JINS/1*) when the per-

former closes his phrases on the highest tone of that tetrachordal or pentachordal segment instead of on its tonic or QARĀR* (d'Erlanger 1949:108).
2. One of the six octave scales mentioned by ʿAbd al Qādir ibn Ghaybī (d. 1435) which were known collectively as the AṢĀBIʿ/1* or MAWĀJIB*. By the time of Ṣafī al Dīn, this categorization was already considered ancient (QĀDĪM) (Wright 1978:249-250). Others were MAZMŪM*, MUṬLAQ/2*, MUSARRAJ*, MAḤMŪL* and MUJANNAB/3*.

MU'ALLIF (pl. MU'ALLIFŪN) ('-l-f) "one who composes"

1. Generic term for author.
2. Author of text or lyrics, often in Egypt a poet specializing in colloquial Arabic poetry for use in music for records and public broadcasting (Racy 1978a:49).
3. Composer of music (al Khwarizmi 1968:236; Hickmann 1958:16).

MUʿALLIM (pl. MUʿALLIMŪN) = MAÁLEM, MAÂLEM (ʿ-l-m) "teacher"

1. Leader of the orchestra or ensemble (Rouanet 1922:2936).
2. Musical performer (Mor.) (Chottin 1939:115).

MUʿALLIM AL ĀLAH (ʿ-l-m) ('-w-l) "teacher of the instrument"

Leader of the orchestra or ensemble (Alg.) (Delphin and Guin 1886: 55).

MUʿALLIM AL AWWAL (ʿ-l-m) ('-w-l) "the first teacher"

Respectful title given to Aristotle by the music theorists of the Classical Period.

MUʿALLIM AL RUBĀʿAH (ʿ-l-m) (r-b-ʿ) "teacher of the quartet"

Leader of the orchestra or ensemble (Alg.) (Delphin and Guin 1886:55).

MUʿALLIM AL THĀNĪ (ʿ-l-m) (th-n-y) "the second teacher"

Name given by music theorists of the Classical Period to al Fārābī, as successor to Aristotle,"the first teacher" or the MUʿALLIM AL AWWAL*.

MUʿANNĀ = MʿANNA, MAʿANNĀ, 'EMʿANNĀ (ʿ-n-w) or (ʿ-n-y) "carefully prepared; much cared for"

A genre of folk song of Lebanon which follows closely the form of the QAṢĪDAH* with its uniformity of rhymes and unity of theme. It has many different forms, but is regularly a solo song in which the last part of the couplet line (BAYT/1*) is repeated as a refrain by a chorus or the audience. Its rhythm is a mixture of free recitative and regular recurrence of equal time values (Jargy 1970:40; 1978:87; Reichow 1971:40).

MUBSIṬ (pl. MUBSIṬŪN) (b-s-ṭ) "one who delights or amuses"

Traveling minstrel who performs in the open air or in the public square (Mor.) (Chottin 1939:163). MUBSITÎN is pl. form in Chottin.

MUBTADA' AL NAGHAM (b-d-') (n-gh-m) "beginning of the tones"

Starting tone, tonal center (al Kindī 1966:156).

MUDĀRĀT AL AWTĀR (d-w-r) (w-t-r) "guidance of the strings"

Tuning of the strings of a musical instrument (Ibn al Munajjim in Shawqī 1976:350).

MUDARRAJ MŪSĪQĪ (pl. MUDARRAJĀT MŪSĪQIYYAH) (d-r-j) (Gr.) "musically graded or classified"

The staff adopted from the West for musical notation by contemporary musicians and theorists (al Ḥafnī 1946:286; Maḥfūẓ 1964:186).

MUDAWWAR = MOUDAOUAR, MEDAWAR (d-w-r) "rounded"

Descriptive name used for several contemporary rhythmic modes which have a simple binary organization of constituent beats.

MUDAWWIN (pl. MUDAWWINŪN) (d-w-n) "recorder"

The transcriber of music (given as MUDAWIN in El-Shawan 1978). Syn. of MUNAWWIṬ*.

MUDDA

Var. of MADDAH* (Farmer EI(Fr), "Musiki":802).

MUDĪR AL JAWQ (d-w-r) (j-w-q) "director of the troupe"

Conductor; bandleader; choir leader (Wehr).

MUDJINAH (pl. MUDJINĀT) (d-j-n) "darkened"

Singing girl of pre-Islamic and early Islamic periods (Farmer EI (Eng), "Ghinā'":1073; 1967:11, n. 4; Ibn ʿAbd Rabbihi 1887:III, 186). Also DĀJINAH*, QAYNAH*.

MUḌLAʿ (ḍ-l-ʿ) "branched out"

A variety of INTIQĀL/1*, according to Ṣafī al Dīn, in which the melodic patterning involves returns to different starting tones (Rouanet 1922:2726, 2808; de Vaux 1891:342). See RĀJIʿ AL MUḌLIʿ* (supp.).

MUFAṢṢAL (f-ṣ-l) "divided, disjunct"

1. A disjunct rhythmic mode, i.e., one in which the time between the last percussion of a cycle and the beginning of the next one is greater than that between any two percussions of the cycle. It can have two percussions (MUFAṢṢAL AL AWWAL*), three percussions (MUFAṢṢAL AL THĀNĪ*), four percussions (MUFAṢṢAL AL THĀLITH*) or more (al Fārābī 1967:428, 999; 1930:31ff). Opp. of MUWAṢṢAL*.
2. Said of a tune (LAḤN*) containing partitions separated by silences (WAQFĀT, s. WAQFAH*) (al Fārābī 1967:1140; 1935:77).

MUFAṢṢAL AL AWWAL (f-ṣ-l) ('-w-l) "first disjunct"

Said of any disjunct (MUFAṢṢAL/1*) rhythmic mode which comprised two percussions per cycle or measure (al Fārābī 1967:458, 1001; 1935:32). See also MUFAṢṢAL AL THĀNĪ*, MUFAṢṢAL AL THĀLITH*.

MUFAṢṢAL AL BASĪṬ (f-ṣ-l) (b-s-ṭ) "simple disjunct"

Said of those disjunct (MUFAṢṢAL/1*) rhythmic modes generated from one conjunct rhythm, i.e., it had only one percussion length within the cycle, the last of which was followed by a rest or separating time unit known as FĀṢILAH/4* which closed the cycle (al Fārābī 1967:999ff; 1935:31ff). See MUFAṢṢAL AL MURAKKAB*.

MUFAṢṢAL AL MURAKKAB (f-ṣ-l) (r-k-b) "complex disjunct"

Said of those disjunct (MUFAṢṢAL/1*) rhythmic modes made out of percussions of two or more different lengths (al Fārābī 1967:1000ff; 1935:31ff). See MUFAṢṢAL AL BASĪṬ*.

MUFAṢṢAL AL THĀLITH (f-ṣ-l) (th-l-th) "third disjunct"

Said of any disjunct (MUFAṢṢAL/1*) rhythmic mode comprising four percussions per cycle or measure (al Fārābī 1967:474-477). See MUFAṢṢAL AL AWWAL*, MUFAṢṢAL AL THĀNĪ*.

MUFAṢṢAL AL THĀNĪ (f-ṣ-l) (th-n-y) "second disjunct"

Said of any disjunct (MUFAṢṢAL/1*) rhythmic mode comprising three percussions per cycle or measure (al Fārābī 1967:462-473). See MUFAṢṢAL AL AWWAL*, MUFAṢṢAL AL THĀLITH*.

MUFRAD = MOUFRAD (f-r-d) "single"

1. A term used to describe a line (BAYT/1*) of poetry or song that has only one segment (el Helou 1965:91). Opp. of MURAKKAB/6*.
2. Descriptive term for a wind instrument with a single pipe.
3. Said of a MUWASHSHAḤ/1* in which the opening musical segment (DAWR/6*) is a setting of only one poetic line or hemistich, the second line or hemistich being set to a repetition of that musical segment (el Helou 1965:91). See diagram in al Faruqi 1975:16.

MUFRADAH (f-r-d) f. of "single"

1. Any tetrachordal division (JINS/1*) which is used without combination with other tetrachordal divisions (al Fārābī 1967:153).
2. Said of a tone which has no octave equivalent in the notes achieved in the finger positions of the ʿŪD/2* (al Fārābī 1967:543). See also QUWWAH/1*.
3. Contemporary equivalent for sixteenth note (Allawerdi 1949:475).
4. Descriptive term for AJNĀS (s. JINS/1*) which are divided into more than the usual number of intervals (Ṣafī al Dīn in Rouanet 1922:2719-2720), e.g., a perfect fourth divided into four rather than three intervals, or a perfect fifth into four intervals.
5. Solo, unaccompanied.

MUFRADAN (f-r-d) "singly"

An adverbial term implying a meaning similar to MUFRAD* or MUFRADAH*.

MUǦANNAB

Var. of MUJANNAB* (d'Erlanger 1939:502-503, n. 12).

MUGHANNĀ (gh-n-y) "place of singing"

The special apartment behind a screen or curtain in which the musician performed. This apartment is mentioned in 1001 Nights (Farmer 1945:17)and was still found in 19th C. Egypt, according to Lane (1973:355).

MUGHANNĪ (pl. MUGHANNŪN) = MOGHANNI, MUGHANNIYY (gh-n-y) "male singer"

1. Male vocalist.
2. Musician (Farmer 1967:9-10).
3. A bowed lute invented by Ṣafī al Dīn ʿAbd al Mu'min, a music theorist of 13th C. Baghdād.

MUGHANNĪ MUFRAD (gh-n-y) (f-r-d) "male vocal soloist"

Male vocal soloist (Ḥāfiẓ 1971:111).

MUGHANNIYAH (pl. MUGHANNIYĀT) (gh-n-y) "female singer"

Female vocalist.

MUGHARRAD (gh-r-d) "twittering, singing (of birds)"

Singing.

MUGHARRID (pl. MUGHARRIDŪN) (gh-r-d) "singing bird"

Vocalist (Maḥfūẓ 1964:22).

MUGHNĪ or MŪGHNĪ = MOGHNI, MUGNĪ, MOĠNĪ (gh-n-y)

An obsolete chordophone said to have been invented by Ṣafī al Dīn ʿAbd al Mu'min (d. 1294) (d'Erlanger 1938:568, n. 1). In the Kanz al Tuḥaf of the 14th C. it was described as a combination of the RUBĀB* (a type of lute), QĀNŪN* (psaltery) and NUZHAH* (another type of psaltery). It had a large convex sound chest like the RUBĀB with a wide, flat neck, and strings arranged over a bridge as in the QĀNŪN (Farmer 1976b:43; 1978:I, 15). According to Sachs (1940: 258), its 39 strings were tuned in triplets. In the 15th C. Jāmiʿ al Alḥān fī ʿIlm al Mūsīqī of ʿAbd al Qādir ibn Ghaybī, it consisted of a soundboard with 24 strings, every second string giving the octave of the preceding one. In the 17th C. it was described as a form of QĀNŪN which had been invented in Magnesia.

MUGNĪ

Var. of MUGHNĪ or MŪGHNĪ* (Sachs 1940:258; Marcuse).

MUḤAJJAR (ḥ-j-r) "petrified"

Descriptive name applied to contemporary rhythmic modes which have a quick repetition of DUMM* strokes at the opening of the cycle.

MUḤĀSIBAH (ḥ-s-b) f. of "bookkeeper"

An instrumental musical segment used as response to the vocal line in the TAḤRĪR* or opening vocal portion of the MAQĀM AL ʿIRĀQĪ* (Tsuge 1972:63-64). In the Maghrib, a term with similar meaning is MUḤASSABAH*.

MUḤASSABAH = MOUHASSABAH, MOHASSABA (ḥ-s-b) "that which is calculated carefully and strongly"

The instrumental repetition of a vocal number or segment, when used as one item within the suite (NAWBAH/1*) of the Maghrib. In Tunisia it is also called RADD AL JAWĀB* (el Mahdi 1972:14, 19). See MUḤĀSIBAH*.

MUḤAYIR

Var. of MUḤAYYIR* (d'Erlanger 1939:47).

MUḤAYYIR = MUḤAYIR, MOUHAYYIR, MOHAYAR (ḥ-y-r) "perplexing, confusing"

A note of the contemporary Arabian scale, D_2  .
Also MAḤBAR*.

MUJENNAB

Var. of MUJANNAB/2* (Smith 1847:206).

MUJANNAB (pl. MUJANNABĀT) = MUǦANNAB, MUJENNAB (j-n-b) "adjoining; neighbor"

1. Name used in the Classical Period for intervals smaller than a major tone (204 c. or 9/8 ratio) and larger than the BAQIYYAH* (90 c. or 256/243). The larger version of this interval was called MUJANNAB AL KABĪR* (182 c.), the smaller, MUJANNAB AL ṢAGHĪR* (112 c.) (al Dāqūqī 1965:84). According to al Jurjānī (1938:238) and al Lādhiqī (1939:302), the former corresponded to the sum of two BAQIYYAH intervals (i.e., two Pythagorean limmas) or a minor tone with approximate ratio of 10/9 (182 c.). The latter was roughly equivalent to the sum of a Pythagorean limma and a comma, with an approximate ratio of 16/15 (112 c.) (d'Erlanger 1939:502-503, n. 12; Anonymous Treatise 1939:38). According to Collangettes (1904:42), it had a ratio of 12/11, one of the possible 3/4 tone ratios.
2. Any of the fret positions between the nut and the first finger fret which produced tones larger than the BAQIYYAH* and smaller than the whole tone. This term was thought to have been introduced by al Kindī to designate a fret producing an interval of 90 cents (the BAQIYYAH) above the open string of the three lowest pitched strings. On the upper two strings of the lute (ʿŪD*), the MUJANNAB fret produced tones too low for this interval, so al Kindī added another anterior fret, thereby producing the interval known as INFIṢĀL* (114 c.) (Farmer 1937a:248). This fret was

also known as ZĀ'ID/1* (al Khwārizmī 1968:238; Shawqī 1976:285). 3. One of the six octave scales mentioned by ʿAbd al Qādir ibn Ghaybī, and known collectively as the MAWĀJIB* or AṢĀBIʿ/1*. The use of this term for melodic mode goes back at least to the 10th C. By the time of Ṣafī al Dīn and ʿAbd al Qādir, it was virtually forgotten (Wright 1978:250). Others of the six were MAZMŪM*, MUSARRAJ*, MUʿALLAQ/2*, MAḤMŪL* AND MUṬLAQ/2*.

MUJANNAB AL KABĪR (j-n-b) (k-b-r) "large neighbor"

An interval of 182 c. and ratio of 10/9, i.e., the minor whole tone. See MUJANNAB/1*, "J"/2*.

MUJANNAB AL SABBĀBAH (j-n-b) (s-b-b) "neighbor of the index finger"

Syn. of MUJANNAB/2*. Al Fārābī designated four different MUJANNAB AL SABBĀBAH fret positions, those producing intervals with 18/17, 256/243, 54/49 and 162/149 ratios (al Fārābī 1967:512-514).

MUJANNAB AL ṢAGHĪR (j-n-b) (ṣ-gh-r) "small neighbor"

An interval of 112 c. and ratio of 16/15. See MUJANNAB/1*, "J"/2*.

MUJANNAB AL WUSṬĀ (j-n-b) (w-s-ṭ) "neighbor of the middle finger"

Classical Period lute fret or fret position producing a tone slightly lower than the WUSṬĀ* positions which yielded various kinds of thirds. The tone produced had a ratio of 32/27 (al Fārābī 1967: 126; Shawqī 1976:972-973). It was also known as WUSṬĀ AL QADĪM*.

MUJASSAD (j-s-d) "embodied"

A tone sounded (Maḥfūẓ 1964:187).

MUJAWWABAH (j-w-b) "answered"

Syn. of MUJAWWABAH ṢAWTIYYAH*.

MUJAWWABAH SAWTIYYAH (j-w-b) (s-w-t) "answered in sound"

Antiphony (Wahba 1968:68). Also MUJAWWABAH*.

MUJAWWAD (j-w-d) "improved; beautified"

Designation for an elaborate style of Qur'ānic cantillation. Opp. of MURATTAL* style.

MŪJIB (pl. MAWĀJIB) (w-j-b) "necessary thing"

According to Ṣafī al Dīn in de Vaux (1891:352), these were six principle finger exercises; in Wright's analysis, scales (1978:249).

MUKĀ' (m-k-w) "whistling"

Whistling, which was regarded as an unlawful form of SAMĀʿ/1* by Ibn Taymiyyah (1966:II, 299).

MUKHĀLIFAH (kh-l-f) "opposing, contradictory"

Said of the percussions of a disjunct (MUNFAṢIL/3*) rhythmic mode with three or more percussions per cycle, when the first two beats were of unequal length (Ibn Sīnā 1930:93). Opp. of MUTASĀWĪ or MUTASĀWIYAH*.

MUKHAMMAS (kh-m-s) "five-sided, quinaire"

1. Name for one of the rhythmic modes described by Ṣafī al Dīn (1938a:494; 1938b:169) and al Jurjānī (1938:494). It was notated somewhat differently in *Al Sharafiyyah* (♪. ♩ 𝅗𝅥) than in *Kitāb al Adwār* (𝅗𝅥. ♩ ♩ 𝅗𝅥. 𝅗𝅥.). Syn. of KHAFĪF AL THAQĪL*. The name has been given as descriptive title to various contemporary rhythmic modes, *e.g.*, MUKHAMMAS TURKĪ, MUKHAMMAS ʻARABĪ, etc.(d'Erlanger 1959:61, 88, 93, 119).
2. A strophic poem of five lines using colloquial rather than classical Arabic. Used in the Mashriq, this contemporary variety of the MAWWĀL/2* is frequently used as poetic base for a vocal setting of non-rhythmed, improvised variety. Earlier the MUKHAMMAS or MUKHAMMASAH was a classical poetic form derived from the QAṢĪDAH/2* but with internal rhymes in each line that divided it into five segments.

MUKHĀNITH (kh-n-th) "the always effeminate"

Male singer (Ibn Taymiyyah 1966:II, 301). See Haq 1944:115, n. 2. Syn. of MUKHANNATH*.

MUKHANNATH (pl. MUKHANNATHŪN) "effeminate person"

Any of a class of professional musicians of the early period of Islamic history who were known for their effeminacy. The first male professional of the period (ṬUWAYS*), as well as many other performers of his time and later, belonged to this class which existed at a low level of society, despite the interest in music shown by the upper classes and the court. Also MUKHĀNITH*.

MUKHASHKHASHĀT (pl. of MUKHASHKHASHAH) (onom.) "rattles"

Clappers used as a percussion instrument (Maḥfūẓ 1964:191).

MUKHĀWAYAH = MEKRAOUÏA (kh-w-y) "action of tuning"

Tuning of a musical instrument (Delphin and Guin 1886:61).

MUKHLÀṢ (kh-l-ṣ) "that which is brought to completion"

Syn. of MAKHLAṢ* (Farmer 1967:200).

MUKHTALIFAH (pl. MUKHTALIFĀT) (kh-l-f) "changing (ones)"

Said of any of the tones (NAGHAMĀT) of the ancient AṢĀBIʻ* scales which varied according to the MAJRĀ* or "course" chosen for that particular tetrachordal collection of tones (Ibn al Munajjim 1950:7), therefore, the different thirds above the open string. Opp. of

MU'TALIFAH*, or those notes which did not vary according to the MAJRĀ.

MULĀ'AMĀT AL ʻASHR (l-'-m) (ʻ-sh-r) "the ten concordances"

Syn. of KAMĀLĀT AL ʻASHR* (al Fārābī 1967:175-178).

MULĀ'AMĀT AL NAGHAM (l-'-m) (n-gh-m) "the fittingnesses of tones"

Consonant intervals, of which al Fārābī writes that there are six: the second (9/8), the perfect fourth (4/3), the perfect fifth (3/2) and the octave (2/1), the octave plus perfect fourth (8/3) and the octave plus fifth (3/1) (al Fārābī 1967:553-580).

MULAḤḤAN (l-ḥ-n) "tuned"

Set to music.

MULAḤḤIN = MOULAHHIN (l-ḥ-n) "he who sets to tune"

1. Composer.
2. One who sets poetry to music.
3. Singer.

MULĀ'IM = MULĀYAM (l-'-m) "harmonizing"

Consonant, a descriptive category for scales containing as many consonant intervals as notes, according to Ṣafī al Dīn. His other categories are MUTANĀFIR* (dissonant) and KHAFĪ AL TANĀFUR* (intermediate) (Wright 1978:97, 98, 288). See MULĀYAM*.

MULAKHKHAṢ (pl. MULAKHKHAṢĀT) (l-kh-ṣ) "that which is abridged, condensed"

Vocal number of the suite (NAWBAH/1*) based on a triple rhythm (Alg.). Each BAYT/1* or line has two or three hemistiches separated by a vocal improvisation (TARANNUM/1*) and an instrumental response (JAWĀB/2*). The MULAKHKHAṢ ends with a non-rhythmed sentence slowly performed (Ḥāfiẓ 1971:127).

MULAWWAN (l-w-n) "colored"

1. The chromatic JINS/1* or tetrachord (i.e., with minor third interval of 6/5 ratio included) according to most theorists of the Classical Period. Al Khwārizmī also called it KHUNTHAWĪ* (1968:243-244).
2. Ibn Sīnā used this term to designate the enharmonic JINS/1* (i.e., the tetrachord with a major third interval of 7/6 or 8/7 ratio) (Ibn Sīnā 1930:90-91; 1935:143ff).

MULĀYAM

Consonant, a term used by d'Erlanger (1939:375) in his translation of al Lādhiqī in order to describe some of the melodic modes of the time of that theorist (16th C.). The word as used must be a colloq. or var. of MULĀ'IM*.

MULĀZIMAH (l-z-m) "necessary"

Syn. of LĀZIMAH*, the instrumental punctuating phrase which marks the end of a musical segment (al Dāqūqī 1965:28).

MÛLÛ'

Amateur musician (Mor.) (Chottin 1939:102), probably a var. of MAWLŪʻ*.

MUNAFFIR (n-f-r) "one who plays the NAFĪR"

The performer on the NAFĪR*, BŪQ* or other instrument of the brass family (El-Kholy 1954:196).

MUNĀSABAH (n-s-b) "appropriateness; correlation"

Proportion or relation. Al Kindī (1965:17) uses this term in describing the correspondence between two tones an octave apart. He says they are equal in MUNĀSABAH (relation to each other) and TANGHĪM* (tune) though not in GHILẒ* (lowness of pitch) or DAQQAH* (highness of pitch).

MUNAWWIṬ (Eng.) "the notator"

Notator of music, being a musician who specializes in transcribing into Western notation items from both the contemporary and older repertoire. He works with the composer, with someone who remembers a former performance, or with a sound recording to produce notated examples for the use of instrumentalists and conductors in contemporary ensembles (MUNAWIT in El-Shawan 1978). Syn. of MUDAWWIN*.

MUNBAT (n-b-t) "cultivated"

According to Ṣafī al Dīn, a variety of INTIQĀL/1* with returns to notes near the point or tone of departure (Rouanet 1922:2726, 2808; de Vaux 1891:342).

MUNCHID

Var. of MUNSHID/2* (Chottin 1939:132).

MUNFARID (f-r-d) "operating or existing singly"

Solo (adj.).

MUNFAṢIL or MUNFAṢILAH = MOUNFAÇIL (f-ṣ-l) "disjunct"

1. A term used by the Ikhwān al Ṣafā' for all musical sounds which are separated by a perceptible silence (Ikhwān al Ṣafā' 1964/65:194; Shiloah 1964/65:140; Farmer EI(Fr), "Rabāb":160); i.e., non-legato.
2. Said of one type of QAWĪ* ("strong") tetrachordal division in which the larger two intervals have ratios which do not increase or decrease consecutively (al Fārābī 1967:304ff), QAWĪ DHŪ AL TAḌʻĪF*.
3. Descriptive term for a rhythmic mode which has percussions of different lengths (Ibn Sīnā 1930:92). Syn. of MUFAṢṢAL/1*,

MUTAFĀḌILAH*, MUKHĀLIFAH*. Opp. of MUTASĀWĪ/1* or MUTTAṢIL/4*. Ibn Sīnā provides two sub-categories for the MUNFAṢIL rhythmic modes:

1) ASRAʿ/2*, if the shorter percussion comes initially;
2) ABṬA'/2*, if the shorter comes after the longer (al Ḥafnī 1930:38).

4. A term used to describe a combination of tetrachords to form a modal scale in which there is no common tone between any two tetrachords (Al Ḥalqah 1964:17; al Kindī 1966:15).

MŪNIS (ʾ-n-s?) perhaps from MU'NIS "entertainer"

Unidentified musical instrument mentioned in a 13th C. treatise from Moorish Spain (Farmer 1926a:247; 1978:I, 11).

MUNSHED

Var. of MUNSHID/5*.

MUNSHID (pl. MUNSHIDŪN = MUNCHID, MUNSHED (n-sh-d) "one who declames or chants"

1. Singer.
2. One who sings poetry.
3. One who sings praises of the Prophet Muḥammad.
4. Chorister.
5. Singer of hymns in the Ṣūfī DHIKR* ceremony. He directs the musical elements of the DHIKR, while the SHAYKH/4* or religious leader attends to the spiritual elements (Poche 1978:65-66).

MUNTAẒIM = MOUNTAD'IM (n-ẓ-m) "ordered"

One of the sub-categories of LAYYIN* ("soft") tetrachordal divisions (AJNĀS, s. JINS/1*). It has its large interval at one extremity (al Fārābī 1967:380ff; Ṣafī al Dīn in de Vaux 1891:309).

MUNŪLŪJ (Eng.) "monologue"

As the name indicates, this is a genre of vocal music adopted from the West, first in Egypt and later in Palestine, Lebanon, Syria and ʿIrāq. Originally it was a vocal solo using a combination of music and words to express a state or feeling, or to describe something or someone. The music was meant to enhance the programmatic content of the words, and it was often used in connection with translations of Western dramatic productions. More recently it has gone through a process of orientalization, of Arabization, which made so many changes in its character that it has become difficult to describe it accurately or simply. Realizing this, many musicians have renamed it LAḤN AL ḤURR*, i.e., "free tune" (el Helou 1961:187-188; Ḥāfiẓ 1971:207).

MUQADDAM

Var. of MUQADDIM* (Jones 1977:44, 51).

MUQADDAM ES-ṢAFF

Var. of MUQADDIM AL ṢAFF* (Jones 1977:44).

MUQADDIM (pl. MUQADDIMŪN) = MOQADDEM, MUQADDAM (q-d-m) "introducer, initiator"

The leader of a troup of ambulant professional musicians (Chottin 1939:33; Jones 1977:44). Among the ʿĪsāwiyyah musicians of Tunisia, this role is usually assumed by a vocalist. Also SHAYKH/1*.

MUQADDIM AL ṢAFF = MUQADDAM ES-ṢAFF (q-d-m) (ṣ-f-f) "leader of the line"

Leader of the dancers (Tun.).

MUQADDIMAH (q-d-m) "introduction"

Instrumental musical introduction with an underlying meter.

MUQADDIMAH AL DŪLĀBĪ (q-d-m) (d-l-b) "wheel introduction"

A short orchestral prelude of well defined rhythm, sometimes used to open a MAQĀM AL ʿIRĀQĪ* performance (Tsuge 1972:63).

MUQĀRIʿ (pl. of MIQRAʿAH) (q-r-ʿ) "instruments for knocking"

Clappers, long pieces of wood or metal that are beaten together as a percussion instrument (Maḥfūẓ 1964:191).

MUQARRAN DUNBALAYĪ (q-r-n) (Turk.) "paired kettledrum"

The paired kettledrums which were played in the processions of 17th C. Istanbul. It was said to have always been played by performers from Makkah (Farmer 1976b:17).

MUQAWWĪ (q-w-y) "strengthener"

Designation for any tetrachordal scalar segment (JINS/1*) in which no interval is larger than the sum of the other two. It includes diatonic tetrachords and those with 3/4 tones. It is described by al Khwārizmī (1968:243) as masculine.

MUQAWWIL (q-w-l) "intensive speaker"

Woodwind player (Madina).

MUQRI' (q-r-') "reader"

Syn. of QĀRI'*, or Qur'ān reader. It can also mean only that reader of the Qur'ān who has memorized the whole work and is a master chanter of the holy scripture (Ibn Khaldūn 1967:II, 388).

MURABBAʿ = MARĀBBA, MURĀBIʿ, MOURABBA', 'EMRABBAʿ, MERABA' (r-b-ʿ) "four-sided"

1. Square tambourine.
2. A small bowed chordophone of the Arabs, mentioned by an 18th C. writer. Its rectangular body which gave it its name had a skin belly and back and a single horsehair string. Marcuse writes that it is obsolete. It is true that the name is no longer current, but

there is a similar viol used today as a folk instrument under various other names, e.g., RABĀB AL SHĀ'IR*, RABĀB or RABĀBAH/3*.
3. According to Farmer, a pre-Islamic flat-chested quadrangular guitar or plucked lute, also known as QĪTHĀRAH* (Farmer 1926a:246; 1967:16; 1978:I, 10). See Def. 2 above.
4. A MAWWĀL* poem with four lines which is set to music of a folkish variety in non-metered, improvised style. This is a popular poetic form in ʿIrāq (Jargy 1970:45; Shiloah 1974:55).
5. A refrain-like repetition of the last hemistich of an initial couplet of the QAṢĪDAH/2* (Alg.), given as MURĀBIʿ* and MERABA'* in Delphin and Guin (1886:36).

MURĀBIʿ

Probably a variant of MURABBAʿ/5* (Delphin and Guin 1886:36).

MURADDAD (r-d-d) "that which is repeated"

Syn. of LĀZIMAH*, the repeated instrumental interjections between segments of a musical composition or improvisation.

MURADDID (pl. MURADDIDŪN) (r-d-d) "one who repeats"

Chorister or secondary singer in a contemporary ensemble. These singers form a group to reply musically to the soloist.

MURAJJIʿ (r-j-ʿ) "that which causes something to return"

The da capo sign borrowed from Western notation (Maḥfūẓ 1964:187).

MURAJJAḤAH (r-j-ḥ) "favored one"

A way of beautifying a melody which involved the widening of the mouth opening for the breath to be emitted, and giving chest emphasis to the tones (al Fārābī 1967:1172; 1935:90).

MURAKKAB or MURAKKABAH (pl. MURAKKABĀT) (r-k-b) "constructed"

1. Said of a melodic mode in which more than one variety of tetrachordal segment (JINS/1*) is used (Ṣafī al Dīn 1938a:387; al Jurjānī 1938:387). It is therefore often described as a derivative rather than a principal mode. In the modern period, the "combinations" of different tetrachords are described as involving 1) the use of different AJNĀS in the different registers (ṬABAQĀT, s. ṬABAQAH/2*) of the modal scale; 2) the alteration of one or more tones within a JINS to create a modulation to another mode beginning from the same tonic; or 3) moving the tonic of the JINS lower or higher without altering the interval relationships (d'Erlanger 1949:101-104). D'Erlanger uses the term "composées" for translation of this Arabic term. Although no Arabic equivalent for this term is available in the d'Erlanger passage, it seems highly probable that MURAKKAB or MURAKKABAH is the Arabic original. In other instances in the same work (La Musique arabe), that Arabic term has been similarly rendered in French. Ṣafī al Dīn and his followers contrasted the MURAKKAB modes to the twelve SHUDŪD (s. SHADD/2*) and the six ĀWĀZĀT (s. ĀWĀZ/2*) modes (Ṣafī al Dīn 1938a:376-392; al Jurjānī 1938:376-392;

see also Wright 1978:90-91). In the Durrah al Tāj ms., its author, Quṭb al Dīn al Shīrāzī (d. 1311), also uses the term TARKĪB/3* for this category of mode (Wright 1978:283, 290) and criticizes his predecessor's looseness in identifying modes of this grouping (Ibid.:168, 170-172).

2. Said of a contemporary melodic mode (MAQĀM/1*) which is regularly used with transpositions to other melodic modes. If the transpositions are consistent enough, the tendency is to think of the MAQĀMĀT combination as constituting a new derived mode or "constructed" mode (al Dāqūqī 1965:33). Such a mode can also be identified as one of TARKĪB/3* (Ibid.).

3. This term is used to describe graces comprising multiple tones rather than a single tone (BASĪṬ or BASĪṬAH/8*) preceding a longer main tone (al Faruqi 1978:24).

4. A sub-category of INTIQĀL/1* or melodic patterning as described by Ibn Sīnā. It included all those types of melodic movement which involved alternating ascending and descending progression (Ibn Sīnā 1930:95; 1935:162ff). MURAKKAB INTIQĀL can include two or more patterns which resemble each other (i.e., are MUTASHĀBIHAH/3*), or others which do not resemble each other (GHAYR MUTASHĀBIHAH*). The resemblance or not may be one of a) movement (i.e., KAYF*); b) the number of notes (KAMM*); and/or c) the ratios of their intervals (NISBAH*).

5. A variety of INSHĀD/2* in which the vocal soloist introduces each new tune, followed by a choral repetition and ending with a return to a TASLĪM/2* section or repeated phrase which acts as a coda (Ḥāfiẓ 1971:199).

6. A line of poetry or song having more than one internal division or segment (el Helou 1965:91). Opp. of MUFRAD/1*.

7. Designation for any MUWASHSHAḤ/1* in which the opening musical section (DAWR/6*) is a setting of more than one poetic segment or BAYT/1*, the second BAYT set to a musical repetition of that used for the first BAYT. Opp. of MUFRAD/1* (al Faruqi 1975:16).

8. A disjunct rhythmic cycle (al Fārābī 1967:1005; 1935:33). When it was composed of two percussions of different length and a FĀṢILAH/4* or time unit separating the last percussion of one cycle from the first percussion of the next, it was called MURAKKAB AL AWWAL*. Other types (MURAKKAB AL THĀNĪ, MURAKKAB AL THĀLITH, etc.) could be formed by increasing the number of percussions to three, four, etc. (al Fārābī 1967:1007; 1935:34).

MURAKKAB AL AWWAL (r-k-b) ('-w-l) "first composed"

See MURAKKAB or MURAKKABAH/8* (al Fārābī 1967:1007).

MURAKKAB AL THĀNĪ (r-k-b) (th-n-y) "second composed"

See MURAKKAB or MURAKKABAH/8* (al Fārābī 1967:1007).

MURAṢṢAʻ (r-ṣ-ʻ) "set, studded, decorated"

1. A genre of composition described by ʻAbd al Qādir ibn Ghaybī which utilized in a single performance Arabic, Persian, as well as Turkish poetry or prose. Performers were permitted many licenses in the performance of this genre which would have been forbidden in others. It was also known as FAṢL/2* (Anonymous Treatise 1939: 246-247). Farmer described it as a fantasy-like genre (1957:452).

2. The interval between ʿIRĀQ* (B𝄳$_1$) and KAWASHT (B$_1$ or Cb$_1$) (Kāẓim 1964:90). The author probably means any quarter tone interval.

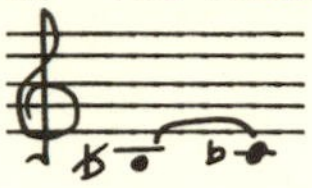

MURATTIL (r-t-l) "singer; reciter; chanter"

1. Reciter of religious music or scriptural chant.
2. A singer.

MURATTAL (r-t-l) "cantillated"

Designation for a simple style of Qur'ānic reading or cantillation. Opp. of MUJAWWAD* style.

MURSAL (r-s-l) "sent out"

1. A contemporary descriptive word for unmetered or free rhythmed music. See also NATHR AL NAGHAMĀT* and al Fāruqi 1974:Chap. II.
2. A variety of performance for the RAMAL* rhythmic cycle which is described in an anonymous treatise of the 15th C. In this performance, only the ḌARB AL AṢL* or fundamental two percussions of the 12-beat cycle were executed (Anonymous Treatise 1939:200).

MURTAJAL (r-j-l) "extemporized"

1. Improvised (Ibn ʿAbd Rabbihi 1887:III, 129, 187).
2. Unaccompanied (Maḥfūẓ 1964:21).

MURŪNAH (m-r-n) "flexibility"

Medium loud, comparable to Mezzo forte (al Ḥafnī 1946:287).

MUSABBAʿ (s-b-ʿ) "seven-ed"

1. One variety of that vocal, free rhythmed, improvised music known as MAWWĀL/1*. It is a richly ornamented setting of a colloquial language poem of the same name. It is popular in ʿIrāq. See MUSABBAʿ AL ZAHRĪ*.
2. A variety of MAWWĀL/2* poetry having seven hemistiches. The lines are grouped in two 3-line segments, each of which has its own rhyme. The seventh line completes the meaning of the first line and rhymes with it.

MUSABBAʿ AL ZAHRĪ (s-b-ʿ) (z-h-r) "radiant seven-ed"

A species of MAWWĀL/1* sung in ʿIrāq (Farmer 1954, "Iraqian and Mesopotamian Music":532).

MUṢADDAR (pl. MUṢADDARĀT) = MECDER, MṢADDAR, MOSADDER, M'SADAR, M'SADDAR (ṣ-d-r) "put at the beginning"

1. A movement of the NAWBAH/1* which opens with a short orchestral overture based on a rhythm of the same name (Def. 3). It follows directly after the prelude of the suite in Tunisia. The opening

refrain-like segment is followed by a slow and solemn vocal recitative sung to a line or strophe of poetry. The orchestral refrain is repeated after each of a series of vocal solos. The MUṢADDAR usually starts with a slow triple rhythm, and is gradually accelerated in order to end with a 3/8 cycle. Two codas are included. The first, called ṬAWQ/1*, ḌURŪB/2* or ḤURŪB*, has a 3/4 or 6/8 rhythmic cycle; the second, called SILSILAH/1*, has a 3/8 rhythm (Touma 1977b:78; d'Erlanger 1959:192; el Mahdi 1972:14), and brings the piece to a piercing and violent finale. According to Rouanet (1922:2852-2854), this is considered the most noble movement of the NAWBAH.

2. Usually in its pl. form, designates the series of MUWASHSHAḤ/1*-type vocal numbers done to a duple rhythm of the same name (MUṢADDAR/4*) as part of the Algerian suite (NAWBAH/1*). It often has an instrumental prelude known as KURSĪ* and refrain-like, rapidly executed instrumental interludes (d'Erlanger 1959:190; el Mahdi 1972:12). See MAṢDAR*.

3. The 6/4 or 12/8 rhythmic mode used for the MUṢADDAR/1* movement of the Tunisian NAWBAH/1*, one version of which follows:

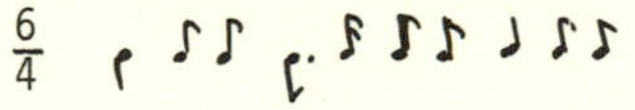

(d'Erlanger 1959:146).

4. The 8/8 rhythmic mode of Algerian practice, which is used in the vocal-instrumental movement of the same name (See def. 2). One version of its rhythmic cycle follows:

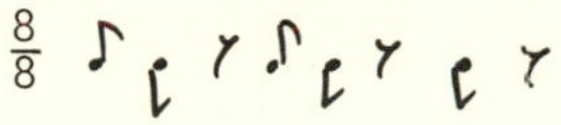

(el Helou 1961:160).

MUṢADDIḤ (pl. MUṢADDIḤŪN) (ṣ-d-ḥ) "singer, instrumentalist"

1. Singer.
2. Musician.
3. Instrumentalist.

MUṢAFFAḤĀT (ṣ-f-ḥ) "those which are shaped into thin plates"

Pl. of MUṢAFFAḤ and defined as clackers used by professional female mourners (Farmer EI(Fr),"Ṣandj":210).

MUṢĀFIQ (pl. of MIṢFAQAH) (ṣ-f-q) "instruments of clapping"

Small, metal cymbals, a designation used for castanets in the early centuries of the Islamic Period (Farmer 1978:II, 28-29; EI(Fr), "Ṣandj":210).

MUṢĀḤABAH (ṣ-ḥ-b) "that which accompanies"

Musical accompaniment (Wahba 1968:68).

MUṢĀḤIB (pl. MUṢĀḤIBŪN) (ṣ-ḥ-b) "accompanying person"

Musical accompanist of a soloist (Wahba 1968:68).

MUṢAKKA (ṣ-k-k) from ṢAKKA, "to beat or strike"

To hump or beat, as a drum, according to Farmer (1943/44:275, n. 7). The ending of the word is indeed a verbal ending, but the opening syllable suggests an adjectival or nominal form. There seems to have been some distortion of the word between its original spelling and its ultimate form in this article.

MUSĀMARAH = MESAMER (s-m-r) "evening conversation or entertainment"

A women's song mentioned by a 19th C. traveler to the Arabian Peninsula (Burckhardt 1967:82-83; 253). Such songs were sung only on happy occasions by two choruses of 6, 8 or 10 women. These antiphonal repetitions were sung in praise of valor and generosity, using either a slow or quick tempo, depending on the wishes of the singers. The first line of the song was repeated 5 or 6 times by the leading chorus and then repeated by the other group of vocalists. Each line was treated successively in the same manner. See ASĀMAR*.

MUSAMMAṬ (s-m-ṭ) "strung like pearls in a necklace"

Any Arabic poetry with strophes and a multiple rhyme scheme (e.g., MUWASHSHAḤ/2*, ZAJAL/2*) rather than a single rhyme as in the traditional QAṢĪDAH/2*. It is often a genre of strophic poetry with a refrain line or lines. Strophes are from 3-10 lines in length. Therefore there are eight types of TASMĪṬ* or MUSAMMAṬ, depending on the number of lines in each strophe (e.g., MUTHALLATH/3* or "three-lined," MURABBAʿ/4* or "four-lined," etc.) (Weil 1913:474). Syn. of TASMĪṬ*.

MUSAMMIʿ (pl. MUSAMMIʿŪN) = MOUSSEMI (s-m-ʿ) "those who make or let hear"

1. A chanter of religious music (Chottin 1939:134).
2. A vocal soloist of the RUBĀʿĪ* ensemble (Mor.) (Chottin 1939:147).

MUṢANNAJ (ṣ-n-j)

Syn. of ṢANJ/2* (Ibn Khurdādhbih 1951:95).

MUṢARRAF (pl. MUṢARRAFĀT) = MUSSARRAF, MESARAF (ṣ-r-f) "that which has been drained or expedited"

Gradual accelerando near the end of a movement of the Maghribī NAWBAH/1*, in preparation for the entry of a faster piece (el Mahdi 1972:12; Jargy 1971:95). Also INṢIRĀF/2*. See MĪZĀN MUṢARRAF*.

MUSARRAJ (s-r-j) "saddled"

One of the six octave scales mentioned by ʿAbd al Qādir ibn Ghaybī (d. 1435) which were known collectively as the AṢĀBIʿ/1* or MAWĀJIB*. By the time of Ṣafī al Dīn (d. 1294), however, this categorization was already considered ancient (QADĪM) (Wright 1978:249-250). The other scales (or modes?) were MUṬLAQ/2*, MUʿALLAQ/2*, MAḤMŪL*, MUJANNAB/3* and MAZMŪM*.

MUSĀWIYAH (pl. MUSĀWIYĀT) (s-w-y) "equalization"

Tuning of a musical instrument (Chottin 1939:144-145).

MUSĀYARAH (s-y-r) "that which adapts and adjusts; adjustment"

Musical accompaniment (Maḥfūẓ 1964:187).

MUSHABBIB (pl. MUSHABBIBŪN) (sh-b-b) "the one who plays the SHABBĀBAH*"

1. Generic for any woodwind instrument performer (Maḥfūẓ 1964:21).
2. A performer on the SHABBĀBAH* or NĀY* (Maḥfūẓ 1964:21).

MUSHAJJIʿ (sh-j-ʿ) "that which incites to bravery"

A type of music which was used in war time and on occasions of great excitement (Ikhwān al Ṣafā' 1957:I, 187).

MUSHṬ (pl. MISHĀṬ, AMSHĀṬ) = MOCHT, MISHṬ (m-sh-ṭ) "comb"

1. The piece of wood attached to the sounding board of a stringed instrument, to which the lower end of the string or strings are attached. It marks the lower end of the vibrating portion of the string or strings (al Fārābī 1967:484; al Masʿūdī 1887:VIII, 99; Ikhwān al Ṣafā' 1957:I, 203; Ṣafī al Dīn 1938a:223; al Jurjānī 1939:222; Anonymous Treatise 1939:27).
2. Bridge of a musical instrument (Wehr; Madina).

MUSHTAQ ṢĪNĪ "Chinese MUSTAQ"

Syn. of MUSTAQ ṢĪNĪ* (Ibn Salamah 1938a:15, n. 4; 1951:86).

MUSIKAR and MUSIKER

Vars. of MŪSĪQĀR* (Kieswetter 1968:94).

MŪSĪQĀ or MŪSĪQĪ (Gr.) "music"

1. General term for music, which was borrowed from the Gr. at least as early as ISḤAQ AL MAWṢILĪ* (d. 850). Al Khwārizmī (d. ca. 976-977) defined the term as one of the four mathematical sciences as well as "the composition of melodies (ALḤĀN) and songs (GHINĀ'* (1968:236). See Roy Choudhury n.d.:54, n. 2, 94.
2. The theory of music as distinguished from the practical art (Farmer 1929a:244, n. 14). Whereas before the 9th C., the Ar. word GHINĀ'* had often been used for both "song" and "music" in general, the former was now more frequently applied to the practical art and MŪSĪQĀ became associated closely with the theory of music (Farmer 1967:152).
3. The music of the ancient Greeks, as distinguished from that of the Arabs (GHINĀ'*) in the 9th C.
4. Melodies (al Fārābī 1967:47; al Jurjānī 1938:190; Ikhwān al Ṣafā' 1957:I, 188).
5. A complex organ, usually known as URGHAN or URGHANŪM*, which was mentioned in a 15th C. anonymous treatise (Farmer 1965b:62; 1954, "Egyptian Music":894).

MŪSĪQĀ ĀLIYYAH (Gr.) ('-w-l) "instrumental music"

Instrumental music.

MŪSĪQĀ ʿAMALIYYAH (Gr.) (ʿ-m-l) "music of practice"

Practical art of music, in contrast to its theory (al Fārābī 1967: 49; al Fārābī in Farmer 1960:10, 14).

MŪSĪQĀ ANDALUSIYYAH (Gr.) (geog.) "Andalusian music"

Art music of the Maghrib (el Helou 1965:9).

MŪSĪQĀ BIDŪN GHINĀ' (Gr.) (gh-n-y) "music without song"

Instrumental music (Chabrier 1978:94).

MŪSĪQĀ FĀRISIYYAH (Gr.) (nat.) "Persian music"

Oriental music, syn. of MŪSĪQĀ SHARQIYYAH* in the terminology of Aḥmad Amīn al Dīk, a 20th C. Egyptian theorist (Shawqī 1969a:37). For most authors it carries its literal meaning, "Persian music."

MŪSĪQĀ GHINĀ'IYYAH (Gr.) (gh-n-y) "vocal music"

Vocal music.

MŪSĪQĀ NAẒARIYYAH (Gr.) (n-ẓ-r) "theoretical music"

The theory of music (al Fārābī 1967:50; al Fārābī in Farmer 1960: 10, 14).

MŪSĪQĀ SHARQIYYAH (Gr.) (sh-r-q) "eastern music"

Music of the Arab and Muslim peoples (Shawqī 1969a:37).

MŪSĪQĀ TAṢWĪRIYYAH (Gr.) (ṣ-w-r) "portrayal music"

Descriptive music, e.g., film music (Racy 1978a:53).

MŪSĪQĀL (Gr.)

Name for panpipes in the Classical Period. This instrument corresponded to the SHUʿAYBIYYAH* of contemporary Egypt (Marcuse). Also MŪSĪQĀR/4* (Sachs 1940:247-248), MITHQĀL* (Farmer 1976b:22).

MŪSĪQĀR = MŪSĪQŪR, MUSIKER, MUSIKAR (Gr.) "musician"

1. Musician (Maḥfūẓ 1964:188), both composer and performer (al Khwārizmī 1968:236).
2. Vocalist (Maʿlūf).
3. Virtuoso in musical performance (Maḥfūẓ 1964:188). See Ikhwān al Ṣafā' (1957:I, 188, 233), where a case could be made for defining MŪSĪQĀR as both "musician" and "vocalist" (see def. 1 and def. 2 above).
4. Syn. of MŪSĪQĀL* (Sachs 1940:247).

MŪSĪQĀR-I-KHATAY "MŪSĪQĀR of Cathay"

Panpipes of Cathay (Farmer EI(Eng.), "Mizmār":541).

MŪSĪQĀT (Gr.)

Any musical instrument (Ikhwān al Ṣafā' 1957:I, 188; 1964/65:133; Farmer 1929a:66; see also Shiloah 1968a:231). The passage in the Risālah of the Ikhwān seems even to include the human vocal "instrument," for it defines the term as "ĀLAH AL GHINĀ'" and then proceeds to define GHINĀ' as all musical sound (see GHINĀ'/1*). The term is used as a singular form by the Ikhwān, despite the plural appearance of its ending. As a result of this ending syllable, Shiloah and Farmer have translated it as plural, i.e., "instruments of music" (Shiloah 1964/65:133; Farmer 1929a:66), without any indication of its being designated as "ĀLAH" in the text.

MŪSĪQŪR (Gr.)

Syn. of MŪSĪQĀR/1* (al Khwārizmī 1968:236).

MUSNAJ

An unidentified musical instrument of the Persians mentioned in one edition of the passage on music in al Mas'ūdī (1951:95). In the de Meynard edition, the word SINJ* is found instead; and in Ibn Khurdādhbih (1969:16), we find MUSTAJ*. The instrument is said to be played with the ṢANJ or ṢINJ*.

MUSSA'

Var. of MUWASSA'* (Chottin 1939:12).

MUSSARRAF

Var. of MUṢARRAF* (el Mahdi 1972:12).

MUSTADĪR (d-w-r) "rounded, circular"

According to Ṣafī al Dīn (13th C.), a variety of melodic movement (INTIQĀL/1*) which involved repeated returns to a particular tone (Rouanet 1922:2726, 2808; de Vaux 1891:342).

MUSTADĪRAH (pl. MUSTADĪRĀT) (d-w-r) "rounded, circular"

Name for the whole note in contemporary notation (el Helou 1961:20).

MUSTAFIQ

Term used to identify the character of any strong (QAWĪ*) or diatonic 4- or 5-tone scalar segment (JINS/1*). The name, we are told, pertains to the "consonant" distance between its end notes, which make the perfect fourth or perfect fifth (Ibn Abī al Ṣalt 1952:34). The Avenary translation, strangely enough, includes the following statement: "mustafiq (which is 'entangled' [sic] in Arabic) applies to the [relatively wide] distance between its end [notes]" (Avenary 1952:34).

MUSTAJ

An unidentified musical instrument of the Persians mentioned by Ibn Khurdādhbih (1969:16) and described as one which was played with the ṢANJ*. See MUSNAJ*.

MUSTAKHBIR (pl. MUSTAKHBIRŪN) = MESTEKBER (kh-b-r) "that which seeks information"

1. A short, free rhythmed instrumental prelude of the Algerian suite (NAWBAH/1*). It makes the initial exposure of the melodic mode to be used in the suite. This overture played in unison is considered one of the most important segments of the NAWBAH (Ḥāfiẓ 1971:122). Syn. of MUSTAKHBIR AL ṢANʿAH*, ISTIKHBĀR*.
2. Syn. of MUSTAKHBIR AL INQILĀBĀT*, that is, a vocal prelude of free rhythmed style which has very elaborate embellishments to show off the voice, as well as to display the singer's technique and artistry. Each series of songs (INQILĀBĀT, s. INQILĀB*) in the NAWBAH INQILĀBĀT*, a variety of semi-classical suite of the Maghribī musical tradition, is introduced by this vocal solo which establishes the new mode to be used in that group. See MUSTAKHBIR AL ṢANʿAH*.

MUSTAKHBIR AL INQILĀBĀT = MUSTAKHBIR NEQLABĀT (kh-b-r) (q-l-b) "that which seeks information about the INQILĀBĀT"

A vocal prelude for soloist which establishes the chosen mode of the series of songs (INQILĀBĀT, s. INQILĀB*) to follow. Each series included in the suite (NAWBAH INQILĀBĀT*), a semi-classical performance of the Maghrib, is governed by one particular melodic mode (Rouanet 1922:2847, 2863-2864). Syn. of MUSTAKHBIR/2*. See also MUSTAKHBIR AL ṢANʿAH*, an instrumental counterpart.

MUSTAKHBIR NEQLABĀT

Var. of MUSTAKHBIR AL INQILĀBĀT* (Rouanet 1922:2847).

MUSTAKHBIR AL ṢANʿAH = MESTEKBER SENÂA (kh-b-r) (ṣ-n-ʿ) "that which seeks information about the art or craft"

One of the two kinds of much appreciated introductory numbers used in the suites of the Maghrib. See also MUSTAKHBIR AL INQILĀBĀT*. This overture played in unison by the ensemble establishes the melodic mode to be used in the numbers of the classical suite (NAWBAH/1*) to follow. It is more traditional in style and bound by rules than the MUSTAKHBIR AL INQILĀBĀT. Syn. of MUSTAKHBIR/1* (Rouanet 1922:2847, 2863-2864).

MUSTAMIʿŪN (pl. of MUSTAMIʿ) (s-m-ʿ) "listeners"

The audience.

MUSTAQ

Panpipes, a musical instrument of the Chinese made from many reed pipes and carrying the Persian name of BĪSHAH MUSHTAH* (al Khwārizmī 1968:237). It was introduced into Persia in the Sasanian period (6th C. of the Christian Era) (Robson 1938a:15, n. 4).

MUSTAQ ṢĪNĪ = MUSHTAQ ṢĪNĪ "Chinese MUSTAQ"

Syn. of MUSTAQ*.

MUSTAQA

In a 14th C. dictionary, defined as an implement for beating or plucking, therefore, a stringed instrument such as the harp, dulcimer or psaltery (Farmer 1978:II, 10, n. 4).

MUSTAQĪM (q-w-m) "direct; straight"

According to Ṣafī al Dīn, a variety of melodic patterning (INTIQĀL/1*) involving movement in one direction only (Rouanet 1922:2726, 2808; de Vaux 1891:342).

MUSTAQIRR (q-r-r) "established, stable"

Contemporary term for the tonic note (el Helou 1961:78).

MUSTAZĀD (z-y-d) "supplement"

A fifth movement of the NAWBAH/1* or suite, which was introduced by ʿAbd al Qādir ibn Ghaybī in 1379. It was a movement containing the melodic motives and the poetic verses of the other four movements (Anonymous Treatise 1939:237).

MUTABĀYINAH (b-y-n) "differing, varying"

Term used by al Fārābī to describe two strings of the ṬUNBŪR/1* when they are tuned to achieve no notes in common. In practice, several notes were generally common to both strings (al Fārābī 1967:638). See MUTAWĀLIYAH*.

MUṬABBIL (t-b-l) "drummer"

Drummer.

MUTADĀKHIL (d-kh-l) "overlapping; interpenetrating"

Term used by contemporary theorists to describe the combination (JAMʿ/1*) of two tetrachordal AJNĀS (s. JINS/1*) which have two or more tones in common (Al Ḥalqah 1964:17).

MUʿTADIL (ʿ-d-l) "evenly balanced"

One of the three kinds or moods of a musical composition (al Kindī in Farmer 1926b:16). See also QABḌĪ* and BASṬĪ*. Cowl uses instead KARAM* in his translation (1966:137) though the Ar. passage has MUʿTADIL (Ibid.:166).

MUTADIQQ (d-q-q) "that which is made thin"

The neck of a stringed instrument (al Fārābī 1930:166; Farmer 1978:II, 65).

MUTAFAḌḌIL (f-ḍ-l) "benefactor"

Syn. of MUTAFĀḌIL or MUTAFĀḌILAH*. Farmer gives MUTAFAḌḌIL (instead of MUTAFĀḌIL) as having been used by al Fārābī (Farmer 1965:xix), but we have found no evidence for this in Kitāb al Mūsīqā al Kabīr (al Fārābī 1967).

MUTAFĀḌIL or MUTAFĀḌILAH (f-ḍ-l) "excelling"

Descriptive term used for the percussions or time units (AZMINAH, s. ZAMĀN/2*) of a disjunct (MUNFAṢIL/3*) rhythmic mode with first two percussions of unequal length (al Fārābī 1967:449, 462; 1930:154). See also de Vaux 1891:347.

MUTAFĀḌILAH AL MUWAṢṢALAH (f-ḍ-l) (w-ṣ-l) "the conjunct excelling"

Any disjunct rhythmic mode in which there is no separating duration (FĀṢILAH/4*) between the end of one cycle (DAWR/1*) and the beginning of the next (al Fārābī 1967:454, and n. 2).

MUTAFĀḌILAH AL MUFAṢṢALAH (f-ḍ-l) (f-ṣ-l) "the disjunct excelling"

Any disjunct rhythmic mode in which the separating duration (FĀṢILAH/4*) between the end of one cycle (DAWR/1*) and the beginning of the next is longer than the percussions surrounding it in either cycle (al Fārābī 1967:454, and n. 3).

MUTAFĀṢIL (f-ṣ-l) "disjunct"

Said of a disjunct rhythmic mode of three or more percussions when its first two beats are of unequal length (Farmer 1943:75).

MUTAKĀTIF (k-t-f) "compact; shoulder-to-shoulder"

Descriptive term for the "weak" (LAYYIN*) tetrachordal or pentachordal segment (JINS/1*) because of the closeness of its tones (Ibn Abī al Ṣalt 1952:38).

MUTAKHALLAṢĀT AL HAWĀ' (kh-l-ṣ) (h-w-y) "escape places for the air"

The side holes or end hole of a woodwind instrument, i.e., any opening from which the air escapes (al Fārābī 1967:772). Later in the same work (Ibid.:781), al Fārābī uses the term for only the lower end opening of the flute.

MUTALĀ'IM or MUTALĀ'IMAH = MOUTALÂÏM (l-'-m) "consonant with"

1. Consonant (al Fārābī 1967:480, 883), pertaining to intervals (s. BUʿD*) or systems (s. JAMʿ/1*) (de Vaux 1891:292). Opp. of MUTANĀFIR*.

2. A descriptive term (syn. of KHAFĪ AL TANĀFUR*) for a category of scales including more consonant intervals than the prime, the perfect fourth and fifth, and the octave, but less than the total number of notes (Wright 1978:98).

MU'TALIFAH ('-l-f) "that which is united or joined"

1. Harmonious (al Kindī 1966:151).
2. Said of any of the six tones (NAGHAM, s. NAGHM or NAGHMAH/1*) or fret positions which do not vary according to the MAJRĀ* or "course" chosen for that particular tetrachordal or pentachordal combination of tones (Ibn al Munajjim 1950:7). See MUKHTALIFAH*.

MUTAMMAM (t-m-m) "that which is complete"

An interval comparable to the semitone with ratio 16/15. It is one of the two kinds of "J"/2* interval, the other being TATIMMAH* (al Jurjānī 1938:238).

MUTANĀFIR (n-f-r) "incompatible"

1. Dissonant, pertaining to intervals (s. BU'D*) or systems (s. JAM'/1*) (Ibn Sīnā 1930:85; Ṣafī al Dīn in de Vaux 1891:292; al Fārābī 1967:883; Maḥfūẓ 1964:187).
2. Dissonant, as a descriptive category for scales containing any of the causes of dissonance specified by Ṣafī al Dīn. The other categories are MULĀ'IM* ("consonant") and KHAFĪ AL TANĀFUR* or MUTALĀ'IM* ("intermediate"). Syn. of ẒĀHIR AL TANĀFUR* (Wright 1978:44).

MUTASĀWĪ or MUTASĀWIYAH (s-w-y) "equal"

Descriptive term used for the percussions or time units (AZMINAH, s. ZAMĀN/2*) of a disjunct (MUNFAṢIL/3*) rhythmic mode of three or more percussions per cycle when its first two beats were of equal length (al Fārābī 1967:449, 462; Farmer 1943:75; Ibn Sīnā 1930:93; al Ḥafnī 1930:37). Opp. of MUTAFĀḌIL or MUTAFĀḌILAH*, and MUKHĀLIFAH*.

MUTASHĀBIH or MUTASHĀBIHAH (sh-b-h) "resembling each other"

1. Said of a "collection" (JAM'/1*) of notes when the tones of its upper octave are similar to those of the lower octave except for being on a higher pitch level (al Fārābī 1967:964).
2. Said of two different intervals which are identical in size or ratio (al Fārābī 1967:358; 540).
3. Said of any two melodic progressions (s. INTIQĀL/1*) which share an identity of movement or direction (i.e., in KAYF*), of number of notes (in KAMM*), or of ratio of their intervals (in NISBAH*). When patterns are identical in all these three ways, the INTIQĀL is designated as INTIQĀL DĀ'IR* (Ibn Sīnā 1930:96). See INTIQĀL/1*.

MUTASHĀBIH AL MUKHTALIF BIL QUWWAH (sh-b-h) (kh-l-f) (q-w-y) "resembling each other [but] with a difference in strength"

Said of any two musical intervals which are similar to each other in ratio, but which differ from each other in their pitches (al Fārābī 1967:358).

MUTAṢIF

Var. of MUTTAṢIF* (Avenary 1952:80).

MUTATĀLĪ (t-l-w) "successive"

1. One of the sub-categories of melodic movement (INTIQĀL/1*) as described by al Kindī (1966:135-136). It included all melodic patterns of ascending or descending stepwise movement. LA MUTATĀLĪ therefore was the designation for all those types of melodic movement with leaps, whether ascending or descending.
2. A variety (ṢINF*) of tetrachordal or pentachordal segment (JINS/1*) in which the constituent intervals are progressively arranged according to size (Ṣafī al Dīn in de Vaux 1891:309).

MUTAWĀLIYAH (w-l-y) "continuing in succession"

Designation for the strings of the ṬUNBŪR/1* when they are tuned to achieve one or more notes in common (al Fārābī 1967:638). Opp. of MUTABĀYANAH*.

MUṬAWWAL (ṭ-w-l) "lengthened and elaborate"

Descriptive term for songs of highly ornamented, melismatic character, and used by the professional musicians of the Yaman (Jargy 1978:81).

MUTHALLATH or MUTHALLITH = MTHELLETH (th-l-th) "tripled or tripling" (resp.)

1. A popular tuning of the KAMĀNJAH KABĪRAH*, which is one octave lower in pitch than that of the KAMĀNJAH ṢAGHĪRAH* tuning (Mor.) (Chottin 1939:144).
2. One of the popular tunings for the ʿŪD/2* (Mor.) (Chottin 1939: 145).
3. Designation for 3-lined poetic strophes. See MUSAMMAṬ*.

MUṬLAQ = MOTLAQ (ṭ-l-q) "freed"

1. Without musical meter, i.e., with free rhythm (Tun.) (Ḥāfiẓ 1971:122; Maḥfūẓ 1964:98).
2. One of the six octave scales mentioned by ʿAbd al Qādir ibn Ghaybī (d. 1435), which were known collectively as the AṢĀBIʿ/1* or MAWĀJIB*. The use of this term as a modal name goes back at least to the 10th C. By the time of Ṣafī al Dīn and ʿAbd al Qādir, this categorization was considered ancient (QADĪM) (Wright 1978:249-250). The other octave scales were MAZMŪM*, MUSARRAJ*, MUʿALLAQ/2*, MAḤMŪL* and MUJANNAB/3*.

3. A drone (Hickmann 1947:10).
4. The open string of a chordophone, or the sound produced on it. (al Fārābī 1967:500).

MUṬLAQ AL WATAR (ṭ-l-q) (w-t-r) "the freed string"

The open string of a chordophone or its sound (al Fārābī 1967:500).

MUṬRIB (pl. MUṬRIBŪN) = MOTHRIB, MOUTRIB (ṭ-r-b) "one who produces ṬARAB* or musical aesthetic delight in the listener"

Though the term is correctly used only for the vocalist of great talent, its meaning is sometimes extended to include both instrumentalists and vocalists and even those of lesser talent. Therefore, it is commonly equated with musician (Wehr), regardless of the specialty in performance.

MUṬRIB AL MUNFARID (ṭ-r-b) (f-r-d) "one who produces ṬARAB* singly"

Male vocal soloist (Ḥāfiẓ 1971:111).

MUTTAFIQ (w-f-q) "agreeing"

Consonant, pertaining to intervals (Ibn Sīnā 1930:85; al Fārābī 1967:481); and generally (al Ḥafnī 1946:288; Maḥfūẓ 1964:187).

MUTTAFIQĀT ṢUGHRĀ (w-f-q) (ṣ-gh-r) "small consonances"

An expression used by Classical Period theorists to designate all intervals smaller than a perfect fourth (al Fārābī 1967:269-270; 1930:101; Ibn Sīnā 1935:119; al Lādhiqī 1939:310). Also AB'ĀD LAḤNIYYAH*, NAGHAM SUGHRA*.

MUTTAFIQĀT 'UẒMĀ (w-f-q) ('-ẓ-m) "large consonances"

An expression used by Classical Period theorists to designate the octave interval, or the double octave. These were not only the largest intervals in size, but also greatest in consonance (al Fārābī 1967:269; 1930:100; Ibn Sīnā 1935:119; al Lādhiqī 1939: 309). Also AB'ĀD MUTTAFIQAH AL NAGHM*, NAGHAM 'UẒMĀ*.

MUTTAFIQĀT WUSṬĀ (w-f-q) (w-s-ṭ) "median consonances"

An expression used by Classical Period theorists to designate the intervals of a perfect fourth and fifth or the octave plus fourth or fifth (al Fārābī 1967:270; 1930:100; Ibn Sīnā 1935:119; al Lādhiqī 1939:309). Also AB'ĀD MUTASHĀKILAH AL NAGHM*, NAGHAM WUSṬĀ*.

MUTTAṢIF (w-ṣ-f) "middle"

The "middle" or WUSṬĀ* fret (Ibn Abī al Ṣalt 1952:36, 54), wrongly transliterated as MUTAṢIF (Avenary 1952:80;, 36, n.23; 54, n.3).

MUTTAṢIL or MUTTAṢILAH = MOUTTAÇIL (w-ṣ-l) "joined"

1. Stepwise progression in melodic movement or patterning (INTIQĀL/1*) (Ibn Sīnā 1930:95; Khashabah in al Fārābī 1967:968, n.1). Opp. of ṬAFIR*, see materials under INTIQĀL/1*.
2. Conjunct, as description of one of the three types of QAWĪ* ("strong") JINS/1*, that in which the two larger intervals have ratios which increase or decrease consecutively (al Fārābī 1967: 299-303).
3. Conjunct, in respect to the way tetrachordal segments or octaves are combined to form a scale. In the MUTTAṢIL combination (JAMʿ/1*), the constituent AJNĀS (s. JINS/1*) or octaves have one note in common, that is, the highest note of the lower segment is at the same time the lowest tone of the higher one (al Kindī in Cowl 1966:155; Ibn Sīnā 1935:159; el Helou 1961:92). According to Ṣafī al Dīn, this scalar combination is one in which the whole tone interval is low in the lower octave, high in the higher octave of a two octave scale. It was called JAMʿ AL IJTIMĀʿ* by his predecessors (de Vaux 1891:323).
4. Designation for a conjunct rhythmic mode (ĪQĀʿ/1*), i.e., one in which all percussions are of equal duration and follow each other at regular intervals (Ibn Sina 1930:92; 1935:185). Syn. of HAZAJ/3*, MUWAṢṢAL*.
5. Continuous, as descriptive term used for all musical sounds which have no perceptible silence between tones of different pitch, as in those produced by woodwind instruments, bowed chordophones, organs, etc. (Ikhwān al Ṣafā' 1964/65:194; Shiloah 1964/65: 140). Syn. of legato.

MUWĀḌAʿ (w-ḍ-ʿ) "mutually put, agreed upon"

A fret, or finger position on the string of a musical instrument (al Kindī 1966:156).

MUWĀFIQ or MUWĀFIQAH (w-f-q) "mutually agreeing"

Consonant.

MUWAJJIHAH (pl. MUWAJJIHĀT) (w-j-h) "that which guides or controls"

The Da Capo sign, borrowed from Western notation by contemporary musicians and theorists (Maḥfūẓ 1964:192).

MUWÂL

Var. of MAWWĀL/1*, as an improvised genre of music in Morocco (Chottin 1939:66, 133, 135-136).

MUWANNAJ (w-n-j)

A kind of harp with seven strings mentioned in the 9th-10th C. and said to have been used by the people of Khurāsān and their neighbors (Ibn Khurdādhbih 1969:16). This open stringed instrument is said to have been played like the ṢANJ*. In al ʿAzzāwī's edition of Ibn Khurdādhbih (1951:95), WANJ* is used instead of the term MUWANNAJ found in the 1969 edition.

MUWASHSHAḤ (pl. MUWASHSHAḤĀT) = MUWAŠŠAḤ, MOUACHCHAH, MUACHCHAH', MU-WASHSHA (w-sh-ḥ) "encircled; ornamented"

1. A composition of vocal, regularly rhythmed variety which is a musical setting of a MUWASHSHAḤ/2* poem. It has been a part of the musical tradition since its poetic development at the beginning of the 10th C. in Moorish Spain. From there it spread to North Africa and the Mashriq. It comprises three main segments: an opening DAWR/6* or BADANIYYAH/1*; a KHĀNAH* or SILSILAH/2* as middle section with contrast in tune, mode and/or register; and a QAFLAH/1*, RUJŪ'/3* or GHIṬĀ'/1*, which is the final segment comprising a musical refrain which repeats the melodic content of the opening DAWR/6. See al Faruqi 1975:1-29. These musical settings are performed as choral numbers of the suites performed in the Maghrib and Mashriq.
2. A genre of strophic poetry invented in Spain about 900 A.C. It has usually been composed in classical Arabic, but not always in classical meters. It has 5-7 strophes with complicated rhyme schemes and a refrain passage known as SIMṬ* or QAFLAH/4*, which contrasts in rhyme scheme from the opening segment or GHUṢN/3*. The final QAFLAH, also known as KHARJAH/1*, generally consists of colloquial or non-Arabic verses which end with the refrain-line rhyme.
3. The term is used by the Lebanese to designate a dance-like tune of the folk tradition which is similar to QARRĀDĪ or QARRĀ-DIYYAH* (Jargy 1970:33, 37, 41).

MUWASSA' = MUSSA' (w-s-') "the enlarged"

1. The slow and solemn first part of each of the five segments (each with its particular rhythmic mode or MĪZĀN/2*) into which a suite or NAWBAH/1* is divided (Mor.). The faster part of each MĪZĀN is known as INṢIRĀF/2* (Schuyler 1978:37).
2. Slow in tempo (Chottin 1939:112).

MUWAŠŠAḤ

Var. of MUWASHSHAḤ* (Reichow 1971:27).

MUWAṢṢAL (w-ṣ-l) "intensely joined"

Any conjunct rhythmic mode (ĪQĀ'/1*), and syn. of HAZAJ/2* and MUTTAṢIL/4*. Some people, according to al Fārābī, divided the conjunct rhythmic modes into three categories: 1) the slowest or THAQĪL/2*, which were the bases from which all rhythmic modes were formed (also known as ĪQĀ' AL JĀMI'AH*); 2) the fastest, which were also known as KHAFĪF/1*; and 3) the ones of medium length percussions, which were called HAZAJ/2*, in distinction from the other two varieties (al Fārābī 1967:449ff). Opp. of MUFAṢṢAL/1* (de Vaux 1891:345).

MUWAṢṢAL AL HAZAJ (w-ṣ-l) (h-z-j) "intensely joined HAZAJ"

A conjunct rhythmic mode with medium length percussions (i.e., of medium tempo) (al Fārābī 1967:449ff). See MUWAṢṢAL*, HAZAJ/2*.

MUWAṢṢAL AL KHAFĪF (w-ṣ-l) (kh-f-f) "light intensely joined"

A conjunct rhythmic mode with short percussions (i.e., with fast tempo) (al Fārābī 1967:449ff). See MUWAṢṢAL*.

MUWAṢṢAL AL THAQĪL (w-ṣ-l) (th-q-l) "Heavy, intensely joined"

A conjunct rhythmic mode with long percussions (i.e., with slow tempo) (al Fārābī 1967:449ff). See MUWAṢṢAL*.

MUWATTAR = MOUATTAR (w-t-r) "stringed"

A leather faced, short necked lute of very early times which was a forerunner of the ʿŪD/2*. According to Ḥāfiẓ (1971:20), it was similar to the ʿŪD and was made either with skin or wooden face. He describes it, however, as having had only two strings, rather than the four of the early examples of the ʿŪD. Robson describes it as an early name for the ʿŪD (Robson 1938b:241; 1938a:11) as mentioned by Ibn Salamah (9th-10th C.). See MAWTIR*.

MUWWĀL

Var. of MAWWĀL* (Schuyler 1978:38).

MUZAMZIM (z-m-z-m) "one who rumbles, murmurs"

A person who chants in a mystical assembly (Majd al Dīn al Ghazālī 1938:112, 176).

MUZĀWAJ (z-w-j) "mutually paired"

1. Another name for the woodwind instrument of the early Classical Period known as DŪNĀY* (Farmer EI(Eng), "Mizmār":541).
2. A contemporary double reed-pipe of Syria, with both pipes having finger holes. In the Maghrib, a similar instrument is known as MAQRŪNAH* (Farmer EI(Eng), "Mizmār":541).

MUZDAWIJ or MUZDAWIJAH (z-w-j) "double, twofold"

1. The practice begun by IBN MUḤRIZ* (d. ca. 715) of using a different melody for the second BAYT/1* or line of a song. Before that, the same melodic phrase was repeated for each BAYT of the song.
2. Descriptive term for any aerophone with double (paired) pipes.
3. Any tonal or durational elements occurring in pairs.
4. A cycle of a rhythmic mode (ĪQĀʿ*) which contains binary organization of beats or percussions.
5. Descriptive term for strings that are tuned in pairs of identical pitch (Ḥāfiẓ 1971:80).

N

NABARA (n-b-r) "to raise; to accentuate"

To sing in a high-pitched voice; to raise one's voice.

NABR or NABRAH (pl. NABRAT) (n-b-r) "elevating of the voice"

1. Short notes with sharp, glottal stop attack, which are thought to beautify the melody (al Fārābī 1967:1173; 1935:90; al Ḥafnī 1946:286). Ibn Ṣalamah (1951:89) writes that it was a characteristic of the SINĀD* genre.
2. Raising the volume suddenly after soft singing (al Zabīdī 1965: III, 552).
3. Very old designation for "interval" (Kitāb al Aghānī) which fell into disuse with the adoption of the term BUʿD* (Farmer 1929a: 67, 239; 1967:51-52, 70).

NABRAH ṢAWTIYYAH (n-b-r) (ṣ-w-t) "sound elevation"

Explosive vocal sounds employed for emphasis (el Helou 1961:193).

NACHAD

Var. of NASHSHĀD* (Poche 1978:65).

NACH'ATKAR

A short necked lute of contemporary Syria which, because of its brass strings, sounds very much like the BUZUQ*. It has five pairs of strings tuned like those of the short necked lute (ʿŪD/2*): G_1, A_1, D_1, G_2 and C_2 (Touma 1977b:103).

NACHÎD

Var. of NASHĪD/4* (Chottin 1939:87, 91).

NADB (n-d-b) "mourning, lamentation"

Songs of lamentation (Jargy 1970:30, 38).

NADDĀB (pl. NADDĀBŪN) "mourner"

A male folk singer (poet-musician) of the contemporary Mashriq who specializes in funeral chants (Shiloah 1974).

NADDĀBAH (pl. NADDĀBĀT) (n-d-b) "female mourner"

Professional female mourner (Farmer 1957:434).

NÂD'IM

Var. of NĀẒIM* (Rouanet 1922:2719).

NĀḎHIM

Var. of NĀẒIM* (Ṣafī al Dīn 1938b:39, d'Erlanger translation).

(AL) NAḌR IBN AL ḤĀRITH (d. 624)

Musician of al Ḥīrah, an important center of Arabian culture in pre-Islamic times, who introduced the lute (ʿŪD/2*) and the new type of artistic song (GHINĀ'/4*) into Makkah and the Peninsula (Farmer 1957:427).

NAFAKHA (n-f-kh) "to blow; to breathe"

To play a wind instrument.

NAFAS (pl. ANFĀS) (n-f-s) "breath"

The short pause which separates each phrase of the TAQĀSĪM* or any other similar performance from that which follows. It gives a chance for the listener to praise the performer as well as for the musician to gather his thoughts and inspiration for the next phrase (Touma 1976:33-34).

NĀFIDHAH ṢAWTIYYAH (pl. NAWĀFIDH ṢAWTIYYAH) (n-f-dh) (ṣ-w-t) "sound opening or window"

One of the two openings on the face of the sound box of any viol type instrument, to the left and right of the strings (Maḥfūẓ 1964:160).

NAFĪR (pl. ANFĀR, ANFIRAH) (n-f-r) "a group, party"

Generic term for any long, straight trumpet with cylindrical bore (Hickmann 1947:15; Farmer EI(Fr), "Būḳ":46. This term is not known to have been used before the 11th C., though use of the instrument may have been much earlier. In that century, it stood for a very long straight trumpet made of metal with cylindrical bore. According to Ibn Ghaybī (d. 1435), it was 168 cm. long (Farmer 1976b:30). This instrument was used as a military trumpet, and therefore is probably the "cor sarrazinois" known to the Crusaders. The word NAFĪR, in fact, implies a connection with war; and it is known to have been popular in the military bands of the Muslims. Even its sound must have been coarse and warlike, for we read that the player "shouted, screamed" (SĀḤA) into the instrument (Farmer, EI(Fr), "Būq":46). The instrument is still used in parts of the Maghrib and the Mashriq.

NAGHAM (n-gh-m) see NAGHM or NAGHAM*

Pl. of NAGHM* (al Fārābī, Ibn al Munajjim, al Zabīdī, etc.); equiv. of NAGHM*.

NAGHAM DAQĪQAH (n-gh-m) (d-q-q) "tiny or intricate tones"

High pitched tones (according to ISḤAQ AL MAWṢILĪ*, d. 850) (Shawqī 1976:346).

NAGHAM GHALĪẒAH (n-gh-m) (gh-l-ẓ) "burly, thick tones"

Bass or low pitched tones (according to ISḤAQ AL MAWṢILĪ*, d. 850) (Shawqī 1976:346).

NAGHAM INSĀNIYYAH MAQRŪNAH BIL AQĀWĪL (n-gh-m) ('-n-s) (q-r-n) (q-w-l) "human sounds joined with words"

Music with words, i.e., vocal music. Al Fārābī designated it as the ṢINF AL THĀNĪ* ("second genre"), the ṢINF AL AWWAL* ("first genre") corresponding to instrumental music (al Fārābī 1967:881, see n. 3).

NAGHAM ʿALĀ IṬLĀQ or NAGHAM BI IṬLĀQ (n-gh-m) (ṭ-l-q) "free sounds or tones"

Music without words, i.e., instrumental music (al Fārābī 1967:881, n. 2, 1056, n. 1, 1063). Syn. of ṢINF AL AWWAL*.

NAGHAM KHĀFITAH (n-gh-m) (kh-f-t) "tones which are dying away or becoming inaudible"

Soft tones (according to ISḤAQ AL MAWṢILĪ*, d. 850) (Shawqī 1976:346).

NAGHAM KIBĀR (n-gh-m) (k-b-r) "large notes"

Bass notes (al Kindī, according to Farmer 1978:II, 91).

NAGHAM LAYYINAH (n-gh-m) (l-y-n) "soft, gentle tones"

Soft tones (according to ISḤAQ AL MAWṢILĪ*, d. 850) (Shawqī 1976:346).

NAGHAM MUKHTALIFAH (n-gh-m) (kh-l-f) "differing tones"

The four tones which are susceptible to variation in a tetrachordal succession of tones when shifting from one MAJRĀ* or course to the other (Ibn al Munajjim 1950:7). These tones include the WUSṬĀ*(minor third) and BINṢIR* (major third) above the open string tone. The WUSṬĀ is the "differing tone" used for the

MAJRĀ AL WUSṬĀ*, the BINṢIR, for the MAJRĀ AL BINṢIR*. See NAGHAM AL MU'TALIFAH*.

NAGHAM MU'TALIFAH (n-gh-m) ('-l-f) "agreeing tones"
The notes of the tetrachordal succession that did not change when shifting from one MAJRĀ* or course to the other. This terminology was used by Ibn al Munajjim in his presentation of the musical theory of ISḤAQ AL MAWṢILĪ* (Ibn al Munajjim 1950:7). There are three NAGHAM AL MU'TALIFAH in each tetrachord as performed on the lute (ʿŪD/2*): MUṬLAQ* (or open string tone); the SABBĀBAH* (major second above the open string) and the KHINṢIR* (perfect fourth above the open string). See NAGHAM AL MUKHTALIFAH*.

NAGHAM NAḤĪFAH (n-gh-m) (n-ḥ-f) "thin, slender tones"

Treble or high notes (according to ISḤAQ AL MAWṢILĪ*) (Shawqī 1976: 349).

NAGHAM QAWIYYAH (n-gh-m) (q-w-y) "strong tones"

Loud notes or tones (according to ISḤAQ AL MAWṢILĪ*) (Shawqī 1976:346).

NAGHAM RĀTIBAH (n-gh-m) (r-t-b) "organizing tones"

The unchangeable tones within a two-octave scalar collection of tones. These are the lowest tone (THAQĪLAH AL MAFRŪḌĀT*), its upper octave equivalent (the WUSṬĀ/3*) and the highest tone, two octaves above the lowest tone (ḤADDAH AL ḤADDĀT*) (al Fārābī 1967: 372).

NAGHAM SHADĪDAH (n-gh-m) (sh-d-d) "strong, powerful tones"

Loud tones (according to ISḤAQ AL MAWṢILĪ*) (Shawqī 1976:346).

NAGHAM AL ṢUGHRĀ (n-gh-m) (ṣ-gh-r) "smallest tones"

The intervals smaller than a perfect fourth, syn. of MUTTAFIQAT SUGHRA* or AB'AD LAHNIYYAH* (al Farabi 1967:269-270; 1930:101; see Ibn Sina 1935:119).

NAGHAM AL ʿUẒMĀ (n-gh-m) (ʿ-ẓ-m) "largest tones"

The intervals of a perfect octave or double octave, syn. of MUTTAFIQĀT ʿUẒMĀ* or ABʿĀD MUTTAFIQAH AL NAGHM* (al Fārābī 1967: 270).

NAGHAM AL WUSṬĀ (n-gh-m) (w-s-ṭ) "intermediate tones"

The intervals of a perfect fourth and perfect fifth, and the octave plus fourth or fifth. Syn. of MUTTAFIQĀT WUSṬĀ* or ABʿĀD MUTASHĀKILAH AL NAGHM*.

NAGHAMAH or NAGHMAH (pl. NAGHAMĀT) (n-gh-m) "a sound; note; melody"

Equiv. of NAGHM or NAGHAM*, but emphasizing the singleness of the item.

NAGHAMA or NAGHIMA (n-gh-m) "to hum or sing"

To hum or sing a tune.

NAGHAMĀT AL BUḤŪR (pl. of NAGHMAH AL BAḤR) = NARHAMÂT-EL-BUH'UR (n-gh-m) (b-ḥ-r) "melodies of poetic meters"

1. Any of the simple vocal formulae corresponding to each of the classical poetic meters and used for scanning lines of poetry (Chottin 1939:127). Each note corresponds to a syllable of the poetry.
2. Melodies with regular rhythm (Farmer, EI(Eng), "Ghinā'":1074).

NAGHAMĀT MAWZŪNAH (n-gh-m) (w-z-n) "measured tones"

Music with regular rhythmic underlay (Ibn Taymiyyah 1966:II, 318). Also see NAGHM MAWZŪN*.

NAGHGHAMA (n-gh-m) "to set to a tune"

To hum a tune or to sing.

NAGHIMA (n-gh-m) "to hum or sing"

Equiv. of NAGHAMA*.

NAGHM or NAGHAM (pl. NAGHAM, ANGHĀM, NIGHAM) = NAR'AM (n-gh-m) "sound; tone; melody"

1. A musical sound, tone, or note.
2. A melody; the vocal or instrumental line for a musical composition or improvization.
3. A song.
4. After the 14th C., this term came to be used for melodic mode (Farmer 1945:45; Ibn Khurdādhbih 1969:15). It carries this meaning to the present century (Lachmann 1929:56). It can also be given to a tetrachordal or pentachordal scale, and therefore has come to mean any scalar succession of tones (d'Erlanger 1949:69-70).
5. Since a chordophone sounded by plucking (ḌARB/3*) was the chief instrument with which the theorists made their experiments and explanations, the word for tone (NAGHM or NAGHMAH) was often used for "beat" or "percussion" (ḌARB/1*) as well as for "note" or "tone" (Farmer 1943:24, 28-37). It was even used with both meanings in the writings of the same theorist, or even in the same work (e.g., the Ikhwān al Ṣafā', see Shiloah 1964/65:128, n. 7). See def. 6.
6. A musical rhythmic mode (Ikhwān al Ṣafā' 1964/65:128, n. 7). See def. 5.

NAGHM AL MAUZŪN

Var. of NAGHM MAWZŪN* (Farmer 1943:78).

NAGHM MAWZŪN (n-gh-m) (w-z-n) "measured tune"

Music with regular rhythmic underlay. Also NAGHAMĀT MAWZŪNAH*.

NAGHMAH (pl. NAGHAMĀT) (n-gh-m) "a sound; note; melody"

Equiv. of NAGHM*.

NAGHMAH AṢLIYYAH (n-gh-m) ('-ṣ-l) "basic tone"

The principal tone embellished by a melodic ornamentation which is known as TARKĪB/1* (Ibn Sīnā 1930:99). See NAGHMAH MUWĀFIQAH*.

NAGHMAH AL ḌIʿF (n-gh-m) (ḍ-ʿ-f) "doubled tone"

Upper octave equivalent of a tone (Ibn al Munajjim 1950:7).

NAGHMAH AL IḌʿĀF (n-gh-m) (ḍ-ʿ-f) "tone of doubling"

Syn. of NAGHMAH AL ḌIʿF* (Ibn al Munajjim 1950:7).

NAGHMAH MUWĀFIQAH (n-gh-m) (w-f-q) "harmonious tone"

The subsidiary or auxiliary tone of the embellishment known as TARKĪB/1* (Ibn Sīnā 1930:99). See NAGHMAH AṢLIYYAH*.

NAGHMAH AL YATĪMAH (n-gh-m) (y-t-m) "isolated tone"

The middle tone of a two octave scalar collection, which marks the last tone of the lower octave and the first tone of the upper octave. It was given this name, according to al Kindī, because it held a unique position in being part of both octaves (al Kindī 1962:21).

NĀḤA (n-w-ḥ) "to weep or lament; to coo (as a pigeon)"

To sing (Ibn Khurdādhbih 1969:15).

NAHĀWAND = NIHĀWAND (geog.) "a Persian city"

1. A note of the contemporary Arabian scale,  . Also called KURD or KŪRD* or KŪRDĪ*. Notated as $D\#_1$ or Eb_1.
2. Contemporary name for a tetrachordal scalar segment (JINS/1*) having the following interval division: 1-½-1.
3. A contemporary melodic mode utilizing the NAHĀWAND JINS (see def. 2 above), with RĀST/3* (C_1) as tonic.

NAḤḤĀM (n-ḥ-m) "one who clears his throat or pants"

Male soloist for a type of folk music in the Arabian/Persian Gulf region, which is known as FIJRĪ* (Touma 1977a:123).

NAḤĪFAH (n-ḥ-f) "thin, slender"

Treble or high in pitch (Shawqī 1976:349).

NAI or NAÏ

Vars. of NĀY* (Lachmann and Fox-Strangways 1938:578; Touma 1977b: 104-105, resp.).

NĀ'IḤ (pl. NĀ'IḤŪN) (n-w-ḥ) "one who laments"

The professional male wailer, or singer of elegies, who was and still is much less common than his female counterpart, the NĀ'IḤAH*.

NĀ'IḤAH (pl. NĀ'IḤĀT) (n-w-ḥ) "female who laments"

Professional female singer of laments or songs of mourning (Ibn Abī al Dunyā 1938:28, 51).

NAKĀKEER

Var. of NAQĀQĪR* (Salvador-Daniel 1976:225).

NAḲĪB

Var. of NAQĪB* (Farmer, EI(Eng), "Mizmār":542).

NAKISH

Var. of NAQSH/3* (Chottin and Hickmann 1949-1951:Band I, col. 594).

NAḲḲĀR KHĀNA

Var. of NAQQĀR KHĀNAH or NAQQĀRAH KHĀNAH* (Farmer EI(Fr), "Ṭabl Khāna":232).

NAKKARA

Var. of NAQQĀRAH* (Marcuse).

NAḲRAZĀN

Var. of NAQRAZĀN* (Farmer EI(Fr), "Ṭabl":232).

NĀḲŪS

Var. of NĀQŪS* (Farmer EI(Fr), "Ṣandj":210).

NANGAH

Syn. of ṬUNBŪRAH SŪDĀNĪ*, a harp-like instrument of Palestine and Upper Egypt (Farmer EI(Eng), "Miʿzaf":529).

NAOUA

Var. of NAWĀ* (Touma 1977b:37).

NAOUBAH

Var. of NAWBAH* (Touma 1977b:75).

NAQAGUÎR

A small barrel drum played with a leather baton or the hand (Hickmann 1958:61). The term seems to be a colloq. of NAQĀQĪR*, but with a different meaning.

NAQALA

Var. of NUQLAH* (Cowl 1966:150).

NAQĀQĪR = NAKĀKEER, NAQAGUÎR (n-q-r) "knockers"

1. General term in the Mashriq for kettledrums (s. NAQQĀR*).
2. Used by the ancient Arabs to designate their warlike songs, perhaps because kettledrums were also associated with war (Salvador-Daniel 1976:225).

NAQARA (n-q-r) "to peck, strike"

1. To pluck a stringed instrument.
2. To strike a percussion instrument.

NAQARAH (n-q-r) "a plucking; a percussion"

Equiv. of NAQRAH*.

NAQARĀT AṢLIYYAH (pl. of NAQRAH AṢLIYYAH) (n-q-r) ('-ṣ-l) "fundamental strikes"

The fundamental beats of accentuation in a rhythmic cycle, contemporary syn. of ḌARB AṢLĪ*.

NAQARĀT MUTAWĀLIYĀT (n-q-r) (w-l-y) "successive strikes"

Consecutive beats or percussions (al Kindī, in Farmer 1943:18, 21).

NAQARYAH (n-q-r)

Large kettle drum of the type which is fastened to the back of a camel, one on the right, one on the left. These drums, like the NAQRAZĀN*, are played by a mounted drummer and are used for processions (Touma 1977b:109). See NAQQĀRAH*, of which this term may be a var. See also NAQQĀRYA*, NAQQARAH or NAQQĀRAH*.

NAQAYRAH

Var. of NUQAYRAH* (Shiloah 1965:I, 30).

NAQĪB = NAḲĪB (n-q-b) "head, leader"

Syn. of MIZMĀR* (14th or 15th C. ms.).

NĀQIR (n-q-r) "one who strikes"

A musical instrument, of woodwind variety (Madina).

NĀQIṢ (n-q-ṣ) "lacking"

Descriptive term for a tetrachordal segment (JINS/1*) in which the two extremities are less than a perfect fourth apart (Ṣalāḥ al Dīn 1950:101). See also TAMM/2* and ZĀ'ID/2*.

NAQQÂRÂ

Var. of NAQQARAH or NAQQĀRAH* (Sachs 1967:85).

NAQQARA (n-q-r) "to strike"

To sound a percussion or stringed musical instrument.

NAQQARAH OR NAQQĀRAH (pl. NAQĀQĪR, NAQQARĀT) = NAKKARA, NAQQÂRÂ (n-q-r) "intense strike"

One of a pair of large kettledrums generally used in religious processions. These two drums are made of metal or clay and are shaped similarly, though one is larger than the other. The larger NAQQĀRAH in the Mashriq in recent centuries is about two feet in diameter, the smaller one about one and a half feet across. The pair is mounted on the saddle of a camel or other riding animal and is played by the mounted drummer. The larger drum is usually mounted on the right, the smaller one on the left (Lane 1973:365). ʿArnīṭah writes that the drums are tuned a fifth apart (1968:49). The membranes are struck with two small wooden sticks, each of which has a small head. The larger instrument sounds the dense DUM* strokes; the smaller one produces the dry TAK* strokes. Pairs of such drums have been known for a long period of Arab history. In those earlier centuries, they were made of metal, wood or clay. Today they are generally made of metal.

NAQQĀRAH KHĀNAH or NAQQĀR KHĀNAH = NAḲḲĀR KHĀNA (n-q-r) (kh-w-n) "house of that which strikes"

The military band, syn. of ṬABL KHĀNAH* (Farmer EI(Fr), "Ṭabl Khāna":232).

NAQQĀRATĀN (n-q-r) "two NAQQĀRĀT"

Pair of kettledrums (see illus. from 15th C. ms. in Farmer 1965b).

NAQQĀRYA (n-q-r) (NAQQARIYYAH?)

Syn. of NAQQARAH or NAQQĀRAH* (Sachs 1940:251).

NAQR (n-q-r) "striking"

Plucking the strings of a chordophone.

NAQRAH (pl. NAQARĀT) (n-q-r) "blow, percussion"

1. Generic for a percussion, made on either a stringed or percussion instrument.
2. More specifically, the term is applied to a percussion on a stringed instrument, as distinguished from the tone made by a percussion instrument (Ikhwān al Ṣafā' 1957:I, 200).
3. Internal division unit, i.e., a percussion, of a rhythmic cycle (al Fārābī 1967:449ff).
4. Any sound duration, whether produced by the human voice or any musical instrument (al Rajab 1967:23).
5. A very strong beat or percussion. Al Fārābī writes that some people of his time distinguished between a very strong beat (NAQRAH), one of medium strength (MASḤAH*), and a light one (GHAMZAH*) (al Fārābī 1967:987).

NAQRAH BASĪṬAH (n-q-r) (b-s-ṭ) "simple percussion"

Contemporary designation for the sixteenth note (Allawerdi 1949: 475).

NAQRAH KHAFĪFAH (n-q-r) (kh-f-f) "light percussions"

A short percussion said to be half the duration of a NAQRAH THAQĪLAH* (al Rajab 1967:23).

NAQRAH LAYYINAH (n-q-r) (l-y-n) "soft percussion"

Any of the supplementary percussions that were added during the separating duration (FĀṢILAH/4*) between the last percussion of one cycle and the first percussion of the next cycle (al Rajab 1967:23).

NAQRAH MUNFARIDAH (n-q-r) (f-r-d) "single percussion"

Said by al Kindī to have been comparable to the NAQRAH THAQĪLAH*, or long percussion (al Rajab 1967:23, n. 3).

NAQRAH MUTAḤARRIKAH (n-q-r) (ḥ-r-k) "moving percussion"

1. Any percussion not followed by a pause (WAQF or WAQFAH/1*), i.e., one which proceeds directly to another percussion (al Fārābī 1967:998; 1935:31; al Rajab 1967:23). Opp. of NAQRAH SĀKINAH/1*.
2. Al Kindī described the NAQRAH MUTAḤARRIKAH as a moving beat, i.e., one marked by a percussion rather than a silence (al Kindī in Farmer 1943:19, 21). Opp. of NAQRAH SĀKINAH/2*.

NAQRAH SĀKINAH (n-q-r) (s-k-n) "silent percussion"

1. Any percussion followed by a pause (WAQF or WAQFAH*) instead of moving immediately to another percussion (al Fārābī 1967:998; 1935:31; al Rajab 1967:23).
2. A quiescent beat, i.e., a rest between percussions of a rhythmic cycle (al Kindī in Farmer 1943:19, 21).

NAQRAH THAQĪLAH (n-q-r) (th-q-l) "heavy percussion"

A long percussion, said to have been twice the duration of a NAQRAH KHAFĪFAH* (al Rajab 1967:23).

NAQRAZĀN = NAḲRAZĀN

A pair of kettle drums used in the contemporary Mashriq (esp. Egypt). They are of the same type as the NAQQARĀT (s. NAQQARAH*), but of medium size. Used primarily in folk music (Sachs 1940:248), these small, nearly hemispherical drums are beaten with two sticks. They are often played while mounted to the back of a donkey (Ibid.: 251).

NAQŠ

Var. of NAQSH (d'Erlanger 1959:175).

NAQSH = NAKISH, NAQŠ (n-q-sh) "variegating; painting; engraving; sculpting"

1. A genre of music resembling an introduction which involves the fantasy-like treatment of various GHAZAL* tunes in a succession (ʿAbd al Qādir ibn Ghaybī in Anonymous Treatise 1939:244).
2. An unidentified vocal number of the NAWBAH/1* which is characterized by much ornamentation (Mor.) (Chottin and Hickmann 1949-1951:Band I, col. 594).
3. Practice of using more than one rhythmic mode (ĪQĀʿ/1*) in a performance of composed or improvised music (Allawerdi 1949:544; d'Erlanger 1959:175).
4. Practice of using more than one melodic mode (MAQĀM/1*) in a performance of composed or improvised music (d'Erlanger 1959:175).

NĀQŪR (pl. NAWĀQĪR) (n-q-r) "that which knocks"

1. A stringed instrument with open strings (zither type) mentioned by al Jurjānī (1938:220). It is said to have furnished a three-octave range (al Jurjānī 1938:412).
2. A horn named as one to be used on Judgment Day (Qur'ān 74:8).

NAQŪS or NĀQŪS (pl. NAWĀQĪS) = NĀḲŪS (n-q-s) "bell; gong"

1. Generic term for any clapper used as a musical instrument (Farmer 1967:6).
2. A hemispheric, clapperless bell on a metal handle, struck with metal rods. It was used as a liturgical percussion instrument by the Copts of Egypt and as a gong by Arab Christians generally (Marcuse).
3. A wooden or metal percussion slab or plate used by Arab Christians (Farmer 1945:37). It has also been described as a long piece of wood which was struck with another piece of wood, with which the early Christians announced the times of prayer (Juynboll 1913:193).
4. A percussion instrument of the Maghrib resembling a gong. It comprises a circular piece of steel which is struck with two metal rods (Grame 1970:85).

NARHAMÂT AL BUH'ÛR

Var. of NAGHAMĀT AL BUḤŪR* (Chottin 1939:127).

NAṢB (n-ṣ-b) "raising, erection"

One of the three kinds of singing in ancient Arabia (Ibn ʿAbd Rabbihi 1941:25; 1887:III, 186; Ibn Salamah 1938a:19; 1938b:249). It was, according to these references, the singing of travelers, or a type of improved camel driver's song which was sung by young people. The other two kinds of singing were SINĀD* and HAZAJ/1*. Other references record that there were three kinds of NAṢB in pre-Islamic times: the RUKBĀNĪ*, the SINĀD AL THAQĪL* and the HAZAJ AL KHAFĪF* (Ibn Khurdādhbih 1969:29; al Masʿūdī 1874:VIII, 93; Collangettes 1904:370).

NASHĀZ (n-sh-z) "discord"

Musical dissonance (d'Erlanger 1949:104).

NASHĪD (pl. NASHĀ'ID, ANSHĀD, ANĀSHĪD) = NASCHÎD (n-sh-d) "declamation of poetry, chanting, singing"

1. Measured song or hymn (Farmer EI(Eng), "Ghinā'":1073).
2. Vocal recitative; nasal, free rhythmed psalming (Farmer 1957: 441).
3. A vocal prelude setting the first hemistich or the first couplet of the lyrics (al Fārābī 1967:1162). In the French translation of this passage in d'Erlanger (1935:85), the word TASHYĪD* is used instead of NASHĪD. Sometimes this vocal setting of poetry was described as having a regular rhythm (al Fārābī 1967:990, n. 3); others described it as being free-rhythmed (al Jurjānī 1938:540). It was of greater length than a similar type of vocal prelude known as ISTIHLĀL* (al Fārābī 1967:1162; d'Erlanger 1935:85; al Jurjānī 1938:540). For the author of a 15th C. treatise, it had alternating regular and free rhythmed segments (Anonymous Treatise 1939:233ff).
4. In Moorish Spain, a recitative to open a concert or NAWBAH/1*, according to the rules of ZIRYĀB*(reported by al Maqqarī (d. 1631), see Chottin and Hickmann, 1949-1951:Band I, col. 589).

NASHĪD AL ʿAJAM (n-sh-d) (ʿ-j-m) "foreign or Persian song"

Musically equivalent to NASHĪD AL ʿARAB*, but utilizing Persian poetry (Anonymous Treatise 1939:235).

NASHĪD AL ʿARAB (n-sh-d) (ʿ-r-b) "Arab song"

A vocal form of the 14th C. to 16th C. which was described by ʿAbd al Qādir ibn Ghaybī (Wright 1979:499) as a musical setting of four couplets of Arabic poetry. It was described in a 15th C. treatise (Anonymous Treatise 1939:233-235) as having alternating segments of free rhythmed (NATHR AL NAGHAMĀT*) and regularly rhythmed (NAẒM AL NAGHAMĀT*) music. See NASHĪD AL ʿAJAM*.

NASHSHĀD (pl. NASHSHĀDŪN) = NACHĀD (n-sh-d) "one who performs the NASHĪD"

One who sings NASHĀ'ID (s. NASHĪD*). Syn. of MUNSHID*.

NASĪB (n-s-b) "a relative"

The opening section of a QAṢĪDAH/2* poem, traditionally comprising an elegy over a past love affair.

NASĪBAH (pl. NASĪBĀT) (n-s-b) "a relative"

The fifth tone of the modal scale, equivalent to GHAMMĀZ* of contemporary terminology (al Kindī 1965:23; see also n. 12).

NĀṢIYAH (pl. NAWĀṢĪ) (n-ṣ-y) "forelock"

The end piece to which the tuning pegs of the KAMĀN or KAMĀNJAH* are affixed (Maḥfūẓ 1964:160).

NATHR AL NAGHAMĀT (n-th-r) (n-gh-m) "prose of tones, i.e., musical prose"

Free rhythmed or parlando rubato music, i.e., vocal or instrumental performance without regularly recurring rhythmic pattern (Anonymous Treatise 1939:233-235; Allawerdi 1949:548). Opp. of NAẒM AL NAGHAMĀT*.

NAUBA

Var. of NAWBAH* (Farmer 1954, "Nauba":VI, 32-34; d'Erlanger 1939: 236-238).

NAUḤ

Var. of NAWḤ* (Farmer 1967:10, 14-15).

NĀʿŪRAH (pl. NAWĀʿĪR) = NA'ÛRA (n-ʿ-r) "waterwheel"

The central part of the three-part SARRĀBAH* genre of vocal music (Mor.) (Chottin 1939:160-161). This part has three lines, each of which is subdivided into three parts, as well as a six-line strophe with lines rhymed two-by-two.

NAWʿ (pl. ANWĀʿ) (n-w-ʿ) "kind, species"

1. Term used for octave, pentachordal, as well as tetrachordal species by Arab theoreticians prior to Ṣafī al Dīn (13th C.) (al Kindī 1966:157; d'Erlanger 1938:581, n. 26). These scalar segments, repeated at different levels without transposition or alteration of tones by accidentals, were later divided into two categories: the octave species (NAWʿ) and the tetrachordal or pentachordal species (BAḤR/6*)(al Jurjānī 1938:351-354; 581, n. 26; Ṣafī al Dīn 1938b:109; de Vaux 1891:330).
2. Derivative rhythmic mode (Farmer 1943:78). See JINS/2*.

NAWʿ AL JAMĀʿAH (n-w-ʿ) (j-m-ʿ) "species of the collection"

The "collection" or scale of tones, from any tone to its upper octave equivalent (al Fārābī 1967:126; 1930:47). The scales were not, at the time of al Fārābī, so fixed as in later practice, and the musicians could choose intervals or tetrachordal units from a veritable infinity of choices. It seems likely that the later theorists (from the 13th C. on), who seemed more concerned with specific though a much more limited number of scales, were not only reflecting a change in theoretizing but also a change in practice. This trend has continued to today when the musician chooses not between various intervals and tetrachordal segments to "create anew" his "collection" (JAMʿ/1* or JAMĀʿAH*) or modal scale, but between the much larger units known as MAQĀMĀT (s. MAQĀM/1*) which comprise fixed two-octave scales. He is further limited to those MAQĀMĀT in favor in his region. As if to increase his options, the Contemporary Period musician has emphasized the practice and increased the incidence of modulations within the composed or improvised performance.

NAWĀ (Pers.) "voice, tune"

1. Melodic mode mentioned by Ṣafī al Dīn (1938b:135).
2. A tetrachordal division (JINS/1*) mentioned by Ṣafī al Dīn (1938b:119).
3. Name for a note of the contemporary Arabian scale, G_2

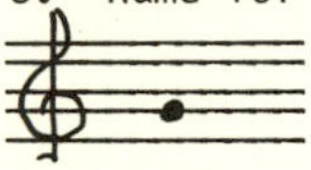
.

NAWAKHT (Pers.)

A genre of instrumental music without regular rhythm (Anonymous Treatise 1939:245-246; al Jurjānī 1938:519, 521-522). See PISHRŪ/1* and TARJĪʿ/3*, other genres of that time.

NAWBAH (pl. NAWBĀT, NUWAB) = NAUBA, NÛBA, NOUBA, NAOUBAH (n-w-b) "turn, rotation"

1. A suite of vocal and instrumental pieces of both composed and improvised variety. The use of this term for the suite seems to have arisen by the end of the 9th C., out of the practice of the musicians of the ʿAbbāsī court who performed their numbers by "turn" (NAWBAH/4*). Eventually the word for this turn of the different performers became the designation for the performance as a whole. Another explanation for this use of the term relates to the performance of certain pieces of music at particular hours (NUWAB, s. NAWBAH) of the day. The military band performed this music (see def. 2) as well as the suite of pieces later known as NAWBAH.

We know little about the integral parts of the NAWBAH suite before the 14th C. At that time it comprised four movements: QAWL/2*, GHAZAL*, TARĀNAH* and FURŪ-DĀSHT*. In 1379, ʿAbd al Qādir ibn Ghaybī introduced a fifth movement known as MUSTAZĀD* (d'Erlanger 1939:236-238). All of these five were vocal movements, each of which was preceded by an instrumental prelude known as ṬARĪQAH/3*. Each was composed according to a specific poetic meter as well as musical rhythmic mode.

Today the term NAWBAH is used primarily for the suite of the Maghrib, though similar phenomena are found in the Mashriq under other names (WAṢLAH/1*, FAṢL/1* and FĀṢIL/2*). The number and kinds of pieces varies from region to region, but each suite or NAWBAH is dominated by a single melodic mode. In the Maghrib, it is said that there were once 24 NAWBĀT, one composed on each of the 24 melodic modes (ṬUBŪʿ, s. ṬABʿ*). Today some of these have been lost. According to el Mahdi (1972:12-15), there are now only 15 different NAWBĀT in Algeria and Tunisia.

The five most popular movements of the NAWBAH (MUṢADDAR/1*, BAṬĀYḤĪ/1*, DARAJ/1*, INṢIRAF/1*, and KHALĀṢ* or MAKHLAṢ*) are named for the rhythmic modes on which they are based. In addition to these movements, a Maghribī NAWBAH often has a vocal prelude (DĀ'IRAH/3*), an instrumental prelude (MUSTAKHBIR/1), a rhythmed instrumental overture (TAWSHIYAH or TŪSHIYAH*) and a short introduction (KURSĪ/1*) which can be added to any or all of the main movements. See el Helou (1965:109-110); Delphin and Guin (1886:64); d'Erlanger (1959:186-197); Chottin (1939:119); Ḥāfiẓ (1971:113-138); and Farmer (EI(Fr), "Nauba":947-948). The vocal numbers are usually sung by a chorus in unison, though occasionally vocal solos alternate with choral segments. There is a gradual acceleration from one section to the next. Each movement has a final section of acceleration called MUṢARRAF* which makes preparation for the faster movement to follow (Jargy 1971:95). See also NŪBAH*.

2. A military band which filled both the military and court ceremonial needs of the various rulers and feudal lords of the Classical Period (See Farmer 1967:206-208; EI(Fr), "Ṭabl Khāna": 217-222). The term was used with this meaning in al Iṣfahānī's <u>Kitāb al Aghānī</u>, as well as in the <u>1001 Nights</u> (Farmer 1945:5). The plural of this word is still used in the Mashriq (Syria) (Wehr) and the Maghrib (el Mahdi 1972:11) to designate a group of musicians. See ṬABL KHĀNAH*.

3. A melodic mode (Alg.) (Delphin and Guin 1886:61).

4. A "turn" of a musician for performing (Wehr). See NAWBAH/1*.

5. A bugle call (Wehr).

6. Military music of the Arabs (Delphin and Guin 1886:43).

NAWBAH ANDALUSIYYAH (n-w-b) (geog.) "Andalusian suite"

Syn. of NAWBAH/1*, or more specifically, the classical suite of the Maghrib (Chottin 1961:Band IX, col. 1561; Farmer 1957:453).

NAWBAH GHARNĀṬAH (n-w-b) (geog.) "suite of Granada"

Var. of NAWBAH GHURNĀṬIYYAH* (Salvador-Daniel 1976:194-195).

NAWBAH GHARNAṬIYYAH (n-w-b) (geog.) "Granadan suite"

Var. of NAWBAH GHURNĀṬIYYAH* (Chottin 1961:Band IX, col. 1561).

NAWBAH GHURNĀṬIYYAH = NAWBAH GHARNĀṬAH, NAWBAH GHARNAṬIYYAH (n-w-b) (geog.) "Granadan suite"

One type of suite (NAWBAH/1*) in the Maghrib. This NAWBAH is the traditional, classical variety, as distinguished from a more recently introduced and less proper form, the NAWBAH INQILĀBĀT*). The classical suite is also called NAWBAH ANDALUSIYYAH*.

NAWBAH INQILĀBĀT = NAWBAH NEKLABĀT (n-w-b) (q-l-b) "rotation of songs"

This Maghribī suite comprises a series of songs (INQILĀBĀT, s. INQILĀB/2*), each introduced by a prelude called MUSTAKHBIR/2*. An orchestral SHANBAR* (given TCHENEBAR*) serves as overture for the series as a whole. This type of NAWBAH is said to have been introduced into the Maghrib (Alg.) at the beginning of the 16th C. by Turkish musicians (Farmer 1976a:194). It is judged as innovative and less proper, less classical, than the NAWBAH ANDALUSIYYAH* or NAWBAH GHURNĀṬIYYAH*. See Rouanet 1922:2863.

NAWBAH KHĀNAH (n-w-b) (kh-w-n) "house of the turn or rotation"

Syn. of ṬABL KHĀNAH* (Farmer EI(Fr), "Ṭabl Khāna":232).

NAWBAH NEKLABĀT (n-w-b) (colloq.)

Var. of NAWBAH INQILĀBĀT* (Farmer 1976a:194; Chottin 1961:Band IX, col. 1561).

NAWḤ = NAUḤ (n-w-ḥ) "lament; lamentation"

1. An elegy, generally sung by women, in the early centuries of the Islamic period. It is said to have been, along with the NAṢB*, one of the only genres of song sung in the Ḥijāz until the end of the 6th or beginning of the 7th C. (Farmer 1967:14-15). 2. More generally, it applies to the song or chant of the professional wailer.

NĀY (pl. NĀYĀT) = NAI, NAÏ (Pers.) "flute"

1. An end-blown cane flute without mouthpiece or reed. This Persian name superseded the term QUṢṢĀBAH* (usually a shorter instrument) about the 9th C. Later it was used for a great variety of flutes of different sizes, borings and materials. Generally, the instrument has been made from cane, occasionally from wood or metal (al Ḥafnī 1971:178). Used throughout the Arab World, this instrument generally has six upper holes and one on the underside for the thumb. It should have nine equal segments between nodes of the reed. It has a range of about two octaves, though skilled performers are able to produce three octaves on this simple instrument (el Mahdi 1972:62). A performer usually uses a set of at least five NĀYĀT with different lengths, thicknesses and hole borings so that he can move easily from one melodic mode to another. This instrument has been used for performing all forms of music: art, folk and religious.

2. In very early times, a generic term for all woodwind instruments (Marcuse). According to Ibn Salamah (1938b:246), this term was used for either the oboe (double reed) or flute types.

NĀY ABYAḌ (Pers.) (b-y-ḍ) "white flute"

A 15th C. name for a variety of woodwind instrument, said to have been more difficult to play than the NĀY ASWAD* and less perfect as an instrument (Anonymous Treatise 1939:25). It was probably an end-blown flute (see NĀY/1*). Also NĀY BAYḌĀ'*.

NĀY ASWAD (Pers.) (s-w-d) "black flute"

A 15th C. name for a variety of woodwind instrument which was equivalent to the NĀY ṢIYĀḤ*. It was probably a reed-blown instrument. It was described as being of half cubit length (i.e., the length of the arm from the elbow to the tip of the middle finger) with a mouthpiece "like that of the SURNĀY*." It had a range of 35 notes, covering a double octave (Anonymous Treatise 1939:25). Also NĀY SAWDĀ'*, NĀY ṢIYĀḤ*.

NĀY BAYḌĀ' (Pers.) (b-y-ḍ) "white flute"

Syn. of NĀY ABYAḌ* (Anonymous Treatise 1939:25).

NĀY AL ʿIRĀQĪ (Pers.) (geog.) "ʿIrāqī flute"

A woodwind instrument mentioned by al Ghazālī (1901:214; Farmer EI(Eng), "Mizmār":541). It probably had a double reed, like a later instrument known as ʿIRĀQIYYAH*.

NĀY JIRĀF (Pers.) (j-r-f)

The shortest Egyptian NĀY/1*, about 50 cm. long (Marcuse).

NĀY MUHADHDHAB (Pers.) (h-dh-b) "refined NAY"

Unidentified woodwind instrument of Moorish Spain (el Helou 1965: 39).

NĀY SAFĪD (Pers.) (s-f-d)

An end-blown flute said to have been invented by shepherds and the Kurds, according to ʿAbd al Qādir ibn Ghaybī (15th C.) (Farmer 1978:I, 67).

NĀY SAWDĀ' (Pers.) (s-w-d) "black flute"

Syn. of NĀY ASWAD* (Anonymous Treatise 1939:25).

NĀY SHĀH (Pers.) (Pers.) "NĀY king"

The largest Egyptian NĀY/1*, about 75 cm. in length (Marcuse).

NĀY ṢIYĀḤ (Pers.) (ṣ-y-ḥ) "shouting NĀY"

Syn. of NĀY ASWAD*. This expression was used for a double-reed aerophone in a 14th C. ms. (Farmer EI(Eng), "Mizmār":540).

NĀY TATARĪ (Pers.) (nat.) "flute of the Tatars"

An unidentified woodwind instrument mentioned in the 1001 Nights The name has not been found mentioned elsewhere in the literature (Farmer 1945:32-33).

NĀY ṬUNBŪR (Pers.) (Pers.)

A ṬUNBŪR/1* with two strings tuned a fourth apart and played with a plectrum. This instrument was described by the 15th C. author, ʿAbd al Qādir ibn Ghaybī (Farmer EI(Fr), "Ṭunbūr":270).

NĀY ZUNĀMĪ (Pers.) (n. of pers.) "flute of ZUNĀM"

The NĀY/1* as improved in the early 9th C. by Zunām (Marcuse).

NĀYĔL

Var. of NĀYALĪ* (Jargy 1970:238).

NĀY-I-C̲HADŪR

A woodwind instrument mentioned by ʿAbd al Qādir ibn Ghaybī (d. 1435) which is thought to have been a reed cornet (Farmer 1976b: 29).

NĀYALĪ (n-y-l) = NĀYĔL, perhaps an adj. form from NĀYAL, "sea and river workers"

1. A folkish variety of MAWWĀL/1* sung in ʿIrāq (el Helou 1961: 197).
2. The poem sung with a variety of improvisatory music known in ʿIrāq (def. 1).

NAẒARĪ (n-ẓ-r) "visual; theoretical"

Theoretical as opposed to the practical art of music (ʿAMALĪ*) (Farmer 1943:15; 1929a:106).

NĀZILAN (n-z-l) "descending"

Descending in pitch (Ibn Sīnā 1930:95).

NĀẒIM = NĀD̲HIM (n-ẓ-m) "ordered"

1. The enharmonic tetrachordal scalar segment (JINS/1*), a variety of soft (LAYYIN/1*) JINS in which the large interval is comparable to the major third (ratio 5/4) (al Fārābī 1967:161; al Khwārizmī 1968:243).
2. The chromatic tetrachordal scalar segment (JINS/1*), a variety of soft (LAYYIN/1*) JINS in which the large interval is comparable

to the minor third (ratio 7/6) (Ibn Sīnā 1930:90-91; Ṣafī al Dīn 1938a:63; al Lādhiqī 1939:346). It is, according to Ṣafī al Dīn, the most dissonant of the soft AJNĀS (1938b:55). See also de Vaux 1891:311).

NAẒĪR (pl. NAẒĀ'IR) (n-ẓ-r) "equivalent; copy; parallel"

Octave equivalent (Ibn al Munajjim 1976:345).

NAẒM (n-z-m) "order"

A syllabic song of simple rhythm (Jargy 1970:31; 1978:81).

NAẒM AL NAGHAMĀT (n-ẓ-m) (n-gh-m) "ordering of tones"

One of two divisions into which music of the Arabs can be divided. This includes all that music based on a traditional or composed melody and having a regularly rhythmed underlay (Anonymous Treatise 1939:232-233; Allawerdi 1949:548; al Faruqi 1974:Chap. II). Opp. of NATHR AL NAGHAMĀT*.

NEÇERAF

Var. of INṢIRĀF/1* (Rouanet 1922:2857-2858).

NEKLAB or NEKLÂB (pl. NEKLÂBAT)

Vars. of INQILĀB* (Farmer 1976a:194; Chottin 1961:Band IX, col. 1561).

NFĪR

Var. of NAFĪR* (Chottin 1961:Band IX, col. 1565).

NIGHAM (n-gh-m) "notes"

Pl. of NAGHM or NAGHAM* (al Fārābī 1960:11, 14; Farmer 1929a:238; Anonymous Treatise 1939:240-243).

NIHĀWAND

Var. of NAHĀWAND* (d'Erlanger 1939:145).

NIHOUFT

Var. of NIHUFT* (Touma 1977b:37).

NIHUFT or NUHUFT = NIHOUFT (Pers.)

1. Melodic mode mentioned from the 15th C. (Anonymous Treatise 1939:139; Ṣafī al Dīn in de Vaux 1891:340).
2. A note of the contemporary Arabian scale, B_2 or Cb_2  .

NIM

Syn. of NĪM/1* (Ṣalāḥ al Dīn 1950:91; Ḥāfiẓ 1971:180).

NĪM (pl. NĪMĀT) (Pers.) "half; lower"

1. A prefix used for naming certain notes of the contemporary Arab scale and indicating that the tone is approximately ¼ tone below the note mentioned, e.g., NĪM KURDĪ 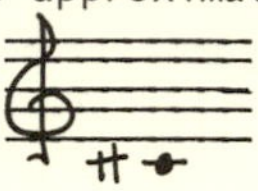 is ¼ tone below KURDĪ* 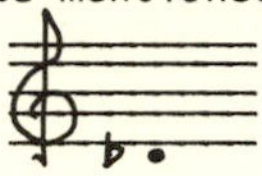 (al Khulaʿī 1904:35). Also NĪM ʿARABAH*.

2. The quarter tone of the contemporary theoretical system. El Helou writes that the whole tone (BARDAH/1*) can be divided into three smaller intervals: the quarter tone (NĪM), the half tone (ʿARABAH/1*), and the three-quarter tone (TĪK*) (el Helou 1961:68). Also NĪM ʿARABAH/2*.

NĪM ʿAJAM (Pers.) (ʿ-j-m) "lowered ʿAJAM"

Name of a note of the contemporary Arab scale, $A\#_2$  .

NĪM ʿARABAH (pl. NĪMĀT ʿARABAH) (Pers.) (ʿ-r-b) "lowered vehicle"

1. The tone ¼ tone below one of the notes of the fundamental scale of the Arabs (Ṣalāḥ al Dīn 1950:89; Collangettes 1904:414). 2. Quarter tone interval. See NIM/2* (Ṣalāḥ al Dīn 1950:89; Collangettes 1904:414).

NĪM BARDAH = NĪM PARDAH (Pers.) (Pers.) "half of the curtain"

The half tone interval of the contemporary theoretical system (al Dāqūqī 1965:25).

NĪM ḤIJĀZ (Pers.) (geog.) "lowered ḤIJĀZ"

Name of a note of the contemporary Arab scale, $F\#_1$  .

NĪM ḤIṢĀR (Pers.) (ḥ-ṣ-r) "lowered ḤIṢĀR"

Name of a note of the contemporary Arab scale, $G\#_2$  .

NĪM KURD (Pers.) (nat.) "lowered KURD"

Name of a note of the contemporary Arab scale, $D\#_1$  . Also NĪM KURDĪ*.

NĪM SHĀHNĀZ (Pers.) (Pers.) "lowered SHĀHNĀZ"

Name of a note of the contemporary Arab scale, $C\#_2$  .

NĪM ZAWĀL (Pers.) (z-w-l) "lowered ZAWĀL"

Name of a note of the contemporary Arab scale, $D\#_2$  .

NĪM ZĪRKŪLAH (Pers.) (Pers.) "lowered ZĪRKŪLAH"

Name of a note of the contemporary Arab scale, $C^{\sharp}_{1}$  .

NĪRA

An end-blown flute or recorder type instrument, syn. of LIRA or LÎRA* (Chottin 1939:34; 1961:Band IX, col. 1565).

NISBAH (pl. NISAB) (n-s-b) "ratio, relationship"

Frequency ratio for a musical interval. See MUTASHĀBIHAH/3* for the use of this term in connection with the comparison of two melodic motifs or progressions (Ibn Sīnā 1930:96).

NIṢF or NUṢF BARDAH = NIṢF PARDAH (n-ṣ-f) (Pers.) "half curtain"

The half step interval, syn. of NĪM BARDAH* (al Dāqūqī 1965:89).

NIṢF or NUṢF BU‘D (n-ṣ-f) (b-‘-d) "half interval"

The half step interval (al Dāqūqī 1965:25).

NIṢF or NUṢF ṬAB‘ (n-ṣ-f) (ṭ-b-‘) "half printing"

The semitone (Farmer 1933b:19; see ṬAB‘/2* and ṬAB‘/3*.

NIṢF ṬANĪNĪ (n-ṣ-f) (ṭ-n-n) "half ṬANĪNĪ"

The semitone which is equiv. to the Limma, i.e., with 90 c. and a ratio of 256/243 (Ḥāfiẓ 1971:95-96).

NIṢF AL WAḤDAH AL ṢAGHĪRAH (n-ṣ-f) (w-ḥ-d) (ṣ-gh-r) "half the small unit"

A note corresponding to the eighth note of European notation (al Khula‘ī 1904; d'Erlanger 1959:23-24).

NIYĀḤAH (n-w-ḥ) "mourning"

Vocal music for mourning, as opposed to the vocal music for enjoyment (GHINĀ'/6*) (al Fārābī 1967:68).

NOQAÎRÂT

Var. of NUQAYRĀT (Chottin 1961:Band IX, col. 1567). See NUQAYRAH*.

NOUAR'ER

Var. of NUWĀGHIR*(Delphin and Guin 1886:44).

NOUBA

Var. of NAWBAH/1* (Chottin 1939:111; Touma 1977b:75).

NOUZHAH

Var. of NUZHAH* (Farmer 1977:98).

NQAIṬĪ

Var. of NUQAYṬĪ* (Chottin 1939:116, n. 1).

NŪBAH (n-w-b)

1. NAWBAH* equiv. (Touma 1977b:75; Jones 1977:68-78). In describing this suite as performed by the ʿĪsāwiyyah(Tun.), Jones designates it as a series of instrumental and vocal solos, and antiphonal selections by vocal soloist, chorus, ZUKRAH/1* player and accompanying instrumentalists. The bulk of the NŪBAH is antiphonal between vocalists and the ZUKRAH. Individual vocal sequences consist of a short segment from the poetic text, usually not more than one line, with possible repetitions or improvisations. Then the ZUKRAH player (ZAKKĀR*) repeats the melodic and rhythmic material of the preceding vocal segment, but sometimes including variations and improvisations in his "response." He may also make an "excursion" (called KHURŪJ/2* or SURŪḤ*) to new materials before returning to the required refrain or "response." This main part of the NŪBAH is preceded by an ISTIKHBĀR* or MUSTAKHBIR/1*. and a QAṢĪDAH/1*. The main part of the NŪBAH is also called NŪBAH (def. 2 below). It begins when other vocalists as well as drums join the ensemble. It generally maintains a rhythmic unity, though a gradual acceleration is evident throughout. The BARWAL/1* is the second main part of the NŪBAH. It is based on a rhythmic mode of the same name and is faster than the preceding section. It resembles that previous part by maintaining a gradual acceleration. Optional segments which can be added after the BARWAL are the DARRĀZĪ*, the KHATM/1* finale or a final KHURŪJ* played by the ZAKKĀR (Jones 1977:68-77).
2. The main part of the suite (NŪBAH/1*) as performed by the ʿĪsāwiyyah musicians of Tunisia. Another main segment is the BARWAL/1*. Other parts are optional. See NŪBAH/1*.

NUFṬAH (n-f-ṭ) f. of "irritable, hot tempered"

A kind of vocal music mentioned in the <u>1001 Nights</u> (Farmer 1945:5).

NUHUFT (Pers.)

Equiv. of NIHUFT*.

NUÎQSÂT (n-q-s) colloq. der. dim. pl. of NAQŪS, NUWAYQASĀT "bell" (?)

Small finger cymbals of copper used by dancers (Chottin 1939:47). See NUQAYSĀT*.

NUḲAIRA

Var. of NUQAYRAH* (Farmer EI(Fr), "Ṭabl":232).

NU'MĀNĪ (n-'-m) "pertaining to Nu'mān, a person and district of 'Irāq"

A type of MAWWĀL/1* (Maḥfūẓ 1964:103).

NUQAYRAH (pl. NUQAYRĀT) = NAQAYRAH, NUḲAIRA, NOQAÎRÂT (n-q-r) dim. of "that which strikes"

Tiny kettledrum made of clay or metal, and used in Syria and in North Africa (Farmer 1957:455). Also called DABLAK*. The term is usually found in its plural form (Farmer 1954, "Syrian Music":256; Shiloah 1965:I, 30), since this drum is played in pairs.

NUQAYSĀT (pl. of NUQAYSAH) = NUÎQSÂT, NÛWÎQSÂT (n-q-s) pl. dim. of NAQŪS "bell, gong"

Finger cymbals of the Berbers (Marcuse). See NUÎQSÂT*, NÛWÎQSÂT*.

NUQAYṬĪ (n-q-ṭ) "pertaining to droplet"

The musician talented with notes (Chottin 1939:116, n. 1).

NUQLAH = NAQALA (n-q-l) "movement; migration; pattern"

Syn. of INTIQĀL/1* (al Fārābī 1967:967-983; al Kindī 1966:150).

NUQLAH 'ALĀ IN'IRĀJ (n-q-l) ('-r-j) "limping movement"

Syn. of INTIQĀL 'ALĀ IN'IRĀJ* (al Fārābī 1967:967-983).

NUQLAH 'ALĀ IN'IṬĀF (n-q-l) ('-ṭ-f) "bending or curved movement"

Syn. of INTIQĀL 'ALĀ IN'IṬĀF* (al Fārābī 1967:967-983).

NUQLAH 'ALĀ ISTIDĀRAH (n-q-l) (d-w-r) "cyclical movement"

Syn. of INTIQĀL 'ALĀ ISTIDĀRAH* (al Fārābī 1967:967-983).

NUQLAH 'ALĀ ISTIQĀMAH or NUQLAH MUSTAQĪMAH (n-q-l) (q-w-m) "direct movement"

Syn. of INTIQĀL 'ALĀ ISTIQĀMAH* (al Fārābī 1967:968).

NUQQĀRIYAH (pl. NUQQĀRIYĀT) (n-q-r) "that which strikes or pecks"

A kettledrum.

NUQQAYRAH (pl. NUQQAYRĀT (n-q-r) dim. of NUQQĀR (?)

A small kettledrum (Madina).

NUQṢĀN (n-q-ṣ) "diminution"

One of the categories of melodic beautification presented by Ibn Sīnā (1930:99). It includes two types: 1) the diminution of the length of every percussion in a rhythmic cycle (ḤATHĪTH/2*); or 2) a decrease in the number of percussions within the cycle while maintaining the overall time span (ṬAYY*). See TAḤSĪN AL LAḤN*.

NUQṢĀN AL ṢAWT BIL TADRĪJ (n-q-ṣ) (ṣ-w-t) (d-r-j) "diminution of the sound by degrees"

Diminuendo, i.e., a gradual softening of volume (el Helou 1971:58).

NUQṬAH (pl. NUQĀṬ) (n-q-ṭ) "point; position"

Finger position (on the neck of a stringed instrument) (al Fārābī 1967:503).

NUQŪṬ (pl. of NAQṬ) (n-q-ṭ) "drippings"

The monetary tips which were given to musicians of the ʿAbbāsī period (Farmer 1945:6).

NŪRAH = NOURA

An unidentified musical instrument which was mentioned in a 13th C. treatise from Moorish Spain (Farmer 1926a:247). It may have been a woodwind instrument, or perhaps a stringed instrument. The term MIZMĀR* with which it was associated in that ms. was used for both categories of instrument.

NUṢF (n-ṣ-f) "half"

Equiv. of NIṢF*, alone or in various compounds, e.g., NIṢF or NUṢF BARDAH*, NIṢF BUʿD*, etc.

NŪTĪ (n-w-t) "apprentice"

The left pipe of a double clarinet type instrument, on which the drone tone is performed while the other pipe or RA'ĪS/4* performs the melody (al Ḥafnī 1971:178). Also SANAD*.

NUWĀGHIR = NOUAR'ER (pl. of NĀGHIR?) (n-gh-r) "Niger" (?)

Pair of kettledrums played with two drumsticks (Alg.) (Delphin and Guin 1886:44).

NUWĀR (Fr.) "black"

Quarter note (Ḥāfiẓ 1971:187).

NUWWĀRAH (pl. NUWWĀRĀT) (n-w-r) colloq. "flower"

Rosette covering for the opening of a stringed instrument (Moorish Spain) (Farmer 1978:I, 44).

NÛWÎQSÂT

Var. of NUQAYṢĀT*(Chottin 1961:Band IX, col. 1567).

NUZHAH = NOUZHAH (n-z-h) "stroll; pleasure ride; entertainment"

A rectangular psaltery invented by Ṣafī al Dīn (d. 1294). It had 32 tuning pegs at the left side of the instrument to control 32 strings of various lengths stretched across the surface of the instrument. In the 14th C. ms., Kanz al Tuḥaf, it was described as twice the size of the QĀNŪN* with the following dimensions: 74.25 cm. x 54 cm., with the depth of its sound box being 27 cm. This later version of the instrument had 108 ctrings, 81 of which were stretched across the whole body of the instrument and tuned trichordally. Between these strings, 27 single treble strings of differing lengths were placed. It was held horizontally and played with both hands (Farmer 1926a:249-250). In the 15th C., the instrument was described as having 81 strings, tuned trichordally and producing 27 different pitches.

O

'OCHAÏRAN

Var. of ʿUSHAYRĀN*(Rouanet 1922:2732).

'OOD

Var. of ʿŪD* (Lane 1973:361).

ORAB

Var. of ʿURAB* (Touma 1977b:96).

'ÖSHEIRÂN

Var. of ʿUSHAYRĀN* (Smith 1847:181).

OUASLAH

Var. of WAṢLAH/1* (Touma 1977b:81).

OUAZN

Var. of WAZN* (Touma 1977b:61).

OUCHAÏRAN

Var. of ʿUSHAYRĀN* (Touma 1977b:36).

OUÇOUL

Var. of UṢŪL* (Rouanet 1922:2770).

OUD

Var. of ʿŪD* (Touma 1977b:94; Salvador-Daniel 1976:239).

OUGNIYA

Var. of UGHNIYAH* (Touma 1972:116).

OUSOUL

Var. of UṢŪL* (Touma 1977b:63).

OUST'A

Var. of WUSṬĀ* (Rouanet 1922:2807).

OUTAR

Var. of WATAR* (Rouanet 1922:2809).

P

PARDAH (pl. PARDĀT) = BARDAH, PURDAH (Pers.) "curtain"

1. Melodic mode, as defined in a 13th C. ms. in the following way: A limited number of notes bounded by a major consonant interval such as an octave, a perfect fifth, a perfect fourth or sometimes a third. It is therefore synonymous with JAMʿ/1* or a scalar combination of tones (Quṭb al Dīn al Shīrāzī 1978:283, tr. on p. 172). At times the term was used by Quṭb al Dīn as a Persian equivalent of the Arabic SHADD/2* (pl. SHUDŪD), i.e., a principal melodic mode. In addition, he made a distinction between the PARDAH, as a principal mode, and the SHUʿBAH*, a derived mode (Wright 1978:169). See also Anonymous Treatise 1939: 101; al Lādhiqī 1939:374. Some theorists further qualified the term by maintaining that it designated a "consonant" combination of intervals making up the modal scale (ʿAbd al Qādir ibn Ghaybī in Wright 1978:169, n. 16).
2. Syn. of BARDAH/1* (Col. Muḥammad Dhākir in 1894, according to Shawqī 1969a:22-24; al Khulaʿī 1904:33, 36).

PASTA or PASTĀ (Pers.) "tie, connection"

Var. of BISTAH or BASTAH* (Tsuge 1972:64; Jargy 1970:246, resp.).

PÉCHEREV

Var. of BASHRAF* (Chottin 1939:105).

PESCHEREFF

Var. of BASHRAF* (Farmer 1976a:201).

PESCHREF

Var. of BASHRAF* (Chottin and Hickmann 1949;1951:Band I, col. 594).

PESTE

Var. of BISTAH or BASTAH* (Tsuge 1972:64).

PĪPĀ

"Balloon" guitar of the Chinese which was introduced into Mesopotamia by the Mughals in the 13th C. According to ʿAbd al Qādir ibn Ghaybī (d. 1435), it was much used by the people of Khaṭā. It had a shallow sound box (KĀSAH/1*) about 9 cm. in depth, a wooden face, and four strings (Farmer 1978:II, 16; EI(Eng), "ʿŪd": 986).

PISHRŪ (pl. PISHRAWĀT)

1. From the 14th C., a genre of vocal or instrumental improvisation among non-Arab musicians (al Jurjānī 1938:519, 522-523). When vocal, it resembled the vocalise, i.e., it had no words or poetic meter. It was, however, based on one of the musical rhythmic cycles. It was indefinite in length, having three, five, seven or even more segments, each of which ended with a return to a refrain motif known as TARJĪʿ BAND or SAR-BAND PISHRŪ* which emphasized as well as marked the divisions of the improvisation. Instrumentalists played the PISHRAWĀT after the NAWAKHT* and the TARJĪʿ/3*. Other types of composition or improvisation could be performed after the PISHRŪ (ʿAbd al Qādir ibn Ghaybī as quoted in Anonymous Treatise (1939:245-246). See BASHRAF/1*, a modern syn.
2. One of the rhythms described by a 15th C. treatise as a conjunct four-beat cycle (Anonymous Treatise 1939:219).

PURDAH (Pers.)

See PARDAH/1* (Anonymous Treatise 1939:101-102). The author of that 15th C. work quotes from an earlier work in which PURDAH applies to any principal melodic mode.

Q

QABĀ = ABA

A large double reed (oboe-type) aerophone of Egypt which was described by Villoteau (d. 1839) as being approximately 58-60 cm. in length (Hickmann 1947:12).

QABĀ DŪDUK

A large recorder-type instrument said to have been invented at Mosul (Farmer 1976b:20).

QABĀ SŪRNĀ

Var. of QABĀ ZŪRNĀ (Farmer EI(Eng), "Mizmār":540).

QABĀ ZŪRNĀ = QABĀ SŪRNĀ

A large oboe described in a 17th C. work. It had seven finger holes and a thumb hole and was about 60 cm. long (Farmer 1976b:24). It seems to have been similar to the QABĀ* described by Villoteau in the early 19th C. It was also known as ZAMR AL KABĪR*.

QABBUṢ

Var. of QABŪṢ* or QUBŪZ* used in ʿUmān (Farmer EI(Eng), "ʿŪd":986).

QABḌĀ

Var. of QABḌĪ*(Cowl 1966:137).

QABḌAH (pl. QIBĀḌ) = QABD'A (q-b-ḍ)"handle, that which is grasped"

The neck of the early short necked lute known as BARBAṬ* as well as of the contemporary RABAB/2* of the Maghrib (Rouanet 1922:2924).

QABḌĪ = QABḌĀ (q-b-ḍ) "contracted; oppressed"

One of the three types of ethos mentioned by al Kindī (Cowl 1966:

137). It could also be defined as one of three moods expressed in music. See also BUSṬĪ*, KARAM*, MUʿTADIL*.

QABŪṢ (q-b-ṣ) or (Turk.), see Farmer 1978:I, 73

A lute made of a single block of wood, with skin face and six strings. It is played with a plectrum of quill. This instrument used today in the ḤIJĀZ is very old and has had many variant names. See QUBŪZ*. According to ʿAbd al Qādir ibn Ghaybī (d. 1435), a similar instrument called QŪPŪZ RŪMĪ* had five double strings. In the 17th C., the QABŪS was a small, hollow instrument with three strings. Other more recent names for this instrument are QABBUṢ in ʿUMĀN; QANBUṢ in Hadramawt; QUPŪZ, QŪPŪZ or QAPŪZ in Turkey (Farmer EI(Eng), "ʿŪd":986; 1978:I, 72).

QAÇBA

Var. of QAṢABAH* (Chottin 1939:34).

QADARIYYAH (pl. QADARIYYĀT) = QADRIAH (q-d-r) "measure"

A women's song of the Maghrib.

QADARIYYAH AL ṢINĀʿAH = KADRIAT SENÂA (q-d-r) (ṣ-n-ʿ) "measure of the art or craft, i.e., measure of art music"

Classical songs (Farmer 1976a:195, where the following spelling is used, KADRIAT SENÂA*).

QADD (pl. QUDŪD) (q-d-d) "cutting into strips"

An instrumental genre of Syria similar to the Egyptian TAḤMĪLAH*. Like the latter, it is made up of 1) a rhythmed refrain tune performed in unison by the orchestra; and 2) segments of solo free rhythmed improvisations by the various solo instruments of the orchestra, each segment followed by a return to the orchestral refrain (d'Erlanger 1959:184-185).

QAḌĪB (pl. QUḌBĀN or QIḌBĀN) = ḲADĪB (q-ḍ-b) "twig, stick"

Wand or stick for beating the rhythm or ĪQĀʿ/l* pattern (Kitāb al Aghānī; Ibn ʿAbd Rabbihi; Ikhwān al Ṣafā' 1957:I, 200; Farmer 1943: 45). It is said to have been used in pre-Islamic times as well as later (Farmer 1967:13). Other authors maintain that it was first used by IBRAHĪM AL MAWṢILĪ* (d. 804) (Ibn ʿAbd Rabbihi 1887: III, 188; and Farmer 1943/44:53). It was popular with those who sang the MURTAJAL/l* improvisations during the ʿAbbāsī period (Farmer 1967:47). It was wrongly described by Laborde, Kiesewetter and Sachs as a woodwind instrument.

QAḌĪB AL QAWL (q-ḍ-b) (q-w-l) "speech stick"

Syn. of QAḌĪB*.

QADĪḤAH (q-d-ḥ) "that which always incepts motion, strikes fire"

A kettledrum played with two drumsticks (Alg.) (Delphin and Guin 1886:37).

QADR (pl. AQDĀR) (q-d-r) "extent; amount"

Bar line used in musical notation (Maḥfūẓ 1964:187).

QADRIAH (pl. QADRIAT)

Probably a var. of QADARIYYAH* (Chottin 1961:Band IX, col. 1563).

QĀFIYAH (pl. QAWĀFĪ) (q-f-w) "rhyme"

Poetic rhyme.

QAFL or QAFLAH (pl. AQFĀL) = QFEL (q-f-l) "key, closing"

1. Last section of the MUWASHSHAḤ/1*, DAWR/5* or other similar composition. It is sung by the chorus and repeats the musical line of the opening section (BADANIYYAH*) but with different lyrics (Ḥāfiẓ 1971:111; el Helou 1965:88; d'Erlanger 1959:179). It terminates with a descent to end on the tonic of the principal mode. It is also called RUJŪʿ/3*, GHIṬĀ'/1* or TAQFIYYAH/2*.
2. A cadence (Wahba 1968:68); or more specifically, the final cadence or coda-like ending.
3. Last MUWASHSHAḤ/1* in the series of these songs found in the NAWBAH/1* or suite of the Maghrib (Maḥfūẓ 1964:106; Chottin 1939:126).

QĀ'ID (pl. QUWWĀD) (q-w-d) "leader"

Syn. of QĀ'ID FIRQAH MŪSĪQIYYAH* (Wahba 1968:68; el-Shawan 1978).

QĀ'ID FIRQAH MŪSĪQIYYAH (q-w-d) (f-r-q) (Gr.) "leader of a musical ensemble"

Conductor of a musical ensemble (Wahba 1968:68).

QĀʿIDAH (pl. QAWĀʿID) (q-ʿ-d) "foundation, base; foot, support"

1. The wooden base of the sound box of the QĀNŪN*. It is usually about 80 cm. long and 32 cm. wide (Ḥāfiẓ 1971:84).
2. The "foot" on which a stick fiddle rests when it is performed (al Fārābī 1967:800).

QÂ'ÎM-or QAÏM-U-NUÇÇ

Vars. of QĀ'IM WA NIṢF* (Chottin 1939:111, 118, resp.).

QĀ'IM WA NIṢF = QĀYIM WA NIṢF, QÂ'IM-U-NUÇÇ, QAÏM-U-NUÇÇ (q-w-m) (n-s-f) "the erect one and a half"

The second of the five movements of the NAWBAH/1* of Morocco

(Chottin 1939:111, 119; Ḥāfiẓ 1971:128; Farmer 1933b:24). It is based on a binary rhythm of eight beats to the cycle, according to Chottin; of sixteen beats, according to Ḥāfiẓ.

QAINAH

Var. of QAYNAH* (Farmer 1967:10).

QALĀQIL = ḲALĀḲIL (q-l-q-l)

Pl. of QALQAL or QALQALAH*. This plural form was the one used to designate the jingles or bells which were hung on animals to create confusion among the enemies during battle, since they were generally used in quantity (Farmer 1945:36).

QALB (q-l-b) "reversal; transformation; overturning"

A musical inversion (Maḥfūẓ 1964:187).

QALB AL ʿIYĀN (q-l-b) (ʿ-y-n) "transformation of the viewing"

Transposition of a melodic mode to a different tonic (al Khulaʿī 1904:38). Also QALB AL LAḤN*, QALB AL QARĀR*, TAṢWĪR*.

QALB AL LAḤN (q-l-b) (l-ḥ-n) "transformation of the tune"

Syn. of QALB AL ʿIYĀN* (al Khulaʿī 1904:38, n. 2).

QALB AL QARĀR (q-l-b) (q-r-r) "transformation of the position"

Syn. of QALB AL ʿIYĀN* (al Khulaʿī 1904:38, n. 2).

QALLABA (q-l-b) "to turn; to invert; to transform"

To perform musically (Farmer 1945:43).

QALLĀL = GUELLAL (q-l-l) "one who lessens or reduces"

Earthenware cylindrical drum of about 30 cm. by 13 cm. One of its openings is covered with skin, and it is played by either a seated or standing drummer(Alg.) (Delphin and Guin 1886:39).

QALQAL or QALQALAH (pl. QALĀQIL) (q-l-q-l) "that which moves or shakes"

Usually found in the plural form to designate the jingles or bells which were hung on animals to create confusion among the enemies during battle. These idiophones were mentioned in the <u>1001 Nights</u> (Farmer 1945:36).

QANĀBIR

Pl. of QANBRĪ* (Delphin and Guin 1886:60).

QANBRĪ

A two-stringed lute used by and perhaps originated by negroes of the Maghrib (Delphin and Guin 1886:60). This seems to be the singular of QANĀBIR*, a term designating musical instruments of the 14th C. Sultan of Mali (Marcuse; Maḥfūẓ 1964:46). See also QUNBURĪ*, GUNBRĪ*

QANBŪṢ

Syn. for a lute similar to the QABŪS* or QUBŪZ* and used in Ḥadramawt (Farmer EI(Eng), "ʿŪd":986). This contemporary instrument has seven strings, one metal and six of gut. The latter are tuned dichordally (Farmer 1978:I, 72).

QANĪBRĪ

Dim. var. of QANBRĪ* (Delphin and Guin 1886:60; Rouanet 1922: 2944). See QUNAYBURĪ*, GUNĪBRĪ*.

QANOUN

Var. of QĀNŪN* (Touma 1977b:77).

QANṬARAH (pl. QANĀṬIR) = QANTRA (q-n-ṭ-r) "arched bridge"

A subsection in each of the five main movements (s. ṢANʿAH/1*) of the NAWBAH/1* or suite (Mor.). This section is marked by a sudden and abrupt change to a faster tempo. The new tempo is signaled to the rest of the ensemble by the frame drum (ṬĀR/1*) performer (Chottin 1939:112). See QANṬARAH AL ŪLĀ*, QANṬARAH AL THĀNIYAH*.

QANṬARAH AL ŪLĀ = QANTRA-1-ʿULA (q-n-ṭ-r) ('-w-1) "first bridge"

The first QANṬARAH* of a movement of the suite (NAWBAH/1*) as performed in Morocco (Maḥfūẓ 1964:106; Chottin 1939:126).

QANṬARAH AL THĀNIYAH = QANTRA-T-TÂNIA (q-n-ṭ-r) (th-n-y) "second bridge"

A second and still more rapid MUWASHSHAḤ/1* than that found in the QANṬARAH AL ŪLĀ*, which is performed in the series (SILSILAH*) of MUWASHSHAḤĀT found in all five movements of the NAWBAH/1* or suite (Mor.) (Maḥfūẓ 1964:106; Chottin 1939:126). See QANṬARAH*.

QANTRA

Var. of QANṬARAH* (Chottin 1939:112).

QĀNŪN (pl. QAWĀNĪN) = KANOUN, QANOUN, K'ANOUN, GHANOUN (Gr.) "law, regulation"

A psaltery-type chordophone made of a trapezoidal box of wood with strings stretched across the top from the rectangular end of the sound box and ending near the opposite or oblique end after passing over bridges and being wrapped around the tuning pegs. It rests in the performer's lap during performance or, more rarely, on a table in front of him/her. Metal plectra are affixed to the index fingers of both hands with ring-like mounts (s. KUSHTUBĀN*). The instrument generally has from 72-75 metal strings strung trichordally, and is thus capable of producing a range of more than three octaves. Some examples of the QĀNŪN, however, have as few as 63 or as many as 84 strings (Touma 1977b:96). Its long parallel side is around 95 cm., its shortest parallel side ca. 25 cm. In the Maghrib the QĀNŪN has the shape of the SANṬŪR*

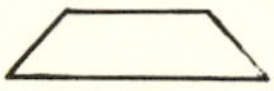 rather than the trapezoidal shape 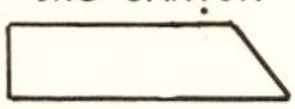

of the Mashriqī instrument. The Maghribī performer is said to attach plectra with rings to both the first and middle fingers of each hand (Salvador-Daniel 1976:112-113).

The QĀNŪN has a history that goes back at least to the 10th C., although it was not generally used until later. Plato as well as al Fārābī have been credited with inventing this instrument. Although the name is derived from a Greek word, the instrument seems to have been of oriental invention (Farmer 1926a:247). It probably was known under another name (MIʿZAF*) before the 10th C. and was only then given its present name. Al Fārābī does not mention this name in his writings, nor is it found in the works of Ibn Sīnā, Ḥusayn ibn Zaylah or the Syriac lexicons of the 9th-10th C. (Ibid.:245). It does appear in one of the tales of the 1001 Nights, a story which is thought to date from the 10th C. (Ibid.:247). In the 10th C. it was depicted with ten strings; by the 13th or 14th C. in Spain the instrument had 64 strings in courses of three. From the 12th-15th C., it was held vertically, one hand carrying it and the other plucking the strings. In the 15th C., an instrument of this name was described as having 105 strings strung trichordally (Farmer 1954, "Qānūn":VI, 1027).

QĀNŪN MIṢRĪ (q-n-n) (nat.) "Egyptian psaltery"

A chordophone mentioned in the 1001 Nights (Farmer 1945:31), and believed to have been a psaltery.

QAOUACHT

Var. of KAWASHT* (Touma 1977b:36).

QAPŪZ

Var. of QABŪS*. This lute is said to have been invented by a 15th C. sultan. Similar instruments were, however, described earlier than that century (Farmer 1978:I, 72).

QARʿ (q-r-ʿ) "striking, beating"

Striking one body with another in order to produce musical sound; therefore, a percussion or beat (al Fārābī 1967:212).

QARAʿA (q-r-ʿ) "to knock, strike or beat"

To strike or beat a musical instrument, especially a percussion instrument (al Fārābī 1967:78).

QARAQAH (q-r-q) "a clucking (of a hen)"

Metal idiophone made of two sticks approx. 30 cm. in length, each one of which carries two metal castanets which produce the sound (Shiloah 1965:I, 30).

QARAQEB

Var. of QARĀQIB* (Chottin 1957:I, 41).

QARĀQIB = QARAQEB (q-r-q-b)

Large metal castanets of the Maghrib. Each castanet is about 30 cm. long and carries two discs at its extremities. The QARĀQIB are played in pairs, one in each hand, and held together with thong loops into which three fingers of each hand are inserted (Rouanet 1922:2935). These folk cymbals made of iron are used by the negro dancers of the Maghrib and the GNAWA, members of a religious brotherhood of Sudanese origin. Pl. of QARQABŪ*.

QARĀR (pl. QARĀRĀT) (q-r-r) "resting place"

1. Contemporary term commonly used for the tonic, i.e., the tone of repose and the lowest tone of the modal scale. It is also the tone on which an improvisation or composition ends (al Khulaʿī 1904:37).
2. Prefix used to name the lower octave equivalents of some of the notes of the fundamental octave or DĪWĀN AL ASĀSĪ*, i.e., C_1 to C_2, of a modal scale (el Helou 1961:69). Thus QARĀR ḤIṢĀR* 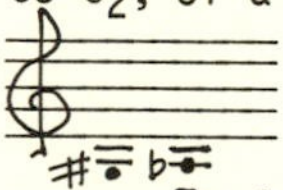 names a note an octave below ḤIṢĀR* 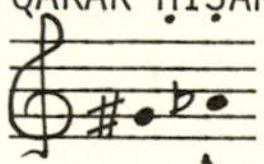; and QARĀR ʿAJAM*  is one octave below ʿAJAM* .

QARĀR ʿAJAM (q-r-r) (ʿ-j-m) "foundation of ʿAJAM"

Syn. of ʿAJAM ʿUSHAYRĀN*, , a note of the contemporary Arab scale, $A\#_1$ or Bb_1.

QARĀR ḤIṢĀR (q-r-r) (ḥ-ṣ-r) "foundation of ḤIṢĀR"

A note of the contemporary Arab scale, $G\#_1$ or Ab_1 .

QARĀR NĪM ʿAJAM (q-r-r) (Pers.) (ʿ-j-m) "foundation of lowered ʿAJAM"

A note of the contemporary Arab scale, $A\#_1$ 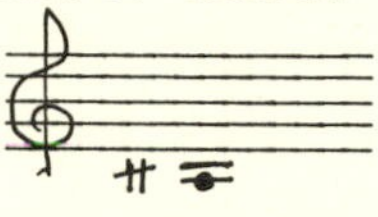.

QARĀR NĪM ḤIṢĀR (q-r-r) (Pers.) (ḥ-ṣ-r) "foundation of lowered ḤIṢĀR"

A note of the contemporary Arab scale, $G^{\ddagger}_{1}$  .

QARĀR TĪK ḤIṢĀR (q-r-r) (Pers.) (ḥ-ṣ-r) "foundation of raised ḤIṢĀR"

A note of the contemporary Arab scale, $A^{\flat}_{1}$  .

QĀRI' (pl. QURRĀ') (q-r-') "reader"

1. A person trained to read and recite the Qur'ān correctly.
2. A vocal soloist of the MAQĀM AL ʿIRĀQĪ* (Touma 1977b:73).

QARĪʿAH = QRÎʿA (q-r-ʿ)

A small variety of Maghribī lute used in the towns (Rouanet 1922: 2924, 2944). See QARĪNADAH*, another syn. of the QUWAYṬARAH*.

QARĪḤAH = GRĪḤAH (q-r-ḥ) "inspiration; natural talent"

Folk song or popular song as opposed to the art song (ʿĀLAH* or ṢANʿAH*). This term is usually colloquialized as GRĪḤAH* (Mor.). It is of three kinds: MUSHARQĪ*, MAQṢŪR AL JANĀḤ* and MAẒLŪQ* (Rouanet 1922:2883).

QARĪNADAH = QRÎNEDA (q-r-n-d)

A small variety of Maghribī lute used in the towns (Rouanet 1922: 2924, 2944). See QARĪʿAH*, another syn. of the QUWAYṬARAH*.

QARĪNAH (pl. QARĪNĀT) (q-r-n) "wife, spouse"

Professional singing girl (Farmer EI(Eng), "Ghinā'":1073).

QARMŪDAH = QARMOUDA (q-r-m-d)

The scroll or ornamental head of a lute- or viol-type chordophone (Farmer 1978:I, 42).

QARN (pl. QURŪN) = ḲARN (q-r-n) "horn; tentacle"

Generic term for any conical brass instrument (Hickmann 1947:15; Farmer EI(Fr), "Būḳ":45).

QARNA (pl. QURUN) (q-r-n) "a horn"

A long S-shaped trumpet in use during and after the 14th C. It was a successor of the NAFĪR*. As QARNĀ, it designated a horn or trumpet of ancient Babylon (Marcuse).

QARQABĀT (pl. of QARQABAH) = KARKABET

Used in its pl. form, this word designates metal idiophones resembling a pair of double castanets made of iron. These instruments, which are approx. 10" long, are shaped like dumbbells sliced in half. One pair is held in each hand, the two pieces of metal being stabilized by means of leather thongs. These Maghribī instruments of itinerant street musicians are also known as SHAQSHAQAH*, TIQERQAWIN*, QARĀQIB* (Grame 1970:79).

QARQABŪ or QARQĀBŪ = K'ERK'ABOU, QERQABOU (q-r-q-b)

S. of QARĀQIB* (Marcuse; Delphin and Guin 1886:61; Rouanet 1922: 2935).

QARRĀḌĪ or QARRĀḌIYYAH = QARRĀDIYYE (q-r-d) "that which is cut short"

One of the principal types of Lebanese folk song, a musical setting for quatrains of colloquial Arabic. Each line of the poem generally comprises seven syllables. Themes vary, but nostalgia for the village and love are common. The tune has a small range and simple, generally binary, rhythm of dancelike quality. Instruments usually provide a simple accompaniment (Jargy 1978:88; 1970:40; Reichow 1971:6).

QASA'

Var. of QAṢʿAH* (Marcuse).

QAṢAB (q-ṣ-b) "reed; cane"

A flute mentioned in the 12th C. treatise of Majd al Dīn al Ghazālī (1938:54;96). See QAṢABAH*.

QAṢABAH (pl. QAṢABĀT) = QAṢĀBAH, QAṢB or QAṢBAH, QASSĀBAH, QUṢṢĀBAH, QAṢĪBAH, GEŚBA, QṢAB, QUSAIBAH, QEÇBA, K'EÇBA (q-ṣ-b) "reed; cane"

1. Generic term for any instrument made from reed cane (al Ḥafnī 1971:25).
2. An end-blown flute of the Maghrib, similar to the NĀY/1* of the Mashriq. It is made of cane, or rarely metal, and has from three to six finger holes in addition to a thumb hole (el Mahdi 1972:49). This name was known for the instrument as early as the 7th C., but it gave way to the Pers. NĀY in the nomenclature of the Mashriq in the 9th C. The term QAṢABAH continued to be used in Moorish Spain (el Helou 1965:39).
3. A percussion instrument of Moorish Spain (el Helou 1965:39).
4. A reed used to play a woodwind instrument (Farmer EI(Eng), "Mizmār":539). Also QASHSHAH*.

QAṢĀBAH (pl. QAṢĀBĀT) (q-ṣ-b) "reed; cane"

Syn. of QAṢABAH/1* and QAṢABAH/2*.

QAṢABAH MATĀʿ AL GHANNĀ'Ī (q-ṣ-b) (m-t-ʿ) (gh-n-y) "reed pipe of the singer"

A woodwind instrument similar to QAṢĀBAH MATAʿ AL MADDAH*, but slightly shorter (Alg.) (Delphin and Guin 1886:45).

QAṢĀBAH MATĀʿ AL MADDĀḤ (q-ṣ-b) (m-t-ʿ) (m-d-ḥ) "reed pipe of the MADDĀḤ"

A woodwind instrument of about 38 cm. in length and having five fingerholes (Alg.) (Delphin and Guin 1886:45). See also QAṢĀBAH MATĀʿ AL GHANNĀ'Ī*.

QAṢĀBAYN (q-ṣ-b) "two reeds"

Double flute (Alg.) (Delphin and Guin 1886:37).

QAṢʿAH (pl. QAṢʿĀT, QIṢAʿ, QIṢĀʿ) = QASA', QAṢAʿAH, QASÂA, GUEÇAʿA, GEṢʿAH, GEṢʿÂAH (q-ṣ-ʿ) "large bowl"

1. A shallow kettledrum made in various sizes and played in the folk music of the Maghrib. It comprises a wooden bowl covered by a single membrane of camel's skin. It is played with two drumsticks, mainly by people of the desert regions (el Mahdi 1972:52). Such drum was mentioned as early as the 10th C. (Sachs 1940:249). In the ʿAbbāsī period, it was used in military bands (Farmer 1967:154). In a 16th C. text (al Lādhiqī 1939:414-415), strangely enough, it is suggested that the instrument was a recent invention.
2. The bulging body of the lute (ʿŪD*), i.e., its sound box (al Ḥafnī 1971:74).

QAṢĀ'IDĪ (pl. QAṢĀ'IDŪN) (q-ṣ-d) "one who recites QAṢĪDAH poems"

1. Chanter or singer of QAṢĪDAH poetry (QAṢĪDAH/2*).
2. Any vocalist.

QAṢB or QAṢBAH = QṢAB (q-ṣ-b) "reed"

1. Syn. of QAṢABAH/1* and QAṢABAH/2*.
2. Blowing reed of a musical instrument.

QAṢBAH ʿASHARIYYAH = QASBA 'ACHARIYA (q-ṣ-b) (ʿ-sh-r) "ten-d reed"

An aerophone of end-blown flute type which has 10 nodes in the cane from which it is made (Mor.). It is seldom used because of its very low tessitura, and is employed chiefly by religious mystical brotherhoods. Its length exceeds 75 cm. (Chottin 1939:35).

QAṢBAH KHUMĀSIYYAH = QASBA KHOMASSIYA (q-ṣ-b) (kh-m-s) "quintuple reed"

An aerophone of end-blown flute type which has five nodes in the cane from which it is made (Mor.). It is smaller than the QAṢBAH ʿASHARIYYAH*or QAṢBAH WASAṬIYYAH* (Chottin 1939:34-36).

QAṢBAH WASAṬIYYAH = QASBA USTIYA (q-ṣ-b) (w-s-ṭ) "median reed"

An aerophone of end-blown flute type (Mor.), which is longer than the QAṢBAH KHUMĀSIYYAH* and less long than the QAṢBAH ʿASHARIYYAH* (Chottin 1939:33).

QĀSHIQ (q-sh-q) "spoon (?)

Unidentified musical instrument mentioned by an early 19th C. traveler (Farmer 1954, "Iraqian and Mesopotamian Music":531).

QASHSHAH (pl. QASHSHĀT) (q-sh-sh) "straw"

The sounding reed of a woodwind instrument (Farmer EI(Eng), "Mizmār": 539; Maḥfūẓ 1964:163).

QĀṢIB (pl. QĀṢIBŪN) (q-ṣ-b) "a player of woodwind instruments"

A woodwind player or, more specifically, a player of the QAṢABAH/2* or NĀY/1*.

QAṢĪBAH (q-ṣ-b) "a piece of reed"

Var. and dim. of QAṢABAH/2* in the Maghrib (Farmer 1954, "Quṣṣába": 1040). This smaller version of the end-blown flute is more generally called JUWĀQ/1*. Also QUṢAYBAH*.

QAṢĪD (q-ṣ-d)

Syn. of QAṢĪDAH/1* (Jargy 1970:32). This term is usually used for the folkish variety of QAṢĪDAH which evidences a melismatic unmetered style of improvisation.

QAṢĪDAH (pl. QAṢĀ'ID) = QASSEEDA, QASIDE, K'ACIDA, QÇIDA, KASEEDAH (q-ṣ-d) "a poem, generally translated as 'ode' and characterized by a monorhythm and monorhyme"

1. A variety of vocal music of ancient origin and widespread provenance in the Arab World. It is a musical rendering of 2, 3, 5 or 7 lines of classical Arabic poem of the same name (see def. 2). It has varied from region to region and from century to century. In ʿAbbāsī times it was a serious type of music which was contrasted (in the Kitāb al Aghānī) to a lighter genre known as QIṬʿAH* (Farmer 1967:153). One Mashriqī writer describes the QAṢĪDAH of contemporary Syria as of three kinds: 1) an unmetered song; 2) a vocal number sung to a rhythmic mode with a short instrumental motif (LĀZIMAH*) to separate the segments into which the vocal part is divided; and 3) a vocal number similar to 2) above, but with long instrumental interludes between vocal segments. Of these, the first is the oldest variety (Ibn Dhurayl 1969:141-144). In Egypt, the QAṢĪDAH is a responsorial number performed by a small instrumental ensemble, chorus and soloist. The chorus repeats a basic melodic refrain which alternates with a freely improvised segment by the soloist. The latter conforms to the rhythmic structure of the repeated choral segment (el-Kholy 1978: 12-13).

The name QAṢĪDAH is also used for numbers which belong to the folk repertoire. In rural regions of Syria and Lebanon, the QAṢĪDAH is even a kind of dance tune in which a poet-singer

(SHĀ'IR*) and chorus alternate in singing the simple melody while a DARABUKKAK* and/or hand clapping provide percussion accompaniment for the singing and dancing (Jargy 1978:84-85). In fact, according to Reichow, any folk song which does not fit into a definite category is called a QAṢĪD* or QAṢĪDAH (Reichow 1971:39-40).

In the Maghrib, the term QAṢĪDAH is also used to name genres in both the classical and folk repertoires. It is the main type of QARĪḤAH* (GRĪḤAH*) popular music of Morocco. Unlike the QAṢĪDAH of the Mashriq, it is a setting of dialect language strophic poetry. There is a preference for strophes comprising an uneven number of lines. Each line of the poem is made of two parts, the opening one called FIRĀSH/1*; the closing, called GHIṬĀ'*(Chottin 1939:155). Delphin and Guin (1886:33-34) describe QAṢĪDAH (K'ACIDA) of Algeria as comprising both serious and light poetry and music. Some singers of the Maghrib apply the term QAṢĪDAH only to serious music, and use the term RIKĀB* for the lighter varieties. In Tunisia, QAṢĪDAH is the name given to an introductory number performed by the ʿĪsāwiyyah musicians.
2. Poem of pre-Islamic origin in which each couplet line (BAYT/1*) is based on a single meter and a single rhyme scheme.
3. A style of performance: non-metric, improvised and performed by a vocal soloist (Racy 1979:21). Opp. of TAWSHĪḤ/2* style.

QAṢṢĀB or QAṢṢĀB ʿARABĪ (q-ṣ-b) or (q-ṣ-b) (ʿ-r-b) "cutter" or "Arab cutter"

A QAṢĀBAH* or woodwind player of the Maghrib.

QAṢṢĀBAH (q-ṣ-b)

Var. of QAṢABAH/1* (Marcuse).

QAṬʿ (q-ṭ-ʿ) "a dividing, a separating"

1. Stopping the breath at the end of a musical line.
2. A line or segment of poetry.
3. The comparable musical entity setting a line or segment of poetry.

QAUL

Var. of QAWL* (Farmer 1978:I, 81).

QAWĀFĪ (q-w-f)

Pl. of QĀFIYAH*.

QAWAL (q-w-l) perhaps a colloq. of QAWL, "speech";or QAWWĀL, "speaker"

A rustic end-blown flute of Morocco and Egypt. The number of its finger holes differs, but normally it has six or seven in addition to a thumbhole. It is said to have been the first musical instrument and to have been invented by Pythagorus (Farmer 1976b:18).

QAWĪ (f. QAWIYYAH) (q-w-y) "strong"

A term used from at least the 10th C. (al Khwārizmī 1968:243-244; al Fārābī 1967:293-309) and designating any tetrachordal scalar segment (JINS/1*) in which no interval is larger than the sum of the other two. It includes the AJNĀS with half, whole and 3/4 tones. Syn. of MUQAWWĪ*.

QAWĪ DHŪ AL TAḌʿĪF (q-w-y) (ḍ-ʿ-f) "strong possessor of doubling"

A variety of QAWĪ* tetrachordal scalar segment (JINS/1*) in which two intervals are of identical size (de Vaux 1891:313). There are three kinds of these according to Ṣafī al Dīn (13th C.): 1) AḤADD*, with the non-repeated interval at the bottom of the segment; 2) MUNFAṢIL/2*, at the middle, or 3) ATHQAL*, at the top (de Vaux 1891:313). Also DHŪ AL TAḌʿĪF*, JINS AL QAWĪ DHŪ AL TAḌʿĪF*.

QAWL (pl. AQWĀL, AQĀWĪL) = QAUL (q-w-l) "speech"

1. Lyrics, i.e., the verbal element in a vocal musical performance, whether that be an example of composed song or an improvisation.
2. One of the movements of the suite as described by Ṣafī al Dīn (d. 1294), who is quoted in the 14th C. commentary of al Jurjānī (1938:552-553). See def. 3 below.
3. A type of extended free rhythmed vocal improvisation setting Arabic poetry. This genre had an instrumental introduction. With Persian instead of Arabic words, such a number was known as a GHAZAL*. An example of the QAWL is given in <u>Durrah al Tāj</u> of Quṭb al Dīn al Shīrāzī (d. 1311) and notated in Wright (1978:233-244). In the 15th C., QAWL was described as a vocal recitative which was the first number of the NAWBAH/1* or suite. It was preceded by a prelude (ṬARĪQAH/3*) and always contained a refrain segment (TASHYĪʿAH*) (<u>Anonymous Treatise</u> 1939:236). See def. 2 above.
4. The thumb hole at the back of a woodwind instrument (Farmer 1978:I, 81).

QAWS (pl. AQWĀS) = QÛS, QOUSS (q-w-s) "bow"

A bow for playing a musical instrument (Maḥfūẓ 1964:160). This term has been used by the Arabs at least since the 10th C. It is originally a borrowing from the Persian language.

QAWS ITTIṢĀL (q-w-s) (w-ṣ-l) "bow of connection"

Contemporary term for a slur or phrase mark.

QAWWA

Probably a var. of QUWWAH*. In connection with a discussion of melodic progression (INTIQĀL*), we find this term in the translation of a 12th C. treatise. It is said to designate the musical technique or device of repeating a tone one or more times (Ibn Abī al Ṣalt 1952:66).

QAWWĀL (pl. QUWWĀL) (q-w-l) "one who speaks"

1. The person who chants poetry or passages from the Qur'ān (Majd al Dīn al Ghazālī 1938:71, 121).
2. Singer, and particularly an itinerant singer.
3. Loosely, any street musician.

QAWWĪL (q-w-l) "one who speaks"

A chanter or "caller" who may perform with the instruments which play for the DABKAH* dancers of Palestine (ʿArnīṭah 1968:65).

QĀYIM WA NIṢF

Var. of QĀ'IM WA NIṢF (Ḥāfiẓ 1971:128).

QĀYINAH

Var. of QAYNAH* (d'Erlanger 1938:606).

QAYLEMI

One of the work songs (AHĀZĪJ, s. HAZAJ/7*) of the sailors of the Arab/Persian Gulf region. It is used to accompany the setting of the large sails. It is one of the genres of FIJRĪ* music (Touma 1977a:122). See also MEYDAF*, BASSEH*, KHRAB*.

QAYNAH (pl. QAYNĀT, QIYĀN) = QAINAH, QAINA, QĀYINAH (q-y-n) "singer; ladies maid"

Pre-Islamic and early Islamic period singing girl. The practice of keeping singing girls for entertainment is said to have been introduced into the Arabian Peninsula from the Arab community of al Ḥīrah in ʿIrāq (Ibn Khurdādhbih 1969:19). The QAYNAH (a slave girl) was distinguished from a MUGHANNIYAH*, who was a free woman. Also JĀRIYAH*, KARĪNAH*.

QÇEM

Var. of QIṢM* (Chottin 1939:155).

QÇÎDA

Var. of QAṢĪDAH/1* (Chottin 1939:165).

QEÇBA

Var. of QAṢABAH* (Rouanet 1922:2943).

QERQABOU

Var. of QARQABŪ*.

QEṢBAH

Var. of QAṢABAH* (Chottin 1961:Band IX, col. 1568).

QFEL

Var. of QAFL or QAFLAH* (Chottin 1939:126).

QIBLAH (q-b-l) "south; direction of the Kaʿbah"

The short side of the soundbox of the QĀNŪN* (Maḥfūẓ 1964:155; al Ḥafnī 1971:48).

QINNĪN (q-n-n) "that which is divided into measured quantities"

A lute or ʿŪD* mentioned in a 9th C. ms. (Ibn Abī al Dunyā 1938: 31, 53). It has also been used to designate the pandore (Robson 1938c:31, n. 8).

QIRĀ'AH (q-r-') "reading"

Qur'ānic reading or cantillation. Shiloah's argument that the Ikhwān al Ṣafā' extend the term to apply to all religiously significant chanting (Shiloah 1964/65:131), n. 19) does not seem to warranted by the Arabic text (Ikhwān al Ṣafā' 1957:I, 186).

QIRĀ'AH BIL ALḤĀN (q-r-') (l-ḥ-n) "cantillation with melodies"

Qur'ānic cantillation making use of popular melodies, a practice that was introduced in the late 7th C. by ʿAbd Allah ibn Abī Bakr. It was much discouraged in later centuries. See Talbi 1958; al Faruqi 1974:274-277).

QĪRĀṬ (pl. QARĀRĪṬ) (q-r-ṭ) "a measure; width of the finger"

One of the 24 intervals into which the octave has been divided by contemporary theorists. Mashāqah is one of the earliest to employ the term with this musical meaning (Mashāqah 1849:214). It was produced by dividing the string of a musical instrument into 48 equal parts and using one of these (a QURṬ*) to produce the theoretical division (see Mashaqah n.d.: fol. 38-41).

QIRBAH (pl. QIRAB) (q-r-b) "waterskin"

A bagpipe(Hickmann 1958:69). According to al Ḥafnī (1971:25), this term is used for any musical instrument utilizing a wind chamber made from skin.

QISĀRA

Var. of QĪTĀRAH/3* (Farmer 1926a:246).

QISM or QISMAH (pl. AQSĀM) = QÇEM (q-s-m) "section, division, share"

1. Either of the two tetrachordal or pentachordal segments into which the octave scale is divided (Ṣafī al Dīn, <u>Kitāb al Adwār</u>, Chap. 5, Chap. 6; al Shīrāzī 1978:170; al Khulaʿī 1904:34). See AQSĀM BUʿD DHĪ AL ARBAʿ*.
2. A strophe or couplet of QAṢĪDAH/2* poetry set to music of a

popular variety (Mor.) (Chottin 1939:155). See GRĪḤAH*, QARĪḤAH*.
3. A part or section of a musical performance. The term has been used with this meaning from as early as the Kitāb al Aghānī (Farmer 1967:106) and is still used today.

QISṬ AL ṢAN'AH (pl. AQSĀṬ AL ṢANĀ'AH) = UST-EÇ-ÇAN'Â (q-s-ṭ) (ṣ-n-') "part or extent of the craft"

Transition or modulation section of the classical performance of the NAWBAH/1* movement (Mor.) (Chottin 1939:128). See ṢAN'AH/2*.

QIṬ' or QIṬ'AH (pl. QIṬA') = QITĀ' (q-ṭ-') "piece"

A musical selection or piece (al Ḥafnī 1946:254). It was used in this general sense as well as more specifically: e.g., a kind of vocal music mentioned in the 1001 Nights (Farmer 1945: 5); in the Kitāb al Aghānī, a type of light piece (in contrast to the more serious QAṢIDAH/1*)which was popular in 'Abbāsī times (Farmer 1967:153). For 'Abd al Qādir ibn Ghaybī (d. 1435), the term was applied to any of the movements of the suite (NAWBAH/1*): QAWL/2*, GHAZAL*, TARANAH*, FURŪDĀSHT*, or MUSTAZĀD* (Farmer 1967:200), thus utilizing, like the contemporary Arabs, a very general meaning for the term.

QITĀR (Gr.)

A contemporary lyre of Egypt and neighboring regions. This folk instrument has a triangular frame and five metal or gut strings attached to a round sound box. The strings are generally tuned to a pentatonic scale (Jargy 1971:123). Also TAMBŪRAH*, SIMSIMIYYAH*.

QĪTĀRAH (pl. QAYĀTĪR) = QITĀR, QĪṬĀRA, QISĀRA, QĪTHĀRA, QĪTĀRA, QITHARAH, CITARA, CITHARA, CHITHARA, KITARA, KAITARA, KAITHĀR, KAITHAR (Gr.) "an open stringed chordophone of the lyre type"

1. A Byzantine open stringed instrument of the lyre type which Ibn Khurdādhbih has described as having 11 strings (1969:19; also al Mas'ūdī 1874:VIII, 91). The term is still used for lyre in contemporary Egypt (Farmer EI(Eng), "Mi'zaf";529; Wahba 1968:69). See QĪTHĀRAH*.
2. A guitar-like lute in North Africa (Sachs 1940:253). In general this term has been applied to a European rather than an oriental lute. From the 10th C., it was a flat-chested instrument with four strings, two of silk and two of metal, in Moorish Spain. This instrument was also known as MURABBA'/3* at that time, so it is thought to have had a quadrangular sound box (Ḥāfiẓ 1971: 82; Farmer 1967:209; 1926a:246).
3. An ancient Greek and Byzantine chordophone similar to the ṬUNBŪR/1*, according to al Khwārizmī (1968:236-237).

QĪTHĀRAH (pl. QAYĀTHĪR) (Gr.)

1. Syn. of QĪTĀRAH/1* (Ibn Khurdādhbih 1969:19; al Mas'ūdī 1874: VIII, 91).

2. Syn. of QĪTĀRAH/2* (Farmer 1926a:246; 1967:209; Ḥāfiẓ 1971: 82).

QITHORO (Gr.)

1. A trapezoidal psaltery of 10 strings used in the 10th C. (Farmer 1926a:245). In Spain of the 13th-14th C. this instrument had many more strings which were strung trichordally like the contemporary QĀNŪN* (Ibid.:245-246).
2. Generic term used in the 10th C. for "stringed instruments" (Farmer 1926a:245).

QIYĀM NĀṬIQ = KIAMI-NATIK (q-w-m) (n-ṭ-q) "eloquent performance"

Unidentified vocal number with much ornamentation (Chottin and Hickmann 1949-1951:Band I, col. 594).

QODDÂM

Var. of QUDDĀM* (Chottin 1939:111, 118).

QOUSS

Var. of QAWS* (Rouanet 1922:2943).

QOUSSAB

Var. of QUṢṢĀB or QUṢṢĀBAH* (Touma 1977b:15).

QOPÛZ

Var. of QABŪS* or QUBŪZ* (Sachs 1967:216).

QRÎʿA

Var. of QARĪʿAH* (Rouanet 1922:2927, 2944).

QRÎNEDA

Var. of QARĪNADAH* (Rouanet 1922:2927, 2944).

QṢAB

Var. of QAṢB or QAṢBAH/2* (Jones 1977:49).

QUBŪZ = QŪPŪZ, QOPŪZ, QABŪS, QANBŪṢ, QABBŪṢ, KABBŪS, ḲŪPŪZ, ḲUPŪZ, KABŪS (Turk.)

A Turkish lute invented in the 10th C. According to ʿAbd al Qādir ibn Ghaybī, it was adopted from the people of the Oxus region during the 14th or 15th C. by the peoples farther to the West (Farmer 1954, "Iraqian and Mesopotamian Music":IV, 530). Others say it was invented in the 15th C. (Farmer 1976b:37; 1978:I, 72). It was introduced into Egypt during the Ayyubī dynasty and remained a popular instrument during Mamluk times (Farmer 1967:209; 1954,

"Egyptian Music":894). It had a large sound chest, wide fingerboard and five double strings. It was played with a wooden plectrum (Ḥāfiẓ 1971:78). See also QUBŪZ ḤIJĀZĪ*, QŪPŪZ RŪMĪ*.

QUBŪZ ḤIJĀZĪ (Turk.) (geog.)

A chordophone similar to the ancient BARBAṬ/1*, which had a wooden sound box with skin face and 6 paired strings (Ḥāfiẓ 1971:78, 80).

QUDAMĀ' (pl. of QADĪM) (q-d-m) "people of ancient times"

The theorists of the Classical Period used this term to designate their forerunners.

QUDDĀM = QUODDAM, QODDÂM (q-d-m) "front part, fore part"

1. A rapid movement of the Moroccan NAWBAH/1* (d'Erlanger 1959: 189). In most theoretical works it is described as the fourth of the five movements of the suite (Chottin 1939:111; Ḥāfiẓ 1971: 128, 132). This movement is performed on a syncopated 6-beat rhythm which carries the same name (Chottin 1939:118). See def. 2.
2. A rhythmic mode of Morocco comprising a syncopated 6-beat cycle on which the fourth movement of the NAWBAH/1* is based (Chottin 1939:118).

QUDŪM (q-d-m) "arrival"

A medium-sized kettledrum, smaller than the KŪS/1*, and larger than the NAQQARAH or NAQQĀRAH*. It is said to have been used on the nuptial night of the Prophet Muḥammad and Khadījah, his first wife, in 595. In the 17th C., this instrument was played in pairs with club-shaped sticks (Farmer 1976b:14).

QULLĀL = GULLĀL, GUELLAL (q-l-l) "larklike; bomblike"

Syn. of QUWWĀL*, a single headed goblet drum of the Maghrib (Alg.) (Farmer 1978:I, 45, n. 3).

QUNBURĪ (q-n-b-r) (?)

This term is hypothesized to be a literary equivalent for a long necked lute of the African folk tradition and its many colloq. variants (ʿArnīṭah 1968:54). Maḥfūẓ includes the entry QANĀBIR (probably a pl. form), but his definition is not precise (1964:46). See GUNBRĪ*.

QUNAYBURĪ (q-n-b-r) (?)

This term is hypothesized to be a literary equivalent for the dim. of QUNBURĪ*, GUNĪBRĪ* and any other colloq. variants.

QUNDHŪRĀT

Var. of GHAYRWĀRĀT (pl. of GHAYRWĀRAH*) an ancient long necked lute (Farmer 1928:512, 515). See also GHUNDŪRAH*.

QUODDAM

Var. of QUDDĀM* (el Mahdi 1972:11).

QUPŪZ or QŪPŪZ (Turk.)

Var. of QUBŪZ*, used in Turkish dominated regions. Since there is no letter for "p" in Arabic, this name was often Arabicized to QUBŪZ*. See also QABŪṢ*.

QŪPŪZ RŪMĪ (Turk.) (nat.) "Roman, i.e., Byzantine, QŪPŪZ"

A long necked lute described by ʿAbd al Qādir ibn Ghaybī (d. 1435) as having a skin face and five double strings (Farmer 1976b:36-37).

QURMAH (q-r-m) "block of wood"

A double clarinet of the ARGHŪL* type, which is characterized by parallel tubes of equal length (Marcuse).

QURNĀṬAH (Eng.) "cornet" (?)

An unidentified aerophone of the Mashriq. In the 17th C. it was made of horn and was said to have been invented in England. It was played by the monks at the Holy Sepulchre (Jerusalem). Both Farmer and Rauf Yekta Bey consider it to have been equivalent to the "clarionet," an obsolete form of clarinet (Farmer 1976b:26-27).

QURNAYṬAH = QURNAIṬA

Generic for all instruments of the reed-pipe family (Syria) (Farmer 1976b:26-27).

QURRIBA (q-r-b) "to draw or make closer"

To shorten the time between the percussion ending one rhythmic cycle and the beginning of the next (al Fārābī 1967:992).

QURṬ (pl. QIRĀṬ) (q-r-ṭ) "earring; hanging cluster"

A minute measure (equal to 1/48 of its entirety) into which any string of a musical instrument is divided in order to achieve the tones of the Arabian contemporary scale. This system was conceived by Mashaqah of Lebanon in the 19th C. (d'Erlanger 1949:35). It produced an octave of 24 intervals, each of which is known as a QĪRĀT*.

QÛS

Var. of QAWS* (Chottin 1939:140).

QUṢAIBA

Var. of QUṢAYBAH* (Farmer 1954, "Quṣṣába": VI, 1040).

QUṢAYBAH = QUSAIBA (q-ṣ-b)"dim. or QAṢABAH"

Small end-blown flute, also known as JUWĀQ/1* (Farmer 1954, "Quṣṣába":VI, 1040). See also QUṢṢĀB or QUṢṢĀBAH/1*.

QUṢṢĀB or QUṢṢĀBAH (pl. QIṢĀB) = QOUSSAB (q-ṣ-b) "(reed) pipe"

Old Ar. name for the end-blown flute (Hickmann 1947:8). Syn. of QAṢABAH/1* and QAṢABAH/2*. This term is still used to designate a folk instrument of the Maghrib. Today instruments of this type have five or six finger holes and sometimes a thumb hole (RAJʿ*) (Farmer 1954, "Quṣṣába":VI, 1040).

QUWĀL

Var. of QUWWĀL* (Marcuse).

QUWÂS

Var. of QUWWĀS* (Chottin 1939:116, n. 1).

QUWAYṮARAH = KOUEITRA, KOUEṮRRA, KOUÎTRA, KOUÏTRA, KŪWAYṮARAH, KWĪTRA, KÛWĪTHRA, KUWAITARA, KUWĪTRA (Gr.) "dim. of QIṬĀRAH"

A small short necked lute of the Maghrib. It has a smaller, narrower body and longer neck than the ʿŪD/2*, and only a slight bend in its neck (Ḥāfiẓ 1971:82). This unfretted instrument, which is also known as the "Tunisian lute," has four pairs of strings tuned to the following tones in Morocco (Chottin 1939:99-100). See ʿŪD/2*.

Despite the variation in spelling, Farmer feels the name is a dim. for the instrument known as KITĀRAH* or KITHĀRAH* (i.e., QITĀRAH* or QITHĀRAH*), an instrument used in Moorish Spain as early as the 10th C. (Farmer EI(Eng), "ʿŪd":987).

QUWWĀ

Var. of QUWWAH* (Wright 1966:46).

QUWWAH (pl. QUWĀ) = QUWWĀ (q-w-y) "strength"

1. The relationship or identity that occurs between two tones one octave apart, i.e., either the upper octave equivalent or the lower octave equivalent of a tone (al Fārābī 1967:114ff).
2. The term also referred to any tone produced on the ʿŪD/2* which had one or more octave equivalent tones within the range of that instrument. Other tones, which had no octave equivalents within the range of the ʿŪD were termed MUFRADAH/2* (see d'Erlanger 1930:313, n. 8, al Fārābī 1967:540).
3. Tension of a string, therefore pitch (Ibn al Munajjim, see Shawqī 1976:343; al Fārābī 1967:122; Ibn Sīnā 1930:95). In translating and interpreting the ms. of Ibn al Munajjim (Kitāb al Nagham), Wright equates this term with aesthetic and emotional effect (Wright 1966:46). Shawqī disagrees with this reading,

arguing that Ibn al Munajjim and his school had not yet been affected by ideas of the Greek theory that this interpretation implies.
4. A tone of identical pitch, i.e., a repetition (see al Jurjānī 1938:231, where the French translation uses "puissance," but the Arabic is not given).
5. Contemporary equivalent of medium loud (mezzo forte) (Maḥfūẓ 1964:181).
6. Contemporary equivalent of loud (forte) (al Ḥafnī 1946:287).

QUWWĀL = QUWĀL (q-w-l) "the one that speaks"

A single headed goblet drum used in the contemporary Maghrib (Alg.) (Farmer EI(Fr), "Ṭabl":231). It is not a tambourine (frame drum), as seems to be meant by Farmer in another reference (1978:I, 45; also Marcuse).

QUWÂS

Var. of QUWWĀS* (Chottin 1939:116).

QUWWĀS = QUWÂS (q-w-s) "user of the bow"

The instrumentalist who is capable with the bow of his instrument.

R

RABĀB or RABĀBAH = REBÂB, RBĀB, REBEB, REBAB, RIBAB, REBEC (r-b-b) "master; that which is assembled"

1. Generic term for bowed unfretted chordophones. Instruments included within this definition have differed in number of strings, length of neck, tuning of strings, as well as in size and shape of soundbox. In addition, a wide range of materials have been used to construct the sometimes primitive, sometimes very sophisticated RABĀBs of the contemporary and historical Arab World. At least six different shapes have been used for instruments included in this category: 1) rectangular (pre-Islamic as well as the contemporary Mashriq; 2) round (contemporary Maghrib, see def. 4); 3) boat-shaped (Maghrib since the 8th C.); 4) pear-shaped (Ibn Khurdādhbih, and see al Mas'ūdī 1874:VIII, 91; and contemporary Maghrib); 5) hemispheric (from about 900); 6) violin-shaped (contemporary Mashriq and Maghrib).

This name is said to have been used since pre-Islamic times for the bowed chordophone (Ḥāfiẓ 1971:22; Farmer 1978:I, 99); but the oldest literary documentation of the term is a 9th C. ms. By the 10th C., the RABĀB was sufficiently well known to cause al Fārābī to describe it carefully (1967:800-822). He wrote that at that time it could have one, two or four strings. If four strings were used, they were tuned in pairs a fourth apart (al Fārābī 1967:801). With instruments of two strings, the most usual tuning put the strings a minor third apart. Other tunings (a major third or a perfect fourth apart) were also used (Ibid.: 811-813). Al Khwārizmī wrote that it was used in Persia and Khurāsān (al Khwārizmī 1968:237). According to Ibn Khurdādhbih (1969:19), an instrument of this type having five strings was used by the Byzantines in pre-Islamic times, though it was called by a different name at that time (LŪR or LŪRA in al Mas'ūdī 1874: VIII, 91).

2. A bowed, unfretted stringed instrument with vault chest which is used for performing the contemporary art music of the Maghrib. It is often described as "boat-shaped" (see def. 1 above). It is held upright on the knee when played. Its two strings are tuned

to one of three different tunings (see Chottin 1939:145-146). As such, it is also called RABĀB AL MAGHRIBĪ*.
3. A bowed, unfretted chordophone with flat chest used for performing folk music of the contemporary Mashriq. In Egypt a stick fiddle carrying this name is made from a coconut shell and has one or two strings. In Greater Syria and ʿIrāq, it has a rectangular body with either straight or concave sides. Skins cover both front and back of the sound box. This RABĀB can have one, two or three strings, according to ʿArnīṭah (1968:53). See RABĀB MUGHANNĪ* and RABĀB AL SHĀʿIR*.
4. A bowed, unfretted chordophone of the folk tradition in the contemporary Maghrib. It has a flat, circular sound chamber covered by a skin.

RABĀB MAGHRIBĪ (r-b-b) (gh-r-b) "Western RABĀB"

The RABĀB or RABĀBAH/2* used in the contemporary Maghrib for performing art music. It has a vault chest and a wide neck with bent back peg box.

RABĀB MIṢRĪ (r-b-b) (geog.) "Egyptian RABĀB"

A bowed chordophone with hemispheric sound box used in the folk tradition of contemporary Egypt. This unfretted instrument is made of a coconut or a gourd with membrane covering its face (Farmer EI(Fr), "Rabāb").

RABĀB AL MUGHANNĪ (r-b-b) (gh-n-y) "singer's fiddle"

A rectangular, flat-chested spike fiddle with quadrilaterial frame and two strings, popularly used to accompany the Arab folk singer (Jargy 1971:123). The frame of the sound box is covered with skin. Its upper and lower sides are parallel, the other two being either straight to form a trapezoid face or curved to produce concave sides.

RABĀB AL SHĀʿIR (r-b-b) (sh-ʿ-r) "poet's fiddle"

Similar to RABAB AL MUGHANNI*, but possessing only one string. It may also have only a single parchment for the face of the instrument and an open back (Lane 1973:364).

RABĀB AL SHARQĪ (r-b-b) (sh-r-q) "Eastern RABĀB"

Syn. of RABĀB or RABĀBAH/3*.

RABĀB AL TURKĪ (r-b-b) (geog.) "Turkish RABĀB"

Pear-shaped bowed chordophone (Egypt) (Farmer EI(Fr), "Rabāb":1161).

RABĀBĪ = RBÂÏBĪ (r-b-b) "player of the RABĀB"

RABĀB or RABĀBAH* performer. In the Maghrib, this musician is often the leader of the performing ensemble (Chottin 1939:142).

RĀBIʿAH (r-b-ʿ) "fourth"

A tetrachordal scalar segment (JINS/1*) (Ṣalāḥ al Dīn 1950:100).

RĀBIʿAH NĀQIṢAH (r-b-ʿ) (n-q-ṣ) "fourth which is missing something"

The tetrachordal scalar segment whose extremities are less than a perfect fourth apart (Ṣalāḥ al Dīn 1950:100).

RĀBIʿAH AL TĀMMAH (r-b-ʿ) (t-m-m) "perfect or complete fourth"

The perfect fourth interval (al Khulaʿī 1904; Shawqī 1976:408).

RĀBIʿAH ZĀ'IDAH (r-b-ʿ) (z-y-d) "the increasing fourth"

1. The tritone interval (Shawqī 1976:408).
2. A tetrachordal scalar segment whose extremities exceed the perfect fourth (Ṣalāḥ al Dīn 1950:100).

RABĪQ

Perhaps a miscopying of ZANBAQ* (Ibn Salamah in ʿAzzāwī 1951:86, n. 2).

RAÇD

Var. of RĀST*.

RADAN EL JAOUAB

Var. of RADD AL JAWĀB* (el Mahdi 1972:19).

RADD (r-d-d) "answer, repetition"

A style of responsorial singing performed for the MAWLID/3*, the birthday celebration for the Prophet Muḥammad. In these performances the group sings the refrain or RADD, and the leader or soloist performs the new poetic lines.

RADD AL JAWĀB = RADAN EL JAOUAB, RADDAN EL JAOUAB (r-d-d) (j-w-b) "bringing back the answer"

An instrumental repetition of a vocal number. It is performed in the Maghribī NAWBAH/1* or suite by one instrument or an ensemble. In the Mashriq, a similar number is called MUḤASSABAH*.

RADD AL NAFAS = RUDD NFESS (r-d-d) (n-f-s) "repetition of breath"

Circular breathing, i.e., the technique of inhaling and exhaling by the woodwind performer without breaking the flow of breath or the sound on his instrument. See Jones 1977:50.

RADDAH (pl. RADDĀT) (r-d-d) "an answer; a repetition"

1. A musical repetition.
2. Repetition of the first section of a melody (al Fārābī 1967: 1163; 1935:85).
3. A refrain.

RADDAN AL JAOUAB

Var. of RADD AL JAWĀB* (el Mahdi 1972:14).

RADḤAH (r-d-ḥ)

A folk dance of the Arabian Peninsula (Jargy 1971:109). Jargy calls it a syn. of the DABKAH*.

RADJAZ

Var. of RAJAZ* (Rouanet 1922:2714).

RADMAH = REDMA (r-d-m) "filler"

The third and final section of the SARRĀBAH*, a genre of popular music of Morocco (Chottin 1939:160). It comprises a musical setting for three poetic lines, each of which has three subsections.

RĀḤAH (pl. RĀḤĀT) (r-w-ḥ) "rest, repose"

A musical rest--the sign, or the period of silence itself (al Ḥafnī 1946:286).

RAICA

Var. of GHAYṬAH*, the double reed aerophone of the Maghrib (Salvador-Daniel 1976:117).

RA'ĪS (pl. RU'ASĀ') = RAYYES, RAÏS (r-'-s) "leader"

1. Leader of a musical ensemble.
2. Vocal soloist of a musical ensemble.
3. Nickname for Ibn Sīnā which was used by later theorists, e.g., Ṣafī al Dīn.
4. The main or melody pipe of a double clarinet aerophone. It generally is the right pipe of the pair. It has four to six finger holes, in contrast to the left or drone pipe (NŪṬĪ) (al Ḥafnī 1971:178).

RAITA

Var. of GHAYṬAH* (Salvador-Daniel 1976:117), the double reed aerophone.

R'AÏTA

Var. of GHAYṬAH* (Delphin and Guin 1886:47, 49), the double reed aerophone.

RĀ'ITH (r-y-th) "slow moving"

Slow in tempo, comparable to Lento (al Ḥafnī 1946:287; Maḥfūẓ 1964: 177).

RAJʿ = REDDJAA' (r-j-ʿ) "return, answer"

Thumb hole of the QUṢṢĀBAH*, an end-blown flute (Farmer 1954, "Quṣṣába":VI, 1040).

RAJAZ = RADJAZ (r-f-z)

A meter of pre-Islamic times, said to correspond with the movement of the camel's feet (Farmer 1967:14).

RĀJIʿ (r-j-ʿ) "returning"

1. Drone string used in performing a TARJĪʿAH* as contrasted from a melody string (SĀYIR AL TARJĪʿAH*) (ʿAbd al Qādir ibn Ghaybī, quoted in Anonymous Treatise 1939:246).
2. The repetition of a single tone or of any combination of tones.

RAKBĀNĪ (r-k-b)

Syn. of RUKBĀNĪ* (Farmer 1967:14).

RAKHĀMAH (r-kh-m) "softness"

Medium soft, comparable to mezzo piano (al Ḥafnī 1946:287; Maḥfūẓ 1964:181).

RAKHĀWAH (r-kh-w) "loosened, relaxed"

Very soft, comparable to pianissimo (al Ḥafnī 1946:287; Maḥfūẓ 1964:181).

RAKHĪM (r-kh-m) "soft, pleasant"

Melodious and pleasant (said of a voice).

RAKHKHAMA (r-kh-m) "to soften"

To soften or mellow the voice.

RAKĪZAH (pl. RAKĀ'IZ) "support"

A slanted piece of ivory fastened by its larger end to the face of the QĀNŪN* near its QIBLAH* or short side. The bridge (FARAS*) rests on the upper, smaller end of the RAKĪZAH (al Ḥafnī 1971: 49; Maḥfūẓ 1964:155).

RAKMAH

Var. of RAQMAH* (Lane 1973:360).

RAMAL = RAML (r-m-l) " poetic meter used from pre-Islamic times"

1. One of the "Famous Rhythmic Modes" (ĪQĀʿĀT AL MASHHŪRAH*) of the Classical Period. Its invention is credited to IBN MUḤRIZ* (7th C.). This ĪQĀʿ/1* was described by al Fārābī as a three-percussion cycle beginning with one long percussion followed by two short ones (al Fārābī 1967:1033-1037; 1930:43-44). Al Kindī, al Khwārizmī and Ibn Sīnā give similar descriptions of the RAMAL cycle. Later theorists described differing and longer cycles for this mode. Today RAMAL is used to designate any ĪQĀʿ of quick tempo. See THAQĪL AL RAMAL*, a syn. of the RAMAL rhythmic mode at the time of al Fārābī.
2. A poetic meter known from pre-Islamic times.
3. Another name for the MATHNĀ* string of the Maghribī ʿŪD/2* (Farmer 1933b:3).

RAMAL ṬŪṬĪ = RAMAL TOUTĪ (r-m-l) (?)

Syn. of JAWĀB NAWĀ* (el Helou 1961:69).

RAMAL TOUTI

Var. of RAMAL ṬŪṬĪ* (Touma 1977b:38).

RANĪN (r-n-n) "sounding"

Wailing, screaming (said of a singer, or a voice).

RANNAH (r-n-n) "sound, reverberation"

Sound, echo, reverberation, twang, ring(ing), scream(ing), as applied to a musical sound (Robson 1938:28, 50-51).

RANNĀM (r-n-m) "musician"

Musician, i.e., the one who does TARANNUM* or who softens his sound and sings in a delightful way.

RANNAMA (r-n-m) "to sing"

To sing or chant.

RANNĀN (r-n-n) "resonant"

Beautiful and melodious (of a musical sound).

RANNANA (r-n-n) "to pluck or twang"

To pluck the strings of a chordophone.

RANNĀNAH (r-n-n) "a resonant thing"

Tuning fork (Wehr).

RAQABAH (pl. RAQABĀT, RIQĀB) (r-q-b) "neck"

Neck of the ʿŪD* or other stringed instrument (al Ḥafnī 1971:75; Maḥfūẓ 1964:151).

RAQAṢA (r-q-ṣ) "to dance"

To dance.

RĀQIṢ (r-q-ṣ) "male dancer"

1. Male dancer.
2. Dance, or dancing.
3. Dancing (adj.).

RAQMAH (r-q-m) "a small area of land; a mark or marking"

1. The piece of fish skin covering the five oblong apertures in the face of the QĀNŪN*, over which the bridge (FARAS*) is placed (Lane 1973:360).
2. The protective covering on the face of the ʿŪD/2*. It is placed directly under the strings at the place where the plectrum strikes (al Ḥafnī 1971:74).

RAQQ or RIQQ = RIḲḲ, RIQ (r-q-q) "parchment"

A round frame drum with one membrane and 10 pairs of cymbals. This instrument is used widely in the Arab World. In Egypt it is known as RAQQ, in ʿIrāq as RIQQ or DUFF SINJĀRĪ*. It varies in size, but a typical example would be approximately 20 cm. in diameter. Expensive models are covered with fish skin while cheaper ones are made with goat skin. Because of its importance as a percussion instrument in the TAKHT* ensemble, it is also sometimes called ḌĀBIT AL ĪQĀʿ (Touma 1977b:105-107).

RAQQĀṢ (r-q-ṣ) "dancer"

Male dancer.

RAQṢ or RAQṢAH (r-q-ṣ) "dancing; a dance (resp.)"

Dancing; a dance (resp.).

RA'S (r-'-s) "head"

1. The end section, beyond the neck of the ʿŪD/2*, which is bent toward the back (Farmer EI(Eng), "ʿŪd":986). It is also known as BANJAQ* (al Ḥafnī 1971:75).
2. The head of the vertical flute, on which the player supports his lip (Farmer 1978:I, 84).

RA'S AL NADFAH = RAS-EN-NEDFA (r-'-s) (n-d-f) "head of the combing"

Major beat with which the rhythmic cycle (DAWR/1*) begins and with which the beginning of a melody is matched (Chottin 1939:115).

RAṢD

Var. of RĀST* in the Maghrib (Rouanet 1922:2941).

RĀSIM (r-s-m) "drawer, tracer"

1. A Classical Period term for "enharmonic" as applied to a tetrachordal scalar segment (JINS/1*), i.e., a JINS in which the largest of the three intervals is an interval of a major third (ratio 5/4) (al Khwārizmī 1968:243-244; Ṣafī al Dīn 1938b:37; al Lādhiqī 1939:346). It is, according to Ṣafī al Dīn, the least dissonant of the "soft" (LAYYIN/1*) AJNĀS (Ṣafī al Dīn 1938b:55). See also de Vaux 1891:309-310.
2. According to some other theorists of the Classical Period, RĀSIM designated a chromatic JINS/1*, i.e., one containing a minor third as one of its intervals (Ibn Sīnā 1935:143ff; Ibn Abī al Ṣalt 1952:40).

RASL (r-s-l) "slow"

A moderate tempo, comparable to <u>Moderato</u> (al Ḥafnī 1946:287; Maḥfūẓ 1964:177).

RASM (r-s-m) "drawing, tracing"

A type of LĀZIMAH*, or instrumental interlude, which includes melodic material from the song to follow (el Helou 1961:180).

RĀST = RAṢD, REÇD, RAÇD, REST (Pers.) "straight, regular"

1. A contemporary tetrachordal scalar segment (JINS/1*) of 1-3/4-3/4 division, mentioned from the 13th C. (Ṣafī al Dīn 1938b: 119).
2. The fundamental melodic mode (MAQĀM/1*) or modal scale of the contemporary Arabs. It has been cited in the works on music with this meaning from the 13th C. (Ṣafī al Dīn 1938b:135). Other names for this mode are MAQĀM AL UMM* or ĀNĀ MAQĀM* (al Dāqūqī 1965:42). It is built on a C_1 to C_2 scale and includes two alterations: E𝄳 and B𝄳.
3. Name for one of the tones of the contemporary Arab scale: C_1

RATTALA (r-t-l) "to be ordered, neat"

1. To recite or chant the Qur'ān slowly and distinctly.
2. To sing or chant.
3. To phrase elegantly.

RAWĀSĪM = RĀWISĪN (r-s-m)

Unmetered, instrumental compositions of Khurāsān and Persia which were mentioned by al Fārābī (1930:17). He wrote that no voice could produce them--probably because of their very complicated melodic line or the unvocal range and leaps. Ibn Zaylah regards them as either vocal or instrumental (Ibn Zaylah 1964:66).

RĀWĪ (r-w-y)

1. Storyteller who usually chants his tales.
2. The reciter who repeats the poet's work for him, and who therefore must have a prodigious memory.

RĀWISĪN

Var. of RAWĀSĪM* in a ms. of Ibn Zaylah (Farmer 1967:199).

RAWM (r-w-m) "wish, desire"

A weak percussion (al Fārābī 1967:987).

RAYYES

Var. of RA'ĪS* (Hickmann 1958:16).

RBĀB

Var. of RABĀB* (Jones 1977:4).

RBÂÏBI

Var. and dim. of RABĀBĪ (Chottin 1939:142).

REBÂ'A

Var. of the regional term RUBĀʿAH* (Mor.), or the literary Ar. RUBĀʿĪ* (Chottin 1939:141).

REBÂB

Var. of RABĀB* (Schuyler 1978:38; Chottin 1939:139, 145-146).

REBEB and REBEC

Vars. of RABĀB* (Salvador-Daniel 1976:119-120).

REÇD

Var. of RĀST* (Rouanet 1922:2941; Chottin 1939:123).

R'EÇEN

Var. of GHUṢN (Delphin and Guin 1886:36).

REDDJAA'

Var. of RAJʿ* (Delphin and Guin 1886:45).

REDMA

Var. of RADMAH* (Chottin 1939:160).

REJEZ

Var. of RAJAZ* (Ribera 1970:91).

REKAB

Var. of RIKĀB* (Delphin and Guin 1886:33).

R'ENNAI

Var. of GHANNĀ'Ī* (Delphin and Guin 1886:31-32).

REQ

Var. of RAQQ or RIQQ* (Chottin and Hickmann 1949-1951:Band I, 598). According to Sachs (1940:247), this version was a small tambourine of approximately 10" diameter without snares.

REST

Var. of RĀST* (Smith 1847:181).

RHÂDÎ BEL-'ÂKS

Var. of GHĀDĪ BIL ʿAKS*(Chottin 1939:147).

RHAÏTA

Var. of GHAYṬAH/1* (Delphin and Guin 1886:47, 49).

RHEITA

Var. of GHAYṬAH/1* (Marcuse).

RHINĀ

Var. of GHINĀ'/2* (Chottin 1939:59).

RHOÇN

Var. of GHUṢN/2* (Chottin 1939:155).

RHONIA

Var. of UGHNIYAH* or song. Chottin describes this UGHNIYAH as a genre of GRĪḤAH* (popular) music, sung to the words of the local dialect and dealing with everyday contemporary topics (Mor.). It is performed in the public squares or streets by traveling or street minstrels known as MUBSITĪN (s. MUBSIṬ*) (Chottin 1939:163). The nominative pl. would be MUBSIṬŪN.

RHTA

Var. of GHIṬĀ'/1* (Chottin 1939:155).

RIBĀB

Var. of RABĀB* among the Sūs-Shluh of Morocco (Farmer EI(Fr), "Rabāb":1160).

RIBĀṬ (pl. RIBĀṬĀT) (r-b-ṭ) "tie or tieing"

1. A musical tie (al Ḥafnī 1946:108).
2. Dividing the strokes of a rhythmic cycle in a way which produces a cross rhythm, e.g., a (4-2) division of the cycle played as (3-3). This is a contemporary Mashriqī performance technique (Allawerdi 1949:547).
3. Any of the chords tied around the neck of a lute which serve as frets for the instrument (al ʿAzzāwī 1951:83, n. 1).
4. The double band of leather tied around the strings and the neck of the KAMĀN or KAMĀNJAH/1* just below the tuning pegs (Lane 1973:356).

RIDJL

Var. of RIJL* (Farmer EI(Fr), "Rabāb":1160).

RIJL (pl. ARJUL) (r-j-l) "foot, leg"

1. Any of the percussions from which the cycle (DAWR/1*) of a rhythmic mode (ĪQĀʿ/1*) is composed (Ibn Sīnā 1930:93; 1935:186; al Rajab 1967:23).
2. Foot of the spiked fiddle.

RIKĀB = REKAB (r-k-b)

1. Syn. of QAṢĪDAH/1* in the Maghrib, both in its serious (KALĀM AL JADD*) and light (KALĀM AL HAZL*) varieties.
2. With some singers of the Maghrib, this term applies only to the light songs (KALĀM AL HAZL*) in contrast to the more serious ones (KALĀM AL JADD*) of the QAṢĪDAH/1* materials (Delphin and Guin 1886:33-34). This music is characterized by many liberties of musical and poetic practice which would not be used in the more classical QAṢĪDAH.

RIḲḲ

Var. of RAQQ or RIQQ* (Farmer EI(Fr), "Duff":80).

RIMAZ or RIMĀZ

Vars. of GHAMMĀZ* (Rouanet 1922:2754, 2809).

RIQ

Var. of RAQQ or RIQQ* (el Helou 1961:135).

RIQQ (r-q-q)

Equiv. of RAQQ* (Touma 1977b:105-107; Lane 1973:363). According to Marcuse and Sachs, this frame drum of the contemporary Middle East is without snares, but this is not always borne out by evidence from other sources.

RĪSHAH (pl. RĪSHĀT) (r-y-sh) "feather"

1. Plectrum. For the ʿŪD/2*, it is made out of an eagle's quill, or in more recent times from plastic produced to resemble its feather prototype. For the QĀNŪN*, there are two plectra, each of which is attached by a metal ring-like apparatus to the forefingers of the hands. These picks are made of bone or ivory and are approx. 5 cm. in length.
2. The blowing reed of a woodwind instrument.

RĪSHAH MIṢRIYYAH (r-y-sh) (geog.) "Egyptian feather"

A manner of plucking the strings of the lute, whereby the plectrum alternates in striking the string once from the top, once from below, in regular succession. See RĪSHAH TURKIYYAH* (Touma 1976:27).

RĪSHAH MUZDAWIJAH (r-y-sh) (z-w-j) "paired (double) reed"

Double reed of an aerophone such as the oboe (al Ḥafnī 1971:178).

RĪSHAH AL NASR = RICHET ENNESSER (r-y-sh) (n-s-r) "eagle's feather"

Plectrum (Farmer 1978:I, 75).

RĪSHAH TURKIYYAH (r-y-sh) (geog.) "Turkish feather"

A manner of plucking the strings of the lute, whereby the plectrum is not regularly applied to the string with alternating up and down strokes as in "Egyptian plucking" (RĪSHAH MIṢRIYYAH*) (Touma 1976:27).

RITHĀ' (r-th-w) or (r-th-y) "lamentation"

Funerary poems or songs, usually performed by women.

ROCBANI

Var. of RUKBĀNĪ* (Ribera 1970:31, n. 2).

ROUAQA

Var. of RUWĀQAH* (Touma 1977b:105).

RUBʿ (pl. ARBĀʿ) "quarter, one-fourth"

The quarter tone interval (Ṣalāḥ al Dīn 1950:84). It has been condiered the smallest division of the theoretical scale of the Arabs from the 18th C. (Ḥāfiẓ 1971:179, 182).

RUBʿ ṬANĪNĪ (r-b-ʿ) (ṭ-n-n) "quarter of a whole tone interval"

Quarter tone interval (al Fārābī 1930:100; 1967:269).

RUBʿ MASĀFAH (r-b-ʿ) (s-w-f) "quarter of a distance"

Quarter tone interval. This term was used by a 19th C. theorist (Shawqī 1969:21).

RUBÂ'A

Var. of RUBĀʿĪ* or the regional RUBĀʿAH* (Chottin 1939:141; Delphin and Guin 1886:55).

RUBĀB or RŪBĀB (r-b-b)

A long necked lute used from the 12th to the 14th C. in Persia and East Turkestan. The instrument had a vaulted soundchest and incurvatures at the waist. The lower part of the soundbox was covered with skin. The instrument usually had three double strings, but these were sometimes increased to four or five pairs (Farmer EI(Eng), "ʿŪd":987; 1954, "Egyptian Music":II, 893; Ḥāfiẓ 1971:80).

RUBĀʿĪ = RUBÂ'A, REBA'A, RUBĀʿAH (r-b-ʿ) "quartet; with four"

Instrumental and vocal ensemble of the Maghrib. It comprises the following instrumental elements: 1) one RABĀB or RABĀBAH*/2* which carries the basic melody and is usually played by the leader of the ensemble 2) two KAMĀN or KAMĀNJAH/2* instruments; 3) two lutes; and 4) percussion instruments--ṬĀR*, DARABUKKAH* and sometimes ṬUBAYLĀT (s. ṬUBAYLAH*) if the ensemble is a women's group. This ensemble provides accompaniment for the vocalist(s) as well as performs the instrumental interludes and refrains. Both of these functions require their own particular style of performance. The interludes and refrains employ much TARʿĪD/1* (trills), DAṢṢAH* (high-pitched embellishments), ZUWWĀQ* (ornaments), T'ÂSKÎRÂT*(variations), TAʿMĪR AL FARĀGH* (repeated notes to fill the durations), and GHĀDĪ BIL ʿAKS (syncopations). The style underlying the vocal line, on the contrary, is much more subdued, homogeneous and continuous. It is known as TABRĪD* (Chottin 1939:147).

RUBĀʿIYYAH AL ASNĀN (r-b-ʿ) (s-n-n) "the one with four teeth"

Hemidemisemiquaver, i.e., a 64th note (𝅘𝅥𝅲) (al Ḥafnī 1946:286; Maḥfūẓ 1964:186).

RUBʿAYN (r-b-ʿ) "dual of RUBʿ, i.e., two quarters"

The semitone interval (Al Ḥalqah 1964:11).

RŪD = RŪḌAH, RŪDAK, RŪṬAH, SHĀHRŪD (Pers.) "string"

An ancient musical instrument. According to ʿAbd al Qādir ibn Ghaybī (d. 1435), it was a lute which had half of its face covered with membrane (Farmer EI(Eng), "ʿŪd":987). This name and variations of it, however, have been used to designate a lute, a pandore, a low pitched KAMĀNJAH* and even a harp.

RŪḌAH

Var. of RŪD* (Farmer 1976b:40).

RŪDAK

Var. of RŪD* (Farmer 1976b:40).

RUDD NFESS

Var. of RADD AL NAFAS* (Jones 1977:50).

RUJŪʿ (r-j-ʿ) "return"

1. Repetition.
2. Refrain phrase, tune or section.
3. Third of the three main sections of the MUWASHSHAḤ/1* or other similar forms. It constitutes a return to the main thematic material and the mode and register of the opening section. Other names for this section are QAFLAH/1* and GHIṬĀ'/1*.

RUKBĀNĪ = RAKBĀNĪ, ROCBANI (r-k-b) "pertaining to riders or cameleers"

A traveller's or caravan song. It was synonymous with ḤIDĀ' or ḤUDĀ'* in the early centuries of the Islamic period (al Zabīdī 1965:I, 276).

RUKŪZ (r-k-z) "leaning point"

1. Contemporary term for the tonic.
2. Contemporary name for the fundamental and lowest tetrachordal scalar segment (JINS/1*) of a melodic mode (MAQĀM/1*) (Ṣalāḥ al Dīn 1950:103).

RŪṬAH

Var. of RŪD* which is known to have been used in 13th C. Moorish Spain (Farmer 1926a:247).

RUWĀQAH (r-w-q) "a vestibule; a canopy"

Bagpipe.

RUWAYḤAH (pl. RUWAYḤĀT) (r-w-ḥ)

Half rest (▬) (Maḥfūẓ 1964:186).

RŪYIN NĀY

Unidentified variety of reed pipe of pre-Islamic times (Farmer 1957:425).

S

ṢABĀ (ṣ-b-w) or (ṣ-b-y) "east wind"

1. A contemporary tetrachordal scalar segment (JINS/1*) of 3/4-3/4-½ interval division.
2. An important contemporary melodic mode (MAQĀM/1*) utilizing the JINS/1* of the same name (see def. 1). This name was used for a melodic mode as early as the 14th C. (al Jurjānī 1938:428).
3. A note of the contemporary Arab scale which is also called ḤIJĀZ/3*, F#$_1$ or Gb$_2$  .

SABʿ AL AWĀ'IL (s-b-ʿ) ('-w-l) "first seven"

The seven-tone scale produced on the two lower strings of the ʿŪD/2* (al Kindī 1965:20). See also SABAʿ AL AWĀKHIR*.

SABʿ AL AWĀKHIR (s-b-ʿ) ('-kh-r) "last seven"

The seven-tone scale produced on the two upper strings of the ʿŪD/2* (al Kindī 1965:20). See also SABAʿ AL AWĀ'IL*.

SABAB (s-b-b) "cause"

A prosodic term borrowed by the Arab musical theorists to indicate the duration of a member (RIJL/1*) within the rhythmic cycle (DAWR/1*). This term stands for a duration which was comparable to a poetic member with two consonants, the one moving and the other quiescent--TAN). It was notated in various ways, and varying tempi of performance (e.g., 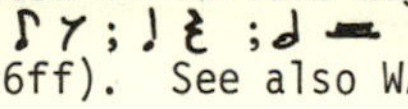 ; etc.) (Farmer 1943:72; al Fārābī 1967:1076ff). See also WATAD*, FĀṢILAH/6*.

ŠABBĀBA

Var. of SHABBĀBAH* (Sachs 1967:302; 1940:247).

SABBĀBAH = SEBĀBEH (s-b-b) "index finger"

Fret position on the ʿŪD/2* or any other lute, which was stopped by the index finger. This fret produced a pitch one whole tone above the open string (ratio 9/8) (Ibn al Munajjim 1950:3; al Fārābī 1967:500; and other theorists of the Classical Period).

ŠABBŪR or ŠABBUR

Vars. of SHABBŪR* (Hickmann 1947; Marcuse, resp.).

ṢADĀ (ṣ-d-w) "echo"

1. A type of LĀZIMAH* or instrumental interlude which repeats the final phrase of the vocal segment just completed. It is also called ISTIDHKĀR* (el Helou 1961:180).
2. The effective musical sound (Kāẓim 1964:67).

ṢADAF = ÇEDEF, ṢDAF (ṣ-d-f) "sea shell"

Round disk of bone, ivory or plastic which holds the double reed of an oboe-type woodwind instrument and serves as a connector of the staple (LAWLĀ*) to the head of the instrument (Alg.) (Delphin and Guin 1886:48). The player usually takes the reed completely into his mouth, and his lips touch the ṢADAF as he plays (Farmer 1978:I, 82).

ṢADAF MUDAWWAR (ṣ-d-f) (d-w-r) "round sea shell"

Syn. of ṢADAF* (Farmer 1978:I, 82).

ṢADAḤA (ṣ-d-ḥ) "to sing, to play"

To sing or play a tune (Madina).

ṢADAḤAH (pl. ṢADAḤĀT) (ṣ-d-ḥ) "a tune"

A musical strain or tune.

ŠADD

Var. of SHADD* (Touma 1976:11, n. 4).

ṢADḤ (ṣ-d-ḥ) "singing"

Raising of the voice in song, singing, chanting (Ibn Salamah 1938a:12; 1938b:243; Maḥfūẓ 1964:82).

ṢĀDIḤ (ṣ-d-ḥ) "singer"

Note raised a semitone; a sharp (Wehr).

SADJDJĀT or ṢADJDJĀT

Vars. of SAJJĀT or ṢAJJĀT* (Farmer EI(Fr), "Ṣandj":209).

ṢADR (pl. ṢUDŪR) (ṣ-d-r) "source, origin; chest"

1. Wooden or skin face of the soundbox of the ʿŪD*, KAMĀN or KAMĀNJAH*, ṬUNBŪR* or other similar instruments (Maḥfūẓ 1964:151, 159).
2. The first of the hemistiches of a line of poetry, also SHAṬR/1*.

SAFĀQIS

Hourglass drum similar to the KŪBAH*. It was mentioned in a 9th C. source (Farmer 1978:II, 32).

ṢAFFĀQĀT (pl. of SAFFĀQAH) (ṣ-f-q) "clappers"

An ancient percussion instrument (idiophone) made of wood or bone (el Helou 1961:163).

ṢAFFĀQATĀN (ṣ-f-q) "dual of ṢAFFĀQAH, a clapper"

Cymbals (a pair) mentioned in the Kitāb al Aghānī (10th C.) but not described until the 16th C. when they were two round brass plates that were struck together (Farmer 1978:II, 29). In Marcuse, we find SAFFAQĀTĀN.

ṢAFFĀRAH (pl. ṢAFFĀRĀT) = ṢUFŪRAH, ṢUFFĀRA, SĀFŪRA, ṢŪFAYRAH, SŪFAĪRA, SUFĪRAH (ṣ-f-r) "whistle"

1. Whistle (Wahba 1968:70).
2. Generic term for flutes (Hickmann 1947:6; Ikhwān al Ṣafā' 1957:I, 202).
3. A recorder-like instrument, according to Villoteau, the 18th C. writer on Egyptian music (Farmer 1954, "Egyptian Music": II, 895).
4. Syn. of NĀY/1* in Egypt and the Maghrib (Jargy 1971:121; al Khwārizmī 1968:236).

ṢAFḤ (ṣ-f-ḥ) "flat surface"

Face of the ʿŪD/2* (Farmer 1978:II, 93).

ṢĀFĪ = ÇĀFĪ (ṣ-f-w) "pure"

Pureness of vocal tone.

ṢAFĪR (ṣ-f-r) "whistling"

Whistling, as an undesirable vocal practice in the SAMĀʿ/1* of the Muslims, according to Ibn Taymiyyah (1966:II, 299). See ṢAFQ*.

ṢAFQ (ṣ-f-q) "clapping"

Hand clapping used as rhythmic accompaniment. This was considered an undesirable performance practice in the SAMĀʿ/1* of the Muslims (Ibn Taymiyyah 1966:II, 299). See also ṢAFĪR*.

SĀFŪRA

Generic for flutes (Marcuse).

SAGĀḤ

Var. of SAJĀḤ/1* (Ibn Abī al Ṣalt 1952:32).

SAGÂT or ṢAĠĀT

Vars. of ṢĀJĀT* in Egypt (Jargy 1971:125; Hickmann 1958:44).

SAGGAT

Var. of ṢAJJĀT* (Marcuse).

ṢAGHĀNAH

Syn. of ZILLĪ MĀSHA* (Farmer EI(Fr), "Ṣandj":210). JAGHĀNAH* is another name used for this type of percussion instrument (small cymbals attached to a mount). It is not known which term is the more correct.

ṢĀḤA (ṣ-y-ḥ) "to cry, shout"

To wail or shout in performing a song or chant (Shawqī 1976:284).

ṢAHBĀ (ṣ-h-b)

A folk song of Egypt which evolved from the MUWASHSHAḤ/1*. It uses colloq. Arabic lyrics. The name may refer to the group of singers kn n as ṢAHBAJIYYAH* who practiced this art in the coffee houses from olden times (Al Ḥalqah 1964:57). Other derivation possibilities link it with ṢAHBĀ' (wine) or ṢAHBAJIYYAH (a quarter of Cairo).

ṢAHBAJIYYAH (ṣ-h-b)

The group of singers who perform the ṢAHBĀ* (Al Ḥalqah 1964:57).

ṢAHJAH = SZABDJE (ṣ-h-j) (?)

A choral song and dance from the Arabian Peninsula sung by a group of men utilizing words of praise for some individual which was followed by other songs (Farmer 1954, "Iraqian and Mesopotamian Music":IV,532). This form is a corrected spelling of the term SZAHDJE* used by the 19th C. traveler Burckhardt (1967:85). It has not been possible to verify the validity of this spelling alteration in Wehr, Madina, Maʿlūf or al Zabīdī, or to find an unquestionable substitute.

SĀH-RŪD

Var. of SHĀHRŪD* (al Jurjānī 1938:240-241).

ṢĀʿID (ṣ-ʿ-d) "that which ascends"

1. The neck of a lute or viol (Ṣafī al Dīn in de Vaux 1891:333). In 19th C. Egypt, it was usually of ebony inlaid with ivory (Lane 1973:356).
2. Sharp sign for raising any note by one semitone (Kāẓim 1964:67).

ṢĀʿIDAN (ṣ-ʿ-d) "ascending"

Ascending in pitch (Ibn Sīnā 1930:95).

SAÏKA

Oboe-like instrument of the Arabs of Moorish Spain. It was used for war songs (Salvador-Daniel 1976:224-225). The claim that this instrument was mentioned by al Fārābī is doubtful, though he did describe a similar instrument under the name SURNĀY* (al Fārābī 1967:787ff).

ṢAJ

Var. of ṢANJ or ṢINJ/1* or ṢĀJĀT*, the metal finger castanets used in the contemporary Mashriq. This var. is used in the Arabian Peninsula (Jargy 1971:125).

SAJʿ (pl. ASJĀʿ) (s-j-ʿ) "a variety of prose often translated as 'rhymed prose'"

A type of poetic expression evidencing occasional, rather than regular, repetitive motifs. These occur most frequently at the ends of lines or strophes, thus increasing the aesthetic excitement and contributing to the emotional relief of the DAFQAH*. See al Faruqi 1974:Chap. II, where this author relates this literary phenomenon to certain types of musical expression in the Arab World. Syn. of TASJĪʿ*.

SAJĀḤ (s-j-ḥ) "the sound of the dove"

1. Name given by the Classical Period theorists to the lower of the two tones of an octave interval (al Khwārizmī 1968:240). ISJĀḤ is a syn. often used but labeled as incorrect by al Khwārizmī (Ibid.). Syn. of SHUḤĀJ* or SHUḤĪJ*. For example, the note produced on the open BAMM* string when combined with that produced by the SABBĀBAH* fret on the MATHNĀ* string. It is such an example which probably caused Maḥfūẓ (1964:90) to define this term as "open string tone," a definition found in no other source.
2. Tonic note (Farmer 1967:52). This is given by Farmer as a "highly probable" meaning for the term in the 7th C.
3. The lowest tone according to Maḥfūẓ (1964:80).

ṢĀJĀT (pl. of ṢĀJAH) = SAGÂT, ṢAGĀT, ṢAJ (s-w-j) "(baking) tins"

Small copper finger cymbals used in pairs, which are fastened to the fingers of a dancer with small string loops (al Ḥafnī 1971:

177). Each dancer has two pairs of these metal castanets attached to thumbs and second fingers (Lane 1973:365). Syn. of SAJJĀT or ṢAJJĀT*.

SAJJALA (s-j-l) "to record"

To record a musical performance (Wahba 1968:68).

SAJJĀT or ṢAJJĀT = SAGGAT (s-j-j) or (ṣ-j-j)

Syn. of SĀJĀT*, the cymbalettes described by Villoteau (Egypt) (Hickmann 1947:21; Farmer 1954, "Egyptian Music":II, 895).

ṢAKKA (ṣ-k-k) "to thump"

To beat a drum or other percussion instrument (Maʿlūf).

SAKT or SAKTAH (pl. SAKTĀT) = SEKTA (s-k-t) "point of silence"

1. A silence or rest (al Ḥafnī 1946:286).
2. A separation between two tones of a melody without taking a breath (Maḥfūẓ 1964:80).
3. A sudden silence for expressive effect in Moroccan art music (Chotttin 1939:114).
4. The silence between one cycle of a rhythmic mode and the next (Chottin 1939:115).

ṢALĀBAH (ṣ-l-b) "hardness, firmness"

Very loud, comparable to fortissimo (al Ḥafnī 1946:287; Maḥfūẓ 1964:181).

SALĀM (s-l-m) "greeting"

A short prelude (Hickmann 1958:42).

ṢALĀṢIL (pl. of ṢALṢAL) = SELĀSIL (ṣ-l-ṣ-l) "ringing, clanking"

Cymbals (Sachs 1940:122).

SALBĀB

Syn. of SALBĀQ*, a small triangular harp of the Byzantines which was also known to the Arabs (Ikhwān al Ṣafā' 1957:I, 202; 1964/65: 148).

SALBĀḲ

Var. of SALBĀQ* (Farmer EI(Eng), "Miʿzaf":529).

SALBĀN

Syn. of SALBĀQ* (Farmer EI(Eng), "Miʿzaf":529; al Masʿūdī 1874: VIII, 91).

SALBĀQ = SALBĀB, ṢALBĀQ, ṢALBĀḲ, SALBĀN, SĪLBĀN, SALYĀK, SHALYĀK, SAMBYKÉ, SULYĀQ, SHULYĀQ, SULYĀNĪ (Gr.) "a thousand voices", according to Ibn Khurdādhbih

An ancient triangular harp known to the Greeks as SAMBYKÉ and to the Arabs as SALBĀQ, SALBĀN*, etc. (Ikhwān al Ṣafā' 1957:I, 202, 1964/65:148, see n. 98). It was described as an instrument of 24 strings, without frets, and having its strings stretched across a space rather than across a surface (Farmer 1926a:243; 1978:I, 56). See SAMBUCA*.

ṢALBĀQ

Var. of SALBĀQ* (Ibn Sīnā, according to Farmer 1926a:244). In Ibn Sīnā 1935:233, we find the var. SULYĀQ*.

ṢALḤĪ = SALHI

A vocal genre of Tunisia with a highly melismatic, florid and nonmetric style (Jones 1977:6, 295). Jones writes that the term is supposed to be derived from a man's name. That author designates it as a type of folk music or a folkish mode. In Racy (1979:21), we find SALHI.

ṢALINJ

Equiv. of ṢILINJ*, a kind of ancient harp (Farmer 1978:I, 60).

ṢALṢAL (pl. ṢALĀṢIL)(ṣ-l-ṣ-l) "clanking"

S. form of a term usually found as a pl. since it designates finger cymbals which are rarely used singly (Farmer EI(Fr),"Ṣandj": 209).

SALSLA

Var. of SILSILAH/1* (Perkuhn 1976:107).

ṢALTIJ

Var. of ṢILINJ*, a kind of ancient open-stringed instrument (Farmer 1978:I, 60; Ibn Khurdādhbih 1969:19; al Masʿūdī 1874: VIII, 91).

SALYĀḲ

Var. of SALBĀQ* (Farmer EI(Eng), "Miʿzaf":529).

SALYĀNĪ

Syn. of SALBĀQ* (Ibn Khurdādhbih 1969:19).

SAMĀʿ (s-m-ʿ) "audition"

1. Listening to the repeated formulas, the poetry and the music of the Muslim mystics (Ṣūfīs); and by derivation, listening to

other types of religious music. See al Ghazālī 1901/1902; Robson 1938c; and Ibn Taymiyyah 1966:293-330 for the traditional arguments for and against SAMĀʿ. SAMĀʿ has always been primarily a vocal music, but instruments are also sometimes included. This is particularly a religious custom of the Ṣūfīs, but it is also participated in by some non-Ṣūfīs. The term includes not only "listening" to this devotional music, but the performance of it as well. It is sometimes expanded to include the instrumental and dance participation associated with the vocal phenomenon. See Farmer 1967:Chap. II.
2. A variety of classical vocal music of the Maghrib which is essentially religious in theme. It is similar to MA'LŪF* or ṢANʿAH* music (Alg., Tun.), but makes less use of instruments (Chottin 1961:Band IX, col. 1559; 1939:108).

SAMA'A (s-m-ʿ) (?)

Clarinet of modern Egypt, with cylindrical tube and six or seven finger holes (Marcuse). It is not known to which literary term this spelling refers: perhaps SAMĀʿAH or SAMMĀʿAH.

SAMAÏ

Var. of SAMĀʿĪ* (Touma 1977b:28).

SAMĀʿĪ (pl. SAMĀʿIYĀT) = SEMAI, SAMAÏ (s-m-ʿ) "heard"

1. An instrumental overture similar to the BASHRAH/1*, but lighter and more spirited. It is performed in both the Mashriq and Maghrib. It follows the rules of the BASHRAF as to composition in four equal parts (KHĀNĀT, s. KHĀNAH*) separated by refrain sections, but differs in the rhythms which it uses. Its first three KHĀNĀT are composed on the SAMĀʿĪ THAQĪL* rhythm (10/8 cycle), while its fourth KHĀNAH (known in Tunisia as ḤARBĪ/2*) makes use of a ternary rhythm (6/8, 6/4 or 3/4 cycle) (el Mahdi 1972:20-21). The SAMĀʿĪ is performed 1) after a BASHRAF based on the same mode; 2) as overture for a suite of pieces; or 3) at the end of the suite (WAṢLAH/1*) (d'Erlanger 1959:182-183).
2. A designation for those rhythmic modes of ternary and quintuple base, which are used by the Ṣūfī derviches while dancing in connection with their DHIKR* recitations, or which are thought to be derived from those rhythms (d'Erlanger 1959:182-183). See SAMĀʿ*.

SAMĀʿĪ THAQĪL (s-m-ʿ) (th-q-l) "heavy (slow) heard"

A rhythmic mode of 10/8 cycle which is believed to have derived its name from the fact that it was associated with the SAMĀʿ/1* performances of the Muslim mystics.

SAMBUCA

Syn. of SANJ/1*, in the translation of al Masʿūdī (1874:VIII, 91). This term, however, is not in the Arabic version of the same edition. It seems likely that this is yet another var. of SALBĀQ*, used by de Meynard, the translator, or found in a different ms. copy.

SAMBYKÉ

See SALBĀQ*.

SAMʿĪ (s-m-ʿ) "auditory"

Auditory or acoustical (al Kindī 1966:153).

SĀMIʿ (pl. SĀMIʿŪN) (s-m-ʿ) "one who listens"

Person who listens to music.

SĀMIR (s-m-r) "companion in evening entertainment; an entertainer"

An Egyptian vocal genre similar to the DAWR/5*, from which it developed. This form was popular in the 19th C. (Al Ḥalqah 1964: 60ff). It comprises two entities: a MADHHAB/1* and a GHUṢN/1* or DAWR/6*. The MADHHAB is divided into three sections: a) beginning in low register of the MAQĀM/1* without exceeding one octave in range upward from the tonic, and often confined to the first five notes of the scale; 2) a melodic passage in a higher range; and c) a passage in which the melody moves from the higher ranges to return to the tonic at the base of the modal scale. There is often an acceleration in the last part of the MADHHAB. It is followed by a LĀZIMAH*, or instrumental interlude which is repeated until the soloist is ready to begin the second section (i.e., the GHUṢN or DAWR). The GHUṢN also has three parts: a) a phrase similar to that of the main melody of the MADHHAB but with different words; 2) another melody, which also may contain elements derived from the MADHHAB, and which is repeated and varied by the soloist; and c) a melody sung by the soloist beginning with the word "AH" or "YĀ LAYL, YĀ ʿAYN." This phrase is repeated many times by the soloist and then by the chorus with improvisational melodic content. The alteration between soloist and chorus, as well as between new and refrain themes, continues. The piece ends with a return to the main MADHHAB tune performed by tne whole ensemble (Ḥāfiẓ 1971:196-198).

ṢĀMIT (pl. ṢUMŪT) (ṣ-m-t) "silent"

Without words, i.e., instrumental rather than vocal (music).

SAN'A

Var. of ṢANʿAH* (Touma 1977b:77; Schuyler 1978:36).

SANAʿA

Var. of ṢANʿAH/2* (Lachmann 1929:56; Lachmann and Fox-Strangways 1938:V, 578).

SANAD (pl. SANADĀT, ASNĀD) (s-n-d) "support"

One pipe of a double clarinet woodwind instrument. This is the tube which produces the drone tone. It is usually the left pipe of the pair (Maḥfūẓ 1964:163). Also NŪTĪ*.

ṢAN'AH (pl. ṢAN'ĀT, ṢANĀ'I') = SANA'A, SAN'A, ÇAN'A (ṣ-n-') "art; craft"

1. Classical music of the Maghrib (Tun.) (Chottin 1961:Band IX, col. 1559).
2. Movement of a NAWBAH/1* suite of the Maghrib (Chottin 1939: 112), which sets one or at most two strophes of a poem to music. The most frequently used strophe has five lines. Each strophe becomes the basis of a musical whole with four parts: 1) a DUKHŪL* or introduction; 2) the KIRSH AL ṢAN'AH* or development; 3) the QIṢT AL ṢAN'AH* or transition/modulation section; and 4) a KHURŪJ/1* or closing (Chottin 1939:127-128).
3. Any of the 19 melodic modes of Algeria (Delphin and Guin 1886:61; Farmer 1933b:33).
4. Syn. of NAWBAH/1* (Alg.).
5. A melodic theme or tune (Maghrib), which is similar to the HAWĀ' *of the Mashriq (d'Erlanger 1959:169).

ṢAN'AH AL 'ŪD (ṣ-n-') ('-w-d) "craft of the lute"

Construction of the lute ('ŪD/2*) (al Kindī in Farmer 1965b:8).

SANCH

Var. of ṢANJ/1* (Ribera 1970:94), the open-stringed instrument. It has also been used for the tambourine with jingles mounted in its frame (ṢANJ/3).

ṢANDJ or SANDJ

Vars. of ṢANJ* (Farmer EI(Fr), "Ṣandj":209-211; Touma 1977b:15, resp.).

ṢANDŪQ (ṣ-n-d-q)

Equiv. of ṢUNDŪQ*, and also possible in ṢUNDŪQ MUṢAWWIT*.

ṢANF (ṣ-n-f)

Equiv. of ṢINF* (de Vaux 1891:308-309).

ṢANǴ

Var. of SANJ/2* (Sachs 1940:259).

ṢĀNI' (pl. ṢĀNI'ŪN) (ṣ-n-') "maker or craftsman"

Composer or tunemaker.

ṢANJ or ṢINJ (pl. ṢUNŪJ) = ṢANǴ, SINJ, ṢANDJ, SANDJ, SANCH (ṣ-n-j) (Perṡ.)

1. An open-stringed harp-like instrument, similar to the Ar. JANK*. This vertical, angular harp had 13-40 strings, sometimes paired, sometimes tuned trichordally. It was plucked by the fingers

of both hands. An instrument of this type was used by the Arabs from pre-Islamic times and was still known in the 16th C. It was designated by many different names (al Fārābī 1967:822; Ibn Sīnā 1935:233; al Khwārizmī 1968:237; al Ḥafnī 1976:41; Ḥāfiẓ 1971:6, illus. on p. 19). See WANJ*, MUWANNAJ*, MUṢANNAJ*, SAMBUCA*.
2. Generic for all types of cymbals. This term is thought to have been borrowed from the Persian language though Farmer argues that it may have its root in Assyrian. It was known in ancient Semitic and Arabic literature and has been used from pre-Islamic times until today to designate castanets or cymbals of various kinds. In the 13th C. the term meant a large cymbal. Today it is found generally in its plural form denoting the finger cymbals which are used as a folk instrument or accompaniment of the dancer (Jargy 1971:125). It is also used often to designate the metal jingles mounted on the rim of the tambourine. See ZINJ*.
3. The tambourine with jingles in its frame (given as SANCH* in Ribera 1970:94). This is the only reference to this meaning known. It therefore needs further verification.

ṢANJ CHINI (ṣ-n-j) (ethn.) "Chinese ṢANJ"

Var. of ṢANJ ṢĪNĪ* (Marcuse).

ṢANJ JĪNĪ (ṣ-n-j) (ethn. ? corruption of SĪNĪ)

Var. of ṢANJ ṢĪNĪ* (mentioned by Ibn Sīnā, according to d'Erlanger 1935:234).

ṢANJ ṢĪNĪ = ṢANJ CHINI, SANJ JĪNĪ, SINJ KHĪNĪ (Pers.)(ethn.) "Chinese ṢANJ"

An open-stringed instrument played with two mallets (MAṬĀRIQ, s. MIṬRAQ*). This dulcimer-like instrument was mentioned by the 11th C. theorists Ibn Sīnā (1935:234) and Ibn Zaylah (Br. Mus. Or. 2361, fol. 235v; 1964:73; also mentioned in Farmer 1926a:243).

ṢANNĀJ (ṣ-n-j) "player of the ṢANJ"

One who performs on the cymbals, dulcimer or harp (ṢANJ*) (Farmer 1967:18, 79).

ṢANNĀJĀT (ṣ-n-j)

Castanets (Wehr).

ṢANNĀJĀT AL JAYSH (ṣ-n-j) (j-y-sh) "cymbals of the army"

Hand cymbals used in the military band (Farmer EI(Fr), "Ṣandj":209).

SANNĪDAH = SNAYYIDAH (s-n-d) "group of supporters"

A chorus of three or four men which supports the male soloist (MUṬRIB*) in the Egyptian instrumental ensemble (TAKHT*) (Racy 1978b:1).

SANT (Eng.) "cent"

Cent, the unit of measurement for musical intervals, i.e., 1/100 of the semitone of the tempered scale. Thus each octave equals 1200 cents and each semitone of the tempered scale equals 100 cents. See DHARRAH ṢAWTIYYAH*, a syn. of SANT.

SANTĪR, SANṬĪR or ṢANṬĪR

Vars. of SANṬŪR* (Farmer 1954, "Santīr":VII, 404-405). Both of the terms ṢANTĪR and SANTĪR are found in Delphin and Guin (1886:58).

SANTŪR

Var. of SANṬŪR*(Ḥāfiẓ 1971:162). Touma uses this spelling to designate the Arab dulcimer used especially in ʿIrāq. He contrasts it with the Persian SANTUR. The latter has 18 groups of strings and two series of bridges, while the ʿIrāqī instrument has 23 groups of strings and three series of bridges (Touma 1977b:100-102).

SANṬŪR (pl. SANĀṬĪR) = ṢANTŪR, SANṬĪR, SUNṬŪR, ṢUNTŪR, SANTĪR, ṢANṬĪR, SANTIR (Pers.)

A dulcimer-type instrument made of wood, with metal (or sometimes silk) strings, and played with two mallets. It is usually in the form of a symmetrical trapezoid, with two sides (rather than one) oblique. It is played in horizontal position like the QĀNŪN*.

Some say that the word is of Persian derivation and means "a quick accent" (al Ḥafnī 1971:54) while others claim that the word is derived from Aramaic and perhaps traceable back to the Greek (Farmer EI(Eng), "Miʿzaf":530; 1954, "Santīr":VII, 404). An instrument of this name is known to have existed by the 14th C. and is still found today in ʿIrāq, as well as in Turkey and Iran. This term is not mentioned in the Classical Period Arabic works on music. The instrument became popular in the 17th C.. Since that time it has been favored more by the foreigners and the minority religious communities living in the Arab World than by the Arab Muslims.

The longest side of the instrument is ca. 75 cm. and the shortest is ca. 35 cm. There are two or three systems of bridges (s. FARAS*) under each group of identically tuned strings which serve to facilitate modulations and increase the range of the instrument. Each group of strings provides three different notes: one when struck to the left, one when struck between the bridges and a third when struck to the right (el Mahdi 1972:64). See further details in Touma 1977:100-102. There are several varieties of this instrument used today with differing size of soundbox, bridges systems, and number of strings. According al Ḥafnī (1971:54), it has between 72 and 100 strings. Others describe it as an instrument with 33-45 strings (el Mahdi 1972:63); or with 69 strings (Touma 1977b:100).

SANŪJ

Var. of ṢUNŪJ, pl. of ṢANJ/2*, the finger cymbals of modern Egypt (Marcuse).

SAOUT

Var. of ṢAWT/2* (Touma 1977b:76, 155).

SAPUT

Var. of SHABŪT* (Ribera 1970:60).

SĀQAH (s-w-q) "rear guard"

The separate company of the army comprising the standard bearers and the military band under the Muwaḥḥid rulers of Moorish Spain (Farmer 1967:208).

ṢAQR (ṣ-q-r) "falcon"

The cymbals mounted in the rim of the tambourines of Moorish Spain (el Helou 1965:39).

ŠARARAH

Var. of SHARARAH* (Shiloah 1972:19).

SARĪʿ or SARĪʿAH (s-r-ʿ) "fast"

A fast tempo comparable to Allegro Vivace (al Ḥafnī 1946:287; Maḥfūẓ 1964:177).

SARĪʿ AL HAZAJ (s-r-ʿ) (h-z-j) "fast HAZAJ"

The fastest sequence of equal percussions possible, i.e., one in which no extra percussion could be fitted between any two percussions (al Fārābī 1967:450).

SARRĀBAH = SERRÂBA (s-r-b) "that which is sent out in groups"

A genre of GRĪḤAH*, the popular music of Morocco. This piece comprises many subdivisions into threes. It has 1) an introduction (ASHṬUR AL ŪLĀ*); 2) a central segment (NAʿŪRAH*); and a final RADMAH*. Each of these parts is made up of three poetic lines, each of which has three subsections. The SARRĀBAH is usually based on a 5-beat rhythm (Chottin 1939:160-162). This vocal genre is often used as an introduction for the QAṢĪDAH/1*.

SARUD

Var. of SHĀHRŪD* (Marcuse).

SARW (s-r-w) "high ranking"

The opening in the top of the soundbox of the QĀNŪN* which is nearest the pointed corner of the instrument (al Ḥafnī 1971:49).

SAṬḤ (pl. SUṬŪḤ, ASṬIḤAH, ASṬUḤ) (s-ṭ-ḥ) "surface; roof"

Top face of the soundbox of the QĀNŪN*, ʿŪD*, RABĀB* or other chordophone (al Fārābī 1967:800; Maḥfūẓ 1964:155).

SAṬṬĀʿAH (s-ṭ-ʿ) "the producer of brilliance"

Plectrum (Moorish Sp.) (Farmer 1954, "Moorish Music":V, 874).

SAṬṬARAH (s-ṭ-r) "promenade; line"

An introductory musical "promenade" performed in the south of Morocco (given SATTARAH in Chottin 1939:46). Also colloquially as AṬSARAH*.

SAUT

Var. of ṢAWT/2* (Touma 1977a:122).

SAWAKĀT = SAWAKET (s-k-t) or perhaps (s-q-ṭ) (?)

A genre of Tunisian music from the NAWBAH/1* or suite repertoire. It comprises a lute improvisation based on a folkish motif or tune (Perkuhn 1976:107). See SAWAKET*.

SAWAKET (s-k-t) or perhaps (s-q-ṭ) (?)

Var. or syn. of SAWAKĀT (el Mahdi 1972:14). This may be a colloq. of SAWAKIT, "silent ones" or a derivative from SAQAṬA, "to fall."

SAWDĀ' (s-w-d) "black" (f.)

Name for the quarter note of contemporary notation (el Helou 1961: 20).

ṢAWT (pl. AṢWĀT) (ṣ-w-t) "sound"

1. Any sound perceptible to the ear, from noise to musical sound (Ikhwān al Ṣafā' 1957:183, 188; Shiloah 1964/65:128, n. 7; Ibn Abī al Dunyā 1938:28, 50). It has sometimes been used to mean "noise" in contrast to the musical sound (Farmer 1967:51).
2. A vocal piece or song as mentioned in the 1001 Nights (Farmer 1945:43). and in other works of Muslim writers (Ibn Khurdādhbih 1969:16; Ibn ʿAbd Rabbihi 1887:III, 189; Ibn al Munajjim 1976:832). This vocal genre had a melody which matched perfectly the length of the poetry to which it was set. No extra words or percussions were needed to fill out either element of the combination (ʿAbd al Qādir ibn Ghaybī in Anonymous Treatise 1939:244). It was described as QALĪL AL AJZĀ'*, i.e.,"with few parts," and similar

to a vocalise (al Jurjānī 1938:552-553; Wright 1978:219). This melismatic vocal number was an optional part of the ancient NAWBAH/1* or suite. As such, it was a syn. of MIYAT KHĀNAH* (Anonymous Treatise 1939:236). This meaning seems to be the one intended by al Nadīm (1970:I, 342), though the translator uses the term "refrain" as equivalent. Ibn Khaldūn equated this genre with the MAWĀLIYĀ/1* of his time (1967:III, 475;476).
3. Note or tone.
4. Voice (Ibn Abī al Dunyā 1938:31, 53).
5. In the early Islamic period, melodic mode (Jargy 1971:32).
6. Vocal suite of the Arabian/Persian Gulf region. It comprises both solo and choral passages based on regular rhythms of extreme complexity. It is performed with accompaniment of percussion instruments and hand clapping (Jargy 1971:93; Touma 1977a:122).
7. An unidentified instrumental/ vocal number in the ancient Arab musical tradition of the Ḥijāz (Touma 197bb:76).

ṢAWT AL ʿĀLIYAH (ṣ-w-t) (ʿ-l-w) or ('-l-y) "high sound"

A tone high in pitch.

ṢAWT DHAYL = ÇÛTU DĪL (ṣ-w-t) (dh-y-l) "sound of the lowermost part"

The male vocal range comparable to bass (Mor.) (Chottin 1939:132). Also ṢAWT JAHĪR* (Ibid.:133).

ṢAWT GHALĪZAH (ṣ-w-t) (gh-l-z) "thick sound"

A tone low in pitch.

ṢAWT ḤĀDDAH (ṣ-w-t) (ḥ-d-d) "sharp or borderline sound"

A tone high in pitch.

ṢAWT ḤUSAYN = ÇÛTU H'SIN (ṣ-w-t) (ḥ-s-n) "sound of ḤUSAYN"

The male vocal range comparable to high tenor (Mor.) (Chottin 1939:132).

ṢAWT INQIBĀḌ (ṣ-w-t) (q-b-ḍ) "sad sound"

Sad music or a sad sound (al Kindī 1966:151).

ṢAWT JAHĪR = ÇÛTU JHIR (ṣ-w-t) (j-h-r) "loud sound"

The lowest male vocal range, comparable to bass (Chottin 1939:133). Also ṢAWT DHAYL*.

ṢAWT MĀ'IYYAH = ÇÛTU MÂÏA (ṣ-w-t) (m-w-h) "juicy sound" (?)

The male vocal range comparable to tenor (Mor.) (Chottin 1939:132).

ṢAWT MUTAWASSIṬAH (ṣ-w-t) (w-s-ṭ) "middle sound"

A tone in the middle range, neither high nor low in pitch.

ṢAWT RAMAL = ṢÛTU RAMAL (ṣ-w-t) (r-m-l) "sound of RAMAL"

The male vocal range comparable to baritone (Mor.) (Chottin 1939: 132).

ṢAWT RAQĪQAH (ṣ-w-t) (r-q-q) "fine sound"

A tone high in pitch.

ṢAWT THAQĪLAH (s-w-t) (th-q-l) "heavy sound"

A tone low in pitch.

ṢAWT AL WASAṬ (ṣ-w-t) (w-s-ṭ) "sound of the middle"

A melismatic section or vocalise said to have been an optional part of the four movements of the NAWBAH/1* or suite of the 15th C. (Anonymous Treatise 1939:236). Syn. of MIYAT KHĀNAH*. See also ʿAMAL*, BASĪṬ/4*.

ṢAWT WĀṬIYAH (ṣ-w-t) (w-ṭ-y) "low sound"

A tone low in pitch.

ṢAWTĪ (ṣ-w-t) "sounding"

Vocal.

SAWURĪ (perhaps from SUWWĀRĪ "grand")

A long necked lute (ṬUNBŪR/1*) of 19th C. Egypt which had three metal strings, of which two were doubles (Farmer EI(Fr), "Ṭunbūr": 270).

SAWWĀ (s-w-y) "to equalize"

To tune the strings of a musical instrument (al Fārābī 1967:123).

ṢAYḤAH (ṣ-y-ḥ) "a cry or shout"

Syn. of ṢIYĀH* (al Khwarizmi 1968:240; Farmer 1965b:20).

SĀYIR AL TARJĪʿAH (s-y-r) (r-j-ʿ)

This may be a var. spelling of SĀ'IR AL TARJĪʿAH ("wanderer of the TARJĪʿAH"--see TARJĪ or TARJĪʿAH*). It designated the melody string which was used to perform the TARJĪʿ or TARJĪʿAH/3* improvisation. It was contrasted with the drone string (LĀZIM AL TARJĪʿ* or RĀJIʿ*) (ʿAbd al Qādir ibn Ghaybī in Anonymous Treatise 1939:245).

ṢAYYĀḤ (ṣ-y-ḥ) "the clamorous one"

Syn. of ṢIYĀḤ* (from 9th C. ms., see Farmer 1965b:20).

SĀZ (Turk.) "rush or reed"

A musical instrument. This term has been used to designate a number of different types, e.g.: the JANK*, the ʿŪD/2* or BARBAṬ/1*, the ṬUNBŪR/1*, QĀNŪN* and even the drum (Maḥfūẓ 1964:35-36).

SĀZ ʿĀLĪ MURAṢṢAʿ (Turk.) (ʿ-l-w) (r-ṣ-ʿ) "high, heavily decorated SĀZ"

A drum with strings which had a drumstick attached to a wheel as in SĀZ DŪLĀB* for mechanically beating the strings attached to the exterior of the membrane (Maḥfūẓ 1964:36).

SĀZ ALWĀḤ AL FŪLĀDH = SĀZ-i ALWĀḤ-i FŪLĀD (Pers.) (l-w-ḥ) (f-l-dh) "SĀZ of steel bars"

A metalophone of the 15th C. with 35 iron bars, each producing a particular pitch (Farmer EI(Fr), "Ṣandj":211). In all works investigated, the last word is FŪLĀD, a colloq. of the Ar. word for "metal" (FŪLĀDH).

SĀZ DŪLĀB (Pers.) (Pers.) "wheel SĀZ"

A drum with strings outside the membrane which were mechanically struck by a drumstick affixed to a wheel in such a way as to regularly beat the strings (Maḥfūẓ 1964:36).

SĀZ FŪLĀDH (Pers.) (f-l-dh) "steel SĀZ"

Shortened name for the metalophone which was known as SĀZ ALWĀḤ AL FŪLĀDH* (Maḥfūẓ 1964:36). Here again we find the text carrying "FŪLĀD" rather than "FŪLĀDH." See SĀZ ALWĀḤ AL FŪLĀDH*.

SĀZ KA'SĀT or SĀZ KĀSĀT (Pers.) (k-'-s) or (k-w-s) "SĀZ of cups or of glasses"

Musical cups, made of earthenware, the pitch being determined by the amount of water in each one. This instrument was mentioned by ʿAbd al Qādir ibn Ghaybī (d. 1435) (Farmer 1957:442; EI(Fr), "Ṣandj":211). Syn. of SĀZ ṬĀSĀT*.

SĀZ ṬĀSĀT (Pers.) (ṭ-w-s) "SĀZ of metal drinking cups"

Syn. of SĀZ KA'SĀT or SĀZ KĀSĀT* (Farmer EI(Fr), "Ṣandj":211).

SĀZ-I ALWĀḤ-I FŪLĀD

Var. of SĀZ ALWĀḤ AL FŪLĀDH* (Farmer EI(Fr), "Ṣandj":211).

SCHEHRUD

Var. of SHĀHRŪD* (Kieswetter 1968:95).

SDAF

Var. of ṢADAF* (Jones 1977:50).

SEBĀBEH

Var. of SABBĀBAH (Smith 1847:206).

SEKTA

Var. of SAKT or SAKTAH* (Chottin 1939:114-115).

SELĀSIL

Var. of ṢALĀṢIL* (Marcuse).

SEMAI

Var. of SAMĀʿĪ/1* (Chottin and Hickmann 1949-1951:Band I, col. 594).

SEMSEMIYYA

Var. of SIMSIMIYYAH* (Jargy 1971:123).

SENED

Var. of SANAD* (Ribera 1970:31, n. 2).

SERRÂBA

Var. of SARRĀBAH* (Chottin 1939:160-162).

SHABĀB (pl. of SHABB) (sh-b-b) "young men"

Syn. of QAṢABAH/2*, a large end-blown flute (Tun.). This instrument is still very popular in rural areas though the ZUKRAH/1* (oboe) has taken over in the more populated northern and eastern littoral (Jones 1977:19).

SHABB or SHĀBB (pl. SHABĀB) (sh-b-b) "young man"

1. The upper tone of an octave interval (Farmer 1933b:25). See SHAYKH/1*.
2. The upper octave equivalent of the open BAMM* or DHAYL/1* string of the ʿŪD/2* (Farmer 1933b:7). The older, more classical name for this tone was ṢIYĀḤ/1*. See SHAYKH/2*.

SHABBĀBAH (pl. SHABBĀBĀT) = CHABBABAH, SABBĀBA, SHABEBA (sh-b-b)

1. A well known end-blown flute made of cane of both Maghrib and Mashriq. It is half the size of the QAṢABAH/2*, and usually has six front finger holes and one rear thumbhole. Maḥfūẓ, however, describes it as an instrument with eight finger holes (1964:38). This term has been used for a great variety of similar instruments. It has even served to name double piped instruments (Shawqī 1976:281).
2. A record-type aerophone according to Villoteau (Egypt, 19th C.). Syn. of ṢAFFĀRAH/3* (Farmer 1978:I:83).

SHABBŪR = Š̌ABBUR (sh-b-r) "trumpet"

A horn with conical bore, and esp. the horn of the Jews (Maḥfūẓ 1964:38). This term may have been derived from the Hebrew "SHŌFAR" (Farmer EI(Fr), "Būḳ":46).

SHABEBA

Var. of SHABBĀBAH* (Ribera 1970:94, n. 33).

SHABĪL = CHEBIL (sh-b-l)

A drumstick held in the left hand (Alg.) (Delphin and Guin 1886: 44).

SHA'BIYYAH = SHA'IBĪYA (sh-'-b) "pertaining to the people"

Panpipes, according to a 15th C. treatise. Equiv. of SHU'AYBIYYAH*.

SHADD (pl. SHUDŪD) = Š̌ADD (sh-d-d) "tightening, tension"

1. Tuning of a musical instrument.
2. A melodic mode encompassing one octave according to Ṣafī al Dīn in his Kitāb al Adwār (d'Erlanger 1938:109, 376, 392). The modes of the time (13th C.) were divided into three categories. Those designated as SHADD modes were the largest in number (12 modes) and the most basic to the system. They all had a scale divisible into two conjunct tetrachords or into a tetrachord and a pentachord (Wright 1978:Chap. III). In the 14th C. this category included 12 primary melodic modes (Badr al Dīn al Irbalī 1951:108, n. 2). It was at that time considered to be an Ar. equiv. of PARDAH/1* and MAQĀM/1*, the words used for basic modes in Persia (Wright 1978:16, n. 15). See also ĀWĀZ/2*, MURAKKAB or MURAKKABAH/1* and DAWR/3*.
3. Tension of the string of a musical instrument, and by extension the pitch of that string (Shiloah 1968:237, 244).

SHADDA (sh-d-d) "to pull or strengthen"

To perform the melody of one melodic mode (MAQĀM/1*) with the notes and organization of another. In defining this term, Kāẓim (1964:63) seems to be describing transposition. He says that the practice has little importance in Arabic music, but is extremely important for Western music.

SHADDĀD (pl. SHADDĀDŪN) = CHEDDÂD (sh-d-d) "one who pulls and strenghthens"

Chorister.

SHADDĀDAH = CHEDDÂDA (sh-d-d) f. of "that which strengthens or doubles"

1. Chorus or choristers.
2. A female chorus member.

SHADDAH (sh-d-d) "pulling, stress"

1. Highness of pitch (Shawqī 1976:305).
2. Loudness (Shawqī 1976:348).
3. Loud and comparable to Forte (Maḥfūẓ 1964:181; al Ḥafnī 1946: 287).

SHĀDH (pl. SHAWĀDH, SHĀDHĀT) = SHĀZ (sh-w-dh)

Any of the three secondary melodic modes derived from the six ĀWĀZ/2* modes, according to Badr al Dīn al Irbalī (1951:109).

SHADHRAH (pl. SHADHRĀT) (sh-dh-r) "insertion"

Short, light embellishing tones added between main tones as a means of beautifying a melody (al Fārābī 1935:90; 1967:1173). These compare to the ISHĀRĀT AL ḤULYAH* mentioned by contemporary theorists (Maḥfūẓ 1964:185), or to grace notes.

SHĀDĪ (pl. SHUDĀH) (sh-d-w) "singer"

Singer (Maḥfūẓ 1964:19; Ibn Salamah 1938a:18; 1938b:248). See SHUDĀH*.

SHADĪDAH (sh-d-d) "stretched"

Loud (Shawqī 1976:346).

SHADW (sh-d-w) "singing"

1. Lengthening the sound in singing or instrumental music.
2. Singing, song or chant (Ibn Salamah 1938a:18; 1938b:248).

SHAERA

Var. of SHAʿĪRAH* (Ribera 1970:94).

SHĀH (Pers.) "king"

An end-blown flute of Egypt (Maḥfūẓ 1964:37). See SHĀHRŪD or SHAHRŪD/2*.

SHĀHĪN (pl. SHAWĀHĪN) (sh-h-n) "an Indian falcon"

1. A kind of fife used in pilgrimage processions of the pre-Islamic and early Islamic times. It was considered a "permissible" instrument because of its association with pilgrimage (Farmer 1967:30, 34).
2. An unidentified chordophone described by al Zabīdī (1888:IX, 257) as corresponding to the harp. See Ribera 1970:90, n. 22.

SHĀHNĀZ or SHAHNĀZ (Pers.) "coquetry of the king"

1. Melodic mode mentioned from the 15th C. (Anonymous Treatise 1939:130).

2. Name for a note of the contemporary Arab scale, $C\#_2$ or Db_2

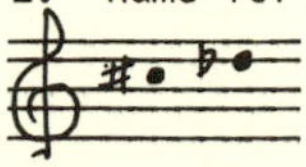

.

SHĀHRŪD or SHAHRŪD = SĀH-RŪD, SHĀHRŪDH, SARUD, SCHEHRUD (Pers.) "king of the RŪD"

1. An ancient open-stringed instrument, archlute, described as an instrument which produced the greatest number of notes of any of the instruments of that time (10th C.). It was said to have been invented by Khulāyṣ ibn al Aḥwaṣ (or Akhwaṣ) al Ṣughdī in 912 (al Fārābī 1967:116-118). Other writers give the inventor's first name as Ḥakīm (al Khwārizmī 1968:237; Maḥfūẓ 1964:39). In the 15th C., it was described by ʿAbd al Qādir ibn Ghaybī as having 10 double strings and being twice as long as the ʿŪD/2* (Farmer EI(Eng), "ʿŪd":987; 1967:209). See also Ṣafī al Dīn 1938b:20; al Jurjānī 1938:240-241; <u>Anonymous Treatise</u> 1939:43; al Lādhiqī 1939:298).
2. A large end-blown flute (Maḥfūẓ 1964:37).

SHĀHRŪDH

Var. of SHĀHRŪD or SHAHRŪD/1* (al Khwārizmī 1968:237; al Lādhiqī 1939:298).

SHAʿIBĪYA

Var. of SHAʿBIYYAH* (Farmer 1954, "Egyptian Music":II, 894).

SHĀʿIR (pl. SHĀʿIRŪN) (sh-ʿ-r) "poet"

Poet and/or vocal improvisor.

SHAʿĪRAH = SHAERA (sh-ʿ-r) "barleycorn; grain"

Mouthpiece of a woodwind instrument which included a contrivance by which the pitch could be lowered by cutting off one finger hole. It was first described by al Fārābī (d. 950). Later it was known as ṬAWQ/3*, FAṢL/4* or ḤABBAH AL MUṢAWWITAH*. See al Fārābī 1967:788; al Khwārizmī 1968:237; and SHAʿRAH*.

SHAʿĪRAH AL MIZMĀR (sh-ʿ-r) (z-m-r) "grain of the MIZMĀR"

Soundbox of the organ according to a 12th C. copy of an earlier ms. (Farmer 1931:136).

SHAKSHĀK

Var. of SHAQSHĀQ* (Delphin and Guin 1886:38).

SHAKSHĪKAH

A percussion instrument comprising two pieces of wood fastened to each other and having a number of small bells attached at the crux of the pieces of wood. The instrument was usually struck with a baton (Farmer EI(Fr), "Ṣandj":211).

SHALIAK

Var. of SHALYĀQ* (Ribera 1970:93).

SHALYĀḲ

Var. of SHALYĀQ* (Farmer EI(Eng), "Miʿzaf":529).

SHALYĀQ = SHALIAK, SHALYĀḲ

A chordophone of ancient Greece and Byzantium which was similar to the harp (al Khwārizmī 1968:236). Syn. of SALBĀQ*.

SHAMBAR

A form of BASHRAF/2* or instrumental overture based on a special rhythmic mode called TSHAMBAR* and formerly performed in Tunisia (d'Erlanger 1959:200). Var. of SHANBAR or SHANBĀR*.

SHAMSAH = CHEMSA (sh-m-s) "sun"

The circular carving covering an opening in the face of the soundbox of any chordophone.

SHAMSIYYAH (sh-m-s) "umbrella; curtain"

Syn. of SHAMSAH*.

SHANĀSHIN (sh-n-sh-n) "things that rustle"

Small metal jingles inserted in the frame of the tambourine (Tun.) (Jones 1977:46). In Rouanet (1922:2944) SHANĀSHIL* (supp.).

SHANBAR or SHANBĀR = SHAMBAR, TCHENBAR, TSHAMBAR

1. An orchestral overture which opens the NAWBAH INQILĀBĀT* (Rouanet 1922:2863).
2. A rhythmic mode which was formerly used in Tunisia as rhythmic underlay of the overture of the same name. See def. 1 above.

SHANGHAL = CHENGAL, SHANQĀL (sh-n-gh-l) "hook"

A curved stick of about 28 cm. in length which is used to play a drum (Alg.) (Delphin and Guin 1886:44). SHANQĀL in Rouanet 1922: 2933).

SHAQAF or SHAQF = SHAQEF (sh-q-f) colloq. for "(pot)sherds"

A late ʿAbbāsī period name for a tambourine with cymbals mounted in its frame (Hickmann 1947:21; Farmer 1967:211).

SHAQIRAH (sh-q-r) "light skinned"

A musical instrument mentioned in a 13th C. treatise of Moorish Spain. It is believed to have been a chordophone (Farmer 1926a: 252ff; 1978:I, 20ff).

SHAQSHĀQ = SHAKSHĀK, CHEKCHEK (sh-q-sh-q) "chirping"

Small round tambourine with metal jingles in the frame (Alg.). It is usually played only by women. More recently it is included in any of the indigenous orchestras of Algeria, whether composed of male or female performers.

SHAQSHAQAH (pl. SHAQSHAQĀT) (sh-q-sh-q) "a chirping"

Elongated metal clappers used by members of a negro Muslim brotherhood of Tunisia (Racy 1979:24). Syn. of QARQABAT*.

SHAʿR (pl. ASHʿĀR, SHUʿŪR) (sh-ʿ-r) "hair"

The hair stretched on the bow of a musical instrument (Maḥfūẓ 1964:159). Rouanet 1922:2924 has CHEʿOUR, a var. pl. form.

SHAʿRAH (pl. SHAʿRĀT) (sh-ʿ-r) "a piece of hair"

Said by Ḥāfiẓ (1971:32) to have been the 10th C. innovation of al Fārābī, this playing reed of a woodwind instrument is in al Fārābī (1967:788) given as SHAʿĪRAH*.

SHARʿAH or SHIRʿAH (pl. SHIRAʿ, SHIRĀʿ) (sh-r-ʿ) "string, thong"

A string of the lute (ʿŪD/2*), according to Ibn Salamah (1938a:12; 1938b:242). The translator of Ibn Salamah's work (Robson 1938a: 12; 1938b:242) uses SHIRʿAH. The term is used for the string of other musical instruments as well (Madina).

SHARĀRAH = ŠARARAH (sh-r-r) "spark"

The highest pitched of the five strings of the SIMSIMIYYAH*, a contemporary harp-like folk instrument. Shiloah suggests that the term may have been chosen for its meaning relationship to ḤADD* ("acute"), the name for the fifth and highest string of the lute in earlier times (1972:19).

SHARGĪ

Var. of SHARQĪ/1* (Jargy 1979:85).

SHARQAH (sh-r-q) "choking"

A long and trembling vocal tone terminating a song (al Fārābī 1967:1154; 1935:86). According to al Jurjānī (1938:541), the name was given to the final tone of a vocal number which did not end on a quiescent "H," but rather, ended abruptly with a sharp cut off. See also ISTIRĀḤAH* and IʿTIMĀD/1*.

SHARQĪ = SHERŪQĪ, SHARGĪ, SHURŪQĪ, ŠRŪQĪ, SHRŪGĪ (sh-r-q) "oriental"

1. Among the Bedouins of Syria, a variety of ʿATĀBĀ or ʿATĀBAH* (an improvised folk song) which is usually accompanied by a bowed chordophone (RABĀB or RABĀBAH/3*. Among the settled peoples,

it is a setting of poetry with generally religious theme (Jargy 1978:85). According to Kāẓim (1964:64), this genre of music is a strophic musical setting for poetry of four, five or six lines per strophe. It usually makes use of short, simple rhythms. It can be included as one of the contemporary genres performed in the WAṢLAH/1* or suite (Farmer 1954, "Nauba":VI, 33).
2. Generic term for any musical genre or piece (al Khulaʿī 1904: 46).
3. A four-string lute or pandore mentioned by a 17th C. Turkish traveler (Farmer 1976b:39). See ṬUNBŪR SHARQĪ*.
4. Adj., pertaining to the musical tradition of the peoples at the eastern end of the Mediterranean Sea, i.e., from Egypt towards the north and east. Syn. of MASHRIQĪ*, and opp. of MAGHRIBĪ*.

SHASHTĀ or SHASHTĀR (Pers.) "six strings"

A small lute with six strings according to the 15th C. theorist, ʿAbd al Qādir ibn Ghaybī. He described it as being of three kinds: 1) a pear-shaped instrument smaller than the ʿŪD/2*; 2) an instrument similar to 1) above, but with a longer neck; and 3) an instrument similar to 2) above, but with 30 sympathetic strings tuned bichordally to give two octaves. In the 17th C., the SHASHTĀR was described as a fretted chordophone with six metal strings (Farmer 1976b:42-43; 1978:II, 97). The various definitions seem to establish that it was a long necked lute similar to the ṬUNBŪR/1*.

SHASHUM

One of the principal melodic modes (UṢŪL, s. AṢL/5*) of Persia which were mentioned by al Kindī (Farmer 1926c:95).

SHAṬḤ = CHATH, CHTIH' (sh-ṭ-ḥ) "escapade"

1. Dance in general or the trembling of the shoulders by dancers (al Zabīdī 1888:II, 173).
2. The unconscious verbalizations that may take place in a state of mystical ecstasy (al Zabīdī 1888:II, 173).

SHAṬḤAH (pl. SHAṬAḤĀT) (sh-ṭ-ḥ) "an escapade"

The dance which accompanies the NAWBAH/1* music among members of the ʿĪsāwiyyah religious brotherhood of Tunisia. Usually it is performed by men and boys, but in more private situations or areas, women also perform (Jones 1977:56).

SHAṬR (pl. ASHṬUR, SHUṬŪR) = CHATR (sh-ṭ-r) "a partition, division; half"

1. The opening hemistich of a line of poetry and, by extension, the musical line accompanying it.
2. A line of poetry (Chottin 1939:155).

SHAUSHAK

Var. of SHĪSHĀK or SHĪSHĀL*. It is thought that this instrument was similar to the Turkish spike fiddle known as GHISHAK* (Farmer 1967:210).

SHAWSHAL or SHAWSHIL (pl. SHAWĀSHIL) (Pers./Turk.)

Vars. of SHĪSHĀK or SHĪSHĀL* (Ikhwān al Ṣafā' 1957:I, 202; 1964/65: 148).

SHAYKH (pl. SHUYŪKH) = SHAIKH, CHÎKH, CHÉKH (sh-y-kh) "old man; elder"

1. Popular singer (Alg.) (Delphin and Guin 1886:2), who is also known as MADDĀḤ*. In Morocco, the term designates a performer who fills a multiple role: as poet, author, actor, administrator, flutist and group leader of a performance group. This person is also known as MUQADDIM*. Among the mountain peoples (Mor.), he is called AMGHAR* or MAWLĀ AL ZAMR* (Chottin 1939:33, 159-160).
2. The lower tone of an octave interval (Farmer 1933b:25).
3. The note produced on the open BAMM* or DHAYL/1* string of the lute (Farmer 1933b:7).
4. Religious teacher to instruct in Qur'ānic cantillation.

(AL) SHAYKH AL RA'ĪS (sh-y-kh) (r-'-s) "elder head"

Nickname given to Ibn Sīnā by later theorists.

SHAYKHAH (pl. SHAYKHĀT) = CHÎKHAH (sh-y-kh) f. of "SHAYKH"

Professional female singer or musician of Morocco . Sometimes the SHAYKHAH is described as a young performer in contrast to the older female professional called ḤAḌḌARAH* (Chottin 1939:40).

SHĀZ (pl. SHĀZĀT) (sh-w-z)

Var. of SHĀDH* (al Irbalī 1951:109).

SHERUQI

Var. of SHURŪQĪ* or SHARQĪ/1* (Jargy 1970:36).

SHIDIRGHU or S̲HIDŪRG̲HŪR

A long necked lute described by ʿAbd al Qādir ibn Ghaybī (d. 1435). Half of its face was covered with skin. It had four strings and was known primarily in China (Farmer 1978:II, 16; EI(Eng), "ʿŪd": 988).

SHIHĀBĪ ZŪRNĀ (n. of pers.) (Turk.) "Shihāb's oboe or reed pipe"

A woodwind instrument invented in the Maghrib by Shaykh Shihāb. It was used commonly in 17th C. Fez. It is thought to have been an oboe-type instrument similar to the GHAYṬAH/1*, i.e., with double reed (Farmer 1976b:25-26).

SHIMSHĀR or SHIMSHĀL

A musical instrument which is described as being made of cane (Kāẓim 1964:65), therefore, probably a woodwind instrument.

SHIʿR (sh-ʿ-r) "that which is felt"

Poetry, a poem.

SHIʿR GHINĀ'Ī (sh-ʿ-r) (gh-n-y) "sung poetry"

Chanted or sung poetry.

SHIRʿAH (sh-r-ʿ)

Equiv. of SHARʿAH*.

SHĪSHĀK or SHĪSHĀL = SHAWSHAL, SHAWSHIL, SHAWSHAK, SHAUSHAL, SHŪSHAK, SHĪZĀN, SHĪZĀK, GHISHAK, GHIZHAK, GHIZAK, GHIČAK (Pers./Turk.)

An ancient bowed chordophone said to have first been mentioned at the beginning of the 10th C. According to Ḥāfiẓ, it generally had 10 strings, yet that it was "smaller than the KAMANJAH" (Ḥāfiẓ 1971:80). If this description of its size is correct, the instrument probably had many fewer strings. See Farmer 1978:II, 32, where he writes that the instrument generally had only two strings. This viol with hemispheric soundbox was made of wood. It had a face of skin, and was played with a horsehair bow.

SHĪZĀK

Var. of SHĪSHĀK or SHĪSHĀL* (Farmer 1978:II, 32).

SHĪZĀN

Var. of SHĪSHĀK or SHĪSHĀL* (Farmer 1978:II, 32).

SHRŪGĪ

Var. of SHURŪQĪ* or SHARQĪ/1* (Jargy 1978:85), a long improvisational form, similar to the ʿATĀBĀ or ʿATĀBAH* (Jargy 1970:36).

SHU'AIBĪYA or SHUʿAIBIYYAH

Vars. of SHUʿAYBIYYAH* (Marcuse; Farmer 1957:443, resp.)

SHUʿAYBIYYAH = SHU'AIBĪYA, SHUʿAIBIYYA (sh-ʿ-b) dim. of "that which has many parts"

Panpipes of Egypt. See SHAʿBIYYAH*.

SHUʿBAH (pl. SHUʿAB, SHUʿBĀT, SHIʿĀB) = CHOʿBA, ŜUʿBAH (sh-ʿ-b) "branch, division"

A derivative melodic mode according to theorists of the 13th-16th C. In Quṭb al Dīn al Shīrāzī's Durrah al Tāj (written about 1300),

SHUʿBAH was a derivative mode whose definable characteristics included emphasis on particular tones, an initial and final, and specific melodic movement on the tones of the parent scale (PARDAH/1*) from which it was derived. It seems to have been equivalent, therefore, to a "melodic type." See Quṭb al Dīn in Wright 1978:143; Wright 1978:Chap. 8, pp. 194-215). In another 14th C. work (the commentary on Ṣafī al Dīn's Kitāb al Adwār) the author uses the term SHUʿAB as equivalent of AWAZAT and describes them as modal combinations derived from the principal scales (al Jurjānī 1938: 377, 388). In the 15th C. (Anonymous Treatise 1939:131-149), these derivative modes numbered 24. They were derived from six MAQĀMĀT or parent modes of the time. Each SHUʿBAH mode shared common tones with the parent mode but employed a different use of those tones. Instead of being, like the ĀWĀZĀT, combinations of parts of different basic scales, the author of that treatise described a SHUʿBAH mode as one which uses the tones of the parent mode (MAQĀM/1*), but with its own peculiar melodic treatment. In the 16th C. treatise of al Lādhiqī (1939:399-413), the 24 SHUʿAB were described as obsolete. By that time, only four modes belonged to this category (Ibid.:440-441).

SHUDĀH (pl. of SHĀDĪ) (sh-d-w) "singers"

Singing or chanting (al Nadīm 1970:I, 310), in the Dodge translation.

SHUGHL (pl. ASHGHĀL) = CHURHL, ECHREUL, ECH-CHREUL (sh-gh-l)"work, occupation"

1. A vocalise-like number of Morocco. It utilizes stock phrases and nonsense syllables which may be added in various ways: 1) in the middle of a word; 2) to the end of a phrase; or 3) as a refrain segment (Chottin 1939:128-129). See TAWSHĪḤ KIĀR*, a syn.
2. A genre of vocal music similar to the MUWASHSHAḤ/1* (Tun.). Not used in the classical suite or NAWBAH/1*, this type of song is usually based on rhythmic modes foreign to the Andalusian rhythmic system. The songs seem to have been influenced by the Mashriq, and many are direct borrowings from the East. They are generally freer in conformance to standard practices than the songs which compose the NAWBAH, and they are considered to be less noble than those of the Andalusian repertoire (d'Erlanger 1959:200-201). A refrain divides the number into several parts (Rouanet 1922:2942).

SHUḤĀJ (sh-ḥ-j) "lowest sounds of some animals or birds"

1. The lower of two tones forming an octave interval (al Fārābī 1967:114-115, 517). Syn. of SAJĀḤ*.
2. A name for the lowest possible pitch (al Fārābī 1967:114, n. 8).
3. A low-pitched sound (al Fārābī 1967:505, 517).

SHUḤĀJ AL AṢGHAR (sh-ḥ-j) (ṣ-gh-r) "smaller low note"

The lower of the two notes which form an interval of a perfect fourth (al Fārābī 1967:505, n. 3).

SHUḤĀJ AL AWSAṬ (sh-ḥ-j) (w-s-ṭ) "median low note"

The lower of the two notes which form an interval of a perfect fifth (al Fārābī 1967:505, n. 3).

SHUḤĀJ AL AʿẒAM (sh-ḥ-j) (ʿ-ẓ-m) "larger low note"

The lower of the two notes which form an interval of an octave (al Fārābī 1967:114-115).

SHUḤĪJ (sh-ḥ-j)

Syn. of SHUḤĀJ* (al Fārābī 1967:114, n. 8).

SHUJĀʿ (sh-j-ʿ) "courageous"

The thumb opening on the lower side of the NĀY/1* or similar instrument (Anonymous Treatise 1939:24; Farmer 1954, "Nāy":37).

SHUḲAIFĀT

Var. of SHUQAYFĀT* (Farmer EI(Fr), "Ṣandj":209).

SHULYĀQ

Var. of SULYĀQ* or SALBĀQ* (d'Erlanger 1935:256-257, n. 63).

SHUQAYFĀT (pl. of SHUQAYFAH) = SHUKAIFĀT (sh-q-f) "little pieces"

Metal cymbals of the dancers of the Mashriq (Hickmann 1947:21). In a 15th C. ms., they were described as clappers (Farmer 1965b, see frontispiece illus.).

SHUQRAH = CHOUQRA (sh-q-r) "blondness"

An unidentified woodwind instrument of Moorish Spain (Chottin 1939:89).

SHURŪQĪ = SHERUQI, SHRŪQĪ, ŠRŪQĪ (sh-r-q) "pertaining to the sunrise"

Syn. of SHARQĪ/1*, a difficult and sophisticated genre of vocal folk music (Ibn Dhurayl 1969:149).

SHŪSHĀK

Var. of SHĪSHĀK or SHĪSHĀL* (Farmer 1978:II, 32).

SIAH

Var. of ṢIYĀḤ* (Ribera 1970:76).

SIBS

Small oboe-type (double reed) aerophone used in contemporary Egypt (Sachs 1940:248; Maḥfūẓ 1964:36).

SÎGÂH

Var. of SĪKĀH/3* (Smith 1849:181).

SĪKĀH (Pers.) "station three"

1. A tetrachordal scalar segment (JINS/1*) of 3/4-1-1 division.
2. An important melodic mode (MAQĀM/1*) utilizing the SĪKĀH tetrachordal division, also called SĪKĀH FAWQ AL TĀMM*.
3. A note of the contemporary Arab scale, E$\not\flat_1$ 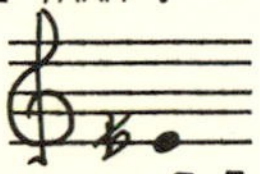 .

SĪKĀH FAWQ AL TĀMM (Pers.) (f-w-q) (t-m-m) "over-complete SĪKĀH"

Syn. of SĪKĀH/2*.

SĪKĀH MUTAWASSIṬ (Pers.) (w-s-ṭ) "median SĪKĀH"

1. A tetrachordal scalar segment (JINS/1*) of 3/4-1-½ division.
2. An important melodic mode (MAQĀM/1*) utilizing this tetrachordal division (see def. 1). Also called ḤUZĀM*.

SĪKĀH TĀMM (Pers.) (t-m-m) "complete SĪKĀH"

1. A tetrachordal scalar segment (JINS/1*) of 3/4-1-3/4 division.
2. An important melodic mode (MAQĀM/1*) utilizing this tetrachordal division (see def. 1). Also called ‘IRĀQ/2*.

SĪKH (pl. ASYĀKH) (s-y-kh) "skewer; iron bolt"

The iron foot which passes through the sounding body and is inserted into the neck of the KAMĀNJAH* or stick fiddle of Egypt (Lane 1973:356).

SĪLBĀN

A harp of Byzantine origin, syn. of SALBĀQ* (al Mas‘ūdī 1874: VIII, 91, n. 2).

ṢILINDJ

Var. of ṢILINJ* (Farmer 1978:I, 60).

ṢILINJ or ṢIRINJ = ṢALTIJ, ṢILINDJ, ṢALINJ

An ancient stringed instrument made of skin of animals (sic), which was believed to have been a Byzantine harp (Ibn Khurdādhbih 1969:19; al Mas‘ūdī 1874:VIII, 91).

SILSILAH = SALSLA (s-l-s-l) "chain, series"

1. The second of two codas for the MUṢADDAR/1*, an instrumental overture of the Tunisian NAWBAH/1* (d'Érlanger 1959:192). It has a 3/8 rhythmic cycle and includes repetitions of a musical phrase in many tonalities. This segment brings the MUṢADDAR to a violent

and piercing finale (el Mahdi 1972:14).
2. One of the segments of the MUWASHSHAḤ/1* which operates as a musical and poetic contrast to the DAWR/6* or opening musical segment, in addition to the contrast found in the KHĀNAH/1* or KHĀNĀT. In the case of there being two musical SILSILAH segments, the first is found between the KHĀNAH and the GHIṬĀ'/1*, the second after the latter. The second SILSILAH will be in the principal melodic mode of the MUWASHSHAḤ and will terminate on its tonic, thereby ending the piece (d'Erlanger 1959:169).
3. A series of MUWASHSHAḤĀT within a NAWBAH/1* or suite (Maḥfūẓ 1964:106).

SILSILAH AṢWĀT (s-l-s-l) (ṣ-w-t) "chain of sounds"

Musical scale (Kāẓim 1964:60).

SIMĀʻĪ (s-m-ʻ)

A variety of SHARQIYYĀT (s. SHARQĪ*) songs in which each line or hemistich of poetry has its own musical setting (therefore, not a strophic song, but through-composed). It is sung near the end of the suite of numbers and is based on a single melodic mode (Kāẓim 1964:61).

SIMSIMAH

Var. of SIMSIMIYYAH* (Ḥāfiẓ 1971:46).

SIMSIMIYYAH = SIMSIMAH, SIMSĪYAH, SUMSUMĪYYA

A five-stringed triangular lyre of the inhabitants of Egypt, the Sūdān and the lands near the Red Sea. It is especially a folk instrument of fishermen and the coffee houses in the coastal towns. The body of this instrument was formerly made of wood in a box-like or bowl-like shape. Today it is sometimes constructed of a small, open rectangular can which has been covered by a stretched camel or sheep membrane. Two wooden arms, either equal or one slightly longer than the other, protrude diagonally from the soundbox, their opposite extremities joined by another wooden stick which closes the triangular frame. The strings extend from the soundbox over a wooden bridge in a fan shape to reach the joining arm or yoke at the opposite end of the instrument. There they are either wound around the yoke itself or around tuning pegs inserted in the yoke for that purpose. The strings are tuned to a diatonic series with either a neutral third, a minor third or a major third. The actual pitch varies to suit the voice of the singer, who often accompanies himself on the instrument. The strings of the SIMSIMIYYAH, from lowest to highest in pitch, are named BŪMA* (BAMM*?), DUKA* (DŪKĀH*?), WATAR*, ḤUSAYNĪ/3*, and SHARARAH* (Shiloah 1972:19). The instrument is held by the seated performer with the soundbox clasped between his left elbow and hip. In Egypt it is played with the fingers, while the people of the Sinai utilize a plectrum (Shiloah 1972:19). A similar instrument is known as TAMBŪRAH* in Upper Egypt and the Sūdān;

in ancient Egypt (where such an instrument was known from about 2000 B.C.), it was called KINNĀR* (al Ḥafnī 1971:45-46). From this word, the Arabs took the name KINNĀRAH*.

SIMSĪYAH

Var. of SIMSIMIYYAH* (Ḥāfiẓ 1971:45-46).

SIMṬ (s-m-ṭ) "string of pearls"

Another name for the refrain segment or QAFLAH/4* of a MUWASHSHAḤ/2* poem (d'Erlanger 1959:165).

ṢINĀʿAH (ṣ-n-ʿ) "art, skill, profession"

1. Singing.
2. Playing a musical instrument.

ṢINĀʿAH AL MALĀHĪ (s-n-ʿ) (l-h-w) "art of diversion"

Translated as "instrumental musical art" by Shiloah (1968a:229; 1964/65:127). In the text of the Rasā'il of the Ikhwān al Ṣafā' (1957:183), it seems to mean "creating diversions" rather than indicating a specifically musical meaning.

ṢINĀʿAH AL MŪSĪQĀ (ṣ-n-ʿ) (Gr.) "art of music"

The art of producing or performing music.

ṢINĀʿAH AL MŪSĪQĀ AL ʿAMALIYYAH (ṣ-n-ʿ) (Gr.) (ʿ-m-l) "art of musical practice"

The art of musical practice, as contrasted to the theoretical art (al Fārābī 1967:49, 174).

ṢINĀʿAH AL MŪSĪQĀ AL NAẒARIYYAH (ṣ-n-ʿ) (Gr.) (n-ẓ-r) "art of music theory"

The art of musical theory, as contrasted to the practical art (al Fārābī 1967:50).

SINĀD (s-n-d) "that which always supports"

One of the three kinds of singing in ancient Arabia. It was characterized by a slow rhythm, a refrain, low pitches and glottal stops (Ibn Salamah 1938a:19; 1938b:249). Ibn ʿAbd Rabbihi adds the characteristic of recurring notes (1941:25). See also NAṢB*, HAZAJ/1*

SINDI (Pers.)

A type of cymbal (Shiloah 1965:I, 20).

ṢINF = ṢANF (ṣ-n-f) "variety; category"

1. Any of the varieties of tetrachordal scale segments (s. JINS/1*) in which the separating intervals are of different sizes. Each ṢINF has a different arrangement or placement of intervals (Ṣafī al Dīn in de Vaux 1891:308-309).
2. Any of the species or varieties of scalar combinations (s. JAMʿ/1*). According to Ṣafī al Dīn, there are four of these "varieties" or "categories". For details of their characteristics, as well as the names given to them by that author of the 13th C., see de Vaux 1891:322-323.

ṢINF AL AWWAL (ṣ-n-f) ('-w-l) "first kind, or species"

Instrumental music (al Fārābī 1967:1063; also 881, n. 2).

ṢINF AL THĀNĪ (ṣ-n-f) (th-n-y) "second kind, or species"

Vocal music (al Fārābī 1967:1963; also 881, n. 3).

SINJ (pl. SUNŪJ) (s-n-j)

An unidentified instrument said to have been invented by the Persians in order to be played with the ṢANJ/1* or harp (Ibn Khurdādhbih 1969:16, n. 16; 1951:95; al Masʿūdī 1874:VIII, 90). See MUSTAJ*, MUSNAJ*.

ṢINJ

Equiv. of ṢANJ/1* and ṢANJ/2* (Jargy 1971:125), large and finger cymbals, or a harp, resp.

ṢINJ JĪNĪ or ṢINJ KHĪNĪ

These seem to be misspellings of ṢANJ ṢINĪ* (Farmer 1926a:243, n. 2; 1978:7, n. 2).

ṢINJ ṢĪNĪ (ṣ-n-j) (geog.) "Chinese ṢINJ"

Equiv. of ṢANJ ṢĪNĪ*.

SINṬĪR (pl. SANĀṬIR)

Syn. of SANṬŪR*, generally a dulcimer, but sometimes a psaltery. As dulcimer, it was mentioned in the <u>1001 Nights</u> (Farmer 1945:5). In 18th C. Egypt, Villoteau reported its use (Farmer 1954, "Egyptian Music": II,895). This term is used to name a psaltery-type instrument in a 15th C. anonymous ms. (Farmer 1965b:62).

ṢIRINJ

Equiv. of ṢILINJ* (Ibn Khurdādhbih 1969:17; al Masʿūdī 1874:VIII, 91).

SITĀRAH or SITĀR (s-t-r) "veil, screen"

1. A large curtain separating the performing musicians from the audience in the caliphal court of the ʿAbbāsī period.
2. A chamber orchestra which played from behind a curtain (ʿAbbāsī period). Also a musical ensemble in Moorish Spain.

ṢIYĀGHAH (ṣ-w-gh) "shaping or setting, like the work of the jeweler"

The composing of music.

ṢIYĀGHAH AL LAḤN (ṣ-w-gh) (l-ḥ-n) "setting the tune"

The composing of music.

ṢIYĀḤ = ṢAYḤAH, ṢIYYAḤ, SIAH (ṣ-y-ḥ) "crying"

1. The upper octave equivalent of a tone, or the upper tone of an octave interval (al Khwārizmī 1968:240); Ṣafī al Dīn 1938a:231; al Fārābī 1967:115). Also ṢAYḤAH* or IḌʿĀF*.
2. The highest tone of any interval.

ṢIYĀḤ AL AṢGHAR (ṣ-y-ḥ) (ṣ-gh-r) "smaller cry"

The higher of the two notes which form an interval of a perfect fourth (al Fārābī 1967:505, n. 3).

ṢIYĀḤ AL AWSAṬ (ṣ-y-ḥ) (w-s-ṭ) "median cry"

The higher of the two notes which form an interval of a perfect fifth (al Fārābī 1967:505, n. 3).

ṢIYĀḤ AL AʿẒAM (ṣ-y-ḥ) (ʿ-ẓ-m) "larger cry"

The higher note of the perfect interval, i.e., the octave (al Fārābī 1967:505, 115).

ṢIYĀḤAH (ṣ-y-ḥ) "tour, journey"

A type of LĀZIMAH* or instrumental interlude which fills in the remaining beats of the unfinished ĪQĀʿ* cycle following the soloist's musical phrase (el Helou 1961:180).

ṢIYYAḤ

Var. of ṢIYĀḤ/1* (Farmer 1967:52).

SNAYYIDAH

Var. of SANNĪDAH*.

SNÛǦ

Var. of ṢUNŪJ, pl. of ṢANJ/2*, metal castanets (Chottin 1961: Band IX, col. 1567).

SOBA

Var. of ṢABĀ* (Rouanet 1922:2732).

SONOUDJ

Var. of ṢUNŪJ, pl. of ṢANJ/2* (Rouanet 1922:2683).

ŠRŪQĪ

Var. of SHURŪQĪ* (Jargy 1970:58; Shiloah 1974:58, 61).

SU'ĀL (pl. AS'ILAH) (s-'-l) "question"

Antiphonal antecedent, usually followed by a consequent phrase or JAWĀB/2* (Ḥāfiẓ 1971:126).

ŠU'BAH

Var. of SHU'BAH* (d'Erlanger 1939:101-102, 123, 131-149- 374, 399-414).

ṢUDĀḤ (ṣ-d-ḥ) "song"

Raising the voice in song or chant, therefore, either singing or a song. By extension, it is reported to also mean an instrumental tune (Maḥfūẓ 1964:83).

SUDĀSĪ = SOUDASSI (s-d-s) "sixfold; consisting of six parts"

The largest of the woodwind instruments of the Algerians. This instrument of southern Algeria is approximately 70 cm. in length, and has six finger holes (Delphin and Guin 1886:45).

ŠUDD

Var. of SHADD* (d'Erlanger 1938:376), a category of melodic mode.

SŪFAĪRA

Dim. and var. of ṢAFFĀRAH/2* (Marcuse).

ṢŪFAYRAH (ṣ-f-r) "dim. of whistle"

Dim. and var. of ṢAFFĀRAH/2* (Hickmann 1947:6).

ṢUFFĀRA

Var. of ṢAFFĀRAH/4* (Jargy 1971:121); or ṢAFFĀRAH/3* (Farmer 1954, "Egyptian Music":II, 295).

ṢUFĪRAH

Var. of ṢAFFĀRAH*.

ṢUFŪRAH (ṣ-f-r)

Var. of ṢAFFĀRAH/2* (Hickmann 1947:6).

ṢUGHRĀ (ṣ-gh-r) f. of "small"

Designation for a category of "small" intervals used by Classical Period theorists. It included three subdivisions: the large (major 3rd, ratio 5/4; minor 3rd, 6/5; large neutral 3rd, 7/6), the medium (small neutral 3rd, 8/7; whole tone, 9/8; minor whole tone, 10/9); and the small (all smaller intervals) (Ṣafī al Dīn 1938b:26-27; al Jurjānī 1938:244-246; see Wright 1978:133).

SUISIN

Tear-drop shaped lute with three strings, originally a folk instrument, but now often added to the radio or television orchestra (Mor.) (Schuyler 1978:40).

SULBĀN

Syn. of SALBĀQ* (Ibn Khurdādhbih 1951:95; 1969:19; al Masʿūdī 1874: 91).

SULLAM (pl. SALĀLIM) (s-l-m) "ladder"

Musical scale.

SULLAM AL ʿARABĪ AL QADĪM (s-l-m) (ʿ-r-b) (q-d-m) "ancient Arab ladder"

The scale of the Arabs in former times which contained 17 tones to the octave (Shawqī 1969:143).

SULLAM AL ʿARABI AL ḤALĪ (s-l-m) (ʿ-r-b) (ḥ-w-l) "contemporary Arab ladder"

The scale of 25 equal quarter tones which is used by contemporary theorists (Shawqī 1969:145).

SULLAM AL ASĀSĪ (s-l-m) ('-s-s) "fundamental ladder"

Syn. of RĀST/2*, the fundamental scale of the Arabs (Shawqī 1969: 62).

SULLAM AL MUʿADDAL (s-l-m) (ʿ-d-l) "balanced ladder"

The tempered scale (ʿArnīṭah 1968:24; Shawqī 1969:141).

SULLAM AL MULAWWAN (s-l-m) (l-w-n) "colored ladder"

The chromatic scale of contemporary Europe (Shawqī 1976:953; Maḥfūẓ 1974:186).

SULLAM AL MUʿTADIL (s-l-m) (ʿ-d-l) "just ladder"

Syn. of SULLAM AL MUʿADDAL* (Shawqī 1969:145).

SULLAM AL NAGHMAH (s-l-m) (n-gh-m) "ladder of the tune"

The scale of a melodic mode (d'Erlanger 1949:99).

SULLAM AL QAWĪ (s-l-m) (q-w-y) "strong ladder"

The diatonic scale (Maḥfūẓ 1964:186).

SULLAM AL RAKHW (s-l-m) (r-kh-w) or (r-kh-y) "ladder of looseness"

The enharmonic scale (Maḥfūẓ 1964:186).

SULLAM AL ŪRUBBĪ ṬABĪʿĪ (s-l-m) (geog.) (ṭ-b-ʿ) "natural European ladder"

The contemporary octave division into twelve half-steps which is the basis for European music (Shawqī 1969:145).

ṢULNAJ

A musical instrument of the lute type, said to have been made from the skin of a calf (Ibn Khurdādhbih 1969:17; 1951:95).

SULṬĀN AL ALḤĀN (s-l-ṭ) (l-ḥ-n) "the king (i.e., the best) of tunes"

Descriptive title given to the MUṢADDAR/1* movement of the NAWBAH/1* (Alg.) (Ḥāfiẓ 1971:144).

SULṬĀNĪ (s-l-ṭ) "pertaining to kingship"

A way of reciting the call to prayer which is popular in Egypt (el Helou 1961:201). It is less recitative-like than the LAYTHĪ* rendering. See ADHĀN*.

SULYĀNĪ

Syn. of SULYĀQ* or SALBĀQ* (Ibn Khurdādhbih 1969:19, see n. 2).

SULYĀQ = SHULYĀQ

An open-stringed Byzantine instrument, said to have had 24 strings and 1000 possible tones. It is mentioned by Classical Period theorists and generally equated with the SALBĀQ* (Ibn Sīnā 1935: 233; Ibn Khurdādhbih 1969:17, n. 2; see d'Erlanger 1935:256, n. 63).

SUMSUMIYYA

Var. of SIMSIMIYYAH* (Shiloah 1972:18).

SUNBULAH (Pers.) "ear of corn"

1. A melodic mode mentioned in the 16th C. (al Lādhiqī 1939:441).

2. Name for one of the tones of the contemporary Arab scale, D#$_2$ or Eb$_2$ 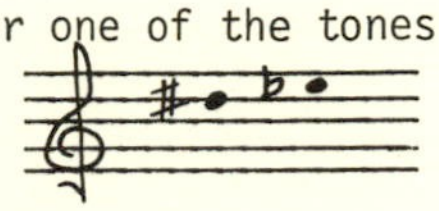 . Also called ZAWĀL*.

ṢUNDŪQ (pl. ṢANĀDĪQ) (ṣ-n-d-q) "box"

The soundbox of any chordophone (al Ḥafnī 1971:67).

ṢUNDŪQ AL MUṢAWWIT (ṣ-n-d-q) (ṣ-w-t) "sounding box"

Syn. of ṢUNDŪQ* (al Ḥafnī 1971:47, 74).

ṢUNNŪJ

Var. of ṢUNŪJ/1* (Farmer 1967:47).

SUNṬŪR or ṢUNTŪR

Vars. of SANṬŪR*(Farmer 1954, "Sanṭīr":VII, 404-405).

ṢUNŪǦ

Var. of ṢUNŪJ*(Perkuhn 1976:175).

ṢUNŪJ (pl. of ṢANJ/1*) = ṢUNNŪJ, SONOUDJ (s-n-j)

1. Small metal castanets held in the hands of a dancer or mounted on a frame drum. They have been used from pre-Islamic times until today.
2. Cymbals used in performances of religious music (Touma 1977b: 110).

ṢUNŪJ AL AṢĀBIʿ or ṢUNŪJ AL YAD (ṣ-n-j) (ṣ-b-ʿ) or (ṣ-n-j) (y-d) "finger cymbals" or "hand cymbals"

Finger cymbals (Maḥfūẓ 1964:40).

SUQQĀRAH

Syn. of ZUKRAH or ZŪKRAH/2* (Marcuse), a kind of bagpipe of the Maghrib.

ṢŪR (ṣ-w-r) "horn; bugle"

1. A horn named ten times in the Qur'ān as one to be used on Judgment Day (Qur'ān 6:73; 23:101; 39:68; 69:13; 78:18, etc.). It was probably the long, straight trumpet variety which later came to be known as the NAFĪR* (11th C.).
2. Bass male vocalist (Maḥfūẓ 1964:186).

SŪR (s-w-r) "wall"

The sidewalls of the soundbox of the QĀNŪN* (Lane 1973:358).

SUR'AH (s-r-') "haste; velocity"

1. Acceleration (al Ḥafnī 1946:287).
2. Tempo (al Ḥafnī 1946:287).

SURNĀ or SŪRNĀ

Var. of SURNĀY/3* (Farmer 1929a:141; al Ḥafnī 1971:179).

SŪRNĀ JURĀ

Syn. of ZAMR AL ṢUGHAYYAR* (Farmer EI(Eng), "Mizmār":540), a small Egyptian oboe.

SURNĀĪ

Var. of SURNĀY/1* (Farmer 1929a:141; 1978:57-58).

SURNĀY (pl. SURNĀYĀT) = SURNĀ, SŪRNĀ, SURNĀĪ, ṢŪRNĀY, SURYĀNĪ, SURYĀNĀY, ZŪRNĀ, SURYĀ NAI (Pers.)

1. A double reed aerophone described by al Fārābī as having eight front finger holes and two side holes near the lower end of the instrument (al Fārābī 1967:788). An instrument of this name and type (though perhaps larger) was used in the 9th C. by the 'Abbāsīs as a martial instrument. It often had a conical bore. In the 11th C. it was found used by the Fāṭimīs, and in the 14th C. by the Mughals. This instrument is still used under this name from the Gulf region to Morocco. It also exists under such names as ZUQRĀ*, ZUKRAH/1* and ZŪRNĀ* (al Ḥafnī 1971:179).
2. An aerophone of the NĀY/1* type (al Fārābī 1967:280), i.e., an end-blown flute similar to the shepherd's flute or YARĀ'* (al Khwārizmī 1968:237; Ibn Sīnā 1935:234).
3. The pipe of an organ, according to a 12th C. copy of an 8th or 9th C. work (Farmer 1931:91-92).

SURŪḤ (s-r-ḥ) "going away, departure"

Syn. of KHURŪJ/2* (Tun.) (Jones 1977:71-72).

SURYĀNĪ

Equiv. of SURNĀY* (al Fārābī 1930:272; al Mas'ūdī 1874:VIII, 90), which was used to accompany the drum in the 9th-10th C. (Ibn Khurdādhbih 1969:16).

SURYĀNĀY or SURYĀNAI

Var. of SURNĀY* (Farmer 1928:513-514; 1978:57-58). See also SURYĀ NAI*.

SURYĀ NAI (SURYĀ NĀY) "Syrian reed" (?)

Var. of SURNĀY*, first mentioned in the 9th C. (Marcuse).

SŪSY

An unidentified form of QAṢĪDAH/1* in the Maghrib (Chottin and Hickmann 1949-1951: Band I, col. 1564).

SŪZDĀK (Pers.)

Syn. of KAWASHT/1*.

SWELHI

An unidentified form of traditional ʿIrāqī music (Bashir 1978:76).

SZAHDJE

Men's songs of praise in the Arabian Peninsula, syn. of ṢAHJAH*, according to the transliteration by Farmer (Burckhardt 1967:85). See Farmer 1954, "Iraqian and Mesopotamian Music":IV,532).

T

"Ṭ" (abbrev. for ṭā', one of the letters of the Ar. alphabet)

An abbreviation for a ṬANĪNĪ* or whole tone interval (al Jurjānī 1938:238; Anonymous Treatise 1939:37; al Lādhiqī 1939:302-303).

TĀ

A percussion stroke, weaker and drier than the TAK*. This stroke is always found followed by the HAK* stroke. This combination of strokes of equal length occurs only in one of the last measures of a long rhythmic cycle in order to announce the end (d'Erlanger 1959:10-11).

ṬĀ' (pl. ṬĀ'ĀT)

Syn. of TIK* or TAK* (Massignon 1913:VIII, 765).

TA'ĀLUF ('-l-f) "self-harmonization with others"

Harmony (al Kindī 1966:151). Cowl (Ibid.) renders it TA'ALLUF.

TAAR

Var. of ṬĀR/1* (Farmer 1976a:201-202, 219).

ṬAB' (pl. ṬUBŪ') = ṬABA' (ṭ-b-') "printing; impression; character"

1. Any of the 24 melodic modes of Maghribī practice and theory. There are five principal modes or UṢŪL (s. AṢL/1*) and nineteen derivative or FURŪ' (s. FAR'/2*) modes. See chart in Chottin 1939:121.
2. A note or tone (Maghrib) (Farmer 1933b:20), syn. of NAGHM or NAGHAM* as used in the Mashriq.
3. Traditional or "classical" music in the Maghrib (Farmer 1933b:19).
4. Any of the four elements (fire, water, air, earth) which were associated with melodic and rhythmic modes during the Classical Period (Farmer 1933b:19).

5. Whole tone interval (Farmer 1933b:19). See also NIṢF ṬAB'*.

TABA

Var. of TAB'* (Touma 1977b:76).

ṬABA'

Var. of ṬAB'* (Lachmann 1929:56; Chottin and Hickmann 1949-1951: Band I, col. 589, 598; Chottin 1939:69).

ṬABALE

Var. of ṬABLAH* (Ribera 1970:94, n. 33).

ṬABAQAH (pl. ṬABAQĀT) (ṭ-b-q) "layer, stage, class"

1. General pitch level of a tone, interval, tetrachordal scalar segment (JINS/1*) or octave (al Fārābī 1930 132; 1967:112, 363-364; al Khwārizmī 1968:241; al Ḥafnī 1936:41; d'Erlanger 1939: 505, n. 8).
2. Each octave of the two-octave scale (al Fārābī 1967:365; Anonymous Treatise 1939:89; al Ḥafnī 1946:286).
3. Each tetrachord or pentachord of the double octave scale (Anonymous Treatise 1939:121). The lowest JINS/1* of the combination is known as ṬABAQAH AL ŪLĀ*, the next higher, but still within the lower octave, is the ṬABAQAH AL THĀNIYAH* (Ṣafī al Dīn 1938b:95-107; al Lādhiqī 1939:313-316; see also d'Erlanger 1939:505-506, n. 18; 509, n. 3).
4. Any of the 17 possible transposition levels for a tetrachordal or modal scale (Ṣafī al Dīn 1938b:138-149; 1938a: 381, 408-430; al Lādhiqī 1939:391ff; d'Erlanger 1938:603). These were presented in the order of transposition through a circle of ascending fourths (Ṣafī al Dīn 1938a:415-429). Also TAMDĪD/2*, according to Ṣafī al Dīn and al Jurjānī (d'Erlanger 1938:603).
5. A scale or tonality (according to Ṣafī al Dīn in 13th C. ms., see Farmer 1965b:49; 1937a:245; Collangettes 1906:170).
6. The tetrachordal span covered by frets or finger positions on each string of the lute or similar instrument (Ibn al Munajjim in Shawqī 1976:222; Shiloah 1968a:242, and n. 140).
7. One strand of silk which was combined with others to form the strings of a chordophone during the Classical Period (al Kindī 1965:15). Al Kindī described the four strings of the lute as made from 1, 2, 3 or 4 such ṬABAQĀT (Farmer 1926b:92; 1928:515). Also ṬĀQAH*.
8. Frame drum of the Maghrib (Marcuse).

ṬABAQAH MUTASĀWIYAH (ṭ-b-q) (s-w-y) "equal layer, stage"

Said of two tones, two intervals, or two tetrachords which are found in the same general pitch level (al Fārābī 1967:365; 1930: 132). Contrasted with TAMDĪD MUTASĀWĪ*.

ṬABAQAH ṢAWTIYYAH (ṭ-b-q) (ṣ-w-t) "sound level"

Although only the word "octave" is given for translating this term in Wahba (1968:69), this expression is generally a syn. of ṬABAQAH/2*, i.e., either the octave or the two-octave gamut.

ṬABAQAH AL THĀNIYAH (ṭ-b-q) (th-n-y) "second level"

The second tetrachord or pentachord (counting from the lowest to highest) of the double octave scale (Ṣafī al Dīn 1938b:95-107; 1938a:298-299, 315-316). See also ṬABAQAH/3*.

ṬABAQAH AL ŪLĀ (ṭ-b-q) ('-w-l) "first level"

The first tetrachord or pentachord (counting from the lowest to highest) of the double octave scale (Ṣafī al Dīn 1938b:95-107). See also ṬABAQAH/3*.

ṬABBĀL (ṭ-b-l) "drummer"

1. Drummer, player of the ṬABL* (Snoussi 1961:143).
2. A kettledrum (Marcuse).
3. In North Africa, a small bass drum played with two sticks, one heavy, one thin.

TABDABA (onom.)

This name has been used in Tripoli (Lībyā) for a DARABUKKAH*-type drum (single headed goblet). Also known in Algeria as GULLĀL* (Perkuhn 1976:178; Farmer EI(Fr), "Ṭabl":231).

TABDĪLAH (pl. TABDĪLĀT) (b-d-l) "an alteration or replacement"

Any of the many variant parts of the religious chant or overture known as ISTIFTĀḤ/2* which is performed by the Muslim brotherhoods of the Maghrib (Tun.) (d'Erlanger 1937:11).

ṬĀBIʿ (pl. ṬAWĀBIʿ) (ṭ-b-ʿ) "follower"

1. Syn. of KHĀNAH* (Maḥfūẓ 1964:86).
2. A part of the Andalusian NAWBAH/1* (Alg.) comprising the musical segments which are performed between the songs known as INṢIRĀFĀT (s. INṢIRĀF/1*) (Maḥfūẓ 1964:86).

ṬABĪʿAH (pl. ṬABĀ'Iʿ) (ṭ-b-ʿ) "nature"

Term used in the Maghrib for the natures (black bile, blood, phlegm and yellow bile) which were associated with one or more of the principal melodic modes (s. AṢL/1*) (Farmer 1933b:11, 39). Al Kindī, al Masʿūdī and the Ikhwān al Ṣafā' used instead the term KHULQ*.

TABʿĪD (b-ʿ-d) "removal, separation"

The lengthening of the time between the percussion of one ZAMĀN

AL MABDA'* and the beginning of the next, i.e., increasing the length of time between a succession of percussions which are otherwise separated from each other by equal durations (al Fārābī 1967:992).

ṬABĪʿĪ (ṭ-b-ʿ) "natural"

Natural, i.e., without accidentals (al Dāqūqī 1965:39).

ṬABĪLAH = T'EBILA, TBILAH (ṭ-b-l) "a drum"

1. A small frame drum with snares and jingles, which is used to accompany vocalists and dancers (Alg.). It is played either with fingers, hand or a short stick (Delphin and Guin 1886:38-39).
2. A small drum said to be used only by women (Mor.) (Chottin 1939:141-142; Farmer 1978:I, 45).

ṬABĪR = TABĪRA (t-b-r)

An hourglass drum mentioned in writings of the 11th C. (Farmer 1929a:18). According to Farmer this drum was used even in pre-Islamic times (Farmer 1957:425).

TAʿBĪR (ʿ-b-r) "interpreting"

Syn. of TAGHBĪR* (Farmer 1952:62; Shiloah 1968b:418). Farmer defines this term loosely as "religious music" (1952:62).

TABĪRA

Var. of ṬABĪR* (Farmer 1957:425).

ṬABL (pl. ṬUBŪL, AṬBĀL) = TABL, THABL, TABELLA, TEBEUL (ṭ-b-l) "drum"

1. Generic term for many kinds of drums used by the Arabs throughout their history. In Egypt, it is a collective term for all instruments of percussion, but especially for drums (Hickmann 1947:19).
2. A cylindrical double headed drum made in various sizes and used in many regions (Touma 1977b:109; ʿArnīṭah 1968:46-47; el Mahdi 1972:52).
3. Kettledrum in the Maghrib. Because it is one of a pair played with two drumsticks, the more usual designation is the plural form, AṬBĀL (see ATABAL*) (Salvador-Daniel 1976:118).

ṬABL BALADĪ (ṭ-b-l) (b-l-d) "village drum"

1. A cylindrical, double headed drum of the folk music tradition in Egypt (Hickmann 1947:20). This shallow drum is made of wood and has its two skins stretched by hoops at either end. The drum hangs from the shoulders of the drummer so that the heads face sideways. Flexible beaters, two sticks, or a stick and a bundle of thongs, are used to produce the sound (Sachs 1940:248).
2. Goblet shaped, single headed drum (Ḥāfiẓ 1971:5).
3. Musical ensemble which performs for wedding and circumcision processions in the Middle East. It usually comprises three oboes

(one small and two large), a pair of kettledrums (NAQRAZĀN*) and the cylindrical double headed drum whose name has been given to the ensemble as a whole. In some numbers the larger oboes are used to play a drone; in others they double the part of the SIBS* (small oboe) in a lower octave (Sachs 1940:248).

ṬABL AL BĀZ = ṬABLĪ-BĀZ (ṭ-b-l) (b-w-z) "falcon drum"

A very small kettledrum of the Mashriq made of metal and used for hawking. It is said to have first been played by the Prophet Ismaʿīl. It was designated simply as BĀZ or BĀZAH* in 19th C. Egypt (Lane 1973:365, 476) and was described as an instrument only 6-7 inches in diameter. It was held in the left hand by a small projection at its center and beaten with a leather strap held in the right hand. A similar drum is used during the month of fasting (Ramaḍān) to awaken the people for the pre-dawn meal. It is then known as ṬABL AL MUSAḤḤIR*.

ṬABL DŪRŪʿĪ (ṭ-b-l) (d-r-ʿ) "shields drum"

Obsolete double headed drum of the Mashriq (Marcuse), which was played while mounted on a stand or tripod (Farmer 197i:II, 13).

ṬABL ǴAWĪǴ

Var. of ṬABL JĀWĪSH* (Sachs 1940:251).

ṬABL ǴAWĪQ

Var. of ṬABL JĀWĪSH* (Marcuse).

ṬABL JĀWĪSH = ṬABL ǴAWĪǴ, ṬABL ǴAWĪQ (ṭ-b-l) (colloq.) "staff sergeant's drum"

A shallow kettledrum of the Mashriq (Egypt), with laced head. This drum is usually carried on horseback, and struck with a single drumstick.

ṬABL KABĪR (ṭ-b-l) (k-b-r) "large drum"

1. A large kettledrum of the Mashriq, similar to the KŪRGAH*. It was mentioned by the 14th C. traveler, Ibn Baṭṭūṭah (Farmer EI(Fr), "Ṭabl":232).
2. Large double headed, cylindrical drum of contemporary Egypt, also ṬABL/2*.

ṬABL KHĀNAH (ṭ-b-l) (kh-w-n) "drum house"

1. A military band of ʿAbbāsī times (Farmer 1967:196, 206-208). See also Farmer EI(Fr), "Ṭabl Khāna":232-237. During wars or raids, the members of this band withdrew from the actual conflict in order to play unceasingly during the fighting. As long as the music continued, the army fought on, often returning to the fight after a moment of defeat because the band was still playing. There were special musical signals for battle and for retreat

which were sounded by the drum (ṬABL*), cymbals (KĀSĀT*) or kettledrums (KŪSĀT*). Sometimes this military band comprised simply drum or cymbals. At other times, reedpipes, horns or a trumpet were added (Farmer 1945:7-8). The value created by the deafening noise of these bands was also well recognized as a factor in the battle. One reads of idiophones attached to the mules and camels to add further to the confusion (Ibid.). In the 1001 Nights the ṬABL KHĀNAH ensemble was known as NAWBAH KHĀNAH* or simply NAWBAH/2*. It took that name because of its chief function in times of peace--to perform at particular hours (NUWĀB) of the day as well as at official ceremonies. This ensemble was also called NAQQĀRAH KHĀNAH* (Farmer EI(Fr), "Ṭabl Khāna":232).
2. The military music of the ṬABL KHĀNAH/1*.

ṬABL AL MARKAB (ṭ-b-l) (r-k-b) "riding drum"

A kettledrum mentioned by the Ikhwān al Ṣafā' (10th C.). It was a large instrument similar to the NAQQĀRAH* (Sachs 1940:250).

ṬABL AL MIDJRĪ

Var. of ṬABL AL MIJRĪ* (Farmer EI(Fr), "Ṭabl":231).

ṬABL MIGRĪ

Var. of ṬABL AL MIJRĪ* (Sachs 1940:251).

ṬABL MIJRĪ (ṭ-b-l) (j-r-y) probably a colloq. of ṬABL MUJRĪ, "drum that makes you run"

A contemporary shallow kettledrum of metal with a laced head and thong beaters (Farmer EI(Fr), "Ṭabl":232).

ṬABL AL MUKHANNATH (ṭ-b-l) (kh-n-th) "drum of the effeminate"

Syn. of KŪBAH*, a drum shaped like an hourglass (Ikhwān al Ṣafā' 1957:I, 193).

ṬABL AL MUSAḤḤIR (ṭ-b-l) (s-ḥ-r) "drum of the person who wakes people for the pre-dawn meal during the month of Ramaḍān"

A small kettledrum beaten with a leather strap which is carried and played by the MUSAḤḤIR or Ramaḍān "crier" who announces, each night, the approaching time of the pre-dawn meal (Lane 1973:476). Also called BĀZ* or ṬABL AL BĀZ*.

ṬABL ŠĀMĪ

Var. of ṬABL SHĀMĪ* (Sachs 1940:251).

ṬABL ŠAWĪŠ

Var. of ṬABL SHĀWĪSH* (Sachs 1940:251).

ṬABL SHĀMĪ (ṭ-b-l) (geog.) "Syrian drum"

A very ancient as well as a contemporary kettledrum of very shallow depth. It is carried by the performer, suspended from his neck by cords or strings tied to two rings on the edge of the instrument. It is about 16 inches in diameter and 4 inches at its deepest point. It is beaten with a pair of slender sticks (Lane 1973:365; Sachs 1940:251).

ṬABL SHĀWĪSH = ṬABL ŠĀWĪŠ (ṭ-b-l) (sh-w-sh) "staff sergeant's drum"

Syn. of ṬABL JAWĪSH* (Sachs 1940:251).

ṬABL AL SŪDĀN (ṭ-b-l) (geog.) "drum of the Sūdān"

A waisted drum similar to the KŪBAH*.

ṬABL ṬAWĪL (ṭ-b-l) (ṭ-w-l) "long drum"

A long drum used in late ʿAbbāsī period (Farmer 1967:210).

ṬABL TURKĪ (ṭ-b-l) (geog.) "Turkish drum"

A large, shallow, cylindrical drum of the Mashriq described by Villoteau (d. 1839). It had two membranes and was carried on donkey back (Marcuse; Farmer EI(Fr), "Ṭabl":231).

ṬABLĀ (ṭ-b-l)

A series of bells attached to a board, chain or cord and tied to the necks of animals. During Mamlūk times it was suspended from the hair of itinerant musicians as well (Farmer EI(Fr), "Ṣandj":210).

ṬABLAH (pl. ṬUBŪL, AṬBĀL) (ṭ-b-l) "a drum"

1. Generic for drum. See ṬABL/1*.
2. The double headed cylindrical drum of contemporary practice. See ṬABL/2*.
3. A single headed drum made of clay, metal or wood, of the DARABUKKAH* type (al Ḥafnī 1946:291; el Helou 1961:163; Hickmann 1958:44; Farmer 1978:I, 86).
4. Small kettledrum of Morocco used for accompanying folk music (GRĪḤAH*). It is usually played in pairs, tuned a fifth apart (Chottin 1939:165).

ṬABLĪ-BĀZ

Var. of ṬABL AL BĀZ* (Farmer 1945:35).

TABRĪD = TEBRID (b-r-d) "cooling, refrigeration"

A homogeneous, continuous orchestral style utilized for accompaniment of vocalists in the performance of Moroccan art music. It involves much use of long sustained-note (TAṬWĪLAH*) playing by the bowed instruments and a way of striking the ṬĀR* or other percussion instrument which allows certain beats to be filled by silence rather than the percussions normally accorded them (Chottin 1939:113, 147). Also called KHĀWĪ*.

TACHERAFT (perhaps colloq. of TASHARRAFTU, "I am honored")

Syn. of TAMAWAÏT*, a solo vocal improvisation of the Berbers (Mor.) (Chottin 1939:22).

TAḌĀDD (ḍ-d-d) "opposition"

Contrary motion (Maḥfūẓ 1964:185).

TADHKĪRAH (pl. TADHKĪRĀT)(dh-k-r) "a reminding"

See T'ÂSKÎRÂT*.

TADHYĪL (dh-y-l) "addition of an appendix (tail)"

1. Coda (Al Ḥalqah 1964:59; Ḥāfiẓ 1971:199).
2. A glissando-like embellishment (Ibn Sīnā in one ms. of Al Najāt, see 1930:98, n. 7). Syn. of TAWṢĪL/1*.

TAʿDĪD (ʿ-d-d) "enumeration; a series"

Multiple repetitions of tones, motifs or musical segments.

TAḌʿĪF (pl. TAḌʿĪFĀT) (ḍ-ʿ-f) "doubling"

1. An embellishment involving the plucking of two strings in such a way as to produce the simultaneous combination of a main note and its octave equivalent (Ibn Sīnā 1930:99; 1935:231).
2. Supplementary percussions added to an ĪQĀʿ* or rhythmic cycle (Ibn Sīnā 1930:99; 1935:176, 181; Anonymous Treatise 1939:165). If the addition occurs before the cycle, it is called IʿTIMĀD/2* or TAṢDĪR*. If the addition occurs in the space after the final beat of the cycle, i.e., within the FĀṢILAH/4*, it is called MAJĀZ* (Ibn Sīnā 1930:99; al Rajab 1967:23).
3. A tonal embellishment involving the fast repetition of a tone or tones to keep the sound moving (see Anonymous Treatise 1939:159, for a description in Fr.). The durations of the tones are too short to be accurately distinguishable (Ṣafī al Dīn in de Vaux 1891:344-345). Other names for this embellishment are MARGHŪLAH/1*, TAKARRUR/3*, TAKRĪR/1*, and TARʿĪD/1*.
4. Doubling the length of a percussion (al Fārābī 1967:1035).

TADJOUID

Var. of TAJWĪD* (Touma 1977b:127).

TADWĪN (d-w-n) "registering, recording"

Musical notation (al Ḥafnī 1946:126; Shawqī 1969:68).

TADWĪR (d-w-r) "act of turning something"

Medium speed recitation of the Qur'ān. It was given as one of three ways of recitation in the 15th C. work by Jalāl al Dīn al Suyūṭī (1941:I, 172). See also TAḤQĪQ*, ḤADR/2*.

ṬĀFIR (ṭ-f-r) "leaping across"

Melodic movement with leaps rather than through stepwise progression (Ibn Sīnā 1930:95-96), a variety of INTIQĀL/1*.

ṬĀFIR AL INTIQĀL (ṭ-f-r) (n-q-l) "leaping movement"

Syn. of ṬĀFIR* (Ibn Sīnā 1930:95).

TAFKHĪM (f-kh-m) "exaggeration; accentuation"

Intensifying the tones and increasing their stateliness by moving them to a higher or lower pitch position. This method of embellishment could use the notes of the new position simultaneously with the original tones or successively (al Fārābī 1967:1059-1061; 1935:50). Al Fārābī writes that these substitutions are best included in the middle part of the piece, rather than in the opening and closing sections (Ibid.:1059).

TAFṢĪL (pl. TAFṢĪLĀT) (f-ṣ-l) "act of dividing in parts; clarification"

1. Syn. of TAFṢĪL AL MUWAṢṢAL/1* (al Fārābī 1967:1013).
2. Dividing larger tonal intervals into smaller ones (al Fārābī 1967:517).

TAFṢĪL AL MUWAṢṢAL (f-ṣ-l) (w-ṣ-l) "dividing the joined"

One of the kinds of alteration (TAGHYĪR/2*) of a rhythmic cycle used to create a new rhythmic mode (ĪQĀʿ*), without additions from outside (GHAYR ZIYĀDAH NAQRĀT*). It involved adding extra space between percussions (al Fārābī 1967:1013; 1935:36-37). See also TAWṢĪL AL MUFAṢṢAL*, TARKĪB/2*, TAKRĪR/2*.

TAGBIR

Var. of TAGHBĪR* (Touma 1977b:129).

TAGHANNĀ (gh-n-y) "to make oneself sing, to enjoy"

1. To sing.
2. To chant.
3. To sing the praises of, to eulogize in song.

TAGHARRADA (gh-r-d) "to twitter as a bird"

To sing.

TAGHAZZUL (gh-z-l) "flirtation"

1. A lyrical, free rhythmed song of the 15th C. (Anonymous Treatise 1939:233).
2. A category of popular music which is based on a poetry of the same name and using metaphorical language to hide its amorous subject matter (Alg.). It is usually included under KALĀM AL HAZL* (Delphin and Guin 1886:28-29).

TAGHBĪR = TAGBIR (gh-b-r) "covering with dust"

Chanting like people will do in the afterlife (AL GHĀBIRAH), i.e., like the sounds of angels (al ʿAzzāwī 1951:7, n. 1). According to Ibn Taymiyyah (1966:II, 304), this is something which originated in Baghdād among the irreligious people known as Zindīqs, a practice which "turns [people] from the Qur'ān" (Ibid.; Haq 1944: 116). Ibn Khaldūn uses the term to designate pre-Islamic religious chanting (1967:II, 403); yet Farmer and others have equated this term with Qur'ānic cantillation (Farmer 1967:33; 1957:439; Touma 1977b:127). There is also a question whether the term should instead be TAʿBĪR* ("expression") since the two terms differ from each other in Arabic orthography only by the inclusion or omission of a single diacritical point.

TAGHĪR (colloq. of TAGHYĪR)

See TAGHYĪR/1* for the equivalent of this colloquialism used by Nettl and Riddle (1973:18, with an added typesetting error making it TAQHĪR).

TAGHRĪD (gh-r-d) "twittering"

1. Singing.
2. Improving vocal sounds.
3. The emotion in chanting.
4. High pitched musical sounds.

TAGHṬIYAH = TRHOTIYA, TRHOTIA (gh-ṭ-w) "cover"

1. A rapid, measured musical segment used to close the MAWWĀL/1*. It usually consists of a fragment heard earlier (Chottin 1939:136).
2. A modulation of pitch or mode near the end of a musical segment of the NAWBAH/1* (Chottin 1939:131).

TAGHYĪR (pl. TAGHYĪRĀT) (gh-y-r) "change"

1. Modulation (Al Ḥalqah 1964:20). See TAGHĪR*.
2. Alteration of the basic cycle to form a new rhythmic mode (ĪQĀʿ/1*) (al Fārābī 1967:1012ff). It was of the following kinds:
   1) By addition of supplementary percussions (i.e., with ZIYĀDAH NAQRĀT*)
   2) Without additional percussions (i.e., GHAYR ZIYĀDAH NAQRĀT*)
      a) TAWṢĪL AL MUFAṢṢAL*: Shortening the FĀṢILAH/4* or eliminating it completely to combine two or more

cycles of a rhythmic mode into one larger one (Ibid.:1012)

b) TAFṢĪL AL MUWAṢṢAL: Division of a conjunct or disjunct cycle by addition of rests (Ibid.:1014).

c) TAKRĪR/2*: Repetition of percussions and the time span between them (Ibid.:1014-1015)

d) TARKĪB/2*: Repeating an opening percussion at the end of a cycle, or an ending percussion at the beginning of the cycle (Ibid.:1016-1017).

3. Variation (al Fārābī 1967:1029).

TAḤĀSĪN (ḥ-s-n) "adornments"

Pl. of TAḤSĪN*. See also TAḤSĪN AL LAḤN*.

TAHLĪL (pl. TAHĀLĪL) (h-l-l) "acclamation; repeating the formula "LĀ ILĀHA ILLĀ ALLAH"

A musical utterance or chant going back to the moon worshippers of pre-Islamic times. This ancient practice was superceded in Islam by the pilgrimage chants associated with the ceremonies around the Kaʿbah. They are also known as TALBIYAH*.

TAHLĪLAH (pl. TAHLĪLĀT) (h-l-l) "an acclamation"

A solo chant accompanied by the frame drum as performed by religious brotherhoods of the Maghrib (d'Erlanger 1937:11).

TAḤMEELA

Var. of TAḤMĪLAH* (El-Kholy 1978:13).

TAḤMĪLAH (pl. TAḤĀMĪL) = TAḤMEELA (ḥ-m-l) "a loading. a shipment"

A popular instrumental number of Egypt which is performed by the instruments of the classical ensemble or TAKHT*. This genre comprises unison orchestral refrains alternating with contrasting free rhythmed improvisations by each of the instruments in turn, the solos being accompanied by the percussion instruments or by a simple ostinato on one of the melodic instruments. The improvised phrases should correspond to the time span of the principal refrain rhythm by being either of the same length, or by being half or twice as long. When played by only two instruments, there is a great deal of competition between the two performers as they respond to each other. Modulations occur in the solo passages, but the soloist consistently leads the group back to the dominant mode in time for the return of the refrain. The piece always begins and ends with the orchestral refrain. (El-Kholy 1978:13-14; d'Erlanger 1959:184).

TAḤQĪQ (ḥ-q-q) "realization; fulfillment; achievement"

Slow cantillation of the Qur'ān, so as to give each letter its due. This style, used for learning drills, was one of the three styles of recitation which were mentioned by the 15th C. writer,

Jalāl al Dīn al Suyūṭī (al Suyūṭī 1941:I, 172). See also TADWĪR*, ḤADR/2*.

TAḤRĪK AL AWTĀR (ḥ-r-q) (w-t-r) "moving the strings"

Playing or plucking the strings of a musical instrument.

TAḤRĪR (ḥ-r-r) "liberation"

The opening improvisatory segment of the MAQĀM AL ʿIRĀQĪ* performance. It acts as a vocal prelude and sets to music one or more lines of poetic text as well as stock phrases from the Arabic, Persian and Turkish languages. These fill out the text and delay each line's musical denouement. The TAḤRĪR includes short or long, vocal or instrumental, improvisatory passages exploring different pitch regions of the chosen melodic mode (MAQĀM/1*). It ends with a TASLĪM* (or TASLŪM*), a short passage descending to the tonic of the dominant melodic mode (Ḥāfiẓ 1971:164, 166). According to Maḥfūẓ, this term can be extended to mean the opening part of any song (Maḥfūẓ 1964:68). The TAḤRĪR section can be preceded by an additional instrumental introduction with well defined rhythm (Touma 1977b:72).

TAḤSĪN (pl. TAḤĀSĪN) (ḥ-s-n) "improvement; beautification"

1. Embellishment, syn. of TAḤSĪN AL ḌARB*, TAḤSĪN AL LAḤN*.
2. Applause, an enlargement of the meaning of the word based on the applause resulting from skillful use of embellishments (Farmer 1954, "Syrian Music":VIII, 255).

TAḤSĪN AL ḌARB (ḥ-s-n) (ḍ-r-b) "improvement of the beating"

Embellishing a tune through use (simultaneously or successively) of tones of different volume and pitch level (Ibn al Munajjim 1976:346).

TAḤSĪN AL LAḤN (ḥ-s-n) (l-ḥ-n) "improvement of the melody"

Improvement or embellishment of the melody (Ibn Sīnā 1930:98-99). There were many different kinds of TAḤSĪN AL LAḤN described by Ibn Sīnā, as is shown in the following table.

TAḤSĪN AL LAḤN ("Improvement of the Melody")
According to Ibn Sīnā

I. TONAL
- IBDĀL* (substitution of one note for another)
- TARʿĪD/1* (repetition of a note or mordent, trill, vibrato treatment to keep the sound)
- TAMZĪJ/5*
  - TASHQĪQ* (placing one finger across two strings at same distance from the nut, and playing them together, either with or without trill)
  - (produced by moving to the finger position of a note above, before the

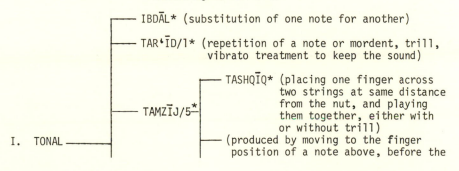

- TAMZĪJ (cont.)
  - vibration of the first string tone is finished)
  - (as above, but moving to the finger position of a lower note)
- TAWṢĪL/1* (glissando-like movement between tones)
- TARKĪB/1* (combination of main tone with another one, preferably one producing a large interval)
- TAḌʿĪF/1* (variety of TARKĪB which uses the octave equivalent as combination tone)

II. DURATIONAL

- BI ZIYĀDAH* ("with addition")
  - According to MAQĀDĪR ("sizes") (changing the size of the percussions or feet of the rhythmic cycle through
    1) TARTĪL/5* (lengthening the percussions); or
    2) TAWĀṢUL* (joining percussions)
  - According to AʿDĀD* ("numbers") (changing the number of feet in the cycle through:
    1) TAḌʿĪF/2* (supplementary percussions added between feet of the cycle)
    2) TAṢDĪR* or ʿIMĀD* (supplementary percussions at beginning of cycle)
    3) MAJĀZ* (supplementary percussions at end of cycle)
- BI NUQṢĀN* ("with diminution")
  - According to MAQĀDĪR ("sizes")
    1) ḤATHĪTH* (acceleration of the tempo)
    2) TAQAṢṢUR* (reduction of space between two cycles)
  - According to AʿDĀD* ("numbers") ṬAYY* (reduction of percussions but retaining the same number of basic units in the cycle)

TAḤWĪR (ḥ-w-r) "alteration"

Variation of musical elements or characteristics.

TAḤZĪN (ḥ-z-n) "causing sadness"

Prohibited Qurʾānic cantillation practice which involves exaggerated expression of sadness (Maḥmūd n.d.:35).

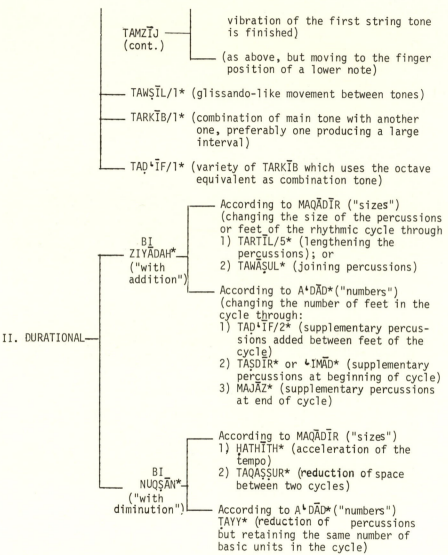

TAḤZĪZ (ḥ-z-z) "indentation, notch"

A notch in the bridge of a chordophone which maintains the distance between the various strings (Ibn Abī al Ṣalt 1952:58).

ṬAI

Var. of ṬAYY* (al Hafni 1930:53).

ṬĀ'IR (ṭ-y-r) "flying; flyer"

Name used by contemporary musicians to designate a fast rhythmic mode (ĪQĀʿ*).

TĀJIRA

Mistaken var. of TAʿRĪJAH* (Marcuse). See Farmer 1954, "Berber Music":I, 633, where the term is TĀRIJA.

TAJNĪS (j-n-s) "correspondence; homogenization"

Syn. of JINS/1*. Al Fārābī used this term for the four AJNĀS (s. JINS) or intervallic divisions of the tetrachord which determine the scalar composition of melodic modes. He calls them TAJNĪS AL AWWAL* (which contains the intervals whole tone--whole tone--half tone, or 1-1-½), TAJNĪS AL THĀNĪ* (1-3/4-3/4), TAJNĪS AL THĀLITH* (1¼-3/4-½), and TAJNĪS AL RĀBIʿ* (1½-½-½) (al Fārābī 1967:150-152).

TAJNĪS AL AWWAL (j-n-s) ('-w-l) "first correspondence"

The Pythagorean diatonic tetrachordal division with the following intervals: whole tone--whole tone--half tone (al Fārābī 1967: 150-152). This is one of the four AJNĀS (s. JINS/1*) used for the scalar composition of the melodic modes, according to al Fārābī. Also called JINS AL AWWAL* by the same author. See TAJNĪS AL THĀNĪ*, TAJNĪS AL THĀLITH*, TAJNĪS AL RĀBIʿ*.

TAJNĪS AL RĀBIʿ (j-n-s) (r-b-ʿ) "fourth correspondence"

The chromatic tetrachordal division, containing the following intervals: 1½-½-½ (al Fārābī 1967:150-152). This is one of the four AJNĀS (s. JINS/1*) used for the scalar composition of the melodic modes, according to al Fārābī. Also called JINS AL RĀBIʿ* by the same author. See TAJNĪS AL AWWAL*, TAJNĪS AL THĀNĪ*, TAJNĪS AL THĀLITH*.

TAJNĪS AL THĀLITH (j-n-s) (th-l-th) "third correspondence"

The tetrachord segment with the following intervals: 1¼-3/4-½ (al Fārābī 1967:150-152). This is one of the four AJNĀS (s. JINS/1*) used for the scalar composition of the melodic modes, according to al Fārābī. Also JINS AL THĀLITH* by the same author. See TAJNĪS AL AWWAL*, TAJNĪS AL THĀNĪ*, TAJNĪS AL RĀBIʿ*.

TAJNĪS AL THĀNĪ (j-n-s) (th-n-y) "second correspondence"

The "Arab" diatonic tetrachord with the following intervals: 1-3/4-3/4 (al Fārābī 1967:150-152). This is one of the four AJNĀS (s. JINS/1*) used for the scalar composition of the melodic modes. Also called JINS AL THĀNĪ* by the same author. See TAJNĪS AL AWWAL*, TAJNĪS AL THĀLITH*, TAJNĪS AL RĀBIʿ*.

TAJWĪD (j-w-d) "improvement"

Qur'ānic cantillation, or the technical science of proper cantillation. There are three kinds according to an important 15th C. writer: TAḤQĪQ*, ḤADR/2* and TADWĪR* (al Suyūṭī 1941:I, 172).

TAJZĪ'AH (j-z-') "partitioning"

The dividing of a melody into parts or segments (Farmer 1967:106).

TAK (pl. TAKŪK) (onom.)

The light accent of the cycle of any rhythmic mode (ĪQĀʿ/1*). This accent or percussion stroke has a dry, crisp sound, in contrast to the wet, deep sound of the DUM* or DUMM* stroke. It is produced by striking a) at the rim of the percussion instrument with the fingers; b) on the back of the closed left hand, if clapping; or c) with the left foot if dancing (el Helou 1961:134; Massignon 1913:VIII, 765-766). Also TIK/1*.

TAKARRUR (k-r-r) "repetition"

1. Repetition.
2. Refrain.
3. A melodic ornament involving repetition of a note to keep the sound and movement continuous. See MARGHŪLAH*, TAKRĪR/1*.

TAKBĪR (pl. TAKBĪRĀT) (k-b-r) "enlargement; exclaiming God is Greater!"

The chanting of "ALLAHU AKBAR" ("God is Greater!") and other religious formulae as a feature of religious and social gatherings among Muslims. Repeating the TAKBĪR formula also serves as an audience response to a moving performance or poetry, music or chant.

TAKHANNUTH (kh-n-th) "effeminacy"

Falsetto voice. This vocal style was first adopted, we are told, by ISḤAQ AL MAWṢILĪ* (767-850), and later by many other singers of the ʿAbbāsī period.

(BI) TAKHAṬṬI (kh-ṭ-ṭ) "exceeding"

Melodic patterning (INTIQĀL/1*) with leaps of various sizes (al Fārābī 1967:968). Syn. of ṬĀFIR*.

TAKHFĪF (kh-f-f) "lightening"

1. Acceleration of the movement in a measured musical performance either through the addition of supplementary percussions (IDRĀJ*) or by increasing the tempo (ḤATHTH*) (al Fārābī 1967:1177).
2. Shortening durational elements within a musical performance.
3. Softening the volume in a musical performance.

TA'KHĪR ('-kh-r) "delaying; postponement"

According to O. Wright (1966:48), this term was used by theorists of the Classical Period ("later" than Ibn al Munajjim) for descending melodic movement. Opp. of TAQDĪM*.

TA'KHIR AL NABR ('-kh-r) (n-b-r) "postponement of the accent"

Syncopation (Maḥfūẓ 1964:185).

TAKHMĪR (kh-m-r) "covering; concealment"

The trance dance performed by members of the ʿĪsāwiyyah brotherhood and their audience (Tun.). This activity provides both a means for achieving spiritual ecstasy and a popular form of entertainment and social interaction. Performed with the musical NAWBAH/1*, it is a line dance in which the participants bend slowly forward and return, then backward and return in time to an eight-beat rhythm (two measures of four beats each). There is a gradual acceleration during the performance. Similar dances can be done with any NAWBAH performance, without conscious trance-induction; but then they are not called TAKHMĪR (Jones 1977:54-56).

TAKHT (t-kh-t) (Pers.) "platform, dais; board"

The traditional orchestral ensemble for performing Arab art music of the Mashriq. In the early part of the 20th C., it comprised a small but flexible number of instruments, the usual ones being the ʿŪD/2*, QĀNŪN*, KAMĀNJAH/2*, NĀY/1*, RIQQ*, and DARABUKKAH*. These instruments played in unison, heterophonically or alternating as soloists. Doubling of instruments was avoided before the early 1930's. The instruments were in general compatible in melodic scope and intensity, but dissimilar in register and tone color. All of them retained therefore a distinct personality which gave the impression of compatible layers of sound interacting with each other rather than a homogeneous unity (Racy 1978b:1). A male or female singer was often added to the instrumental group, or even a choir of male and/or female voices. Today the TAKHT is often somewhat larger and includes doublings of the traditional instruments as well as the addition of Western instruments such as the violin and cello.

TAKIL

Var. of THAQĪL* (Ribera 1970:79).

TAKK (onom.)

Light percussion stroke, syn. of TAK* or TIK/1*(Racy 1978b:1).

TAKRĪR (k-r-r) "repetition"

1. Repetition of notes, used as a melodic embellishment.
2. One of the four kinds of alteration (TAGHYĪR/2*) without additional percussions from outside (GHAYR ZIYĀDAH NAQRĀT*) which may affect a rhythmic cycle in order to create a new rhythmic mode. It involves repetition(s) of one of the percussions within the cycle (al Fārābī 1967:1015). See also TAWṢĪL AL MUFAṢṢAL, TAFṢĪL AL MUWAṢṢAL*, TARKĪB/2* (al Fārābī 1967:1014-1015).
3. A refrain.

TAKTHĪR (k-th-r) "enrichment; multiplication"

Enrichment of a melody with notes of other octave species, other AJNĀS (tetrachordal scalar segments), or other TAMDĪDĀT (registers) (al Fārābī 1967:1059; 1935:50).

TAKTHĪR AL ṬABAQĀT (k-th-r) (ṭ-b-q) "enrichment of the levels"

Extension of the melodic range or tessitura (Shawqī 1976:354).

TAKTĪF (k-t-f) "binding or tieing up"

The basic percussion and silence pattern of a rhythmic mode without rhythmic embellishment or improvisation (Mor.) (Chottin 1939:116). Also called MĪZĀN MUṬLAQ*.

ṬĀLAʿ

Var. of ṬĀLIʿ* (Jones 1977:84; d'Erlanger 1959:200).

ṬĀLIʿ = ṬALAʿ (ṭ-l-ʿ) "riser; emergent entity"

1. The name given to the KHĀNAH* section, which provides thematic, modal and/or register contrast in the SHUGHL/2* composition (Tun.) (d'Erlanger 1959:200). It also designates the KHĀNAH in the Algerian NAWBAH/1*, especially in the INṢIRĀF/1* movement (Ḥāfiẓ 1971:126; Maḥfūẓ 1964:86). In this use of the term, the literal meaning "riser" is pertinent; for this part is usually characterized by modulations or by higher pitch levels of the modal scale.
2. Syn. of MAṬLAʿ/2* and MAṬLAʿ/3*, i.e., the opening ("emergent") musical or poetic segment of various forms or genres of music in the Maghrib (al Rizqī 1967:371).

TALĀ'IM (l-'-m) "mending, correction"

Consonance (Farmer 1925:10).

TALBIYAH (l-b-y) "obeying, compliance"

Religious chanting performed in connection with the pilgrimage rites of the Muslims to the Kaʿbah in Makkah. This religious chant is of very ancient origin, and is said to have been practiced by Adam and Noah (Farmer 1957:438). See TAHLĪL*.

TALḤĪN (pl. TALḤĪNĀT, TALĀḤĪN) (l-ḥ-n) "musical composition"

1. A musical composition.
2. The act of composing.
3. Poetic or religious cantillation.
4. The singing of the Ṣūfī brotherhoods (Maḥfūẓ 1964:71).
5. Melodious sound.
6. A free rhythmed composition sung by popular or folk vocalists (Alg.) (Delphin and Guin 1886:2).
7. Melodic mode, according to the 13th C. ms. of al Shustarī (Farmer 1965b:46).

TALḤĪNĀT AL INSĀNIYYAH (l-ḥ-n) ('-n-s) "human musical compositions"

Vocal music; singing (al Fārābī 1967:879).

TALḤĪNĪ (l-ḥ-n) "pertaining to music"

Singable.

TA'LĪF ('-l-f) "composition"

1. Musical composition.
2. Any combination of two or more different tones (Maḥfūẓ 1964:68).
3. Harmony (see Shiloah 1964/65:127, n. 2).

TA'LĪF AL ĀLĪ ('-l-f) ('-w-l) "instrumental composition"

Musical composition for instruments (Maḥfūẓ 1964:185). See TA'LĪF AL GHINĀ'Ī*.

TA'LĪF AL AWTĀR ('-l-f) (w-t-r) "composition of strings"

The combination of tones of different pitch levels (i.e., on different strings of the lute) as a kind of musical embellishment (Ibn al Munajjim 1976:346-347).

TA'LĪF AL GHINĀ'Ī ('-l-f) (gh-n-y) "composition of singing"

Vocal composition (Maḥfūẓ 1964:185). See TA'LĪF AL ĀLĪ*.

TA'LĪF MURTAJAL ('-l-f) (r-j-l) "improvised composition"

1. The act of improvising.
2. An improvisation.

TA'LĪF AL NĀṬIQ ('-l-f) (n-ṭ-q) "composition with words"

Vocal composition, opp. of TA'LĪF AL ṢĀMIT*.

TA'LĪF AL ṢĀMIT ('-l-f) (ṣ-m-t) "silent composition"

Instrumental composition, i.e., without words, opp. of TA'LĪF AL NĀṬIQ*.

TA'LĪF AL ṢAWTĪ ('-l-f) (ṣ-w-t) "sound composition"

Musical composition (al Kindī 1966:153).

TA'LĪFĪ or TA'LĪFIYYAH ('-l-f) "composed"

One of the categories of AJNĀS (JINS/1*) used by theorists of the Classical Period. Most of these theorists equated this term with the designation "enharmonic," a JINS in which one interval of the tetrachord equals a major third (al Khwārizmī 1968:243). Other terms for the same tetrachordal division were NĀẒIM/1* and RĀSIM/1*. Strangely enough, Ibn Sīnā uses these terms, as well as RAKHW, for the chromatic JINS (i.e., the one with a minor third) (Ibn Sīnā 1930:90-91; 1935:143). See also d'Erlanger 1935: 273-276. According to the 10th C. writer, al Khwārizmī, this tetrachordal combination produces mournfulness, grief and reserve. He also designated it as effeminate (al Khwārizmī 1968:244). See JINS AL RAKHWĪ*.

TALLĀ' (t-l-w) "one who always recites or chants"

The reciter of poetry or the Qur'ān, therefore, the chanter (Farmer 1945:4). The term is used in this way in the 1001 Nights.

TÂ'MAR EL-FARÂRH

Var. of TA'MĪR AL FARĀGH* (Chottin 1939:147).

TAMAWAÏT

A solo, improvised, unmetered Berber song used in the AHIDOUS* music-poetry-dance performance (Mor.). It is also called TACHERAFT* (Chottin 1939:22).

TAMAWWUJ (pl. TAMAWWUJĀT) (m-w-j) "vibration; swaying"

Sound wave or musical vibration (Ikhwān al Ṣafā' 1957:I, 190).

TAMBOUR or TAMBOURAH

Vars. of ṬAMBŪR/2* (Olsen 1967:28).

ṬAMBŪR = TAMBOUR, TAMBUR, TAMBOURAH, ṬAMBŪRAH

1. A lyre of the contemporary Arabian/Persian Gulf and Peninsula regions. In the 19th C. in Makkah, an instrument of this name had six strings and a large wooden plectrum which seems to have been seldom used (Olsen 1967:28-29). Syn. of ṬAMBŪRAH*.
2. A long necked, fretted lute. As such, it is probably equivalent to the ṬUNBŪR/1*, the word more commonly used for this instrument. It has been documented with a great variety of soundbox and neck dimensions, number of strings, as well as of tunings. According to Mashāqah (1847:210), the ṬAMBŪR generally had eight strings, four tuned to G_1, the others to G_2.

ṬAMBŪRAH = TOUMBOURAH, TAMBOURAH, TIMBOURA, ṬANBŪRAH

A lyre of the contemporary folk tradition of the Arabian/Persian Gulf region and the Arabian Peninsula, as well as of the Sūdān and East Africa. Different examples are known to have had five or six strings which are tuned according to different systems (al Ḥafnī 1971:45-46; Jargy 1971:123).

TAMDĪD (pl. TAMDĪDĀT) (m-d-d) "extension, prolongation"

1. General pitch level, syn. of ṬABAQAH/1* (al Fārābī 1967:785; Ibn Sīnā 1935:161; Collangettes 1906:170).
2. Any of the pitch levels to which a melodic mode is transposed (al Fārābī 1930:133; 1967:374-383; Ṣafī al Dīn and al Jurjānī in d'Erlanger 1938:603).
3. Pitch (al Fārābī 1967:365, 961; 1930:132).

TAMDĪD MUTASĀWĪ (m-d-d) (s-w-y) "equal extension"

Said of two tones, two intervals, or two tetrachords which reveal an identity of notes (al Fārābī 1967:365; 1930:132). Contrasted with ṬABAQAH MUTASĀWIYAH*.

TAMEDIAZT

A solo, improvised, vocal setting of a poem dealing with bravery, generosity, satire, panegyric or religion and performed as part of the AHIDOUS* music-poetry-dance performance of the Berbers of the Middle Atlas (Mor.). A very developed example of this genre is called ZEDAYET* (ZIYĀDAH/2* ?) rather than TAMEDIAZT (Chottin 1939:22).

TAMHAWST

Name for a kind of AHIDOUS* in which rhythmic underlay is supplied by beating of hands and feet (Berbers of Mor.) (Chottin 1939:21). See TAMSERALIT*.

TAʿMĪR (ʿ-m-r) "filling, loading"

Equiv. of TAʿMĪR AL FARĀGH*.

TAʿMĪR AL FARĀGH = TÂ'MAR EL-FARÂRH (ʿ-m-r) (f-r-gh) "filling the empty space"

Filling of empty spaces between beats of a rhythmic cycle with additional percussions (Mor.) (Chottin 1939:147). Also TAʿMĪR*.

TAMKHĪR (m-kh-r) "act of lightening"

1. Shortening of some or all of the percussions of a rhythmic cycle, and thus, a process of acceleration (al Fārābī 1967:1052-1055).
2. Descriptive term for a rhythmic mode when it is of medium tempo (al Fārābī 1967:999; 1935:31).

TĀMM (t-m-m) "complete"

1. Descriptive of a MUWASHSHAḤ/1* that opens with the refrain section (al Ṣafadī 1966:21). Opp. of AQRAʿ*.
2. Said of a tetrachordal scalar segment (JINS/1*) whose two extremities are at a distance from each other of a perfect fourth (Ṣalāḥ al Dīn 1950:101). See also NĀQIṢ* and ZĀ'ID/2*.

TĀMM BARDAH (t-m-m) (Pers.) "complete curtain"

A whole tone interval (al Dāqūqī 1965:25).

TAMSERALIT

Name for a kind of AHIDOUS* in which rhythmic underlay is supplied by percussion instruments rather than by the beatings of hands and feet (Mor.) (Chottin 1939:21). See TAMHAWST*.

TAMWĪLAH = TEMUÎLA (m-w-l) "an enrichment"

That part of the QAṢĪDAH/1* (Mor.) devoted to stock phrases and formulae which are sung first by the soloist, then repeated by the chorus (SHADDĀDAH/1*) (Chottin 1939:160). Chottin's hypothesis that the word is derived from the term MAWLATĪ (MÛLÂTÎ) which is often used in the lyrics is not tenable.

TAMZĪJ (m-z-j) "mixing"

1. Combination of two or more notes (al Fārābī 1930:136; 1967:389; Ibn Abī al Ṣalt 1952:50).
2. Combination of intervals (al Fārābī 1930:136; 1967:391; Ibn Abī al Ṣalt 1952:50).
3. Combination of melodic AJNĀS (s. JINS/1*). Al Fārābī has described this TAMZĪJ as one involving different tetrachordal scalar segments which start on the same base note or lowest tone (al Farabi 1967:397-414; see also al Jurjānī 1938:448-450). In another place in the same work, TAMZĪJ of AJNĀS is described as involving tetrachordal segments starting from different tones (al Fārābī 1930:144; 1967:389). For Ibn Abī al Ṣalt, the combination of AJNĀS known as TAMZĪJ is a joining which produces a larger scalar combination. He writes that it can be of two kinds: 1) DIRECT, in which the largest interval of one JINS joins, or is connected to, the largest interval of the other JINS; or 2) CHANGING, in which the largest interval of one JINS connects to the smallest interval of the other JINS (Ibn Abī al Ṣalt 1952:50).
4. A combination of cycles to create new rhythmic modes (al Fārābī 1930:156; 1967:477). Also known as MAMZŪJAH*.
5. An embellishment which involves plucking a string stopped at one position with one finger and then rapidly raising and lowering a second finger at another position on the same string (Ibn Sīnā 1935:230). There are three kinds of TAMZĪJ, according to Ibn Sīnā in another work:

1) Sliding the finger to the higher fret position of a new note before the vibration of the first tone is finished;
2) Similar to 1), but moving to a lower fret position;

3) Placing the finger across two strings at the same distance from the nut and then sounding the two together, either with or without trilling with another note. This type of TAMZĪJ is also known as TASHQĪQ*. Ibn Sīnā writes that TASHQĪQ is more effective if the main note is higher than the embellishing tone added to it (1930:98).

TANĀFUR (n-f-r) "dissonance"

Musical dissonance (al Fārābī 1967:112), Ikhwān al Ṣafā' 1958:194ff; Maḥfūẓ 1964:124).

TANAGHGHUM (n-gh-m) "act of making oneself sing/enjoy/put to notes"

Given the literal meaning of this term, it can be used for humming, singing or even playing on an instrument (Maḥfūẓ 1964:71).

TANĀGHUM (n-gh-m) "reciprocal melodizing"

Harmony (al Kindī 1966:157).

TANĀWĪḤ (pl. of TANĀWUḤ) (n-w-ḥ) "lamentation with reciprocal action"

Vocal lamentations.

TANBAK

Syn. of DARABUKKAH* (Farmer EI(Fr), "Ṭabl":231).

TANBOUR

Var. of ṬUNBŪR/1* (Rouanet 1922:2711).

TANBOUR BAR'DĀDI

Var. of ṬUNBŪR AL BAGHDĀDĪ* (Rouanet 1922:2711).

ṬANBŪR (pl. ṬANĀBĪR)

Var. of ṬUNBŪR/1*. Also see constructs of ṬANBŪR and ṬUNBŪR.

ṬANBŪR-I SHIRWĪNĀN

According to ʿAbd al Qādir ibn Ghaybī (d. 1435), one of two kinds of long necked lute of the time, the other being ṬANBŪR-I TURKĪ*. It had a pear-shaped soundbox and two strings (Farmer 1976b:36; EI(Fr), "Ṭunbūr":270).

ṬANBŪR-I TURKĪ

One of two kinds of long necked lute mentioned by ʿAbd al Qādir ibn Ghaybī (d. 1435). It had a small soundbox and a longer neck than the ṬANBŪR-I SHIRWĪNĀN*, and either two or three strings. See ṬUNBŪR TURKĪ*.

ṬANBŪRAH

Var. of ṬAMBŪRAH* (Hickmann 1958:49), the large triangular lyre of the Sudanese folk tradition. It is also used in the Arabian/ Persian Gulf region. An illustration in Hickmann 1958:50 reveals an instrument with six strings.

TANGHĪM (n-gh-m) "intoning"

1. Pitch "identity," i.e., two tones of octave equivalency are said to be equal in TANGHĪM (al Kindī 1965:17).
2. Solfeggio (Maḥfūẓ 1964:185); the sounding of pitches.
3. This term and other terms generally pertaining to melody (e.g., NAGHM or NAGHAM*, LAḤN*) are accorded rhythmic and durational meanings in the work of Saadyah Gaon (see Farmer 1943:30-37). In that work, TANGHĪM applies to the sounding of percussions rather than the sounding of pitches.

ṬANĪN (pl. ṬANĪNĀT) (ṭ-n-n) "ringing, resounding"

1. A tone (see Shiloah 1964/65:147, n. 91).
2. The whole tone interval (al Kindī 1966:134, 146, Shiloah 1964/65:147, n. 91).
3. A tonal or melodic pattern (INTIQĀL/1*) (al Kindī 1966:144ff, 162ff), i.e., a melodic motif (motive).
4. Melodic mode (al Kindī as reported in Shawqī 1969:66). Cowl also translates a use of this term by al Kindī as melodic mode (Cowl 1966:144, 162ff); but in that instance, definition 3 above seems more fitting. The same passage uses LAḤN* for melodic mode.
5. Resonance (Ikhwān al Ṣafā' 1964/65:147, n. 91; Ibn ʿAbd Rabbihi 1887:III, 28).

ṬANĪNĪ = T'ĀNĪNI (ṭ-n-n) "resonant"

1. Classical and Modern Period name for the whole tone interval (ratio 9/8). It has had many other names as well (see chart under BUʿD*). It was abbreviated as "T"*.
2. The diatonic tetrachordal scalar segment (JINS/1*) (al Khwārizmī 1968:243), also given the names of QAWĪ* and MUQAWWĪ* by the same theorist. He described it as masculine and as affecting towards nobleness, strength and joy.

T'ĀNĪNI

Var. of ṬANĪNĪ/1* (Rouanet 1922:2715).

TANQĪR (n-q-r) "beating"

Producing the percussions or beats of a rhythmic mode (Farmer 1943: 35).

ṬANṬANAH ASĀS AL MAQĀM (onom.) ('-s-s) (q-w-m) "to make ṬAN ṬAN ṬAN on the base tone of the melodic mode"

A drone or pedal point on the tonic (Al Ḥalqah 1964:53).

TANWĪʻAH (pl. TANWĪʻĀT) (n-w-ʻ) "act of varying"

Musical variation, the act and the product (Al Ḥalqah 1964:60).

TANẒĪM AL ALḤĀN (n-ẓ-m) (l-ḥ-n) "organization of the melodies"

Musical composition (Kāẓim 1964:32).

TANẒĪM DHŪ AL ABʻĀD AL MUTASĀWIYAH (n-ẓ-m) (b-ʻ-d) (s-w-y) "organization of the possessor of equal intervals"

The tempered scale (al Dāqūqī 1965:29).

TANẒĪM MIN THUNĀ'IYYĀT AL MUTASĀWIYAH (n-ẓ-m) (th-n-y) (s-w-y) "organization from equal seconds"

Syn. of TANẒĪM DHŪ AL ABʻĀD AL MUTASĀWIYAH* (al Dāqūqī 1965:29).

TAPDEBA

Var. of DABDABAH/2* (Rouanet 1922:2794).

ṬĀQAH (pl. ṬĀQĀT) (ṭ-w-q) "power, strength"

The thread or strand which is twisted together with others of its kind to make one of the strings of the lute (ʻŪD/2*) or of any other chordophone (Ikhwān al Ṣafā' 1957:I, 203).

TAQĀSĪM (q-s-m) "divisions; dividings"

Pl. of TAQSĪM*. This term is also used to designate the single performance of this genre of solo improvisational instrumental music known as TAQSĪM. Since each performance of these improvisations is an open-ended series of segments (or "divisions"), the plural form is perhaps even more apt than the singular. It should be noted that the comparable vocal genre is always designated with a plural name (LAYĀLĪ*).

TAQAṢṢUR (q-ṣ-r) "act of shortening"

A technique of rhythmic embellishment which involved eliminating the space (FĀṢILAH/4*) between the cycles (Ibn Sīnā 1930:99). Ibn Sīnā treated TAQAṢṢUR as one of the two kinds of embellishment involving the FĀṢILAH. See TAWĀṢUL*.

TAQDĪM (q-d-m) "presentation"

According to Wright, a term used by Classical Period theorists (after Ibn al Munajjim) for ascending melodic movement (Wright 1966:48). See also TA'KHĪR*.

TAQFĪLAH (pl. TAQFĪLĀT) (q-f-l) "closing"

1. Coda (al Ḥafnī 1946:290; Maḥfūẓ 1964:192).
2. The last section of the MUWASHSHAḤ/1* (Egypt).

TAQFIYYAH (pl. TAQFIYYĀT) (q-f-w) "closing"

1. Final cadence.
2. Closing section of many musical compositions. Also QAFL or QAFLAH/1*.

TAQLĪB (q-l-b) "overturning"

Combination of one melodic mode (MAQĀM/1*) with another, i.e., substituting in performance the tones of one melodic mode for those of a second, while maintaining the manner of usage of the first mode (Kāẓim 1964:33).

ṬAQM (pl. AṬQĀM) (ṭ-q-m) "set, series"

Cycle of a rhythmic mode (ĪQĀʿ/1*) (el Helou 1961:195; 1965:90).

TAQRĪB (q-r-b) "shortening"

The shortening of the time between percussions of equal duration (al Fārābī 1967:992), i.e., a process having the effect of increasing the tempo if done consistently.

TAQSĪM (pl. TAQĀSĪM) (q-s-m) "act of dividing repeatedly; division"

A solo instrumental improvisation of unmetered variety, which is an important and popular genre of performance in the Arab World. This genre of contemporary music comprises a series of "divisions" or phrases separated from each other by silences of varying lengths. Each division explores the tones of a limited segment of the modal scale in use and provides a new, usually self-contained unit with a return at the end to a point of melodic stability or tonal rest. Each is a new excursion or arabesque in sound, in which there is a building of tension, followed by a resolution experienced at the return to melodic "home base." The TAQSĪM begins with the tones of the basic tetrachord/pentachordal scalar segment (JINS/1*) of the melodic mode. But other AJNĀS of the basic mode as well as modulations to new MAQĀMĀT (s. MAQĀM/1*) are treated in subsequent phrases before the improvising performer returns near the end of the genre to the tones of the basic JINS in order to end on the tonic of the mode. Historically the TAQSĪM is said to have been an introductory piece (Gerson-Kiwi 1970:68), but today it may appear in any position in a musical performance of pieces. It is often used as forerunner to a vocal or instrumental number with regular rhythm. In addition, it is used as a kind of intermezzo between contrasting numbers of the suites in both Maghrib and Mashriq. See Touma 1971; and 1976.

TAQSĪM ʿALĀ AL WAḤDAH (q-s-m) (w-ḥ-d) "division on the one"

A TAQSĪM* which is performed with a simple rhythmic accompaniment based on the WAḤDAH/2* rhythmic mode. The beats of the rhythmic cycle are performed by any of the percussion instruments or even, at times, by a stringed instrument which provides an underlying ostinato (Nettl and Riddle 1973:12).

TAQṬĪʿ (q-ṭ-ʿ) "division"

Distribution of the hemistiches of poetry on the tones to which it is sung according to the meter of the poetry (Kāẓim 1964:33).

ṬAQṬŪQAH (pl. ṬAQĀṬĪQ) (onom.)

A light, pre-composed piece of the Mashriq which might be compared to a folkish version of the MUWASHSHAḤ/1* or DAWR/5*. It was originally a women's song, but is now also performed by men. It is a strophic and metered genre, with an amorous text in colloquial Arabic. It utilizes a new melodic mode (MAQĀM/1*) for each GHUṢN/2* or poetic segment. The rhythmic modes used are the simple ones without extended cycles (Ḥāfiẓ 1971:204-205). UHZŪJAH* is a more proper name for this genre, according to Ḥāfiẓ (1971:204).

TAQUÎD ES-SANAYA

Var. of TAQYĪD AL ṢANʿAH* (el Mahdi 1972:12).

TAQWĪM AL AWTĀR (q-w-m) (w-t-r) "resetting the strings"

Tuning the strings of a musical instrument. This term is used more in the sense of improving the tuning after the strings have been tuned once, e.g., during the course of a performance (Shawqī 1976:352).

TAQYĪD AL ṢANʿAH = TAQUÎD ES-SANAYA (q-y-d) (ṣ-n-ʿ) "restraining, defining the limits of the art or craft"

An opening unmetered instrumental prelude of the NAWBAH/1* or suite (Alg.) (el Mahdi 1972:12). This hypothesis regarding the origin of the colloq. terms of el Mahdi (TAQUÎD ES-SANAYA*) might be challenged by arguments for the first term's being derived from TA'KĪD ("confirmation") or TAʿQĪD ("complexity"). There seems to be little doubt that the second term is derived from ṢANʿAH.

TĀR (Pers.) "string"

A long necked lute of al Khwārizm and Turkestan (Farmer EI(Fr), "Ṭunbūr":270). This name is often combined with a Persian number to indicate the number of strings on the instrument, e.g., SITTĀR, DŪTĀR, etc.

ṬĀR (pl. ṬIRAN) = TIRR, T'AR, TARR, ṬARR (ṭ-w-r) "hoop; wheel"

1. Small, round frame drum in the Maghrib and Mashriq with single head and metal cymbals affixed in the frame (Delphin and Guin 1886:42; Lane 1973:188, 366, 512). It is used in both art and folk music. It has been known in many parts of the Arab World from the ʿAbbāsī period to the present day (Farmer 1967:211; 1945:34). The instrument achieves three different kinds of tones: 1) the clear TAK* stroke when struck on its edge with single finger or bottom of the thumb; 2) the rich and deep DUM* or DUMM*

stroke made with the palm or flat fingers on the outer third of the membrane; and 3) the BAYN AL ZUNŪJ* at the center of the skin with the fist or the palm. It is the chief instrument of percussion in use for the classical music of the Maghrib and is therefore a most respected instrument there (Chottin 1939:116-117). It is often the instrument played by the leader of the ensemble in the Maghrib (el Mahdi 1972:64). It exists in different sizes from 11-25 cm. in diameter, with depths of approximately 7-8 cm.
2. A large frame drum used in upper Egypt (Hickmann 1947:21) and the Arabian/Persian Gulf region, where it can reach up to a diameter of 70 cm. (Touma 1977a:124). It is more often about 40 cm. in diameter. According to al Rizqī (1967:363), a smaller version is found in Tunisia; but it is not known if that particular variety is other than the one described in def. 1 above.

T'AR

Var. of ṬĀR/2* (Delphin and Guin 1886:42), which is described as a large instrument which never accompanies the vocalist because of its loud sound.

ṬĀR AL JĀHILĪ (ṭ-w-r) (j-h-l) "pre-Islamic tambourine"

Probably the square frame drum used in pre-Islamic times since Farmer relates that it has been described as "different from" the round frame drum (Farmer EI(Fr), "Duff":79).

ṬARAB (pl. AṬRĀB) (ṭ-r-b) "delight, pleasure"

1. Aesthetic delight created through music, therefore, the effect of music. According to the Tāj al ʿArūs of al Zabīdī, it means "the stirring of both joy and sorrow in the listener" (al Zabīdī 1965:I, 354).
2. Entertainment.
3. Singing or music (Farmer 1967:51).

ṬARAB AL FUTŪḤ (ṭ-r-b) (f-t-ḥ) "delight of wide compass"

A variety of lute (ʿŪD/2*) described by ʿAbd al Qādir ibn Ghaybī (d. 1435) as having six double strings (Farmer EI(Eng), "ʿŪd": 987). The instrument is believed to have been a short necked variety of the lute.

ṬARAB RABB = ṬARABRAB, ṬARABRŪB (ṭ-r-b) (r-b-b) "owner or possessor of delight"

A variety of small, short necked lute (ʿŪD/2*) with six strings which was mentioned by ʿAbd al Qādir ibn Ghaybī (d. 1435) (Farmer 1978:II, 97, and n. 1). Syn. of SHASTĀ or SHASHTĀR*.

ṬARAB ZŪR (ṭ-r-b) (z-w-r) or (z-y-r) "powerful delight"

A variety of short necked lute (ʿŪD/2*) mentioned by ʿAbd al Qādir ibn Ghaybī (d. 1435) (Farmer EI(Eng), "ʿŪd":987).

ṬARABA (ṭ-r-b) "to delight or give pleasure"

To excite and please through the means of sound.

ṬARABRAB

Var. of ṬARAB RABB* (Farmer 1978:II, 97, n. 1).

ṬARABRUB

Var. of ṬARAB RABB* (Farmer 1978:II, 97, n. 1).

TARADDUD (r-d-d) "recurrence"

Musical vibrations (of strings, air columns, etc.) (al Fārābī 1967:365; Shawqī 1976:277).

ṬARĀ'IQ

Pl. of ṬARĪQAH/3*.

ṬĀRĀJĪ (ṭ-w-r) Turk. colloq. ending

Performer on the ṬĀR* (Jones 1977:44).

TARĀNAH

One of the four movements of the ancient NAWBAH/1* or suite. According to ʿAbd al Qādir ibn Ghaybī (d. 1435), this vocal movement set either Arabic or Persian quatrains to music. It was designated as the third movement of the NAWBAH at that time. It utilized THAQĪL AL AWWAL*, THAQĪL AL THĀNĪ*, or Double RAMAL* rhythms, and was said to have started on the seventh percussion when the THAQĪL rhythms were used, on the ninth percussion when the Double RAMAL was used (Anonymous Treatise 1939:236; Farmer 1967:200). In the 14th C. commentary on the Kitāb al Adwār, it was a musical number in which there was an alternation between vocal and instrumental segments and in which several syllables might occur with a single melody tone (al Jurjānī 1938:553).

TARANNAMA (r-n-m) "to sing, chant"

1. To sing or cantillate (Ibn ʿAbd Rabbihi 1887:III, 189; Madina; Farmer 1943-1944:55).
2. The term sometimes takes on a more general meaning of "producing musical sound," for it is even used in connection with stringed instruments (al Kindī in Yūsuf 1965:22).
3. To sing softly, pleasantly, and with ṬARAB* (Maḥfūẓ 1964:69).

TARANNUM (pl. TARANNUMĀT) (r-n-m) "cantillation"

1. Singing or cantillation which resembles vocalise rather than actual song (Shiloah 1968a:241, n. 137), i.e., syn. of NATHR AL NAGHAMĀT*. Such chanting of poetry was practiced from pre-Islamic times.
2. Vocalizing a tune with stock words and syllables or with humming (el Helou 1961:193).
3. In al Nadīm (1970:I, 319), it means musical sound produced

either by singing or by a musical instrument.

4. Lowering the voice and using vocal repetitions (al Fārābī 1967:990, n. 4; 1160, n. 4).

TARASSUL BIL QIRĀ'AH (r-s-l) (q-r-') "leisurely paced in recitation"

Giving extra time and gravity to the chanting of the Qur'ān (Maḥfūẓ 1964:69).

TARASSUL FĪ AL GHINĀ' (r-s-l) (gh-n-y) "leisurely paced in singing"

Treating various tones of a song with lengthenings and shortenings not prescribed in the rhythmic mode (Maḥfūẓ 1964:68-69). This seems to be an equiv. of Tempo rubato.

TARDĪD (pl. TARDĪDĀT) (r-d-d) "repetition"

1. Repetition of musical tones, intervals, motifs, etc.
2. A refrain.

TARDĪD AL ALḤĀN (r-d-d) (l-ḥ-n) "repetition of tunes"

Singing (al Ghazālī n.d.: I, 287).

TARDĪD AL ṢAWT (r-d-d) (ṣ-w-t) "repetition of sound"

Singing (al Ghazālī n.d.:I, 287).

ṬARDJAHĀRĀT

A variety of idiophone comprising pots which were played with sticks. This instrument was mentioned by the Ikhwān al Ṣafā' (10th C.) (Farmer EI(Fr), "Ṣandj":211).

TARHIULT

Syn. of IZLI*, a Berber song (Chottin 1939:21).

ṬARIBA (ṭ-r-b) "to be moved"

To be affected or moved by singing or music (al Zabīdī 1965:I, 354).

TARʿĪD (r-ʿ-d) "thundering"

1. A mordent, trill or wide vibrato as a tonal embellishment (Ibn Sīnā 1930:98; Chottin 1939:66). Ibn Sīnā writes that it is so fast a succession of tones thatone does not feel the disjunction between them.
2. Rapid percussions, so short that the length of their duration is imperceptible. These repetitions keep the sound and movement continuous (al Lādhiqī 1939:459).
3. A prohibited cantillation practice which involves making the voice sound like thunder or like it is shivering from cold or pain (Maḥmūd n.d.:35).

TARʿĪDAH = TERʾÎDA (r-ʿ-d) "a thundering"

A trill or tremolo (el Helou 1961:56; Chottin 1939:147).

TAʿRÎǦAH

Var. of TAʿRĪJAH/1* (Chottin 1961:Band IX, col. 1564, 1567).

TÂRÎJA or TA'RÎJA

Vars. of TAʿRĪJAH/1* (Farmer 1954, "Berber Music":I, 633; Chottin 1939:39, resp.),

TAʿRĪJAH (pl. TAʿĀRĪJ, TAʿRĪJĀT) = TÂRÎJA, TA'RÎYA, TAʿRÎǦAH, TA'RÎJA (ʿ-r-j)

1. A cylindrical, waisted, single headed drum usually made of pottery and having the assymetrical form of a tube more spread at one end than the other. It is probably the most popular drum of Morocco. It is played solo or in pairs. In the former case, it is held horizontally on the left arm and played with the right hand. In the latter case, the two drums (known as UMM WA ḤASHIYAH*) are held vertically from their waists, the heads pointing downward. On one instrument, the UMM or "mother" drum, the DUM* strokes are played; on the other, the ḤASHIYAH* or "margin" drum, the TAK* strokes are played (Chottin 1939:39-40).
2. Farmer calls this instrument a tambourine in 1978:I, 45.

ṬARĪQ = TRÎQ (ṭ-r-q) "way, method"

A suite of Hebraic songs of North African Jews (Chottin 1939:149).

ṬARĪQ AL MULŪKIYYAH (pl. ṬURŪQ AL MULŪKIYYAH) (ṭ-r-q) (m-l-k) "royal path"

Any one of the set of seven melodic modes mentioned by Ibn Khurdādhbih (d. ca. 912) (al ʿAzzāwī 1951:95).

ṬARĪQAH (pl. ṬARĀ'IQ, ṬURUQ, ṬIRĀ'IQ, ṬURŪQ, ṬURUQĀT, ṬARĀYIQ) = ṬURQAH (pl. ṬURAQ) (ṭ-r-q) "a way, a method"

1. Rhythmic mode (al Kindī 1965:26; al Masʿūdī 1874:VIII, 99; al Ghazālī 1901:222).
2. Melodic mode (al Ghazālī 1901:220, 742; al Kindī, Berlin ms. Ahlwardt 5530, fol. 30, quoted by Farmer 1967:151; al Masʿūdī 1874: VIII, 98).
3. An instrumental composition used as a prelude for a vocal number. Al Fārābī mentions that it was common to the musical tradition of Khurāsān and Persia and that it was without the definite parts found in the ALḤAN AL JUZ'IYYAH* (al Fārābī 1967: 69, 880; 1930:17). By the 14th C. this instrumental prelude with regular rhythm was called PISHRŪ/1* by non-Arab musicians (al Jurjānī 1938:519, 522-523). It was obligatory for every movement of the NAWBAH/1* or suite, according to a 15th C. theorist (Anonymous Treatise 1939:235-236). Ṣafī al Dīn (d. 1294) supplied

notation for ṬARĪQAHs in the last pages of Al Sharafiyyah (Ṣafī al Dīn 1938b:181-182) and in the Kitāb al Adwār (Ṣafī al Dīn 1938a: 552ff). Wright hypothesizes that these short examples may have served as teaching materials for beginners rather than as fully developed pieces for professional performance (Wright 1978:254). Transcribed examples of this genre can be found in Wright 1978:218-231).
4. Manner of performance (al Fārābī 1967:516, and see n. 2; Maḥfūẓ 1964:87). Al Lādhiqī expands on this meaning of the term by saying it is a method of producing a melody that is melodically and rhythmically pleasing (al Lādhiqī 1939:484). This would also seem to be the meaning of the term as used by al Ghazālī (1901: 201, n. 1), though the translator, Duncan B. Macdonald, has rendered it as "a musical phrase, part or section of a melody."
5. Any of the 36 possible combinations produced through the alliance of the six melodic modes (AṢĀBIʿ*) and the rhythmic modes (ĪQĀʿĀT, s. ĪQĀʿ/1*) with which they were associated for musical performance (Wright 1978:254).

TA'RÎYA

Var. of TAʿRĪJAH/1*, the clay cylindrical, single headed drum of North Africa (Marcuse).

TARJAMAH (t-r-j-m) "translation"

1. A form of accompaniment exemplified in a soft mimicking "shadowing" of the vocal or instrumental solo by the ensemble (Racy 1978b:8).
2. One of the varieties of LĀZIMAH* or instrumental interlude which comprises a repetition of that music which has just been sung or played by the soloist.

TARJĪʿ or TARJĪʿAH (pl. TARJĪʿĀT) (r-j-ʿ) "act of causing to return"

1. Repetition of tones or motifs.
2. Refrain (al Masʿūdī 1874:VIII, 92; Ibn ʿAbd Rabbihi in Farmer, 1941:25). Farmer writes that this term was used for a refrain sung by singing girls in pre-Islamic times (Farmer 1967:12). It is probably this meaning which best fits its use in the works of Ibn Salamah (1951:89) and Ibn Khurdādhbih (1951:96), where it is found as a characteristic of the early Arab song, SINĀD*. See also Farmer 1957:424
3. An improvisatory number, the melody of which is played on a single string of the instrument with repeated returns to a drone tone executed on a different open string. The string on which this improvisation is played is known as SĀYIR AL TARJĪʿAH*; the drone string, as LĀZIM AL TARJĪʿAH* or RĀJIʿ*. The TARJĪʿ was designated as "equal" when each entrance of the drone consisted of the same number of tones as had just been executed in the melody; "unequal" when the drone tones were more or less than the number of melody tones just performed. This combination of melody and drone tones was performed without destroying the rhythmic cycle (Anonymous Treatise, drawing from the writings of ʿAbd al Qādir ibn Ghaybī 1939:245-246). See also al Lādhiqī (1939:427).

TARJĪḤ (r-j-ḥ) "act of favoring"

Trembling the tones in the chest while singing (al Fārābī 1967:1173; 1935:91).

TARKHĪM (r-kh-m) "softening, mellowing"

Beautifying the musical sound.

TARKĪB (pl. TARĀKĪB, TARKĪBĀT) (r-k-b) "combination, superpositioning"

1. A tonal embellishment which involved plucking two strings at the same time in such a way as to produce the simultaneous combination of the main and the embellishing tones. Most desirable was the embellishing tone at a distance of an octave from the main tone, and next best was the one at a perfect fourth, according to Ibn Sīnā (1930:99). In another work by the same author, we read that both the fourth and fifth intervals are listed as ones to be combined with a main tone to produce TARKĪB, while a similar embellishment using the octave interval is known as TAḌʿĪF/1* (Ibn Sina 1935:230-231).
2. One of the four kinds of TAGHYĪR/2* or alteration of a rhythmic cycle to produce a new mode which is described by al Fārābī. This type of TAGHYĪR, which is without additional percussions from outside (GHAYR ZIYĀDAH NAGRĀT*) involved repetition of the opening percussion at the end of a cycle or of the ending percussion at the beginning of the cycle (al Fārābī 1967: 1016-1017). See also TAFṢĪL AL MUWAṢṢAL*, TAWṢĪL AL MUFAṢṢAL*, TAKRĪR/2*.
3. One of the categories of melodic modes discussed by theorists of the 13th-16th C. (Quṭb al Dīn al Shīrāzī in Wright 1978:168; Anonymous Treatise 1939:102). With this meaning, the term probably equates with MURAKKAB or MURAKKABAH/1*, a category of derivative modes (Ṣafī al Dīn 1938:387; see also Wright 1978:90ff). There is, according to al Lādhiqī (1939:413), no essential difference between a TARKĪB and a SHUʿBAH* mode. According to the musicians of his time (16th C.), 30 of these derivative modes were created from the 12 principal modes or MAQĀMĀT (s. MAQĀM/1*) (al Lādhiqī 1939:441-452; see also al Jurjānī 1938:387). For Quṭb al Dīn al Shīrāzī, the TARKĪB was a modal combination less integrated than the octave scales. It contained two units which did not necessarily form a unity (Wright 1978:199-200), as, for example, in a MUTADĀKHILAH* combination of AJNĀS.
4. Combination of tetrachordal segments to form a modal scale (al Fārābī 1930:137ff; 1967:393ff; Ṣafī al Dīn 1938b:387; Quṭb al Dīn in Wright 1978:192).
5. Combination of different kinds of tetrachordal segments within a single MAQĀM/1* (d'Erlanger 1949:101).
6. Modulation (d'Erlanger 1949:104ff). The melodic mode composed of a number of modes used in succession is sometimes given this name in contemporary practice. A MAQĀM/1*-governed performance can include excursions to various other MAQĀMĀT considered suitable as transposition modes in connection with the main mode. Not only is the modal combination thus generated called TARKĪB or a MAQĀM MURAKKAB*, but this act of modal transposition and combination

is itself known as TARKĪB (al Dāqūqī 1965:33).
7. Changing a tone or tones of a tetrachordal scalar segment (JINS/1*) in the course of performing a single melody (al Jurjānī 1938:448-450; see also d'Erlanger 1938:584, n. 39).
8. Adaptation of new words to a known melody (Chottin 1939:150).

TARKĪB BI ISTIQĀMAH (r-k-b) (q-w-m) "combination with straightness"

Combination of different AJNĀS (s. JINS/1*) in which the placement of small and large intervals in one is similar to the placement of the intervals in the other (al Fārābī 1967:394; 1930:137). See TARKĪB MUNAKKAS*.

TARKĪB MUNAKKAS (r-k-b) (n-k-s) "inverted combination"

Combination of different AJNĀS (s. JINS/1*) in which the placement of small and large intervals in one is not similar to that in the other (al Fārābī 1967:137; 1967:394). See TARKĪB BI ISTIQĀMAH*.

TARNĪM (r-n-m) "singing; chanting"

1. Singing, chanting or humming.
2. Beautification of musical sound.

TARNĪMAH (pl. TARĀNĪM) (r-n-m) "a singing or chanting"

1. A hymn or song.
2. A variety of MAWWĀL/1* sung in Egypt (Al Ḥalqah 1964:52).

ṬARQ (pl. ṬURŪQ) (ṭ-r-q) "a knock"

1. A sounding of a tone on the lute (ʿŪD*) or similar instrument, by striking the string or plucking it (Maḥfūẓ 1964:87; al Zabīdī 1965:VI, 418).
2. A tone sounded on the lute or similar instrument which is in some way unique, whether in volume, pitch, or some other aspect (al Zabīdī 1965:VI, 418).
3. A tune or melody (Maḥfūẓ 1964:87).

ṬARQAH (ṭ-r-q) "hammering"

Syn. of ṬARQ/1* (Maḥfūẓ 1964:87).

TARQĪM AL MĪZĀN (r-q-m) (w-z-n) "marking the balance or scale"

Beating out a musical rhythm (Maḥfūẓ 1964:185).

TARQĪṢ (r-q-ṣ) "dancing"

A prohibited Qur'ānic cantillation practice which involves making the voice "dance" (al Saʿīd 1967:345) or spurt after a long stop, as if running and galloping (al Suyūṭī 1941:I, 175).

ṬARR or TARR

Syn. of ṬĀR/1*, a round frame drum with cymbals (Chottin 1961:

Band IX, col. 1564; Touma 1977b:106, resp.).

TARRA

Clay or gourd pot drum of Morocco, with goatskin head (Marcuse).

ṬARRĀB (ṭ-r-b) "one who affects listeners with a musical performance"

Anyone who produces ṬARAB*, therefore the minstrel, vocalist, instrumentalist, musician.

ṬARRABA (ṭ-r-b) "to make something pleasing and moving"

1. To perform musically.
2. To perform music with repetitions and embellishments (al Zabīdī 1965:I, 354).

ṬARRĀR = TERRÂR, TURAR

Player of the ṬĀR* or ṬARR* (Chottin 1939:112, 147).

TARTĪL (r-t-l) "rendering musically"

1. Cantillation of the Qur'ān or any religious chant.
2. Slow cantillation of the Qur'ān for thought and meditation, with each syllable clearly and correctly pronounced (Shiloah 1968a: 241, n. 136).
3. Slow, clear enunciation of a song (al Fārābī 1967:1177).
4. Unmetered song, therefore, the vocal equivalent of TAQSĪM* or TAQĀSĪM*, according to Mashāqah (n.d.:fol. 46). The term has been used in this sense over a long period of time (Farmer 1954, "Syrian Music":VIII, 257).
5. A way of embellishing a melody through durational means which involve slowing down its tempo (Ibn Sīnā 1930:99).

TARTĪL DĪNĪ (r-t-l) (d-y-n) "religious musical rendering"

Chanting or singing of religious texts or words.

TARTĪLAH (pl. TARĀTĪL) (r-t-l) "a musical rendering"

A hymm (Madina).

TASAH

Var. of ṬĀSAH*.

ṬĀSAH (pl. ṬĀSĀT) = TASAH (ṭ-w-s) "drinking vessel made of metal"

Small kettledrum of pre-Islamic times.

TAṢDĪR (ṣ-d-r) "preface"

A supplementary percussion anterior to the rhythmic cycle (Ibn Sīnā 1935:181; see also <u>Anonymous Treatise</u> 1939:165). It is described by Ibn Sīnā as a durational embellishment which was also known as ʿIMĀD* (1930:99). According to al Rajab (1967:23), it is also syn. with IʿTIMĀD/2*.

TAṢDĪRAH (pl. TAṢDĪRĀT) = TÇDÎRA (ṣ-d-r) "that which is advanced"

1. Any introductory piece.
2. The opening part of any of the five main movements of the NAWBAH/1* or suite (Mor.). It has a slow tempo and is followed by a series of MUWASHSHAḤĀT (s. MUWASHSHAḤ/1*) which undergo a gradual acceleration in tempo at fixed junctures (Chottin 1939: 112, 126; Maḥfūz 1964:106).

TAṢDIYYAH (ṣ-d-y) "hand clapping"

Rhythmic accompaniment of hand clapping considered to be an unacceptable form of SAMĀʿ/1* by Ibn Taymiyyah (1966:II, 299).

TASFĪQ (s-f-q) "banging, slapping"

Syn. of TAṢFĪQ*.

TAṢFĪQ (ṣ-f-q) "hand clapping"

Hand clapping or beating to provide rhythmic underlay to a performance of music.

TASHĀBUH FĪ AL KAYFIYYAH (sh-b-h) (k-y-f) "resemblance in nature"

The lower or upper octave equivalent of a tone (al Kindī 1969:44, 74).

TASHQĪQ (sh-q-q) "cutting in two"

An embellishment technique, one of the forms of TAMZĪJ/5*, which is executed by placing the finger across two strings at the same distance from the nut of a lute (ʿŪD/2*) and then plucking the two strings together. It can be done with or without an additional embellishing trill between the two main tones and third tone produced by a second finger. Ibn Sīnā adds that the embellishment is more beautiful without this additional trill (Ibn Sīnā 1930:98). See chart under TAḤSĪN AL LAḤN*.

TASHYĪʿAH

A refrain section contained in every movement of the NAWBAH/1* or suite, according to a 15th C. theorist. It could also be found in the genre of that time known as BASĪṬ/4* (Anonymous Treatise 1939:235-236).

TASHYĪD (?)

Syn. of NASHĪD/3* (d'Erlanger 1935:85). The al Fārābī passage (1967:1162) has NASHĪD.

TASJĪʿ (s-j-ʿ) "rhyming"

Poetic rhyme, see SAJʿ*.

TASJĪL (s-j-l) "recording"

Musical notation, the act or the product (Shawqī 1969:68).

T'ÂSKÎRÂT (?) perhaps a var. of TADHKĪRAH (pl. TADHKĪRĀT) (dh-k-r)

Orchestral embellishments or variations in which the lutes multiply the strokes of the plectrum in order to fill the duration (Mor.) (Chottin 1939:147). See RUBĀʿAH* or RUBĀʿĪ*.

TASLĪM (pl. TASLĪMĀT) = TASLŪM, TASLOUM (s-l-m) "presentation, greeting"

1. The refrain section of a BASHRAF/1*, LUNGHAH*, SAMĀʿĪ/1* or other metered instrumental compositions, which is repeated after each KHĀNAH* or section of contrast. Therefore, any refrain-like instrumental segment or interlude to emphasize the division of a performance (Maḥfūẓ 1964:69-70).
2. The concluding cadential passage of a musical segment or a song. It usually comprises a descending vocal passage leading back to the tonic of the principal melodic mode of the performance (Jargy 1971:92; Touma 1977b:72). See TAḤRĪR*.

TASLOUM

Var. of TASLĪM/2* (Touma 1977b:72).

TASLŪM (s-l-m)

Syn. of TASLĪM* (Ḥāfiẓ 1971:166).

TASMĪṬ (s-m-ṭ) "stringing of pearls"

Poetic refrain recurrence was a characteristic of this genre of strophic poetry developed early in the Islamic period. Strophes could be composed of from three to ten lines each. Therefore there were eight types of TASMĪṬ poetry, depending on the size of the strophe (e.g., MUTHALLATH/3*, 3 lined; MURABBAʿ/4*, 4 lined; etc.) (Weil 1913:I, 474). Syn. of MUSAMMAṬ/2*.

TAṢWĪR (ṣ-w-r) "painting, figurizing"

Transposition of a modal scale to a new tonic. Usually such transpositions move up or down a perfect fourth or fifth (d'Erlanger 1949:109-110; al Khulaʿī 1904:38, n. 2; Al Ḥalqah 1964:18). See also syn. QALB AL ʿIYĀN*.

TAṢWĪT (ṣ-w-t) "production of artificial sounds"

Production of musical sounds, especially instrumental sounds (Ikhwān al Ṣafā' 1957:I, 192; Shiloah 1964/65:137, n. 47).

TASWIYAH (s-w-y) "equalizing"

1. Tuning of a musical instrument.
2. The accordature or tuning pattern of a stringed instrument (al Kindī 1965:7; al Fārābī 1967:597, 608-618).

TASWIYAH AL ĀLAH (s-w-y) ('-w-l) "perfecting or equalizing the instrument"

Tuning the strings of a musical instrument (Maḥfūẓ 1964:151).

TASWIYAH AL MURAKKABAH (s-w-y) (r-k-b) "constructed equalizing or perfecting"

A tuning or accordature in which both strings of a ṬUNBŪR/1* are tuned to the same pitch (al Fārābī 1967:724).

TASWIYAH AL MUZĀWAJ (s-w-y) (z-w-j) "equalizing of the reciprocally joined pair"

A tuning or accord in which both strings of a ṬUNBŪR* are tuned to the same pitch (al Fārābī 1967:724).

TASWIYAH AL ʿUẒMĀ (s-w-y) (ʿ-ẓ-m) "greater equalizing or perfecting"

The tuning of the strings of the lute (ʿŪD*) in fourths as described by al Kindī (1965:16; Yūsuf 1965:7).

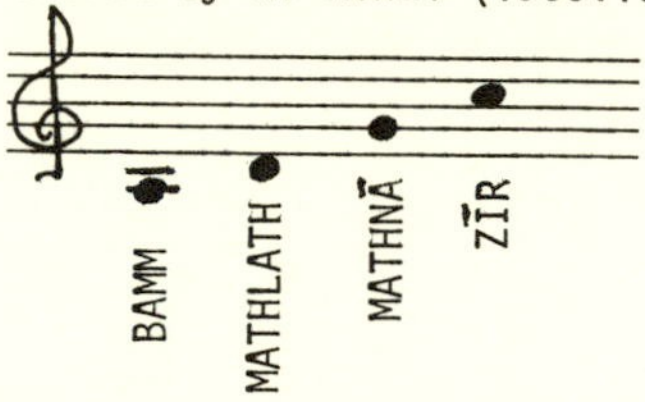

TAṬARRUB (ṭ-r-b) "making oneself pleased and moved with sound"

To sing (al Zabīdī 1965:I, 354).

TA'THĪR ('-th-r) "influence"

The elaborate theory linking the various strings of the lute, the melodic and rhythmic modes, and musical sounds with the humors, the elements, the seasons, the winds, the planets, the zodiac, the colors, etc. (al Kindī in Berlin ms. 5530, fol. 30; see Farmer 1943:4-9; 1967:109-110). This was similar to the "ethos" doctrine of the Greeks.

TATHQĪL (th-q-l) "slowing"

Slowing the tempo (al Fārābī 1967:1177).

TATIMMAH (t-m-m) "complement; conclusion"

The double limma or minor tone of 10/9 ratio (al Jurjānī 1938:238).

TAṬRĪB (ṭ-r-b) "pleasing or moving the listener through music"

1. Singing.

2. Performing music with prolongation and improvement of the sound (al Zabīdī 1965:I, 354), therefore, to perform beautifully and effectively, whether vocally or instrumentally.
3. The performance of Qur'ānic chant, according to Farmer 1952: 64; 1954, "Mohammedan Music":V, 817. There is no bibliographical material accompanying this claim to indicate the geographic location or the time for this use of the term. It seems very unlikely, however, that this term with its "baggage" of secular ideas could ever have been attributed to Qur'ānic chant. See def. 4 below.
4. A prohibited Qur'ānic cantillation practice involving the improper use of the long and short vowels (al Suyūṭī 1941:I, 175).

TAṬWĪLAH

The long, sustained notes played by the KAMĀNJAH* or bowed instruments which are used in the TABRĪD* style of accompaniment for vocal melodies performed as part of the NAWBAH/1* or suite (Mor.) (Chottin 1939:147).

TAÛÇIL

Var. of TAWṢĪL/1* (Chottin 1939:66).

TAUQĪʿ

Var. of TAWQĪʿ/1* (Cowl 1966:150).

TAUŠIYA

Var. of TAWSHIYAH or TŪSHIYAH* (Perkuhn 1976:107).

TAWĀFUQ (w-f-q) "mutual agreement"

Harmony (al Ḥafnī 1946:286).

TAWĀṢUL (w-ṣ-l) "mutual connection or joining"

A durational embellishment involving the FĀṢILAH/4* or separating space between the cycles. According to Ibn Sīnā, it was of two kinds:

1) TAQAṢṢUR: Elimination of the FĀṢILAH between cycles of the rhythmic mode;
2) TAWĀṢUL : Lengthening of the FĀṢILAH between cycles (Ibn Sīnā 1930:99).

See chart under TAḤSĪN AL LAḤN*.

TAWCHÎH'

Var. of TAWSHĪḤ* (Chottin 1939).

TAWḌĪḤ AL ḌARB (w-ḍ-ḥ) (ḍ-r-b) "clarification of rhythm"

A type of LĀZIMAH* instrumental interlude that comprises repetition of the DUMŪM (s. DUM*) and TAKŪK (s. TAK*) strokes of the ĪQĀʿ/1* (el Helou 1961:180).

ṬAWQ (pl. AṬWĀQ) (ṭ-w-q) "ability; power; collar, necklace"

1. A first coda (of two) of the MUṢADDAR/1*, the ternary rhythmed orchestral overture of the Tunisian NAWBAH/1* (d'Erlanger 1959: 192). Also called ḌURŪB/2*. KHURŪJ/1* is the name for the coda(s) part of this number.
2. The wooden collar around the neck of the short necked lute (ʿŪD*) (Maḥfūẓ 1964:42).
3. A mouthpiece for a woodwind instrument and including the blowing reed (Farmer EI(Eng), "Mizmār":540).

TAWQĪʿ (w-q-ʿ) "dropping; execution"

Playing or performing on a musical instrument, i.e., musical performance (al Kindī 1966:150; al Rizqī 1967:62). In Maḥfūẓ, the term is limited to performance on any of the stringed instruments (Maḥfūẓ 1964:155).

TAWQĪʿĪ (w-q-ʿ) "rhythmic"

Rhythmic (al Kindī 1966:150).

ṬAWR (ṭ-w-r) "condition, limit, phase"

Syn. of ṬAWR al MAQĀM*.

ṬAWR AL MAQĀM (ṭ-w-r) (q-w-m) "limit of the MAQĀM"

The order of AJNĀS (s. JINS/1*) exposition, the melodic progression characteristics, and possible modulations which determine the use of tones of the scale in any melodic mode (MAQĀM/1*) (d'Erlanger 1949:100; al Dāqūqī 1965:65).

ṬAWR AL NAGHMAH (ṭ-w-r) (n-gh-m) "path of the tune or note"

Syn. of ṬAWR AL MAQĀM* (d'Erlanger 1949:99-100).

TAWSHĪḤ (pl. TAWĀSHĪḤ) (w-sh-ḥ) "act of adorning something"

1. Syn. of MUWASHSHAḤ/1* and MUWASHSHAḤ/2*. According to Chottin, this term is a "new" name for the genre of strophic-refrain poetry and the musical setting of it (Chottin 1939:101). Actually, the term has been used since the 16th C. and probably even earlier (al Lādhiqī 1939:432; see also d'Erlanger 1939:520-521, n. 42).
2. A musical style described as metric, precomposed and sung by a soloist in alternation with a chorus, as opposed to QAṢĪDAH/3* style (Racy 1979:21).

TAWSHĪḤ ḌARBAYN (w-sh-ḥ) (ḍ-r-b) "TAWSHĪḤ of two strikes"

A variety of MUWASHSHAḤ/1* which is based on a combination of two rhythmic modes (s. ḌARB/2*). This may comprise a combination of the two cycles to form a new mode; or perhaps the two rhythms alternate with each other, first a series of cycles of one, then a change to several cycles of the second, and so on until the end of the piece (d'Erlanger 1959:174-175).

TAWSHĪḤ KIĀR (w-sh-ḥ) (Turk.) "work of art TAWSHĪḤ"

A variety of MUWASHSHAḤ/1* which begins with an improvised vocalise utilizing nonsense or stock words and phrases. Sometimes these expressions are organized to conform to the poetic meter of the lyrics being sung. This variety of MUWASHSHAḤ is generally very long and difficult to sing. In Tunisia it is also known as SHUGHL/1* (d'Erlanger 1959:176-177).

TAWSHĪḤ MA'LŪF (w-sh-ḥ) ('-l-f) "popular TAWSHĪḤ"

A popular type of MUWASHSHAḤ/1* characterized by short rhythmic periods which can be transcribed in simple binary or ternary measures. It is based on a single melodic mode with possible modulations to related modes (d'Erlanger 1959:173-174).

TAWSHĪḤ NAQSH (w-sh-ḥ) (n-q-sh) "chiseled, decorated TAWSHĪḤ"

A variety of MUWASHSHAḤ/1* composed on several different rhythmic cycles which have been combined to form a new longer cycle or are used successively in the performance of the number. In the latter case, each rhythmic mode is represented by a repetition of two or more cycles (d'Erlanger 1959:175).

TAWSHĪḤ NĀṬIQ (w-sh-ḥ) (n-ṭ-q) "speaking TAWSHĪḤ"

A variety of MUWASHSHAḤ/1* which, while beginning and ending in the principal melodic mode, makes use of a series of different modes. The name of each mode is mentioned in the words of that portion of the performance which utilizes it. If more than one rhythmic mode is used, the names of these are also cited in the lyrics of the corresponding rhythmic phases (d'Erlanger 1959: 177-178).

TAWSHĪḤ ZANJĪR (w-sh-ḥ) (Turk.) "chain TAWSHĪḤ"

A variety of MUWASHSHAḤ/1* for which the rhythm constitutes a combination of five, or occasionally six, different rhythmic cycles. The rhythmic modes are arranged consecutively from longest to shortest (d'Erlanger 1959:175-176).

TAWSHĪḤAH (w-sh-ḥ) "act of adorning"

1. Syn. of TAWSHIYAH or TŪSHIYAH/1* (Farmer 1933b:11, 24).
2. Syn. of TAWSHIYAH or TŪSHIYAH/2* (Delphin and Guin 1886:64).

TAWSHIYAH or TŪSHIYAH = TOUCHIA, TOUCHYAH, TAUŠIYA, TOUCHIAT, TŪSHIAH, TŪSHĪYA (w-sh-y) "embellishment; embroidery"

1. A measured orchestral overture of the Maghribī NAWBAH/1*. In Algeria it has a binary rhythm and rather slow tempo, according to d'Erlanger (1959:190). Others describe it as having a medium tempo with an acceleration near the end, before concluding in a slower manner, on the tonic (QARĀR/1*) (Ḥāfiẓ 1971:124). Some writers say that it is performed on a ternary rhythm of moderate

tempo (Mor.) (d'Erlanger 1959:189); others describe the Moroccan version of this number as having a binary rhythm (el Mahdi 1972:11). It can be used to begin any of the five movement of the NAWBAH. Sometimes there are more than one of these short introductory pieces to begin a performance. It is performed in unison.
2. A prelude for solo violin or RABĀB/2* used in the NAWBAH/1* which emphasizes the principal motifs of the melodic motifs of the melodic mode to be used (Alg.) (Delphin and Guin 1886:64).
3. In the Tunisian NAWBAH/1*, an orchestral intermezzo which is combined with an improvised, unmetered solo on RABĀB/2* or ʿŪD/2* known as MASHADD*. A lute MASHADD or TAWSHIYAH is sometimes underlaid with a duple rhythm (MĪZĀN AL MASHADD*) (Ḥāfiẓ 1971:120).

TAWSHIYAH AL INṢIRĀFĀT (w-sh-y) (ṣ-r-f) "adornment of the departures"

A rapid solo instrumental intermezzo of ternary rhythm used in the Maghribī NAWBAH/1* (d'Erlanger 1959:191; Ḥāfiẓ 1971:126). In Tunisia, this portion of the suite opens with an improvised, non-rhythmed solo executed by a bowed string instrument (RABĀB/2*) and closes with a similar solo. It is performed to give the singers a period of rest between series of vocal numbers. See TAWSHIYAH/3*.

TAWṢĪL (pl. TAWṢĪLĀT) (w-ṣ-l) "liason"

1. A tonal embellishment which involves gliding on the strings of an instrument from one finger position to another higher or lower position (glissando) (Ibn Sīnā 1930:98; 1935:231). See chart under TAḤSĪN AL LAḤN*.
2. One of the four kinds of TAGHYĪR/2* ("alteration") used to create new rhythmic modes, as described by al Fārābī (1967:1012-1013; 1935:36-37). This variety is without additional percussions from outside the original cycle (GHAYR ZIYĀDAH NAQRĀT*). It involves combining two or more cycles of the original mode to form a single new one. Also known as TAWṢĪL AL MUFAṢṢAL*. See also TAFṢĪL AL MUWAṢṢAL*, TAKRĪR/2*, TARKĪB/2*.

TAWṢĪL AL MUFAṢṢAL (w-ṣ-l) (f-ṣ-l) "liason of the separated"

Syn. of TAWṢĪL/2* (al Fārābī 1967:1012-1013).

TA'WWADIT (ʿ-w-d)

Colloq. var. of ʿAWWĀDAH/3*, the end-blown flute of the Moroccan Berbers (Chottin 1939:20).

TAWZĪʿ (w-z-ʿ) "distribution; division, allotment"

Orchestration, i.e., the division for the sake of performance of the melody in homophonic music between the various instruments. This TAWZĪʿ involves the assignment of segments of solo performance to the various instruments as well as the determination of which segments will be done in ensemble.

TAWZĪN (w-z-n) "weighing"

The art of fitting words and music rhythmically (al Rajab 1967: 22, n. 5).

ṬAY

Var. of ṬAYY* (al Ḥafnī 1930:53).

ṬAYY = ṬAY, ṬAI, (ṭ-w-y) "folding up together; hiding"

A durational embellishment which involves eliminating one or more percussions of a cycle but maintaining the same number of beats, i.e., the overall duration (Ibn Sīnā 1930:99). If the elimination takes place at the beginning of the cycle, it is known as JAZM*. ṬAYY is the opp. of TAḌʿĪF/2*, which involves addition rather than elimination of percussions (al Rajab 1967:23).

TĀZĪ

The generally accepted tessitura of a melodic mode, e.g., the tessitura of the RĀST MAQĀM (see RĀST/2*), or C_1 to C_2, was called TĀZĪ RĀST, according to the 14th C. theorist, Shams al Dīn ibn al Afkānī (Shiloah 1968a:237, 244).

TAZYĪDAH (pl. TAZYĪDĀT) (z-y-d) "addition"

A musical ornament or embellishment (al Fārābī 1967:965).

TAZYĪNAH (pl. TAZYĪNĀT) (z-y-n) "improvement"

Ornamentation or embellishment of the melody by addition of extra notes (al Fārābī 1967:965, 1060; 1935:51).

TBÂ'

Var. of ṬABʿ* (Chottin 1939:122).

TBAL or TBEL

Vars. of ṬABL/2* (Grame 1970:79; Chottin 1939:166, resp.).

TBÎLÂT

Pl. Var. of ṬABĪLAH*. It is used by Chottin to designate a pair of small drums made of pottery and having a single membrane. They are generally played by women and used in the folk music of Morocco (Chottin 1939:141, illus. on Planche XVII).

TÇDÎRA

Var. of TAṢDĪRAH/2* (Chottin 1939:112, 126).

TCHENBAR or TCHENEBAR

Vars. of SHANBAR or SHANBĀR*, the overture of the NAWBAH INQILĀBĀT* According to Maqrīzī (1364-1442) such a term was used in the Maghrib for an orchestral number with duple rhythm, of Persian or Turkish origin (Farmer 1976a:194; Rouanet 1922:2863).

T'EBEL

Var. of ṬABL/2* (Delphin and Guin 1886:37).

T'EBILA

Var. of ṬABĪLAH* (Delphin and Guin 1886:38).

TEBRID

Var. of TABRĪD* (Chottin 1939:113, 147).

TEK

Var. of TAK* (Chottin 1957:I, 41).

TEMUÎLA

Var. of TAMWĪLAH* (Chottin 1939:160).

TER'ÎDA

Var. of TARʿĪDAH* (Chottin 1939:147).

TERRÂR

Var. of ṬARRĀR* (Chottin 1939:147).

TETUÎLA

Var. of TAṬWĪLAH* (Chottin 1939:147).

THĀBIT (th-b-t) "something which stands firm"

1. Any of the fixed tones of a scale, i.e., the starting tone, the fourth, the fifth, the octave (Ṣafī al Dīn as described by Wright 1978:97).
2. The dominant (in the Western music sense) of a scale (Maḥfūẓ 1964:185).

THĀBIT AL ṢAWT (th-b-t) (ṣ-w-t) "fixed of sound"

Said of any instrument whose intervals cannot be altered in pitch (e.g., the organ) (Kāẓim 1964:36).

THABL

Var. of ṬABL* (Kieswetter 1968:93).

THĀLITH (th-l-th) "third"

Syn. of MATHLATH* (Ibn Salamah 1938a:31, 34; 1938b:242, 244).

THĀNĪ (th-n-y) "second"

Syn. of MATHNĀ* (Ibn Salamah 1938a:12, 14, 34).

THĀNIYAH AL ZĀ'IDAH (th-n-y) (z-y-d) "the increased second"

The augmented second interval (Ḥāfiẓ 1971:185).

THANIYYAH = TNIA (th-n-y) "a bend"

An embellishing musical passage played at a high pitch level by the KAMĀNJAH/2* (Chottin 1939:147). It is also known as DASSAH* or JUMLAH/1*.

THAQB or THUQB (pl. THUQŪB, ATHQĀB) (th-q-b) "hole, opening"

Any opening in the woodwind instrument, an expression sometimes used for finger or thumb hole, sometimes for the end openings of the instrument as well (al Fārābī 1967:787). For Maḥfūẓ (1964:163), it is only those openings which can be designated as finger holes for altering the pitch of the tone.

THAQĪL (th-q-l) "heavy"

1. Slow in tempo.
2. Slowest of the conjunct (MUWAṢṢAL*) rhythmic modes of the Classical Period.
3. One of three categories of rhythmic modes, according to Kāẓim (1964:25). This one contains all the slow modes. See also KHAFĪF AL THĀNĪ/2*, KHAFĪF AL AWWAL*, the other two categories.

THAQĪL AL AWWAL (th-q-l) ('-w-l) "first heavy"

1. One of the "Famous Rhythmic Modes" (ĪQĀʿĀT AL ʿARABIYYAH AL MASHHŪRAH*). It was described by Classical Period theorists as having three long percussions, sometimes equal in duration, but more often the third one being longer than the other two (e.g., 4 beat - 4 beat - 8 beat cycle in al Fārābī 1967:1045ff).
2. One of the four basic time units described by the Ikhwān al Ṣafā' (1957:I, 200; also see Shiloah 1964/65:146). Syn. of ʿAMŪD AL THĀLITH*, which has been notated as "O.." (Shiloah 1964/65:146).

THAQĪL AL HAZAJ (th-q-l) (h-z-j) "slow HAZAJ"

A sequence of equal percussions performed at a tempo which allows of three extra beats between any two percussions (al Fārābī 1967: 452) in order to produce a rhythmic mode.

THAQĪL AL RAMAL (th-q-l) (r-m-l) "slow RAMAL"

Syn. of RAMAL/1*, one of the "Famous Arabian Rhythmic Modes" (ĪQĀʿĀT AL ʿARABIYYAH AL MASHHŪRAH*) of the Classical Period. According to theorists of the 13th to 15th C., it was also called ḌARB AL AṢL/2* (Ṣafī al Dīn and al Jurjānī in d'Erlanger 1938:499; *Anonymous Treatise* 1939:196-199).

THAQĪL AL THĀNĪ (th-q-l) (th-n-y) "second heavy"

1. One of the "Famous Arabian Rhythmic Modes" (ĪQĀʿĀT AL ʿARABIYYAH AL MASHHŪRAH*) described by Classical Period theorists. According to al Fārābī, it had three slow percussions, each one of one of progressively longer duration (4 - 6 - 8) (al Fārābī 1967:1038-1041); but the name was used by other theorists to designate other slow meters.
2. One of the four basic time units described by the Ikhwān al Ṣafā' (1957:I, 200, also see Shiloah 1964/65:146). Syn. of ʿAMŪD AL RĀBIʿ* which has been notated as "0..." (Shiloah 1964/65: 146, n. 89).

THAQĪLAH AL MAFRŪḌĀT (th-q-l) (f-r-ḍ) "lowest of the necessary"

The lowest tone in the two octave scalar collection of tones. It was considered one of the three unchangeable tones (NAGHAM AL RĀTIBAH*) within the collection (JAMʿ/1*) (al Fārābī 1967:372).

THIQL (pl. ATHQĀL) (th-q-l) "heaviness"

1. Slowness of tempo.
2. Lowness of pitch.

THULĀTHIYYAH AL ASNĀN (th-l-th) (s-n-n) "with three teeth or prongs"

Demisemiquaver (𝅘𝅥𝅰) (el Helou 1961:20).

THUNĀ'IYYAH (th-n-y) "dualism"

A duet or duo (Madina).

THUNĀ'IYYAH AL ASNĀN (th-n-y) (s-n-n) "with two teeth or prongs"

Semiquaver (𝅘𝅥𝅯) (el Helou 1961:20).

THUQB (th-q-b)

Equiv. of THAQB*.

TIDINIT

A lute of Mauritania, which women are excluded from playing (Grame 1972:26). It has a shallow, oblong body, lambskin belly and four strings. The neck is surmounted by a metal plaque with copper rings. Normally plucked, this instrument is also sometimes bowed (Marcuse).

TIK (pl. TIKĀT) (onom.)

1. Syn. of TAK*, the light percussion stroke (Massignon 1913:765).
2. Syn. of TĪK* (Ṣalāḥ al Dīn 1950:91; Ḥāfiẓ 1971:180; Touma 1977b:36-37).

TĪK (pl. TĪKĀT) (Pers.) "elevated, raised; larger (according to Ṣafī al Dīn)"

A prefix used in naming notes in contemporary practice which indicates that the tone is one ARABAH/1* above the note mentioned, e.g., TĪK ḤIJĀZ 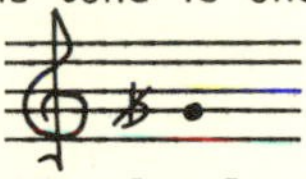 is one ARABAH above ḤIJĀZ 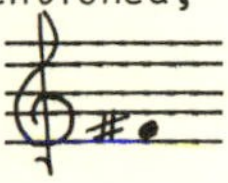 (al Khulaʿī 1904:35; el Helou 1961:69). See also NĪM/1*.

TĪK ʿARABAH (Pers.) (ʿ-r-b) "elevated vehicle"

1. The note ¼ tone below any note of the fundamental scale of the Arabs (Ṣalāḥ al Dīn 1950:89; Collangettes 1904:414).
2. The 3/4 tone interval (Farmer EI(Fr), "Mūsīkī":805).

TĪK BŪSALĪK (Pers.) "raised BŪSALĪK"

Name for a note of the contemporary Arab scale, E𝄲$_1$ or F𝄳$_1$  .

TĪK ḤIJĀZ (Pers.) (ḥ-j-z) "raised ḤIJĀZ"

Name for a note of the contemporary Arab scale, G𝄳$_2$  .

TĪK ḤIṢĀR (Pers.) (ḥ-ṣ-r) "raised ḤIṢĀR"

Name for a note of the contemporary Arab scale, A𝄳$_2$  .

TĪK ḤUSAYNĪ SHADD (Pers.) (ḥ-s-n) (sh-d-d) "raised, pulled ḤUSAYNĪ"

Name for a note of the contemporary Arab scale, E𝄲$_2$ or F𝄳$_2$ 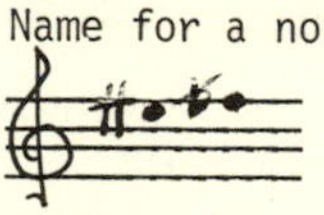

TĪK KAWASHT (Pers.) (Pers.) "raised KAWASHT"

Name for a note of the contemporary Arab scale, B𝄲$_1$ or C𝄳$_1$  .

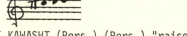

TĪK NUHUFT (Pers.) (Pers.) "raised NUHUFT"

Name for a note of the contemporary Arab scale, B𝄲$_2$ or C𝄳$_2$

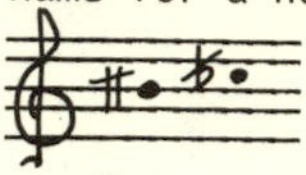 .

TĪK ZĪRKŪLAH (Pers.) (Pers.) "raised ZĪRKŪLAH"

Name for a note of the contemporary Arab scale, D𝄳$_1$  .

TILĀWAH (t-l-w) "recitation"

Qur'ānic cantillation.

ṬINBĀL

A drum used by Muslim bands at the time of the Crusades (Farmer 1929a:8).

ṬINBĀR

Var. of ṬUNBŪR* (Farmer EI(Fr), "Ṭunbūr":269).

TIQERQAWIN

Syn. of QARQABĀT* or QARĀQIB* (Grame 1970:79).

TIRBĀL

Large drum in Northwest Africa.

TIRR

Var. of ṬĀR* found in an 18th C. ms. of Morocco (Farmer EI(Fr), "Duff":79).

TIRYĀL

Tambourine with cymbals in the frame (Hickmann 1947:21). It was used in late ʿAbbāsī times (Farmer 1967:211).

TĪZ (Pers.) "high in pitch"

1. High in pitch.
2. Fast.
3. The higher of two tones, and also the upper octave equivalent (Kāẓim 1964:34; al Khulaʿī 1904:46). Also DĪK* (Kāẓim 1964:34).

TNIA

Var. of THANIYYAH* (Chottin 1939:147).

TOBOL

Var. of ṬABL/3* in Mauretania (Marcuse).

TÔM

Lyre of Egypt (Hickmann 1958:70).

TOMBUR

Var. of ṬUNBŪR* (Ribera 1970:44).

TOUCHIA

Var. of TAWSHIYAH OR TŪSHIYAH* (Delphin and Guin 1886:64).

TOUCHIAT

Var. of TAWSHIYAH OR TŪSHIYAH* (Farmer 1976a:194-195; Rouanet 1922: 2848-2852).

TOUCHIYA

Var. of TAWSHIYAH OR TŪSHIYAH* (Touma 1977b:78).

TOUCHYAH

Var. of TAWSHIYAH OR TŪSHIYAH* (el Mahdi 1972:11-12, 14).

TOUNBOUR

Var. of ṬUNBŪR* (Chottin 1939:68).

TOÛZAH

A double headed cylindrical drum used in folk music of the Sūdān (Hickmann 1958:49, illus. p. 50).

TRHOTIA or TRHOTIYA

Vars. of TAGHṬIYAH* (Chottin 1939:131, 136).

TRÎQ

Var. of ṬARĪQ* (Chottin 1939:149).

TSHAMBAR

A special rhythmic mode which was formerly performed in Tunisia as rhythmic underlay of the SHANBAR or SHANBĀR* instrumental overture (d'Erlanger 1959:200), thus a var. of SHANBAR or SHANBĀR.

TUBAILE

Var. of ṬUBAYLAH* (Marcuse).

TŪBAL

Unidentified Sūdānī folk drum (Hickmann 1958:49).

ṬŪBAL IBN LAMAK = YŪBĀL IBN LAMAK

ṬŪBAL, son of LAMAK*, and traditionally regarded as inventor of the drum (ṬABL*) and tambourine (DAFF*) (al Mas'ūdī 1874:VIII, 89; Ibn Khurdādhbih 1969:14; Collangettes 1904:369).

ṬUBAYLAH (pl. ṬUBAYLĀT) = TUBAILE (ṭ-b-l) "a small drum"

A small kettledrum of the 18th C. Maghrib. It was made of a metal shell about 14 cm. in diameter (Farmer 1954, "Maghribi Music": V, 506).

TUBBEL (probably a var. of ṬABL)

Word occasionally used for drum by the Tuareg (Marcuse).

ṬUBŪ' (ṭ-b-')

Pl. of ṬAB'*.

TÛCHÎA

Var. of TAWSHIYAH OR TŪSHIYAH* (Chottin 1939:126).

TUDHRĪ or TUDRĪ (dh-r-w) (?) perhaps der. from DHARWAH, "summit"

A high trill on the final vowels of a vocal number. This embellishment was mentioned by the Arab poets of the pre-Islamic period (Farmer 1957:424; 1967:14).

TUḤFAH AL 'ŪD (t-ḥ-f) ('-w-d) "gift of the 'ŪD; best of the 'ŪD"

A half-sized, short necked lute, according to 'Abd al Qādir ibn Ghaybī (d. 1435) (Farmer EI(Eng), "'Ūd":987).

TUM

Var. of DUM* or DUMM* (Massignon 1913:VIII, 765).

TUMBAK

Variety of drum of pre-Islamic times (Farmer 1957:426).

TUMBUL

Tuareg word for drum (Marcuse).

ṬUNBŪR (pl. ṬANĀBĪR) = TUNBŪR, TOUNBOUR, ṬANBŪR, ṬINBĀR (ṭ-n-b-r)

1. A fretted, long necked stringed instrument (lute) whose metal strings are played with a plectrum. It has been known as an instrument with a smaller body than the 'ŪD/2*. It is strung with a variable number of thin metal strings. A two-string instrument of this type and name existed in 'Irāq at least as early as the 7th C. (Ibn 'Abd Rabbihi 1887:III, 181), and is traditionally

thought to have been invented much earlier by the people of Sodom and Gomorrah (Ibn Khurdādhbih 1969:14; al Masʿūdī 1874:VIII, 89). In the 10th C. two types of ṬUNBŪR were known and described: the ṬUNBŪR MĪZĀNĪ* or ṬUNBŪR BAGHDĀDĪ*; and the ṬUNBŪR KHURĀSĀNĪ*. The former type was used in ʿIrāq and southward and westward, while the latter was known in Khurāsān and northward and eastward. Normally both instruments had two strings, but sometimes the ṬUNBŪR KHURĀSĀNĪ had three.

A comparable contemporary instrument in the Mashriq is the BUZUQ* (al Ḥafnī 1971:83); in the Maghrib, the GUNBRĪ* or QUNBURĪ*. According to al Ḥafnī, the ṬANĀBĪR used by contemporary Arabs are of two kinds: a larger instrument known as ṬUNBŪR AL TURKĪ*, which that author equates with the ṬUNBŪR AL KHURĀSĀNĪ described by Classical Period theorists and a smaller instrument commonly known as BUZUQ* or ṬUNBŪR AL SHARQĪ*. Al Ḥafnī equates the second of these two types with the ṬUNBŪR AL BAGHDĀDĪ of the Classical Period (al Ḥafnī 1971:83). The ṬUNBŪR AL TURKĪ generally has four strings, the first and third tuned to C_2, the second to G_2 and the fourth to C_1 (al Ḥafnī 1971:81-85). The BUZUQ has two or three strings pitched an octave higher than those of the ṬUNBŪR AL TURKĪ. See also al Fārābī 1967 629ff; 1930:218ff; al Jurjānī 1938:363ff).
2. A variety of harp (Madina). Claiming that it is a lyre, Marcuse equates the ṬUNBŪR with SIMSIMIYAH*(i.e., SIMSIMIYYAH*).
3. A drum (Madina).

ṬUNBŪR AL BAGHDĀDĪ = TANBOUR BAR'DĀDI (ṭ-n-b-r) (geog.) "Baghdād ṬUNBŪR"

A long necked lute used in ʿIrāq and in the countries to the south and west in the Classical Period (al Fārābī 1967:630; al Jurjānī 1938:366). It was also known as ṬUNBŪR AL MĪZĀNĪ* (al Khwārizmī 1968:237). According to al Fārābī, its frets and tuning needed revision in order to increase its range and the performance of more consonant AJNĀS (al Fārābī 1967:696-698).

ṬUNBŪR BAGHLAMAH (ṭ-n-b-r)(Turk.) "tied ṬUNBŪR" (in Farmer, "young man's ṬUNBŪR" ?)

A small, long necked lute which was mentioned by Villoteau (Egypt of the early 19th C.) (Kieswetter 1968:91; Farmer 1929a:144). It had a pear-shaped body and three metal strings. It was smaller than the ṬUNBŪR BUZURK*. The name is said to have been given to this instrument by the Greeks of Cairo.

ṬUNBŪR BUZURK (ṭ-n-b-r) (Pers.) "large ṬUNBŪR"

A large, long necked lute mentioned by Villoteau (Egypt of the early 19th C.) (Rouanet 1922:2711; Farmer 1929a:144, EI(Fr), "Ṭunbūr": 270; 1945:29). It had three metal strings.

ṬUNBŪR KABĪR TURKĪ (ṭ-n-b-r) (k-b-r) (geog.) "large Turkish ṬUNBŪR"

A large, long necked lute with round sound chest and four double strings (Farmer EI(Fr), "Ṭunbūr":270).

ṬUNBŪR KHURĀSĀNĪ (ṭ-n-b-r) (geog.) Khurāsānī ṬUNBŪR"

A long necked lute used in Khurāsān and the countries to the north and east during the Classical Period (al Fārābī 1967:630; al Jurjānī 1938:366). It shape, length and size varied from country to country, though it was consistently larger than the ṬUNBŪR BAGHDĀDĪ*. It had two strings of equal thickness which were attached to a button (ZABĪBAH*) on the base of the instrument, after which they passed over the notched bridge and the nut and were twisted around the two tuning pegs. Some of the fret positions for this instrument were common to all such instruments: others varied from country to country (al Fārābī 1967:698-699). Its two strings were tuned according to various systems (Ibid.: 724; 1930:250), but the lower string was usually one whole tone below the higher (Ibid.:731). This instrument is said to have been comparable to the ṬUNBŪR AL TURKĪ* (al Ḥafnī 1971:83) and also to the ṬUNBŪR BUZURK* and ṬUNBŪR AL SHARQĪ* (Ibid.:698, n. 1).

ṬUNBŪR MĪRĀTHĪ (ṭ-n-b-r) (w-r-th) "hereditary ṬUNBŪR"

A long necked lute mentioned in some manuscripts of al Fārābī's Kitāb al Mūsīqā al Kabīr, the precise definition of which is not known (see d'Erlagner 1930:312; al Fārābī 1967:120, n. 2). Farmer thinks the name may result from a misreading or miscopying of ṬUNBŪR MĪZĀNĪ* (Farmer 1978:II, 34-35).

ṬUNBŪR MĪZĀNĪ (ṭ-n-b-r) (w-z-n) "measured ṬUNBŪR"

This seems to have been an early name for the ṬUNBŪR AL BAGHDĀDĪ* (al Khwārizmī 1968:237). The length of its two strings was divided theoretically into 40 equal parts. The first five of these, approximating a series of unequal quarter tones were the only ones used in performance. The second string was tuned to the second fret of the first string, that is, less than a semitone higher, giving the range of the instrument no more than a minor third if only the mentioned frets were used. This limited tuning was already considered obsolete by the 10th C. (al Fārābī 1967: 631-697).

ṬUNBŪR AL SHARQĪ (ṭ-n-b-r) (sh-r-q) "eastern ṬUNBŪR"

A contemporary instrument of the long necked lute variety which is said to be comparable to the Classical Period ṬUNBŪR AL KHURĀSĀNĪ* (al Ḥafnī 1971:83).

ṬUNBŪR AL TURKĪ (ṭ-n-b-r) (geog.) "Turkish ṬUNBŪR"

The largest long necked lute of the contemporary Arabs. It has a round body and is usually fitted with four strings (or eight tuned in pairs). The first and third strings or pairs are tuned to C_2, the second to G_2 and the fourth to C_1 (al Ḥafnī 1971: 81-85). It is thought to be comparable to the ṬUNBŪR AL KHURĀSĀNĪ* of the Classical Period. See also ṬANBŪR-I TURKĪ* for a description of an earlier long necked lute with a similar name.

ṬUNBŪRAH SŪDĀNĪ (ṭ-n-b-r) (geog.) "Sudanese ṬUNBŪR"

A harp with lower sound chest which is used in contemporary Palestine and Upper Egypt. Also known as NANGAH*. See also ṬANBŪRAH*.

ṬUNBŪRĪ or ṬUNBŪRIYY (ṭ-n-b-r)

Player of the ṬUNBŪR* or long necked lute, as mentioned in a 9th C. ms. (Farmer 1965b:10, 26, 33).

TURĀTH (w-r-th) "heritage"

The heritage of Arabian music. Sometimes this refers to musical stylistic features which were common prior to the 1930's, others put the 1920's as its temporal limit. Sometimes contemporary works which are similar stylistically to the earlier works are included in this category, regardless of their date of performance or composition (el-Shawan 1978).

ṬURQAH (pl. ṬURAQ) (ṭ-r-q) "road; passageway"

1. Melodic mode (Farmer 1967:151).
2. Rhythmic mode, as well as melodic mode (Farmer 1945:44).

ṬURŪQ AL MULŪKIYYAH (ṭ-r-q) (m-l-k) "royal modes or means"

Name given to the seven melodic modes, genres or styles of performance (?) which are only cursorily described by Ibn Khurdādhbih in this address delivered for the Caliph al Muʿtamid (1951:95; in al Masʿūdī 1874:VIII, 90).

ṬŪS (ṭ-w-s) "basin"

Cymbals of the Arabian/Persian Gulf Region used to accompany folk music. Touma(1977a:124) has TUS.

TŪSHIA

Var. of TAWSHIYAH or TŪSHIYAH* (Schuyler 1978:38).

TŪSHĪYAH

Var. of TAWSHIYAH OR TŪSHIYAH* (Farmer 1933b:11, 24).

ṬUSŪT (pl. of ṬAST or ṬIST) (ṭ-s-t) "basins"

Musical glasses played with little sticks, a 15th C. instrument mentioned by ʿAbd al Qādir ibn Ghaybī (d. 1435) (Farmer EI(Fr), "Ṣandj":211; Marcuse).

ṬUWAYS (ṭ-w-s) dim. of "peacock"

Nickname for Abū ʿAbd al Munaʿʿam ʿĪsā ibn ʿAbdullah al Dhā'ib (632-710), a freedman of the Banū Makhzūm who lived in Madīnah and was brought up in the household of the mother of the third caliph, ʿUthmān. ṬUWAYS was generally considered to have been the first to sing the GHINĀ' AL MUTQAN*, the new music of his time. In addition, he is said to have been the first professional singer of Madīnah during the Islamic period (Ibn ʿAbd Rabbihi 1887: III, 26), as well as the first to use the HAZAJ* and RAMAL* rhythms (Maḥfūẓ 1964:135). He accompanied himself on a square tambourine called a DUFF (DAFF or DUFF/4*). As a homosexual, he was a social outcast, yet was highly esteemed for his musical talents by the wealthy and nobles. He had many notable students (Farmer 1967:52-53).

U

ʿŪD (pl. ʿĪDĀN, AʿWĀD) = 'OOD, OUD (ʿ-w-d) "flexible stick; branch"

1. Generic name for various types of lutes.
2. The short necked lute played with a plectrum which has been the most important musical instrument of the Arabs. LAMAK* (Lamech of Genesis IV) was generally considered to be the inventor of this instrument, although credits for it have sometimes been given to such famous Greeks as Pythagorus, Plato, Euclid and Ptolemy (Farmer EI(Eng), "ʿŪd":985). Until the end of the 6th C., the short necked lute of the Arabs was an instrument whose soundbox and neck were made of a single piece of wood faced with skin. At that time the wooden face was introduced from Al Ḥīrah in ʿIrāq into the Peninsula, perhaps giving rise to a change of name from the earlier "MIZHAR"(see MIZHAR/2*) to "ʿŪD" (al Khwārizmī 1968:238). Other early names for the short necked lute were KIRĀN* and MUWATTAR* for skin-bellied lutes, and the Persian name "BARBAṬ" (see BARBAṬ/1*) which was used for early varieties of wood-faced lutes (Ibn Salamah 1938b:241; Farmer 1978:I, 91ff). The ʿŪD with separately constructed neck was introduced by ZALZAL in 8th C. Spain. The instrument is unfretted today, and probably always was, although there are many references to the word DASĀTĪN (s. DASTĀN/1* or "fret") or ʿUTUB (s. ʿATAB or ʿATABAH/1*, "fret" or "tie"). These were probably finger positions for stopping the strings or chords tied around the neck for instruction purposes. See Farmer 1937b for another view.

The early ʿŪD or ʿŪD QADĪM* had four strings which were known as BAMM*, MATHLATH*, MATHNĀ*, and ZĪR/1*, from lowest to highest in pitch. The early tuning of these four strings was C_1, D_1, G_2 and A_2. Probably during the Umawī period, Persian influence caused the Arabs to adopt a new tuning in fourths: A_1, D_1, G_2 and C_2. ZIRYĀB* is said to have added the fifth string in 9th C. Spain, and both al Kindī (d. 874) and al Fārābī (d. 950) included it in their descriptions of this instrument (al Kindī 1966:133; 1965:inside of cover; al Fārābī 1967:592). The five-stringed instrument was known as ʿŪD KĀMIL* or "complete ʿŪD", in contrast to the ʿŪD QADĪM*, the slightly smaller instrument with four string. In the 19th C., the ʿŪD was reported by Lane (1973:362) and Mashāqah (1849:208; n.d.:fol. 10) to have had seven double strings. It had three sound holes and a bent neck. It has today, as in earlier times, a bulging wooden body with a thin wooden soundboard, a frontal stringholder, lateral tuning pegs and double stringing.

There are two types of ʿŪD used today: 1) an oriental ʿŪD known as ʿŪD SHARQĪ* or ʿŪD MIṢRĪ*, which is found all over the Arab World; and 2) a Maghribī type used only in North Africa. The ʿŪD MAGHRIBĪ* is smaller and less bulging than the oriental type, and its neck is somewhat longer. It has four double strings. Both instruments have bent necks. The ʿŪD MAGHRIBĪ is also called QUWAYṬARAH*, KWĪTRA*, etc. in Morocco and ʿŪD ʿARABĪ* in Tunisia. Names for the four double strings of the ʿŪD MAGHRIBĪ are DHAYL/1*, ḤUSAYN/1*, MĀʾIYAH/1* and RAMAL/3* (Chottin 1939:145). Al Ḥafnī describes the ʿŪD SHARQĪ as having five pairs of strings (or four pairs and a single one at the lowest pitch). These are usually tuned to G_1, A_1, D_1, G_2 amd C_2. An additional pair sometimes added is tuned to F_2 (al Ḥafnī 1971:77). The strings are usually named by contemporary theorists and musicians with the Arabic pitch names to which they are tuned, e.g., YAKĀH*, ʿUSHAYRĀN/1*, DŪKĀH/3*, NAWĀ/3*, KARDĀN/2* and JAWĀB JIHĀRKĀH*.

ʿŪD ʿARABĪ (ʿ-w-d) (ʿ-r-b) "Arabian lute"

Syn. of ʿŪD MAGHRIBĪ* (Tun.), as distinguished from the ʿŪD MASHRIQĪ* or ʿŪD MIṢRĪ* (d'Erlanger 1938:607).

ʿŪD FĀRISĪ (ʿ-w-d) (nat.) "Persian ʿŪD"

Persian lute said to have been first used for performing Arabian music in Makkah by IBN SURAYJ* (Farmer 1967:73). The "Persianness" of this instrument probably referred to its tuning in fourths instead of the older Arab system (see ʿŪD/2*). It may also have referred to its wooden, rather than skin face.

ʿŪD ʿIRĀQĪ (ʿ-w-d) (geog.) "ʿIrāqī ʿŪD"

A short necked lute mentioned in 1001 Nights and believed to have been a lute of Damascus (Farmer 1945:29-30). It was also known as ʿŪD JILLIQĪ*.

ʿŪD JILLIQĪ (ʿ-w-d) (j-l-q)

Syn. of ʿŪD ʿIRĀQĪ* (Farmer 1945:25-26), and thought to have been a lute of Damascus (Ibid.:29-30).

ʿŪD KĀMIL (ʿ-w-d) (k-m-l) "complete ʿŪD"

The five-stringed lute said to have been perfected by ZIRYĀB*. It was used in both Mashriq and Maghrib from the 9th C. with various specifications and sizes. It was the principal instrument of performance and theory for the Classical Period. By the time of al Lādhiqī (16th C.), it had six strings, all tuned at distances of a perfect fourth (al Ladhiqī 1939:422-423). It was contrasted to the ʿŪD QADĪM*, an earlier four-string instrument.

ʿŪD MAGHRIBĪ (ʿ-w-d) (gh-r-b) "western ʿŪD"

A small contemporary, short necked lute used in the Maghrib. See ʿŪD/2*. It is also known as ʿŪD ʿARABĪ* and QUWAYTARAH* (KUWĪTRA*, KŪWAYTARAH, etc.), and is contrasted with ʿŪD MASHRIQĪ*.

ʿŪD MASHRIQĪ (ʿ-w-d) (sh-r-q) "eastern ʿŪD"

The contemporary short necked lute of the Mashriq, a larger and deeper bodied instrument than the ʿŪD MAGHRIBĪ*. Also known as ʿŪD SHARQĪ* or ʿŪD MIṢRĪ*. See ʿŪD/2*.

ʿŪD MIṢRĪ (ʿ-w-d) (geog.) "Egyptian ʿŪD"

Syn. of ʿŪD MASHRIQĪ*, as distinguished from the ʿŪD MAGHRIBĪ* (d'Erlanger 1938:607). It is used all over the Arab World, but is particularly associated with the countries at the eastern end of the Mediterranean Sea.

ʿŪD QADĪM (ʿ-w-d) (q-d-m) "ancient ʿŪD"

The ancient short necked lute with four strings which was introduced early in the Islamic period to replace the earlier skin faced lutes known as KIRĀN* and MUWATTAR*. This instrument continued to be used as late as the 15th C., long after the five stringed instrument (ʿŪD KĀMIL*) had become known (Farmer 1967: 208ff). See ʿŪD/2*.

ʿŪD AL RABĀB = 'UD-ER-RBAB (ʿ-w-d) (r-b-b)

An ancient bowed lute of the Berbers with one or two strings and a skin face (Mor.) (Chottin 1939:33).

ʿŪD AL SHABBŪṬ (ʿ-w-d) (sh-b-ṭ)

A lute introduced by the court musician ZALZAL* (d. 791), which soon replaced the ʿŪD FĀRISĪ* in the second half of the 8th C. It is thought to have been an instrument in which the neck and fingerboard were constructed separately from the body. It had four strings (Farmer 1967:108; 1930:771-772). It was named after a species of fish which was slender in the tail, wide at the middle and small headed.

ʿŪD SHARQĪ (ʿ-w-d) (sh-r-q) "oriental ʿŪD"

A contemporary short necked lute used all over the Arab World but particularly associated with the MASHRIQ*. It has a bent neck, a bulging wooden body with a thin wooden soundboard, a frontal stringholder, lateral tuning pegs and double stringing. It is played with an eagle's quill or plastic facsimile. It generally has five pairs of strings, or four pairs with a single string tuned to the lowest pitch. See ʿŪD/2*.

ʿŪD TŪNISĪ (ʿ-w-d) (geog.) "Tunisian ʿŪD"

A variety of short necked lute used in the Maghrib. It is distinguished from the ʿŪD SHARQĪ* or ʿŪD MIṢRĪ* by having four rather than five pairs of strings. It is also somewhat smaller than the instrument commonly used in the Mashriq. It has a fretted neck. Its strings are tuned in different ways in different countries (el Mahdi 1972:55; Racy 1979:2).

UDHAN or UDHN (pl. ĀDHĀN) ('-dh-n) "ear"

Tuning peg of the lute, or of any other chordophone.

ʿUFFÂTAH

An end blown aerophone of modern Egypt and Morocco, which has a very wide bore, and a length of ca. 52 cm. (Hickmann 1958:29).

UGHNIYAH (pl. UGHNIYĀT, AGHĀNĪ) = OUGNIYA (gh-n-y) "song"

1. Song or tune.
2. Melodic mode.

UGHNIYAH SHAʿBIYYAH (gh-n-y) (sh-ʿ-b) "song of the people"

Folksong (Wahba 1968:68).

UGHRŪDAH (pl. AGHĀRĪD) (gh-r-d) "twittering"

Song.

UHZŪJAH (pl. AHĀZĪJ) (h-z-j) "an intonation"

Syn. of ṬAQṬŪQAH*, and a more correct name, according to Ḥāfiẓ, for that popular genre of contemporary song (Ḥāfiẓ 1971:204).

ÛJEH

Var. of WAJH* (Chottin 1939:138).

ʿULUWW AL ṢAWT (ʿ-l-w) (ṣ-w-t) "height of the sound"

Volume, intensity of sound (al Kindī 1966:154).

UMM AL ZULUF = UMM-Z-ZELUF ('-m-m) (z-l-f) "mother of ZULUF" or "mother of coming close"

Syn. of ABŪ AL ZULUF* (Jargy 1971:40).

UMM WA ḤĀSHIYAH = UM-U-H'ACHIA, UMM-U-HACHIA ('-m-m) (ḥ-sh-y) "mother and border"

1. A rhythm characterized by an alternation between strokes made at the center and at the edge of the ṬĀR/1* (frame drum of Morocco) (Chottin 1961:Band IX, col. 1564; 1939:158) or between two per-

cussion instruments.
2. A pair of drums of goblet shaped, single headed type, usually made of pottery. The drums are held vertically from their waists, the heads pointing downward. On one instrument, the UMM or "mother" drum, the DUM* or DUMM* strokes are played; the other, the ḤĀSHIYAH* or "border" drum, is used for the TAK* strokes (Chottin 1939:39-40). See TAʿRĪJAH*.

UMM-U-HACHIA

Var. of UMM WA ḤĀSHIYAH*(Chottin 1939:40).

UMM-Z-ZELUF

Var. of UMM AL ZULUF* (Jargy 1971:40).

UM-U-H'ACHIA

Var. of UMM WA ḤĀSHIYAH* (Chottin 1939:158).

ʿUMŪD

Var. of ʿAMŪD/2* (Farmer 1978:II, 63).

UNBŪB or UNBŪBAH (pl. ANĀBĪB) (n-b-b) "tube; joint of a knotted stem"

1. Generic name for woodwind instruments made of reed. They are of two kinds according to some writers: 1) with blowing reed; or 2) without reed (Kāẓim 1964:21; al Khwārizmī 1968:237).
2. The pieces of cane used to make wind instruments (Maḥfūẓ 1964: 163).
3. The tube of an aerophone, including the organ.

UNBŪB or UNBŪBAH MUTAṢAWWIT(AH) (n-b-b) (ṣ-w-t) "sounding reed"

Syn. of UNBŪB or UNBŪBAH/1* (Kāẓim 1964:21).

ʿUNNAIZ

Var. of ʿUNNAYZ* (Hickmann 1958:69 and illus.).

ʿUNNAYZ = ʿUNNAIZ (ʿ-n-z) "little goats"

Bagpipe (Egypt).

ʿUNQ (pl. AʿNĀQ) (ʿ-n-q) "neck; trunk (of a tree)"

The neck and fingerboard of the ʿŪD/2* or other chordophone. Also IBRĪQ* (Farmer EI(Eng), "ʿŪd":986).

UNSHŪDAH = ANSHŪDAH (n-sh-d) "a recitation"

Syn. of NASHĪD/1*, i.e., a metered vocal genre (Farmer EI(Eng), "Ghinā'":1073). Also INSHĀD*.

UQṢŪṢAH (pl. AQĀṢĪṢ) (q-ṣ-ṣ) "narrative, tale"

Any one of the chanted poetic narratives described by al Jurjānī as being similar to the cantillation of the Qur'ān and the ADHĀN* (call to prayer), since they did not conform to regular periods matching the hemistiches of a metered poem (al Jurjānī 1938:531, 586, n. 50).

ʿURAB (pl. of ʿARABAH) = ORAB (ʿ-r-b) "vehicles"

Small metal pieces fastened near the strings at the left side of the QĀNŪN* which permit the performer to lower or raise the pitch of the strings (al Ḥafnī 1971:49-50; Touma 1977b:96, and illus. 12). See ʿARABAH/2*.

URGHAN or URGHANŪN (pl. ARĀGHIN) = ARGHAN, ARGHANUM, URGHĀNŪM, URGHUN, URGHĪN, ŪRGHĀNUM, URGHUNN (Gr.) "organ"

1. The Byzantine organ which was used by the Arabs to distract and confuse their enemies during times of war (al Lādhiqī 1939: 269; Ibn Sīnā 1935:234; Ibn Khurdādhbih 1969:17). It was said to have been audible for 60 miles (al Nadīm 1970:II, 643) and was made of skin and metal (Ibn Khurdādhbih 1969:17; al Masʿūdī 1874:VIII, 92; Ibn Salamah 1951:101). Both hydraulic and reed organs were known (see Farmer 1931).
2. A harp-like instrument of the Byzantines with 26 strings and a wide compass. Other manuscripts say 16 strings (Farmer 1928: 512; Ibn Khurdādhbih 1969:17; al Masʿūdī 1874:VIII, 91).
3. As used by the Persians, a kind of vocal composition described by Farmer as "somewhat analogous to the medieval European _organum_" (Farmer EI(Fr), "Urghan":274).
4. A bagpipe-like instrument described by al Khwārizmī (1968:236). See URGHĀNŪM*.

ŪRGHĀNUM

Var. of URGHAN or URGHANUN* (Farmer 1931:52).

URGHĀNŪM

Equiv. of URGHAN or URGHANŪN/4*. An instrument described by al Khwārizmī as comprising three large skins of the water buffalo which were joined together with another big skin on the top (head) of the middle skin. To this, ANĀBĪB (s. UNBŪB*) with fingerholes were fastened (al Khwārizmī 1968:236).

URGHANUM AL BŪQĪ = URGHĪN AL BŪQĪ (Gr.) (b-w-q) "horn organ"

The hydraulic organ (from a 9th C. ms. in Farmer 1965b:18-19).

URGHANUM AL ZAMRĪ (Gr.) (z-m-r) "blowing organ"

The reed pipe organ (from a 9th C. ms. in Farmer 1965b:18-19).

URGHĪN AL BŪQĪ

Var. of URGHANUM AL BŪQĪ* (from a 9th C. ms. in Farmer 1965b:18-19).

URGHŪL

Equiv. of ARGHŪL* (al Ḥafnī 1971:178; Lane 1973:367-368; Wehr).

URGHUN (Gr.)

1. Contemporary term for organ (Madina, Wehr).
2. Equiv. of URGHAN OR URGHANŪN/1* (Ibn Khurdādhbih 1969:17).

URGHUNN

Contemporary term for organ (Maʿlūf).

ʿUṢFŪR (pl. ʿAṢĀFĪR) = AASFOUR, AÇFOUR (ʿ-ṣ-f-r) "bird"

Tuning peg (Farmer 1978:I, 74).

ʿUSHAYRĀ' (ʿ-sh-r) "the ten"

Syn. of ʿUSHAYRĀN/2* (al Lādhiqī 1939:441).

ʿUSHAYRĀN = ÖSHEIRÂN, OUCHAÏRAN, 'OCHAÏRAN, ʿUSHAYRĀ', ACHÈRANE (ʿ-sh-r) "two small tens"

1. Name for one of the notes of the contemporary Arab scale, A_1

.

2. In the 15th C., the name for a melodic mode described in an anonymous work (Anonymous Treatise 1939:135). In the 16th C. the term ʿUSHAYRĀ'* was an equivalent (al Lādhiqī 1939:441).

USLŪB AL MAQĀM (s-l-b) (q-w-m) "method of the MAQĀM"

The rules for melodic progression of a melodic mode (MAQĀM/1*). It includes the order for treating AJNĀS (JINS/1*), their respective importance, the modulations allowed, and the characteristic use of QARĀR/1*, GHAMMĀZ*, MABDĀ'/1*, ẒAHĪR* and MARĀKIZ (s. MARKAZ/1*) tones--that is, everything but the modal scale.

UST-EÇ-ÇAN'Â

Var. of QISṬ AL ṢANʿAH* (Chottin 1939:128).

USṬŪKHŪSIYYAH = ASṬŪKŪSIYA (Gr.)

Syrian music theorists of the early Islamic period (Farmer 1957: 447; 1954, "Syrian Music":VIII, 255; al Kindī 1965:26).

UṢŪL = OUSOUL ('-ṣ-l)

Pl. of AṢL*.

ʿUTAB (ʿ-t-b)

Var. pl. of ʿATABAH*, used by Ibn Salamah (1938a:13).

ʿUYŪN (ʿ-y-n)

Pl. of ʿAYN*, a sound hole of a musical instrument.

ŪZĀN = UZAN, ŪZAN

A long necked lute of the Timūrī period. The name was adopted from the Oxus region by ʿAbd al Qādir ibn Ghaybī (d. 1435) (Farmer 1954, "Iraqian and Mesopotamian Music:IV, 530). This term was also used for an Egyptian lute during the Mamlūk period (Farmer 1954, "Egyptian Music":II, 894).

W

"W" (abbrev. for "waw," one of the letters of the Ar. alphabet)

Abbreviation for the WUSṬĀ AL ZALZAL* fret (al Jurjānī 1938:372-373; also see d'Erlanger 1938:595-597).

WADJH

Var. of WAJH* (Farmer EI(Eng), "ʿŪd":986).

WAḤDAH (pl. WAḤDĀT) (w-ḥ-d) "unit"

1. The shortest time unit used to produce a musical rhythmic cycle. This basic beat can vary in actual duration from cycle to cycle, or from performance to performance. All longer beats in the cycle are multiples of this basic beat (Allawerdi 1949:533).
2. A contemporary rhythmic mode, syn. of WAḤDAH AL ṢAGHĪRAH/1*, which is used for simple folk or traditional songs and to underlay the unmetered improvisations of vocalists and instrumentalists (d'Erlanger 1959:32). This rhythm is also used in the music of the Ṣūfī DHIKR* ceremony (Poche 1978:68).

WAḤDAH AL KABĪRAH (w-ḥ-d) (k-b-r) "large unit"

Note corresponding to the whole note (𝅝) of European notation (al Khulaʿī 1904; d'Erlanger 1959:23-24).

WAḤDAH AL KUBRĀ (w-ḥ-d) (k-b-r) "largest unit"

Note corresponding to the whole note (𝅝) of European notation (Allawerdi 1949:534).

WAḤDAH AL MUTAWASSIṬAH (w-ḥ-d) (w-s-ṭ) "median unit"

1. Note corresponding to the half note (𝅗𝅥) of European notation (al Khulaʿī 1904; d'Erlanger 1959:23-24).
2. Note corresponding to the quarter note (♩) of European notation (Ḥāfiẓ 1971:187; Allawerdi 1949:539).

WAḤDAH AL ṢAGHĪRAH (w-ḥ-d) (ṣ-gh-r) "small unit"

1. A contemporary rhythm with a 4/8 or 2/4 (𝅘𝅥 𝄾 𝅘𝅥 ♪) cycle. Syn. of WAḤDAH/2*. It is used for folk and traditional songs and to underlay unmetered improvisations by soloists.
2. Note corresponding to the quarter note (♩) of European notation (al Khulaʻī 1904; d'Erlanger 1959:23-24).
3. Note corresponding to the eighth note (♪) of European notation (Ḥāfiẓ 1971:187).

WAḤDAH SARĪʻAH (w-ḥ-d) (s-r-ʻ) "rapid one"

Note corresponding to the sixteenth note (𝅘𝅥𝅯) of European notation (Allawerdi 1949:475).

WAḤDAH AL ṢUGHRĀ (w-ḥ-d) (ṣ-gh-r) "smaller unit"

Note corresponding to the eighth note (♪) of European notation (Allawerdi 1949:534).

WAḤĪ (w-ḥ-y) "inspiration"

A very rapid tempo, comparable to Presto (Maḥfūẓ 1964:177; al Ḥafnī 1946:287).

WĀḤID BIL QUWWAH (w-ḥ-d) (q-w-y) "one (i.e., identical) in strength"

1. Term used to describe tones that are octave equivalents (Shawqī 1976:845). Also QUWWAH/1*.
2. Term used to describe intervals which are identical in pitch (al Fārābī 1967:358). See QUWWAH/4*.

WĀḤIDAH (pl. WĀḤIDĀT) (w-ḥ-d) "unit"

Syn. of WAḤDAH/2* (Racy 1978b:6-7).

WAJH (pl. WUJŪH) = WADGH, ÛJEH (w-j-h) "face"

1. The face of the soundbox of the ʻŪD*, ṬUNBŪR*, QĀNŪN* or other stringed instrument.
2. Head of a drum.

WANADJ

Var. of WANJ* (Farmer EI(Eng), "Miʻzaf":529).

WANAJ

Var. of WANJ* (al Khwārizmī 1968:237; Ibn Khurdādhbih 1969:16).

WĀNIN (w-n-y) "tired one"

A tempo comparable to Andante (Maḥfūẓ 1964:177; al Ḥafnī 1946:287).

WANJ = MUWANNAJ, WANADJ, ZANADJ, WANNAJ

An open-stringed musical instrument with seven strings. It was used in ancient times by the people of Khurāsān and Persia. It is said to have been played like the ṢANJ/1* (Ibh Khurdādhbih 1969:17; al Khwārizmī 1968:237). IBRĀHĪM AL MAWṢILĪ* is sometimes claimed to have been the first to play this instrument (al ʿAzzāwī 1951:5). According to al Zabīdī, it was like the MIZHAR*, ʿŪD*, ṢANJ* and MIʿZAF*; probably this meant only that it belonged to the category of chordophones. Syn. of WANN* (al Zabīdī 1965: IX, 393).

WANN (w-n-n) "buzzing"

1. A stringed instrument of the ṢANJ/1* type (harp), although it is believed that the WANN had a lower sound chest, while the ṢANJ had an upper sound chest (Robson 1938a:14). The WANN was played with the fingers (al Zabīdī 1965:IX, 393). Syn. of WANJ*.
2. A stringed instrument of the ṬUNBŪR* (long necked lute) type (Maḥfūẓ 1964:53).
3. A cymbal (Maḥfūẓ 1964:53).

WANNAJ

Var. of WANJ* (Farmer 1957:425).

WAQʿ (w-q-ʿ) "falling"

1. Loudness (Maḥfūẓ 1964:188).
2. Act of sounding the rhythm stick (QADĪB*).

WAQF or WAQFAH (pl. WAQFĀT) "stop"

1. A rest, i.e., the beat(s) of silence within the basic rhythmic cycle (al Fārābī 1967:992, 995).
2. A silence between the musical phrases or sections of a performance of TAQSĪM*, LAYĀLĪ*, Qur'ānic cantillation, etc.

WARDAH (w-r-d) "a rose"

The decorative covering of the openings or sound holes on the face of the lute or other chordophone.

WASAṬ (or WASṬ) AL ṢANʿAH (w-s-ṭ) (ṣ-n-ʿ) "midst of the work"

Syn. of KARSH AL ṢANʿAH* (Ḥāfiẓ 1971:130).

WAṢLAH (pl. AWSAL) = OUASLAH (w-ṣ-l) "a connection"

1. A vocal-instrumental suite performed in the Mashriq, which is comparable to the NAWBAH/1* of the Maghrib (d'Erlanger 1959:185; el Mahdi 1972:16). The melodies of any WAṢLAH are based on a single melodic mode (MAQĀM/1*), but they differ in their rhythmic modes. Any modulations within a piece are followed by a return to the

principal mode before concluding the number. There is an order in the rhythms of the successive pieces which puts the slowest at the beginning of the suite and a gradual progression to the faster rhythms (d'Erlanger 1959:186-188). The WAṢLAH was a much more popular type of performance in Egypt prior to World War I than it is today (Racy 1978a:49), but it is still heard there and in other parts of the Mashriq. It may comprise all or some of the following genres: BASHRAF/1*, SAMĀ'Ī*, MUWASHSHAH/1*, TAQĀSĪM* or TAQSĪM*, LAYĀLĪ*, QAṢĪDAH/1*, MAWWĀL/1*, TAḤMĪLAH*, DAWR/5* and DĀRIJ/2*.
2. A tie (el Helou 1961:55).

WASSA'A (w-s-') "to make wider"

To lower in pitch (al Khwārizmī 1968:237), opp. of DĀQA*.

WATAD (w-t-d) "peg, pin, stake"

A prosodic term borrowed by the Arab music theorists of the Classical Period to indicate a duration of a member or percussion (RIJL/1*) within the rhythmic cycle (DAWR/1*). This term stands for a member with three beats (comparable to a poetic member with three consonants, the two moving and the third quiescent--TANAN), and notated in various ways at various tempi (al Fārābī 1967: 1076ff). See also SABAB* and FĀṢILAH/6*.

WATAR (pl. AWTĀR) (w-t-r) "string"

1. A string for a musical instrument.
2. The piece of lamb's gut which lengthens each of the two horse-hair strings of the KAMĀNJAH* near the tuning pegs and by which the playing string is attached to the tuning peg (Egypt) (Lane 1973:356).
3. Name for the middle of the five strings of the SIMSIMIYYAH*, a contemporary harp-like folk instrument (Shiloah 1972:19).

WATAR AL KHĀMIS (w-t-r) (kh-m-s) "fifth string"

The fifth string, added by ZIRYĀB* to the originally four-stringed lute ('ŪD/2*). It was also called ḤADD* or ZĪR AL THĀNĪ*. See AWTĀR AL 'ŪD*.

WAZN (pl. AWZĀN) = OUAZN (w-z-n) "weight"

1. A rhythmic mode or the pattern of its cycle.
2. Rhythm.

WAZZĀN (pl. WAZZĀNAH) (w-z-n) "the one who measures (performs) the WAZN"

Drummer (Jones 1977:53).

WILWĀL (w-l-w-l)

The wailing of funerary singers (usually women). Although considered unlawful in many cases, it remained part of the cultural tradition through the centuries of Islamic history (Farmer 1957:434).

WUSʿAH (w-s-ʿ) "wideness; extent"

Range, the distance between the highest and lowest sound possible on a musical instrument or for a particular human voice (al Dāqūqī 1965:77).

WUSṬĀ (pl. WUSṬIYĀT) (w-s-ṭ) "middle finger"

1. Any of the fret positions of the lute (ʿŪD/2*) which were stopped by the middle finger. They produced various thirds above the open string. This term was known from the time of ISḤAQ AL MAWṢILĪ* (d. 850) (Ibn al Munajjim 1950:3) and continued in use throughout the Classical Period. Three different WUSTA frets known. From lowest to highest in pitch, they were WUSṬĀ AL QADĪM* (also called MUJANNAB AL WUSṬĀ*); WUSṬĀ AL FURS* and WUSṬĀ AL ZALZAL* (also called WUSṬĀ AL ʿARAB*).
2. One of the three categories of intervals described by Ṣafī al Dīn (Ṣafī al Dīn 1938a:243; al Jurjānī 1938:243; Wright 1978:133). It included the perfect fourth and perfect fifth.
3. The tone at the mid-point of the two-octave scalar collection (JAMʿ/1*) of tones known to the Classical Period theorists. It was one of the three unchangeable tones within the collection which were known as NAGHAM AL RĀTIBAH* (al Fārābī 1967:372; Ṣafī al Dīn 1938b:81).

WUSṬĀ AL ʿARAB (w-s-ṭ) (ʿ-r-b) "Arab WUSṬĀ"

Syn. of WUSṬĀ AL ZALZAL*, a fret position which produced a tone at an interval approximately 1 and 3/4 steps above the open string tone (a neutral third with ratio of 27/22).

WUSṬĀ AL FURS (w-s-ṭ) (nat.) "Persian WUSṬĀ"

The Classical Period fret position for producing a tone approximately 1½ steps above the open string (a minor third with ratio of 81/68).

WUSṬĀ AL QADĪM (w-s-ṭ) (q-d-m) "ancient WUSṬĀ"

The Classical Period fret position for producing a tone approximately 1½ steps above the open string (ratio of 32/27). It was slightly lower in pitch than the WUSṬĀ AL FURS*. Also known as MUJANNAB AL WUSṬĀ*.

WUSṬĀ AL ZALZAL or WUSṬĀ AL ZULZUL (w-s-ṭ) (n. of pers.) "WUSṬĀ of ZALZAL"

The Classical Period fret position for producing a tone approximately 1 and 3/4 tones above the open string, at a comma or ¼ tone below the major third. This fret position, the so-called "neutral third," is said to have been introduced by the famous musician and lutenist ZALZAL* (d. 791). Both al Fārābī and Ibn Sīnā incorporated this fret into their systems but assigned to it slightly variant placements on the strings of the ʿŪD/2*. According to Ṣafī al Dīn and the theorists who followed him, this fret (abbreviated as "W"*) was sometimes placed to produce a major (384 c.) rather than a neutral third. Ṣafī al Dīn, however, after establishing that interval, added a passage which countered his earlier theoretical placement and reinstated the neutral third fret under the name WUSṬĀ AL FURS*, a name which he and others more commonly assigned to the fret producing the minor third (Ṣafī al Dīn 1938a:596-597; Anonymous Treatise 1939:40; al Lādhiqī 1939:483; Wright 1978:31-32). Also known as the WUSṬĀ AL ʿARAB*.

X

XANAT (pl. XAANAAT)

Var. of KHĀNAH* (Bulos 1971:35).

Y

YAKĀH = YEGAH (Pers.) "station one"

Name for one of the notes of the contemporary Arab scale, G_1

. It probably got its name from being the first or lowest tone of the Arab scale (al Dāqūqī 1965:98).

YARĀʿ or YARĀʿAH (y-r-ʿ) "cane, reed"

1. An end-blown flute, often associated with shepherds. In the work of al Khwārizmī, it was equated with the SURNĀY* (1968:237).
2. Generic term for any reed flute.

YARGHOUL

Var. of YARGHŪL* (Touma 1977b:105). See also ARGHŪL or URGHŪL*.

YARGHŪL = YARGHOUL

A wind instrument with single reed. It is of various types, sometimes single piped, sometimes with double pipes (ʿArnīṭah 1968: 60).

YATĀYIM (pl. of YATĪMAH) = ITÂMAH (y-t-m) "orphans"

The vocal numbers of the ancient Andalusian classical music of Morocco which do not belong to a specific NAWBAH/1*. These are often fitted into those NAWBAHs which have corresponding or nearly corresponding melodic modes (Chottin 1939:124; Maḥfūẓ 1964:108).

YĀTŪGHĀN

According to ʿAbd al Qādir ibn Ghaybī (d. 1435), a stringed instrument made of a long, hollowed piece of wood. It had strings on its surface supported by movable bridges. These strings were plucked with the fingers of the right hand while the left hand adjusted the pitch of the notes by pressure on the strings or by moving the bridges. It is believed to have been a psaltery with a neck (Farmer 1978:II, 15-16, and no. 1 on p. 16).

YEGAH

Var. of (Smith 1847:181).

YIQA'

Var. of ĪQĀʿ/1* (Rouanet 1922:2706).

YŪBĀL

Var. of ṬŪBAL IBN LAMAK*, whom tradition has regarded as the inventor of the drum and tambourine (Maḥfūẓ 1964:143).

YŪRUK (Turk.) "rapid"

Syn. of DĀRIJ/1*, a descriptive term used in the titles for certain contemporary rhythmic modes of rapid tempo.

Z

ZABĪBAH (z-b-b) "raisin"

The button at the base of the ṬUNBŪR/1* or other similar instrument to which the strings are fastened (al Fārābī 1967:630, 801; al Jurjānī 1938:366).

ZAFFAH (z-f-f) "procession"

Nuptial procession which is the occasion for extensive musical activities.

ZĀFINAH (pl. ZAFŪN) (z-f-n) f. of "one who kicks or dances"

Dancing girl.

ZAFN (z-f-n) "dancing"

Dancing; described by al Fārābī (1967:78) as moving the body in time with the rhythm but without making sound. Also in Ibn Zaylah 1964:71, 73).

ZAǦAL

Var. of ZAJAL* (Jargy 1970:58).

ZAĠARĪṬ

Var. of ZAGHĀRĪD or ZAGHĀRĪṬ* and pl. of ZAGHRADAH or ZAGHRAṬAH/3* (Jargy 1970:10).

ZAGHĀRĪD or ZAGHĀRĪṬ = ZALĀGHĪT, ZAĠARĪṬ (z-gh-r-d) or (z-gh-r-ṭ)

Pl. of ZAGHRADAH or ZAGHRAṬAH*.

ZAGHRADA (z-gh-r-d) "to trill the voice in joy"

To produce a prolonged and shrill vocal trill, to ululate.

ZAGHRADAH or ZAGHRAṬAH (pl. ZAGHĀRĪD or ZAGHĀRĪṬ) (z-gh-r-d) or (z-gh-r-ṭ) "a shrill and trilling vocal sound"

1. A prolonged and shrill tongue trill produced by women as a musical exclamation and/or ornament (Maḥfūẓ 1964:180, 196; al Ḥafnī 1946:287). It is heard in combination with the music performed at joyous occasions such as weddings and circumcisions.
2. Vibrato or tremolo (al Ḥafnī 1946:287).

ZAGHRAṬAH (pl. ZAGHĀRĪṬ) (z-gh-r-ṭ) "a shrill and trilling vocal sound"

Equiv. of ZAGHRADAH* (Wehr).

ẒĀHIR = DHĀHIR (ẓ-h-r) "apparent, obvious"

Designation for a melodic modal scale which reveals obvious dissonance (al Jurjānī 1938:336; al Lādhiqī 1939:375). This term is given as DHĀHIR* in these translations, and abbreviated as "DH". It is not known if that spelling comes from the original manuscript or from its translation and transliteration. Syn. of ẒĀHIR AL TANĀFUR*.

ẒAHĪR = DHAHĪR (ẓ-h-r) "assistant; something that appears"

The one or more tones below the tonic which are sounded in melodic progressions to the cadence (QAFLAH/2*) on the tonic. D'Erlanger uses the spelling DHAHIR*to transliterate this term (d'Erlanger 1949:106-108). The ẒAHĪR acts as leading tone(s).

ẒĀHIR AL TANĀFUR (ẓ-h-r) (n-f-r) "evidencing dissonance"

Dissonant (Ṣafī al Dīn in Kitāb al Adwār, as discussed in Wright 1978:98). This term, like MUTANĀFIR*, is applied to a group of scales in which consonant intervals occur only between the "fixed notes," i.e., the first, fourth, fifth and eighth scale steps. Syn. of ẒĀHIR*.

ẒAHR (pl. ẒUHŪR, AẒHŪR) (ẓ-h-r) "back"

1. Convex back of the ʿŪD*, ṬUNBŪR* RABĀB* or other chordophone.
2. The top side of a woodwind instrument where the main finger holes are bored (al Fārābī 1967:781).

ZĀ'ID = ZĀYID (z-y-d) "increaser" (masc.)

1. A fret or fret position on the lute (either long- or short-necked) which was comparable to the MUJANNAB/1* fret and gave a tone 256/243 or 90 c. above the open string (MUṬLAQ/4*) tone (Collangettes 1904:410; al Khwārizmī 1968:238; de Vaux (1891:382-333). A passage in the work of al Khwārizmī (1968:238) reads that the ZĀ'ID fret is "stretched above" the SABBĀBAH* or whole tone fret; but this certainly refers to the relative position on the neck of the instrument as it is raised for performance, rather than to pitch relationship.
2. A term which is used for any tetrachordal scalar segment (JINS/1*) whose two extremities are at a distance from each other of more than a perfect fourth (Ṣalāḥ al Dīn 1950:101).

ZĀ'IDAH (pl. ZAWĀ'ID) (z-y-d) "increaser" (f.)

The embellishment or gloss of a melody (Farmer 1929a:5, 157).

ZAJAL (pl. AZJĀL) (z-j-l) "the release (esp. of a bird)"

1. The musical setting of the strophic poetry of the same name (see def. 2). Its musical setting is similar to that of the MUWASHSHAḤ/1*, though it is usually a lighter music to match the more popular style of the poetry.
2. A genre of lyric poetry which has flourished from the 9th C., according to d'Erlanger (1959:635). Other writers attribute its rise to somewhat later. It originated in Spain but later was popular in other parts of the Arab-Islamic World as well. It is related to the MUWASHSHAḤ/2* from which it differs in being entirely in the colloquial language. This poetry was meant to be sung by one or more vocalists as a series of four-lined stanzas, each followed by a refrain of two lines called a MARKAZ/3*. Lines of this refrain are composed to rhyme with the fourth line of each stanza. See Appendix in d'Erlanger (1959:635-639).
3. Soft humming sound of the JINN at night (Madina).
4. Musical sound (Maḥfūẓ 1964:116).

ZAJALA (z-j-l) "to release (esp. a bird)"

To sing or perform music (Maḥfūẓ 1964:79, 116).

ZĀJIL (z-j-l) "one who releases"

Reciter or singer of ZAJAL* (Maḥfūẓ 1964:79).

ZAJJĀL (z-j-l) "one who releases always"

Syn. of ZĀJIL*.

ZAKHMAH (pl. ZAKHMĀT) (z-kh-m) "that which pushes forward"

1. A plectrum for a chordophone. It could be a loose piece held in the hand or any of the plectra which are fastened to the tips of the fingers.
2. Any striking instrument, such as a bow of a stringed instrument, a mallet for a dulcimer, or a drumstick (Farmer 1945:35; Madina).
3. A genre of instrumental or vocal improvisation. It is described as similar to the PISHRŪ* improvisation. When set to poetry, it becomes identical with the improvised musical genre known as HAWĀ'Ī* (ʿAbd al Qādir ibn Ghaybī in Anonymous Treatise 1939:246).
4. According to Maḥfūẓ (1964:79), a sound (ṢAWT*) or tone (NAGHAM*).

ZAKKĀR (z-k-r) "one who plays the ZUKRAH"

A player of the ZUKRAH, an oboe-like, double reed instrument with conical bore (Snoussi 1961:143, 145; Jones 1977:71-72). The

ZAKKĀR is often the leader of a folk or religious musical ensemble (Tun.) and is the paid performer of the group. He is therefore considered as a professional who maintains an independence from the FIRQAH* with which he plays (Jones 1977:297).

ZALĀGHĪT

Probably a colloq. var. of ZAGHĀRĪD or ZAGHĀRĪṬ* (Jargy 1970: 38, 82; 1978:82).

ZALZAL, MANṢŪR (d. 791) = ZULZUL

A famous musician of the 8th C. who was known for his performance on the ʿŪD/2*, with which he accompanied the singing of his brother-in-law, IBRAHĪM AL MAWṢILĪ*. He is credited with initiating use of a fret position called the WUSṬĀ ZALZAL* or WUSṬĀ AL ʿARAB* which produced the neutral third (ca. 350 c.) above the open string tone (al Fārābī 1967:127, n. 2). He also invented the ʿŪD AL SHABBŪṬ*, which took the place of the Persian lute (BARBAṬ/1*) formerly in use. He spent many years in prison after incurring the displeasure of the Caliph Hārūn al Rashīd.

ZAMAN (pl. AZMĀN) or ZAMĀN (pl. AZMAN, AZMINAH, AZMUN) (z-m-n) "time, period of time"

1. A musical time value; the duration of a beat.
2. The time allotted to one percussion or foot (RIJL/1*) of a rhythmic cycle (al Fārābī 1967:999).

ZAMĀN AL AQALL (z-m-n) (q-l-l) "least time"

Syn. of ZAMĀN AL AWWAL* (Wright 1979:491).

ZAMĀN AL AWWAL (pl. AZMINAH AL ŪLĀ) (z-m-n) ('-w-l) "first time"

For the theorists of the Classical Period, it was the smallest perceptible duration, the fundamental and indivisible time unit from which all rhythmic patterns were made. It was therefore the shortest as well as the basic unit of the rhythmic mode (ĪQĀʿ/1*) (al Fārābī 1930:151; 1967:440). It was abbreviated as "A"/1* time (Ṣafī al Dīn 1938a:161). See also ZAMĀN AL THĀNĪ*, ZAMĀN AL THĀLITH*, etc.

ZAMĀN AL MABDA' (z-m-n) (b-d-') "principal or fundamental time"

The basic meter from which all others were said to be derived. It was for the early theorists of the Classical Period a conjunct (MUTTAṢIL/4*) rhythm (i.e., one in which every percussion within the cycle is of the same length). Its longest possible variety consisted of eight percussions followed by two beats of rest, thereby totaling ten beats (al Fārābī 1967:983-991; 1935:27ff).

ZAMĀN AL MIʿYĀR (z-m-n) (ʿ-y-r) "measuring time"

Syn. of ZAMAN AL AWWAL*. This expression was used by the theorists of the Classical Period (d'Erlanger 1959:6).

ZAMĀN MUTAFĀḌIL (z-m-n) (f-ḍ-l) "surplus time"

A disjunct(MUFAṢṢAL/1*)rhythmic mode (al Rajab 1967:25).

ZAMĀN AL RĀBIʿ (z-m-n) (r-b-ʿ) "fourth time"

A percussion four times the length of ZAMĀN AL AWWAL* or "A"/1* time (Ṣafī al Dīn 1938b:161; 1938a:478). It was abbreviated as "D"*.

ZAMĀN AL THĀLITH (z-m-n) (th-l-th) "third time"

A percussion three times the length of ZAMĀN AL AWWAL* or "A"/1* time (Ṣafī al Dīn 1938b:161; 1938a:478). It was abbreviated "J"/1*.

ZAMĀN AL THĀNĪ (z-m-n) (th-n-y) "second time"

A percussion two times the length of ZAMĀN AL AWWAL* or "A"/1* time (Ṣafī al Dīn 1938b:161; 1938a:478). It was abbreviated as "B"/2*.

ZĀMAR (z-m-r) probably a var. of ZAMR*

A double hornpipe of Morocco with two cane pipes ca. 42 cm. in length which are tied together at top and bottom and inserted in two large cow-horn bells. Each pipe has a single reed and six front finger holes, opposite one another in two groups of three. It is played by the Berbers of the Riff Mountains (Marcuse).

ZAMARA (z-m-r) "to blow or play"

To play a woodwind or brass instrument.

ZAMBRAH (Sp.) corruption of SAMRAH, "an evening entertainment"

1. A musical gathering; an evening concert of Andalusian Spain (Chottin 1939:88). Syn. of LAYLAH*.
2. A certain dance of the Moors in Spain (Farmer 1954, "Zambra": IX,396).

ZĀMILAH (z-m-l) f. of "companion"

A bridge for a chordophone, according to Farmer (1926a:249, 251). Could this be a misreading or miscopying of ḤAMILAH*?

ZĀMIR = ZAMER (z-m-r) "one who blows or plays"

1. A woodwind instrument described as a version of the oboe-like GHAYṬAH/1* (Alg.) (Delphin and Guin 1886:48).
2. A wind instrument player, a flutist or piper (Madina; Ibn ʿAbd Rabbihi 1889:III, 188; Farmer 1943-44:53).

ZAMĪR (z-m-r) "act of blowing or playing a wind instrument"

Performing on a wind instrument.

ZAMJARAH (pl. ZAMĀJĪR or ZAMĀJIR) (z-m-j-r) "that which roars"

A large woodwind instrument made from cane (Maḥfūẓ 1964:35).

ZAMKHAR (z-m-kh-r) (?) This is probably a miscopying of ZAMJAR.

1. A large black woodwind instrument (MIZMĀR/1*) (Maḥfūẓ 1964:35).
2. Syn. of NĀY/1* (Maḥfūẓ 1964:35). See ZAMJARAH*.

ZAMM (z-m-m) "tieing up, tightening"

A very nasal vocal tone, said to be more nasal than the GHUNNAH* sound (al Fārābī 1967:1070, esp. n. 2).

ZAMMĀR (z-m-r) "one who blows or plays"

1. Generic term for any woodwind performer.
2. The NĀY/1* player.
3. A single piped, folkish woodwind instrument of ʿIrāq.

ZAMMARA (z-m-r) "to blow or play"

Syn. of ZAMARA*.

ZAMMĀRAH (pl. ZAMMĀRĀT) (z-m-r) "that which one blows or plays"

1. A double piped folk instrument of Egypt and the Peninsula (Farmer 1978:I, 78). This aerophone made from cane is more often called ZUMMĀRAH* today. In earlier times, the term was also used for a single piped instrument similar to a shepherd's pipe (Ibn Abī al Dunyā 1938:29, 52, n. 6; Ibn Salamah 1938a:22; 1938b:246).
2. A female singer or musician according to Lane, Lexicon, cited in Farmer 1978:I, 77-79).

ZAMR (pl. ZUMŪR) = ZEMR (z-m-r) "blowing instrument"

1. Generic term for any wind instrument. In this sense, it (like the term MIZMĀR*) is used most commonly for a reed-blown instrument rather than for a pipe-blown or brass instrument.
2. A double clarinet of the Maghrib (Chottin 1939:33, 37-38). This folk instrument consists of two cylindrical pipes, each of which has finger holes and a single reed. It is found in many different sizes.
3. According to Lane (1973:365), it was an oboe-like instrument used for wedding processions and other folk festivals in Egypt of the 19th C. It is described as a conical wooden instrument with flaring bell and five to eight front fingerholes and a rear thumb hole. Its double reed is attached to a removable neck. Also see Rouanet 1922:2792.
4. According to a 9th C. treatise, an organ (Farmer 1926a:256).
5. Act of playing a wind instrument (Madina).

ZAMR AL BŪQĪ (z-m-r) (b-w-q) "horn wind instrument"

A horn-like reed instrument, according to a 9th C. ms. (Farmer 1965b:21).

ZAMR AL KABĪR (z-m-r) (k-b-r) "large wind instrument"

A large, oboe-type instrument described by Villoteau (18th C. Egypt) (Farmer EI(Eng), "Mizmār":540). It was also known as QABĀ SŪRNĀ*, QABĀ ZŪRNĀ*.

ZAMR AL RĪḤĪ (z-m-r) (r-y-h) "air wind-instrument"

A reed-pipe instrument mechanically supplied with air, which was mentioned in a 9th C. ms. (Farmer 1965b:21).

ZAMR AL SOGHAIR

Var. of ZAMR AL ṢUGHAYYIR* (Marcuse).

ZAMR AL ṢUGHAYYIR = ZAMR AL SOGHAIR (z-m-r) (ṣ-gh-r) "small wind instrument"

A small Egyptian oboe-like instrument (18th C.) (Farmer EI(Eng), "Mizmār":540). Also known as SŪRNĀ JURĀ* or JŪRĀ ZŪRNĀ* (Farmer 1976b:24-25).

ZAMZAMA (z-m-z-m) "to rumble; to murmur"

To chant (Majd al Dīn al Ghazālī 1938:112, 176).

ZAMZAMAH (z-m-z-m) "a rumble; a murmur"

1. A chant (Majd al Dīn al Ghazālī 1938:112, 176).
2. A musical sound emitted while keeping the mouth closed (d'Erlanger 1939:510, n. 5).

ZANADJ or ZANAJ

Vars. of ZANJ* (Farmer EI(Eng), "Miʿzaf":529).

ZANBAQ (z-n-b-q) colloq. "lily; iris"

A woodwind instrument, probably reed-blown, which was used in the early centuries of the Islamic period (Ibn Salamah 1951:86; Farmer 1929a:143). Farmer suggests that its name may derive from the sambucus wood from which it was made (Farmer 1957:425).

ZĀNDĀLĪ

A refined folk tune sometimes utilized in the final movement (KHATM/1*) of the NAWBAH/1* (Tun.) (Ḥāfiẓ 1971:122). Probably ZENDANI* or ZANDĀNĪ* (found in Rouanet 1922:2845) are equivalents.

ZANDĀNĪ = ZENDANI

A variety of popular song in the Maghrib (Rouanet 1922:2845). See ZĀNDĀLĪ*.

ZANDJ or ZANG

Vars. of ZANJ* or ZINJ* (de Meynard 1874:VIII, 91).

ZANJ (pl. ZUNŪJ) = ZANDJ, ZANG (z-n-j) colloq. of "negro"

1. Equiv. of ZINJ/1*, a word used for cymbal.
2. A stringed instrument of the people of Khurāsān which was used for accompanying a vocalist. It is believed to have been of the open-stringed type known as WANJ* or MUWANNAJ* (Ibn Khurdādhbih 1951:95; al Masʿūdī 1874:VIII, 90). Equiv. of ZINJ/2*.

ZĀR (z-w-r)

1. A religious musical gathering for women, or both men and women, in which songs of exorcism are sung and many different percussion instruments and woodwinds of the end-blown variety are used (Egypt). The songs are generally divided between solo parts and choral refrains (Hickmann 1958:44-46). Farmer uses ẒAR (1952:61), perhaps a printer's mistake.
2. The music performed at the ZĀR/1*, therefore, songs of exorcism.

ZAWĀḤIM (pl. of ZĀḤIM) (z-ḥ-m) "those which push or press"

Drumsticks used to play the NAWĀGHIR* drum (Alg.) (Delphin and Guin 1886:44).

ZAWĀ'ID (pl. of ZĀ'IDAH) (z-y-d) "appendices"

Ornaments of the melodic line (al Kindī 1965:19; Farmer 1967:14).

ZAWĀL (z-w-l) "disappearance; end"

Name for one of the notes of the contemporary Arab scale, $D\#_2$ or Eb_2

, also called SUNBULAH*.

ZAWĀQ

Musical ornament or ornamentation.

ZAWBAʿĪ (z-w-b-ʿ) "stormy"

A vocal improvisatory genre of the Bedouins of Syria, said to be similar to the SHARQĪ* (SHRŪGĪ*) (Jargy 1970:34).

ZAWJ (z-w-j) "pair"

1. Any pair of drums, such as the NAQQĀRĀT* (Ḥāfiẓ 1971:7).
2. The musical rendering of couplets with new melodic material for the second line, a practice said to have been first used by IBN MUḤRIZ* (Farmer 1967:79).

ZAWWĀDAH (z-w-d)

Colloq. var. of ZUWWĀDAH* (Rouanet 1922:2932).

ZĀYID

Var. of ZĀ'ID/1* (d'Erlanger 1938:596).

ZEDAYET

Var. of ZIYĀDAH/2* (Chottin 1939:22).

ZEMR

Var. of ZAMR/3* (Lane 1973:365).

ZENDANI

A variety of popular song in the Maghrib (Farmer 1976a:189, 195), probably a var. of ZANDALĪ*. It is said to be similar to QARĪḤAH* (Rouanet 1922:2883).

ZIKĀRAH (z-k-r)

An instrument of Tunis said to be synonymous with the BŪQ* (Maḥfūẓ 1964:35). This is the only reference for a derivative of this root used to designate a brass instrument.

ZIKR

Var. of DHIKR* (Touma 1977b:134).

ZIKRAH (z-k-r)

Syn. of ZIKĀRAH* (Maḥfūẓ 1964:35).

ZIL or ZĪL

Vars. of ZILL* (Shiloah 1965:30; Farmer EI(Fr), "Ṣandj":209 resp.).

ZILL = ZIL, ZĪL

Small cymbals of brass fastened to thumb and index or second fingers (Farmer EI(Fr.), "Ṣandj":209). Syn. of ṢUNŪJ/1*.

ZILLĪ MĀSHA

Syn. of JAGHĀNAH or ṢAGHĀNAH*, small cymbals or bells mounted on some form of carrier (Farmer EI(Fr), "Ṣandj":209).

ZINJ (pl. ZUNŪJ) equiv. of ZANJ* (z-n-j)

1. Syn. of ṢANJ/1*. In the 13th C., the word stood for cymbal. Today in the Maghrib, ZUNŪJ are metal cymbals or castanets.
2. Syn. of ṢANJ/2*, the seven-stringed harp of the Classical Period (Ibn Khurdādhbih 1951:95; Farmer 1928:514-515; al Mas'ūdī 1874: VIII, 90).

ZIQQ (pl. AZQĀQ) (z-q-q) "a skin as a receptable"

The bellows of the organ or bagpipe (Farmer 1931:107).

ZĪR (Pers.) "below; high pitched"

1. One of the strings of the 'ŪD*, according to the Classical Period theorists. It was the highest pitched string when the lute had four strings, the fourth (counting from the lowest pitched) when the instrument was altered to carry a fifth string (al Fārābī 1967:126; Ibn al Munajjim 1950:4-5; al Kindī 1965:17; Ibn Abī al

Ṣalt 1952:79). Its name was fitting since it was both "below" as far as position, and "high" as far as pitch was concerned.
2. A single pipe end-blown flute mentioned by a 13th-14th C. writer (Shawqī 1976:281).

ZĪR AL THĀNĪ (Pers.) (th-w-n) "second ZĪR"

The name given to the fifth and highest string of the lute (ʿŪD/2*) by al Kindī. Other Classical Period writers called it ḤADD/1*. The use of a fifth string is mentioned by Ibn Munajjim, al Kindī, Ibn Salamah, Ibn Sīnā, al Fārābī and Ibn Zaylah (al Rajab 1967:9 n. 1).

ZĪRKŪLAH or ZIRKŪLĀH = ZENKALA, ZERKALA, ZINKULĀH (Pers.) "gold crown"

1. Name of note of the contemporary Arab scale, C#1, Db1  .
2. Name of a melodic mode.

ZIRR (pl. AZRĀR) (z-r-r) "button"

A swelling protrusion at the bottom of the sound box of the KAMĀN or KAMĀNJAH* (Maḥfūẓ 1964:159).

ZIRYĀB, nickname for Abū al Ḥasan ʿAlī ibn Nāfiʿ (9th C.) (Pers.) "blackbird"

The most famous musician of Muslim Spain. He was a client of the ʿAbbāsī caliph, al Mahdī, and started his musical career as the protege of ISḤAQ AL MAWṢILĪ* in Baghdād. Later rivalry with his teacher forced ZIRYĀB to emigrate to North Africa, where he won fame in the service of the Aghlabī sultan of Qayrawān, and thence went to Spain where he became the leading musician of the Spanish Umawī court. He was gifted and well educated in every branch of the art of music as well as learned in literature, astronomy and geography. He founded a music school in Cordova which was the center of musical life in Spain. He is credited with introducing the eagle's feather plectrum for the ʿŪD/2*, a more heavily constructed instrument, a fifth string, and gut (for the lower) strings in place of the silk (see Farmer 1967:108-109; 129-130; d'Erlanger 1949:388-391). His nickname was given to him because of his black complexion and the eloquence of his speech.

ZIYĀDAH (z-y-d) "increase, surplus; addition"

1. A way of beautifying a melody through durational means, according to Ibn Sīnā. See chart under TAḤSĪN AL LAḤN*. It could involve increasing the length of percussions (e.g., TARTĪL*, in which every percussion is made longer; or TAḌʿĪF/2* in which the number of percussions increases without changing the time span (Ibn Sīnā 1930:99).
2. In Morocco it refers to a very refined rendition of the Berber vocal improvisation known as TAMEDIAZT* (Chottin 1939:22).
3. A tube(s) added to the drone pipe of a double reed-pipe to lower the pitch (Farmer EI(Eng), "Mizmār":541).

ZIYĀDAH NAQRĀT MIN KHĀRIJ (z-y-d) (n-q-r) (kh-r-j) "addition of supplementary percussions from outside"

One of the two types of alteration (TAGHYĪR/2*) of a basic rhythm in order to form new rhythmic modes (ĪQĀʿĀT). This alteration involved the addition of supplementary percussions of various lengths. It was generally done to slow rhythms where the space between percussions was considerable. The other way of altering was GHAYR ZIYĀDAH* (al Fārābī 1967:1012-1017).

ZIYĀDAH SHADDAH AL ṢAWT TADRĪJIYYAN (z-y-d) (sh-d-d) (ṣ-w-t) (d-r-j) "increasing the strength of the sound by degrees"

Crescendo (el Helou 1961:58).

ZIYĀDAH SURʿAH BIL TADRĪJ (z-y-d) (s-r-ʿ) (d-r-j) "increasing the speed by degrees"

Accelerando (el Helou 1961:58).

ZNOUDJ

Var. of ṢUNŪJ/1* (Shiloah 1965:I, 29; Farmer 1976a:189, 243), the finger cymbals used in the Mashriq and Maghrib.

ZORNA

Var. of ZURNA* (el Mahdi 1972:49).

ZOUKRAH

Var. of ZUKRAH/1* (d'Erlanger 1937:9).

ZOUMMÂRAH

Var. of ZUMMAR or ZUMMARAH* (Hickmann 1958:27).

ZÛÂQ

Var. of ZUWĀQ* (Chottin 1939:114, 147).

ZUBAYDAH (z-b-d) dim. of "cream; prime; essence"

The lower peg to which strings were fastened at the base of the TUNBUR* or of the stick fiddle (Farmer 1945:13).

ZUGRA

Var. of ZUKRAH or ZŪKRAH* (Farmer 1978:I, 45, n. 6).

ZUKHRUF (pl. ZAKĀRIF) (z-kh-r-f) "ornament"

Embellishment, ornamentation.

ZUKHRUFAH (z-kh-r-f) "ornament"

A musical embellishment or ornament.

ZUKKRĀ

Var. of ZUKRAH or ZŪKRAH* (Farmer 1978:I, 45, n. 6).

ZUKRAH or ZŪKRAH (pl. ZUKAR) = SUQQĀRAH, ZUKHRA, ZOUKRAH, ZŪQRA, ZŪQQARA, ZUQQĀRA (z-k-r) "wineskin"

1. A double reed aerophone used in the Maghrib (esp. Tun.) (Touma 1977:105; Snoussi 1961:147; Jones 1977:6). This oboe-type, conical bored instrument is used particularly in folk music performances.
2. A bagpipe-like instrument of the Maghrib, mouth-blown with kidskin bag, two parallel pipes, each furnished with a single reed and five fingerholes (Marcuse).
3. Generic term for bagpipe (Farmer EI(Eng), "Mizmār":541).

ZULĀMĪ = ZULLĀMĪ, ZUNĀMĪ (z-l-m) "pertaining to the cut one"

An oboe-type instrument invented in Baghdād at the end of the 8th C. or beginning of the 9th C. (al Zabīdī 1965:VIII, 326; Hickmann 1947: 8). According to Ibn Khaldūn (d. 1406), it was a woodwind instrument with a double reed and a conical bore. Its single pipe (Maḥfūẓ 1964:35) had finger holes and produced a high pitched sound (Ibn Khaldūn 1967:II, 396).

ZULLĀMĪ

Var. of ZULĀMĪ* which was important in Moorish Spain and the Maghrib (Farmer EI(Eng), "Mizmār":540).

ZULZUL

Var. of ZALZAL* (d'Erlanger 1930).

ZUMMĀR or ZUMMĀRAH (pl. ZAMMĀMĪR) = ZOÛMMARAH (z-m-r) "blowing instrument"

1. A double piped, clarinet-type instrument which has been used in Egypt and other parts of the Arab World. It consists of two parallel, cylindrical pipes of the same length with equidistant finger holes. Each tube has a single reed and is ca. 18-43 cm. in length. One pipe is used as a drone, the other as melody producer. Varying numbers of finger holes are found on the melody pipe, and the instrument is often named accordingly (e.g., ZUMMĀRAH RUBĀʿIYYAH*, ZUMMĀRAH KHAMSAWIYYAH*, etc. (al Ḥafnī 1971:178).
2. A single pipe, double reed woodwind instrument of folkish variety (al Ḥafnī 1971:178).
3. Generic term for any woodwind instrument.
4. A small horn for children (Tun.).

ZUMMĀRA ARBAWIJA (z-m-r) (colloq.) "four-ed blowing instrument"

Var. of ZUMMĀRAH RUBĀʿIYYAH* (Marcuse).

ZUMMĀRA CHAMSĀWIJA (z-m-r) (colloq.)

Var. of ZUMMĀRAH KHUMĀSIYYAH* (Marcuse).

ZUMMĀRAH KHUMĀSIYYAH = ZUMMĀRA CHAMSĀWIJA (z-m-r) (kh-m-s) "five-ed blowing instrument"

A ZUMMĀRAH* with five finger holes on each pipe (al Ḥafnī 1971: 178).

ZUMMĀRAH AL ḲIRBA (z-m-r)

Var. of ZUMMĀRAH AL QIRBAH* (Farmer EI(Eng), "Mizmār":541).

ZUMMĀRAH AL MUZDAWAJAH (z-m-r) (z-w-j) "paired blowing instrument"

Syn. of ZUMMĀRAH/1* (al Ḥafnī 1971:178).

ZUMMĀRAH AL QIRBAH = ZUMMĀRAH AL ḲIRBA (z-m-r) (q-r-b) "water skin blowing instrument"

Bagpipes. Also ZUMMĀRAH BI SUʿN* (Farmer EI(Eng), "Mizmār":541).

ZUMMĀRAH RUBĀʿIYYAH = ZUMMĀRA ARBAWIJA (z-m-r) (r-b-ʿ) "four-ed blowing instrument"

A double piped clarinet with four finger holes on each pipe (al Ḥafnī 1971:178).

ZUMMĀRA SATTAWIJA (z-m-r) (colloq.)

Var. of ZUMMARAH SUDĀSIYYAH* (Marcuse).

ZUMMĀRAH BI-SOẠN (z-m-r)

Var. of ZUMMĀRAH BI SUʿN* (Lane 1973:368).

ZUMMĀRAH SUDĀSIYYAH = ZUMMARA SATTAWIJA (z-m-r) (s-d-s) "six-ed blowing instrument"

A double piped clarinet with six finger holes on each pipe (al Ḥafnī 1971:178).

ZUMMĀRAH BI SUʿN = ZUMMĀRAH BI-SOẠN (z-m-r) (s-ʿ-n) "blowing instrument with skins"

A rude kind of bagpipe seen occasionally in Egypt (Farmer EI(Eng), "Mizmār":541).

ZUNĀMĪ

Syn. of ZULĀMĪ* (Ibn Khurdādhbih 1969:15). In al Masʿūdī (1874: VIII, 90), we find DIYĀNĪ*. See Farmer 1954, "ZAMR":396. Farmer writes that this instrument was named after a famous wind instrument player at the the caliphal court named Zunām.

ZUNŪJ (z-n-j)

Pl. of ZANJ* or ZINJ*.

ZŪQQARA (z-q-r)

Var. of ZUKRAH or ZŪKRAH/2* (Farmer 1978:I, 45, n. 6; EI(Eng), "Mizmār":541).

ZŪQRA (z-q-r)

An oboe-type aerophone of the Maghrib (Libyā and Tun.) (Sachs 1940: 248). Var. of ZUKRAH or ZŪKRAH/1*.

ZŪRNĀ, ZŪRNA or ZURNĀY

1. Generic term for any double reed aerophone (Farmer 1976b:23-24).
2. A double reed, conical aerophone of the Maghrib which normally has seven finger holes on the top and a rear thumb hole (Marcuse, al Dāqūqī 1965:38). This name is used for folk instruments of the type in the Maghrib. In the Mashriq it is known as MIZMĀR*; in Tun., as ZUKRAH, in Libyā as GHAYṬAH/1*. Its length varies from 30-40 cm. Its range is approximately 1½-2 octaves.

ZUWWĀDAH (z-w-d) colloq. for "that which is extra, the addition"

The embroidered covering of a single headed terra-cotta drum of the Maghrib (GUELLAL*) (Rouanet 1922:2932). Another colloq. form is ZAWWĀDAH*.

Supplement

AARBI or ʿARBI

Var. of ʿARABĪ* (Rouanet 1922:2865).

AASFOUR

Var. of ʿUṢFŪR* (Rouanet 1922:2925).

AÇFOUR

Var. of ʿUṢFŪR* (Rouanet 1922:2844).

ACHERANE

Var. of ʿUSHAYRĀN* (Rouanet 1922:2754).

ʿALĀ AL KHILĀF (kh-l-f) "with difference, inequality"

A variety of melodic patterning (INTIQĀL/1*) in which successive tones in a motif are repeated differing numbers of times (Ibn Zaylah 1964:42). For example: 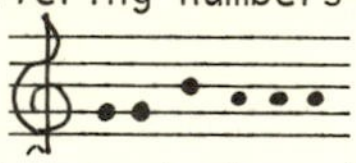 .

ʿALĀ AL MUSĀWĀH (s-w-y) "with equality, equivalence"

A variety of melodic patterning (INTIQĀL/1*) in which successive tones in a motif are repeated the same number of times (Ibn Zaylah 1964:42). See also the opp. ʿALĀ AL KHILĀF*.

ĀLAH MUṬRIBAH ('-w-l) (ṭ-r-b) "instrument of musical delight"

Musical instrument (Farmer 1945:21).

ʿARABĪ = ʿARBI, AARBI (ʿ-r-b) "Arab (adj.)"

A category of Maghribī music comprising tunes of the village or peasant musicians as distinguished from those of the more classical ṢANʿAH/2* or INQILĀB/2* repertoires. It is a category which is felt to be inferior to these two types, but superior in quality of musical and poetic expression to the ḤAWZĪ* music. Like the other repertoires, it comprises suites of vocal and instrumental numbers. See Rouanet 1922:2865, where this term is spelled AARBI or ʿARBI*.

ARBAʿAH AL AḌʿĀF (r-b-ʿ) (ḍ-ʿ-f) "the quadrupled"

Double octave interval (Ibn Zaylah 1964:23).

(AL) AWSĀṬ (w-s-ṭ) "the medium or average ones"

The medium sized intervals, i.e., the perfect fourth and perfect fifth (Ibn Zaylah 1964:23). See also (AL) KIBĀR*, (AL) ṢIGHĀR*, WUSṬĀ/2*.

BŪḌIYA

Var. of ABŪDHIYYAH* (Tsuge 1972:64).

DANDŪN = DENDOUN

A drum (ṬABL/2*) of the negroes of the Sūdān. Although it is a double headed drum, only one of its faces is used for playing. A hooked drumstick is manipulated by the right hand, while the left hand makes use of a straight stick or the fingers. It is also known as GUENGOU* (Rouanet 1922:2934).

ḌARB (ḍ-r-b)

7. Open-string execution of a tone on the lute (ʿŪD/2*). Opp. of DASS* (stopped-string execution) (Farmer 1933b:3).

DARDABAH

Syn. of DABDABAH/2* (Marcuse).

ḌARRĀB (ḍ-r-b) "one who always strikes"

A drummer, syn. of ḌĀRIB*.

DAWR (d-w-r)

8. Any of the three octave scales making up the complete scale or "collection" (JAMʿ/1*) of Arabian musical theory or of a melodic mode. The lowest of these was known as DAWR AL AWWAL, the middle one as DAWR AL THĀNĪ, and the highest as DAWR AL THĀLITH (al Fārābī 1967:124).

DENDOUN

Var. of DANDŪN* (Rouanet 1922:2934).

ḌIʿF (ḍ-ʿ-f)

2. Octave interval (Ibn Zaylah 1964:23).

ḌIʿF AL ḌIʿF (ḍ-ʿ-f) (ḍ-ʿ-f) "doubling of the doubling"

Double octave interval (Ibn Zaylah 1964:23).

DONBAG

A goblet-shaped single headed drum of modern ʿIrāq (Tsuge 1972:63). DŪMBŪK, DUNBŪK or DUMBUK* and DUMBALAK* are other names for this drum.

FÂÇIL

Var. of FĀṢILAH/4*, the separating time between the cycles of a rhythmic mode (Rouanet 1922:2727).

FAḌLĀT LAḤNIYYAH (pl. of FAḌLAH LAḤNIYYAH) (f-ḍ-l) (l-ḥ-n) "melodic remainders"

The smallest of the three sizes of intervals, i.e., all those smaller than the interval with ratio 16-15 (Ṣafī al Dīn in de Vaux 1891:297).

FAḌLĀT AL SAWĀQIṬ (pl. of FAḌLAH AL SĀQIṬAH) (f-ḍ-l) (s-q-ṭ) "falling remainders"

All those intervals of a size that, when they are doubled and subtracted from a perfect fourth, they leave a remainder smaller than a single interval of their size (Safi al Din in de Vaux 1891: 321). For example, a whole tone interval; when doubled and subtracted from a perfect fourth, a semitone remains.

FARSHAH = FERCHA (f-r-sh) "bed; mattress"

The fingerboard of a chordophone.

FERCHA

Var. of FARSHAH* (Rouanet 1922:2926).

GIRBAL

Var. of GHIRBĀL* (Shiloah 1965:I, 30).

GUEDRA

1. Cooking pot drum of the Maghrib.
2. A dance performed by Chleuh women in the southern part of Morocco.

HAOUZI

Var. of ḤAWZĪ* (Rouanet 1922:2866).

ʿILM AL ĪQĀʿ (ʿ-l-m) (w-q-ʿ) "knowledge of rhythms"

One of two branches into which ʿILM AL MŪSĪQĀ*, or the science of music, can be divided: the study of durations and rhythms (Yūsuf 1964:8). Opp. of ʿILM AL TA'LĪF*.

ʿILM AL TA'LĪF (ʿ-l-m) ('-l-f) "knowledge of composition"

One of two branches into which ʿILM AL MŪSĪQĀ*, or the science of music, can be divided: the study of tones and melodies (Yūsuf 1964:8). Opp. of ʿILM AL ĪQĀʿ*.

IQĀMAH (q-w-m) "establishment; stay"

Melodic patterning (INTIQĀL/1*) in which a tone is touched or sounded several times (Rouanet 1922:2726, 2808; de Vaux 1891:342). See also Ibn Zaylah 1964:42.

I'TILĀF (pl. I'TILĀFĀT) ('-l-f) "union; agreement"

Consonance (al Kindī 1966:151).

ITTIFĀQ AL AWWAL (w-f-q) ('-w-l) "first agreement"

The consonance of intervals smaller than an octave (de Vaux 1891:300; Ibn Zaylah 1964:24-25). See ITTIFĀQ AL THĀNĪ*.

ITTIFĀQ AL THĀNĪ (w-f-q) (th-n-y) "second agreement"

The consonance formed by the interval smaller than an octave when added to another sound which is the octave equivalent of one tone of the initial interval (de Vaux 1891:301).

JAMĀʿAH (j-m-ʿ)

2. Any of the three octave scales making up the complete scale or "collection" (JAMʿ/1*) of Arabian musical theory or of a melodic mode. The lowest of these was known as JAMĀʿAH AL ŪLĀ, the middle one as JAMĀʿAH AL THĀNIYAH, and the highest as JAMĀʿAH AL THĀLITHAH (al Fārābī 1967:124).

JINS AL MUʿTADIL (j-n-s) (ʿ-d-l) "straight or harmonious genus"

The enharmonic tetrachordal scalar segment (JINS/1*) (Ibn Zaylah 1964:27).

KARNĪṬAH

A musical instrument made of brass which resembles the GHAYṬAH/1*. It is longer than that popular oboe-type wind instrument (al Rizqī 1967:365).

(AL) KIBĀR (k-b-r) "the large ones"

Syn. of KUBRĀ*, but using a masculine form. The large intervals, i.e., the octave (ḌIʿF*), the octave plus fifth (THALĀTHAH AL AḌʿĀF*), and the double octave (ḌIʿF AL ḌIʿF*) (Ibn Zaylah 1964:23). See also (AL) AWSAṬ*, (AL) ṢIGHĀR*.

MAQṢŪR AL JANĀḤ = MAKSŪR AL ǦENÂH, MEQÇOUR EL DJENAH (q-ṣ-r) (j-n-ḥ) "shortened wing; broken wing"

A QAṢĪDAH/1*-type song of the folk repertoire (GRĪḤAH* or QARĪḤAH*) of the Maghrib with a love theme and usually marked by a stock phrase which begins each strophe. It is one of three varieties of folksong (Rouanet 1922:2883). See also MUSHARQĪ*, MAZLŪQ*.

MARTABAH (r-t-b)

2. Any of the three octave scales making up the complete scale or "collection" (JAMʿ/1*) of Arabian musical theory or of a melodic mode. The lowest of these was known as MARTABAH AL ŪLĀ, the middle one as MARTABAH AL THĀNIYAH, and the highest as MARTABAH AL THĀLITHAH (Mashāqah n.d.:fol. 3).

MAZLŪQ = MESLOUQ (z-l-q) "made slippery"

One of the three types of folksong of the GRĪḤAH* or QARĪḤAH* repertoire of the Maghrib. This term applies to the humorous songs (Rouanet 1922:2883). See also MAQṢŪR AL JANĀḤ*, MUSHARQĪ*, and MASLŪQ*.

MCHERQI

Var. of MUSHARQĪ* (Rouanet 1922:2883).

MEÇDER

Var. of MUṢADDAR/2*, one of the most noble parts of the NAWBAH/1* or suite (Rouanet 1922:2852-2854).

MEFTEL

Var. of MIFTĀL* (Rouanet 1922:2925).

MEQÇOUR EL-DJENAH

Var. of MAQṢŪR AL JANĀḤ* (Rouanet 1922:2942). MEQÇOUR EL-DJENAD, as found on p. 2883 of the same work, is undoubtedly a printer's error.

MESTEKBER SENÂA

Var. of MUSTAKHBIR AL ṢANʿAH* (Farmer 1976a:202).

MEZLOUQ

Var. of MAZLŪQ* (Rouanet 1922:2884).

MIFTĀL (pl. MAFĀTĪL) = MEFTEL (f-t-l) "instrument of twisting"

Tuning peg.

MUKHILLAN (kh-l-l) "that which comes short of"

A variety of melodic patterning (INTIQĀL/1*) in which the melody returns a single time to a tone other than the starting tone or MABDA'/3* (Ibn Zaylah 1964:42).

NAR'AM

Var. of NAGHAM* (Rouanet 1922:2756).

NAWBAH ʿARABĪ (n-w-b) (ʿ-r-b) "rotation or suite of the Arab"

A suite belonging to an inferior category of folk music (Alg.). This music is sung by the village people of the interior. It is less refined in both words and music than the NAWBAH GHURNĀṬIYYAH* or the somewhat less classical NAWBAH INQILĀBĀT*. In Rouanet (1922:2865), we find NAWBAH AARBI or ʿARBI.

NAWWARAT

Var. pl. of NUWWĀRAH* (Rouanet 1922:2924).

QABD'A

Var. of QABḌAH* (Rouanet 1922:2924).

QŪRQAH

Equiv. of KŪRKAH* (Farmer 1978:II, 12, n. 4).

RĀJIʿ AL FARD (r-j-ʿ) (f-r-d) "return which is single"

A category of melodic patterning (INTIQĀL/1*) involving a single return to the starting tone (MABDA'/3*) or near it (Ibn Zaylah 1964:41). See RĀJIʿ AL MUTAWĀTIR*.

RĀJIʿ AL MUDLA' (r-j-') (d-l-') "ribbed return"

A category of melodic patterning (INTIQĀL/1*) involving returns to other than the starting tone (MABDA'/3*) (Ibn Zaylah 1964:42; Ṣafī al Dīn in de Vaux 1891:342).

RĀJIʿ AL MUSTADĪR (r-j-ʿ) (d-w-r) "circular return"

A category of melodic patterning (INTIQĀL/1*) involving exact return to the starting tones (MABĀDI') (Ibn Zaylah 1964:42).

RĀJIʿ AL MUTAWĀTIR (r-j-ʿ) (w-t-r) "successive return"

A category of melodic patterning (INTIQĀL/1*) involving many returns to the starting tone (MABDA'/3*) or near it (Ibn Zaylah 1964:41). See RĀJIʿ AL FARD*.

RICHET ENNESSER

Var. of RĪSHAH AL NASR* (Rouanet 1922:2926).

RŪḤ AFZĀ (r-w-ḥ) (?)

A long necked lute with a hemispherical sound chest and six double strings of silk and metal (Farmer EI(Eng), "ʿŪd":988).

RUJŪʿ (r-j-ʿ)

4. This term is used to designate those categories of melodic patterning (INTIQĀL/1*) in which the melody moves in both directions and makes returns to tones heard earlier (Ṣafī al Dīn in de Vaux 1891:342). It replaces RĀJIʿ in compounds such as RĀJIʿ AL FARD*, RĀJIʿ AL MUTAWĀTIR*, etc. in the writing of Ṣafī al Dīn (de Vaux 1891:342).

RUJŪʿ MUKHTALIF AL NISAB (r-j-ʿ) (kh-l-f) (n-s-b) "return with ratios which differ"

A category of melodic patterning (INTIQĀL/1*) involving returns to tones sounded earlier through use of intervals of different sizes (Ṣafī al Dīn in de Vaux 1891:342).

RUJŪʿ MUNBAT (r-j-ʿ) (n-b-t) "grown or developed return

A category of melodic patterning (INTIQĀL/1*) involving returns to various tones other than the starting tone (MABDA'/3*), but near to it (Ṣafī al Dīn in de Vaux 1891:1891:342). Syn. of RĀJIʿ AL MUḌLAʿ*.

RUJŪʿ MUTASĀWĪ AL NISAB (r-j-ʿ) (s-w-y) (n-s-b) "return with ratios which are equal"

A category of melodic patterning (INTIQĀL/1*) involving returns to tones sounded earlier, through use of intervals of identical sizes (Ṣafī al Dīn in de Vaux 1891:342).

SCHENACHEK

Var. of SHANĀSHIK* (Rouanet 1922:2793).

SHANĀSHIK = SCHENACHEK

The rattles or castanets which are used by street musicians (Rouanet 1922:2793).

SIAH'

Var. of ṢIYĀḤ/3* (supp.) (Rouanet 1922:2865).

(AL) ṢIGHĀR (ṣ-gh-r) "the small ones"

The small intervals, i.e., the major third (ratio 5/4) and every smaller interval (Ibn Zaylah 1964:23). See also (AL) AWSAṬ*, (AL) KIBĀR*, ṢUGHRĀ*.

ṢIYĀḤ (ṣ-y-ḥ)

3. A recitative-like vocal solo which terminates a choral number in the NAWBAH ʿARABĪ*, a type of folkish suite of Algeria (Rouanet 1922:2865).

TABELLA

Var. of ṬABL/2*. It is described as a large drum which is only used in open air performance and for accompanying the ZAMR*. It is a double headed instrument, about 35-50 cm. in diameter, which is carried suspended from the neck. Two flexible drumsticks are used in its performance (Rouanet 1922:2793).

TCHNATCHEL

Var. of SHANĀSHIL, the jingles mounted in the rim of the tambourine (Rouanet 1922:2934, 2944). See SHANĀSHIN*.

TEBEUL

Var. of ṬABL/2* (Rouanet 1922:2933).

THALĀTHAH AL AḌʿĀF (th-l-th) (ḍ-ʿ-f) "three doublings"

The interval of an octave plus perfect fifth (Ibn Zaylah 1964:23).

TURAR

Var. of ṬARRĀR*, player of the ṬĀR* (Rouanet 1922:2910).

YAD = YED (y-d) "hand"

The neck of the violin or other similar chordophone.

YED

Var. of YAD* (Rouanet 1922:2925).

ZĀ'ID JUZ'AN (z-y-d) (j-z-') "increaser by a segment"

Ratio as indicator of interval size (Yūsuf 1964:11).

ZĀ'ID NIṢFAN (z-y-d) (n-ṣ-f) "increaser by a half"

The ratio of the perfect fifth interval (ratio 3/2) (Yūsuf 1964:11).

ZĀ'ID RUBʿAN (z-y-d) (r-b-ʿ) "increaser by a quarter"

The ratio of the major third interval (5/4) (Yūsuf 1964:11).

ZĀ'ID THULTHAN (z-y-d) (th-l-th) "increaser by a third"

The ratio of the perfect fourth interval (4/3) (Yūsuf 1964:11).

ZĀ'ID TUSʿAN (z-y-d) (t-s-ʿ) "increaser by a ninth"

The ratio of the minor whole step interval (10/9) (Yūsuf 1964:11).

ZENKALA

Var. of ZĪRKŪLAH or ZIRKŪLĀH* (Rouanet 1922:2740, 2809).

ZERKALA

Var. of ZĪRKŪLAH or ZIRKŪLĀH* (Rouanet 1922:2740, 2809; Collangettes 1904:412).

ZINKULĀH

Var. of ZĪRKŪLAH or ZIRKŪLĀH* (Maḥfūẓ 1964:79).

Appendix I: Index of English Musical Terms

ACCELERANDO
ghāyah al surʿah, muṣarraf, ziyādad surʿah bil tadrīj
ACCELERATE, TO
ʿajjala
ACCELERATION
ḥadr/1, ḥathīth/2, ḥathth, surʿah/1, takhfīf/1, tamkhīr/1, taqrīb, see idrāj
ACCENT
hamzah/2, see nabr or nabrah/1, /2
ACCIDENTAL
ʿalāmah al taḥwīl
ACCOMPANIED (of a vocal or instrumental solo)
maqrūn or maqrūnah/2
ACCOMPANIMENT
iṣṭiḥāb/2, musāḥabah, musāyarah, see tarjamah, taṣdiyyah
ACCOMPANIST(s)
areddad, muṣāḥib
ACCORDATURA
iṣṭiḥāb/1, taswiyah/2, see taswiyah al murakkabah, taswiyah al muzāwaj, taswiyah al ʿuẓmā
ACOUSTICAL
samʿī
ADAGIO
amhal
AEROPHONE
ālah nafkh, ālah dhāt al nafkh, miʿzaf or miʿzafah/3, see BRASS INSTRUMENTS, ORGAN, WOODWIND INSTRUMENTS
(unidentified) būq bil qaṣabah, ghāb or ghābah/2, hanbaqah, hunbūqah, ʿirān, kerift, manṣūrī/2, mazāmīr, mizmār al ʿirāqī, naqīb, nāqir, nāy muhadhdhab, nāy tatarī, qaṣab, qashiq, rūyin nāy, shimshār or shimshāl, shuqrah, sudāsī, zamjarah, zamkhar/1, zammār/3, zamr al būqī, zanbaq
ALLEGRETTO
ʿājil
ALLEGRO
aʿjal
ALLEGRO VIVACE
sarīʿ or sarīʿah
AMBITUS
āhang or āhank/1, /2
ANDANTE
wānin
(slower than)awnā
ANTECEDENT (phrase or segment)
su'āl
ANTIPHONAL RESPONSE
jawāb/2
ANTIPHONY
mujawwabah, mujawwabah ṣawtiyyah, radd
APOTOME (major semitone of 2187/2048, 114 c.)
faḍlah al ṭanīnī, infiṣāl, mujannab al ṣaghīr, see mutamman (16/15, 112 c.) which d'Erlanger equates with the apotome
APPLAUSE
taḥsīn/2
ARCHLUTE
shāhrūd or shahrūd/1

ASCENDING (in pitch)
ṣāʿidan, see taqdim
AUDIENCE
mustamiʿūn
AUDITION
samāʿ/1
AUGMENTED SECOND
buʿd al zā'id, thāniyah al zā'idah

BACK (of sound chest of a chordophone)
qā'idah (qānūn), ẓahr/1, see ḍahr
BAGPIPES
ghayṭah/3, jirbah, mizmār al jirāb, mizwad, mizwij/2, ruwāqah, qirbah, suqqārah, ʿunnayz, urghan or urghanūn/4, urghānūm, zukrah or zūkrah/2, /3, zummārah al qirbah, zummārah bi suʿn
BAND (military)
naqqār khānah, naqqārah khānah, nawbah/2, ṭabl khānah/1, see ENSEMBLE
BAR LINE (notation)
qadr
BASS
ghalīẓah, see VOCAL RANGES (male)
BEAT
see PERCUSSION
(followed by a pause) naqrah sākinah/1
("moving," i.e., marked by a percussion rather than a silence) naqrah mutaharrikah/2
(not followed by a pause) naqrah mutaḥarrikah/1
(opening of a rhythmic cycle) ra's al nadfah
BEATING TIME
ḍarb/5, naqr, qarʿ, ṭarqīm al mīzān
BELL(s)
ajrās, darā, jalājil/1, jaras, juljul/1, naqūs or nāqūs/2, qalāqil, qalqal or qalqalah, see dabbūs, jaghānah, khalākhil or khalākhīl, khalkhal or khalkhāl, ṣaghānah, zillī māsha
BELLOWS (of organ or bagpipes)
ziqq
BLOWING REED
balūṣā, lisān, qaṣabah/4, qaṣābah, qaṣb or qaṣbah/2, qashshah, rīshah/2, see DOUBLE REED
BOW (of a chordophone)
ʿaṣā, majrūr, qaws
BOW, TO
jarra
BOWED CHORDOPHONES
amez'ad, amz'ad, arnabah, arrabil, ghishak, ghūghā, gughe, iqliq, jarānah, jawz, kamān or kamānjah/1, /2, /3, kamān al awsaṭ, kamān al jahīr, kamānjah al ʿajūz, kamānjah al ʿarabī, kamānjah al farkh, kamānjah al frānjī, kamānjah kabīrah, kamānjah rūmī, kamānjah ṣaghīrah, kamānjah taqṭīʿ, līr, lira or lîra/1, lūr or lūrā/1, majrūrah, murabbaʿ/2, /3, rabāb or rabābah, rabāb maghribī, rabāb miṣrī, rabāb al mughannī, rabāb al shāʿir, rabāb al sharqī, rabāb al turkī, rūd, shīshāk or shīshāl, tidinit, ʿūd al rabāb, see LUTE(s)
BRASS INSTRUMENTS
see HORNS, TRUMPETS
BRIDGE (of a chordophone)
anf/2, dāmā (qānūn), faras, ghazāl or ghazālah, ḥāmil or ḥāmilah, ḥimār, kharaq, kursī/3, mushṭ/2, ẓāmilah (?), see taḥzīz
BUGLE CALL
nawbah/5

CADENCE
maḥaṭṭ/1, qafl or qaflah/2
(final) qafl or qaflah/2, taqfiyyah/1, taslīm/2, taslūm
CALL TO PRAYER (Islamic)
adhān
CAMEL DRIVERS' MUSIC/SONG
ghinā' al ʿarab, ghinā' al rukbān, ḥadw/2, ḥidā' or ḥudā'/1, hujaynī, khabab/1, rakbānī, rukbānī
CANTILLATION
see CHANT/CHANTING, QUR'ĀNIC CANTILLATION
CASTANETS
aqligh, muṣāfiq, qaraqāt, qarāqib, qarqabāt, qarqabū or

qarqābū, ṣannājāt, ṣannājāt al jaysh, shanāshik (supp.), ṣunūj/1, ṣunūj al aṣābiʿ or ṣunūj al yad, ṭiqerqawin, see IDIOPHONE(s)
CENT
dharrah ṣawtiyyah, sant
CHANT/CHANTING
ḥawj, ṣadḥ, shadw/2, shudāh, taʿbīr, taghbīr, tarannum/1, tarnīm/1, /2, zamzamah/1
(genres of) adhān, ahellel, ḥidā' or ḥudā'/2, ibtihāl, inshād/3, madīḥ, madīḥ nabawī, mawlid/2, takbīr, talbiyah, talḥīn/3, /4, tartīl/1, tartīl dīnī
CHANT, TO
anshada/2, ghannā/2, jawwada, laḥḥana/2, rannama, rattala/1, /2, taghannā/2, tarannama/1, zamzama
CHANTER
hallāl, ḥazzāb, maddāh/1, mu'adhdhin, munshid, musammiʿ/1, muzamzim, qawwāl/1, qawwīl, tallā', see VOCALIST
CHIME(s)
juljul/2, juljul al ṣayyāḥ, juljul al ṣiyāḥ
CHIN REST (of bowed chordophone)
dhāqinah
CHORDOPHONES
ālah watariyyah, ālah dhāt al awtār, awtār/1, dhāt al awtār, miʿzaf or miʿzafah/1, /3, mizmār/5, qithoro/2, see BOWED CHORDOPHONES, LUTE(s), OPEN-STRINGED INSTRUMENTS
(unidentified) dandafah, kennara, kinnīrah, shaqirah
CHORISTER(s)
madhhabjī, madhhabjiyyah, munshid/4, muraddid, shaddād, shaddādah/1, /2
CHORUS
jawq ghinā'iyyah, kabar/2, kūrus, madhhab/3, sannīdah, shaddādah/1
CHROMATIC
mulawwan/1, see TETRACHORDAL/PENTACHORDAL SCALAR SEGMENT (chromatic), SCALE (chromatic)
CIRCULAR BREATHING
radd al nafas
CLACKERS/CLAPPERS
dabbūs, faqqāshāt, mukhashkhashāt, muqāriʿ muṣaffaḥāt, naqūs or nāqūs/1, shakshīkah, shaqshaqah, shuqayfāt, see IDIOPHONES
CLAPPING
see APPLAUSE
(to execute a rhythm) safq, tasdiyyah, tasfīq, taṣfīq
CLARINET (single reed woodwind instrument)
arghūl or urghūl, būq/3
ghayṭah/2, gheta, ghanam, ghīṭah, mawṣūl, sama'a, urghūl, yarghūl, see qurnāṭah
CLARIONET
qurnāṭah
"CLASSICAL" (ART) MUSIC
ālah, ālah andalusiyyah, ghurnāṭī or ghurnāṭiyyah, kalām al jadd, ma'lūf/1, mūsīqā andalusiyyah, qadariyyah al ṣināʿah, samāʿ/2, ṣanʿah/1, ṭabʿ/3, see khamsah wa khamsīn
CLEF
miftāḥ/4, see F CLEF, G CLEF
CODA
khurūj/1, silsilah/1, tadhyīl/1, taqfīlah/1, ṭawq/1, see āhang or āhank/3, āhāt/2, ḍurūb/2, hank/1,taqfiyyah/2
COMBINATION
(of intervals) tamzīj/2
(of rhythmic cycles) tamzīj/4
(of tetrachordal scalar segments to form a modal scale) jamʿ/1, jamāʿah, tamzīj/3, tarkīb/4, /5, see tarkīb bi istiqāmah, tarkīb munakkas
(of tones) tamzīj/1
COMMA (interval of approx. 81/80 ratio)
"B"/2, Baqiyyah, kūma or kūmā, faḍlah
COMPOSE, TO
laḥḥana/1
COMPOSER
(of lyrics) mu'allif/2
(of music) laḥḥān/1, mu'allif/3, mulaḥḥin/1, /2, ṣāniʿ
COMPOSING/COMPOSITION (the act)
ikhtirāʿ, mu'allaf, talḥīn/2, ta'līf/1, ta'līf al ṣawtī, tanẓīm al alḥān, ṣiyāghah, ṣiyāghah al laḥn

COMPOSING/COMPOSITION (the product)
talḥīn/1, ta'līf al ṣawtī
(instrumental) ta'līf al ālī,
ta'līf al ṣāmit
(vocal) ta'līf al ghinā'ī,
ta'līf al nāṭiq
CONCERT
ḥaflah, ḥaflah mūsīqiyyah
CONDUCTOR
See LEADER (of ensemble)
CONJUNCT
muttaṣil/2, /3, /4, muwaṣṣal
CONSEQUENT (phrase or segment)
jawāb/2, see ANTECEDENT (phrase or segment)
CONSONANCE
imtizāj/2, i'tilāf (supp.), ittifāq/1, talā'im, see HARMONY (concordance), OCTAVE(consonance)
CONSONANT
mulā'im, mulāyam (colloq.), mutalā'im or mutalā'imah/1, /2, muttafiq, muwāfiq or muwāfiqah
CONSONANT INTERVALS
mulā'amāt al nagham, mutalā'im or mutalā'imah/1
CONTRAFACTURA
tarkīb/8, see qirā'ah bil alḥān
CONTRARY MOTION
taḍādd
COUPLET
baytān/2, baytayn
(musical setting of) baytān/1
"COURSE" (modal)
majrā, see majrā al binṣir, majrā al wusṭā, mukhtalifah, mu'talifah/2, nagham mukhtalifah, nagham mu'talifah
CRESCENDO
ziyādah shaddah al ṣawt tadrījiyyan
CRESCENDO SIGN
ʿalāmah al taṣaʿʿud
CURTAIN (separating performers from audience)
sitārah or sitār/1
CYCLE (of a rhythmic mode)
dā'irah/6, ḍarb/3, dawr/1, ṭaqm
(basic) mīzān muṭlaq, taktīf, zamān al mabda'
CYMBALS
fuqayshāt, jaghānah, kās or ka's, kāsah/2, kūs/2, ku'ūs, muṣāfiq, muṣannaj, naqūs or nāqūs, nuīqsât, nuqaysāt, ṣaffāqatān, ṣaghānah, ṣājāt, sajjāt or ṣajjāt, ṣalāṣil, ṣalṣal, ṣanj or ṣinj/2, ṣaqr, shanāshik, shanāshil, shuqayfāt, sindi, ṣinj, ṣunūj/2, ṭūs, wann/3, zanj/1, zill, zillī māsha, zinj/1, zunūj, see zang

DA CAPO (sign)
murajjiʿ, muwajjihah
DANCE/DANCING
raqṣ, shaṭḥ/1, zafn
DANCE, TO
raqaṣa
DANCE (genres)
ʿarāḍah, ʿarḍah, ardha, ayala, dabkah, daḥḥiyyah, guedra/2 (supp.), lūnjah/3, radḥah, ṣahjah, shaṭḥah, takhmīr, zambrah/2
DANCER
ʿālim/2, rāqiṣ/1, raqqāṣ
DANCING GIRL
zāfinah
DECRESCENDO SIGN
ʿalāmah al tanazzul
DEMISEMIQUAVER
thulāthiyyah al asnān
DESCENDING (in pitch)
nāzilan, see ta'khīr
DIMINUENDO
ikhtiṣār/2, nuqṣan al ṣawt bil tadrīj
DISJUNCT
mufaṣṣal, munfaṣil or munfaṣilah
DISSONANCE
ikhtilāf, nashāz, tanāfur
DISSONANT
ghayr mutalā'im, mutanāfir/1, /2, ẓāhir al tanāfur
DOMINANT (in Western sense)
thābit/2
"DOMINANT" (modal)
ghammāz, nasībah
DOTTED (notation)
manqūṭah
DOTTED NOTE
ʿalāmah manqūṭah
DOUBLE, TO (at the octave)
aḍʿafa
DOUBLE CLARINET
arbāb, arghūl, ghanam, juzule, maqrūn or maqrūnah/1, mashūrah, māsūl or māsūlah, mawṣūl, muzāwaj/2, qurnah, urghūl, zāmar,

zamr/2, zukrah or zūkrah/2, zummār or zummārah/1, zummārah khumāsiyyah, zummārah al muzdawajah, zummārah rubā‘iyyah, zummārah sudāsiyyah
DOUBLE OCTAVE
arba‘ah al aḍ‘āf (supp.), bu‘d alladhī bil kull marratayn, bu‘d bil kull marratayn, ḍi‘f al ḍi‘f (supp.) ḍi‘f alladhī bil kull, ḍi‘f dhū al kull, see ab‘ād muttafiqah al naghm, muttafiqāt ‘uẓmā, nagham ‘uẓmā
DOUBLE PIPED
muzdawij or muzdawijah/2
DOUBLE PIPED AEROPHONES
dūnāy, mijwiz, mizmār al muthannā, mizmār muzāwaj or mizmār al muzawwaj, mizwad, mizwij/1, /2, muthannā, muzāwaj/2, muzdawij or muzdawijah/2, qaṣabayn, yarghūl, see DOUBLE CLARINET
DOUBLE REED
rīshah muzdawijah
DOUBLE REED AEROPHONES
see OBOE
DOUBLE SHARP or DOUBLE FLAT
‘alāmah al taḥwīl al muḍā‘af
DOUBLE STRUNG
muzdawij or muzdawijah/5
DOUBLING (at the octave)
iḍ‘af/1
(the length of a percussion)
taḍ‘īf/4
DRONE
ṭanṭanah asās al maqām, tarjī‘ or tarjī‘ah/3
DRONE PIPE
nūtī, sanad
DRONE STRING
lāzim al tarjī‘ah, muṭlaq/3, rāji‘/1
DRUM
ṭabl/1, ṭablah/1
(barrel) duhul, naqaquîr, see DRUM (double headed)
(double headed) atambor, dandūn (supp.), duhul, guangua (?), guengou, naqaquîr, ṭabbāl/3, tabella (supp.), ṭabl/2, ṭabl baladī/1, ṭabl dūrū‘ī, ṭabl kabīr/2, ṭabl turkī, ṭablah/2, toûzah
(pot) guedra (supp.), qaṣ‘ah/1, tarra
(single headed)abrûâl, aqwāl, aṣaf, barbakh, dabdāb, dabdabah/2, danbak, darabukkah, darbūkah/2, dardabah (supp.), derdeba, dirrīj, donbaq (supp.), dumbalak, dūmbūk, dunbak, durraij or durrayj, guellal, gullāl, kabar/1, khashabah, kūbah, qallāl, qullāl, quwwāl, safāqis, tabdaba, ṭabl baladī/2, ṭabl al mukhannath, ṭabl al sūdān, ṭablah/3, tanbak, tbîlât, umm wa ḥāshiyah/2 (pair)
(unidentified) ‘air, allûn, ‘atīdah, ‘artabah (?), awzān (?), ḥallah or ḥillah, sāz, sāz dūlāb, ṭabīlah/2, ṭabl tawīl, tinbāl, ṭirbāl, ṭūbāl, tubbel, tumbak, tumbul, ṭunbūr/3
(waisted) kūbah, ṣafāqis, ṭabīr, ṭabl al mukhannath, ṭabl al sūdān, ta‘rījah/1
see FRAME DRUM, KETTLEDRUM(s)
DRUM COVERING (embroidered)
zawwādah, zuwwādah
DRUM STROKES
dik, dum, dumm, kā, kah, hak, mah, tā, tā', tak, takk, tik/1
DRUMS (paired)
umm wa ḥāshiyah/2, zawj/1
DRUMMER
ḍārib, ḍarrāb, ḍurrāb, ṭabbāl, wazzān
DRUMSTICK
dainak, shabīl, shanghal, zawāhim
DULCIMER
ṣanj ṣīnī, sanṭūr, ṣinj jīnī or ṣinj khīnī, sinṭīr
DURATION
naqrah/4, zaman or zamān/1, see PERCUSSION

EASTERN
mashriqī, sharqī
ECHO
rannah, ṣadā
EIGHTH NOTE
dhāt al sinn/1, kurush, niṣf al waḥdah al ṣaghīrah/3, waḥdah al ṣughrā
EIGHTH REST (notation)
laḥīẓah
ELEMENTS/TEMPERAMENTS
‘anāṣir al arba‘, ṭab‘/3, ṭubū‘
EMBELLISHMENT (of a melody)
taḥāsin, taḥsīn/1, taḥsīn al

ḍarb, taḥsīn al laḥn, tarkhīm, tarnīm/2, tazyīdah, tazyīnah, zawā'id, zawāq, zukhruf, zukhrufah

EMBELLISHMENTS
(durational) ḥathīth/2, ʿimād, iʿtimād/2, majāz, tadhkīrāt or t'âskîrât, taḍʿīf/2, taʿmīr, taʿmīr al farāgh, taqaṣṣur, tartīl/5, taṣdīr, tawāṣul, ṭayy, ziyādah/1
(involving repetitions of a tone) marghūl or marghūlah/1, mukassarah, qawwa, zā'idah
(tonal) ibdāl, ibdāl al shuḥājāt, (bi)izlāq mah'âsin al lah'n, mahzūzah, mālsh, marghūl or marghūlah/1, mukassarah, nuqṣan, qawwa, shadhrah, tadhyīl/2, taḍʿīf/1, /3, tafkhīm, takarrur/3, takrīr/1, takthīr, ta'līf al awtār, tamzīj/5, tarʿīd/1, /2, tarʿīdah, tarkīb/1, tashqīq, tawṣīl/1, tudhrī or tudrī

EMBELLISHMENT SEGMENTS
dassah, jumlah/1, tafkhīm, thaniyyah

END-BLOWN FLUTE
See FLUTE (end-blown)

END OPENING (of aerophone)
maʿṭif, ra's/2, see thaqb or thuqb

ENHARMONIC
mulawwan/2

ENSEMBLE (musical)
ʿAwwādah/2, dammamāt, firqah/1, /2, imdyazen, jālghī baghdādī, jawq, madhhabjiyyah, rubāʿī, ṣahbajiyyah, sitārah or sitār/2, ṭabl baladī/3, takht, see BAND (military)

EQUIVALENT (in pitch)
mutashābih, quwwah/4, tamdid mutasawi, wahid bil quwwah, see mutashabih al mukhtalif bil quwwah

"ETHOS" DOCTRINE
ṭabʿ/3, ta'thīr, see busṭī, karam, muʿtadil, qabḍī

EXTENSION OF MELODIC RANGE
takthīr al ṭabaqāt

F CLEF
miftāḥ fā, miftāḥ jahīr

FACE (of musical instrument)
baṭn, bayāḍ, dā'irah/7, fusḥah/1, jildah, ṣadr/1, ṣafḥ, saṭḥ, wajh/1

FALSETTO
takhannuth

FAST (in tempo)
khabab/2, khafīf/1, sarīʿ, ṭā'ir, ṭīz/2

FASTER
asraʿ/1, see sarīʿ al hazaj

FINGERBOARD (of plucked or bowed chordophone)
farshah(supp.), see malmas, ʿunq

FINGER EXERCISES
see mūjib

FINGER HOLE(s) (of aerophones)
maʿṭif, mutakhallaṣāt al hawā', thaqb or thuqb

FINGER POSITION
nuqṭah, see FRET(s)/FRET POSITION(s)

FIXED TONES (of the scale)
thābit/1

FIXED TONE INSTRUMENT
thābit al ṣawt

FLAT SIGN
ʿalāmah al khafḍ

FLUTE
ṣaffārah/2, sāfūra, sūfaīra, sūfayrah
(end-blown) abbūbah, ʿawwād/2, ʿawwādah/3, faḥl, ghāb or ghābah/1, imbūbū, janjīrah, juwāq/1, lira or līra/4, manjārah, manjīrah, manṣūr, manṣūrī/2, mizmār/4, nāy/1, nāy abyaḍ, nāy bayḍā', nāy jirāf, nāy safīd, nāy shāh, nāy zunāmī, nīra, qaṣabah/2, qaṣabah, qaṣabah matāʿ al ghannā'ī, qaṣabah matāʿ al maddah, qaṣb or qaṣbah/1, qaṣbah ʿashariyyah, qaṣbah khumāsiyyah, qaṣbah wasaṭiyyah, qaṣībah, qaṣṣābah, qawal, quṣaybah, quṣṣāb or quṣṣābah/1, ṣaffārah/4, shabāb, shabbābah/1, shāh, shāhrūd or shahrūd, ṣuffāra, surnāy/2, ta'wwadit, ʿuffâtah, yarāʿ or yarāʿah/1, zamkhar/2, zīr/2
(transverse) shāhīn/1, see TRANSVERSE (said of a flute), WHISTLE FLUTE

FOLK MUSIC (genres)
abū al zuluf, abūdhiyyah, aferdi,

aferdi, ahāzīj, ahellel, ʿamal/1, ʿarabī (supp.), ʿarūbī/2, /3, asāmar, ashghāl/1, /2, ʿatābā or ʿatābah, atemchi, ʿaytah, badwah, barwal/1, barwālah, basīṭ or basīṭah/4, /5, /7, basīṭ al murakkab, basseh, bistah or bastah, baṭāyḥī/1, baṭīḥ, baytayn, billīq, burĝel, daḥḥiyyah, dā'irah/4, daraj/1, ḍarb/6, dārij/2, /4, darrāzī, ḍawr/5, dūbayt/2, fijrī, fundu, furūdāsht, ghazal, ghinā' al mawqiʿ, ghinā' al mutqan, ghinā' al raqīq, hadayā or hadāye, hadī, ḥadw/1, /2, ḥamās, ḥamd, ḥanafī, hawā'ī, hazaj/1, /4, /7, ḥidā' or ḥudā'/1, /3, hiğğon, hijjaniyye, hijā', ḥimyarī, ḥiwār, ḥōrāb, hōsā, hujaynī, infirād, inqilāb/2, inshād/1, /2, inṣirāf/1, istiftāḥ/2, istihlāl, izli, jamʿ al jamʿ/2, kalām malḥūn, kānkān, khābāriyyah, khalās, khatm/1, khrab, kiami-natik, kull al ḍurūb, kull al ḍurūb wal nigham kull al nigham, laḥn al ḥurr, laiwah, laṭm, layālī, lmaït, madḥ, makhāzinī, makhlaṣ, makhūrī/2, malḥūn/1, maqām/3, maqām al ʿirāqī, maqṣūr al janāḥ (supp.), mardamzād, maslūq, maṭāyḥī, mawāliyā/1, mawāt, mawlid/2, mawwāl/1, mayjanā, mazlūq (supp.), miyāt khānah, mrâria, muʿannā, mukhlaṣ, mūnūlūj, murakkab or murakkabah/5, muraṣṣaʿ/1, musabbaʿ/1, musabbaʿ al zahrī, musāmarah, mushajjiʿ, musharqī (supp.), mustakhbir/2, mustakhbir al inqilābāt, mustazād, muwashshaḥ/1, nadb, naqāqīr/2, naqsh/2, naṣb, nashīd, nashīd al ʿajam, nashīd al ʿarab, nawḥ/1, /2, nāyalī/1, naẓm, niyāḥah, nuftah, nuʿmānī, pishrū/1, qadariyyah, qadariyyah al ṣināʿah, qarrāḍī or qarrāḍiyyah, qaṣīd, qaṣīdah/1, qawl/3, qaylemi, qiyām nāṭiq, quddām/1, rikāb, rithā', ṣahbā, ṣahjah, samāʿ/2, sāmir, sarrābah, ṣawt/2, /7, ṣawt al wasaṭ, sharqī/1, shughl/1, /2, shurūqī, simāʿī, sināḍ, ṣiyāḥ/3 (supp.), sūsy, szahdje, tacheraft, taghazzul/1, /2, tahlīl, tahlīlah, taḥrīr, talḥīn/6, tamawait, tamediazt, tamhawst, tamseralit, taqṭūqah, tarānah, tarhiult, tarnīmah/1, /2, tashyīd, tawshīḥ/1, umm al zuluf, unshūdah, urghan or urghanūn/3, yatāyim, zajal/1, zakhmah/3, zawbaʿī, ziyādah/2, zedayet (ziyādah ?)

(vocal religious)
adhān, ahellel, dārij/3, dhikr, ḥamd, ḥizb/1, ibtihāl, istiftāḥ/2, madīḥ, madīḥ nabawī, mawlid/2, samāʿ/2, taʿbīr, taghbīr, tahlīl, tahlīlah, takbīr, talbiyah, tartīl dīnī, see QUR'ANIC RECITATION

GENUS
see TETRACHORDAL/PENTACHORDAL SCALAR SEGMENT

GLISSANDO
(bi) izlāq, tadhyīl/2, tawṣīl/1

GLOTTAL STOP
hamzah/1, nabr or nabrah/1, nabrah ṣawtiyyah

GONG
naqūs or nāqūs/4

GRACE NOTE(s)
ʿalāmah ʿāriḍah, ishārah ḥulyah, shadhrah, see basīṭ or basīṭah/8, murakkab or murakkabah/3

GRAVE
baṭī'

HAIR (of bow)
shaʿr

HALF NOTE
bayḍā', waḥdah al mutawassiṭah/1

HALF REST(notation)
ruwayhah

HANDLE(of bow)
maqbiḍ or miqbaḍ, see lawlab

HARMONIOUS
mu'talifah/1

HARMONIZE, TO
māshā

HARMONY (concordance) insijām. ta'alluf, ta'līf/3, tanāghum, tawāfuq, see CONSONANCE

HARMONY (coordination of vocal and instrumental parts)
ittifāq/2

bib/1, /2, qāṣib, qaṣṣāb, qaṣṣāb ʿarabī, zakkār, zāmir/2, zammār/1, /2
(skilled on chordophones) aḍrab al nās bil watar
(soloist) ʿāzif munfarid
INTERMEZZO
tawshiyah or tūshiyah/3, tawshiyah al inṣirāfāt
INTERVAL
bardah/1, buʿd, nabr or nabrah/3, pardah/2, see APOTOME, AUGMENTED SECOND, COMMA, DOUBLE OCTAVE, LIMMA, THIRD (interval), OCTAVE, PERFECT FIFTH, PERFECT FOURTH, QUARTER TONE, SEMITONE, THREE-QUARTER INTERVAL, WHOLE TONE
(categories) abʿād laḥniyyah, abʿād mutashābihah al naghm, (al) awsāṭ (supp.), faḍlāt laḥniyyah (supp.), faḍlāt al sawāqiṭ (supp.), (al) kibār (supp.), kubrā, mulā'amāt al nagham, mutashābih al mukhtalif bil quwwah, muttafiqāt ṣughrā, muttafiqāt ʿuẓmā, muttafiqāt wusṭā, (al) ṣighār (supp.), wusṭā/2
(consonant) mulā'amāt al ʿashr, see CONSONANT
(dissonant) buʿd mutanāfir, see DISSONANT
(highest tone of) ṣiyāḥ/2
(larger than one octave) ittifāq al thānī
(lowest tone of) sajāḥ/3, see constructs of shuḥāj
(smaller than one octave) ittifāq al awwal
INTRODUCTION
see PRELUDE
INVENTOR (traditional)
(of drum and tambourine) Ṭūbal
(of harp) Ḍalāl
(of lute) Lamak or Lamk ibn Mutawshīl
INVERSION
qalb

KETTLEDRUM(s)
aṭabal, bāz or bāzah
chūmlak, dunbalagī, dabdāb, dabdabah/1, deblak, kurjah, kurkatū, kūs/1, miʿzaf or miʿzafah/6, muqarran dunbalayī, naqāqīr/4, naqaryah, naqqarah or naqqārah, naqqāratān, naqqārya, naqrazān, nuqayrah, nuqqāriyah, nuqqayrah, nuwāghir, qadīḥah, qaṣʿah/1, qudūm, ṭabbāl/2, ṭabl/3, ṭabl al bāz, ṭabl jawīsh, ṭabl kabīr/1, ṭabl al markab, ṭabl mijrī, ṭabl al musaḥḥir, ṭabl shāmī, ṭabl shawīsh, ṭablah/4, ṭāsah, ṭubaylah
KEY SIGNATURE
dalīl, dalīl al maqām, see dalīl al kabīr al ʿamm, dalīl al kabīr al ʿarabī

LAMENT/LAMENTATION
bukā', laṭm, marāthī, marthāh or marthiyah, nadb, nawḥ/1, /2, niyāḥah, tanāwīḥ, wilwāl, see aswat muhzinah, qabḍī, ṣawt inqibāḍ
LARGHETTO
(ʿalā) mahil
LARGO
aryath
LEADER (of dancers)
muqaddim al ṣaff
LEADER (of ensemble)
abū ghanam, amghar, mawlā al zamr, muʿallim/1, muʿallim al ālah, muʿallim al rubāʿah, mudīr al jawq, muqaddim, qā'id, qā'id firqah mūsīqiyyah, ra'īs/1, shaykh/1
LEADING TONE(s)
ḥassās, ẓahīr
LEGATO
muttaṣil or muttaṣilah/5
LEGENDARY FIGURES
Ḍalāl, Lamak or Lamk Ibn Mutawshīl, Ṭūbal Ibn Lamak
LIMMA (256/243 , 90 c.)
"B"/2, baqiyyah, faḍlah, niṣf ṭanīnī, see SEMITONE
LISTENER
sāmiʿ
LOUD
jahīr/1, jahwarī. jihārah, shadīdah, see FORTE, FORTISSIMO
LOUDER
ajhar
LOUDNESS
shaddah/2, thiql/2, waqʿ/1

or nagham/4, nawbah/3, ṣanʿah/3, ṣawt/5, ṭabʿ/1, talḥīn/7, ṭanīn/4, ṭarīqah/2, ṭurqah, ughniyah/2
(basic) ānā maqām, maqām al umm, see also rāst, MELODIC MODE (primary)
(categories of) dalīl al kabīr al ʿarabī, dalīl al kabīr al ʿamm, khafī, khafī al tanāfur, maqām al mutashābih, murakkab or murakkabah/1, /2, mutanāfir, ẓāhir, ẓāhir al tanāfur, see also kurūf, ṭuruq al mulūkiyyah
(creation of) ikhtirā'/2, mawḍiʿ al nagham
(derivative) āwāz/2, farʿ/2, murakkab or murakkabah/1, /2, shādh, shuʿbah, tarkīb/3,
(primary) aṣl/1, bardah/3, dawr/2, pardah/1, purdah, shadd/2
(rules of progression) ijrā' al ʿamal, ṭawr, ṭawr al maqām, ṭawr al naghmah, uslūb al maqām
(transposition to different tonic) qalb al ʿiyān, qalb al laḥn, qalb al qarār

MELODIC MODES
(collective) jamʿ al jamʿ/1
(famous ones) jamā'āt al mashhūrah
(names of) ʿajam/2, ʿardawī/2, awj, bayātī, būsalīk/1, buzurk/1, dhayl/2, dūkāh/2, ḥijāz/2, ḥiṣār/1, ḥusaynī/1, huzām/2, ʿirāq/2, jihārkāh/2, kawasht/2, kurd or kūrd/2, māhūr or māhūrī/3, mā'iyyah/2, nahāwand/3, nawā/1, nihuft or nuhuft/1, rāst/2, ṣabā/2, shāhnāz or shahnāz/1, shashum, sīkāh/2, sīkāh fawq al tāmm, sīkāh mutawassiṭ/2, sīkāh tāmm/2, sunbulah/1, ʿushayrā', ʿushayrān/2, zīrkūlah or zirkūlāh/2

MELODIC MOVEMENT
ḥarakah/1, intiqāl/1, nuqlah, see kamm, kayf, mutashābihah
(stepwise) ittiṣāl, muttaṣil or muttaṣilah/1
(types of) ʿalā ittiṣāl, ʿalā al khilāf (supp.), ʿalā al musāwah (supp.), ʿawd or ʿawdah/2, basīṭ/9, ḍāfir, dā'ir, ghayr mutashābihah, inḥirāf, intiqāl ʿalā inʿirāj, intiqāl ʿala inʿiṭāf, intiqāl ʿalā istidārah, intiqāl ʿalā istiqāmah, iqāmah (supp.), ittiṣāl, la mutatālī, lāḥiq, lawlabī, muḍlaʿ, mukhillān (supp.), mukhtalif, munbat, murakkab or murakkabah/4, mustadīr, mustaqīm, mutasāwī al nisab, mutashābih or mutashābihah/3, mutatālī/1, muttaṣil or muttaṣilah, nuqlah ʿalā inʿirāj, nuqlah ʿalā inʿiṭāf, nuqlah ʿalā istidārah, nuqlah ʿalā istiqāmah or nuqlah mustaqīmah, rājiʿ al farḍ (supp.), rājiʿ al muḍlaʿ (supp.), rājiʿ al mustadīr (supp.), rājiʿ al mutawātir (supp.), rujūʿ/4 (supp.), rujūʿ mukhtalif al nisab (supp.), rujūʿ munbat (supp.), rujūʿ mutasāwī al nisab (supp.), ṭāfir, ṭāfir al intiqāl, (bi) takhaṭṭī
(with leaps) ṭāfir, ṭāfir al intiqāl, (bi) takhaṭṭī

MELODIOUS
aghann, aṭrab/1, ghannā', manghūm, rakhīm, rannām
(comparative) aṭrab

MELODY/MELODIES
āwāz/3, dastān/2, hawā', laḥn/1, maghnā, mūsīqā or mūsīqī/4, naghm or nagham/2, ṣadaḥah, ṣanʿah/5, ṣudāḥ, ṭarq/3, ughniyah/1
(fundamental, without ornament) aṣl/4
(melismatic) kathīr al tarannum, see ORNAMENTED (heavily)
(with segments) alḥān juz'iyyah
(without segments) alḥān bil iṭlāq

MELODY PIPE (of an aerophone)
ra'īs/4

MEMBRANOPHONE
ālah dhāt al riqq, see DRUM, FRAME DRUM, KETTLEDRUM(s)

MEMORIZER (of music)
ḥāfiẓ

METALOPHONE
sāz alwāḥ al fulādh, sāz fulādh

METRICAL
ʿarūḍī

MEZZO FORTE
quwwah/5, see MEDIUM LOUD
MEZZO PIANO
rakhāmah
MILITARY BAND
naqqārah khānah or naqqār khānah, nawbah/2, ṭabl khānah/1
MILITARY MUSIC
naqqārah khānah or naqqār khānah, ṭabl khānah/2
MODAL SCALE
see SCALE, OCTAVE (scale)
(fundamental or lower octave) dīwān asāsī, dīwān awwal, dīwān qarārī, sabʻ al awā'il
(upper octave) dīwān farʻī, dīwān jawābī, dīwān thānī, sabʻ al awākhir, see mabādi' al alḥān, mabānī al alḥān
MODERATO
rasl
MODULATION
intiqāl/2, intiqāl min laḥn ilā laḥn, taghyīr/1, tarkīb/6, see taghṭiyah/2, taqlīb
MOOD (of a composition)
basṭī, muʻtadil, qabḍī
MORDENT
tarʻīd/1
MOTIF(s)
jamʻ/2, mawḍūʻah, ṭanīn/3, see intiqāl, nuqlah, MELODIC MOVEMENT
MOUTHPIECE (of an aerophone)
faṣl/4, ḥabbah, ḥabbah al muṣawwitah, lisān, manfakh, minfākh, mathqūb, maʻṭif, ra's/2, shaʻīrah, ṭawq/3, see also lawlā, lūlā, ṣadaf, ṣadaf mudawwar, shaʻrah
MOVED, TO BE (by music)
ṭariba
MOVEMENT
(melodic) see MELODIC MOVEMENT
(of a suite)
abyāt/2, ashghāl/2, barwal/1, bashraf/1, /2, bashraf samāʻī, basīṭ or basīṭah/5, baṭāyḥī/1, daraj/1, dā'irah/4, dārij/2, /4, darrāzī, faṣl/2, /3, furūdāsht, ghazal, inṣirāf/1, khalāṣ, khatm, makhlaṣ, maṣdar, mashadd/1, mashāliyah, maṭāyḥī, mīzān/3, mukhlaṣ, mulakhkhaṣ, muṣaddar/1, /2, mustazād, nūbah/2, qā'im wa niṣf, qawl/2, quddām/1, ṣanʻah/2, see dukhūl, dūlāb, fārighah, firāsh/3, inṣirāf/2, sulṭān al alḥān, ṭābiʻ/2
MUSIC
aṣwāt al muṭribāt, ghinā'/1, lahw, mūsīqā or mūsīqī, samāʻ/1 ṭarab/3
(classical) see "CLASSICAL" (ART) MUSIC
(descriptive) mūsīqā taṣwīriyyah
(measured) see MEASURED MUSIC, MEASURED/UNMEASURED MUSIC
(of ancient Greeks) mūsīqā or mūsīqī/3
(of the Arabs) ghinā'/5, ghinā' al ʻarab, nashīd al ʻarab
(of the Persians) mūsīqā fārisiyyah, nashīd al ʻajam
(oriental)
mūsīqā fārisiyyah, mūsīqā sharqiyyah
(practical art) fann al nagham, ghinā'/2, mūsīqā ʻamaliyyah, ṣināʻah al mūsīqā al ʻamaliyyah
(ten basic principles of)
kamālāt al ʻashr
(unmeasured) see UNMEASURED MUSIC, MEASURED/UNMEASURED MUSIC
(vocal) see VOCAL MUSIC, GENRES (vocal)
(with segments) mufaṣṣal/2, see istiftāḥ/2
(without segments) masrūdah/1
MUSIC/DANCE EVENT
laylah, zambrah/1, see DANCE (genres)
MUSICAL APTITUDE
miḍmār
MUSICAL ENTERTAINMENT
lahw, ṭarab/2
MUSICAL EVENT
ḥaflah, ḥaflah mūsīqiyyah, zaffah, zambrah/1, zār/1
MUSICAL GLASSES
sāz ka'sāt or sāz kāsāt, sāz ṭāsāt, ṭusūt
MUSICAL HERITAGE
turāth
MUSICAL PIECE
faṣl mūsīqī, maqṭūʻah, qiṭʻ or qiṭʻah
MUSICAL PROCESSION
kharjah/2
MUSICAL RENDERING OF POETIC LINE
bayt/2

MUSICAL SEGMENT
juz', qism or qismah/3, tabdīlah, see PERIOD, PHRASE
MUSICALLY INDUCED DELIGHT
ṭarab/1
MUSICIAN
ʿālim/2, ʿālimah, laḥḥān/2, mawlūʿ, muʿallim/2, mubsiṭ, mughannī/2, mûlû', muṣaddiḥ/2, mūsīqār/1, mūsīqūr, muṭrib, rannām, ṭarrāb, see INSTRUMENTALIST, VOCALIST
(talented with notes) nuqayṭī
MUSICIANS FAMOUS IN HISTORY
Bārbad or Bārbud, (al) Gharīd, Ibn Misjaḥ, Ibn Muḥriz, Ibn Shuklah, Ibn Surayj, Ibrahīm Ibn al Mahdī, Ibrahīm al Mawṣilī, Isḥaq Ibn Ibrahīm al Mawṣilī, Jarād, Jarādatān, Maʿbad, al Mawṣilī, Naḍr Ibn al Ḥārith, Ṭuways, Zalzal or Zulzul, Ziryāb

NATURAL SIGN
ʿalāmah ilghā'
"NATURE(s)"
akhlāq, khulq or khulūq, ṭabīʿah
NECK (of chordophone)
ʿamūd/2, dastah, ḥalq/1, ibrīq, mutadiqq, qabḍah, raqabah, ṣāʿid/1, ʿunq, yad
NON-LEGATO
munfaṣil or munfaṣilah/1
NOTATED
dīwānī
NOTATION
tadwīn, tasjīl
(durational system) ʿadadī
(pitch system) abjadī
NOTATOR
mudawwin, munawwit
NOTE(s)
ʿalāmah mūsīqiyyah, ʿarabah/1, naghm or nagham, naghamah, nigham, naghmah, ṣawt/3, ṭabʿ/2, see TONE(s)
(contemporary names)
ʿajam/3, awj/2, būsalīk/2, buzurk/2, dūkāh/1, ḥijāz/3, ḥiṣār/2, ḥusaynī, ḥusaynī shadd, ʿirāq/3, jawāb ḥijāz, jawāb nawā, jawāb nīm ḥijāz, jawāb tīk ḥijāz, jawāb yakāh, jihārkāh/1, kardān, kawasht/1, kurd or kūrd/3, kūrdī, maḥbar, māhūr or māhūrī/1, /2, māhūrān, mā'iyyah/1, muḥayyir, nahāwand/1, nawā/3, nihuft or nuhuft/2, nīm ḥijāz, nīm ḥiṣār, nīm kurd, nīm shāhnāz, nīm zawāl, nīm zīrkūlah, qarār ʿajam, qarār ḥiṣār, qarār nīm ʿajam, qarār nīm ḥiṣār, qarār tīk ḥiṣār, rāst/3, ṣabā/3, shāhnāz or shahnāz/2, sīkāh/3, sunbulah/2, sūzdāk, tīk būsalīk, tīk ḥijāz, tīk ḥiṣār, tīk ḥusaynī shadd, tīk kawasht, tīk nuhuft, tīk zīrkūlah, ʿushayrān/1, yakāh, zawāl, zīrkūlah or zirkūlāh/1, see nim, nīm/1, nīm ʿarabah, qarār/2, tīk, tīk ʿarabah/1
(important or "dominant")
ghammāz
(letter names of) ḥurūf al hijā', ḥurūf al jumal
(of the scale)
ʿarabah/1, bardah/2, burj, darajah/2, see nīm ʿarabah, tīk ʿarabah
NUT (of chordophone)
anf/1, ʿatab or ʿatabah/2

OBOE(s)
aba, ʿarabī zūrnā, asafī zūrnā, balabān, būq/3, būq zamrī, dūnāy, ghayṭah/1, ʿirāqiyyah, jawrā, jūrā zūrnā, jīrah, karjah, karnīṭah (supp.) mizmār/3, mizmār al baladī, mizwij/1, muzāwaj/1, nāy aswad, nāy al ʿirāqī, nāy sawdā', nāy siyāḥ, qabā, qabā sūrnā, qabā zūrnā, sa'ika, shihābī zūrnā, sibs, sūrnā jurā, surnāy/1, suryānī, zāmir/1, zamr/3, zamr al kabīr, zamr al ṣughayyir, zukrah or zūkrah/1, zulāmī, zummār or zummārah/2, zūrnā, zūrna or zurnāy
OCTAVE
buʿd alladhī bil kull, buʿd al aʿẓam, buʿd bil kull, buʿd muttafiq al awwal, buʿd al thamān, dhū al kull, ḍiʿf (supp.), see abʿād mutashākilah al naghm, abʿād muttafiqah al

naghm, (al) kibār (supp.), munāsabah, muttafiqāt ʿuẓmā, nagham ʿuẓmā, tanghīm/1
(consonance) ittifāq al aʿẓam
(equivalent) quwwah/1, tashābuh fī al kayfiyyah, wāḥid bil quwwah/1, see also naghmah al yatīmah, naẓīr, tanghīm/1
(equivalent-lower) isjāḥ, qarār/2, sajāḥ/1, shaykh/2, shuḥāj/1, shuḥāj al aʿẓam, shuḥīj
(equivalent-upper) ḍiʿf, dīk, jawāb/1, naghmah al ḍiʿf, naghmah al idʿāf, ṣayḥah, ṣayyāḥ, shabb or shābb/1, /2, ṣiyāḥ/1, ṣiyāḥ al aʿẓam, tīz/3
(scale)dawr/8 (supp.), dīwān, dīwān kāmil, jamāʿah/2 (supp.), martabah/2 (supp.), nawʿ al jamāʿah, ṭabaqah/2, ṭabaqah ṣawtiyyah, see MODAL SCALE, SCALE
(span in vocal or instrumental range) dawr al quwā
(species) dawr/4, intiqāl/3, nawʿ/1, see ṭabaqah/4, tamdīd/2

OPEN STRING(s)
awtār muṭlaqah, muṭlaq, muṭlaq al watar

OPEN STRINGED INSTRUMENTS
miʿzaf or miʿzafah/2, see ARCHLUTE, DULCIMER, HARP, PSALTERY

ORCHESTRATION
tawzīʿ

ORGAN
ālah zamr, magrefah, mūsīqā or mūsīqī/5, urghan or urghanūn/1 urghanum al būqī (hydraulic), urghanum al zamrī (reed pipe), urghun, urghunn, zamr/4, see zamr al rīḥī

ORIENTAL
mashriqī, sharqī/4

ORNAMENT ORNAMENTATION
see EMBELLISHMENT

ORNAMENTED (heavily)
kathīr al tarannum, mutawwal

OVERTURE
see PRELUDE

PAIRED
muzdawij or muzdawijah/3

PANEGYRIC (poem or song)
madḥ, madīḥ, madīḥ nabawī, ṣahjah, szahdje

PANPIPES
armūnīqī, bīshah, chubchiq, janāḥ, mithqāl, mūsīqāl, mūsīqār/4, mūsīqār-i-khatay, mushtaq ṣīnī, mustaq, mustaq ṣīnī, shaʿbiyyah, shuʿaybiyyah

PAUSE (silence)
nafas, maqṭaʿ/1, rāḥah, sakt or saktah, waqf or waqfah
(after last percussion of the rhythmic cycle) fâçil (supp.), fāṣilah/4, sakt or saktah/4
(between phrases or sections) fāṣilah/1, /3, nafas, sakt or saktah/3, waqf or waqfah/2
(between tones) fāṣilah/2, mabtūrah, rāḥah, sakt or saktah/1, /2, see REST, RESTS (of various lengths)

PEDAL POINT
ishārah al istimrār, ṭanṭanah asās al maqām

PEGBOX (of chordophone)
banjaq, bayt al malāwī, ibzīm, khaznah, nāṣiyah

PENTACHORD (scalar segment
see TETRACHORD/PENTACHORD (scalar segment)

PERCUSSION(s)
ḍarb/1, īqāʿ/2, naghamah or naghmah, naghm or nagham/5, naqarah, naqrah/1, /2, /5, qarʿ, see constructs of naqrah, BEAT
(basic or fundamental) ʿamūd/1, ʿamūd al awwal, ʿamūd al rābiʿ, ʿamūd al thālith, ʿamūd al thānī, ḍarb aṣlī, iferred, khafīf/4, khafīf al thānī/1, thaqīl al awwal/2, thaqīl al thānī/2, waḥdah/1, zamān al aqall, zamān al awwal, zamān al miʿyār
(consecutive) naqarāt mutawāliyat
(elimination of opening) jazm
(light) ğamrah, ghamzah, rawm
(long) naqrah munfaridah (?), naqrah thaqīlah
(medium) ishmām, mashah
(on percussion instrument) ḍarb/1, īqāʿ/2

(on stringed instrument) ḍarb/1, naqrah/2
(strong) naqrah/5
(supplementary) ḥashw, idrāj, ʿimād/2, ithelleth, iʿtimād/2, majāz, naqrah layyinah, taḍʿīf/2, taṣdīr, ziyādāt min khārij
(various time units) "A"/1, "B"/1, "D", fāṣilah/6, fāṣilah ṣughrā, fāṣilah kubrā, fāṣilah ʿuẓmā, fāṣilah wusṭā, "H"/2, "J"/1, see (basic or fundamental)
(very rapid) marghūl or marghūlah/2, naqrah khafīfah, see mukassarah, shadhrah, tarʿīd
PERFECT FIFTH
bu'd alladhī bil khams, buʿd bil khams, buʿd dhū ittifāq al thānī, buʿd muttafiq al thānī, dhū al khams, dhū quwā al khams, khāmis al tāmmah, zā'id niṣfan (supp.), see abʿād mutashākilah al naghm, muttafiqāt wusṭā, nagham wusṭā, (al) awsāṭ (supp.)
(higher tone of) ṣiyāḥ al awsaṭ
(lower tone of) shuḥāj al awsaṭ
PERFECT FOURTH
buʿd alladhī bil arbaʿ, buʿd bil arbaʿ, buʿd dhū ittifāq al thālith, buʿd muttafiq al thālith, dhū al arbaʿ, dhū quwā al arbaʿ, zā'id thulthan (supp.), see abʿād mutashākilah al naghm, muttafiqāt wusṭā, nagham wusṭā, (al) awsāṭ (supp.)
(higher tone of) ṣiyāḥ al asghar
(lower tone of) shuḥāj al asghar
PERFORM, TO
ʿamila, aṭlaqa, ḍaraba, ghannā bi ____, qallaba, ṣadaḥa, ṭarraba, zajala
(on any aerophone) nafakha, zamara, zammara
(on the būq) bawwaqa
(on a chordophone) ḍaraba, naqara, naqqara, ṭarq/1, ṭarqah
(on musical instrument) aṭraba, ʿazafa/1, /2, daqqa/1, ḥasaba, laʿiba, ṣadaḥa, tarannama/2
(on a percussion instrument) daqqa/3, ḍaraba, muṣakka (?), naqara/2, naqqara, qaraʿa, ṣakka
PERFORMANCE/PERFORMING
adā' al alḥān, ʿamal/2, ʿazf/1, ḍarb/4, īqāʿ/3, iṭlāq, iṭrāb/2, ṣināʿah/2, ṣināʿah al malāhī, ṣināʿah al mūsīqā, tanaghghum, tanghīm/2, /3, tanqīr, tawqīʿ
(of musical rhythm) ḍarb/5, tarqīm al mīzān
(on lute) barbaṭ/4, ḍarb/1
(on percussion instrument) ḍarb/1
(stage position of) maqām/2
(style - instrumental) ghādī bil ʿaks, khāwī, rīshah miṣriyyah, rīshah turkiyyah, tabrīd, tadhkīrah or t'âskîrât, see kurūf, ṭuruq al mulūkiyyah
(style - vocal) fārigh al nagham, laythī, mamlū' al nagham, mujawwad, murattal, radd, takhannuth, tarannum/2, /4, tarassul bil qirā'ah, tarassul fī al ghinā', tawshīḥ/2
(style - vocal/instrumental) ṭarīqah/4, tartīl/2, /3
PERFORMANCE TECHNIQUES
basm, ḍarb/7 (supp.), dass, dayalūj, ghilẓ/2, ḥadhf, halāhil, hamzah/1, /2, hathīth/1, ibdāl, ibdāl al shuḥājāt, istiʿādah, istirāḥah, iʿtimād/1, jass, mālsh, maqām/3, murajjaḥah, mursal/2, muzdawij or muzdawijah/1, naqsh/3, /4, qurriba, ribāṭ/2, sakt or saktah/3, shadw/1, sharqah, tabʿīd, tarjīḥ, tatwīlah, zawj/2
PERIOD (musical)
juz'/2, maqṭaʿ/2
PHRASE
fikrah mūsīqiyyah, ʿibārah, ʿibārah mūsīqiyyah, jamʿ/2, jumlah/2, jumlah mūsīqiyyah, juz'/2, maqṭaʿ/2, see MELODY, THEME
PHRASE MARK
qaws ittiṣāl
PIANISSIMO
rakhāwah
PIPE OF AN ORGAN
mizmār/6, surnāy/3
PIPE OF A WIND INSTRUMENT
See DRONE PIPE, MELODY PIPE

QUARTER NOTE
nuwār, sawdā', waḥdah al mutawassiṭah/2, waḥdah al ṣaghīrah/2
QUARTER REST
laḥẓah
QUARTER TONE (interval)
ʿarabah/1, buʿd al irkhā', irkhā'/1, masāfah sharqiyyah al ṣughrā, masāfah sharqiyyah al asghar, muraṣṣaʿ/2 (?), nīm/2, nīm ʿarabah/2, rubʿ, rubʿ masāfah, rubʿ ṭanīnī
QUR'ĀN RECITER
ḥazzāb, muqri', murattil/1, qāri'/1, qawwāl/1, shaykh/4, see ʿālim/1
QUR'ĀNIC CANTILLATION
qirā'ah, tilāwah, tartīl/1, tajwīd, tarassul bil qirā'ah, see ḥadr/2, tadwīr, taḥqīq, taḥzīn, tarʿīd, tarqīṣ, taṭrīb/3, /4, qirā'ah bil alḥān

RANGE
wusʿah
(of a mode) āhang or āhank/1
(of a voice) āhang or āhank/2, see VOCAL RANGES
RATIO
nisbah, zā'id juz'an (supp.), see zā'id niṣfan, zā'id thulthan, zā'id tusʿan, zā'id rubʿan (all in supp.)
RECITE THE QUR'ĀN, TO
rattala/1
RECITER
(of poetry) shāʿir
(of zajal poetry) zājil, zajjāl, see QUR'ĀN RECITER
RECORD, TO
sajjala
RECORDER
see WHISTLE FLUTE
REED
see BLOWING REED
REED CORNET
nāy-i-chadūr
REFRAIN
ʿawd or ʿawdah/3, bāzkisht, ḥarbah, markaz/2, /3, radd, radd al jawāb, raddah/3, rujūʿ/2, simṭ, takarrur/2, takrīr/3, tardīd/2, tarjīʿ or tarjīʿah/2, tashyīʿah, taslīm/2, taslūm, see madhhab/1, maṭlaʿ/2, mayjanā, muʿannā, ṭāliʿ/2
RELIGIOUS MUSIC
see GENRES (vocal religious)
REPETITIONS(s)
ʿawd or ʿawdah/3, hank/2, iqāmah (supp.), marghūl or marghūlah/1, muḥāsibah, muḥassabah, mukassarah, qawwa, quwwah/4, radd, radd al jawāb, raddah/1, /2, rājiʿ/2, rujūʿ/1, taʿdīd, takarrur/1, takrīr/1, tardīd/1, tarʿīd/2, tarjīʿ or tarjīʿah/1, zā'idah, see ʿalā al khilāf(supp.), ʿalā al musāwah (supp.), dhāt ʿawdāt, taḍʿīf/3
REPETITION SIGN
ishārah al rujūʿ, ishārah al takrār
RESONANCE
ṭanīn/5
REST
maqṭa', naqrah sākinah/2, rāḥah, sakt or saktah/1, waqf or waqfah/1, see EIGHTH REST, HALF REST, PAUSE (silence), QUARTER REST, SIXTEENTH REST, THIRTY-SECOND REST
RHYME
qāfiyah, qawāfī, tasjīʿ
RHYMED PROSE
see PROSE (rhymed)
RHYMED VERSE
dhāt qawāfī
RHYTHM
aṣl/5, īqāʿ/4, mawqiʿah, mīzān/1, wazn/2
RHYTHM STICK(s)
aʿwād/1, naqūs or nāqūs/3, qaḍīb, qaḍīb al qawl, see waqʿ/2
RHYTHMIC
tawqīʿī
(alteration to form new modes) taghyīr/2, various forms of this are ghayr ziyādah naqrāt, idʿāf/2, tafṣīl/1, tafṣīl al muwaṣṣal, takrīr/2, tarkīb/2, tawṣīl/2, tawṣīl al mufaṣṣal, ziyādah naqrāt min khārij
(movement)
ḥarakah/1
RHYTHMIC MODE(s)
aṣl/5, baḥr/4, ḍarb/2, īqāʿ/1, laḥn/4, mīzān/2, naghm or nagham/6, naghmah, ṭarīqah/1, ṭurqah/2, uṣūl, wazn/1

(basic percussion and silence pattern) ḍarb aṣlī/1, mīzān mutlaq, see CYCLE (of a rhythmic mode)
(binary) basīṭ/2
(binary and ternay subdivision) aqṣāq, aʿraj
(conjunct) hazaj/2, īqāʿāt muwaṣṣalah, muttaṣil or muttaṣilah/4, muwaṣṣal, zamān al mabda'
(derivative) nawʿ/2
(disjunct) īqāʿāt mufaṣṣalah, mufaṣṣal/1, munfaṣil/3, murakkab/8, zamān mutafāḍil
("famous Arab modes" of the Classical Period) īqāʿāt al ʿarabiyyah al mashhūrah, see khafīf al ramal, khafīf al thaqīl al awwal, khafīf al thaqīl al thānī, mākhūrī/1, ramal/1, thaqīl al awwal/1, thaqīl al ramal, thaqīl al thānī/1
(fundamental or basic) jins/2, zamān al mabda'
(names of) ʿardāwī/3, barwal/2, basīṭ/3, /6, baṭāyḥī/2, baṭīḥ, daraj/3, ḍarb aṣlī/2, dārij/5, hazaj/2, hazaj khafīf, hazaj khafīf al thaqīl, hazaj sarīʿ, hazaj thaqīl, inṣirāf/3, khafīf/3, khafīf al thaqīl, khafīf al thaqīl al hazaj, khatm, mashadd/2, mukhammas/1, /2, muṣaddar/3, /4, pishrū/2, samāʿī thaqīl, shanbar or shanbār/2, quddām/2, thaqīl al hazaj, tshambar, waḥdah/2, waḥdah al ṣaghīrah/1, wāḥidah, see RHYTHMIC MODES ("famous Arab modes" of the Classical Period)
RIB (of the body of the lute)
ḍilʿ
RING (for attaching finger plectra)
kustabān
RING, TO (a bell)
daqqa/2
RITARDANDO
ibtidā' bi tamahhul tadrījī, ikhtiṣār/1, see SLOWING (the tempo)
ROSETTE (covering of soundhole)
ḥijāb, nuwwārah, raqmah/1, shamsah, shamsiyyah, wardah
SAD MUSIC
ṣawt inqibāḍ, see LAMENT/LAMENTATION
SATIRICAL SONG
hijā', maslūq
SCALAR COMBINATION
jamʿ/1, jamāʿah, and their constructs, see also jumūʿ ṣighar, kāmil fī al talā'um, khafī al tanāfur, mawājib, mulā'im, munfaṣil or munfaṣilah/4, mutalā'im, mutanāfir/1, /2, mutashābih or mutashābihah/1, muttaṣil or muttaṣilah/3, ẓāhir al tanāfur
SCALAR SEGMENT
See TETRACHORDAL/PENTACHORDAL SEGMENT
SCALE
jadwal/1, jamʿ/1, silsilah aṣwāt, sullam, sullam al naghmah, ṭabaqah/5, see OCTAVE (scale) MODAL SCALE, mawājib, mawjib, mūjib, sullam al ʿarabī al ḥālī, sullam al ʿarabī al qadīm, ṭabaqah/2
(chromatic) sullam al mulawwan
(diatonic) sullam al qawī
(enharmonic) sullam al rakhw
(fundamental) rāst/2, sullam al asāsī
(tempered) sullam al muʿaddal, sullam al muʿtadil, sullam al ūrubbī ṭabīʿī, tanẓīm dhū al abʿād al mutasāwiyah, tanẓīm min thunā'iyyāt al mutasāwiyah
(tetrachordal or pentachordal) baḥr/1, jamʿ/1, jins/1, pardah, ṭabaqah/3, see jumūʿ ṣighār
SCALE STEP
bardah/2, burj, darajah/1
"SCHOOL" OF MUSICAL PERFORMANCE
madhhab/2
SCROLL (ornamental head of chordophone) jabhah, qarmūdah
SEMIQUAVER
thunā'iyyah al asnān
SEMITONE
ʿarabah/1, bardah ṣaghīrah, buʿd ṣaghīr, nīm bardah, niṣf or nuṣf bardah, niṣf or nuṣf buʿd, niṣf or nuṣf ṭabʿ, rubʿayn
(major - 2187/2049, 114 c.)
faḍlah al ṭanīnī, infiṣāl

see APOTOME, COMMA, LIMMA

SEQUENTIAL PATTERNS
intiqāl ʿalā inʿirāj

SET TO MUSIC
mulaḥḥan, see COMPOSING/COMPOSITION (the act)

SHARP SIGN
ʿalāmah rafʿah, diyayz, diyayz al kūmā, diyayz al baqiyyah, diyayz al mujannab al ṣaghīr, ṣādiḥ, ṣāʿid/2

SHORTENING (of durations)
takhfīf/2, taqrīb

SING, TO
anshada/1, aṭraba, ghannā/1, ghannā bi _____, gharrada, istahalla, jahara, jahura, laḥḥana/2, nabara, naghama or naghima, naghghama, nāḥa, rannama, rattala/2, ṣadaḥa, taghannā, tagharrada, tarannama/1, taṭarrub, see awqaʿa/2, ghannā/3, żajala

SINGABLE
talḥīnī

SINGER
see VOCALIST

SINGING
gharad, ghinā'/3, ghirrīd, iṭrāb/1, mugharrad, ṣadaḥah, shadw/2, shudāh, ṣināʿah/1, ṣudāḥ, taghrīd/1, tanaghghum, ṭarab/3, tarannum, tardid al ālhan, tardīd al ṣawt, tarnīn/1, taṭrīb/1, see VOCAL MUSIC, constructs of ghinā'
(pertaining to) ghinā'ī

SINGING GIRL
dājinah, jāriyah, juwayriyah, karīnah, madjina, qarīnah, qaynah

SIXTEENTH NOTE
dhāt sinnayn, mufradah/3, naqrah basīṭah, waḥdah sarīʿah, see SEMIQUAVER

SIXTEENTH REST (notation)
lamḥah

SLOW (in tempo)
muwassa'/2, rā'ith, thaqīl/1, see TEMPI

SLOWER
abṭa'/1

SLOWING
tathqīl

SLOWNESS
thiql/1

SLUR
qaws ittiṣāl

SMALL INTERVALS
(al) ṣighār (supp.), ṣughrā

SNARES
awtār/2

SOFT
khafīf/5, khāfitah, layyin/2, see MEZZO PIANO, PIANISSIMO

SOFTEN, TO
khafḍ al ṣawt, rakhkhama, takhfīf

SOLFEGGIO
tanghīm/2

SOLO
(n.) infirād
(adj.) munfarid

SONG(s)
aghānī, laḥn/1, naghm or nagham/3, naghmah, shadw/2, tarnīmah/1, ughniyah/1, ughrūdah, see SINGING, GENRES (vocal)
(pre-Islamic) ḥanafī, ḥimyarī, hazaj/1, ḥidā' or ḥudā'/1, ikhtiyārī, naṣb, sinād, hazaj/1, rukbānī, sinād al thaqīl, hazaj al khafīf, nawḥ/1

SOUND (musical)
darajah/3, ḥiss or ḥass/1, naghm or nagham/1, naghmah, rannah, ṣawt/1, talḥīn/5, tarannum/3, żajal/4, zakhmah/4, see āwāz/4, ṣadā/2
(production of musical) taṣwīt
(end of) ʿaqīrah/2
(of jinn) ʿazf/4, miʿzaf or miʿzafah/7, zajal/3

SOUND CHEST
(of chordophone)
ḥuqqah, kāsah/1, jism, khaznah, makhzinah, qaṣʿah/2, ṣandūq, ṣundūq, ṣundūq muṣawwit
(of organ) ḥabbah, ḥabbah al muṣawwitah, shaʿīrah al mizmār

SOUND HOLE(s)
ʿayn, sarw, ʿuyūn

SOUNDING BOARD
haykal ṣawtī

STAFF
mudarraj mūsīqī

STAPLE (of a double reed instrument) lawlā

STRAND (of silk for strings of chordophone)
ṭabaqah/7, ṭāqah
STRING (for musical instrument)
ʻirq, sharʻah or shirʻah, watar/1, /2, see also mutabāyinah, mutawāliyah
(division of) qurṭ
(drone) lāzim al tarjīʻah, rājiʻ
(melody) sāyir al tarjīʻah
(names) bāj, bamm, būma, dhayl/1, dūkāh/3, ḥādd/1, ḥusayn/1, ḥusaynī/3, jawāb/3, maḥbad, māʻiyyah/1, mathlath or mithlath, mathnā, māya, ramal/3, shararah, thālith, thānī, watar/3, watar al khāmis, zīr/1, zīr al thānī
(to lower in pitch) wassaʻa, see TUNING
(to raise in pitch) daqqa, see TUNING
STRINGING A MUSICAL INSTRUMENT
ḥazq/2, madd
SUITE
ʻardāwī/1, chālghī/1, fāṣil/2, faṣl/1, fiqrah, maḥaṭṭ/2, maqām/4, nawbah/1, nawbah andalusiyyah, nawbah ʻarabī (supp.), nawbah ghurnāṭiyyah, nawbah inqilābāt, ṣanʻah/4, ṣawt/6, nūbah/1, ṭarīq, waṣlah/1, see MOVEMENT (of a suite)
SUPPLEMENTARY PERCUSSION(s)
see PERCUSSION(s) (supplementary)
SYNCOPATION
Ta'khīr al nabr

TAILPIECE (of a chordophone)
kursī/4, masṭarah (?), misṭarah, mushṭ/1
TAMBOURINE
see FRAME DRUM
TEMPO
ḥarakah/2, surʻah/2
TENSION (of a musical string)
madd, madd al watar, shadd/3, quwwah/3
TESSITURA (of a melodic mode)
tāzī, see RANGE
TETRACHORDAL/PENTACHORDAL SCALAR SEGMENT
ʻaqd/1, arbaʻah mutatāliyah, baḥr/1, janāḥ/1, jins/1, jins al tāmm, ʻiqd, qism or qismah/1, rābiʻah, tajnīs, see constructs of jins, tajnīs
(chromatic) jins al lāwinī, jins al lawnī, jins al mulawwan/1, jins al muntaẓim, jins al nāẓim/2, jins al rābiʻ, jins al rakhwī, jins al rāsim/2, jins al ta'līfī, lāwinī, lawnī, mulawwan/1, nāẓim/2, rāsim/2, ta'līf or ta'līfiyyah
(diatonic) jins al awwal, jins al qawī dhū al taḍʻīf, jins al ṭanīnī
(enharmonic) jins al muntaẓim, jins al muʻtadil (supp.), jins al nāẓim/1, jins al rāsim/1, jins al mulawwan/2, jins al muntaẓim, jins al rāsim, jins al ta'līfī/1, mulawwan/2, nāẓim/1, rāsim/1, ta'līfī or ta'līfiyyah
(exactly perfect fourth) tāmm/2
(lower segment of scalar octave) aṣl/2, jidhʻ, jins al adnā, jins al asfal, jins al suflā, qism or qismah/1, rukūz/2, ṭabaqah al ūlā
(names) ʻajam/1, bayāṭī/1, ḥijāz/1, huzām/1, ʻirāq/1, kurd or kūrd/1, nahāwand/2, nawā/2, rāst/1, ṣabā/1, sīkāh/1, sīkāh mutawassiṭ/1, sīkāh tāmm/1
("soft") jins al layyin, layyin/1, see khunthā and khunthāwī, and constructs of jins al layyin
("strong") jins al muqawwī, jins al qawī, jins al qawī dhū al taḍʻīf, qawī, qawī dhū al taḍʻīf, ṭanīnī/2, see muqawwī, constructs of jins al qawī
(upper segment of scalar octave) farʻ/1, jins al aʻlā, qism or qismah/1, ṭabaqah al thāniyah
(with extremities greater than a perfect fourth) rābiʻah zā'idah/2, jins al zā'id, jins al zā'id nawʻan, zā'id/2

(with extremities less than a perfect fourth) rābiʻah nāqiṣah
(with 3/4 tones) jins al sharqī
(without 3/4 tones) jins khāliyah min arbaʻ al ṣawt
TETRACHORDAL SPAN (of each string of a chordophone)
ṭabaqah/6
TETRACHORDAL SPECIES
aqsām buʻd dhī al arbaʻ, baḥr/6, dā'irah/3, nawʻ/1
THEME
fikrah mūsīqiyyah, hawā', ʻibārah, ʻibārah mūsīqiyyah, jumlah/2, jumlah mūsīqiyyah, laḥn/2, mawḍūʻah, see MELODY, PHRASE
(main) jumlah ra'īsiyyah
THEORETICAL
naẓarī
THEORISTS (of ancient Greece)
usṭūkhūsiyyah
THEORY
ʻilm al mūsīqā, mūsīqā or mūsīqī/2, mūsīqā naẓariyyah, ṣināʻah al mūsīqā al naẓariyyah, see ʻilm al īqāʻ (supp.), ʻilm al ta'līf (supp.), MUSIC PRACTICE
THICKNESS
(of sound) ghilẓ/2
(of string)ghilẓ/1, see STRAND
(of silk for strings of chordophone)
THIRD (interval)
buʻd al thulāthī, dhū al thalāthah
(major) buʻd kull wa rubʻ, zā'id rubʻan (supp.)
(minor) see mujannab al wusṭā, wusṭā al furs, wusṭā al qadīm
(neutral) see wusṭā al ʻarab, wusṭā al zalzal or wus ṭā al zulzul
THIRTY-SECOND NOTE
see SEMIQUAVER
THIRTY-SECOND REST
lamīḥah
THREE-QUARTER TONE INTERVAL
buʻd al ʻarabī, buʻd mutawassiṭ, masāfah sharqiyyah mutawassiṭah, tīk ʻarabah/2
THUMB HOLE (of a woodwind instrument)
qawl/4, rajʻ, shujāʻ
TIE
maddah/2, ribāṭ/1, waṣlah/2
TITLES OF RESPECT
muʻallim al awwal (Aristotle), muʻallim al thānī (al Fārābī)
TONE(s)
naghm or nagham/1, ṣawt/3, ṭanīn/1, ṭarq/1, zakhmah/4
(auziliary or embellishing) naghmah muwāfiqah
(bass) nagham kibār
(combination of) imtizāj/1, iqtirān, ta'līf/2
(connecting) waṣlah/3
(ending or final) maqṭaʻ al ṣawt, martabah/1
(fineness or smallness of) diqqah/1
(initial) bidāyah, darajah al bidāyah, darajah al ibtidā', ibtidā', mabādi' al alḥān, mabādi' al intiqālāt, mabda'/1, /3, madkhal, martabah/1, mubtada' al nagham
(high in pitch) nagham naḥīfah, ṣawt al ʻāliyah, ṣawt ḥāddah, ṣawt raqīqah, see also HIGH PITCHED
(loud) nagham qawiyyah, nagham shadīdah
(of median pitch) ṣawt mutawassiṭah
(other than tonic, also used for modal resolution) markaz/1
(low in pitch) ṣawt ghalīẓah, ṣawt thaqīlah, ṣawt wāṭiyah, shuḥāj/3
(lowest) "A"/2, ʻimād/1, mabda'/2, mafrūdah/1, see sajāḥ/3
(principle instead of embellishing) naghmah aṣliyyah
(soft) nagham khāfitah, nagham layyinah
TONIC
arāḍī, asās, darajah al istiqrār, darajah al rukūz, mabda'/2, mafrūdah/2. martabah/1, mustaqirr, qarār/1, rukūz/1, sajāḥ/2 (?), see darajah bidāyah, darajah al ibtidā', mubtada' al nagham
(moving to a new) intiqāl/3, see TRANSPOSITION
TONIC DRONE
ṭanṭanah asās al maqām

TRANSCRIBER
mudawwin, munawwit
TRANSPOSITION
intiqāl/2, qalb al ʿiyān, qalb al laḥn, qalb al qarār, taṣwīr
TRANSVERSE (said of a flute)
ʿalā inʿiṭāf
TREMOLO
mālsh, tarʿīdah, zaghradah or zaghraṭah/2
TRILL
mālsh, tamzīj/5, tarʿīd/1, tarʿīdah, tudhrī or tudrī, zagharīd or zagharīṭ, zaghradah or zaghraṭah/1
TRITONE (interval)
rābiʿah zā'idah/1
TRUMPET
būq/1, būq al nafīr, karna or karna, karranāy or karranā, nafīr, qarnā, ṣūr
TUNE, TO
awqaʿa/1, baḏḏa, ḏabaṭa, dawzana, khawā, sawwā
TUNING FORK
rannamah
TUNING KEY
miftāḥ/2
TUNING MECHANISM(s) (of qanun)
ʿarabah/2, ʿurab
TUNING PEG(s)
adhān al ʿūd, malāwī, malwā or milwā, miftāḥ/1, miftāl (supp.), udhan or udhn, ʿuṣfūr
"TURN" (in performance)
dawr/7, nawbah/4

ULULATE, TO
zaghrada
ULULATION
zagharīd or zagharīṭ, zaghradah or zaghraṭah/1
UNACCOMPANIED
mufradah/5, munfarid, murtajal/2
UNIT(s) OF SCALAR MEASUREMENT
daqīqah, dharrah ṣawtiyyah, fāṣil/1, qīrāṭ, sant
UNMEASURED MUSIC
ikhtiyārī, manthūr/1, maqām/3, mursal/1, muṭlaq/1, nathr al naghamāt
(genres) abū al zuluf, abūdhiyyah, ahellel, ʿatābā or ʿatābah, baytayn, bughyah, dā'irah/4, inshād/1, istiftāḥ/1, istikhbār, layālī, lmaīt, mashāliyah, mawāliyā/1, mawlid/2, mawwāl/1, miyāt khānah muʿannā, musabbaʿ/1, mustakhbir/1, /2, mustakhbir al inqilābāt, mustakhbir al ṣanʿah, nashīd/2, /4, nawakht, nuʿmānī, qaṣīd, qaṣīdah/1, qawl/3, ṣalḥī, ṣawt/2, ṣawt al wasaṭ, sharqī/1, shughl/1, shurūqī, simaʿī, ṣiyāḥ, tacheraft, taghazzul/1, tamawaīt, talḥīn/6, tamediazt, taqāsīm, taqsīm, taqyīd al ṣanʿah, tarnīmah/2, umm al zuluf, ziyādah/2
VARIATION
taghyīr/3, taḥwīr, tanwīʿah
VIBRATION (musical)
dhabdhabah, ihtizāz, tamawwij, taraddud
VIBRATO
tarʿīd/1, zaghradah or zaghraṭah/2
VIOL
see BOWED CHORDOPHONES
VIRTUOSO
mūsīqār/3, see aḍrab al nās bil watar
VOCAL
ṣawtī
VOCAL MUSIC
alḥān kāmilah, ghinā'/2, maqrūnah bil aqāwīl, maqrūnah bil kalām, mūsīqā or mūsīqī/4, mūsīqā ghinā'iyyah, nagham insāniyyah, ṣinf al thānī, talḥīnāt al insāniyyah, see SINGING
VOCAL RANGES (male)
(baritone) ṣawt ramal
(bass) ṣawt dhayl, ṣawt jahīr
(high tenor) ṣawt ḥusayn
(tenor) ṣawt mā'iyyah
VOCAL SOUND (types of)
ʿaqīrah/1, ghunnah, hazaj/5, /6, ḥiss or ḥass/2, ṣāfī, zamm, zamzamah/2
VOCALIST
amessad, chālghī/2, ghannā'ī, ghannāyah, h'addarah, ḥādī, hallāl, ḥazzāb, juwayriyyah, maddāḥ/2, mughannī/1, mughannī mufrad, mughanniyah, mugharrid, mukhānīth, mukhannath, mulaḥḥin, munshid, murattil/2, muṣaddiḥ/1,

musammiʿ/2, mūsīqār/2, muṭrib, muṭrib al munfarid, naddāb, naddābah, naḥḥām, nā'iḥ, nā'iḥah, nashshād, qāri'/2, qaṣā'idī, qawwāl/2, qawwīl, ra'īs/2, shādī, shaykh/1, shaykhah, ṣūr/2, zājil, zajjāl, see CHANTER, CHORISTER, QUR'ĀN RECITER SINGING GIRL, WAILER

VOICE
ṣawt/4

VOLUME
ʿuluww al ṣawt

VOLUME (decreasing the)
see SOFTEN, TO and DECRESCENDO SIGN

WAILING
see LAMENT/LAMENTATION

WAIST (of a chordophone)
khaṣr

WAR SONG(s)
ḥadw/1, ḥamās, ḥōrāb, mushajjiʿ, naqāqīr

WESTERN (i.e., west from Lībyā to the Atlantic)
maghribī

WHISTLE
ṣaffārah/1

WHISTLE FLUTE
ʿarabī dūduk, juwāq/2, lira or līra/3, nīra, qabā dūduk, ṣaffārah/3, shabbābah/2, ṣuffāra

WHISTLING
mukā', ṣafīr

WHOLE NOTE
mustadīrah, waḥdah al kabīrah, waḥdah al kubrā

WHOLE TONE (interval)
ʿawd or ʿawdah/1, bardah kabīrah, buʿd kabīr, buʿd kāmil, buʿd ṭanīnī, maddah/1, "T", ṭabʿ/5, tāmm bardah, ṭanīn/2, ṭanīnī/1
(minor whole tone - 10/9, ca. 182 c.) buʿd kāmil al aqall, mujannab/1, mujannab al kabīr, tatimmah, zā'id tusʿan (supp.)
(plus quarter tone) masāfah sharqiyyah al akbar, masāfah sharqiyyah al kubrā

WINDCHEST (of panpipes)
jawf

WOODEN COLLAR (around neck of lute)
ṭawq/2

WOODWIND INSTRUMENT(s)
mizmār/1, nāy/2, qurnayṭah, zamr/1, zummār or zummārah/3, see AEROPHONE, BAGPIPES, CLARINET, CLARIONET, DOUBLE CLARINET, DOUBLE PIPED AEROPHONE, FLUTE, OBOE, PANPIPES, WHISTLE FLUTE
(made of reed cane) ghāb or ghābah/2, qaṣabah/1, qaṣb or qaṣbah/1, unbūb or unbūbah mutasawwiṭah, yarāʿ or yarāʿah/2
(with blowing reed) dhāt al sinn, mizmār/2
(single piped) mufrad/2, zammār/3, zammārah/1, zīr/2, zummār or zummārah/2

WORK SONG(s)
ahāzīj, basseh, hazaj/7, khrab, meydaf, qaylemi

ZITHER-TYPE INSTRUMENT
nāqūr/1

Appendix II: Index of Arabic Roots

أ

'-b-w

Abū Ghanam
Abū Qurūn
Abū Zuluf
Abūdhiyyah (Abu Adhiyyah)

'-th-r

Ta'thīr

'-kh-r

Sabʿ al Awākhir
Ta'khīr
Ta'khīr al Nabr

'-d-y

Adā' al Alḥān

'-dh-n

Adhān
Ādhān al ʿŪd
Mu'adhdhin
Udhan or Udhn

'-dh-y

Abūdhiyyah (Abū Adhiyyah)

'-r-ḍ

Arāḍī

'-s-s

Asās
Dīwān al Asāsī
Sullam al Asāsī
Ṭanṭanah Asās al Maqām

'-ṣ-l

Aṣl
Ḍarb al Aṣl
Naghmah al Aṣliyyah
Naqarāt Aṣliyyah
Uṣūl

'-l-f

ʿIlm al Ta'līf (supp.)
I'tilāf (supp.)
Jins al Ta'līfī
Ma'lūf
Mu'allaf
Mu'allif
Mu'talifah
Nagham al Mu'talifah
Ta'alluf
Ta'līf
Ta'līf al Ālī
Ta'līf al Awtār
Ta'līf al Ghinā'ī

Ta'līf Murtajal
Ta'līf al Nāṭiq
Ta'līf al Ṣāmit
Ta'līf al Ṣawtī
Ta'līfī
Ta'līfiyyah
Tawshīḥ Ma'lūf

'-m-m

Maqām al Umm
Umm wa Ḥāshiyah
Umm al Żuluf

'-n-s

Aḍrab al Nās bil Watar
Mūnis(?)
Nagham al Insāniyyah Maqrūnah bil Aqāwīl
Talḥīnāt al Insāniyyah

'-n-f

Anf

'-w-j

Awj

'-w-l

Ālah
Ālah Andalusiyyah
Ālah Dhāt al Awtār
Ālah Dhāt al Nafkh
Ālah Dhāt al Riqq
Ālah Īqāʿ
Ālah Īqāʿiyyah
Ālah Lahw
Ālah Malāhī
Ālah Muṣawwitah bi Dhātihā
Ālah Mūsīqā
Ālah Mūsīqāriyyah
Ālah Mūsīqiyyah
Ālah Muṭribah (supp.)
Ālah Nafkh
Ālah Naqr
Ālah Ṣināʿiyyah
Ālah Ṭabīʿiyyah
Ālah Ṭarab
Ālah Watariyyah
Ālah Zamr
Ālat al Ḥarakāt
Ālātī
ʿAmūd al Awwal
Ashṭur al Ūlā
Basīṭ al Awwal
Buʿd Dhū Ittifāq al Awwal
Buʿd Muttafiq al Awwal
Dīwān al Awwal
Ghināʾ al Awwal al Thaqīl
Ittifāq al Awwal (supp.)
Jins al Awwal
Khafīf al Awwal
Khafīf al Thaqīl al Awwal
Mufaṣṣal al Awwal
Murakkab al Awwal
Mūsīqā Āliyyah
Qanṭarah Ūlā
Sabʿ al Awāʾil
Ṣinf al Awwal
Ṭabaqah al Ūlā
Tajnīs al Awwal
Ta'līf al Ālī
Taswiyah al Ālah
Thaqīl al Awwal
Zamān al Awwal

'-w-y

Āyah

ب

b-t-r

Mabtūrah

b-ḥ-ḥ

Abaḥḥ

b-ḥ-r

Baḥr
Naghamāt al Buḥūr

b-d-'

Badwah (?)

Buʻd Ṣaghīr
Buʻd Ṭanīnī
Buʻd bil Thaman
Buʻd al Thulāthī
Buʻd al Zā'id
Niṣf Buʻd
Tabʻīd
Tanẓīm Dhū al Abʻād al Mutasāwiyah

b-gh-y

Bughyah

b-q-y

Baqiyyah
Diyayz al Baqiyyah

b-k-y

Bukā'

b-l-b-l

Bulbul

b-l-d

Mizmār al Baladī
Ṭabl Baladī

b-l-ṣ

Balūṣā

b-l-q

Billīq

b-n-d-r

Banādrī

b-n-ṣ-r

Binṣir
Binṣir al Mashhūrah
Majrā al Binṣir

b-n-y

Mabānī al Alḥān

b-h-l

Ibtihāl

b-w-z

Bāz or Bāzah
Ṭabl al Bāz

b-w-q

Abwāq
Bawwāq
Bawwaqa
Būq
Būq al Nafīr
Būq bil Qaṣabah
Būq Zamrī
Urghanūm al Būqī
Zamr al Būqī

b-y-t

Abyāt
Bayātī
Bayt
Bayt al Malāwī
Baytān
Baytayn
Dūbayt

b-y-ḍ

Bayāḍ
Bayḍā'
Nāy Abyaḍ

b-y-n

Mutabāyinah

th-m-n

Buʿd bil Thamān

th-n-y

ʿAmūd al Thānī
Badaniyyah al Thāniyah
Basīṭ al Thānī
Buʿd Dhū Ittifāq al Thānī
Buʿd Muttafiq al Thānī
Dīwān al Thānī
Ittifāq al Thānī (supp.)
Jins al Thānī
Khafīf al Thānī
Khafīf al Thaqīl al Thānī
Mathānī
Mathnā
Mizmār al Muthannā
Muʿallim al Thānī
Mufaṣṣal al Thānī
Murakkab al Thānī
Qanṭarah al Thāniyah
Ṣinf al Thānī
Ṭabaqah al Thāniyah
Tajnīs al Thānī
Tanẓīm min Thunā'iyyāt Mutasāwiyah
Thānī
Thāniyah al Zā'idah
Thāniyyah
Thaqīl al Thānī
Thunā'iyyah al Asnān
Zamān al Thānī
Zīr al Thānī

ج

j-b-h

Jabhah

j-d-d

Kalām al Jadd

j-d-w-l

Jadwal

j-dh-b

Jadhb
Jādhbiyyah al Laḥniyyah

j-dh-ʿ

Jidhʿ

j-r-b

Jirbah
Mizmār al Jirāb

j-r-d

Jarād
Jarādatān

j-r-r

Jarra
Majrūr
Majrūrah

j-r-s

Ajrās
Jaras

j-r-f

Nāy Jirāf

j-r-n

Jarānah
Jarrāynī

j-r-y

Ijrā' al ʿAmal
Jāriyah
Juwayriyyah
Majrā
Majrā al Binṣir
Majrā al Wusṭā
Ṭabl Mijrī

j-n-s

Ajnās mufradah
Jins
Jins al Adnā
Jins al A'lā
Jins al Asfal
Jins al Awwal
Jins Khāliyah min Arbā' al Ṣawt
JIns al Lāwinī
Jins al Lawnī
Jins al Layyin
Jins al Layyin Ghayr al Muntaẓim
Jins al Layyin al Muntaẓim al Mutatālī
Jins al Mu'allaq
Jins al Mufrad
Jins al Mulawwan
Jins al Muntaẓim
Jins al Muqawwā
Jins al Mu'tadil (supp.)
Jins al Mutawassiṭ
Jins al Nāqiṣ
Jins al Nāẓim
Jins al Qawī
Jins al Qawī Dhū al Taḍ'īf
Jins al Qawī al Munfaṣil
Jins al Qawī al Muttaṣil
Jins al Rābi'
Jins al Rakhwī
Jins al Rāsim
Jins al Sharqī
Jins al Suflā
Jins al Ta'līfī
Jins al Tāmm
Jins al Ṭanīnī
Jins al Thālith
Jins al Thānī
Jins al Zā'id
Jins al Zā'id Naw'an
Tajnīs
Tajnīs al Rābi'
Tajnīs al Thālith
Tajnīs al Thānī

j-n-k

Jank
Jank 'Ajamī
Jank Miṣrī

ḥ-d-d

Aḥadd
Ḥādd
Ḥāddah al Ḥāddāt
Ḥiddah
Ḥiddah al Ṣawt
Ṣawt Ḥāddah

ḥ-d-r

Ḥadr

ḥ-d-w or ḥ-d-y

Ḥādī
Ḥadw
Ḥidā' or Ḥudā'
Ḥudā'

ḥ-dh-f

Ḥadhf

ḥ-r-b

Ḥarbah
Ḥarbī
Ḥōrāb
Ḥurūb

ḥ-r-r

Laḥn al Ḥurr
Taḥrīr

ḥ-r-f

Ḥurūf al Hijā'
Ḥurūf al Jumal
Inḥirāf

ḥ-r-q

Taḥrīq al Awtār

ḥ-r-k

Ālāt al Ḥarakāt
Ḥarakah
Ḥarakāt
Naqrah Mutaḥarrikah

ḥ-z-b

Ḥazzāb
Ḥizb

ḥ-z-z

Taḥzīz

ḥ-z-q

Ḥazq

ḥ-z-n

Aṣwāt al Muḥzinah
Taḥzīn

ḥ-s-b

Ḥasaba
Muḥāsibah
Muḥassabah

ḥ-s-s

Ḥass
Ḥassās
Ḥiss

ḥ-s-n

Ḥusaynī
Ḥusaynī Shadd
Mah'âsin al Lah'n (Maḥāsin al Laḥn)
Ṣawt Ḥusayn
Taḥāsīn
Taḥsīn
Taḥsīn al Ḍarb
Taḥsīn al Laḥn
Tīk Ḥusaynī

ḥ-sh-w

Ḥashw

ḥ-sh-y

Umm wa Ḥāshiyah

ḥ-ṣ-r

Ḥiṣār
Maḥṣūrah
Nīm Ḥiṣār
Qarār Ḥiṣār
Qarār Nīm Ḥiṣār
Qarār Tīk Ḥiṣār
Tīk Ḥiṣār

ḥ-ḍ-r

Ḥaḍḍārah

ḥ-ṭ-ṭ

Aḥaṭṭ
Ḥaṭṭ
Ḥaṭṭaṭa
Maḥaṭṭ

ḥ-f-ẓ

Ḥāfiẓ

ḥ-f-l

Ḥaflah
Ḥaflah Mūsīqiyyah

ḥ-q-q

Ḥuqqah
Taḥqīq

ḥ-l-q

Ḥalq

ḥ-l-l

Ḥallah
Ḥillah

ḥ-l-w

Ishārah Ḥulyah

ḥ-m-d

Ḥamd

ḥ-m-s

Ḥamās

ḥ-m-l

Ḥāmil or Ḥāmilah
Maḥmūl
Taḥmīlah

ḥ-n-f

Ḥanafī

ḥ-n-n

Ḥannānah

ḥ-w-j

Ḥawj

ḥ-w-r

Ḥiwār
Taḥwīr

ḥ-w-z

Ḥawzī

ḥ-w-sh

Aḥwāsh

ḥ-w-l

ʿAlāmah al Taḥwīl
ʿAlāmah al Taḥwīl al Muḍāʿaf
Istiḥālah
Istiḥālah al Ṣawtiyyah
Sullam al ʿArabī al Ḥālī

ḥ-y-r

Muḥayyir

خ

kh-b-b

Khabab

kh-b-r

Khābāriyyah
Mustakhbir
Mustakhbir al Inqilābāt
Mustakhbir al Ṣanʿah

kh-t-m

Khatm

kh-r-b

Khrab

kh-r-j

Khārij al Dasātīn
Kharjah
Khurūj
Ziyādah Naqrāt min Khārij

kh-r-s

Kharas

kh-r-ʿ

Ikhtirāʿ

kh-r-q

Kharaq

kh-z-n

Khaznah
Makhāzinī
Makhzinah

kh-sh-b

Khashabah

kh-ṣ-r

Khaṣr
Ikhtiṣār

kh-ṭ-ṭ

Takhaṭṭī

kh-t-w

(bi) Takhaṭṭī

kh-f-t

Khāfitah
Nagham Khāfitah

kh-f-ḍ

ʿAlāmah al Khafḍah
Khafḍ al Ṣawt

kh-w-y

Khawā
Khāwī

kh-y-r

Ikhtiyārī

kh-y-l

Khiyāl

د

d-b-k

Dabkah

d-b-s

Dabbūs

d-j-n

Dājinah
Mudjinah (Mujinah)

d-ḥ-w

Daḥḥiyyah

d-kh-l

Dukhūl
Jamʿ Mutadākhil
Madkhal
Mutadākhilah

d-r-b-k

Darābkī
Darabukkah
Darbūkah

d-r-j

Daraj
Darajah
Darajah al Bidāyah
Darajah al Ibtidā'
Darajah al Iltiqā'
Darajah al Istiqrār
Darajah al Rukūz
Dārij
Dirrīj
Durraij or Durrayj
Ibtidā' bi Tamaḥḥul Tadrījī
Idrāj
Mudarraj Mūsīqī
Nuqṣan al Ṣawt bil Tadrīj
Ziyādah Shaddah al Ṣawt Tadrījiyyan
Ziyādah Surʿah bil Tadrīj

d-r-d-b

Dardaba (supp.)
Derdeba

d-r-ʿ

Ṭabl al Dūrūʿī

d-s-t

Dastah

d-s-s

Dass
Dassah

d-f-f

Daff or Duff
Daff Mudawwar
Daff Murabbaʿ
Daff Sinjārī
Daffāf
Duff

d-f-q

Dafqah

d-q-q

Adaqq
Daqīqah
Daqqa
Daqqāq
Daqq-il-Ḥabb
Diqqah
Nagham Daqīqah
Mutadiqq

d-l-b

Muqaddimah al Dūlābī

d-l-l

Dalīl
Dalīl al Kabīr al ʿAmm
Dalīl al Kabīr al ʿArabī
Dalīl al Maqām

d-n-w

Jins al Adnā

d-w-r

Daff Mudawwar
Dā'irah
Dawr (also supp.)
Dawr al Quwwah
Intiqāl ʿAlā Istidārah
Mudārāt al Awtār
Mudawwar
Mudīr al Jawq
Mustadīr
Mustadīrah
Nuqlah ʿAlā Istidārah
Rājiʿ al Mustadīr (supp.)
Ṣadaf Mudawwar

d-w-z-n

Dawzana
Dawzanah
Dūzān

d-w-n

Dīwān
Dīwān
Dīwān Awwal
Dīwān Farʿī
Dīwān Jawābī
Dīwān Kāmil
Dīwān Qarārī
Dīwān Thānī
Dīwānī
Mudawwin
Tadwīn

d-y-n

Tartīl Dīnī

ذ

dh-h-b

Madhhab
Madhhabjī
Madhhabjiyyah

dh-k-r

Dhikr
Istidhkār
Tadhkīrah

dh-q-n

Dhāqinah

dh-r-r

Dharrah Ṣawtiyyah

dh-r-w

Tudhrī (or tudrī)?

dh-y-l

Dhayl
Tadhyīl

ر

r-'-s

Jumlah Ra'īsiyyah
Ra'īs
Ra's
Ra's al Nadfah
(al) Shaykh al Ra'īs

r-'-y

Mir'āh

r-b-b

Arbab
Rabāb or Rabābah
Rabāb Maghribī
Rabāb Miṣrī
Rabāb al Mughannī
Rabāb al Shāʿir
Rabāb al Sharqī
Rabāb al Turkī
Rabābah
Rabābī
Rubāb or Rūbāb
Ṭarab Rabb
ʿŪd al Rabāb

r-b-ṭ

Ribāṭ

r-b-ʿ

ʿAmūd al Rābiʿ
ʿAnāṣir al Arbaʿ
Aqsām Buʿd Dhī al Arbaʿ
Arbaʿah al Aḍʿāf (supp.)
Arbaʿah Mutatāliyah
Buʿd Alladhī bil Arbaʿ
Buʿd bil Arbaʿ
Daff al Murabbaʿ
Dhū al Arbaʿ
Dhū Quwā al Arbaʿ
Jins Khāliyah min Arbāʿ al Ṣawt
Jins al Rābiʿ
Marbūʿah
Murabbaʿ
Rābiʿah
Rābiʿah al Tāmmah
Rābiʿah al Zā'idah
Rubʿ
Rubʿ Masāfah
Rubʿ al Ṭanīnī
Rubāʿī
Rubāʿiyyah al Asnān
Rubʿayn
Tajnīs al Rābiʿ
Zamān al Rābiʿ
Zummārah Rubāʿiyyah

r-t-b

Martabah (also supp.)
Nagham Rātibah

r-t-l

Murattal
Murattil
Rattala
Tartīl
Tartīl Dīnī
Tartīlah

r-th-w or r-th-y

Marāthī
Marthiyyah
Rithā'

r-j-ḥ

Murajjaḥah
Tarjīḥ

r-j-z

Rajaz

r-j-ʿ

Ishārah al Rujūʿ
Lāzim al Tarjīʿah
Murajjiʿ
Rājiʿ
Rājiʿ al Fard (supp.)
Rājiʿ al Muḍl ʿ (supp.)
Rājiʿ al Mustadīr (supp.)

r-q-q

Ghinā' al Raqīq
Raqq or Riqq
Riqq
Ṣawt Raqīqah

r-q-m

Raqmah
Tarqīm al Mīzān

r-k-b

Basīṭ al Murakkab
Ghinā' al Rukbān
Juz' al Murakkab
Mufaṣṣal al Murakkab
Murakkab
Murakkab al Awwal
Murakkab al Thānī
Rakbānī
Rikāb
Rukbānī
Ṭabl al Markab
Tarkīb
Tarkīb bi Istiqāmah
Tarkīb Munakkas
Taswiyah al Murakkabah

r-k-z

Darajah al Rukūz
Markaz
Rukūz

r-m-l

Khafīf al Ramal
Ramal
Ramal Tūtī
Ṣawt Ramal
Thaqīl al Ramal

r-n-m

Kathīr al Tarannum
Rannām
Rannama
Tarannama
Tarannum
Tarnīm
Tarnīmah

r-n-n

Ranīn
Rannah
Rannan
Rannana

r-w-ḥ

Istirāḥah
Mirwaḥah
Rāḥah
Rūḥ Afzā (supp.)
Ruwayḥah

r-w-s

Mirwās

r-w-q

Ruwāqah

r-w-m

Rawm

r-w-y

Rāwī

r-y-th

Aryath
Rā'ith

r-y-h

Zamr al Rīḥī

r-y-sh

Rīshah
Rīshah Miṣriyyah

Rīshah Muzdawijah
Rīshah al Nasr
Rīshah Turkiyyah

ز

z-b-b

Zabībah

z-b-d

Zubaydah

z-j-l

Zajal
Zajala
Zājil
Zajjāl

z-ḥ-m

Zawāḥim

z-kh-r-f

Zukhruf
Zukhrufah

z-kh-m

Zakhmah

z-r-r

Zirr

z-gh-r-d

Zaghārīd
Zaghrada
Zaghradah

z-gh-r-ṭ

Zaghārīṭ
Zaghraṭah

z-f-f

Zaffah

z-f-n

Zāfinah
Zafn

z-q-r

Zūqqara
Zūqra

z-q-q

Ziqq

z-k-r

Zakkār
Zikārah
Zikrah
Zukrah

z-l-f

Abū al Zuluf
Umm al Zuluf

z-l-q

Mazlūq

z-l-m

Zulāmī

z-m-j-r

Zamjarah

z-m-kh-r

Zamkhar (?)

z-m-r

Ālah al Zamr
Būq Zamrī
Mawlā al Zamr
Mazāmīr
Mizmār
Mizmār al Baladī
Mizmār ʻIrāqī
Mizmār al Jirāb
Mizmār al Muthannā
Mizmār Muzāwaj
Shaʻīrah al Mizmār
Urghanūm al Zamrī
Zāmar
Zamara
Zāmir
Zamīr
Zammār
Zammara
Zammārah
Zamr
Zamr al Būqī
Zamr al Kabīr
Zamr al Rīḥī
Zamr al Ṣughayyir
Zummār or Zummārah
Zummāra Arbawija
Zummāra Bi-Soan
Zummāra Chamsawija
Zummārah Khumasiyyah
Zummāra al Kirba
Zummārah al Muzdawajah
Zummārah al Qirbah
Zummārah Rubāʻiyyah
Zummāra Sattawija
Zummārah Sudāsiyyah
Zummārah bi Suʻn

z-m-z-m

Muzamzim
Zamzama
Zamzamah

z-m-l

Zāmilah

z-m-m

Mazmūm or Mazmūmah
Zamm

z-m-n

Zaman or Zamān
Zamān al Aqall
Zamān al Awwal
Zamān al Mabda'
Zamān al Mi'yār
Zamān Mutafāḍil
Zamān al Rābiʻ
Zamān al Thālith
Zamān al Thānī

z-n-b-q

Zanbaq

z-n-j

Zanj
Zinj
Zunūj

z-h-r

Mazhar
Mizhar
Musabbaʻ al Zahrī

z-w-b-ʻ

Zawbaʻī

z-w-j

Mizmār Muzāwaj
Mizwij
Muzāwaj
Muzdawaj
Rīshah Muzdawijah
Taswiyah al Muzāwaj
Zawj
Zummārah al Muzdawajah

z-w-d

Mizwad
Mizwid
Zawwādah
Zuwwādah

s-ḥ-r

Masḥūrah
Ṭablah al Musaḥḥir

s-d-s

Sudāsī
Zummārah Sudāsiyyah

s-r-b

Sarrabah

s-r-j

Musarraj

s-r-ḥ

Surūḥ

s-r-d

Masrūdah

s-r-ʿ

Asraʿ
Ghāyah al Surʿah
Hazaj Sarīʿ
Sarīʿ or Sarīʿah
Sarīʿ al Hazaj
Surʿah
Waḥdah Sarīʿah
Ziyādah Surʿah bil Tadrīj

s-r-w

Sarw

s-ṭ-ḥ

Saṭḥ

s-ṭ-r

Aṭsara (?)
Masṭarah
Misṭarah
Saṭṭarah

s-ṭ-ʿ

Saṭṭāʿah

s-ʿ-n

Zummārah bi Suʿn

s-f-d

Nāy Safīd

s-f-l

Jins al Asfal
Jins al Suflā

s-q-ṭ

Faḍlāt al Sawāqiṭ (supp.)
Sawakāt (?)
Sawaket (?)

s-k-t

Sakt or Saktah
Sawakāt (?)
Sawaket (?)

s-k-n

Naqrah Sākinah

s-l-b

Uslūb al Maqām

s-w-f

Masāfah Sharqiyyah al Akbar
Masāfah Sharqiyyah al Aṣghar
Masāfah Sharqiyyah al Kubrā
Masāfah Sharqiyyah Mutawassiṭah
Masāfah Sharqiyyah al Ṣughrā
Rubʻ Masāfah

s-w-q

Sāqah

s-w-y

ʻAlā al Musāwāh (supp.)
Musāwiyah
Mutasāwī
Rujūʻ al Mutasāwī al Nisab (supp.)
Sawwā
Ṭabaqah Mutasāwiyah
Tamdīd Mutasāwiyah
Tanẓīm Dhū al Abʻād al Mutasāwiyah
Tanẓīm min Thunā'iyyāt al
  Mutasāwiyah
Taswiyah
Taswiyah al Ālah
Taswiyah al Murakkabah
Taswiyah al Muzāwaj
Taswiyah al ʻUẓmā

s-y-kh

Sīkh

s-y-r

Musāyarah
Sāyir al Tarjīʻah (?)

ش

sh-b-b

Mushabbib
Shabab
Shabb or Shabb
Shabbabah

sh-b-r

Shabbūr

sh-b-ṭ

ʻŪd al Shabbūṭ

sh-b-h

Abʻād Mutashābihah al Naghm
Buʻd Mutashābih al Naghm
Ghayr Mutashābihah
Maqām al Mutashābih
Mutashābih or Mutashābihah
Mutashābih al Mukhtalif bil
  Quwwah
Tashābuh fī al Kayfiyyah

sh-j-ʻ

Mushajjiʻ
Shujāʻ

sh-ḥ-j

Shuḥāj
Shuḥāj al Aṣghar
Shuḥāj al Awsaṭ
Shuḥāj al Aʻẓam
Shuḥīj

sh-d-d

Ḥusaynī Shadd
Mashadd
Mīzān al Mashadd
Nagham Shadīdah
Shadd
Shadda
Shaddād

Shaddādah
Shaddah
Shadīdah
Ziyādah Shaddah al Ṣawt Tadrījiyyan

sh-d-w

Shādī
Shadw
Shudāh

sh-dh-r

Shadhrah

sh-r-r

Sharārah

sh-r-ʿ

Sharʿah or Shirʿah

sh-r-q

Jins al Sharqī
Masāfah Sharqiyyah al Akbar
Masāfah Sharqiyyah al Aṣghar
Masāfah Sharqiyyah al Kubrā
Masāfah Sharqiyyah Mutawassiṭah
Masāfah Sharqiyyah al Ṣughrā
Mashriqī
Musharqī
Mūsīqā al Sharqiyyah
Sharqah
Sharqī
Shurūqī
Ṭunbūr al Sharqī
ʿŪd Mashriqī
ʿŪd Sharqī

sh-ṭ-ḥ

Shaṭḥ
Shaṭḥah

sh-ṭ-r

Ashṭur al Ūlā
Shaṭr

sh-ʿ-b

Shaʿbiyyah
Shuʿaybiyyah
Shuʿbah
Ughniyah Shaʿbiyyah

sh-ʿ-r

Rabāb al Shāʿir
Shāʿir
Shaʿīrah
Shaʿīrah al Mizmār
Shaʿr
Shaʿrah or Shiʿrah
Shiʿr
Shiʿr Ghinā'ī
Shirʿah

sh-gh-l

Ashghāl
Shughl

sh-q-r

Mishqar
Shaqirah
Shuqrah

sh-q-sh-q

Shaqshāq
Shaqshaqah

sh-q-f

Shaqaf or Shaqf

sh-q-q

Tashqīq

sh-k-l

Abʿād Mutashākilah al Naghm
Buʿd Mutashākil al Naghm

sh-m-s

Shamsah
Shamsiyyah

sh-m-m

Ishmām

sh-n-gh-l

Shanghal

sh-n-sh-n

Shanāshin

sh-h-r

Binṣir al Mashhūrah
Īqāʿāt al Mashhūrah
Jamāʿāt al Mashhūrah

sh-h-n

Shāhīn

sh-w-dh

Shādh

sh-w-r

Ishārah Ḥulyah
Ishārah al Istimrār
Ishārah al Rujūʿ
Ishārah al Takrār

sh-w-z

Shāz

sh-w-sh

Ṭabl Shāwīsh

sh-y-kh

Shaykh
Shaykh al Ra'īs
Shaykhah

sh-y-l

Mashāliyah

ص

ṣ-b-ʿ

Aṣābiʿ
Iṣbaʿ

ṣ-b-w or ṣ-b-y

Ṣabā

ṣ-j-j

Ṣajjāt

ṣ-ḥ-b

Iṣṭiḥāb
Muṣāḥabah
Muṣāḥib

ṣ-d-ḥ

Muṣaddiḥ
Ṣadaḥa
Ṣadaḥah
Ṣadḥ
Ṣādiḥ
Ṣudaḥ

ṣ-d-r

Maṣdar
Muṣaddar

ṣ-l-ṣ-l

Ṣalāṣil
Ṣalṣāl

ṣ-m-t

Ṣāmit
Ta'līf al Ṣāmit

ṣ-n-ʿ

Ālah Ṣināʿiyyah
Kirsh al Ṣanʿah
Mustakhbir al Ṣanʿah
Qadariyyah Ṣināʿah
Qisṭ al Ṣanʿah
Ṣanʿah al ʿŪd
Ṣāniʿ
Ṣināʿah
Ṣināʿah al Malāhī
Ṣināʿah al Mūsīqā
Ṣināʿah al Mūsīqā al ʿAmaliyyah
Ṣināʿah al Mūsīqā al Naẓariyyah
Taqyīd al Ṣanʿah
Wasaṭ al Ṣanʿah

ṣ-n-j

Muṣannaj
Ṣanj
Ṣanj Chini
Ṣanj Jīnī
Ṣanj Sīnī
Ṣannāj
Ṣannājāt al Jaysh
Ṣinj
Ṣunūj

ṣ-n-d-q

Ṣundūq
Ṣundūq al Muṣawwit

ṣ-n-f

Ṣinf al Awwal
Ṣinf al Thānī

ṣ-h-b

Ṣahbā (?)
Ṣahbajiyyah

ṣ-h-j

Ṣahjah

ṣ-w-t

Ālah Muṣawwitah bi Dhātihā
Aṣwāt
Aṣwāt Muḥzinah
(al) Awsāṭ
Dharrah Ṣawtiyyah
Ḥabbah al Muṣawwitah
Ḥiddah al Ṣawt
Haykal Ṣawtī
Istiḥālah al Ṣawtiyyah
Jins Khāliyah min Arbāʿ al Ṣawt
Khafḍ al Ṣawt
Maqṭaʿ al Ṣawt
Mujawwab Ṣawtiyyah
Nabrah Ṣawtiyyah
Nāfidhah al Ṣawtiyyah
Nuqṣān al Ṣawt bil Tadrīj
Ṣawt
Ṣawt al ʿĀliyah
Ṣawt Dhayl
Ṣawt Ghalīẓah
Ṣawt Ḥāddah
Ṣawt Ḥusayn
Ṣawt Inqibāḍ
Ṣawt Jahīr
Ṣawt Mā'iyyah
Ṣawt Mutawassiṭah
Ṣawt Ramal
Ṣawt Raqīqah
Ṣawt Thaqīlah
Ṣawt al Wasaṭ
Ṣawt Wāṭiyah
Ṣawtī
Silsilah Aṣwāt
Ṣundūq Muṣawwit
Ṭabaqah Ṣawtiyyah
Ta'līf al Ṣawtī
Taṣwīt,
Thābit al Ṣawt
ʿUluww al Ṣawt
Unbūb or Unbūbah Mutaṣawwit(ah)
Ziyādah Shaddah al Ṣawt Tadrījiyyan

ḍ-m-r

Miḍmār

ḍ-y-q

Ḍāqa
Dayyaqa

ط

ṭ-b-r

Ṭabīr

ṭ-b-ʿ

Ālah Ṭabīʿiyyah
Niṣf Ṭabʿ
Sullam al Ūrubbī Ṭabīʿī
Ṭabʿ
Ṭābiʿ
Ṭabīʿah
Ṭabīʿī
Ṭubūʿ

ṭ-b-q

Athqal Ṭabaqatan
Ṭabaqah
Ṭabaqah Mutasāwiyah
Ṭabaqah Ṣawtiyyah
Ṭabaqah al Thāniyah
Ṭabaqah al Ūlā
Takthīr al Ṭabaqāt

ṭ-b-l

Muṭabbil
Ṭabbāl
Ṭabīlah
Ṭabl
Ṭabl Baladī
Ṭabl al Bāz
Ṭabl Dūrūʿī
Ṭabl Jāwīsh
Ṭabl Kabīr
Ṭabl Khānah
Ṭabl al Markab
Ṭabl Mijrī
Ṭabl al Mukhannath
Ṭabl al Musaḥḥir
Ṭabl Shāmī
Ṭabl Shāwīsh
Ṭabl al Sūdān
Ṭabl al Tawīl
Ṭabl Turkī
Ṭablā (?)
Ṭablah
Ṭubaylah

t-r-b

Alah Mutribah (supp.)
Ālah al Ṭarab
Aṭrab
Aṭraba
Iṭrāb
Muṭrib
Muṭrib al Munfarid
Ṭarab
Ṭarab al Futūḥ
Ṭarab Rabb
Ṭarab Zūr
Ṭaraba
Ṭariba
Ṭarrāb
Ṭarraba
Taṭarrub
Taṭrīb

ṭ-r-q

ʿAmūd Ṭarīqah
Maṭāriq
Miṭraq
Miṭraqah
Ṭarīq
Ṭarīq al Mulūkiyyah
Ṭarīqah
Ṭarq
Ṭarqah
Ṭurqah
Ṭurūq al Mulūkiyyah

ṭ-s-t

Ṭusūt

ṭ-f-r

Ṭāfir
Ṭāfir al Intiqāl

ṭ-q-m

Ṭaqm

ṭ-l-ʿ

Maṭlaʿ
Ṭāliʿ

ṭ-l-q

Alḥān bil Iṭlāq
Aṭlaqa
Awtār Muṭlaqah
Iṭlāq
Jamʿal Kāmil ʿalā Iṭlāq
Maṭlūq
Mīzān Muṭlaq
Muṭlaq
Muṭlaq al Watar
Mazmūm Muṭlaq
Nagham ʿalā Iṭlāq

ṭ-n-b-r

Nāy Ṭunbūr
Ṭunbūr
Ṭunbūr Baghdādī
Ṭunbūr Baghlamah
Ṭunbūr Buzurk
Ṭunbūr Kabīr Turkī
Ṭunbūr Khurāsānī
Ṭunbūr Mīrāthī
Ṭunbūr Mīzānī
Ṭunbūr al Sharqī
Ṭunbūr al Turkī
Ṭunbūrah Sūdānī
Ṭunbūrī or Ṭunbūriyy

ṭ-n-n

Buʿd Ṭanīnī
Faḍlah al Ṭanīnī
Jins al Ṭanīnī
Niṣf Ṭanīnī
Rubʿ al Ṭanīnī
Ṭanīn
Ṭanīnī

ṭ-w-r

Ṭār
Ṭār al Jāhilī
Ṭarājī
Ṭawr
Ṭawr al Maqām
Ṭawr al Naghmah

ṭ-w-s

Sāz Ṭāsāt
Ṭāsah
Ṭūs
Ṭuways

ṭ-w-q

Ṭāqah
Ṭawq

ṭ-w-l

Muṭawwal
Ṭabl al Ṭawīl
Taṭwīlah

ṭ-w-y

Ṭayy

ṭ-y-r

Ṭā'ir

ظ

ẓ-h-r

Ẓāhir
Ẓahīr
Ẓāhir al Tanāfur
Ẓahr

ع

ʿ-b-r

ʿIbārah Mūsīqiyyah
Taʿbīr

ʿ-t-b

ʿAtab or ʿAtabah
ʿAtābā or ʿAtābah
ʿUtab

ʿ-t-d

ʿAtīdah

ʿ-j-z

ʿAjz
Kamānjah al ʿAjūz

ʿ-j-l

ʿAjal
ʿĀjil
ʿAjjala

ʿ-j-m

ʿAjam
Jank ʿAjamī
Nashīd al ʿAjam
Nīm ʿAjam
Qarār ʿAjam
Qarār Nīm ʿAjam

ʿ-d-d

Aʿdād
ʿAdadī
Adid (?)
Taʿdīd

ʿ-d-l

Jins al Muʿtadil (supp.)
Muʿtadil
Sullam al Muʿaddal
Sullam al Muʿtadil

ʿ-r-b

Aarbi or ʿArbi (supp.)
ʿArabah
ʿArabī
ʿArabī Dūduk
ʿArabī Zūrnā
ʿArūbī
ʿArūbiyyah
Buʿd al ʿArabī
Dalīl al Kabīr al ʿArabī
Ghinā' al ʿArab
Kamānjah al ʿArabī
Nashīd al ʿArab
Nawbah ʿArabī
Nīm ʿArabah
Qaṣṣāb ʿArabī
Sullam al ʿArabī al Ḥālī
Sullam al ʿArabī al Qadīm
ʿŪd ʿArabī
ʿUrab
Wusṭā al ʿArab

ʿ-r-j

Aʿraj
Intiqāl ʿalā Inʿirāj
Juz' al Aʿraj
Nuqlah ʿalā Inʿirāj

ʿ-r-ḍ

ʿAlāmah ʿArīḍah
ʿArāḍah
ʿArḍah
ʿArīḍah
ʿArūḍ
ʿArūḍī

ʿ-r-q

ʿIrq

ʿ-z-f

ʿAzafa
ʿAzafī
ʿAzf
ʿĀzif
ʿĀzif Munfarid
Maʿzūfah
Miʿzaf
Miʿzafah

ʿ-m-l

ʿAmal
ʿAmalī
ʿAmila
Ijrā' al ʿAmal
Mūsīqā ʿAmaliyyah
Ṣināʿah al Mūsīqā al ʿAmaliyyah

ʿ-m-m

Dalīl al Kabīr al ʿĀmm

ʿ-n-z

ʿUnnayz

ʿ-n-ṣ-r

ʿAnāṣir al Arbaʿ

ʿ-n-q

ʿAnqa'
Dhū al ʿAnqā'
ʿUnq

ʿ-n-w or ʿ-n-y

Muʿannā

ʿ-w-d

Ādhān al ʿŪd
ʿAwd
ʿAwwād
ʿAwwadah
Dhāt ʿAwdāt
ʿIdān
Ṣanʿah al ʿŪd
Ta'wwadit
Tuḥfah al ʿŪd
ʿŪd
ʿŪd ʿArabī
ʿŪd Fārisī
ʿŪd ʿIrāqī
ʿŪd Jilliqī
ʿŪd Kāmil
ʿŪd Maghribī
ʿŪd Mashriqī
ʿŪd Miṣrī
ʿŪd Qadīm
ʿŪd al Rabāb
ʿŪd al Shabbūṭ
ʿŪd Sharqī
ʿŪd Tūnisī

ʿ-w-ḍ

Istiʿāḍah

ʿ-y-b

Mīzān ʿĀyib

ʿ-y-r

Zamān al Miʿyār

ʿ-y-ṭ

ʿAyṭah

ʿ-y-n

ʿAyn
Qalb al ʿIyān
ʿUyūn

غ

gh-b-r

Taghbīr

gh-d-w

Ghādī bil ʿAks

gh-r-b

Gharbī
Maghribī
Rabāb al Maghribī
ʿŪd Maghribī

gh-r-b-l

Ghirbāl

gh-r-d

Gharad
Gharrada
Mugharrad
Mugharrid
Tagharrada
Taghrīd
Ughrūdah

gh-z-l

Ghazal
Ghazāl
Taghazzul

gh-ṣ-n

Ghuṣn

gh-ṭ-w

Ghiṭā'
Taghṭiyah

gh-l-ẓ

Ghilẓ
Nagham Ghalīẓah
Ṣawt Ghalīẓah

gh-m-z

Ghammāz

gh-n-m

Abū Ghanam

gh-n-n

Aghann
Ghannā'
Ghunnah

gh-n-y

Aghānī
Ghannā'
Ghanna bi ________
Ghannā'ī
Ghannāyah
Ghannāyāt
Ghinā'
Ghinā' al ʿArab
Ghinā' al Awwal al Thaqīl
Ghinā' al Mawqiʿ
Ghinā' al Murtajal
Ghinā' al Mutqan
Ghinā' al Raqīq
Ghinā' al Rukbān
Ghinā'ī
Jawq Ghinā'iyyah
Maghnā
Mughannā
Mughannī
Mughannī Mufrad
Mughanniyah
Mughnī or Mūghnī
Mūsīqā Bidūn Ghinā'
Mūsīqā Ghinā'iyyah
Qaṣabah Matāʿ al Ghannā'ī
Rabāb al Mughannī
Shiʿr Ghinā'ī
Taghannā
Ta'līf al Ghinā'ī
Tarassul fī al Ghinā'
Ughniyah
Ughniyah Shaʿbiyyah

gh-y-b

Ghābah

gh-y-r

Ghayr Muntaẓim
Ghayr Mutalā'im
Ghayr Mutashābihah
Ghayr Ziyādah Naqrāt
Jamʿ al Mutaghayyir
Jins al Layyin Ghayr al Muntaẓim
Jins al Layyin al Muntaẓim
Ghayr Mutatālī
Taghyīr

gh-y-ṭ

Ghayṭah

gh-y-y

Ghāyah al Surʿah

ف

f-t-ḥ

Iftitāḥ
Istiftāḥ
Miftāḥ
Miftāḥ Fā
Miftāḥ Jahīr
Miftāḥ al Kamān
Miftāḥ Sūl
Ṭarab al Futūḥ

f-t-l

Miftāl

f-kh-m

Tafkhīm

f-ḍ-l

Faḍlah
Faḍlah al Ṭanīnī
Faḍlāt Laḥniyyah (supp.)
Faḍlāt al Sawāqiṭ (supp.)
Mutafaḍḍil
Mutafāḍil or Mutafāḍilah
Mutafāḍilah al Mufaṣṣalah
Mutafāḍilah al Muwaṣṣalah
Zamān Mutafāḍil

f-r-kh

Kamānjah al Farkh

f-r-d

Aferdi (?)
Ajnās Mufradah
ʿAzif Munfarid
Fardiyyah
Infirād
Jins al Mufrad
Mufarrad or Mufarradah
Mufrad
Mufradah
Mughannī Mufrad
Munfarid
Muṭrib al Munfarid
Naqrah Munfaridah
Rājiʿ al Fard (supp.)

f-r-ḍ

Thaqīlah al Mafrūḍāt

f-r-s

Faras

f-r-sh

Farshah (supp.)
Firāsh

f-r-ʿ

Dīwān al Farʿī
Farʿ

f-r-gh

Fārigh al Nagham
Fārighah
Taʿmīr al Farāgh

f-r-q

Firqah
Jamʿ Iftirāq
Qā'id Firqah Mūsīqiyyah

f-s-ḥ

Fusḥah

f-ṣ-l

Fāṣil

Fāṣilah
Fāṣilah Kubrā
Fāṣilah Ṣughrā
Fāṣilah ʿUẓmā
Fāṣilah Wusṭā
Faṣl
Faṣl Mūsīqī
Infiṣāl
Īqāʿāt al Mufaṣṣalah
Jamʿ Infiṣāl
Jamʿ al Munfaṣil
Jins al Qawī al Munfaṣil
Mufaṣṣal
Mufaṣṣal al Awwal
Mufaṣṣal al Basīṭ
Mufaṣṣal al Murakkab
Mufaṣṣal al Thālith
Mufaṣṣal al Thāni
Munfaṣil or Munfaṣilah
Mutafāḍilah al Mufaṣṣalah
Mutafāṣil
Tafṣīl
Tafṣīl al Muwaṣṣal
Tawṣīl al Mufaṣṣal

f-q-r

Fiqrah

f-q-sh

Faqqāshāt
Fuqayshāt

f-k-r

Fikrah Mūsīqiyyah

f-l-dh

Sāz al Alwāḥ al Fūlādh
Sāz Fūlādh

f-n-n

Fann al Nagham

f-w-q

Sīkāh Fawq al Tāmm

ق

q-b-ḍ

Maqbiḍ or Miqbaḍ
Miqbaḍ
Qabḍah
Qabḍī
Ṣawt Inqibāḍ

q-b-ṣ

Qabūṣ

q-b-l

Qablī or Qabliyyah
Qiblah

q-d-ḥ

Qadīḥah

q-d-d

Qadd

q-d-r

Miqdār
Qadariyyah
Qadariyyah Ṣināʿah
Qadr

q-d-m

Muqaddamah
Muqaddamah al Dūlābī
Muqaddim
Muqaddim al Ṣaff
Qudamā'
Quddām
Qudūm
Sullam al ʿArabī al Qadīm
Taqdīm
ʿŪd Qadīm
Wusṭā al Qadīm

q-dh-f

Meydaf (?)

q-r-'

Muqri'
Qāri'
Qirā'ah
Qirā'ah bil Alḥān
Tarassul Bil Qirā'ah

q-r-b

Qirbah
Qurriba
Taqrīb
Zummārah al Qirbah

q-r-ḥ

Grīḥah (?)
Iqtirāḥ
Qarīḥah

q-r-d

Qarrādī

q-r-r

Darajah al Istiqrār
Dīwān Qarārī
Istiqrār
Mustaqirr
Qalb al Qarār
Qarār
Qarār ʿAjam
Qarar Ḥiṣār
Qarār Nīm ʿAjam
Qarār Nīm Ḥiṣār
Qarār Tīk Ḥiṣār

q-r-ṭ

Qīrāṭ
Qurṭ

q-r-ʿ

Aqraʿ
Muqāriʿ
Qarʿ
Qaraʿa
Qarīʿah

q-r-q-b

Qarqabū or Qarqābū

q-r-m

Qurmah

q-r-m-d

Qarmūdah

q-r-n

Abū Qurūn
Iqtirān
Karnā or Ḳarnā
Karranāy or Karranā
Maqrūnah
Maqrūnah bil Kalām
Muqarran Dunbalayī
Nagham al Insāniyyah Maqrūnah bil Aqāwīl
Qarīnah
Qarn
Qarna

q-r-n-d

Qarīndah

q-s-ṭ

Qisṭ al Ṣanʿah

q-s-m

Aqsām Buʿd Dhī al Arbaʿ
Aqsām Buʿd Dhī al Khams
Qism
Qismah

q-l-l

Bu'd al Kāmil al Aqall
Qallāl
Qullāl

q-n-b-r

Qunayburī (?)
Qunburī (?)

q-n-ṭ-r

Qanṭarah
Qanṭarah al Thāniyah
Qanṭarah al Ūlā

q-n-n

Qānūn
Qinnīn

q-w-d

Qā'id
Qā'id Firqah Mūsīqiyyah

q-w-s

Qaws
Qaws Ittiṣāl
Quwwās

q-w-l

Aqāwīl
Aqwāl
Muqawwil
Nagham al Insāniyyah Maqrūnah bil Aqāwīl
Qaḍīb al Qawl
Qawal
Qawl
Qawwāl
Qawwīl
Quwwāl

q-w-m

Ānā Maqām
Dalīl al Maqām
Intiqāl 'alā Istiqāmah
Iqāmah (supp.)
Maqām
Maqām al 'Irāqī
Maqām al Mutashābih
Maqām al Umm
Nuqlah 'alā Istiqāmah
Nuqlah Mustaqīmah
Qā'im wa Niṣf
Qiyām Nāṭiq
Ṭanṭanah Āsās al Maqām
Taqwīm al Awtār
Tarkīb bi Istiqāmah
Ṭawr al Maqām
Ṭawr al Naghmah
Uslūb al Maqām

q-w-y

Dawr al Quwā
Dhū Quwā al Arba'
Dhū Quwā al Khams
Jam' al Kāmil bil Quwwah
Jins al Muqawwī
Jins al Qawī
Jins al Qawī Dhū al Taḍ'īf
Jins al Qawī al Munfaṣil
Jins al Qawī al Muttaṣil
Muqawwī
Mutashābih al Mukhtalif bil Quwwah
Nagham Qawiyyah
Qawī
Qawī Dhū al Taḍ'īf
Quwwah

Sullam al Qawī
Wāḥid bil Quwwah

q-y-d

Taqyīd al Ṣan'ah

q-y-n

Qaynah

ك

k-'-s

See Kās or Ka's
Sāz Ka'sāt

k-b-r

Bu'd al Kabīr
Dalīl al Kabīr al 'Āmm
Dalīl al Kabīr al 'Arabī
Fāṣilah Kubrā
Kabar (?)
Kamānjah Kabīrah
(al) Kibār (supp.)
Kubrā
Masāfah Sharqiyyah al Akbar
Masāfah Sharqiyyah al Kubrā
Mujannab al Kabīr
Nagham Kibār
Ṭabl Kabīr
Takbīr
Ṭunbūr Kabīr Turkī
Waḥdah al Kabīrah
Waḥdah al Kubrā

k-t-f

Mutakātif
Taktīf

k-th-r

Kathīr al Tarannum
Takthīr
Takthīr al Ṭabaqāt

k-r-r

Ishārah al Takrār
Takarrur
Takrīr

k-r-s

Kursī

k-r-sh

Kirsh al Ṣan'ah

k-r-m

Karam

k-r-n

Karīnah
Kirān

k-s-r

Maḥzūzah Mukassarah

k-'-b

Ka'b

k-l-l

Bu'd Alladhī bil Kull
Bu'd Alladhī bil Kull Marratayn
Bu'd bil Kull
Bu'd bil Kull Marratayn
Dhū al Kull
Dhū bil Kull
Ḍi'f Alladhī bil Kull
Ḍi'f Dhū al Kull
Kull al Ḍurūb
Kull al Ḍurūb wal Nagham
Kull al Nigham

k-l-m

Kalām al Hazl
Kalām al Jadd
Kalām Malḥūn
Maqrūnah bil Kalām

k-m-l

Alḥān al Kāmilah
Bu'd al Kāmil
Bu'd al Kāmil al Aqall
Dīwān Kāmil
Jam' al Akmal

Jamʻ al Kāmil
Jamʻ al Kāmil ʻalā Iṭlāq
Jamʻ al Kāmil bil Quwwah
Kamālāt al ʻAshr
Kāmil fī al Talā'um
ʻŪd Kāmil

k-m-m

Kamm
Kammiyyah
Kammiyyāt al Nagham

k-w-b

Kūbah

k-w-s

Kās or Ka's
Kūs
Kūssī
Ku'ūs

k-y-f

Kayf
Kayfiyyāt al Nagham
Tashābuh fī al Kayfiyyah

ل

l-'-m

Ghayr Mutalā'im
Kāmil Fī al Talā'um
Mulā'amāt al ʻAshr
Mulā'amāt al Nagham
Mulā'im
Mutalā'im or Mutalā'imah
Talā'im

l-b-y

Talbiyah

l-ḥ-ẓ

Laḥīẓah
Laḥẓah

l-ḥ-n

Abʻād Laḥniyyah al Naghm
Adā' al Alḥān
Alḥān
Alḥān bil Iṭlāq
Alḥān Juz'iyyah
Alḥān Kāmilah
Buʻd Laḥnī
Faḍlāt Laḥniyyah (supp.)
Intiqāl min Laḥn ilā Laḥn
Jādhbiyyah Laḥniyyah
Kalām Malḥūn
Laḥḥān
Laḥḥana
Laḥn
Laḥn al Ḥurr
Laḥn Mawzūn
Mabādi' al Alḥān
Mabānī al Alḥān
Mah'âsin al Lahn
Malḥūn
Mulaḥḥan
Mulaḥḥin
Qalb al Laḥn
Qirā'ah bil Alḥān
Ṣiyāghah al Laḥn
Sulṭān al Alḥān
Taḥsīn al Laḥn
Talḥīn
Talḥīnāt al Insāniyyah
Talḥīnī
Tanẓīm al Alḥān
Tardīd al Alḥān

l-ḥ-q

Lāḥiq

l-z-m

Lāzim al Tarjīʻah
Lāzimah
Mulāzimah

l-ṭ-m

Laṭm

l-ʻ-b

Laʻiba

Madīḥ
Madīḥ Nabawī
Qaṣabah Matā' al Maddāḥ

m-d-d

Dhū al Maddatayn
Madd
Madd al Watar
Maddah
Tamdīd
Tamdīd Mutasāwī

m-r-t

Bu'd Alladhī bil Kull Marratayn
Bu'd bil Kull Marratayn

m-r-r

Ishārah al Istimrār

m-r-n

Murūnah

m-z-j

Imtizāj
Mamzūjah
Tamzīj

m-s-ḥ

Masḥah

m-sh-ṭ

Mushṭ

m-sh-w or m-sh-y

Māshā

m-'-ṭ

Lma'it (?)

m-'-n

Mā'ūn

m-k-w

Mukā'

m-l-k

Ṭarīq al Mulūkiyyah
Ṭurūq al Mulūkiyyah

m-l-w

Bayt al Malāwī
Mamluwwah al Nagham

m-h-l

Mahil

m-w-t

Mawāt

m-w-j

Tamawwuj

m-w-l

Mawāliyā
Mawwāl
Tamwīlah

m-w-h

Mā'iyyah
Māya
Miyāt Khānah
Ṣawt Mā'iyyah

ن

n-b-b

Anābīb
Unbūb or Unbūbah
Unbūb or Unbūbah Mutaṣawwit(ah)

n-b-t

Rujūʿ Munbat (supp.)

n-b-r

Nabara
Nabr
Nabrah Ṣawtiyyah
Ta'khīr al Nabr

n-b-w

Madīḥ Nabawī

n-th-r

Manthūr
Nathr al Naghamāt

n-j-r

Manjīrah

n-ḥ-f

Nagham Naḥīfah
Naḥīfah

n-ḥ-m

Naḥḥam

n-d-b

Naddāb
Naddābah

n-z-l

ʿAlāmah al Tanazzul
Nāzilan

n-z-h

Nuzhah

n-s-b

Munāsabah
Nasīb
Nasībah
Nisbah

n-s-r

Rīshah al Nasr

n-sh-d

Anshada
Anshūdah
Inshād
Munshid
Nashīd
Nashīd al ʿAjam
Nashīd al ʿArab
Nashshād
Unshūdah

n-sh-z

Nashāz

n-ṣ-b

Naṣb

n-ṣ-r

Manṣūr
Manṣūrī

n-ṣ-f

Niṣf or Nuṣf Bardah
Niṣf or Nuṣf Buʿd
Niṣf or Nuṣf Ṭabʿ
Niṣf Ṭanīnī

Niṣf al Waḥdah al Ṣaghīrah
Nuṣf
Qā'im wa Niṣf

n-ṣ-y

Nāṣiyah

n-ṭ-q

Qiyām Nāṭiq
Ta'līf al Nāṭiq
Tawshīḥ Nāṭiq

n-ẓ-r

Mūsīqā Naẓariyyah
Naẓarī
Naẓīr
Ṣinā'ah al Mūsīqā al Naẓariyyah

n-ẓ-m

Ghayr Muntaẓim
Jins al Layyin Ghayr al Muntaẓim
Jins al Layyin Muntaẓim Ghayr Mutatālī
Jins al Layyin al Muntaẓim al Mutatālī
Jins al Muntaẓim
Jins al Nāẓim
Manẓūm
Muntaẓim
Nāẓim
Naẓm
Naẓm al Naghamāt
Tanẓīm al Alḥān
Tanẓīm Dhū al Ab'ād al Mutasāwiyah
Tanẓīm min Thunā'iyyāt al Mutasāwiyah

n-'-r

Nā'ūrah

n-'-m

Nu'mānī

n-gh-r

Nuwāghir (?)

n-gh-m

Ab'ād Mutashābihah al Naghm
Ab'ād Mutashākilah al Naghm
Ab'ād Muttafiqah al Naghm
Anghām
Bu'd Mutashābih al Naghm
Bu'd Mutashākil al Naghm
Bu'd Muttafiq al Naghm
Fann al Nagham
Fārighah al Nagham
Iṣlāḥ al Nagham
Kammiyyāt al Nagham
Kayfiyyāt al Nagham
Kull al Ḍurūb wal Nagham
Kull al Nigham
Mamluwwah al Nagham
Manghūm
Mawḍī' al Nagham
Mubtada' al Nagham
Mulā'amāt al Nagham
Nagham
Nagham Daqīqah
Nagham Ghalīẓah
Nagham al Insāniyyah Maqrūnah bil Aqāwīl
Nagham 'alā Iṭlāq or Nagham bi Iṭlāq
Nagham Khāfitah
Nagham Kibār
Nagham Layyinah
Nagham al Mukhtalifah
Nagham Mu'talifah
Nagham Naḥīfah
Nagham Qawiyyah
Nagham Rātibah
Nagham Shadīdah
Nagham al Ṣughrā
Nagham al 'Uẓmā
Nagham al Wusṭā
Naghama or Naghima
Naghamah or Naghmah
Naghamah al Ḍi'f
Naghamah al Iḍ'af
Naghamah al Yatīmah
Naghamāt al Buḥūr
Naghamāt Mawzūnah
Naghghama
Naghima
Naghm or Nagham

n-q-l

Intiqāl ʿalā Inʿirāj
Intiqāl ʿalā Inʿiṭāf
Intiqāl ʿalā Istidārah
Intiqāl ʿalā Istiqāmah
Intiqāl min Laḥn ilā Laḥn
Mabādi' al Intiqālāt
Nuqlah
Nuqlah ʿalā Inʿirāj
Nuqlah ʿalā Inʿiṭāf
Nuqlah ʿalā Istidārah
Nuqlah ʿalā Istiqāmah
Nuqlah Mustaqīmah
Ṭāfir al Intiqāl

n-k-s

Tarkīb Munakkas

n-w-b

Nawbah
Nawbah Andalusiyyah
Nawbah ʿArabī (supp.)
Nawbah Gharnāṭah
Nawbah Gharnaṭiyyah
Nawbah Ghurnāṭiyyah
Nawbah Inqilābāt
Nawbah Khānah
Nawbah Neklabāt
Nūbah

n-w-t

Nūtī

n-w-ḥ

Nāḥa
Nā'iḥ
Nā'ihah
Nawḥ
Niyāḥah
Tanāwīḥ

n-w-r

Nuwwārah

n-w-ʿ

Anwāʿ
Jins al Zā'id Nawʿan
Nawʿ
Nawʿ al Jamāʿah
Tanwīʿah

n-w-w

Jawāb Nawā

n-y-l

Nāylī

ه

h-j-n

Hujaynī

h-j-w

Hijā'
Ḥurūf al Hijā'

h-d-d

Haddah

h-d-w or h-d-y

Ahidous (?)

h-d-y

Hadayā or Hadāye (?)
Hadī

h-dh-b

Nāy Muhadhdhab

Waḥdah Sarīʿah
Waḥdah al Ṣughrā
Wāḥid bil Quwwah
Wāḥidah

w-ḥ-y

Awḥā
Waḥī

w-r-th

Ṭunbūr Mīrāthī
Turāth

w-r-d

Wardah

w-z-ʿ

Tawzīʿ

w-z-n

Awzān
Laḥn Mawzūn
Mawzūn
Mîâzeni (?)
Mīzān
Mīzān ʿĀyib
Mīzān al Khafīf
Mīzān al Mashadd
Mīzān Muṣarraf
Mīzān Muṭlaq
Naghamāt Mawzūnah
Naghm Mawzūn
Tawzīn
Ṭunbūr Mīzānī
Wazn
Wazzān

w-s-ṭ

(al) Awsāt (supp.)
Buʿd Mutawassiṭ
Fāṣilah Wusṭā
Jins al Mutawassiṭ
Kamān al Awsaṭ
Majrā al Wusṭā
Masāfah Sharqiyyah Mutawassiṭah
Mujannab al Wusṭā
Muttafiqāt Wusṭā
Nagham al Wusṭā
Qaṣbah Wusṭiyyah
Ṣawt Mutawassiṭah
Ṣawt al Wasaṭ
Shuḥāj al Awsaṭ
Sīkāh Mutawassiṭ
Ṣiyāḥ al Awsaṭ
Waḥdah al Mutawassiṭah
Wasaṭ (or Wasṭ) al Ṣanʿah
Wusṭā
Wusṭā al ʿArab
Wusṭā al Furs
Wusṭā al Qadīm
Wusṭā Zalzal or Wusṭā Zulzul

w-s-ʿ

Muwassaʿ
Wassaʿa
Wusʿah

w-sh-ḥ

Muwashshaḥ
Tawshīḥ
Tawshīḥ Ḍarbayn
Tawshīḥ Kiār
Tawshīḥ Ma'lūf
Tawshīḥ Naqsh
Tawshīḥ Nāṭiq
Tawshīḥ Zanjīr
Tawshīḥah

w-sh-y

Tawshiyah or Tūshiyah
Tawshiyah al Inṣirāfāt

w-ṣ-l

ʿAlā Ittiṣāl
Īqāʿāt al Muwaṣṣalah
Ittiṣāl
Jamʿ al Muttaṣil
Jamʿ al Muttaṣil al Nāqiṣ
Jins al Qawī al Muttaṣil

w-n-y

Awnā
Wānin

ي
y-d

Ṣunūj al Aṣābiʻ or Ṣunūj al Yad
Yad

y-r-ʻ

Yarāʻ or Yarāʻah

y-t-m

Naghmah al Yatīmah
Yatāyim

Appendix III: Guide to Pronunciation and Transliteration

Arabic Letter	Name	Transliteration	Pronunciation
ا	alif	ā	long "ā"
ب	bā'	b	as in "baby"
ت	tā'	t	as in "table"
ث	thā'	th	as in "think"
ج	jīm	j	soft "j"
ح	ḥā'	ḥ	strongly aspirant "h" made in the throat
خ	khā'	kh	as in German "nacht"
د	dāl	d	as in "dog"
ذ	dhāl	dh	as "th" in "this"
ر	rā'	r	as in "rag"
ز	zayn	z	as in "zip"
س	sīn	s	as in "hiss"
ش	shīn	sh	as in "ship"
ص	ṣād	ṣ	a darkening of corresponding undotted letter made with a flat, broad tongue placement
ض	ḍād	ḍ	"
ط	ṭāh	ṭ	"
ظ	ẓāh	ẓ	"

Arabic Letter	Name	Transliteration	Pronunciation
ع	ʿayn	ʿ	a very strong guttural produced by the compression of the throat and the expulsion of the breath
غ	ghayn	gh	a sound like the gargling pronunciation between "g" and "r"
ف	fā'	f	as in "fish"
ق	qāf	q	a "k" sound produced far back in the throat
ك	kāf	k	as in "kit"
ل	lām	l	as in "lemon"
م	mīm	m	as in "mail"
ن	nūn	n	as in "nod"
ه	hā'	h	as in "hat"
و	waw	w or ū	as in "world" (the consonant form) long "ū" as in "clue" (the long vowel)
ي	yā'	y or ī	as in "yet" (the consonant form) as in "feet" (the long vowel)
ء	hamzah	'	the glottal stop, as in the initial vowel of "absolutely". The "'" will not be included when the hamzah appears at the beginning of a word.

Diacritical Signs for Short Vowels	Name	Transliteration	Pronunciation
ـَ	fatḥah	a	as in "bat"
ـُ	dammah	u	as in "put"
ـِ	kasrah	i̧	as in "pit"

Diphthongs	Designation	Transliteration	Pronunciation
ـَيْ	yā' sukūn preceded by fatḥah	ay	as in cockney "pain"
ـَوْ	waw sukūn preceded by fatḥah	aw	as in "ouch"

Long vowels will be indicated by a line over the letter (e.g., Ā, Ī, Ū), except in the case of variant spellings found in the Western language sources. These will retain the vowel and consonant markings used by their authors or translators. A table of variant forms for letters encountered during this study appears at the end of this Guide to Pronunciation and Transliteration.

All instances of the definite article shall be transcribed "AL" without regard to the case of the noun they modify or their assimilation with the so-called "sun letters" (t, th, d, dh, r, z, s, sh, s, d, t, z, l, n). The definite article shall be disregarded completely in matters of alphabetical ordering. The definite article "AL," prepositions, conjunctions and other prefixes will not be connected by a hyphen to the following word as is specified in the Library of Congress Bulletin (Rule 16b, 17, 20). Particles ending with short vowels (e.g., "WA," "BI," etc.) will be joined to the definite article "AL" when it follows them immediately, the latter's short vowel being lost to that of the particle (e.g., "WAL," "BIL," etc.). Particles ending with long vowels (e.g., "ʿALĀ," "FĪ," etc.) will maintain their separate status in all instances. Tā' marbūṭah (ة) will be rendered "H" in all cases, to distinguish it from tā' tawīlah (ت , "t") (see Rule 7). Even transliterated forms omitting this "H" have been altered to conform with this rule.

There is little evidence of accent in Arabic pronunciation. Whatever accent there is generally falls on the long-vowelled syllable, i.e., the one marked ¯ . If there is more than one long syllable in a word, the accent will rest on the last of these long syllables, with the exception of the final syllable. A word without long syllable will have its accent on the first syllable.

Some variance from the guide will be found in proper names where the common usage or the personal preference of the individual in question has prevailed.

VARIANT TRANSLITERATIONS ENCOUNTERED IN THE SOURCES FOR THE ANNOTATED ARABIC-ENGLISH GLOSSARY OF MUSICAL TERMS

Arabic Letter	Transliterations Encountered (The initial form is the one used in this work.
ا	ā, á, â
ب	b, p
ت	t
ث	th, ṯ

Arabic Letter	Transliterations Encountered
ج	j, č, ch, dj, g, ǵ, ǧ, ğ, ĝ
ح	ḥ, ẖ, h'
خ	kh, h
د	d
ذ	dh, d̲h̲, d̲
ر	r
ز	z
س	s, ç
ش	sh, ch, ś, š
ص	ṣ, ç, s
ض	ḍ, d
ط	ṭ, t
ظ	ẓ, z, d̲h̲
ع	ʻ, ', ʼ
غ	gh, g, ḡ, ǵ, rh
ف	f
ق	q, ch, k, ḳ
ك	k, c
ل	l
م	m
ن	n
ه	h
و	w or ū, o, oo, ou, oû, ú, û
ي	y or ī, ï, î, í

Diphthongs are rendered variously: يْ as ay, aï, ai, é, î and وْ as aw, au, aû, ou

Short vowels of the first syllable are often dropped as in MRABBAʻ for MURABBAʻ, RBĀB for RABĀB, etc. The tā' marbūṭah is rarely transliterated.

Appendix IV: List of Abbreviations

abbrev.	abbreviation
abrg.	abridged
acc.	accusative
adj.	adjective
Alg.	Algeria/Algerian
approx.	approximately
Ar.	Arab/Arabic
c.	cents, the units of measurement for musical intervals
C.	century
ca.	about
chap.	chapter
cm.	centimeter(s)
col.	column(s)
colloq.	colloquialization/colloquial
comp.	comparative
d.	died
dat.	dative
def.	definition
der.	derivation from
descr. of des	descriptive of
dim.	diminutive
Eng.	England/English
equiv.	equivalent, used for equally correct transliterations of a term or expression
esp.	especially
ethn.	ethnic group
f.	feminine
fol.	folio
Gr.	France/French
gen.	genitive
geog.	geographic term
Ger.	Germany/German
illus.	illustration
l.h.	left hand
Lib.	Libya/Libyan
lit.	literally
m.	meter
masc.	masculine
Mor.	Morocco/Moroccan
ms.	manuscript
n.	footnote
n. of pers.	name of a person
nat.	nation or state
onom.	onomatopoetic
opp.	opposite
Pal.	Palestine/Palestinian
Pers.	Persia/Persian
pl.	plural
pron.	pronounced
pt.	part
rac.	racial designation
resp.	respectively
r.h.	right hand
s.	singular
sp.	spelling
Sp.	Spain/Spanish
supp.	existing in the Supplement
syn.	synonym
tr.	translated
Tun.	Tunisia/Tunisian
Turk.	Turkey/Turkish
var.	variant spelling or transliteration

Appendix V: Authors and References Cited

Allawerdi, Michael
1949 Falsafah al Mūsīqā al Sharqiyyah. Damascus: Ibn Zaydūn, first pub. 1948.

Anonymous Treatise (15th C.)
1939 Fr. tr. in Baron Rodolphe d'Erlanger, La musique arabe. Paris: Paul Geuthner, IV.

ʿArnīṭah, Yusrā Jawhariyyah
1968 Al Funūn al Shaʿbiyyah fi Filisṭīn. Beirut: Munaẓẓamah al Taḥrīr al Filisṭīniyyah, Markaz al Abḥāth.

Avenary, Hanoch
1952 "The Hebrew Version of Abū L-Ṣalt's Treatise on Music," Yuval, III, 7-81.

al ʿAzzāwī, ʿAbbās
1951 Al Mūsīqā al ʿIrāqiyyah fī ʿAhd al Mughūl wal Turkumān. Baghdād: Sharikah al Tijārah wal Ṭibāʿah al Maḥdūdah.

Bashir, Mounir
1978 "Musical Planning in the Developing Country: Iraq and the Preservation of Musical Identity," The World of Music, XX, No. 1, 74-78.

Bulos, Afif Alvarez
1971 Handbook of Arabic Music. Beirut: Librairie du Liban.

Boubakeur, Si Hamza
1968 "Psalmodie Coronique," Encyclopédie de musiques sacrées, ed. Jacques Porte. Paris: Éditions Labergerie, I, 388-403.

Burckhardt, John Lewis
1967 Notes on the Bedouins and Wahabys. London: Henry Colburn and Richard Bentley, first pub. 1831.

Chabrier, Jean-Claude
1978 "New Developments in Arabian Instrumental Music," World of Music, XX, No. 1, 94-109.

Chottin, Alexis
1939 Tableau de la musique marocaine. Paris: Paul Geuthner.

1957 "Arabe (Musique)," Larousse de la Musique. Paris: Larousse, I, 40-42.

1961 "Nordafrikanische Musik," Die Musik in Geschichte und Gegenwart, tr. Hans Hickmann, IX, col. 1558-1569.

Chottin, Alexis, and Hans Hickmann
1949/51 "Arabische Music," Die Musik in Geschichte und Gegenwart, I, col. 577-601.

Collaer, Paul
1958 "Arabe (Musique)," Encyclopédie de la Musique. Paris: Fasquelle, I, 284-289.

Collangettes, M.
1904 "Étude sur la musique arabe," Journal asiatique, (November-December), 365-422.

1906 "Étude sur la musique arabe," Journal asiatique, (July-August), 149-190.

Cowl, Carl
1966 "The Risāla fī Khubr Ta'līf al Alḥān of al-Kindi," The Consort, Annual Journal of the Dolmetsch Foundation, III, 129-166.

al Dāqūqī, Ibrahīm, ed.
1965 Al Mustadrak ʿalā Kitāb al Iṣṭilāḥāt al Mūsīqiyyah. Baghdād: Maṭbaʿah Dār al Jumhūriyyah.

Delphin, G. and L. Guin
1886 Notes sur la poésie et la musique arabes dans le Maghreb algérien. Paris: Ernest Leroux.

Elias, Antoine Elias, and Edward E. Elias
1959 Al Qāmūs al ʿAṣrī. Cairo: Elias' Modern Press, first pub. 1913.

d'Erlanger, Baron Rodolphe
1930-1959 La musique arabe, six vols. Paris: Librairie Orientaliste Paul Geuthner, I (1930), II (1935), III (1938), IV (1939), V (1949), VI (1959).

1937 Mélodies tunisiennes. Paris: Librairie Orientaliste Paul Geuthner.

al Fārābī, Abū Naṣr Muḥammad Ibn Muḥammad Ibn Ṭarkhān (d. 950)
1930 Kitāb ʿal Mūsīqā al Kabīr, Book I, II, tr. in Baron Rodolphe d'Erlanger, La musique arabe, I. Paris: Paul Geuthner.

1935 Kitāb al Mūsīqā al Kabīr, Book III, tr. in Baron Rodolphe d'Erlanger, La musique arabe, II. Paris: Paul Geuthner.

1967 Kitāb al Mūsīqā al Kabīr, ed. Ghaṭṭās ʿAbd al Malik Khashabah. Cairo: Dār al Kātib al ʿArabī.

Farmer, Henry George

1913-1938 Articles in Encyclopaedia of Islam. Paris, Leyde, London: Picard, E. J. Brill, Luzac, French and English editions, "Būk," "Duff," "Al Ġarīḍ," "Ghinā'," "Ibn Misdjah," "Isḥaḳ al Mawṣilī," "Kitāra," "Miʿzaf," "Mizmār," "Mūsīkī," "Nawba," "Rabāb," "Ṣandj," "Ṭabl," "Ṭabl Khāna," "Ṭunbūr," "Ṭuwais," "ʿUd," "Urġhan," "Zalzal," "Ziryāb."

1925 The Arabic Musical Manuscripts in the Bodleian Library. London: William Reeves.

1926a "The Canon and Eschaquiel of the Arabs," Journal of the Royal Asiatic Society, 239-256.

1926b The Influence of Music from Arabic Sources. London: Harold Reeves.

1926c "The Old Persian Musical Modes," Journal of the Royal Asiatic Society, 93-95.

1928 "Ibn Khurdādhbih on Musical Instruments," Journal of the Royal Asiatic Society, 509-518.

1929a Historical Facts for the Arabian Musical Influence. London: William Reeves.

1929b "Meccan Musical Instruments," Journal of the Royal Asiatic Society, Part III, 489-505.

1930 "The Origin of the Arabian Lute and Rebec," Journal of the Royal Asiatic Society, Part II, 307-322.

1931 The Organ of the Ancients from Eastern Sources. London: William Reeves.

1933a "A Further Arabic-Latin Writing on Music," Journal of the Royal Asiatic Society, Part II, 307-322.

1933b An Old Moorish Lute Tutor: Being Four Arabic Texts from Unique Manuscripts. Glasgow.

1937a "The Lute Scale of Avicenna," Journal of the Royal Asiatic Society, 245-257.

1937b "Was the Arabian and Persian Lute Fretted?", Journal of the Royal Asiatique Society, pp. 453-460.

1941 "Music: The Priceless Jewel," Journal of the Royal Asiatic Society, 22-30; 127-144.

1943 Sa'adyah Gaon on the Influence of Music. London: Arthur Probsthain.

1943/44 "The Minstrels of the Golden Age of Islam," Islamic Culture, XVII, No. 3, 273-281; XVIII, No. 1, 53-61.

1944 "An Anonymous English-Arabic Fragment on Music," Islamic Culture, XVIII, 201-215.

1945 The Minstrelsy of "The Arabian Nights". Bearsden, Scotland: Hinrichsen Edition.

1952 "The Religious Music of Islam," Journal of the Royal Asiatic Society, 60-65.

1954 Articles in Grove's Dictionary of Music and Musicians, ed. Eric Blom. New York: St. Martin's Press, Inc. "Arabian Music," "Barbaṭ," "Berber Music," "Búq," "Egyptian Music," "Iraqian and Meṣopotamian Music," "Kamáncha," "Maghribí Music," "Mi'zaf," "Mohammedan Music," "Moorish Music," "Nafír," "Nauba," "Náy," "Pandur or Pantur," "Qánún," "Quṣṣába," "Rabáb," "Sanṭír," "Syrian Music," "Úd," "Zambra," "Zamr (Mizmár)."

1957 "The Music of Islam," New Oxford History of Music, Vol. I: Ancient and Oriental Music, ed. Egon Wellesz. London: Oxford University Press, 421-477.

1960 Al-Farabi's Arabic-Latin Writings on Music. New York, London, Frankfurt: Hinricksen Edition Ltd., first pub. 1934.

1965a "A Guess at the Origin and Meaning of Conductus," Islamic Culture, XXXIX, 27-28.

1965b The Sources of Arabian Music. Leiden: E. J. Brill.

1967 A History of Arabian Music to the XIIIth Century. London: Luzac and Co., Ltd., first pub. 1929.

1976a Edition of Salvador-Daniel, Francesco, The Music and Musical Instruments of the Arab. Portland, Maine: Longwood Press, first pub. 1915.

1976b Turkish Instruments of Music in the Seventeenth Century: As Described in the Siyāḥat Nāma of Ewliyā Chelebī. Portland, Maine: Longwood Press, first pub. 1937.

1978 Studies in Oriental Musical Instruments. Br. Virgin Islands and Boston: Longwood Press, Series I, first pub. 1931, Series II, first pub. 1939.

al Faruqi, Lois Ibsen
1974 The Nature of the Musical Art of Islamic Culture: A Theoretical and Empirical Study of Arabian Music. Ph.D. diss., Syracuse University, Syracuse, New York.

1975 "Muwashshaḥ: A Vocal Form in Islamic Culture," Ethnomusicology, XIX, No. 1, 1-29.

1978 "Ornamentation in Arabian Improvisational Music: A Study of Interrelatedness in the Arts," The World of Music, XX, No. 1, 17-32.

Gardet, L.
1965 "Dhikr," The Encyclopaedia of Islam. Leyden and London: E. J. Brill and Luzac, II, 223-227.

Gerson-Kiwi, Edith
1970 "On the Technique of Arab Taqsīm Composition," Musik als Gestalt und Erlebnis. Wien-Köln-Graz: Hermann Böhlaus Nachf, 66-73.

al Ghazālī, Abū Ḥāmid Muḥammad Ibn Muḥammad (1058-1111)
1930 "Adāb al Samā‘ wa al Raqṣ," Iḥyā ‘Ulūm al Dīn. Cairo: Maṭba‘ah al Istiqāmah, II, 236-269.

1901/02 "Emotional Religion in Islam as Affected by Music and Singing," tr. from Iḥyā' ‘Ulūm al Dīn by Duncan B. MacDonald, Journal of the Royal Asiatic Society, Part I, 195-252; and Part II, 705-748 (1901); and Part III, 1-28 (1902).

al Ghazālī, "Majd al Dīn" Abū al Futūḥ Aḥmad Ibn Muḥammad Ibn Aḥmad al Ṭūsī (d. 1126)
1938 "Bawāriq al Ilmā‘," Ar. text and Eng. tr. in Tracts on Listening to Music, tr. and ed. James Robson. London: The Royal Asiatic Society.

Grame, Theodore C.
1970 "Music in the Jma al-Fna of Marrakesh," The Musical Quarterly, LVI, No. 1, 74-87.

1972 "The Symbolism of the ‘Ūd," Asian Music, III, No. 1, 25-34.

Ḥāfiẓ, Muḥammad Maḥmūd Sāmī
1971 Tārīkh al Mūsīqā wal Ghinā' al ‘Arabī. Cairo: Maṭba‘ah al Fanniyyah al Ḥadīthah.

al Ḥafnī, Maḥmūd Aḥmad
1930 Ibn Sina's Musiklehre. Berlin-Wilmersdorf: Otto Hellwig, doctoral dissertation.

1946 Al Mūsīqā al Naẓariyyah. Cairo, first pub. 1937.

1971 ‘Ilm al Ālāt al Mūsīqiyyah. Cairo: Al Hay'ah al Miṣriyyah al ‘Ammah lil Ta'līf wal Nashr.

Al Ḥalqah al Thāniyah li Baḥth al Mūsīqā al ‘Arabiyyah
1964 Cairo: Al Majlis al A‘lā li Ri‘āyah al Funūn wal Ādāb wal ‘Ulūm al Ijtimā'iyyah.

Haq, Sirajul
1944 "Samā‘ and Raqṣ," Islamic Culture, XVIII, 111-130.

el Helou, Selim
1961 Al Mūsīqā al Naẓariyyah. Beirut: Dār Maktabah al Ḥayāt.

1965 Al Muwashshaḥāt al Andalusiyyah. Beirut: Dār Maktabah al Ḥayāt.

Hickmann, Hans
1947 Terminologie arabe des instruments de musique. Cairo.

1958 Catalogue d'enregistrements de musique folklorique egyptienne. Strasbourg/Baden-Baden: Éditions P. H. Heitz/ Verlag Heitz GMBH.

Ibn ʿAbd Rabbihi, Aḥmad Ibn Muḥammad (860-940)
1887 Al ʿIqd al Farīd. Cairo: Būlāq, III, 176-209.

1943/44 Al ʿIqd al Farīd, Section on Music, tr. in H. G. Farmer, "The Minstrels of the Golden Age of Islam," Islamic Culture, XVII (1943), No. 3, 273-281; XVIII (1944), No. 1, 53-61.

Ibn Abī al Dunyā al Qurashī al Baghdādī Abū Bakr ʿAbdullah Ibn Muḥammad Ibn Ubayd (d. 894)
1938 "Dhamm al Malāhī," Ar. text and Eng. tr. in Tracts on Listening to Music, tr. and ed. James Robson. London: The Royal Asiatic Society.

Ibn Abī al Ṣalt, ʿUmayyah Ibn ʿAbd al ʿAzīz (1067-1134)
1952 Treatise on Music, translation and edition in Hanoch Avenary, "The Hebrew Version of Abū L-Ṣalt's Treatise on Music," Yuval, III, 7-81.

Ibn Dhurayl, ʿAdnān
1969 Al Mūsīqā fī Suriyyah. Damascus.

Ibn Khaldūn, Abū Zayd ʿAbd al Raḥman Ibn Muḥammad (d. 1406)
n.d. Al Muqaddimah. Cairo: Muṣṭafā Muḥammad.

1967 The Muqaddimah: An Introduction to History, tr. Franz Rosenthal. Princeton: Princeton University Press, Bolingen Series, first pub. 1958, II, 395-405; III, 440-480.

Ibn Khurdādhbih, ʿUbayd Allah Ibn ʿAbdullah (d. 912)
1951 "Fī al Lahw wal Malāhī," included in ʿAbbās al ʿAzzāwī, Al Mūsīqā al ʿIrāqiyyah fī ʿAhd al Mughūl wal Turkumān. Baghdād: Sharikah al Tijārah wal Ṭibāʿah al Maḥdūdah, 91-101.

1969 Mukhtār min Kitāb al Lahw wa al Malāhī, ed. Ighnāṭyūs ʿAbduh Khalīfah al Yasūʿī. Beirut: Maṭbaʿah al Kāthūlīkiyyah.

Ibn al Munajjim, Yaḥyā Ibn ʿAlī Ibn Yaḥyā Ibn Abī Manṣūr (856-912)
1950 Kitāb al Nagham, ed. Muḥammad Bahjat al Atharī. Baghdād: Maṭbaʿah al Rābiṭah.

1976 Kitāb al Nagham, in Yūsuf Shawqī, Risālah Ibn Munajjim fī al Mūsīqā wa Kashf Rumūz Kitāb al Aghānī. Cairo: Wizārah al Thaqāfah.

Ibn Salamah, Abū Ṭālib al Mufaḍḍal (d. 902)
1938a "Kitāb al Malāhī," Ar. text and Eng. tr. in Ancient Arabian Musical Instruments, tr. and ed. James Robson. Glasgow: The Civic Press.

1938b "Kitāb al Malāhī," Ar. text and Eng. tr. in Journal of the Royal Asiatic Society, tr. and ed. James Robson (April), 231-249.

1951 "Kitāb al Malāhī," included in ʿAbbās al ʿAzzāwī, Al Mūsīqā al ʿIrāqiyyah fī ʿAhd al Mughūl wal Turkumān. Baghdād: Sharikah al Tijārah wal Ṭibāʿah al Maḥdūdah, 73-89.

Ibn Sīnā, Abū ʿAlī al Ḥusayn Ibn ʿAbdullah (980-1037)
1930 "Al Najāt," Ar. text and Ger. introduction in Ibn Sina's Musiklehre, ed. Maḥmūd A. al Ḥafnī. Berlin: Otto Hellwig.

1935 "Al Shifā'," tr. in Baron Rodophe d'Erlanger, La musique arabe. Paris: Paul Geuthner, II, 103-245.

Ibn Taymiyyah, Taqī al Dīn Abū al ʿAbbās Aḥmād Ibn ʿAbd al Ḥalīm Ibn ʿAbd al Salām (1263-1328)
1966 "Kitāb al Samāʿ wal Raqṣ," Majmūʿah al Rasā'il al Kubrā Cairo: Maṭbaʿah Muḥammad ʿAlī Ṣubayḥ, II, 295-330.

Ibn Zaylah, Abū Manṣūr al Ḥusayn (d. 1038)
1964 Al Kafī fī al Mūsīqā, ed. Zakariyyā Yūsuf. Cairo: Dar al Qalam.

al Ikhtiyār, Nasīb (20th C.)
n.d. Al Fūlklūr al Ghinā'ī ʿind al ʿArab. Damascus: Maṭbaʿah al Jarīdah al Rasmiyyah, Al Jumhūriyyah al ʿArabiyyah al Sūriyyah.

Ikhwān al Ṣafā' (10th C.)
1957 Rasā'il, Fifth Risālah of the Section (Qiṣm) on Mathematics (Riyāḍī). Beirut: Dār Ṣādir - Dār Bayrūt, I, 183-257.

1964/65 Rasā'il, Section on Music tr. in Amnon Shiloah, "L'épître sur la musique des Ikhwān al-Ṣafāʾ," Revue des études islamique XXXII, 125-162.

al Irbalī, Badr al Dīn Muḥammad Ibn ʿAlī al Khaṭīb (14th C.)
1951 "Arjūzah al Anghām," included in ʿAbbās ʿAzzāwī, Al Mūsīqā al ʿIrāqiyyah fī ʿAhd al Mughūl wal Turkumān. Baghdād: Sharikah al Tijārah wal Ṭibāʿah al Maḥdūdah, 103-113.

Jargy, Simon
1970 La poésie populaire traditionnelle chantée au Proche-Orient arabe. Beirut: Mouton and Co., and École Pratique de Hautes Etudes, I.

1971 La Musique arabe. Paris: Presses Universitaires de France.

1978 "The Folk Music of Syria and Lebanon," The World of Music, XX, No. 1, 79-93.

Jones, Lura JaFran
1977 The 'Īsāwiya of Tunisia and Their Music, Ph.D. dissertation, University of Washington, Seattle, Washington.

al Jurjānī, ʿAlī Ibn Muḥammad al Sayyid al Sharīf (1340-1413)
1938 Commentary on Kitāb al Adwār of Ṣafī al Dīn, tr. in Baron Rodolphe d'Erlanger, La musique arabe. Paris: Paul Geuthner, III, 183-566.

Juynboll, Theodore W.
1960 "Adhān," The Encyclopaedia of Islam. Leyde and Paris: E. J. Brill and G.-P. Maisonneuve, I, 193-194.

Kāẓim, A.
1964 Al Iṣṭilāḥāt al Mūsīqiyyah, tr. Ibrahīm al Dāqūqī. Baghdād Maṭbaʿah Dār al Jumhūriyyah.

El-Kholy, Samha Amin
1954 The Function of Music in Islamic Culture, Ph.D. dissertation, University of Edinburgh.

1978 The Tradition of Improvisation in Arab Music. Giza: Imprimerie Rizk.

al Khulaʿī, Muḥammad Kāmil
1904 Kitāb al Mūsīqā al Sharqī. Cairo: Maṭbaʿah al Taqaddum.

al Khwārizmī, Abū ʿAbdullah Muḥammad Ibn Aḥmad Ibn Yūsuf (d. 980)
1968 Kitāb Mafātīḥ al ʿUlūm, ed. G. von Vloten as Liber Mafātīḥ al-olūm. Leyden: E. J. Brill, first pub. 1895, section on music, 236-246.

Kiesewetter, R. G.
1968 Die Musik der Araber. Wiesbaden: Dr. Martin Sandig, first pub. 1842.

al Kindī, Abū Yūsuf Yaʿqūb Ibn Isḥāq (790-874)
1962 Tamrīn lil Ḍarb ʿalā al ʿŪd, ed. Zakariyyā Yūsuf. Baghdād.

1965 "Risālah fī al Luḥūn wal Naghm," in Zakariyyā Yūsuf, Risālah al Kindī fī al Luḥūn wal Naghm. Baghdād: Maṭbaʿah Shafīq.

1966 "Risālah fi Khubr Ta'līf al Alḥān," Ar. text and tr. in Carl Cowl, "The Risāla fī Ḥubr Tā'līf al-Alḥān of al-Kindī," The Consort, III, 129-166.

1969 "Risālah fī Khubr Ta'līf al Alḥān," in Yūsuf Shawqī, Risālah al Kindī fī Khubr Ṣināʿah al Ta'līf. Cairo: Dār al Kutub, Ar. text, 71-113, Eng. tr. 12-25.

Lachmann, Robert
1929 Musik des Orients. Breslau: Ferdinand Hirt.

Lachmann, Robert, and E. M. Hornbostel
1933 "Asiatische Parallelen zur Berbermusic," Zeitschrift fur Vergleichende Musikwissenschaft, I, 4-11.

Lachmann, Robert, and A. H. Fox Strangways
1938 "Muhammedan Music," Grove's Dictionary of Music and Musicians, ed. H. C. Colles, first pub. 1927. New York: The Macmillan Co., III, 575-579.

al Lādhiqī, Muḥammad Ibn ʿAbd al Ḥamīd (late 15th C.)
1939 "Al Risālah al Fatḥiyyah," tr. in Baron Rodolphe d'Erlanger, La Musique arabe. Paris, Paul Geuthner, IV.

Lane, Edward William (19th C.)
1973 An Account of the Manners and Customs of the Modern Egyptians. New York: Dover, first pub. 1836.

Madina, Maan Z.
1973 Arabic-English Dictionary of the Modern Literary Language. New York: Pocket Books.

el Mahdi, Salah
1972 La Musique arabe. Paris: Alphonse Leduc.

Maḥfūẓ, Ḥusayn ʿAlī
1964 Muʿjam al Mūsīqā al ʿArabiyyah. Baghdād: Dār al Jumhūriyyah.

Maʿlūf, Father Louis
1927 Al Munjid fī al Lughah wal Adab wal ʿUlūm. Beirut: Catholic Press, first pub. 1908.

Marcuse, Sibyl
1975 Musical Instruments: A Comprehensive Dictionary. New York: W. W. Norton and Co., Inc., first pub. 1964.

Mashāqah, Mīkhā'īl Ibn Jirjīs (1800-1888)
n.d. Al Risālah al Shihābiyyah fī al Ṣināʿah al Mūsīqiyyah, ms AP7, Near East School of Theology, Beirut, Lebanon.

1847 Al Risālah al Shihābiyyah fī al Ṣināʿah al Mūsīqiyyah, Eli Smith as "A Treatise on Arab Music," Journal of the American Oriental Society, I, No. 3, 171-217.

Massignon, Louis
1913-1934 "Tik," Encyclopédie de l'Islam. Leyde and Paris: E. J. Brill and Picard, VIII, 765-766.

al Masʿūdī, Abū al Ḥasan ʿAlī (d. ca. 956)
1874 Murūj al Dhahab wa Maʿādin al Jawhar, Ar. text and Fr. tr. by C. Barbier de Meynard (Les Prairies d'Or). Paris: L'Imprimerie Nationale, VIII, 88-100.

de Meynard, C. Barbier (19th C.)
1874 Les Prairies d'Or, tr. and ed. of Abū al Ḥasan ʿAlī al Masʿūdī, Murūj al Dhahab wa Maʿādin al Jawhar. Paris: L'Imprimerie Nationale, VIII, 88-100.

al Nadīm, Abū al Faraj Muḥammad Ibn Isḥāq Ibn Muḥammad Ibn Isḥāq (d. 990)
1970 The Fihrist of al-Nadīm, ed. and tr. by Bayard Dodge. New York: Columbia University Press, I, II.

Nettl, Bruno and Ronald Riddle
1973 "Taqsīm Nahawand: A Study of Sixteen Performances by Jihad Racy," Yearbook of the International Folk Music Council, 11-50.

Olsen, Paul Rovsing
1967 "La musique africaine dans le golfe persique," Journal of the International Folk Music Council, XIX, 28-36.

1977 "Melodic Structures in Traditional Music," paper delivered at International Musicological Society Conference, Berkeley, California, August, 1977.

Perkuhn, Eva Ruth
1976 Die Theorien zum arabischen Einfluss auf die europäischen Musik des Mittelalters. Walldorf-Hessen: Verlag für Orientkünde, Bd. 26 of Beitrage zur Sprach und Kulturgeschichte des Orients.

Poche, Christian
1978 "Zikr and Musicology," The World of Music, XX, No. 1, 59-73.

Racy, ʿAli Jihad
1978a "Arabian Music and the Effects of Commercial Recording," The World of Music, XX, No. 1, 47-58.

1978b "The Egyptian Takht," unpublished paper delivered at the Annual Meeting, Society for Ethnomusicology, St. Louis.

1979 "Music of Tunisia: A Contemporary Perspective," Arabesqué, V, No. 1, 18-24, 28.

al Rajab, Hāshim Muḥammad
1967 Ḥall Rumūz Kitāb al Aghānī lil Muṣṭalaḥāt al Mūsīqiyyah al ʿArabiyyah. Baghdād: Maṭbaʿah al ʿĀnī.

Randel, Don M.
1976 "Al-Fārābī and the Role of Arabic Music Theory in the Latin Middle Ages," Journal of the American Musicological Society, XXIX, No. 2 (Summer), 173-188.

Reichow, Jan
1971 Die Entfaltung eines Melodiemodells in Genus Sikah, Band LXI of Kölner Beiträge zur Musikforschung. Regensburg: Gustav Bosse Verlag.

Ribera Y Tarragó, Julián
1970 Music in Ancient Arabia and Spain, tr. and abrg., Eleanor Hague and Marion Leffington. New York: DaCapo Press, first pub. 1929.

al Rizqī, Ṣādiq
1967 Al Aghānī al Tūnisiyyah. Tūnis: Al Dār al Tūnisiyyah lil Nashr.

Robson, James
1938a Ancient Arabian Musical Instruments. Glasgow: The Civic Press.

1938b "Kitāb al-Malāhī of Abū Ṭālib al-Mufaḍḍal Ibn Salama. Translated with Introduction and Notes, Including notes by H. G. Farmer on the Instruments," Journal of the Royal Asiatic Society (April), 231-249.

1938c Tracts on Listening to Music. London: The Royal Asiatic Society.

Rouanet, Jules
1922 "La musique arabe" (I, v, 2676-2812), and "La musique arabe dans le Maghreb" (I, v, 2813-2944), in Albert Lavignac, ed., Encyclopédie de la musique et dictionnaire du conservatoire. Paris: Librairie Delagrave.

Roychoudhury, M. L. (20th C.)
n.d. Music in Islam, reprinted from Journal of the Royal Asiatic Society, Letters. Calcutta: H. Bhattacharya.

Sachs, Curt
1940 The History of Musical Instruments. New York: W. W. Norton and Co., Inc.

1967 Handbuch der Musikinstrumentenkunde. Wiesbaden: Breitkopf and Hartel.

al Ṣafadī, Ṣalāh al Dīn Khalīl Ibn Aybak (d. 1363)
1966 Tawshīʿ al Tawshīḥ, ed. Albert Ḥabīb Muṭlaq. Beirut: Dār al Thaqāfah.

Ṣafī al Dīn ʿAbd al Mu'min Ibn Fākhir al Urmawī (d. 1293)
1938a Kitāb al Adwār, excerpts tr. with commentary in Baron Rodolphe d'Erlanger, La musique arabe. Paris: Paul Geuthner, III.

1938b Al Risālah al Sharafiyyah, tr. in Baron Rodolphe d'Erlanger, La musique arabe. Paris: Paul Geuthner, III.

Ṣalāḥ al Dīn, Muḥammad
1950 Miftāḥ al Alḥān al ʿArabiyyah. Cairo: Aḥmad, 2nd printing.

Salvador-Daniel, Francesco
1976 The Music and Musical Instruments of the Arab, ed. Henry George Farmer. Portland, Maine: Longwood Press, first pub. 1915.

Schuyler, Philip D.
1978 "Moroccan Andalusian Music," The World of Music, XX, No. 1, 33-46.

el-Shawan, Salwa
1978 "Transmission and Musical Change: Cases from Arabic Music in Egypt," unpublished paper delivered at the Annual Meeting, Society for Ethnomusicology, St. Louis.

Shawqī, Yūsuf
1969a Qiyās al Sullam al Mūsīqā al ʿArabī. Cairo: Dār al Kutub.

1969b Risālah al-Kindī fi Khubr Ṣināʿah al Ta'līf. Cairo: Dār al Kutub.

1976 Risālah Ibn Munajjim fī al Mūsīqā wa Kashf Rumūz Kitāb al Aghānī. Cairo: Wizārah al Thaqāfah.

Shiloah, Amnon
1964/65 "L'Épître sur la Musique des Ikhwān al-Ṣafā'," Revue des Études islamiques, XXXII, 125-162.

1965 "Monde arabe et juif," La musique: Les hommes, les instruments, les oeuvres. Paris: Librairie Larousse, I, 25-32.

1968a "Deux textes arabes inédits sur la musique," Yuval (Jerusalem), 221-248.

1968b "L'Islam and la musique," Encyclopédie de musiques sacrées, ed. Jacques Porte. Paris: Éditions Labergerie, I, 414-421.

1972 "The Simsimiyya: A Stringed Instrument of the Red Sea Area," Asian Music, IV, No. 1, 15-26.

1974 "Le poète-musicien et la creation poético-musical au Moyen Orient," International Folk Music Council Yearbook, 52-63.

al Shīrāzī, Quṭb al Dīn Maḥmūd Ibn Masʿūd (1236-1311)
1978 Durrah al Tāj (excerpt from), Ar. text and Eng. tr. in O. Wright, The Modal System of Arab and Persian Music, A.D. 1250-1300. Oxford University Press, tr. 168-192, text in Appendix II, 282-292.

Smith, Eli
1847 "A Treatise on Arab Music" (being a translation of Mīkhā'īl Ibn Jirjīs Mashāqah, Al Risālah al Shihābiyyah fī al Ṣināʿah al Mūsīqiyyah), Journal of the American Oriental Society, I, No. 3, 171-217.

Snoussi, Manoubi
1961 "Folklore tunisien, musique de plein-air: l'orchestre de Tabbal et Zokkar," Revue des études islamiques, No. 1, 148-157.

Spector, Johanna
1970 "Classical ʿŪd Music in Egypt with Special Reference to

Maqāmāt," Ethnomusicology, XIV, No. 2, 243-257.

al Suyūṭī, Jalāl al Dīn (1445-1505)
1941 Al Itqān fī ʿUlūm al Qur'ān. Cairo: Maṭbaʿah Ḥijāzī.

Talbi, M.
1958 "La Qirā'a bi-l-Alhān," Arabica, V, 183-190.

Touma, Habib Hassan
1971 "The Maqam Phenomenon: An Improvisation Technique in the Music of the Middle East," Ethnomusicology, XV, No. 1, 38-48.

1976 Der Maqam Bayati im arabischen Taqsim. Hamburg: Verlag der Musikalienhandlung Karl Dieter Wagner, Beitrage zur Ethnomusikologie, Band III.

1977a "The Fidjrí, a Major Vocal Form of the Bahrain Pearl-divers," The World of Music, XIX, No. 3/4, 121-133.

1977b La musique arabe, tr. Christine Hetier. Paris: Editions Buchet/Chastel.

Tsuge, Gen'ichi
1972 "A Note on the Iraqi Maqam," Asian Music, IV, No. 1, 59-66.

al Ṭūsī, Naṣīr al Dīn (1201-1274)
1964 Risālah fī ʿIlm al Mūsīqā, ed. Zakariyyā Yūsuf. Cairo: Dār al Qalam.

de Vaux, Baron Carra
1891 "Le Traité des rapports musicaux de Safi ed-Dîn," Journal Asiatique, pt. II, 279-355.

Wahba, Magdi
1968 An English-Arabic Vocabulary of Scientific, Technical and Cultural Terms. Cairo: L. D. F.

Wehr, Hans
1976 A Dictionary of Modern Written Arabic, ed. J. Milton Cowan. Ithaca, New York: Spoken Language Services, Inc., first pub. in Ger. in 1961.

Weil, G.
1913-1934 "ʿArūḍ," Encyclopédie de l'Islam. Leyde and Paris: E. J. Brill, Picard and Fils, I, 469-477.

Wright, Owen
1966 "Ibn al-Munajjim and the Early Arabian Modes," The Galpin Society Journal, XIX (April), 27-48.

1978 The Modal System of Arab and Persian Music, A.D. 1250-1300. London Oriental Series, Vol. 28. Oxford: Oxford University Press.

1979 "Music," The Legacy of Islam, Second Edition, ed. Joseph Schacht with C. E. Bosworth. Oxford: Oxford University Press, 489-505.

Yūsuf, Zakariyyā, ed.
1962 Tamrīn lil Ḍarb ʻalā al ʻŪd, Baghdād.

1964 Risālah Naṣīr al Dīn al Ṭūsī fī ʻIlm al Mūsīqā. Cairo: Dār al Qalam.

1965 Risālah al Kindī fī al Luḥūn wa al Naghm, Second Supplement (Mulḥaq) to the book: Mu'allafāt al Kindī al Mūsīqiyyah. Baghdād: Maṭbaʻah Shafīq.

al Zabīdī, Al Sayyid Murtaḍā (d. 1791)
1965 Tāj al ʻArūs. Beirut: Dār Maktabah al Ḥayāt, first published 1306 A.H./1888 A.C., 10 volumes.

About the Compiler

LOIS IBSEN al FARUQI, Professor of Religion and the Arts, Temple University has published widely on Islamic music, art, and culture.